Lecture Notes in Computer Science 5068

Commenced Publication in 1973
Founding and Former Series Editors:
Gerhard Goos, Juris Hartmanis, and Jan van Leeuwen

T0223130

Seongil Lee   Hyunseung Choo   Sungdo Ha
In Chul Shin (Eds.)

Computer–Human Interaction

8th Asia-Pacific Conference, APCHI 2008
Seoul, Korea, July 6-9, 2008
Proceedings

 Springer

Volume Editors

Seongil Lee
Sungkyunkwan University
Department of Systems Management Engineering
300 Chunchun-Dong, Jangan-Gu, Suwon, 440-746, Korea
E-mail: silee@skku.edu

Hyunseung Choo
Sungkyunkwan University
School of Information and Communication Engineering
300 Chunchun-Dong, Jangan-Gu, Suwon, 440-746, Korea
E-mail: choo@ece.skku.ac.kr

Sungdo Ha
Korea Institute of Science and Technology
Intelligent System Research Division
39-1 Hawolgok-Dong, Seongbuk-Gu, Seoul, 136-791, Korea
E-mail: sungdo@kist.re.kr

In Chul Shin
Korea Agency for Digital Opportunity & Promotion
Office of Digital Access Promotion
188 Gonghang-ro, Gangseo-gu, Seoul, 157-715, Korea
E-mail: icshin@kado.or.kr

Library of Congress Control Number: 2008930157

CR Subject Classification (1998): H.5.2, H.5.3, H.5, C.2.4, H.4, H.3, I.2, I.3.6, K.4.3, K.8

LNCS Sublibrary: SL 3 – Information Systems and Application, incl. Internet/Web and HCI

ISSN 0302-9743

ISBN 978-3-540-70584-0 Springer Berlin Heidelberg New York

Springer is a part of Springer Science+Business Media

springer.com

© Springer-Verlag Berlin Heidelberg 2008

Typesetting: Camera-ready by author, data conversion by Scientific Publishing Services, Chennai, India
Printed on acid-free paper   SPIN: 12322947   06/3180   5 4 3 2 1 0

Preface

Welcome to the proceedings of APCHI 2008, the 8th Asia-Pacific Conference on Computer–Human Interaction held in Seoul, Korea. Following the success of the preceding APCHI conferences, in Singapore (1996, 2000), Australia (1997), Japan (1998), China (2002), New Zealand (2004) and Taiwan (2006), the 8th APCHI brought together the researchers, developers, practitioners, and educators in the field of human–computer interaction. APCHI has been a major forum for scholars and practitioners in the Asia-Pacific region on the latest challenges and developments in HCI. Theoretical breakthroughs and practical systems and interfaces were presented at this 2008 conference, thanks to the support of KADO, the HCI ITRC of Sungkyunk-wan University, and KIST.

APCHI 2008 featured a comprehensive program including keynote speeches, regular paper presentations, poster, demos, and special panel sessions. To address the challenge of socially blending ubiquitous computing technologies and a wider spectrum of people with a variety of skills, knowledge, and capabilities, APCHI 2008 set "Universal and Ubiquitous" as the conference theme. APCHI 2008 attracted a total of 151 paper submissions. Among such a large number of submissions, 45 full papers were accepted as submitted or with minor revisions. All papers were reviewed by at least two reviewers. For the remaining submissions, 41 were recommended to change according to the reviews and were submitted as extended abstracts and posters. One special session with six invited papers was organized to support the conference theme of "Universal and Ubiquitous." This proceeding volume presents 51 full technical contributions which are from many different countries: China, Czech Republic, Hong Kong, Japan, Korea, Malaysia, Singapore, Taiwan, the UK, and USA.

We kindly acknowledge the great support provided in the reviewing of submissions by the Program Committee members, as well as the additional reviewers who generously gave their time. We greatly appreciate the support of our strong Organizing Committee Chairs and International Program Committee members. We are also grateful for the contribution of all the sponsors and cooperating organizations. Special thanks go to members of the conference secretariat, Min Kyoung Kim, Jung Ae Park, Jiho Choi, and Kyohyun Song for their smooth handling of the publication of the proceedings with Springer. Byung Geun Kim and Jiho Choi did a fabulous job as our Web masters.

May 2008

Seongil Lee
Hyunseung Choo
Sungdo Ha
In Chul Shin

Organization

Organization Committee

General Chair

Son,Y.   KADO, Korea

Co-organizing Chair

Lee, S.   Sungkyunkwan University, Korea
Shin, I.C.   KADO, Korea

Program Chairs

Smith, M.J.   University of Wisconsin-Madison, USA
Choo, H.   Sungkyunkwan University, Korea
Ha, S.   KIST, Korea

Treasurer and Registration

Hong, K.S.   KADO, Korea

Publicity Chair

Hyun, J.H.   KADO, Korea

Extended Abstract Chair

Jung, K.T.   KUT, Korea

Posters Chair

Min, H.   University of Incheon, Korea

Workshop and Panel Chair

Yun, M.H.   Seoul National University, Korea

Student Volunteers Chair

Kong, Y.K.   Sungkyunkwan University, Korea

International Program Committee

Fels, S.	University of British Columbia, Canada
Fang, K.Y.	Sun Yat-sen University, China
Fu, X.	Institute of Psychology, China
Ma, C.	Institute of Software, China
Rau, P.L.P.	Tsinghua University, China
Tao, L.	Tsinghua University, China
Wang, H.	Institute of Software, China
Chan, A.	City Univeristy of Hong Kong, Hong Kong
Goonetilleke, R.	The Hong Kong University of Science and Technology, Hong Kong
Iridiastadi, H.	Bandung Institute of Technology, Indonesia
Manuaba, A.	Udayana University, Indonesia
Pawitra, T.	University of Surabaya, Indonesia
Sutalaksana, I.	Bandung Institute of Technology, Indonesia
Fukumoto, M.	NTT DoCoMo Inc., Japan
Hirose, M.	University of Tokyo, Japan
Ko, K.	University of Yamanashi, Japan
Sekine, C.	UDIT, Japan
Tanaka, J.	University of Tsukuba, Japan
Yamaoka, T.	Wakayama University, Japan
Yamazaki, K.	Chiba Institute of Technology, Japan
Seong, D.S.K.	University of Nottingham, Malaysia
Weng, K.C.	Multimedia University, Malaysia
Yin, W.C.	Multimedia University, Malaysia
Chong, J.	De LaSalle University, Philippines
Gutierrez, J.	De LaSalle University, Philippines
Mutuc, J.	De LaSalle University, Philippines
Seva, R.	De LaSalle University, Philippines
Cheok, A.D.	National University of Singapore, Singapore
Chuan, T.K.	National University of Singapore, Singapore
Leng, T.Y.	Nanyang Technological University, Singapore
McLoughlin, I.	Nanyang Technological University, Singapore
Lee, T.	National Taiwan University of Science and Technology, Taiwan
Lin, C.J.	Chung-Yuang Christian University, Taiwan
Lin, D.Y.M.	I-Shou University, Taiwan
Tang, E.K.H.	Feng-Chia University, Taiwan
Wang, E.	National Tsing Hua University, Taiwan
Jones, M.	Swansea University, UK
Braiterman, J.	GiantAnt, USA
Kim, J.B.	University of Pittsburgh, USA
Moallem, A.	San Jose State University, USA

Local Program Committee

Eom, Y.I.	Sungkyunkwan University, Korea
Hong, K.S.	Sungkyunkwan University, Korea
Lee, E.	Sungkyunkwan University, Korea
Lee, S.	Sungkyunkwan University, Korea
Jeon, B.	Sungkyunkwan University, Korea
Jeon, J.W.	Sungkyunkwan University, Korea
Yi, J.H.	Sungkyunkwan University, Korea
Byun, H.	Yonsei University, Korea
Cho, S.B.	Yonsei University, Korea
Seo, Y.H.	Chungbuk National University, Korea
Yoon, W. C.	KAIST, Korea
Han, S.H.	POSTECH, Korea
Hwang, M.C.	Sangmyung University, Korea
Jung, J.H.	Kookmin University, Korea
Choi, D.J.	KADO, Korea
Shin, K.W.	KADO, Korea
Ahn, S.C.	KIST, Korea
Ko, H.D.	KIST, Korea
Park, J.H.	KIST, Korea
Rhee, Y.	Samsung Electronics, Korea
Hwang, B.C.	Samsung Electronics, Korea

Steering Committee

Kurosu, M.	National Institute of Multimedia Education, Japan
Lim, K.Y.	Nanyang Technological University, Singapore

Sponsors

HCI ITRC (Intelligent HCI Research Center, Sungkyunkwan University)

www.security.re.kr/~atrc/

KADO (Korea Agency for Digital Opportunity & Promotion)

www.kado.or.kr

KIST (Korea Institute of Science and Technology)

www.kist.re.kr

Table of Contents

Human-Robot Interaction

Virtual/Augmented Environment

Vision-Based System

Mobile Interaction Design

Novel Interaction Technique

Usability

Web Accessibility

The Elderly

Experience of Enhancing the Space Sensing of Networked Robots Using Atlas Service-Oriented Architecture

Sumi Helal[1], Shinyoung Lim[1], Raja Bose[1], Hen-I Yang[1], Hyun Kim[2],
and Young-Jo Cho[2]

[1] Department of Computer & Information Science & Engineering,
University of Florida, Gainesville, FL 32611, USA
{helal,lim,rbose,hyang}@cise.ufl.edu
[2] Intelligent Robot Research Division
ETRI, Daejeon, Korea
{hyunkim,youngjo}@etri.re.kr

Abstract. In this paper, we describe how we enhance the space sensing capabilities of the Ubiquitous Robotic Companion (URC) developed by ETRI Korea, by utilizing the plug-and-play service-oriented architecture provided by University of Florida's Atlas Platform. Based on our experience in deploying services using the Atlas Platform in smart houses, for the elderly and people with special needs, a requirement emerged for utilizing networked robots to assist elderly people in their activities of daily living. Networked robots consisting of sensors, actuators and smart devices can collaborate as mobile sensing platforms with the other networked robots in a smart space, providing a complex and sophisticated actuator and human interface. This paper describes our experience in designing and implementing system architecture to integrate URC robots into pervasive computing environments using the Atlas Platform. We also show how the integrated system is able to provide better services which enhance the space sensing capabilities of URCs in the smart space.

Keywords: Ubiquitous computing, Pervasive computing, Embedded design, Service-oriented architecture, Assistive technology for elderly people.

1 Introduction

A Ubiquitous Robotic Companion (URC) is a new design concept developed at ETRI, Korea for networked robotic systems. The fundamental concept behind URC is to share the robot's three core functions – sensing, processing and actuation – over the network. URC robots typically only have sensing and actuation capabilities and outsource their processing tasks over the network to a URC server. Furthermore, URC robots use external sensors in the URC environment rather than solely depending on on-board sensors. The URC server communicates with the robots via a broadband network, and enables them to overcoming their on-board memory and processor constraints [1]. The external sensor nodes which are deployed in the environment transmit sensor data to the URC server which then provides device-specific control data to

S. Lee et al. (Eds.): APCHI 2008, LNCS 5068, pp. 1–10, 2008.

the URC robots. ETRI has been using URC technology for real-world applications since 2004, and the URC concept has been verified by the field tests. During this process, it was recognized that in order for the URC to fully utilize external sensors and actuators in the environment, it is critical to reduce the effort in configuration. The plug-and-play service oriented features of the Atlas Platform, developed at the University of Florida, offers a comprehensive solution for easy extension and integration of URC. Furthermore, when augmented by embedded sensor platforms such as Atlas, the space sensing capability of the URC robot can be dramatically improved. However, it is not easy to deploy URC robots in smart spaces, because robotic environments are diverse and subject to dynamic changes especially since, URC robots are moving around in the smart space.

The University of Florida Mobile and Pervasive Computing Laboratory has accumulated significant experience in designing and building smart spaces over the years. In particular, the technology developed has culminated in the grand opening of the Gator Tech Smart House (GTSH) project, a 2,500 sq. ft. stand-alone intelligent house designed for assistive independent living for elderly residents. The primary technical component of GTSH is the Atlas Platform [2], which includes plug-and-play Atlas sensor and actuator nodes, Atlas middleware that embraces service-oriented architecture, and a set of intuitive tools for easy configuration and fast implementation of smart spaces.

The collaboration between ETRI and the University of Florida fuses together the streamlined embedded framework of the URC robots with service-oriented architecture of the Atlas Platform. The result is a fast and easily deployable smart space where robots can collaborate with embedded sensors and each other to enhance the space sensing and processing capabilities and provide better assistant services. Moreover, the introduction of the URC into smart houses brings unforeseen capabilities for performing complex actuations on mobile platforms that can provide better assistance to the elderly, who require mobility and human interaction. In this paper, we present our experience of designing and implementing the system architecture that integrates URC robots and Atlas service-oriented architecture in the smart space to enhance space sensing capabilities of URC robots.

The remainder of the paper is organized as follows. We discuss related work in Section 2, proposed framework architecture in Section 3, implementation of the framework in Section 4 and conclusion in Section 5.

2 Related Work

There are projects that attempt to enhance robots using pervasive computing technologies. A mobile kitchen robot uses Player/Stage/Gazebo software library to create a middleware and supports integration into ubiquitous sensing infrastructures to enhance the interfacing, manipulation and cognitive processing of the robot [9]. The networked robot project of the Japanese Network Robot Forum [10] has been carried out since 2004. It considers sensors and actuators in the environment as unconscious robots which collaborate with software robots and physical robots. The ETRI URC project also is one of major efforts to improve robots' intelligence using pervasive computing technologies. It enables robots to reduce costs and improve service qualities by taking full advantage of ubiquitous network environment and the networked server framework.

Pervasive computing technologies have opened up new opportunities for providing robots with interactive spaces, in which sensors, actuators and smart devices can collaborate with robots. Examples of pervasive computing technologies have been deployed to create intelligent environments include homes [3, 4, 5], offices [6], classrooms [7] and hospitals [8]. Depending on the environment that they have been deployed in and the primary goals of the system, pervasive computing technologies provide services in location tracking, context gathering and interpretation, human gesture recognition, activity planning and many more. These services have been created to gather data in intelligent environments, process and make decisions based on the collected data and information, and then direct the actions of devices and actuators in the same environment.

3 Proposed Framework Architecture

3.1 Experience of ATLAS in the Gator Tech Smart House

During the process of building the full-scale, 2,500 sq. ft. freestanding Gator Tech Smart House, we designed and implemented the ATLAS architecture. This architecture includes the ATLAS sensor and actuator hardware platform as the bridge between the physical and digital worlds; the ATLAS middleware, and the service authoring tool. It supports self-configuration and facilitates programmability of services in smart spaces, and the implementation has become the central core component in our smart homes.

Requirements of system support for pervasive computing environments are extremely diverse depending on the application domains. For instance, a pervasive computing system in assistive living would be vastly different from habitat monitoring in a remote forest. Since our work is primarily concerned with assistive living in smart homes, the design of the ATLAS architecture follows certain assumptions.

First, we assume that there is a light-weight centralized home server with capabilities similar to set-top boxes or access points, that has a global view of the smart home and management capabilities for the various entities and services under the roof. We also assume that the underlying network runs TCP/IP protocol, with most of the entities located inside a private network, with a NAT-enabled gateway for connections to and from any outside services and entities. The abundance of power in regular households means low power design and power management would not be a primary concern in the design.

To make ATLAS middleware the foundation of the kind of pervasive computing systems we envisioned, it is important that it should be able to fulfill the following functionalities and objectives. First of all, this middleware architecture has to be modular and extensible; it should based on a service-oriented architecture, in which each application and device is represented as a service entity, so their entrance, departure and movement can be interpreted and handled more easily; the services can utilize other software components, but they must be built in a modular fashion such that the modules can be shared and reused, and the system should be able to determine if the required modules are present before initiating any service; the system should be easily programmable so its capability is extensible and customizable, meaning that it allows programmers to write new software while utilizing the services provided by existing modules.

Other key functionalities and objectives include the adherence to existing and upcoming standards, the provision of security, safety and privacy features and the mechanism to support scalable concurrent operations by hundreds of components.

At the bottom of the ATLAS architecture are sensor nodes with plug-and-play capabilities. The nodes connect to physical devices such as sensors and actuators, and provide a bridge between the physical world and the digital realm. The ATLAS middleware is implemented as a collection of collaborating modules. The middleware running on the central server is based on OSGi, which is an open standard that defines and provides facilities for service registry, life cycle management and dynamic binding.

On top of OSGi are several service modules in the form of software bundles. Bundle repository manages the collection of service bundles for the various devices that can connect and be integrated into the smart environment; Network Manager keeps track of all the nodes in the network and the services they provide; Configuration Manager is responsible for retrieving the various service bundles required by the nodes and for remotely configuring them over the network; Context manager and safety monitor uses a context-driven model that is independent of the active services to monitor the context changes and alerts users of the occurrence of any unsafe or undesirable context; Communication modules provide an array of standard protocols that can be used for the external communication with other business software, front-end portal, or any other collaborating system and stand-alone software. These modules can also facilitate the inter-bundle communication between various components residing in the same OSGi framework should the need arise; ATLAS Developer API provides a unified interface for programmers to interface and control diverse sensor, actuator and service entities; Service authoring tool is provided in the form of an ATLAS plug-in for Eclipse, and it provides the capability for programmers to browse through the available entities, choose the components they need, and create and deploy new services by simply specifying the application logic.

3.2 Framework Design

The collaboration between ETRI and University of Florida led to the design of a programmable sensor framework for the URC system that bridges real world sensing and actuation. The result is a fast and easily deployable smart space that networked robots can collaborate with and surrogate to, which can offer and extend its sensing and processing capabilities. On the other hand, the introduction of the URC into smart houses brings unforeseen capabilities for performing complex actuations on mobile platforms that can provide better assistance to the elderly that require mobility and human interaction. We present the design of a framework architecture which integrates URC robots with smart spaces in order to enhance the sentience of the URC.

3.2.1 Motivation
We consider sensors and actuators in the environment as unconscious robots which collaborate with software robots and physical robots. The ETRI's URC project is

regarded as one of major efforts to improve robots' intelligence using pervasive computing technologies. It enables robots to reduce cost and improve service qualities by taking full advantage of ubiquitous network environment and the networked server framework. When we tried to integrate the programmable sensor framework into the URC system, the first thing we encountered was the difference in architecture and implementation environment.

As ATLAS is implemented on top of OSGi, the integration of the framework into the URC system requires adaptation, new interfaces or change in its architecture. To resolve these issues, we had intense discussions with the ETRI team on the design of the framework with minimum implementation effort and modification in each system's architecture.

3.2.2 Functions in the Framework

To integrate the ATLAS service-oriented middleware into the URC's middleware, *i.e.*, Context-Aware Middleware for URC Systems (CAMUS), we discussed two different approaches from the perspective of architecture; (1) Comply with the ETRI URC architecture and (2) Build interface of OSGi in the ETRI URC side. The task of CAMUS is to connect and control many different kinds of robots. It acquires sensing information from robots and environments, plans tasks based on the current context and finally sends command messages to robots. Additional functions including voice recognition, voice synthesis and image recognition are heretofore executed in a robot itself.

Figure 1 shows a conceptual architecture based on the ETRI URC architecture. We found that the architecture in Figure 1 would give two different architectures with considerable changes in each other's architecture for integrating the programmable sensor framework into the URC system. For instance, if we design the system that operates on top of OSGi, the OSGi will serve as a bridge between the two different architectures at the cost of the redundancies and seemingly influences possible delay in response time.

For optimized design of the framework, we found out that the CAMUS [1] consists of three main modules: Service Agent Managers, the CAMUS server and the Planet. The Service Agent Manager (SAM) is the robot-side framework to send robot's sensing data to the CAMUS server and receive control commands from the CAMUS server. The CAMUS server is the server-side framework to manage the information delivered from SAMs, generate and disseminate appropriate events according to the context changes, and finally execute server-based robot tasks. And we also found that the Planet is the communication framework between the SAMs and the CAMUS server.

Based on this architectural information and our discussions, we decided to integrate the ATLAS service-oriented middleware with the architecture of SAM. The *service agent* is a software module which acts as a proxy to connect various sensors and devices to the CAMUS server. It raises software events to notify the CAMUS server that its device detects some noticeable changes and receives requests from the CAMUS server to actuate its device. The SAM is a software container of these service agents that resides on a robot or in a space, and manages them. SAM plays a central role in the integration of the ATLAS and the CAMUS systems. The collaboration between smart spaces and robots are facilitated by the communication between the ATLAS middleware and the SAM.

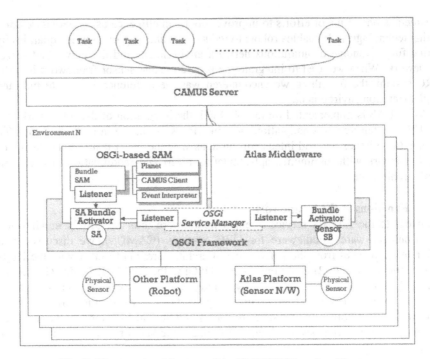

Fig. 1. Conceptual architecture of the ETRI URC based architecture

When a new device is deployed in the space, the plug-and-play capability ensures that a service bundle is activated in the ATLAS middleware; at the same time, the *Service Agent Loader* detects this event from the ATLAS Middleware and registers this service to the CAMUS server so that the CAMUS tasks use this service. Similarly, when an existing device is removed from the space, the corresponding service bundle automatically expires; while the service agent loader also detects this event and un-registers them from the CAMUS server.

In the updated architecture of the SAM, the ATLAS service-oriented middleware is being monitored by the *Listener* in the *Service Agent Loader*. When the sensing event happens in each *Bundle Activator*, then the *Listener* sends an activation signal to the *Sensor Interpreter*. The *Sensor Interpreter* then, receives sensed data from the *Bundle Activator*. After the CAMUS sends commands information regarding the situational response of the sensed data, the *Service Agent Invocator* transmits it to the *Bundle Activator* to activate the ATLAS platform to run the target actuator. Therefore, the ATLAS service-oriented middleware has communication channels with the *Listener*, the *Service Interpreter* and the *Service Agent Invocator* to each *Bundle Activator*.

The integration between the systems requires service bundles to implement interfaces to communicate with the other service in the ATLAS middleware, as well as the SAM. The bundles run in the OSGi framework, but also have the capabilities of regular service agents.

The *Service Agent Invocator* allows the tasks at the CAMUS server to invoke methods at service agents. A key feature of the Service Agent Invocator is supporting the asynchronous method invocation. It participates in necessary scheduling and threads management activities for handling asynchronous invocation. The *Connection Monitor* plays a key role in handling the disconnection. It continuously monitors the connection to the CAMUS server and takes appropriate actions for the reconnection whenever it detects a disconnection. Any events raised by a service agent run through the *Sensor Interpreter* in the SAM. The sensor interpreter examines each event, passing, dropping, refining or aggregating them. Sometimes the Event Interpreter inserts new events based on the event it examines. By this way, any duplicated or unnecessary events are filtered out at the SAM, reducing network and computational overhead at the CAMUS server. The event that survives the run-through is sent to the Event Publisher. The event publisher delivers it to the corresponding event queue at the CAMUS server. Any subscriber to the queue then receives notification of that event.

4   Implementation

The service oriented architecture of Atlas is hosted on an OSGi framework. The URC framework called CAMUS (Context Aware Middleware for URC Systems) from ETRI on the other hand runs outside OSGi and does not come with OSGi based components. Hence, the main task of this integration effort was to create a bridge between the two systems in a manner which fully utilizes both, the plug-and-play features of Atlas and the context-aware backend provided by CAMUS.

4.1   Integration Process

The Atlas Platform represents every sensor connected to it as an OSGi service object. Regardless of a sensor's type and manufacturer, Atlas provides a uniform interface (declared as a Java interface called *AtlasService*) to every sensor. This ensures that application developers are abstracted away from low-level details and variations between different sensors and can use a single set of high-level methods to access multiple heterogeneous sensors.

The CAMUS is responsible for acquiring sensing information from robots and environments, planning tasks based on the current context and sending control messages to robots. The Service Agent Manager (SAM) is the robot-side component of CAMUS which sends a robot's sensing data to the CAMUS server and receives control commands from the CAMUS server. As described earlier, it was decided to integrate by modifying SAM to become the link between the two systems.

First, SAM was ported to OSGi to enable it to run as a bundle inside the service framework. The OSGi version of SAM is split into two parts: The *Service Agent Loader* component and data acquisition components. The data acquisition components implement the *AtlasService* interface to enable them to become Atlas device bundles which can represent hardware devices connected to the Atlas Platform. Hence, as shown in Figure 2, SAM implements interfaces for both CAMUS and Atlas and bridges the connection between the two.

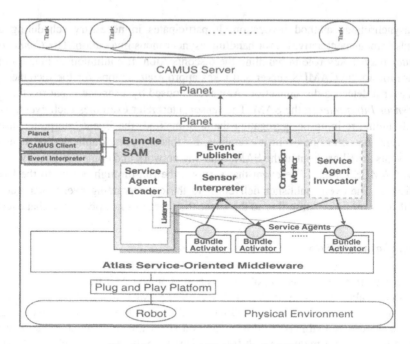

Fig. 2. Integrating ATLAS with CAMUS

Implementing the *AtlasService* interface enables SAM to become an integral part of a sensor service. In our example below, SAM components are present as part of a Pressure Sensor bundle, which enables them to be automatically loaded by Atlas whenever the hardware sensor is powered on. This bundle on being loaded also establishes connection with the *Service Agent Loader* and is able to send data to the CAMUS server and receive commands from it.

4.2 System Execution

When a new device is deployed in the space, the plug-and-play capability of Atlas ensures that a service bundle representing that sensor or actuator is automatically activated in the OSGi framework. The service bundle also contains the data acquisition components of SAM, which automatically seek out the service agent loader using native OSGi calls. The *Service Agent Loader* then registers this service to the CAMUS server so that CAMUS tasks can use this service. Similarly, when an existing device is removed from the space, the corresponding service bundle automatically expires and the service agent loader on detecting this event un-registers them from the CAMUS server.

The integration between the systems requires service bundles to implement interfaces to both communicate with other services in the Atlas middleware, as well as SAM. The bundles run in the OSGi framework, but also have the capabilities of regular service agents.

The *Service Agent Invocator* allows the tasks at CAMUS server to invoke methods at service agents. A key feature of the *Service Agent Invocator* is supporting the asynchronous method invocation. The *Connection Monitor* plays a key role in handling the disconnection. It continuously monitors the connection to the CAMUS server and takes appropriate actions for the reconnection whenever it detects a disconnection.

Any events raised by a service agent run through the *Sensor Interpreter* in SAM. The *sensor interpreter* examines each event, passing, dropping, refining, or aggregating them. Sometimes the event interceptor inserts new events based on the event it examines. By this way, any duplicated or unnecessary events are filtered out at SAM, reducing network and computational overhead at CAMUS server. The event that survives the run-through is sent to the Event Publisher. The event publisher delivers it to the corresponding event queue at CAMUS server. Any subscriber to the queue then receives the event notification.

5 Conclusions

The integration between robots and smart spaces makes robots more intelligent, and also makes a smart space more interactive. However, the major difficulties in integrating the two systems are due to heterogeneity and dynamicity.

Heterogeneity exists in the form of different sensors and actuators, software platforms, communications, data formats and semantics. Dynamicity exists in the form of a rapidly changing environment where multiple devices can enter or leave at various points in time. In this paper, we proposed a four-layer architecture for integrating robots and smart spaces which efficiently addresses these difficulties. This architecture enables devices available in a smart space to be represented as software services. It provides applications with a homogeneous interface to heterogeneous hardware, such as sensors and actuators deployed in the smart space. Applications are automatically notified whenever new devices are introduced into the space or existing devices leave the space. Representing devices as services also allows easy modification of existing applications to enable it to make use of newly available devices. Finally, we discussed the integration of URC with the Atlas Platform, which implements this architecture and provides better services, which enhances the sentience of URC and improves physical interaction between the smart space and the users.

Acknowledgments. This paper has been supported by the Korean Ministry of Information and Communication (Grant No. 2007-S-026-01) which is a part of ETRI's URC research project.

References

1. Kim, H., Cho, Y.-J., Oh, S.-R.: CAMUS: A middleware supporting context-aware services for network-based robots. In: IEEE Workshop on Advanced Robotics and Its Social Impacts, Nagoya, Japan (2005)
2. King, J., Bose, R., Yang, H., Pickles, S., Helal, A.: Atlas - A Service-Oriented Sensor Platform. In: Proceedings of the first IEEE International Workshop on Practical Issues in Building Sensor Network Applications (SenseApp 2006), Tampa, Florida (2006)

3. Helal, A., Mann, W., Elzabadani, H., King, J., Kaddourah, Y., Jansen, E.: Gator Tech Smart House: a programmable pervasive space. IEEE Computer magazine, 66–74 (March, 2005)
4. Kidd, C., et al.: The Aware Home: A living laboratory for ubiquitous computing research. In: Proceedings of Cooperative Buildings, pp. 191–198 (1999)
5. Hagras, et al.: Creating an ambient-intelligence environment using embedded agents. IEEE Intelligent Systems 19(6), 12–20 (2004)
6. Addlesee, M., Curwen, R., Hodges, S., Newman, J., Steggles, P., Ward, A., Hopper, A.: Implementing a Sentient Computing System. IEEE Computer Magazine 34(8), 50–56 (2001)
7. Chen, A., Muntz, R.R., Yuen, S., Locher, I., Park, S., Srivastava, M.B.: A Support Infrastructure for the Smart Kindergarten. IEEE Pervasive Computing 1(2), 49–57 (2002)
8. Hansen, T., Bardram, J., Soegaard, M.: Moving out of the lab: deploying pervasive technologies in a hospital. IEEE Pervasive Computing 5(3), 24–31 (2006)
9. Kranz, M., Rusu, R.B., Maldonado, A., Beetz, M., Schmidt, A.: A Player/Stage System for Context-Aware Intelligent Environments. In: Dourish, P., Friday, A. (eds.) UbiComp 2006. LNCS, vol. 4206, Springer, Heidelberg (2006)
10. Network Robot Forum, http://www.scat.or.jp/nrf/English/

A Formal Model of Coordination for Supporting Community Computing in a Ubiquitous Environment

Jingyu Nam[1], Hyunwoo Kim[1], Dongmin Shin[2], and Jaeil Park[3]

[1] Department of Industrial Engineering, Hanyang University, Seoul, Korea
[2] Department of Information and Industrial, Hanyang University, Ansan, Korea
[3] Division of Industrial and Information Systems, Ajou University, Suwon, Korea
{jgnam,hkim,dmshin}@hanynag.ac.kr, jipark@ajou.ac.kr

Abstract. Recent advances in mobile computing technologies and platform-independent information systems have enabled to realize a ubiquitous environment. Community computing is developed to as a useful tool for realizing collaborative services in a ubiquitous environment. In this paper, we present a formal model of a ubiquitous space that takes community concept into consideration and propose two management frameworks that prevent conflicts among communities. To demonstrate the validity of the proposed frameworks, a prototype system for coordinating medical emergency system is provided.

1 Introduction

Recent advances in mobile computing technologies and platform-independent information systems have enabled to realize ubiquitous environments for humans to entertain the benefits provided by a variety of services. More often than not, the services are provided to users in a collaborative manner in which multiple devices are involved simultaneously. Several users can also be involved in a certain collection of services at the same time, resulting in forming a community among them which refers to a collection of services that cooperates one another to achieve common goals [1][2].

Most of communities have their own specific goals and strategies to meet their participants' requirement in an effective and efficient way. To achieve a community's goal it is necessary to address challenges imposed by limitations of devices and conflict-prone users' preferences. For this reason, several community computing models have been suggested to deliver cooperative and adaptive services to users.

Two principal approaches have widely been adopted which include community system *development* based on a model-driven architecture and service *composition* with existing sets of services [1][3][4]. They, however, tend to put focus on technical aspects and social cognitive issues. Although they are important, it is desirable to construct a formal methodology to represent a community model and specify its operational behavior. A formal model can contribute to analyze and validate a complex system by providing rigorous and robust mathematical representations [5][6].

This paper presents a modeling framework for describing a community and prescribing its behavior to support participants' demands by means of collaborative services. Because a community has one goal and several actions for satisfying human

S. Lee et al. (Eds.): APCHI 2008, LNCS 5068, pp. 11–20, 2008.
© Springer-Verlag Berlin Heidelberg 2008

requirement, conflicts are revealed among goals and actions of the communities. Based on this, we propose a mechanism that coordinates the interactions between inter-community and/or intra-community in which several dynamically changing communities are activated to achieve each goal. Furthermore, the framework is constructed to guarantee the non-blocking property by use of supervisory control theory.

The remainder of this paper is organized as follows: Section 2 identifies elements within a community and presents a model to describe it. In Section 3, a non-blocking mechanism of service collaboration is presented. An implemented prototype is provided to illustrate the execution of the proposed framework in Section 4. Section 5 concludes the paper and suggests possible directions for the future work.

2   Community Computing Model for a Ubiquitous Environment

A ubiquitous environment consists of several services which are invoked by detecting a certain collection of events and one or more participants. It needs to be constructed to be able to provide appropriate services to users while dynamic services are organized in a way that conflicts among them are prevented.

As more than one user and service are involved, a community is formed where each participant can achieve his or her goals by use of services available in it. It needs to be noted that participants (e.g., users and services) play a dynamically changing role in response to a certain event. For a role to be performed, a binding between the role and a participant needs to be established to take required actions by the participant.

We propose a formal model to represent components of a community and describe their behavior in the community. More specifically, we construct a tuple-based ubiquitous environment model $\mathbb{S}$ as shown below:

$$\mathbb{S} = \langle \Sigma, G, E, R, M, A, \theta, \chi, \lambda, \beta, \sigma, \eta \rangle, \text{ where}$$

Σ is a set of events,
G is a set of goals,
E is a set of constraints for selecting an appropriate participants,
R is a set of roles to contribute to achieve a goal of a community,
M is a set of participants which constitute a community,
A is a set of actions that a participant performs,
$\theta : \Sigma \to G$ is a function that generates a goal,
$\chi : G \to E$ is a function that generates a constraint for selecting participants and actions,
$\lambda : G \to R$ is a function that generates a role allocated to a participant,
$\beta : E \to M$ is a function that selects participants that are appropriate by use of the constraints to achieve a goal of a community,
$\sigma : R \to R \times M$ is a function that binds participants into roles,
$\eta : R \times M \to A$ is a function that assigns actions to participants in accordance with their roles.

Based on the ubiquitous environment model, each community can be constructed as follows:

$$\mathbb{C} = < G, E, M, A >,$$

where each element remains the same as defined above.

Note that a community is formed only with the elements that constitute a ubiquitous environment. Therefore, the model can accommodate the dynamics of a community.

3 Frameworks for Supporting Community Operation

As aforementioned, each community has its own goals that can be achieved by services which are, again, realized by actions performed by participants in it. The actions of participants are significantly related to the roles that the participants play in accordance with goals. Therefore, the goals of a community play an important role in determining participants' actions.

Considering the dynamics of a community in terms of its lifecycle, different goals at a certain moment of time need to be considered so that they can be realized in a collaborative way. More specifically, multiple communities with different goals in a ubiquitous environment require a special care in a case that conflicts among goals can be caused. It is considerably important when a participant is involved several communities simultaneously.

The actions taken by participants to achieve their goals can, therefore, cause conflicts among them. To address this problem we devise frameworks each of which coordinates goals of communities and actions of participants, respectively. The two analogous finite state automata (FSA)-based management frameworks prevent actions and goals from causing conflicts as shown in Fig. 1(a) and (b).

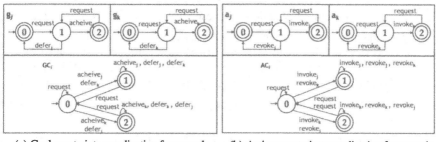

(a) Goal constraints coordination framework   (b) Action constraints coordination framework

Fig. 1. Conflict prevention frameworks

Each of actions and goals is represented by a finite state automaton of which states transition is made in response to events caused by them. Multiple actions and goals are considered by the parallel composition, respectively. A conflict prevention mechanism, then, constructed as shown in the lower of Fig. 1.

In order to represent goals and actions formally, let us define the following finite state automata (FSA).

Definition 1. A goal g_j and an action a_j are expressed, respectively, as follows.

- $g_j = \langle Q_j^g, \Sigma_j^g, \delta_j^g, q_{j,0}^g, Q_{m,j}^g \rangle$, where

$Q_j^g = \{0,1,2\}$: a state set of a goal of a community,

$\Sigma_j^g = \Sigma_{c,j}^g \cup \Sigma_{uc,j}^g$: a set of input alphabets,

$\Sigma_{c,j}^g = \{acheive_j, defer_j\}$: a set of controllable alphabets,

$\Sigma_{uc,j}^g = \{request\}$: a set of uncontrollable alphabets,

request : an input event notification to a community,

$\delta_j^g : Q_j^g \times \Sigma_j^g \to Q_j^g$: a partial state transition function,

$q_{j,0}^g = 0$: an initial state of a goal, $Q_{m,j}^g = \{0,2\}$: a set of accepting states.

$- a_j = \langle Q_j^a, \Sigma_j^a, \delta_j^a, q_{j,0}^a, Q_{m,j}^a \rangle$, where

$Q_j^a = \{0,1,2\}$: a state set of an action of a participant,

$\Sigma_j^a = \Sigma_{c,j}^a \cup \Sigma_{uc,j}^a$: a set of input alphabets,

$\Sigma_{c,j}^a = \{invoke_j, revoke_j\}$: a set of controllable alphabets,

$\Sigma_{uc,j}^a = \{request\}$: a set of uncontrollable alphabets,

request : an input event notification to a participant,

$\delta_j^a : Q_j^a \times \Sigma_j^a \to Q_j^a$: a partial state transition function,

$q_{j,0}^a = 0$: an initial state of a goal, $Q_{m,j}^a = \{0,2\}$: a set of accepting states.

Definition 1 indicates that a goal and an action have finite number of states as a community and a participant process those, respectively. When a community (a participant) receives an event notification (request) that is incurred by a user in a ubiquitous space, the state of a goal (an action) is changed to state 1. If a goal (an action) does not conflict with other goals (actions), the state is varied to state 2 and the goal (action) is achieved (invoked). Otherwise, the state of the goal (action) is changed to state 0. Whether a goal g_j (action a_j) receives $acheive_j$ ($invoke_j$) or $defer_j$ ($revoke_j$) is determined by a conflict prevention mechanism as depicted in the lower of Fig 1.

Since many communities and participants can be emerged in a ubiquitous space, it is necessary to organize all goals and actions, respectively, as follows.

Definition 2. Let us define FSA that represent whole goals and actions that can be in a ubiquitous space by using parallel composition of g_j and a_j, respectively.

GOAL $= \|\{g_j \mid j = 1,...,l\}$, where

$$\Sigma^g = \bigcup_{j=1}^l \Sigma_j^g = \Sigma_c^g \cup \Sigma_{uc}^g, \ \Sigma_c^g = \bigcup_{i=1}^l \Sigma_{c,j}^g, \ \Sigma_{uc}^g = \bigcup_{i=1}^l \Sigma_{uc,j}^g,$$

l : the number of goals of communities in a ubiquitous space.

ACTION $= \|\{a_j \mid j = 1,...,m\}$, where

$$\Sigma^a = \bigcup_{j=1}^l \Sigma_j^a = \Sigma_c^a \cup \Sigma_{uc}^a, \ \Sigma_c^a = \bigcup_{i=1}^l \Sigma_{c,j}^a, \ \Sigma_{uc}^a = \bigcup_{i=1}^l \Sigma_{uc,j}^a,$$

m : the number of actions of participants in a ubiquitous space.

Goals (actions) of communities have to be checked whether conflicts between goals (actions) emerge or not before performing them. We propose conflict prevention mechanism for goals and actions with mutually exclusive relationships as follows.

Definition 3. Let us define FSA for goal constraint and action constraint for conflict prevention as follows.

- Goal constraint for conflict prevention

$$GC_i(j,k) = \langle X_i^g, \Sigma_i^g, \eta_i^g, x_{i,0}^g, X_{m,i}^g \rangle, \text{ where}$$

$X_i^g = \{0,1,2\}$: a state set of goal constraints with respect to goal j and k,

$\Sigma_i^g = \Sigma_j^g \cup \Sigma_k^g$, $\eta_i^g : X_i^g \times \Sigma_i^g \rightarrow X_i^g$: a state transition function,

$x_{i,0}^g = 0$: an initial state, $X_{m,i} = \{1,2\}$: a set of accepting states.

- Action constraint for conflict prevention

$$AC_i(j,k) = < X_i^a, \Sigma_i^a, \eta_i^a, x_{i,0}^a, X_{m,i}^a >, \text{ where}$$

$X_i^a = \{0,1,2\}$: a state set of action constraints with respect to action j and k,

$\Sigma_i^a = \Sigma_j^a \cup \Sigma_k^a$, $\eta_i^a : X_i^a \times \Sigma_i^a \rightarrow X_i^a$: a state transition function,

$x_{i,0}^a = 0$: an initial state, $X_{m,i}^a = \{1,2\}$: a set of accepting states.

The lower of Fig.1 shows the state transition diagram of goal constraint and action constraint for conflict prevention, respectively.

Given the FSA for goals(actions) and goal(action) constraint, we discuss the coordinator within a ubiquitous space and prove its non-blocking property. First, we explain the non-blocking property of a goal constraint coordinator.

Theorem 1. [Modular supervisor] Each FSA $GC_i(j,k), i = 1,\ldots,|\Omega|$ is a modular supervisor for the finite state automaton model of goals, where Ω is a set of constraints among goals in a ubiquitous space.

Proof. A supervisory controller in the control theory is an automaton that, at arbitrary states, controls only the controllable inputs. For an automaton $GC_i(j,k)$, let RC_i be a function such that $RC_i : X \rightarrow 2^{\Sigma}$. $RC_i(x)$ is a set of inputs which are included in Σ but not defined for η_i at any state x. It is a set of invalid inputs when $R_i(j,k)$ is in state x. By the definition of η_i, it can be inferred following results:

$$RC_i(0) = \varnothing, \ RC_i(1) = \{acheive_k\} \subseteq \Sigma_c, \ RC_i(2) = \{acheive_j\} \subseteq \Sigma_c$$

These results indicate that $R_i(j,k)$ can enable and disable only the controllable inputs. Therefore, $R_i(j,k)$ is a modular supervisor for goals. ∎

The goal constraints coordinate goals within the ubiquitous space in such a way that no conflict is caused among goals. When conflicted goals are simultaneously invoked, there is at least one controllable input that is disabled by goal constraints. The controlled behavior of goals of communities in a ubiquitous space, denoted by W, with the goal constraints can be described with a finite state automaton obtained by the parallel composition of the goal of communities and the goal constraints. It is easily verified that the obtained automaton generates the following marked and closed languages:

$$L_{\mathrm{m}}(W) = L_{\mathrm{m}}(\mathrm{GOAL}) \cap \left(\bigcap_{i=1}^{n} L_{\mathrm{m}}(R_i) \big| n = |\Omega| \right), \quad L(W) = L(\mathrm{GOAL}) \cap \left(\bigcap_{i=1}^{n} L(R_i) \big| n = |\Omega| \right)$$

To show the non-blocking property of W, we first prove the following lemma.

Lemma 1. $L(W) \cap L_{\mathrm{m}}(\mathrm{GOAL}) = L_{\mathrm{m}}(W)$

Proof. We prove the following two cases.

Case 1. $L(W) \cap L_{\mathrm{m}}(\mathrm{GOAL}) \supseteq L_{\mathrm{m}}(W)$ and

Case 2. $L(W) \cap L_{\mathrm{m}}(\mathrm{GOAL}) \subseteq L_{\mathrm{m}}(W)$

Case 1 is trivial. $L_{\mathrm{m}}(W) \subseteq L(W) \Rightarrow L_{\mathrm{m}}(W) \cap L_{\mathrm{m}}(\mathrm{GOAL}) \subseteq L(W) \cap L_{\mathrm{m}}(\mathrm{GOAL})$
$\Rightarrow L_{\mathrm{m}}(W) \subseteq L(W) \cap L_{\mathrm{m}}(\mathrm{GOAL})$

In the case 2, we only need to show that for an arbitrary string $s \in L(W) \cap L_{\mathrm{m}}(\mathrm{GOAL})$, it always holds that $s \in L_{\mathrm{m}}(W)$. Assume that string s is included in $L(W) \cap L_{\mathrm{m}}(\mathrm{GOAL})$ and that string $s_j \in L_m(\mathrm{GOAL}_j)$ is a substring of s. Likewise, let string $s_k \in L_m(\mathrm{GOAL}_k)$ be a substring of s, where GOAL_j and GOAL_k are subject to control of $R_i(j,k)$. Since $s_j \in L_m(\mathrm{GOAL}_j)$, we know that $\delta_j^g(0, s_j) = 0$ or $2 \in Q_{m,j}^g$ $j = 1,...,l$. The same holds for string s_k. $R_i(j,k)$, however, requires that if $\delta_k^g(0, s_k) = 0$ $\left(\delta_j^g(0, s_j) = 0 \right)$, then $\delta_j^g(0, s_j) = 0$ or 2 $\left(\delta_k^g(0, s_k) = 0 \text{ or } 2 \right)$. We denote the number of occurrences of alphabet β in a string s as $\beta(s)$. By the transition function for GOAL_j and GOAL_k, the following results are obtained.

request$(s_j) = $ achieve$_j(s_j) + $ defer$_j(s_j)$, request$(s_k) = $ achieve$_k(s_k) + $ defer$_k(s_k)$ or

request$(s) = $ achieve$_j(s) + $ defer$_j(s) + $ achieve$_k(s) + $ defer$_k(s)$

By the definition of η_i^g, we know that $\eta_i^g(0, s) = 1$ or $2 \in X_{m,i}^g, i = 1,...,|\Omega|$ and $s \in L_{\mathrm{m}}(R_i)$. Therefore, string s is included in $L_{\mathrm{m}}(\mathrm{GOAL})$ and $\left(\bigcap_{i=1}^{n} L_{\mathrm{m}}(R_i) \big| n = |\Omega| \right)$ simultaneously, which means $s \in L_{\mathrm{m}}(W)$. ∎

Theorem 2. [Non-blocking coordinator] FSA W has the non-blocking property.

Proof. In order to prove that FSM W is non-blocking, we show that for an arbitrary string $s \in L(W)$, there always exists a string $u \in \Sigma^{g*}$ such that $su \in L_{\mathrm{m}}(W)$. Given a string $s \in L(W)$, it can be inferred the following equations hold considering δ_j^g, $j = 1,...,l$.

1) request$(s_j) = $ achieve$_j(s_j) + $ defer$_j(s_j)$ or

2) request$(s_j) = $ achieve$_j(s_j) + $ defer$_j(s_j) + 1$

In case of equation (1) $\delta_j^g(0, s_j) = 0$ or 2 , for $s_j \in L_m(GOAL_j)$ indicates $s \in L_m(GOAL)$. Therefore, $s \in L(W) \cap L_m(GOAL)$ and by the Lemma1, $L(W) \cap L_m(GOAL) = L_m(W)$, we know $s \in L_m(W)$.

In equation 2), since $\delta_j^g(0, s_j) = 1$, we know $s_j achieve_j \in L_m(GOAL_j)$ or $s_j refer_j \in L_m(GOAL_j)$, and $sachieve_j \in L_m(GOAL)$ or $srefer_j \in L_m(GOAL)$. We also know $sachieve_j \in L(W)$ and $srefer_j \in L(W)$. Extending to a string, there is a string u_j such that $s_j u_j \in L_m(GOAL_j)$, whose last alphabet is always controllable. Also, there exists a string u such that $su \in L_m(GOAL)$. Since $su \in L(W)$, $su \in L(W) \cap L_m(GOAL)$ holds. By Lemma1, we know $su \in L_m(W)$ and that there exists always string u . Therefore, FSA W is non-blocking.   ∎

In the same manner, the non-blocking property of an action constraint coordinator also can be proved. The proof is omitted because of the limitation for the quantity of a paper.

4 Prototype: Medical Emergency System

For the illustrative purpose, we consider three different communities which include traffic management, rescue service, and medical emergency system as depicted in Fig. 2. Although individually running community has no conflicts, there can be cases in which unanticipated conflicts can occur when running simultaneously as shall be described.

1. A traffic management community is created with members of policeman and patrol cars. Its goal is to secure safe traffic and prevent violation of traffic regulation.
2. A rescue service is formed with several ambulances and staffs including firemen. When a car accident is reported they are dispatched to rescue the injured.
3. A medical emergency system is responsible for taking care of patients arrived by a rescue service. Several doctors, nurses, and medical devices constitute the system.

In this environment, the first two communities can have a conflict between them. When a rescue service drives an ambulance, it can violate traffic regulations for the fast service. Obviously, this contradicts to the goal of the traffic management community. On the contrary, if the traffic management community insists that traffic regulations should be observed regardless of any situations, it hinders the fast recue service. Even though this situation is somewhat simple and straightforward, we note that this is considered one of typical cases of goal conflicts that can usually not be predicted beforehand.

Fig. 2. Community Computing Scenario

To address this situation, we develop a prototype to coordinate two communities. Fig. 3 shows simplified communities with their goals, constraints, and members.

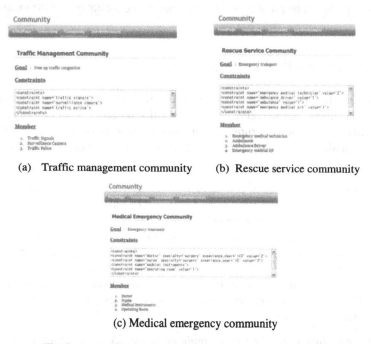

(a)   Traffic management community   (b)   Rescue service community

(c) Medical emergency community

Fig. 3. Communities in a ubiquitous environment prototype

Three communities are coordinated by the proposed framework. While running the communities, the framework detects the conflicts described above and alerts for prevention. Fig. 4 represents the state transitions of the goal, denoted by g_{tmc}, of traffic management community. Initially, the state of g_{tmc} is set to 0. After it detects an event that requests organizing the community, its state changes from 0 to 1. Then goal g_{tmc} is referenced by the goal constraint coordinator $GC_{tmc\ vs\ rsc}$ for information about any conflicts. If no conflict is guaranteed, the state of g_{tmc} changes from 1 to 2, and the state of $GC_{tmc\ vs\ rsc}$ changes from 0 to 1 at the same time. This state change means that the community is activated, and the goal can be achieved without conflicts. If the rescue service community is requested at this time, the state of its goal g_{rsc} changes from 0 to 1. Accordingly, g_{rsc} is reported to $GC_{tmc\ vs\ rsc}$ for information about any conflict. Since the traffic management community has already been activated, $GC_{tmc\ vs\ rsc}$ alerts the conflict to the overall ubiquitous system or the involved participants. This is shown in Fig. 5. Based on this, traffic management community can be adjusted to operate rescue service community or vice versa.

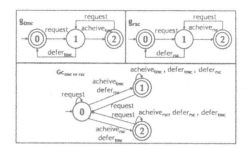

Fig. 4. Goal constraints coordination framework for the prototype

Fig. 5. A case of preventing conflicts between two communities

5 Conclusion

In a ubiquitous service system, one of the most crucial issues is closely related to conflicts which are frequently incurred at runtime when several services are invoked for realizing a specific community's goal that is organized by human's demand. This paper presents a formal model for describing a ubiquitous environment and a community and specifying actions of an individual community by means of finite state automata. For coordinating multiple communities, action and goal constraint coordination frameworks are developed.

A conflict prevention mechanism is constructed in such a way the non-blocking property is attained. With formal methodologies based on the finite state automata, the overall behavior of multiple communities is specified. The behavior is emerged by humans' demand. Therefore, the mechanism that we develop may play an important role in satisfying human's desires by controlling communities' goals.

To develop a reliable and robust ubiquitous service system while preventing conflicts incurred when two or more services are invoked. A prototype is implemented to support emergency rescue service in consideration with traffic management system.

As one of the direction for the future work, a more detailed elaboration of the proposed model is desired. In particular, the relationships among the components of a ubiquitous environment need to be specified with a temporal logic to accommodate the time-variant characteristics of services and participants.

Acknowledgement

This work was supported by Seoul R&BD and the UCN project, the ministry of Information and Communication 21st century frontier R&D program.

References

1. Kim, H., Shim, Y., Choi, D., Kim, S., Cho, W.: Community Manager: A Dynamic Collaboration Solution on Heterogeneous Environment. In: 2006 ACS/IEEE International Conference on Pervasive Services, Lyon, France, pp. 39–46. IEEE Press, Los Alamitos (2006)
2. Shim, Y., Kim, H., Kim, M., Cho, W.: A Ubiquitous System Architecture Based on the Community Computing Model. In: 2006 International Conference on Hybrid Information Technology, Cheju, Korea (2006)
3. Jung, Y., Lee, J., Kim, M.: Multi-agent based community computing system development with the model driven architecture. In: Proceedings of the fifth international joint conference on Autonomous agents and multiagent, Hakodate, Japan, pp. 1329–1331 (2006)
4. Jung, Y., Lee, J., Kim, M.: Community based Ubiquitous System Development in Multi-agent Environment. In: CAiSE 2006 Workshop Ubiquitous Mobile Information and Collaboration Systems(UMICS 2006), Luxembourg, Grand-Ducy of Luxembourg (2006)
5. Hopcroft, J.E., Motwani, R., Ullman, J.D.: Introduction to Automata Theory, Languages, and Computataion, 2nd edn. Addison-Wesley, New York (2001)
6. Castillo, I., Smith, J.S.: Formal Modeling Methodologies for Control of Manufacturing Cells: survey and comparison. Journal of Manufacturing Systems 21(1), 40–57 (2002)

A User-Centered Approach for Ubiquitous Service Evaluation: An Evaluation Metrics Focused on Human-System Interaction Capability

Joohwan Lee[1], Joobong Song[2], Hyungsup Kim[2], Junyoung Choi[2], and Myung Hwan Yun[2]

[1] POSDATA Co., LTD., Seoul, Korea
[2] Department of Industrial Engineering, Seoul National University
Seoul, 151-744 Korea
mhy@snu.ac.kr

Abstract. As the ubiquitous era took off, the interactions between ubiquitous services and users have come to take an important position. So it is necessary to develop new evaluation method that evaluates interactivity with a user-centered perspective. The main objective of this study is the development of user-centered interactivity evaluation metrics of ubiquitous service attributes. For this objective, first, existing ubiquitous service evaluation methodologies are reviewed to define the evaluation attributes for ubiquitous service evaluation. Second, user oriented interactive metrics that can overcome the limitations of those service evaluation methodologies, such as personal service evaluation techniques, usability evaluation techniques and psychometrics based evaluation techniques, are developed. As a validation study, suggested evaluation metrics is utilized to evaluate the u-home service, and priority of each metrics is derived. The suggested evaluation metrics can be used to evaluate the interactivity level of ubiquitous service and identify the potential users and their requirements at the stage of service development.

Keywords: User-Centered Design Evaluation, ubiquitous Service, Interactivity, Usability Evaluation Method (UEM).

1 Introduction

The term "ubiquitous computing" means "computing exists everywhere" and this represents the direction of the changes and development in computing that have become prominent in 2000s [1]. The services in ubiquitous computing environments changed the subjects of marketing from developers to users. That is, "consumers" as "users" have come to emerge as principal actors to create changes in today's societies along with their great influences. Consequently, the interactions between ubiquitous services and users have come to take an important position in ubiquitous industry and new approaches to practical evaluations are required due to the emergences of unverified services.

The emergence of ubiquitous services that has been transformed into the arena of state-of-the-art is being fingered as a cause adding the economic burden to users due

S. Lee et al. (Eds.): APCHI 2008, LNCS 5068, pp. 21–29, 2008.
© Springer-Verlag Berlin Heidelberg 2008

to temporary services neglecting the choices of users and one-sided services at the convenience of service providers. Commenced to overcome that vicious circle, the approach to large-scaled projects related to diverse ubiquitous services initially brought about communications among humans as well as between humans and computers. Moreover the theoretical and technological advancements of service designs to support collaborations between users [7, 8, 9], and activated user studies relating to the selections of ubiquitous services (service matching/selection method) issues for the provision of the services complying with implicit needs of users focusing on the human factors such as usability, service awareness, trust [10]. On the other hand, it brought about visual advancements in complex viewpoints such as the performances of diverse components for the evaluation of the levels and qualities of ubiquitous services that have been progressing in many places, system usability and interactions between users and systems [11, 12]. This expansion of ubiquitous industry scope resulted in the need of the development of the techniques that will enable the evaluation of new and diversified ubiquitous services from the users–centered views.

Especially, as an approach to the evaluation of the levels and qualities of ubiquitous services, a small number of researchers attempted to apply an evaluation methodology using an extension of existing service quality evaluation methodology, an application of software quality evaluation methodology and usability among core concepts of UCD (User-Centered Design). Nevertheless these approaches revealed its limitation by birth of a partial evaluation method that could not reflect the characteristics of ubiquitous services on appropriate places and evaluated only certain components of ubiquitous services. That is, excluding the attributes such as experience, motivation and engagement given importance in ubiquitous, it grafted existing service evaluation methodologies to ubiquitous environments and thereby it had the limitation that it could not evaluate the essence of ubiquitous services [13].

The main objective of this study is the development of user-centered interactivity evaluation metrics reflecting ubiquitous service attribute. For this objective, first, existing ubiquitous service evaluation methodologies are reviewed to define the evaluation attribute for ubiquitous service evaluation. Second, user oriented interactive metrics that can overcome the limitations of those service evaluation methodologies such as personal service evaluation techniques, usability evaluation techniques and psychometrics based evaluation techniques is to be developed. As a validation study, suggested evaluation metrics is utilized to evaluate u-home service.

2   The Development of Interactivity Evaluation Metrics

2.1   Development Procedures and Methodology

Figure 1 shows the processes of the development of interactivity metrics in this study. The approach to this study was composed in two parts, the development of ubiquitous service interactivity attribute index and the development of interactivity performance measurements.

The models of appropriate reference examples were too insufficient to define ubiquitous services component. Thus this study analyzed the components of the services to constitute ubiquitous services such as IT services, inter-personal services, mobile services and system services.

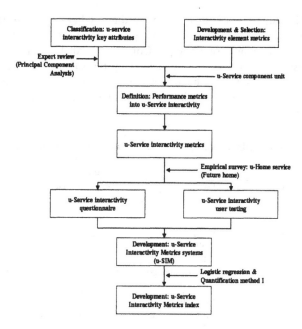

Fig. 1. Development procedures of interactivity evaluation metrics

The indices collected in literature review were integrated to define ubiquitous attribute indices and expert group (policy maker, order placer, designer, developer, standard researcher) reviews were executed to select and structuralize the indices. Interactivity measurement definitions were executed by classifying related indices by analyzing the researches related to usability measurements and ubiquitous service evaluation methods.

The indices and measurements constituted the evaluation areas (EA) of ubiquitous service components to finalize final metrics indices. Large scaled user surveys were executed on U-Home services for validation and priority weight estimation. The final metrics were developed as evaluation systems so that they can be readily applied to practices by designers to maximize utility.

2.2   Interactivity Attributes in Ubiquitous Service Environments

The interactivity attributes in ubiquitous service environments can be defined as the concept of "How easily the tasks for ubiquitous service can be executed and the user can be satisfied with results in user environments [15]". The concept of interactivity attributes can be explained in the objective aspects related to the works executed within the integrated service consisting of ubiquitous service environments, relevant services and users. The results of the researches related to users' subjective aspects were implemented in the areas such as HCI and human factor.

In order to define the interactivity attributes of ubiquitous services, extraction of interactivity attributes through literature review, selection and integration of interactivity attributes and hierarchical classification of interactivity attributes were executed.

Thirty-one ubiquitous service interactivity attribute indices first selected and integrated were structuralized through expert survey method. Those were mathematically interpreted through the results of Principal Component Analysis (PCA) and Correspondence analysis. The surveys were executed by the same evaluators in order to maintain consistency in indices deducing and relation analyses. By analyzing major components, four attribute indices with the explanation ability of 79.3% were extracted like Table 1.

Table 1. The attribute indices deduced with major component analyses

Attribute	Description
Contextualization support	· The level of the interactions considering the relations between services and users · The level of the provision of customized services through status perceptions
Service Capability support	· The level of ubiquitous service user protection and error prevention · The level of the performance, speed, security and storage ability of service systems
Ubiquity support	· The extent of the ubiquity of ubiquitous services · Ubiquitous connectivity of services and convenience in carrying devices etc
User-experience support	· User participation and the degree of effort for use of ubiquitous services · The communication direction/response level of ubiquitous service users

Figure 2 shows the structure for the proposed interactivity evaluation metrics in this study. Each sub-construct(Service capability, User experience, Ubiquity, Contextualization) is consist of detail measure metrics, and each measure metric is comprised of 10 subjective metrics and 40 objective metrics.

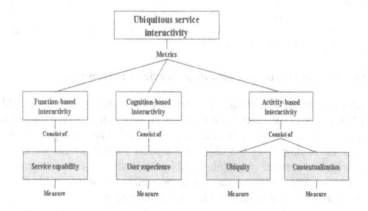

Fig. 2. Structure for ubiquitous interactivity evaluation metrics

2.3 Development of Metrics for Ubiquitous Service Interactivity

Interactivity attributes of ubiquitous services have been defined, the measurement values that can evaluate the interactivity of ubiquitous services are required. Interactivity metrics means the measures to determine the levels of interactivity factors comprising the indices indicating what measurement values should be used to evaluate the extents of interactivity. Table 2 show an example of interactivity evaluation metrics suggested in this study

Table 2. An example of interactivity evaluation metrics

Component	Attribute	Indicator	Metrics	Derived measure	Source (modified/adopted)
u-Service user	User expectation level (Perception) in relation with u-service functions	Agreement degree of service functions (SC: service concordance): ratio of expected service functions and the results. (u_1)	SC (Service Concordance) = A/B	A=Number of expected and comprehended service functions B=Number of functions provided from ubiquitous service	Constantine and Lockwood (1999)
		Participation degree of bidirectional communication, while using service. (u_2)	degree (questionnaire & user testing)	User's participating degree for bidirectional communication of ubiquitous service.	-
		Immersion degree in the service without own location-awareness, while using service. (u_3)	degree (questionnaire & user testing)	User's immersion degree in ubiquitous service.	Scholtz (2006)
		The degree of understanding input data and expecting output at service request. (u_4)	A/B or degree (questionnaire & user testing)	A=Number of expectable and performable I/O B=Number of I/O provided from ubiquitous service	ISO 25000 (2005)
		The degree of receiving unexpected service by providing unrequested service functions. (u_5)	degree (questionnaire & user testing)	Whether the implicit needs of ubiquitous service user is to be provided or not	-
		Recognized degree of wasting time while service use. (u_6)	degree (questionnaire & user testing)	Recognized degree of wasting time during using ubiquitous service	-

Table 3. An example for evaluation factors of ubiquitous service interactivity attribute

Measurable criteria		The characteristics indicator of ubiquitous service interactivity (characteristic factor)	y_1 (user experience) Participation or effort level of user to use the service	y_2 (contextualization) Provides services adequate to the situation, considered the relation of service and user	y_3 (ubiquity) Portability and pervasive connectedness	y_4 (service capability) Level of user protection and error prevention
u-Service user	User expectation level (Perception) in relation with u-service functions	Agreement degree of service functions (SC: service concordance) : ratio of expected service functions and the results. (u_1)	O	-	-	-
		Participation degree of bidirectional communication, while using service. (u_2)	S	-	-	-
		Immersion degree in the service without own location-awareness, while using service. (u_3)	S	-	-	-
		The degree of understanding input data and expecting output at service request. (u_4)	S/O	-	-	-
		The degree of receiving unexpected service by providing unrequested service functions. (u_5)	-	S	-	-
		Recognized degree of wasting time while service use. (u_6)	-	S	-	-
	User's efforts (Perception) required within u-service use	User's approved time before using the service. (u_7)	O	-	-	-
		Learning time to use new service functions. (u_8)	O	-	-	-
		Time of user spending in hesitation or hold to use the service. (u_9)	O	-	-	-
		Number of user out-of-controls during service use. (u_{10})	O	-	-	-
		Ratio to change the service contents properly to user's preference or habit automatically. (u_{11})	-	O	-	-
		Required time / degree for user to modify the service function procedure in user's convenience. (u_{12})	-	S/O	-	-
	Cognizance degree of economical response to u-service (Perception)	Distance degree that user must move additionally to receive the service at proper place and time. (u_{13})	-	S/O	-	-
		Range degree of physical spaces to recognize the status of the service. (u_{14})	-	S	-	-
		Ratio of error occurrence during service use. (u_{15})	-	O	-	-

The most important in extracting the measurement values of interactivity is whether the measurement values are suitable to evaluate the levels of relevant factors because if uncorrelated measurement values are selected, the evaluations of interactivity factors become insignificant. This study was executed in the fashion of existing studied where measurement values were analyzed to extract all the lists selectable as measurement values and subsequently determine their correlations with factors. Table 3 shows the correlations between evaluation factors and ubiquitous service interactivity attribute.

3 Case Study

The experimental subject consists in the dimension of $125.6m^2$ and provides 17 ubiquitous service items. The items consist of the three parts, i.e. facial recognitions for entrance, the door of future, UPIS (Ubiquitous Parking Information System), etc., media table relating to home network control, bidirectional TV relating to multimedia, medical camera relating to health, u-Health, intelligence healthy menu system, therapy music, light control, custom short message relating to living, magic mirror, digital frame, product information built-in OLED (Organic Light Emitting Diodes), Family collaborated learning system relating to education, etc. (figure 3). 118 participants (59 males, 49 females) evaluated the service, the evaluation was conducted by interactivity evaluation metrics for PDA.

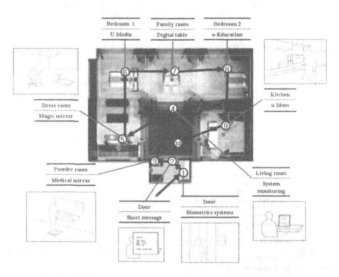

Fig 3. U-Home service evaluation process (10 stages)

The process of reasoning influence variable and deducing the model analyzing data gathered by interactivity evaluation of ubiquitous service is executed as follows. First, the basic statistical characteristics which the data itself includes will be analyzed through descriptive statistic analysis. In addition to, the characteristics of metrics are investigated based on the result of objective and subjective evaluation. Second, using cronbach alpha value and ANOVA, it is checked whether measured data of design value and subjective measured factors gathered for interactivity evaluation, provide meaning result or not. Third, establishing design variable level by K-mean grouping method, it is analyzed whether each group has statistical meaning influence. Fourth, result and model of design variable defined by using I-type quantification analysis, are defined. It is figurable how each design variable level influence interactivity by analysis, and the size of influence power between design variables which effects to interactivity as deducing partial correlation will be established.

Figure 4 is the result of computing the importance of the factors deduced by the experiment. Since the results of the importance of each dependent variable are different from each other, estimate value of each descriptive variables were converted into normalized-value. By the result of the modeling, the most important variable of the ubiquitous service interactivity properties was contextualization support attributes, 'perception: time ratio(correcting time for service procedure)' metrics had the largest importance as a dependent variable, and 'perception: user control level using service manipulation' metrics was a dependent variable containing negative effects.

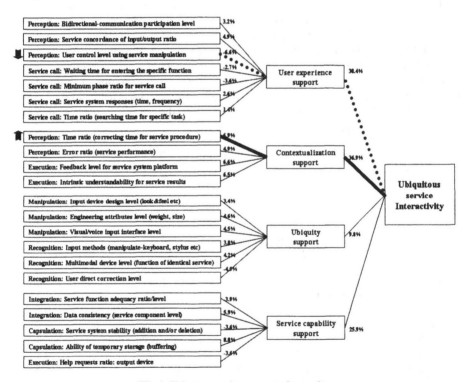

Fig 4. U-home service case study results

4   Conclusion and Discussion

The summary of results in this study is as follows. First, we have suggested the metrics for the ubiquitous service that are experienced in real life, and introduced the concept of ubiquitous service interactivity. Second, as a validation of the developed metrics, we applied the proposed metrics at the evaluation of the interactivity of U-home service. Through the statistical analysis of evaluation data, the subjective satisfaction model of interactivity was developed with the various components of interactivity of ubiquitous service using I-type quantification analysis. As a result, the 22 main components which are consist of contextualization, ubiquity, user experience and service capability and the relationships between each main component and their sub-components were identified.

As referred previously, there have been many attempts to develop the design guideline, metrics, and evaluation techniques for the ubiquitous computing, but there were no contents for the user's evaluation on the service. Most of research methods concerning the ubiquitous environment are the same as conventional ones in the IT era. Therefore, they cannot fully reflect the characteristics of ubiquitous service. To select a space-time, that is necessary for the realization of ubiquitous service among many space-times that the user comes to confront and to serve a service appropriate to the characteristics of each space-time, we need the evaluation methodology that comprehends the importance of space-time and reflects its characteristics. The conventional user evaluation techniques cannot satisfy this condition. It is because the conventional techniques have focused on evaluating the quality of specific applications [14].

It can be used to analyze the potential users of the service by evaluating the interactive level of ubiquitous service. Its application to the stage of service development can be helpful in collecting the demands of potential service users and apprehending their levels. In this situation that the boundary between product and service is disappearing, we may extend the utility evaluation concept of "everyday product" to the evaluation concept of interactivity.

Acknowledgments. This work was supported in part by the Seoul R&BD program at Seoul National University.

References

1. Norman, D.A.: Invisible Computing; Why Good Products Can Fail. In: The Personal Computer Is So Complex and Information Appliances Are the Solution, MIT Press, Cambridge (1999)
2. Jo, W.D., Lee, K.J., Lee, H.K., Kwon, O.B., Kim, K.G., Lee, E.J.: Ubiquitous Paradigm and u-Society, Jinhan M&B Inc. Korea (2006)
3. Aarts, E., Marzano, S.: The New Everyday: Views on Ambient Intelligence. Uitgeverij 010 Publishers, Rotterdam, Netherlands (2003)
4. Lyytinen, K., Yoo, Y.: Issues and challenges in Ubiquitous Computing. Communications of the ACM 45(12), 63–65 (2002)
5. Langheinrich, M.: A privacy awareness system for ubiquitous computing environments. In: Borriello, G., Holmquist, L.E. (eds.) UbiComp 2002. LNCS, vol. 2498, Springer, Heidelberg (2002)
6. Hull, R., Reid, J., Kidd, A.: Experience Design in Ubiquitous Computing. Client and Media Systems Laboratory, HP Technical Report: HPL-2002-115 (2002)
7. Resnick, P.: Beyond Bowling Together; SocioTechnical Capital. In: Carroll, J.M. (ed.) Human-Computer Interaction in the New Millennium, Addison-Wesley, ACM Press, NY (2001)

8. Takemoto, M., Sunage, H., Tanaka, K., Matsumura, H., Shinohara, E.: The Ubiquitous Service-Oriented Network (USON) An approach for a ubiquitous world based on P2P technology. In: Proceedings 2nd International Conference on Peer-to-Peer Computing (2002)

9. Blaine, A.P., Karim, A., Bashar, N.: Keeping ubiquitous computing to yourself: A practical model for user control of privacy. International Journal of Human-Computer Studies 63, 228–253 (2005)

10. Lindenberg, J., Pasman, W., Kranenborg, K., Stegeman, J., Neerincx, M.A.: Improving service matching and selection in ubiquitous computing environments: a user study. Personal and Ubiquitous Computing 11, 59–68 (2007)

11. Williams, J.R.: Developing Performance Support for Computer Systems: a Strategy for Maximizing Usability and Learnability. CRC Press, Boca Raton (2004)

12. Iqbal, R., Sturm, J., Kulyk, O., Wang, J., Terken, J.: User-Centered Design and Evaluation of Ubiquitous Services. In: 23rd Annual International Conference on Design of Communication (SIGDOC 2005), Coventry, UK, pp. 138–145 (2005)

13. Abowd, G.D.: Software design issues for ubiquitous computing. In: Proceedings of VLSI(Very Large Scale Integration) System Level Design, IEEE Computer Society Workshop 1998, USA (1998)

14. Bing, J.W.: Developing a Consulting Tool to Measure Process Change on Global Teams: The Global Team Process QuestionnaireTM. In: Proceedings of Academy of Human Resource Development Conference 2001, UK (2001)

15. Siewiorek, D.P.: New frontiers of Application Design. Communication of the ACM (CACM) 45, 79–82 (2002)

On Generating Backbone Trees through Robust Multi-hop Clusters in Wireless Sensor Networks

Inyoung Shin[1], Moonseong Kim[2], and Hyunseung Choo[1,*]

[1] School of Information and Communication Engineering
Sungkyunkwan University, Korea
yamaco3826@skku.edu, choo@ece.skku.ac.kr
[2] Electrical and Computer Engineering
Michigan State University, USA
mkim@msu.edu

Abstract. Routing through a backbone, which is responsible for performing and managing multipoint communication, reduces the communication overhead and overall energy consumption in wireless sensor networks. However, the backbone nodes will need extra functionality and therefore consume more energy compared to the other nodes. The unbalanced power consumption among sensor nodes may cause a network partition and failures. Hence optimal construction of the backbone is one of the pivotal problems in sensor network applications. In this paper a distributed algorithm is proposed to generate backbone trees through robust multi-hop clusters in wireless sensor networks. The main objective is to form a properly designed backbone through multi-hop clusters by considering energy level and degree of each node. Comprehensive computer simulations have indicated that the newly proposed scheme gives approximately 58.6% and 79.42% improvements in the performances related to the residual energy level and the degree of the cluster heads respectively.

Keywords: Wireless sensor networks, Backbone, Clustering, Energy efficient, Robustness, Load balancing.

1 Introduction

Wireless sensor networks have a wide range of potential applications, including environment monitoring, military uses, and remote medical systems [1]. Although establishing correct routes for the communications between the nodes is an important research topic in sensor networks, energy-efficient routing is the more recent key issue since the node's battery is the most critical limitation factor. Power failure of a node affects its ability to forward data packets of others as well as its own, thus the overall network lifetime will be seriously reduced. For this reason, many related schemes for energy-efficient routing have been proposed.

Since sensor nodes are severely constrained by the amount of battery power available, extensive research has focused on how to prolong the lifetime of a network. The

---

*Corresponding author.

S. Lee et al. (Eds.): APCHI 2008, LNCS 5068, pp. 30–39, 2008.
© Springer-Verlag Berlin Heidelberg 2008

lifetime of a sensor network is defined as the time after which one sensor node depletes its batteries, resulting in a routing hole within the network. A single-hop clustering algorithm can reduce the power consumption since only a fraction of the nodes, called cluster heads, communicate with the sink in one hop.

However, a single-hop clustering algorithm is impractical because nodes at a greater distance than one hop from the sink do not have adequate transmission power to communicate with the sink [2]. Even though the multi-hop model would be a more practical approach to solving this problem, it can increase the communication overhead and costs required to obtain the routing information in large-scale networks. In view of these issues, routing through a backbone could reduce the communication overhead and overall energy consumption in wireless sensor networks [3].

However, backbone nodes require extra functionality and therefore consume more energy compared to the other ordinary nodes in the network. The unbalanced power consumption among the sensor nodes may cause a network partition and failures where transmission from some sensors to the sink node could be blocked. Since the traffic load and power consumption of the backbone nodes is high, the lifetime of a sensor network can be limited by the nodes with heavier traffic load.

Hence optimal construction of the backbone is one of the pivotal problems in sensor network applications and can drastically affect the network's communication energy dissipation. In this paper, we describe a modification of the Max-Min D-Cluster's cluster head selection [6] by considering the residual energy level and the degree of each node in the head selection process. The main objective is to avoid choosing nodes with lower residual energy and degree as cluster head by considering two additional parameters for each node. Since evenly consumed energy among the nodes in the network is the desired objective of our scheme its use could extend the lifetime of the sensor network.

The rest of this paper is organised as follows: in section 2, related works are introduced and discussed; this is followed in section 3 where a robust multi-hop cluster formation scheme for wireless sensor networks is presented. The performance of the proposed scheme is evaluated in section 4 and section 5 concludes with the main findings and contributions of the research.

2   Related Work

2.1   Traditional Energy Efficient Routing Protocol

LEACH (Low Energy Adaptive Clustering Hierarchy) [7] has been proposed which is a clustering-based protocol that randomly rotates cluster-heads to evenly distribute the energy load among the sensors in the network. In addition, LEACH is able to incorporate data fusion into the routing protocol to reduce the amount of information that must be transmitted to the sink. This achieves a large reduction in the energy dissipation, as computation requires negligible amount of energy than communication. However, LEACH uses single-hop routing where each node can transmit directly to the cluster head and the sink. Therefore, in a large-scale sensor networks, comprised of thousands of sensors, this is infeasible due to the limited transmission power.

The multi-hop model is a more practical approach to solve this problem. In this model, data hops from one node to another until it reaches the sink. In view of the limited transmission range of the sensor nodes, this is a viable approach and most nodes can connect to the network and transmit their message to the sink. Therefore, the coverage area of the sensor and sink in this model is an improvement over the one-hop model. However, since all nodes in the sensor network participate in the route discovery phase, the conventional multi-hop routing protocols cause data communication problems, such as unnecessary communication overhead and broadcasting storm .

2.2 Routing Protocol through a Backbone

Routing through a backbone, which is responsible for performing and managing multipoint communication (routing, multicasting and broadcasting), reduces the communication overhead and overall energy consumption in wireless sensor networks. The advantage of a backbone is that the generation and spreading of the routing information can be restricted in a set of particular nodes rather than through all the nodes in the network. Therefore the increase in the additional overhead for transmitting the extra communications through the network is considerably less than the traditional flooding methods of multi-hop models.

Several protocols for constructing the required backbone have been proposed [4]. The HCDD method (Hierarchical Cluster-based Data Dissemination) [8] has been proposed to form the backbone just adopting Max-Min D-Cluster in wireless ad hoc network. In large networks the single-hop cluster may generate a large number of cluster heads and eventually lead to the same problem of flooding. Since the flooding is energy consuming and should be avoided whenever possible in energy-scarce wireless sensor networks, the formation of D-hop cluster which consists of nodes at most d hops from a cluster head is appropriate. Additionally, this heuristic provides load balancing among cluster heads to insure a fair distribution of load among cluster heads. However, there are many differences between ad hoc network and sensor network, so applying ad hoc protocol to wireless sensor network generally is unsuitable for several reasons; these include the following:

A. The sensor nodes are limited in power, computational capacities, and memory;
B. In most works, all sensor nodes are assumed to be homogeneous, having equal capacity in terms of computation, communication and power;
C. Aside from the very few setups that utilize mobile sensors, most of the networks assume that sensor nodes are stationary.

The selection of a cluster head nodes based on Max-Min D-Cluster for the backbone follows a pre-assigned node ID. There is a high possibility to elect nodes with lower residual energy and degree as cluster heads and this significantly affects the overall network performance. In this case, since backbone nodes require extra functionality and therefore consume more energy than the other ordinary nodes, this result in earlier routing hole within the network.

Moreover this clustering approach is effective in the field of ad-hoc networks where the nodes are constantly moving. In unattended sensor networks the location of the sensors is normally fixed once they are deployed. Since cluster head selection on

Max-Min D-Cluster is based on highest IDs and sensor are normally stationary, the same node will be picked as the cluster head every time, resulting in a rapid energy drain on this sensor. Therefore the proposed scheme considers other parameters such as residual energy and degree of each node rather than only node's ID for selecting the cluster head candidates and we have modified the existing routing protocol for wireless sensor network by solving the above-mentioned difficulties.

3   Proposed Scheme

3.1   Network Model and Basic Scheme

This paper considers routing through a backbone which is restricted in a set of particular nodes to reduce the communication overhead for route discovery and the number of active nodes in wireless sensor networks. A typical approach to backbone formation is to partition the network into clusters made up of a cluster head and ordinary nodes. Then the cluster heads are linked to form the connected backbone. As the cluster heads, which are mostly made up of the backbone, consume more energy than the ordinary nodes, it is important to construct a robust backbone and balance the power consumption of all nodes in order to prolong the network lifetime in the wireless sensor network.

The robustness of the nodes in the backbone and the balance of energy consumption can be improved by choosing nodes with the higher residual energy level or degree as the cluster heads. Constructing a robust backbone by selecting nodes with higher energy level could extend the lifetime of the network. Additionally, choosing nodes with higher degree as the cluster heads could distribute the responsibility of packet forwarding among neighbors of the cluster heads and even out the power consumption.

In the proposed scheme each node propagates the flooding value for 2D rounds to form a D-hop cluster in which the node is at most D hops from a cluster head. The algorithm selects a cluster head based on the flooding value of each round, and then they are connected to form the backbone. The flooding value function takes both the node's residual energy level and degree into account by using the following criterion:

$$f(Node\_ID,\omega) = \omega(\frac{E_{residual}}{E_{initial}}) + (1-\omega)(\frac{Degree}{\max\{Degree\ in\ neighbor\ set\}}) \qquad (1)$$

Let $f(Node\_ID,\omega)$ denote the flooding value of the node with $Node\_ID$; ω is the weight factor which adjusts the priority and $\omega \in [0,1]$. A large ω gives more weight to the node's residual energy level than to the degree. $E_{initial}$ is the initial energy of the node and $E_{residual}$ is the residual energy. Degree is the number of nodes which are within the node's transmission range, namely its neighbors and $\max\{Degree\ in\ neighbor\ set\}$ is the largest degree among the neighbor set of the node with $Node\_ID$. Note that $\frac{E_{residual}}{E_{initial}} \in [0,1]$ and $\frac{Degree}{\max\{Degree\ in\ neighbor\ set\}} \in [0,1]$.

Suppose $\dfrac{E_{residual}}{E_{initial}}$ remains constant; in this case, the flooding value increases when the degree increases. On the other hand, suppose $\dfrac{Degree}{\max\{Degree\ in\ neighbor\ set\}}$ and $E_{initial}$ are constant; in this case, the flooding value increases as $E_{residual}$ increases.

3.2 Cluster Formation

The proposed cluster formation mainly consists of three steps. Firstly, each node calculates its initial flooding value, as mentioned in the previous section, and maintains the 2D sized flooding value array. This is used to set the selecting flooding value into the arrays of the nodes for each round. Secondly, this is followed by the FloodMax and FloodMin stages; each stage is D round run, which is made to propagate the flooding value in each node's d-neighborhood. At the FloodMax stage, each node broadcasts its flooding value to all of its 1-hop neighbors, and then it chooses the largest flooding value from the received values and its own flooding value. Each node then sets this as its new flooding value. This procedure continues for D rounds. The FloodMin stage is the same as FloodMax except a node chooses the smallest rather than the largest value as its new flooding value. Finally, after the FloodMax/FloodMin stage, each node looks at the round's flooding value to best determine their cluster.

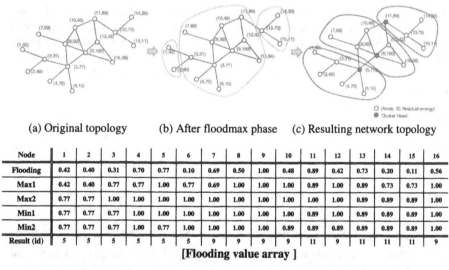

(a) Original topology   (b) After floodmax phase   (c) Resulting network topology

Node	1	2	3	4	5	6	7	8	9	10	11	12	13	14	15	16
Flooding	0.42	0.40	0.31	0.70	0.77	0.10	0.69	0.50	1.00	0.48	0.89	0.42	0.73	0.20	0.11	0.56
Max1	0.42	0.40	0.77	0.77	1.00	0.77	0.69	1.00	1.00	1.00	0.89	1.00	0.89	0.73	0.73	1.00
Max2	0.77	0.77	1.00	1.00	1.00	1.00	1.00	1.00	1.00	1.00	1.00	1.00	0.89	0.89	0.89	1.00
Min1	0.77	0.77	0.77	1.00	1.00	1.00	1.00	1.00	1.00	1.00	0.89	1.00	0.89	0.89	0.89	1.00
Min2	0.77	0.77	0.77	1.00	0.77	1.00	1.00	1.00	1.00	0.89	0.89	0.89	0.89	0.89	0.89	1.00
Result (id)	5	5	5	5	5	5	9	9	9	9	11	9	11	11	11	9

[Flooding value array]

Fig. 1. The step by step demonstration for 2-hop clustering (Weight factor= 1)

Fig. 1 shows a step by step demonstration of 2-hop clustering. Fig. 1(a) shows a network topology generated with 16 nodes. For simplicity it is assumed that the weight factor is 1. After the FloodMax phase, in Fig. 1(b), eleven nodes among the sixteen nodes keep node 9's flooding value which is the largest value in the network. Since the FloodMax is a kind of greedy algorithm then similar-sized clusters should be formed throughout the FloodMin phase for a balanced load of each cluster head.

Fig. 1(c) shows the resulting network topology. Here it can be seen that there are three cluster heads of which the energy level is higher than those of other nodes, namely nodes 5, 9, 11 and three similar-sized clusters.

3.3 Cluster Head Selection

After completion of the FloodMin, each node checks its 2D logged entries for the 2D rounds of flooding to best determine their cluster head based on four rules. The following rules explain the steps that each node runs. Firstly, if a node receives its own flooding value in the FloodMin stage, it declares itself a cluster head and skips the rest. All nodes that are active during the last round of the Floodmax elect themselves as cluster heads. In other words, since these nodes have the largest flooding values, they have higher residual energy level or degree. Secondly, once a node has the same flooding value appearing in both the FloodMax and FloodMin stages, its cluster head is node having this flooding value as its initial flooding value. If there are more than two, the minimum value is selected. Thirdly, each node selects the maximum flooding value in the FloodMax stage and it choose node having this flooding value as its initial flooding value as cluster head. After the cluster head selection, each node broadcasts its elected cluster head's ID to all of its neighbors. If a node receives a different node ID, this node becomes a gateway node. Finally, in the case of a cluster head being on the path between an ordinary node and its elected cluster head, the ordinary node chooses the cluster head with the shortest hops.

4 Performance Evaluation

4.1 Simulation Environment

The network simulation is implemented in C and the simulations refer to scenarios in which 500 static wireless nodes with a maximum transmission radius of 30 metres are randomly and uniformly scattered in a geographic square area of 300 x 300 metres. We make the assumption that two nodes are neighbors if and only if their Euclidean distance is $\leq 30m$. We call the network topology a graph and the topologies generated by drawing edges between each pair of nodes as neighbors. Each node has the same initial energy and its residual energy level is randomly assigned. The equation of $N \approx \frac{a}{r^2} \times d$ holds for the common case where N is the number of nodes in the network, r is transmission range, d is the node density which is the average number of nodes in the network field and a is the length of one side of the network field. We measure four different properties of the system based on a variety of metrics.

A. The average residual energy (or degree) of the cluster heads: Constructing robust clusters by selecting nodes with higher energy level as a cluster head could prolong the network's lifetime. Moreover the cluster heads with higher degree could distribute their responsibility of packet forwarding. Consequently, the power consumption of all the sensors in wireless sensor network is as balanced as possible and the network lifetime will be extended.

B. The standard deviation of the cluster heads' residual energy (degree): The standard deviation of residual energy (degree) gives a good evaluation of distribution of cluster heads' residual energy (degree). The $\sigma = \sqrt{\dfrac{\sum_{i}^{N}(x_i - \bar{x})^2}{N}}$ equation holds for the common cases where 'σ^2' is the variance in the system, N is the number of nodes, x is sample value and $\bar{x}$ is the average value. In order to keep the system close to the average value, we choose an objective function that minimizes the variance of the cardinality of each cluster head in the system.

C. The standard deviation of the cluster size: The cluster size means the number of noes in a cluster and therefore the deviation of the cluster size shows the spread of the number of nodes in each cluster. A small standard deviation indicates that there is a tendency to evenly distribute the load among the cluster heads, that is, the network is divided into similar sized sub-networks and hence the responsibility is distributed evenly across the cluster heads.

D. Backbone robustness: This metric is important for assessing the application of clustering and backbone formation to networks whose nodes are energy constrained. This provides an indirect measure on how long the network will be operational before requiring backbone reorganization. Since backbone recomputation may impose a non-negligible burden to the network constructing robust backbone could eliminate unnecessary energy consumption for frequent backbone reorganization.

4.2 Simulation Results

In this section, we present the results obtained from the simulation. To evaluate the performance of our algorithm, the results are compared with the Max-Min D-Cluster (ID Based clustering).

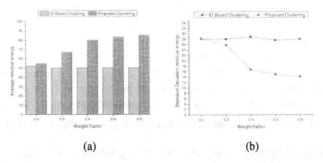

(a)   (b)

Fig. 2. Residual energy of cluster heads. (a) Average residual energy (b) The standard deviation of residual energy.

As shown in Fig. 2(a), the proposed scheme elects the cluster heads with the higher residual energy level than the Max-Min as the weight factor increases. It is clearly seen that a cluster head consumes more energy compared to the other nodes in the network because they handle all inter-cluster traffic as has been mentioned already. Therefore it is important to construct a robust cluster for the backbone based network

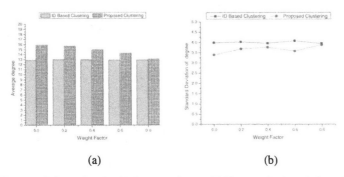

(a)   (b)

Fig. 3. Degree of cluster heads. (a) Average degree (b) The standard deviation of degree

to maximize network lifetime. Fig. 2(b) compares the standard deviation of the residual energy of the cluster heads with Max-Min where it is seen that in our proposed scheme nodes with higher residual energy level are selected as the cluster heads when the weight factor is close to 1.

As shown in Fig. 3(a), the proposed scheme selects the cluster head with higher degree than the Max-Min as the weight factor decreases. Nodes closer to the cluster head have heavier traffic load for packet forwarding, therefore cluster heads with higher degree will relieve the unbalanced power consumption by distributing their loads among their neighboring nodes. Fig. 3(b) shows the standard deviation of the degree of the cluster heads comparing with those obtained via the Max-Min where we can see that the result of the proposed scheme is lower than the Max-Min.

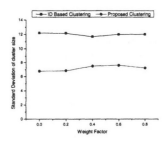

Fig. 4. The standard deviation of the cluster size

Fig. 4 indicates that the proposed scheme provides good load balancing among the cluster heads and ensures a fair distribution of load among them because the difference of the number of nodes in each cluster is small even for large scale sensor networks. Moreover, the weight factor does not affect the cluster size in any significant way. The proposed scheme guarantees even cluster sizing and hence network partition problems and shortening of the network lifetime caused by unbalanced power consumption among clusters will be avoided.

We measure the number of messages that are forwarded by the backbone node that depletes its power supply and, hence, causes backbone disconnection or the uncovering of ordinary nodes. This is the metric that provides an indirect measure on how

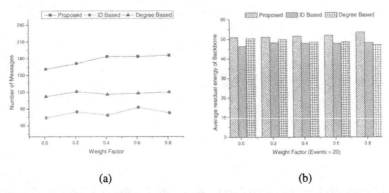

(a)   (b)

Fig. 5. Backbone robustness. (a) Results for the number of messages associated with the nodes that consume the maximum amount of power and, hence, causes the network partition (b) Average residual energy of backbone after 20 events occur.

long the network will be operational before requiring backbone recomputation. Fig 5(a) shows the proposed scheme with the highest number of message followed by Degree Based [5] then finally the ID Based. The backbone network of proposed scheme will be operational for long time, so the overhead cost for backbone reorganization could be reduced. Fig 5(b) shows the average residual energy of backbone after 20 events occur. The proposed method can always perform better than the Degree-based and ID-based method because of backbone node with higher residual energy and degree.

5   Conclusion

In this paper, we describe a modification of the Max-Min D-Cluster's cluster head selection by considering the residual energy level and the degree of each node. This enables us to select favor nodes with higher energy level or degree in the cluster head selection process. An optimal cluster head selection is the pivotal problem in sensor network applications for various reasons. First, since the cluster heads have extra functionality and consume more energy compared to the other nodes in the network. Therefore construction of robust clusters by selecting nodes with higher energy level as the cluster heads could prolong the network lifetime. Second, the sensors transmit their sensed information to the cluster heads in a multi-hop manner. As a result, the sensor nodes closer to the cluster heads tend to exhaust their energy earlier due to their power consumption for packet forwarding. However cluster heads with higher degree can distribute the responsibility of the data packet forwarding to their neighbors. Consequently, the power consumption of all sensors in the wireless sensor network is balanced. Simulation results have revealed that the proposed scheme can construct robust multi-hop clusters and provide the method which can balance each sensor node's power consumption and prolong the network lifetime.

Acknowledgments. This research was supported by MKE, Korea under ITRC IITA-2008-(C1090-0801-0046).

References

1. Akyildiz, I.F., Su, W., Sankarasubramaniam, Y., Cayirci, E.: A Survey on Sensor Networks. IEEE Communications Magazine, 102–114 (August, 2002)
2. Akkaya, K., Younis, M.: A Survey of Routing Protocols in Wireless Sensor Networks. Elsevier Ad Hoc Network Journal 3(3), 325–349 (2005)
3. Cheng, X., Du, D.-Z.: Virtual Backbone-Based Routing in Multihop Ad Hoc Wireless Networks. IEEE Transactions on Parallel and Distributed Systems (2001)
4. Cheng, X., Narahari, B., Simha, R., Cheng, M.X., Liu, D.: Strong Minimum Energy Topology in Wireless Sensor Networks: NP-Completeness and Heuristics. IEEE Transactions on Mobile Computing 2(3) (July-September, 2003)
5. Gerla, M., Tsai, J.T.-C.: Multicluster, mobile, multimedia radio network. ACM Baltzer Journal of Wireless Networks 1(3), 255–265 (1995)
6. Amis, A.D., Prakash, R., Huynh, D., Vuong, T.: Max-Min D-Cluster Formation in Wireless Ad Hoc Networks. In: Proceedings of IEEE INFOCOM 2000, March 2000, pp. 32–41 (2000)
7. Heinzelman, W.R., Chandrakasan, A., Balakrishnan, H.: Energy-Efficient Communication Protocol for Wireless Microsensor Networks. In: Proceedings of IEEE HICSS (Hawaii International Conference on System Sciences) (January 2000)
8. Lin, C.-J., Chou, P.-L., Chou, C.-F.: HCDD: Hierarchical Cluster-based Data Dissemination in Wireless Sensor Networks with Mobile Sink. In: Proceedings of ACM International Conference on Wireless Communications and Mobile Computing, pp. 1189–1194 (2006)

Denial of Sleeping: Performance Analysis and Counteracting Strategy

Vladimir Shakhov[1] and Hyunseung Choo[2]

[1] Institute of Computational Mathematics and Mathematical Geophysics,
Siberian Branch of Russian Academy of Science,
Novosibirsk, 630090, Russia
shakhov@skku.edu
[2] School of Information and Communication Engineering,
Sungkyunkwan University,
Suwon 440-746, South Korea
choo@ece.skku.ac.kr

Abstract. Denial of Sleeping is a novel type of potential attacks in wireless network. The object of the attack is a sensor node's power supply. To make sensors inexpensive so that they can be economically deployed in large numbers, they generally have very limited battery capability. Thus, a lifetime of a sensor is degraded under Denial of Sleeping attack. In this paper a mathematical model for performance evaluation of the attack is offered. Counteracting against the intrusion is discussed.

Keywords: Wireless sensor networks, Denial of Service, Denial of sleeping, Energy consumption.

1 Introduction

Enhancement of wireless sensors is a trend of modern IT industry. Sensors become smart and get new features. Users receive an additional service. On the other hand the vulnerability of sensors is also grows. The wireless sensors area is attractive for malefactor by the following reasons:

- This technology is relatively new and corresponding defense tools are poor.
- A sensor is usually open for environment.
- A sensor can contact with huge number of other mobile devices. It is a good facility for infection extension.
- A malefactor can easy keep anonymity.

Thus, it is very important to investigate potential attacks against sensors. It helps us to counteract future threats. In this paper we consider a relatively novel type of attack named Denial of Sleeping at which the object of the attack is a sensor node's power supply. To make sensors inexpensive so that they can be economically deployed in large numbers, they generally have very limited battery capability. Thus, a lifetime of a sensor is degraded under Denial of Sleeping attack. In the literature there are a lot of examples of attacks against electronic devices or personal data. Most of investigations

S. Lee et al. (Eds.): APCHI 2008, LNCS 5068, pp. 40–47, 2008.

are focused on data confidentiality and network integrity. Facilities of Denial of Service (DoS) attack in sensor networks are considered in [1]. Jamming attacks, when a jammer block the channel and prevent data transmission, is investigated in [2]. DoS attacks against a battery-powered device's energy supply are mentioned in [3]. A paper provides some description for the effect of Denial of Sleeping. But this does not contain an adequate model for performance analysis. Moreover, attacks based on possibility of unauthorized increase of transmitting power for wireless communication devices have not been considered. The Denial of Sleeping attack can be organized like jamming. But in the case of jamming a channel is blocked and sensors cannot communicate. Under novel attack, sensor can communicate but they have to spend a lot of energy. It also can be reason of noise and degradations to the electromagnetic compatibility of neighbor sensors. Thus, the goal of intrusions is Denial of Service.

The rest of the paper is organized as follows. In Section II we analyze possible scenarios of the intrusion and provide models for performance analysis of the attack. In Section III we discuss a method for intrusions counteracting. Finally, we conclude the paper with Section IV.

2 Denial of Sleeping

There are a few ways for organizing Denial of Sleeping attack. Energy loss can be caused by collisions, control packet overhead, overhearing, idle listening etc. If a sensor cannot adaptively change a power of transmission then the intrusion is equivalent to well-known DDoS attack in sensor networks named jamming [2]. If a sensor can counteract against a noise by increasing of power transmission then the object of attack is a battery of sensor. As we mentioned before, a cost of sensor components is a critical consideration in the design of practical sensor networks. A cost of sensor network increases with sensor battery power. It is often economically advantageous to discard a sensor rather than sensor recharging. By this reason a battery power is usually a scare component in wireless devices. It causes wireless sensor networks vulnerability.

A success of the attack depends on embedded algorithm of sensor power control. Other important factor is a protocol of sensor remote control in centralized network. A possible goal of intrusion can be a batteries discharge of some core nodes, which results in violation of network connectivity. Let us estimate an effect of the attack.

2.1 Mathematical Model

We offer a model of sensors behavior based on Markov chain with an absorbing state. Assume a firmware of sensors supports sleeping/idle mode. It is a wide used approach of energy consumption. Thus, a sensor can get three following stages:

Sleep/idle stage – sensor does not transmit any data;
Transmit stage – a sensor transmits some data;
OFF stage – a battery of sensor is exhausted and a sensor is failed.
Let us remark that a sensor is vulnerable in the Trans-mission stage only.

Let the function $a(t)$ be the intensity of sensors activating. This function is defined by MAC protocols for lifetime prolongation. Here and below, t is current time. Let the intensity of sensors deactivating and placing in the sleep/idle mode be $d(t)$. The function $d(t)$ is defined by target behavior and current capacity of sensor battery. The failure rate is $f(t)$. It is defined by offered load and power of a noise generator (intrusion intensity). The properties of introduced function of intensities are defined by concrete applications. The state diagram is given in Figure 1.

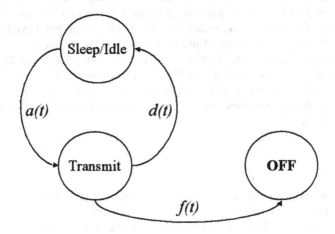

Fig. 1. The state diagram of a sensor under the attack

Thus, probabilities of sensor states are described by the following system of differential equations:

$$\frac{dp_{sleep}(t)}{dt} = -a(t)p_{sleep}(t) + d(t)p_{Tr}(t),$$

$$\frac{dp_{Tr}(t)}{dt} = a(t)p_{sleep}(t) - (d(t) + f(t))p_{Tr}(t),$$

$$\frac{dp_{off}(t)}{dt} = f(t)p_{Tr}(t).$$

To solve the system we have to use the normalization condition:

$$p_{sleep} + p_{Tr} + p_{off} = 1.$$

2.2 Analytical Solution

Assume that the intensities of sensor activating/deactivating and failure rate are deterministic functions. Combining the normalization condition, third and second equations of the system above, we obtain

$$\frac{1}{f} p''_{off} + \left(1 + \frac{a+d}{f}\right) p'_{off} + a p_{off} = a$$

If we replace $p_{off} - 1$ by z we obtain the homogeneous linear differential equation as follows:

$$\frac{1}{f} z''_{off} + \left(1 + \frac{a+d}{f}\right) z'_{off} + a z = 0.$$

The corresponding characteristic equation is

$$\frac{1}{f} \lambda^2 + \left(1 + \frac{a+d}{f}\right) \lambda + a = 0.$$

It is clear that $a>0$, $d>0$, $f>0$. Therefore

$$\left(\left(1 + \frac{a}{f}\right) + \frac{d}{f}\right)^2 - \frac{4a}{f} > \left(1 + \frac{a}{f}\right)^2 - \frac{4a}{f} = \left(1 - \frac{a}{f}\right)^2 \geq 0$$

Hence, the characteristic equation has two distinguish real roots. From here, the general solution of the equation above:

$$z = C_1 e^{-\lambda_1 t} + C_2 e^{-\lambda_2 t},$$

where C_1 and C_2 are some constants and

$$\lambda_1 = \frac{1}{2}\left(\beta f + \sqrt{(\beta f)^2 - 4af}\right),$$

$$\lambda_2 = \frac{1}{2}\left(\beta f - \sqrt{(\beta f)^2 - 4af}\right),$$

$$\beta = 1 + \frac{a+d}{f}.$$

Thus,

$$p_{off}(t) = C_1 e^{-\lambda_1 t} + C_2 e^{-\lambda_2 t} + 1.$$

It is reasonable to assume that

$$p_{off}(0) = 0.$$

Therefore,

$$C_1 + C_2 = -1.$$

From the last equation of the initial system of differential equations we get

$$p_{Trf}(t) = -\frac{1}{f}\left(C_1\lambda_1 e^{-\lambda_1 t} + C_2\lambda_2 e^{-\lambda_2 t}\right).$$

Hence

$$p_{Tr}(0) = -\frac{1}{f}\left(C_1\lambda_1 + C_2\lambda_2\right).$$

From here we find the constants:

$$C_1 = \frac{fp_{Tr}(0) - \lambda_2}{\lambda_2 - \lambda_1}; \quad C_2 = \frac{fp_{Tr}(0) - \lambda_1}{\lambda_1 - \lambda_2}.$$

We can define the probabilities $p_{sleep}(t)$ and $p_{Tr}(t)$. But for our purpose it is enough to know the function $p_{off}(t)$ only. Actually, remark that the $p_{off}(t)$ is the probability that a sensor has failed at or before time t. Thus, the reliability of a sensor is

$$R(t) = 1 - p_{off}(t).$$

Hence, the average sensor lifetime LT under attack is given by

$$LT = \int_0^\infty R(t)dt.$$

It is a main security performance metric.

2.3 Numerical Example

Assume, $a=f=2$, $d=2.5$ (events per a time unit), $p_{Tr}(0)=1$. Then

$$p_{off}(t) = 1 - \frac{2}{3}e^{-t} - \frac{1}{3}e^{-4t}.$$

The mean time to failure

$$LT\Big|_{p_{Tr}(0)=1} = \int_0^\infty \left(\frac{2}{3}e^{-t} + \frac{1}{3}e^{-4t}\right)dt = 0.75.$$

For the same intensity and $p_{Tr}(0)=1$ (i.e. given that at the initial time a sensor is sleeping) we get

$$p_{off}(t) = 1 - \frac{4}{3}e^{-t} + \frac{1}{3}e^{-4t},$$

and

$$LT\Big|_{p_{Tr}(0)=0} = \int_0^\infty \left(\frac{2}{3}e^{-t} + \frac{1}{3}e^{-4t}\right)dt = 1.25.$$

The corresponding sensor reliability functions are shown on Figure 2.

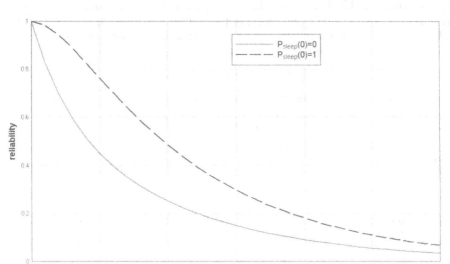

Fig. 2. Effect of initial states

In the first case the expected lifetime is 1.67 times less. Thus, the initial sensor state is a critical factor of reliability.

3 Counteracting

A sensor can be equipped by firmware of sleeping mode activation depending on observed Bit Error Rate, battery capacity and the requested sensor lifetime. For detection of the considered intrusion an algorithm of discord detection can be used. Let us consider a random sequence of transmitted bits $\{b_i\}$. Assume that the probability of error bit is constant. The probability of error in the normal state differs from the probability of error under intrusion. Thus, we have to detect a change point t in a sequence of random variables distributed by Bernoulli: $b_0, b_1, ..., b_t$: before intrusion; $b_{t+1}, b_{t+2}, ..., b_A, ...$: after intrusion.

In above random variable b_i takes a value 0 (correct bit) or 1 (error bit), change point MD is a time of attack beginning (a moment of discord), A is a time moment when a discord is detected (an alarm is generated). It needs to minimize difference $A-MD$. If $A<MD$ then a false alarm is generated. Let us remark that an attacked system can work without significance losses during some expected time, LT. Thus, inequality $A < MD+LT$ is admissible. If the false alarm probability is given then we can use the algorithm for detection of change point with admissible lag. This approach is very effective. The explicit criterions for change point detection and performance analysis have been offered in [4].

In the previous section we demonstrate that the sensor lifetime is essentially increased, if the sensor sleep mode is increased. Hence, an obvious action under the Denial of Sleeping detection is to deactivate a reasonable number of sensors (place to sleep mode). It causes to QoS degradation but it increases WSNs survivability. Let N

be a number of sensor in a cluster of WSNs, n be the number of active sensors in the same cluster. The blocking probability of request can be calculated by Erlang B-formula. Assume the admissible blocking probability B is given. It is clear that the utilization factor of active sensors is increased. Then, the minimal number of active sensors can be estimated as

$$n \approx B(1-\rho),$$

here ρ is an offered load in the cluster. Actually, if

$$\rho > n + \frac{1}{\varepsilon} \quad \forall \varepsilon > 0,$$

then

$$1 - \frac{n}{\rho} < B < 1 - \frac{n}{\rho} + \varepsilon.$$

We omit the proof of this proposition but illustrate the quality of approximation on Figure 3. Thus, the number of deactivated sensors of a cluster can be defined as follows

$$N - B(1-\rho).$$

The total WSNs lifetime is proportional to the multiplication of LT and n.

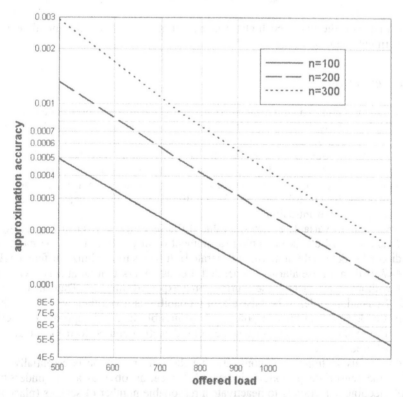

Fig. 3. Performance evaluation of the approximation for the Erlang loss function

4 Conclusion

The intrusion investigated in this paper can be classified as some type of DDoS. In contrast of previously considered attacks the object of the considered potential attack is a sensor node's power supply. The goal can be DDoS caused by violation of wireless network connectivity or monitoring failures. Very effective counteracting technology is a sensor behavior analysis based on the special method of discord detection with admissible lag.

Acknowledgments. This research was supported by MKE(Ministry of Knowledge Economy), Korea under ITRC (Information Technology Research Center) IITA-2008-(C1090-0801-0046) and ITFSIP (IT Foreign Specialist Inviting Program) IITA-2008-(C1012-0801-0006).

References

1. Wood, A.D., Stankovic, J.A.: Denial of service in sensor networks. Computer 35(10), 54–62 (2002)
2. Xu, W., Ma, K., Trappe, W., Zhang, Y.: Jamming Sensor Networks: Attack and Defense Strategies. IEEE Network 20, 41–47 (2006)
3. Raymond, D., Midkiff, S.: Denial-of-Service in Wireless Sensor Networks: Attacks and Defenses. IEEE Pervasive Computing 7, 74–81 (2008)
4. Shakhov, V.V., Choo, H., Bang, Y.: Discord model for detecting unexpected demands in mobile networks. Future Generation Comp. Syst. 20(2), 181–188

Eye, Robot: A Network Control System for Ophthalmologic Examination

Kentaro Go[1], Kenji Kashiwagi[1], Yuki Ito[1], Yu Nakazawa[2], and Jumpei Arata[3]

[1] Interdisciplinary Graduate School of Medicine and Engineering, University of Yamanashi,
4-3-11, Takeda, Kofu 400-8511 Japan
go@yamanashi.ac.jp, kenjik@yamanashi.ac.jp, ito@golab.org
[2] Faculty of Engineering, University of Yamanashi, 4-3-11, Takeda, Kofu 400-8511 Japan
nakazawa@golab.org
[3] Graduate School of Engineering, Nagoya Institute of Technology, Gokiso-cho, Showa-ku,
Nagoya 466-8555 Japan
jumpei@nitech.ac.jp

Abstract. This paper reports an iterative design project of a network control system to support ophthalmologic examination, for use in support of telemedicine. The project is a case study of development and deployment of a telemedicine system through human-centered design approaches. At the early stage of design, we carried out field research and paper prototyping on the network control system with ophthalmologists. Then, we developed working prototypes for conducting usability tests and field tests. We examine lessons learned from the design process and the designed product.

Keywords: Computer-Supported Cooperative Work (CSCW), Groupware, Human-Centered Design (HCD), Interaction design, Ophthalmology, Telemedicine, Usability.

1 Introduction

The number of medical specialists, especially ophthalmology specialists, is decreasing in secluded mountain areas in Japan. Telemedicine has been studied and is expected to be used to ameliorate the situation. In a telemedicine model, a large medical center sets up a network connection to rural health care facilities so that they can perform diagnoses and treatments using a videoconferencing system. For current ophthalmologic telemedicine, general practitioners in a rural health care facility record patients' medical information, typically as still images or moving pictures of eyes, and send it to eye specialists at a large medical center to receive technical advice from a specialist's viewpoint. The current telemedicine process does not fully leverage a slit lamp microscope, which is indispensable for eye diagnostics. Consequently, detailed diagnostics cannot be conducted via current telemedicine in ophthalmology.

For ophthalmologic examination, a slit lamp microscope (Fig. 1) is generally used as a fundamental diagnostic device. The microscope consists of a slit lamp unit (the top round shape) and a microscope unit (binocular-shaped). The microscope-unit position is adjusted using the joystick (the bottom stick shape). An eye doctor sits at

S. Lee et al. (Eds.): APCHI 2008, LNCS 5068, pp. 48–57, 2008.

the front in Fig. 1 and a patient sits at the back. The patient puts her forehead at the forehead rest and chin on the chin rest (the frame at the back).

With the slit lamp microscope, the eye specialist's basic tasks include adjustment of the microscope position using the joystick to find a focal position and to switch slit types using the knobs on the slit lamp unit to set an appropriate diagnostic condition. The eye specialist might use a fronting lens and a blue filter together with the microscope to conduct further examinations. The organization of these special devices requires great skill and experience for microscope control in addition to knowledge of clinical medicine.

The purpose of the project is to design, develop, and deploy "Eye, Robot": a network control system for ophthalmologic examination. The project is a case study of human-centered design [4, 7] of groupware system. We elicited requirements from ophthalmology specialists and designed several versions together with them. Then we developed and deployed the systems.

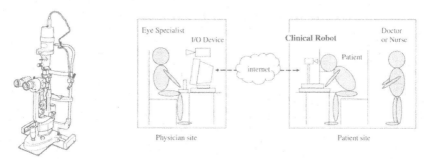

Fig. 1. Slit-lamp microscope (Model SM-70N; courtesy of Takagi Seiko Co., Ltd.) [10]

Fig. 2. Overview of the *Eye, Robot* system: a network control system for ophthalmologic examination [3]

2   A Network Control System for Ophthalmologic Examination

A conventional and common approach to ophthalmologic telemedicine is to capture high-quality still or video images of eyes at the patient's local site and send them to a remote site to ask for a specialists' diagnosis [8]. In this approach, however, the specialist uses no slit lamp microscope. Consequently, it is difficult to conduct an expert diagnosis; an opportunity to find serious eye problems might be missed. We convert a slit lamp microscope into a remote control robot to resolve this shortcoming. An eye specialist can control the robotized slit lamp microscope from a geographically remote site and conduct a diagnosis directly.

Figure 2 portrays an overview of *Eye, Robot*: a network control clinical system for ophthalmology. The system consists of an input and output (I/O) device at the specialist's site and a clinical robot at the patient's site. The specialist's site is assumed to be a central hospital of a region such as a university hospital; the patient's site is a clinic in a remote area. The remote area clinic is assumed to have a doctor who is not an eye specialist, or perhaps a nurse, who would support the specialist's robot operation and assist the patient.

The eye specialist operates the I/O device and inputs the parameters of the micro-scope position and slit light. The I/O device transmits the parameters to the robot and the robot changes its appropriate function levels. The robot has a video camera and captures still and moving images; then it transmits them to the I/O device at the specialist's site using the internet. The eye specialist examines the received images using the I/O device, then conducts a diagnosis.

Figure 3 depicts the system architecture of the *Eye, Robot* system, which was planned and illustrated in 2006. The left box represents the physician site, in which the ophthalmologist stays and diagnoses the eye problem of the patient at a remote site. The right box shows the patient site, from which a patient's eyes are examined by the doctor in the physician site. Both sites are connected through an IP network such as the internet, or a dedicated line network.

A unique feature of the *Eye, Robot* system is that the doctor remotely controls three-dimensional positions and adjusts the light intensity of a slit lamp microscope shown at the top right box of the patient site using the microscope controller and con-trol panel shown at the two top left boxes at the physician site.

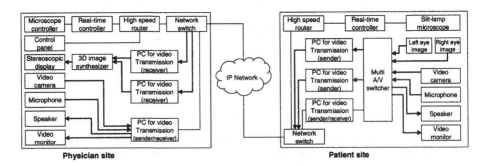

Fig. 3. System architecture of the *Eye, Robot* system

3   Interaction Design, Development and Deployment

We conducted iterative design of the network control system. The first activity for design was a series of interviews with ophthalmology specialists working at a univer-sity hospital. Additionally, we visited their office to observe their work on ophthalmo-logic examination. Following Holtzblatt's Contextual Inquiry technique [5], we stayed in the room, observed their activities, and asked questions to understand what they did in context. Figure 4 shows an eye specialist describing how he conducts eye examinations using a slit lamp microscope. Figure 5 depicts the same room from a different perspective. A video monitor is placed behind the patient; it can display a video and still image captured from the slit lamp microscope. It is useful to explain a diagnosis to the patient. During the visits, we learned that examination rooms for eye specialists at the university hospital are typically small and are already equipped with several medical devices and tools. In contrast, an examination area requires an open

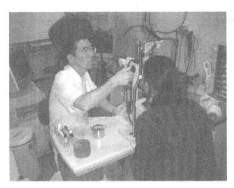
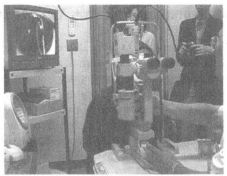

Fig. 4. An eye doctor describes how to examine a patient's eyes using the slit lamp microscope

Fig. 5. Eye doctor's view of the slit lamp microscope and the patient

space for nurses to provide support for the doctor and the patient. There seemed to be no available space in the examination room to install a set of a new device and terminals to control a remote clinical device. For this reason, we concluded that miniaturization, uniformity, and portability of the doctor's system should be our engineering goals for the *Eye, Robot* project.

Through those activities, we identified eye specialists' requirements. To avoid inflation of the rating of a specific design [11], we created several versions of mock-ups and paper prototypes and showed them to the eye specialists. We discussed the characteristics of interaction with the system.

Additionally, we conducted a *rapid technology immersion* session with the eye doctor. To eye doctors, we brought several hardware parts of a solid user interface, such as push buttons, sliders, volume controls, and joysticks, as well as images of a graphical user interface component. We had assumed that eye doctors used various medical devices, including PCs, for their daily examination, but the variety of user interfaces they had access to might have been biased. We sought to explore a wide range of design spaces and did not abandon the possibility of using completely new user interface elements when we designed the doctor's terminal together with eye doctors. We believe that it was important to get the right design [11], not merely to get the design right.

The idea of *rapid technology immersion* was inspired by Druin's concept of technology immersion [1, 2]. Druin provided many technologies to children over a short period to obtain and understand many activity patterns with technologies to design children's technologies together with children. Usually, each child has a limited access to technology. Consequently, it gives the children a chance to encounter technologies they had never seen before.

We carried out paper prototyping [12] on the system (ER-0 version) designed with eye specialists. Subsequently, we developed working prototypes (ER-1 version) and conducted usability tests. Based on the test results, we created a new version of a working prototype (ER-2 version).

4 Evolution of the *Eye, Robot* System

Figure 6 depicts the *Eye, Robot* system evolution. Actually, ER-0 was designed to demonstrate how the system is used in the form of paper-based prototype. The ER-1 was designed as a rapid working version of the prototype by modifying current technologies such as a slit lamp microscope so that it is useful for laboratory tests. The ER-2 is a refined version of the prototype, which is intended for field testing. During the process, iterative design by an interdisciplinary team of specialists with continuous user testing is useful for identifying hidden needs and requirements of uses and obtaining a right design.

4.1 Version ER-0: Paper-Based Design

Figure 7 shows the basic design of the I/O interface (paper-based version) for ER-0. We decided to use a dual display for the interface because of the requirements of the maximum eye images on the video display terminal (VDT). For this design, the left screen (main display) displays the video image transmitted from the slit lamp microscope robot on the remote site. The right screen (sub-display) displays information other than the video image of the eye, such as the camera position and various parameters.

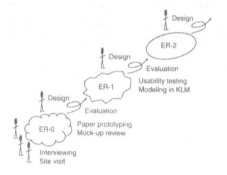

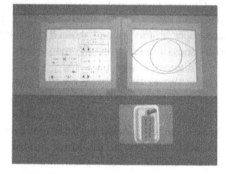

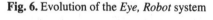

Fig. 6. Evolution of the *Eye, Robot* system

Fig. 7. Mock-up and paper prototype of ER-0: a combination of dual monitors and joystick

Figure 8 shows a paper prototype of the doctor's control panel interface for the ER-0, which is selected and modified by eye doctors. At this stage, we prepared three design proposals: (1) a solid user interface (SUI) design, (2) a graphical user interface (GUI) design, and (3) an SUI and GUI combination design [3].

Through the paper-prototyping session with ER-0 versions (see Fig. 9) and the subsequent debriefing session, we created the idea of a jump button (the two eye-shaped buttons at the bottom of the bottom left panel) and a reset button (at the top left corner). The jump button sends a command to the robot so that it toggles the camera position from the pre-assigned right eye center to the pre-assigned left eye center, and vice versa. The reset button changes all robot parameters to the initial settings so that the eye specialist can always start routine diagnostic examinations in the same manner.

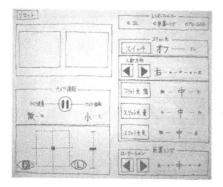

Fig. 8. Paper prototype of the doctor's control panel interface for ER-0

Fig. 9. Paper prototyping session with ER-0

4.2 Version ER-1: The Initial Working Prototype for Laboratory Test

We implemented the jump button and the reset button into a working version of the system (ER-1). Figure 10 depicts the eye doctor's terminal for ER-1. It consists of dual monitors and a joystick. The left monitor is a touch-sensitive LCD and the right monitor is a CRT monitor. We used a CRT monitor for the ER-1 at an eye doctor's request because of his preference for the quality of the video display.

Figure 11 shows the remote-control slit lamp microscope. We designate it as the *robotized* slit lamp microscope because we expected to add autonomous functions to it in future versions. However, because it is the initial working prototype, most parts of the microscope are reused from a conventional slit lamp microscope. We added stepping motors for remote control of its three-dimensional position and switching circuits for remote control of the on/off and intensity of lamps. This rapid prototyping strategy using conventional technologies follows Buxton's design concept: "Let's do smart things with stupid technology today, rather than wait and do stupid things with smart technology tomorrow." [6].

Using the ER-1, we conducted usability tests to evaluate the design of ER-1 against eye specialists' requirements [3]. The purpose of the usability test is to see how effectively eye doctors control the remote slit lamp microscope from the doctor's terminal using the joystick. We implemented ER-1's operation method to be as simple as possible. Each dimension of the xyz position of the slit lamp microscope is controlled independently. For example, when moving from position (0, 0) to (1, 1), one must do it by two steps: move from (0, 0) to (0, 1) to (1, 1), or move from (0, 0) to (1, 0) to (1, 1). We used this *straight move* approach because eye doctors reported that they did not move a slit lamp microscope using a *diagonal move* approach. In other words, they had understood themselves that they did not control the microscope, for example from the (0, 0) to (1, 1) directory. We needed to confirm the effectiveness of the joystick operation.

Two senior eye doctors and three interns participated in the usability test. They controlled the remote slit lamp microscope from the doctor's terminal using the joystick. The observation and debriefing interview results indicated a new requirement; in fact, the eye specialists require diagonal movement of joystick control even though

Fig. 10. Eye doctor's terminal for ER-1 in use

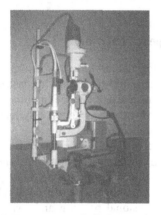

Fig. 11. Remote-control slit lamp microscope for ER-1

Fig. 12. PCs for video transmission and slit lamp microscope control for ER-1

they expressed that they did not usually control it in that manner. Therefore, we started to redesign the operation scheme to include diagonal movement.

In addition, one eye doctor at the university hospital reported that a chief nurse in the emergency department did not like the ER-1 units because they occupy an important corner of the examination room and can hinder a nurse's activity. As presented in Fig. 11 and Fig. 12, the ER-1 units are large. The doctor's report supports our observation during the site visit. The downsizing, uniformity, and portability of doctor's system had become a more specific engineering goal for the *Eye, Robot* project.

4.3 Version ER-2: A Working Prototype for Field Test

The ER-2 version of our *Eye, Robot* system is designed as a revised working prototype for field testing use.

Figure 13 shows an eye doctor's terminal for ER-2. We created an original chassis for our robotized slit lamp microscope for ER-2 (Fig. 14) and prepared a smaller PC box for video transmission and slit lamp microscope control (Fig. 15).

Fig. 13. Eye doctor's terminal for ER-2 in use

Fig. 14. Remote-control slit lamp microscope for ER-2

Fig. 15. PC box for video transmission and slit lamp microscope control for ER-2

The right monitor of the eye doctor's terminal is replaced from CRT monitor to LCD. We brought a CRT monitor and a LCD to the eye doctors, presented them and compared the quality of video images of ER-2. In fact, the eye doctors replied that the quality of video images of LCD is sufficient to conduct remote diagnostic examinations.

Fig. 16. Overview of the *Eye, Robot* system at an annual convention for local ophthalmologists

Fig. 17. Scene from the ER-2 demonstration

We did not implement the diagonal movement of joystick control for ER-2. Instead, we developed a doctor's terminal simulator so that we can conduct a usability test of a new way of joystick control [9].

To obtain a wider spectrum of comments and ideas from eye specialists, we demonstrated ER-2 of the *Eye, Robot* system at an annual convention for local ophthalmologists. Figures 16 and 17 portray scenes from the ER-2 demonstration.

5 Conclusion

This paper presented an evolution of our *Eye, Robot* system design from ER-0 to ER-1 to ER-2. First, ER-0 demonstrated how the system is used in the form of a paper-based prototype. The ER-1 was designed as a rapid working version of the prototype by modifying current technologies such as a slit lamp microscope. Intended for field testing, the ER-2 is a refined version of the prototype. Its evolution was an iterative process of design and evaluation, which are at the heart of human-centered design. Our HCD process, iterative design by an interdisciplinary team of specialists with continuous user testing, was useful for identifying hidden needs and requirements of users and obtaining an appropriate design.

The *Eye, Robot* project is in the third stage. We are now conducting a formative evaluation of ER-2 and are ready to use it at the university hospital's emergency department. We plan to set up the doctor's terminal in an examination room at the department and the remote-control slit lamp microscope in an examination room at a local hospital in a secluded mountain area. We will undertake iterative continuous design through its actual use.

Acknowledgments. We wish to thank Yasuhisa Tsuchiya and Yo'ichi Fukasawa for developing robots for ER-1 and ER-2. This project is partially supported by the Grant-in-Aid for Scientific Research (C), 19500105, 2007, from the Ministry of Education, Culture, Sports, Science and Technology, and by the Strategic Information and Communications R&D Promotion Programme, 2008, in the Ministry of Internal Affairs and Communications.

References

1. Boltman, A., Druin, A., Miura, A.: What Children Can Tell Us about Technology: The CHIkids Model of Technology Immersion. In: CHI 1998 Conference Summary on Human Factors in Computing Systems, pp. 135–136 (1998)
2. Druin, A.: Cooperative Inquiry: Developing New Technologies for Children with Children. In: Proceedings of the SIGCHI conference on Human factors in computing systems: The CHI is the limit, pp. 592–599 (1999)
3. Go, K., Ito, Y., Kashiwagi, K.: Interaction Design of a Remote Clinical Robot for Ophthalmology. In: Smith, M.J., Salvendy, G. (eds.) HCII 2007. LNCS, vol. 4557, pp. 840–849. Springer, Heidelberg (2007)
4. Gould, J.D.: How to Design Usable Systems. In: Buxton, W., Grudin, J., Greenberg, S., Baecker, R.M. (eds.) Readings in Human-Computer Interaction: Toward the Year 2000, pp. 93–121. Morgan Kaufmann, San Francisco (2000)

5. Holtzblatt, K., Beyer, H.: Contextual Design: Principles and Practice, Field Methods Casebook for Software Design. John Wiley & Sons, Inc., New York (1996)
6. Ishii, H., Kobayashi, M., Arita, K.: Iterative Design of Seamless Collaboration Media. Communications of the ACM 37(8), 83–97 (1994)
7. ISO 13407:1999 Human-centred design processes for interactive systems (1999)
8. The Medical Information System Development Center: Telemedicine Report—Revised in March, 1997 (Last accessed: April 4, 2008), http://square.umin.ac.jp/~enkaku/96/Enkaku-RepSoukatu-nof-eng.html
9. Nakazawa, Y., Go, K., Kashiwagi, K.: Ease of learning the operation of a remote clinical robot for ophthalmology. In: The 70th Annual IPSJ Convention, (4), 5ZD-4, pp. 275–276 (Japanese, 2008)
10. Takagi Seiko Ltd. Slitlamp microscope, Model SM-70N. (Last accessed: April 4, 2008), http://www.takagi-j.com/seihin_e/seihin_e.html
11. Tohidi, M., Buxton, W., Baecker, R., Sellen, A.: Getting the Right Design and the Design Right: Testing Many is Better than One. In: CHI 2006, Proceedings of the SIGCHI conference on Human Factors in computing systems, pp. 1243–1252 (2006)
12. Snyder, C.: Paper Prototyping: The Fast and Simple Techniques for Designing and Refining the User Interface. Morgan Kaufmann, San Francisco (2003)

A Study of a Loosely-Coupled Groupware System for Supporting Collaboration and Coordination

Tiffany Y. Tang and Hareton K.N. Leung

Department of Computing, Hong Kong Polytechnic University
{cstiffany,csleung}@comp.polyu.edu.hk

Abstract. A number of researches have focused on the usability aspect of groupware in supporting collaborative work. Unfortunately, our understandings on their impact on supporting collaborative learning are still limited due to a lack of attention on this issue. Furthermore, the majority of educators and designers in CSCL expect that interactions and collaborations would come naturally, as a result, we are too busy with how versatile the tools in educational groupware systems shall have in order to provide a wide variety of interaction opportunities for both learners and educators, and largely ignore whether or not these features are valuable from learners' as well as educators' perspective. To bridge this gap, in this paper, we describe our experiences with loosely-coupled collaborative software called GroupScribbles, in its potential of supporting cooperation and coordination among learners as well as its failures. Our study suggests that it is not the versatility of the tools in these educational groupware systems, but how they can provide a seamless and focused distributed learning environment determines the overall pedagogical appropriateness of the software in CSCL. That is, the learning environment, although distributed, and fragmented, should be capable of sticking learners, their activities and meta-cognitive problem solving skills cohesively so as to continuously construct a relatively compact learning space where coordination and collaborations can be made cheap, lightweight, effective and efficient.

Keywords: Cooperative/collaborative learning, Groupware.

1 Introduction

Imagine several groups of learners in a large class are working collaboratively on a task, what do learners in each group want to look over in order to collaborate effectively? What are learners between each group curious about the progress, or activities of other groups? How can tutors virtually participate and appropriately 'cut in' to provide help or suggest hints? How would the activity visualizations affect group forming for learners? These issues (which are often considered as 'awareness' in the CSCW research community [5,14]) facing educators and educational groupware system designers alike are fundamental to build effective and efficient collaborative learning environments (known as Computer Supported Collaborative Learning, or CSCL in short). Fortunately, CSCL has been benefited from many active research studies attempting to understand and provide technological support for learners to

S. Lee et al. (Eds.): APCHI 2008, LNCS 5068, pp. 58–67, 2008.

cooperate with each other, coordinate their behaviors and learn collaboratively. These educational groupware systems/tools range from discussion forums in iHelp [2], threaded bulletin board [4], a collaborative editor known as SASSE (Synchronous Asynchronous Structured Editor) [1], to a range of annotation tools to support collaborative interpretation [3] etc.

Additionally, there are a number of systems supporting either synchronized or asynchronized learning activities, such as WebCT, Blackboard, Moodle, etc. These interactive technologies are particular essential in distance learning environments [7], where learners are often situated across different physical locations and are unable to perceive the subtle cues that are prevalent in the traditional F2F teaching settings. While technology-equipped collaborative classroom/learning systems/tools aim at encouraging learner interactions [10, 13], their usability remains to be unknown, partly due to the fact that the majority of us, educators and designers alike, hoped that *'interactions among students would occur naturally', though sadly, 'this was not what took place'*, as observed in [9, p.105]. That is, we are too busy with how versatile the tools in educational groupware systems shall have in order to provide a wide variety of interaction opportunities for both learners and educators [2], and largely ignore whether or not these features are valuable from learners' as well as educators' perspective. In this paper, we report our experiences with a loosely-coupled educational groupware system called GroupScribbles (GS), developed by SRI International and released in June 2006, with a particular focus on learners' perceptions of it in supporting the social awareness and interactions. We will also examine whether GS provide some mechanisms to preserve learner privacy.

The rest of this paper is divided into four sections. Related work is presented in section 2, followed by some background information on GS in Section 3. The detailed usability study of GS appeared in section 4. We conclude this paper by briefly pointing out our future work.

2 Related Work

2.1 Social Presence and Collaboration in Educational Groupware Systems

Providing computer-mediated communication (CMC) channels such as emails, discussion forums and chatting [2], bulletin boards [4], instant messengers, could have a great impact on the level of social presence which is considered to be one of the most critical factors in technology-driven social learning environment [16]. Criticisms were heard over the lack of learners' social context support of CMC tools [16], as well as group-oriented tasks to 'force' collaboration. Therefore, it is realized that no matter how powerful and varied educational groupware promises to be appropriate educator interventions are still needed. Unfortunately, existing usability studies or design experience reports have been focusing on the design part of the education groupware [2, 16], and the use of various tools to understand and document social interaction and collaboration [13, 16], and therefore are weak in assessing the perceived value by learners over these features; that is, the usage and patterns of these features, and how they have been used to affect coordination and collaboration are needed. [7] is one of the exceptions focusing on the usability of the tools in CSCL. In particular, they studied various awareness support widgets in CSCL. Four major types of awareness were identified for supporting collaborative learning, i.e. social, task, concept, and workspace awareness. For instance, in a group work, learners might want to know who is the most active as one way to identify the most knowledgeable person to seek help; they might also be interested in knowing their fellow learners activities in the workspace, so as to anticipate their intentions, predict their next move especially in some cases when they are competitors, etc. In synchronized learning workspace, educators sometimes work as moderators to initiate discussions, post questions for learners to make reflections, keep them from being distracted. As such, it is demanding for both learners and educators to take advantage of the social learning environments for effective learning and teaching. Our evaluation study attempts to make up for these drawbacks. The study is set in a two-week laboratory sessions as well as mass lectures involving the groupware system, GS. This paper intends to outline a set of design issues with respect to how far both learners and educators are willing to go in order to micro-construct a more effective learning environment within the system framework.

2.2 Awareness Support in Groupware System

Users of groupware systems would certainly want to obtain more awareness information regarding the working artifact, other users, the tasks etc in order to formulate their own actions accordingly. Additionally, some awareness information (either in the audible or visual form) could cause disruption to users' current information activity [12]. In order to make a compromise between awareness and interruption, the selectivity of awareness information becomes essential. The selection is normally based upon the mechanisms of the workspace applications. For instance, if the awareness mechanism is designed to give the users the overall state of the application, then, only the affected information will be projected and shown.

3   GroupScribbles: A Lightweight Collaborative System

3.1   General System Descriptions

GS is a lightweight distributed environment for documenting and sharing ideas and concepts in both graphical and textual forms (known as 'scribbles'). It is created for tutors to design group learning activities. GS typically presents users with a two paned window (Figure 1, left). The upper pane is a public board which logged users can all see. The lower pane is the private working area, where users can choose between textual or graphical inputs to write down their notes. Once completed, users can simply drag their scribbles to the public board for others to see. A user can arbitrarily re-arrange his/her scribbles by simply dragging them in the public window, or put it back to his/her private work area for edits. The functional flow of this note-taking and sharing is a metaphoric design of the small yellow 'Post-It'. In additions, users can also change the scribbles color in order to be differentiated from others. To facilitate multiple group work, users can turn on more than two sharable boards, including private, group-wide and global boards, as seen in Figure 1 (right), where the upper window is split into two panes: the left one is the group view (local view), while the right one is the public view (global view), the lower pane is again the learner's private view.

3.2 Supporting Awareness in GS

GS has been shown to be effective, lightweight and flexible for learners to create, share and edit their ideas in collaborative work, especially for brain-storming, when users involved can quickly scratch their ideas and share with other group members. [11] documents another usability studies on GS for a college-level Java programming

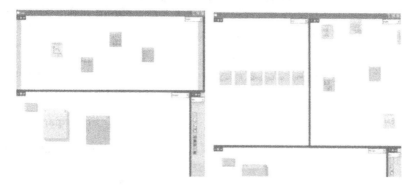

Fig. 1. GS screen shots

class. Experiment results were encouraging, demonstrating the lightweight-ness, yet effectiveness of GS to support CSCL. These evaluation studies only evaluate system capabilities assuming under the system framework, collaboration and interaction would come naturally. In other words, these studies fail to probe the extent to which the system supports collaboration and coordination among learners. [7, 8] remain to be two of the very few works uncovering the usability of educational groupware system based on the notion of awareness. Our study aims at furthering our understanding on the general support of educational groupware, to implicate the design elements required to foster efficient collaborations in CSCL. To better understand awareness, we assess a set of awareness elements loosely based on Gutwin and Greenberg's workspace awareness framework [6] in the single-level and multiple-level group tasks. The aspect of awareness we considered encompass those basic elements due to the nature of GS, in terms of presence, activities and activity levels, changes that are essential for learners. These elements were more under investigated in the CSCW community than in the CSCL area. But we believe if we would want to see a full proliferation of more educational groupware tools in CSCL, a better understanding of its impact on learning and teaching is necessary.

4   Evaluation Study

4.1 Study Goals

In our study, we are interested in examine four major issues regarding GS to support collaborative learning at various levels. First, easiness of system use including ease of manipulating the scribbles, information interpretation; Second, the system's potential to support collaborative learning and awareness; Third, the system's capabilities to support learner coordination and reflection; Fourth, the system's capabilities to pre-serve privacy. In this paper, we will not describe our fourth goal due to the page constraints.

To study it, we designed several learner activities at two main levels. At the lower-level, learners within a group work at their private areas separately, and later brain-storm it through several rounds of discussions at the group-level. At the higher-level, once the consensus within the group is reached regarding the task, they can submit it to the public board, so as to initiate a class-wide discussion. Figure 2 de-picts the flows of the views associated with the levels of activity.

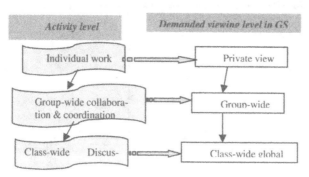

Fig. 2. Learning task-level and required view-level in GS

4.2 Participants

The experiment was car-ried out in an undergradu-ate course in CHI. There are altogether 94 regis-tered students who had experiences with groupware systems before (including instant messenger, etc); al-though they are not familiar with the notion of groupware.

The experiments were carried out in all 5 groups, involving 86 students in total spanning two weeks. In the 1st week, they were asked to complete the exercise, while in the 2nd week, learners are asked to make reflections on the issue of awareness and associate it with their experiences of GS and other groupware systems in general. Our findings reported here are mainly drawn from the results of their first week's activi-ties. The finding we will discuss reflected the 74 valid reports.

4.3 Tasks and Study Procedure

Both individual as well as group tasks were included and carried out in the mass lec-ture room as well as the laboratory. Findings reported here were drawn from our study in the laboratory where there are two kinds of tasks:

✓   One-level task. Each learner will complete the assigned task individually (in-dividual view) before submitting answers to the class public board (global view) as shown in Figure 3 left where the lower pane is learners' individual or private view, where the upper pane is the class-wide view.

✓   Two-level task. Each learner begins to complete the task through the private group board (local view, Figure 4 upper left pane). After completion, the final group work will be submitted to the class public board (global view, Figure 4 upper right pane). Learners can access their private working pane as well (Figure 4 lower pane)

At the beginning, each learner is required to complete the one-level task. After posting their answers to the class public board, they are also required take a screen-shot of their submissions and highlight it accordingly. Once completed, learners are

Fig. 3. The views involving one-level tasks   **Fig. 4.** The views involving two-level tasks

needed to take some time providing their views (on a Likert-scale of 0 to 5) on some essential awareness elements in GS. A class discussion is initiated after it. Next, learners take part in two two-level tasks involving both group and individual activities. To begin with, learners were asked to complete the task by first forming a group, constructing a private group board and then making their discussions there accordingly. Since each learner from a group might sit side-by-side in the lab room, in order to prevent them from exchanging utterances, actions, or even gathering around, they are reminded to keep silent, turn off any on-going chatting sessions such as MSN messengers, and use GS only to make consensus as a group. Once the agreement is reached, they submit their work to the class public board (global view), take screenshots, and highlight their group submission accordingly. Upon completion, each learner is again required to evaluate the extent to which GS support awareness in this round of the task.

During the lab sessions, one tutor was at the lab room with the learners, providing support and initiating class discussions. Another tutor was working remotely in another room of the same building, and also logged on to GS, and occasionally made comments to learners' work. All the entries are included in the lab file which is required to submit when the lab session ends.

4.4 Evaluation Strategies

Throughout the course of the study, we used observations, self-report and interviews to gather data as a basis for our study. The evaluation is not a traditional controlled experiment, but was a structured investigation study similar to others including, too name a few [7, 8, 11]. In accordance to group and individual tasks, sufficient awareness support and a smooth switch from one view to another are highly demanded. As such, the awareness requirements for collaborative learning shall be built upon the view and task separations. In this regard, we will adopt Gutwin et al's framework [7]: view/task matrix which is loosely drawn upon the time/space matrix in groupware. Fig. 5 draws the view and task in a two-dimensional matrix to illustrate it. In our study, only two of the scenarios are relevant (as highlighted in Fig. 5): same task, different view settings and same task, mixed view settings. Refer to Fig. 1 again for the two learning scenarios when (i) learners are involved in the one-level task in the left screenshot; (ii) learners are involved in the two-level tasks in the right screenshot. In the latter, learners have to gain a multiple view in the global and local levels respectively.

In the left screenshot in Fig. 1, the upper window is one of the screenshots taken by the learner in his self-report: the upper pane is his group's local view; the lower one is his private view. While in the right screenshot in Fig. 1, the upper window is split into two panes: the left one is the group view (local view), while the right one is the class public view (global view), the lower pane is again the learner's private view. In this setting, the learner tries to connect with his group as well as monitor other groups' progress, which demands more information in order to make coordination timely and accordingly.

4.5 Evaluation Results and Analysis

Awareness support. Participants all felt very strong over the lack of sufficient support to recognize some critical information such as who is writing on which scribble, who will be responsible to submit the group scribble (the role). As lamented by one, '… we could not know exactly which answer is provided by whom.., though there were someone written "ME" on the public board, again, we did not know which "ME" were they referring to' (Figure 6). This problem highlights the lack of effective ways to reveal 'identity' in the one-level task in GS.

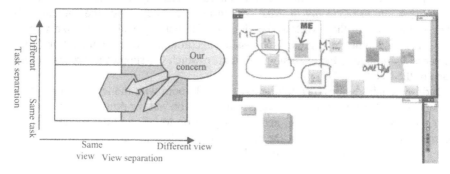

Fig. 5. The view/task matrix for educational groupware   **Fig. 6.** Graffiti-ing 'ME' in discussion board

Color cues have been useful to distinguish participants and their activities such as colored messages in MSN messengers [7, 8]. We observed that some subjects quickly noticed that the color of the scribbles can be used to distinguish them from others. Meanwhile, from the tutor's perspective, when noticing one inaccurate answer and wanting to clear it with the individual students, it is not easy to 'find' them, and provide follow-up helps. However, since there are only 6 colors available, the ability of color cues is extremely limited. Subjects strongly indicated that it is difficult to know who are talking in the group board, who owns the messages etc. A couple of participants suggested the inclusion of name tag on each scribble to identify its owner, or allowing users to set up and attach personalized signatures to each scribble they made. The problems that incurred from the insufficient color cues are less severe than when the time group members engage in discussions. Specifically, the insufficiency of annotating scribbles with time-stamp leads to various negative feedbacks from subjects: subjects strongly agreed that it is much easier to notice what changes are being made to the boards than when and where (sphere of influence) it is made, which results in poor coordination from inaccurate work-flow formulation, and therefore collaboration. It is not difficult for subjects to assess their abilities in these different boards.

For instance, subjects can create as many boards as possible, given that they have to communicate through the previously known board in order to inform others of the new active board. Once the communication is established, they can move around within the boards. We are interested in whether or not learners' evaluation on the issue of awareness changed when they continue to use GS in the classroom. Our analysis here focuses on subjects' completion of the two-level tasks, where coordination and cooperation are more demanding. Figure 7 draws a comparison between subjects' view after completing task 1 and task 2 respectively.

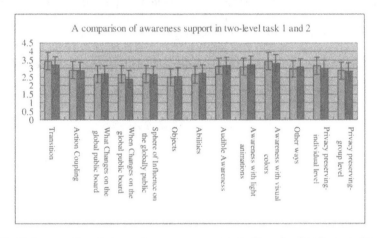

Fig. 7. A comparison between the awareness support of two-level task one and two

As shown in Figure 7, six categories of feedbacks dropped, i.e. easiness and smoothness of window transition (from group-level to class-level and vice versa), when changes were made (the temporal element attached to a scribble), where

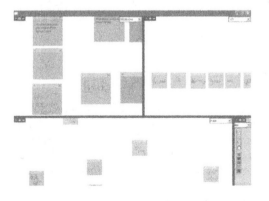

Fig. 8. A switch between group view (upper left) and class view (upper right)

changes were made (sphere of influence), visual awareness cues (for instance, providing more options for learner to declare the ownership of their scribbles), privacy preserving at both individual and group levels. Among them, the largest drop is related to the lack of temporal feature needed to be attached to each scribble, from 2.66 to 2.37.

Meanwhile, it also poses greater challenge for each group to not only engage in their interactions but also keep an eye on others' progress, which requires to switch between group-level and class-level windows, as shown in Figure 8. Notice that the upper level of GS is spitted into two parts: the level part is the group view, whereas the right is the class view. Without some additional audible or visual support, it is hard to spot the changes made in the global view. As a result, many disadvantages come along, not only from learners', but also from tutor's perspective, as explained previously. We performed a t test on the two groups of results. Our results suggest that there was a significant difference in perceived value of awareness quality, increasing from a mean of 0.57 after the first two-level task to a mean of 0.64 after completion of the second two-level task, $t(73) = 2.048$, $p < 0.05$, two tailed. As shown in Table 1, 70% of the correlations among key awareness elements increase after subjects completed the second two-level task. The results indicated that learners expressed more positive views regarding the awareness support GS provides. However, since our current study only concerns adopting GS in one course, we will not make any stronger comments over the long-term usage of GS at this stage.

Table 1. Awareness elements for supporting multiple-level task ($n=73$, $p<0.05$)

	Objects		Abilities		Action coupling		when changes on public board	
	Task 1	Task 2	Task 1	Task 2	Task 1	Task 2	Task 1	Task 2
what changes on public board	-	-	0.617	0.523	0.615	0.601	0.665	0.652
when changes on public board	0.529	0.561	0.578	0.686	0.473	0.606		
sphere of influences (where changes can be made)	0.561	0.796	0.613	0.687	0.510	0.535	0.506	0.619

We also attempted to examine the correlations among the awareness elements. Our results suggest several strong correlations between some awareness elements when learners engaged in the two two-level tasks. For instance, we observe very close relationships among unconventional awareness cues, including audible, light animated scribbles and colorings. Generally, learners indicated that although they will not suggest the over-use of these unconventional cues, they would be happy to see more applications of these in GS; for instance, light animations team up with audible clues, and light animations with visual colorings.

5 Concluding Remark

Stahl [15] has argued that for making collaborative learning effective and successful it is vital to make the learning processes visible to educators. However, it stresses the necessity of understanding the features of interactions from educator and researchers' perspective and largely ignores the needs of learners, which motivates our study here. In particular, we are interested in understanding what types of information learners have to gather during social interaction and collaborations in order to recognize others' intentions, goals, etc. We document our experiences in conducting a usability testing on an educational groupware system called GS in this paper. Our study finds out that it is not the versatility of tools embedded in the educational software system that makes collaborative learning effective, but how it is capable of providing valuable information for learners to formulate their actions and coordinate their activities.

References

1. Baecker, R.M., Glass, G., Mitchell, A., Posner, I.: SASSE: The collaborative editor. In: CHI 1994, pp. 459–460 (1994)
2. Brooks, C., Panesar, R., Greer, J.: Awareness and collaboration in the iHelp courses content management system. In: Nejdl, W., Tochtermann, K. (eds.) EC-TEL 2006. LNCS, vol. 4227, pp. 34–44. Springer, Heidelberg (2006)
3. Cox, D., Greenberg, S.: Supporting collaborative interpretation in distributed groupware. In: CSCW 2000, pp. 289–298 (2000)
4. Dos Santos, B., Wright, A.: Using bulletin boards in an educational setting. CACM 49(3), 115–118 (2006)
5. Dourish, P., Bellotti, V.: Awareness and coordination in shared workspaces. In: CSCW 1992, pp. 107–113 (1992)
6. Gutwin, C., Greenberg, C.: A descriptive framework of workspace awareness for real-time groupware. J. CSCW 11, 411–446 (2002)
7. Gutwin, C., Stark, G., Greenberg, S.: Support for workspace awareness in educational groupware. In: Proc. of CSCL 1995, pp. 147–156 (1995)
8. Gutwin, C., Roseman, M., Greenberg, S.: A usability study of awareness widgets in a shared workspace groupware system. In: CSCW 1996, pp. 258–267 (1996)
9. Hallet, K., Cummings, J.: The virtual classroom as authentic experience. In: Proc. Annual Conference on Distance Teaching and Learning, pp. 103–107 (1997)
10. Hiltz, S., Turoff, M.: What makes learning network effective. CACM 45(4), 56–59 (2002)
11. Hou, M., Austin, T.: Use of CSCL tool in Java applications programming: a case study. In: ACM Southeast Regional Conference, pp. 122–125 (2007)
12. Hudson, S.E., Smith, I.: Techniques for addressing fundamental privacy and disruption tradeoffs in awareness support systems. In: CSCW 1996, pp. 248–257 (1996)
13. Lee, S.-H., Magjuka, R., Liu, X., Bonk, C.J.: Interactive technologies for effective collaborative learning. J. of Instructional Tech. and Distance Learning 3(6) (June, 2006)
14. Schmidt, K.: The problem with 'awareness'. J. CSCW 11, 285–298 (2002)
15. Stahl, G.: Rediscovering CSCL. In: Koschmann, T.D., Hall, R., Miyake, N. (eds.) CSCL 2: Carrying Forward the Conversation, pp. 169–181. Erlbaum, Mahwah (2002)
16. Tu, C.-H.: Strategies to increase interaction in online social learning environments. In: SITE 2000, pp. 1662–1667 (2000)

RIKI: A Wiki-Based Knowledge Sharing System for Collaborative Research Projects

Sang Keun Rhee, Jihye Lee, and Myon-Woong Park

Intelligence and Interaction Research Center
Korea Institute of Science and Technology,
39-1 Hawolgok-dong, Seongbuk-gu, Seoul, Korea
{greyrhee,bluesea,myon}@kist.re.kr

Abstract. During a collaborative research project, each member's knowledge and progress need to be managed and shared with other members. For effective knowledge sharing, each member needs to be able to express their own knowledge within the given project context and easily find and understand other members' knowledge. In this paper, we present our RIKI prototype that supports group communication and knowledge sharing in research projects via the Wiki-based platform. The main aim of RIKI implementation is to manage the shared knowledge semantically and to provide users with straightforward access to necessary information.

Keywords: Collaborative Tools, Knowledge Sharing, Wikis, Semantic Wikis.

1 Introduction

There are various knowledge management systems to support the collaborative work and they typically have three different approaches or combination of them. First, there is a project management system approach, concentrating on the management of people and scheduling. Second approach is document-based system that collects, manages, and sometimes recommends the previously created documents to reduce the time and efforts that researchers and developers spend on seeking for the necessary information. Third, there are systems that concentrate on effective communication and knowledge sharing among members.

Since most academic research projects are performed with team-based collaboration, and knowledge sharing and communication are important factors for innovation, our system is following the third approach to provide collaborative contents creation and sharing medium. This paper presents our RIKI[1] prototype implementation, a Wiki-based portal that supports knowledge management and sharing within a collaborative research project. First, the knowledge sharing within a academic project is briefly discussed. Second, our approach on knowledge management and access methods are explained followed by a brief description on RIKI implementation. Finally, it is concluded with discussions.

---

[1] http://riki.kist.re.kr

S. Lee et al. (Eds.): APCHI 2008, LNCS 5068, pp. 68–76, 2008.

2 Knowledge Sharing and Semantic Wikis

In academic research projects, knowledge sharing means more than simple exchange of documents. During a collaborative project, each member's own ideas, findings, or progress needs to be shared, even if it may be incomplete or undocumented. Apart from e-mail exchange or meetings, for effective sharing of such knowledge via a computer-based system, we see that there are three main requirements. First, each member should be able to express and represent their own knowledge in a sharable form. Second, the members need to find and access the necessary or relevant knowledge easily and quickly. Third, one should be able to interpret and understand others' knowledge with the knowledge creators' own intention and understanding within a same context. Here, the context means the structure of a project, including the tasks, related topics, participating people, and so on.

From this point of view, the knowledge sharing system should provide a decentralised communication platform, hence the Wiki[1]-based collaborative authoring tool would satisfy the first requirement described above. In addition, to enable both easy access to resources and sharing the context which is dependent on a project, the overall knowledge, including the resources and the context which is closely linked to the resources should be represented and managed, and the ontology-based semantic technology provides the necessary structuring and representation of the semantic relationships of knowledge.

There are several researches on applying semantic technology to Wikis, commonly known as the Semantic Wiki[2][3][4]. However, whereas other Semantic Wikis concentrate on annotation and representation of resources, we applied ontology mainly to provide convenient knowledge access within a project-specific context. The details of our knowledge management and access methods are described in the following sections.

3 Knowledge Management

To represent and manage the resource objects with the context information, a semantic structure and representation is required. Before describing our ontology implementation, let us first present the concept of our knowledge management method with a layer model.

3.1 Layer Model

In order to achieve the shared knowledge representation and constant management which can be frequently updated, we designed the knowledge structure in three layers, as shown in Fig. 1: *Base Layer*, *Domain Knowledge Layer*, and *Resource Layer*, representing the fundamental concepts and relations, the context knowledge, and the resource objects, respectively.

Base Layer. On this first layer, the abstract concepts and relations that are necessary and common to all generic research projects are defined. This layer is fixed, and to build this layer, we need to define the characteristics of the knowledge to be shared. Here, the 'knowledge to be shared' includes both the resource objects and domain context.

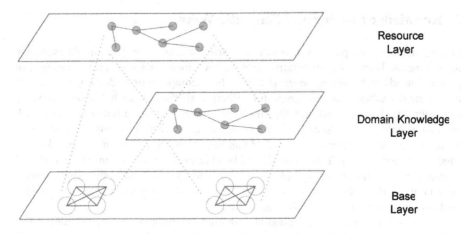

Fig. 1. The layer model

In our opinion, the knowledge resource that needs to be shared in an academic project can be classified as four distinctive categories, and they form the basic four concepts of this *Base Layer*. First, the ideas, opinions, approaches, progress, or results regarding the current project are defined as *ProjectResource*. Second, technical facts or results from external projects that can be referenced or consulted are classified as *TechnicalResource*. Third, the information regarding relevant events including meetings, seminars and conferences are classified as *EventResource*, and finally, the participants' profiles are defined as *PersonResource*.

Then, each concept representing the resource type is connected to another concept representing the domain context. Hence, there are four additional concepts in this layer. The *ProjectResource* is connected to *Task*, which represents the task hierarchy. Similarly, the *TechnicalResource* is connected to *Topic*, the *EventResource* is connected to *Event*, and *PersonResource* is connected to *Person*. Also, these four additional concepts are linked to each other, representing the relation between them. In addition, the *Person* concept is linked to all four resource concepts since every resource needs to be created or modified by a certain person.

Therefore, these eight concepts and the relations between them form our *Base Layer* (Fig. 2), and this layer becomes the basic structure of our ontology. More details on the implemented structure are described in *Section 3.2*.

Domain Knowledge Layer. On this second layer, the domain and context knowledge which is specific to the current project is stored. This layer consists of the hierarchical structure of tasks, topics, events, and people, with the relation between them. The contents of this layer can be regarded as the instances of the four context concepts described in the *Base Layer* (i.e. *Task, Topic, Event, Person*), and we applied different approaches to manage the contents for those four different concepts.

The information on people needs to be managed by the project manager or system administrator. Also, each user is allowed to edit his or her own profile. The contents on events are created and modified automatically by the system, based on the event related resource creation and modification. The topic hierarchy can be constructed by

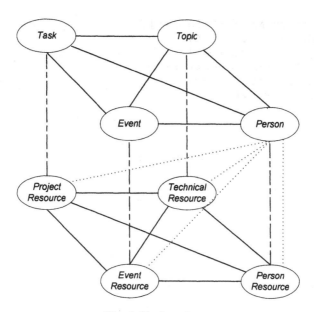

Fig. 2. The Base Layer

adopting existing hierarchies (e.g. the ACM Computing Classification System[5]), but in our opinion, for effective communication and knowledge sharing in the middle of a research project, the topic hierarchy should be constructed to be more specific to a given project. To accomplish this, we propose that any member of the given project should be able to create and edit the hierarchy. Similarly, the task hierarchy is also modifiable by all members. Upon creating or editing the hierarchies, the relations between different hierarchies can also be modified.

Regarding the topic and task hierarchy, it may seem reasonable that only the project manager can create and edit those structures, but we allowed the creation and modification for every member since each member often has the best knowledge on his or her own area. Also, in case of a mistake, it can be quickly fixed by other members. Yet, the justification would be made after further testing.

An example content of this layer is described below in F-Logic[6].

```
#TOPIC34[#topicName->"Wireless_Network"].
#TOPIC34[#hasParentTopic->#TOPIC26].
#TOPIC34[#isRelatedTo->#PERSON3].
#TOPIC34[#isRelatedTo->#TASK51].
#TOPIC34[#isRelatedTo->#TASK76].
```

Resource Layer. This layer contains the actual resource objects – or data – to be shared. The contents of this layer can be regarded as instances of the four resource concepts described in the *Base Layer* (*ProjectResource, TechnicalResource, EventResource, PersonResource*), and each resource is connected to the corresponding content(s) in the *Domain Knowledge Layer*. An example resource in this layer is described below in F-Logic.

```
#A27[#resourceName->"ZigBee"].
#A27[#isAbout->#TOPIC34].
#A27[#isAbout->#TOPIC41].
#A27[#hasContributor->#PERSON3].
#A27[#hasContributor->#PERSON4].
#A27[#hasLinkTo->#A31].
```

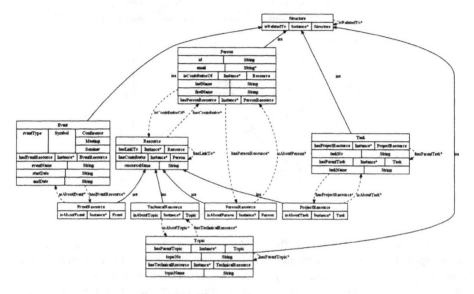

Fig. 3. The ontology design

3.2 Ontology

The 3-layer model described above is implemented as an ontology. The eight concepts in the *Base Layer* form our ontology classes with two additional upper classes – *Resource Class* and *Structure Class*. The relations and attributes are also defined based on that layer. Then, the hierarchical structure of the *Domain Knowledge Layer* is stored in the *Structure Class* and its subclasses as instances. By storing the hierarchies as instances rather than subclasses, frequent modifications by any users can be managed without endangering the consistency of the whole ontology. Finally, each resource is stored in the *Resource Class* and its subclasses.

The ontology can be expanded to provide more service, but currently, it is designed in a simplest way to fit our fundamental purpose – shared knowledge management and knowledge access. Fig. 3 describes our ontology structure.

4 Knowledge Access

Within a knowledge sharing system, easy access to the necessary knowledge is also important as well as consistent knowledge management. Traditional Wiki-based systems[7][8] typically provide two methods for accessing knowledge – searching by keywords and navigating by following hyperlinks within the contents. However, the keyword search is efficient only if users know the matching keywords. Also there may be some resources without links, which is not accessible via hyperlinks. Therefore, in our system, we implemented two more ways to access knowledge – structured browsing and recommendation.

4.1 Structured Browsing

The structured browsing provides a tree-based browsing, based on the *Domain Knowledge Layer*. It provides users with full control on navigation so that users can see the overview structure of the whole contents within the system and they can reach the exact location of a resource they want.

RIKI provides four hierarchies – *Task, Topic, Event, Person* – based on the contents of the subclasses of the Structure class in our ontology. Each node of the hierarchies is presented with a number representing the number of resources related to the node, and the relations to the nodes in other hierarchies are also indicated, if any. Finally, when a user opens a resource page, the node(s) related to the current resource is highlighted to display the context information regarding the resource.

4.2 Recommendation and Semantic Relevance Measure

Along with the structured browsing, RIKI also recommends a list of resources that are potentially necessary to users. More precisely, when a user is viewing a particular resource page, the system provides a list of resources that are closely related to the current page. The list is instantly generated when a user opens a resource page by calculating the relevance value between resources. The relevance value is determined based on the semantic relevance measure [9].

Rule Definition. Upon measuring the relevance, only the relations between resources are considered and all other relations connecting non-resource instances are ignored. However, within our ontology, the only direct relation defined between resources is the *hasLinkTo* relation. Therefore, additional rules are created to define all the indirect relations between resources.

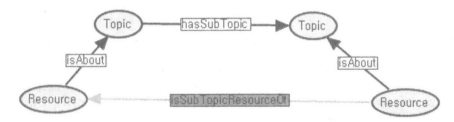

Fig. 4. An example illustration of rule definition

For example, let us consider that we have a resource *R1* which is about topic *T1*, and another resource *R2* which is about topic *T2*, a subtopic of *T1*. Then, there exists an indirect relation between resource *R1* and *R2*: *R2* is a subtopic resource of *R1* (Fig. 4). This example case is expressed in F-Logic as following:

```
RULE #"027_SubTopicResource": FORALL R1, R2, T1, T2,
    R2[#isSubTopicResourceOf->>R1]
    <-
    R1:#Resource AND R2:#Resource AND
    T1:#Topic AND T2:#Topic AND
    R1[#isAbout->>T1[#hasSubTopic->>T2]] AND
    R2[#isAbout->>T2].
```

Overall, there are 50 rules defined in our system to express full semantic relations between resources.

Semantic Relevance Measure. The semantic relevance values between resources are measured based on the *Resource Layer*. First, a numeric value is assigned to each relation or rule, representing the semantic distance, which is determined after a few testing. Then, the content of the layer is interpreted as a directed graph, such that each resource becomes a node and each relation or rule between resources becomes an edge. When a user opens a resource page, the node representing that page becomes the starting node, and the system calculates the relevance value to all other nodes.

The fundamental assumption of this method is that more relations mean more closeness. For example, if resource X has the same topic as resource Y, and Z, and resource A also has same author with resource Z, then resource Z is considered to be closer to resource X than resource Y (see Fig. 5).

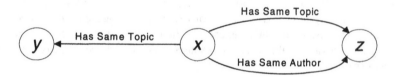

Fig. 5. An example illustration of relation between resources

Therefore, instead of simply considering the distance of the shortest path between two nodes to measure the relevance, all possible paths between them are considered. The full description of the algorithm is in [9].

5 Implementation

Fig. 6 shows the overall structure of the RIKI implementation, which consists of two servers. The *Knowledge Server* manages the semantic structure of resources and analyses the contents, and the *Interface Server* provides the Wiki-based web interface.

The ontology is located within the *Knowledge Server*, and it is interpreted by the OntoBroker[2]. The *Knowledge Controller* accesses the contents of the ontology by querying the OntoBroker, and generates the contents' structure for the structured browsing or the list of the relevant resources for the recommendation. It also controls modification of ontology instances and their properties. The *Semantic Recommender* performs the actual calculation of relevance value between resources.

---

[2] http://www.ontoprise.de

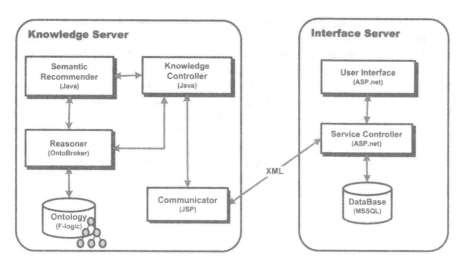

Fig. 6. RIKI system structure

The *Interface Server* contains a database, where the actual pages are stored. The *Service Controller* communicates with the *Knowledge Server* and generates the actual service contents, which are provided to users via Web interfaces. Fig. 7 shows the main pages of RIKI.

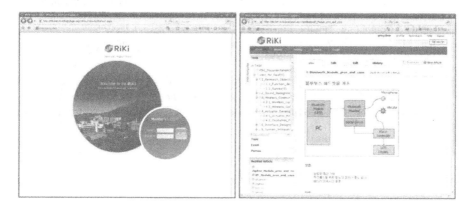

Fig. 7. RIKI pages

6 Discussion and Further Works

The RIKI system supports academic research projects by providing an environment for collaborative knowledge sharing. Not only the resource objects but also the context information are semantically connected and stored with the ontological representation, and the tree-based structured browsing and relevant resource recommendation allow easy navigation. However, there still are several issues to consider to improve the system. First, the scheduling feature would be practical for common project process, but it is excluded in our current prototype to concentrate on the knowledge management and access. It can also provide easier management of the task hierarchy. Second, the similarity measure between resources can be improved by applying a text-based comparison method. Applying tags can provide easier annotation to resources and it would also be utilised in relevance calculation to improve the recommendation results. In addition, making the resource pages compatible with other Wikis, especially the Wikipedia[10], would simplify the process of collecting external technical resources. Finally, a graphical visualization of the structure and resources will provide another easy navigation on resources. The system introduced in this paper is our first prototype, and its usability will be validated in a future user study.

Acknowledgments. This work was supported by the Korea Institute of Science and Technology(KIST) with the project IRS(Intelligent Responsive Space), which is a part of Tangible Space Initiative) project.

References

1. Leuf, B., Cunningham, W.: The Wiki Way: Collaboration and Sharing on the Internet. Addison-Wesley, Reading (2001)
2. Krötzsch, M., Vrandecic, D., Völkel, M., Haller, H., Studer, R.: Semantic MediaWiki. Journal of Web Semantics 5, 251–261 (2007)
3. Oren, E.: SemperWiki: A Semantic Personal Wiki. In: Semantic Desktop Workshop (2005)
4. Schaffert, S.: IkeWiki: A Semantic Wiki for Collaborative Knowledge Management. In: 1st International Workshop on Semantic Technologies in Collaborative Applications (2006)
5. The ACM Computing Classification System, http://www.acm.org/class/
6. Kifer, M., Lausen, G., Wu, J.: Logical Foundations of Object-Oriented and Frame-Based Languages. Journal of the ACM (1995)
7. MediaWiki, http://www.mediawiki.org
8. TWiki, http://twiki.org
9. Rhee, S.K., Lee, J., Park, M.-W.: Ontology-based Semantic Relevance Measure. In: 1st International Workshop on Semantic Web and Web 2.0 in Architectural, Product and Engineering Design (2007)
10. Wikipedia, http://wikipedia.org

Unconsciously Harmonized Online Communication Based on Uninterruptibility Estimation of Interaction Partners

Takahiro Tanaka, Kyouhei Matsumura, and Kinya Fujita

Tokyo University of Agriculture and Technology
2-24-16 Nakacho, Koganei, Tokyo, 184-8588, Japan
{takat,kfujita}@cc.tuat.ac.jp, 50004258054@st.tuat.ac.jp

Abstract. The current users of real-time online communication tools have a problem in recognizing the status of interaction partners. Therefore, the start of dialogue has a risk of unintended interruption of the partner. To overcome the problem, we focused on application-switching (AS) as a potential intelligent activity discontinuity for uninterruptibility estimation. The preliminary experiments revealed the uninterruptibility reduction effect of AS. Therefore, we developed an online communication system which allows users to naturally recognize the uninterruptibility of interaction partners, by estimating uninterruptibility using AS, keystroke, mouse click and presenting uninterruptibility as avatar posture and motion.

Keywords: Online communication, Interruptibility, Human-Agent-Interaction.

1 Introduction

In recent years, the instant messaging tools such as MSN Messenger or Yahoo Messenger have become popular for daily online communication. The feature of the communication style with these tools is "communicate while doing another thing". The most of the messaging tools have a function that shows user status, Busy / Away from Keyboard (AFK) and so on. However, the status is manually set by users and users tend to set the status as AFK to avoid being interrupted by dialogues even while they are using the tool for communication. This unreliable status operation causes a problem that the user can not recognize that the interaction partners are really busy or not. Therefore, automatic status estimation and ambient display of the status is expected to assist the avoidance of unintended interruption.

One potential method for estimating user busyness is to count keystroke or mouse click [1]. However, the physical activity indexes do not reflect the intelligent activity that should not be interrupted, because the intelligent activity has no observable output. Another approach is specifying the purpose of the PC usage from the utilized application. However, multi-purposes application such as WEB browser prevents the estimation. Numbers of recent researches attempt to estimate user context using various sensors set in the living space or on the users. It appears they still require further study to estimate user intelligent activity [2][3].

S. Lee et al. (Eds.): APCHI 2008, LNCS 5068, pp. 77–85, 2008.
© Springer-Verlag Berlin Heidelberg 2008

Text-based or voice-based real-time chat systems are widely used for online communication. Most of the chat systems provide no or very limited non-verbal communication functions in spite of its importance in expression and recognition of emotion, intension, attention and so on. The avatar-mediated communication systems are also getting popular in recent years. The embodied avatar has a potential for assisting non-verbal communication. Facial expression is an essential component for emotional expression. Numbers of systems provide facial expression control functions, however most of them require manual operation. Gaze has rich communication control functions such as turn-requesting, turn-yielding and so on. There are some studies for trying automatic control of avatar's gaze by using eye-tracking cameras [4].

The expression of the uninterruptibility must be intuitive for reducing the cognitive load of the user. There are some researches on ambient awareness using non-verbal information. The movements of head, face and body demonstrated their effectiveness in expressing nonverbal behavior [5]. It was also demonstrated that the user can recognize emotional states of virtual character through head movement and body posture during gaze shifts [6]. The anthropomorphic motions assisted the user understanding the robot's status [7]. The expression of the uninterruptibility using non-verbal information through an avatar appears promising for intuitive recognition of the uninterruptibility.

In attempt to overcome the intelligent activity interruption problem, we focused on the application-switching (AS) as a potential intelligent activity discontinuity. We also have developed an online communication system that estimates user uninterruptibility and expresses it as avatar motion. This paper reports the system concept in section 2, the uninterruptibility estimation method in section 3 and uninterruptibility expression design in section 4.

2 Unconsciously Harmonized Online Communication System

The developed unconsciously harmonizing communication system is based on a three-stage interaction model, "before dialogue", "during dialogue" and "closing dialogue". This paper is focused on the estimation and the expression of user uninterruptibility during "before dialogue" stage for assisting pleasantly-acceptable dialogue start.

Fig. 1 shows an overview of the prototyped unconsciously harmonized online communication system. The developed system consists of two main modules, user uninterruptibility estimation module and user uninterruptibility expression module. The estimation module monitors the keystroke, mouse click and application-switching (AS) of the user, and estimates the uninterruptibility based on the experimentally-acquired rules. The estimation module sends the user uninterruptibility to the interaction partners over the Internet. The expression module at the partner side expresses the uninterruptibility as the animation of his/her avatar.

Fig. 2 shows a screenshot of the user desktop using this system. The user selects interaction partners to show their uninterruptibility from his/her friend list, then the system displays avatar windows to each selected partners. Avatars of interaction partners are displayed on screen corner small, and these avatars aware the partner's uninterruptibility by the posture and motion.

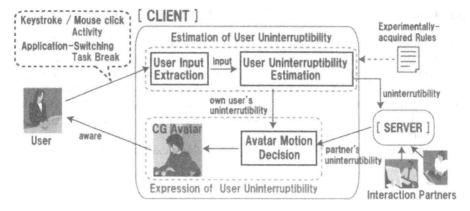

Fig. 1. Overview of the Unconsciously Harmonized Online Communication System

Fig. 2. Screenshot of the User Desktop using System

3 Estimation of User Uninterruptibility

The system estimates the uninterruptibility of PC users based on three kinds of information, keystroke, mouse click and AS. The transition of focused application is considered as the intentional switching of working space or working target by the users. Therefore, the user concentration at AS may be instantaneously lowered at high probability compared to the continuous work. To examine the assumption, we experimentally collected the user operation and subjective interrupt evaluation logs.

3.1 Experimental Evaluation of AS Effect in Uninterruptibility

We implemented a logging tool which records keystroke, mouse click and AS every 500ms. Fig.3 shows an architecture of this logging tool. The tool interrupts the user when AS occurs or every 5 minutes during continuous work (NAS), and requests the user to subjectively evaluate how much the user do not want to be interrupted. The evaluation is scaled from 1: "No problem" to 5: "Absolutely uninterruptible". Over 20 hours evaluation logs during daily PC activity were collected from 10 university students with no limitation in purpose of PC usage. The main purposes of the PC use were "programming", "web browsing", "report writing" and "data arranging".

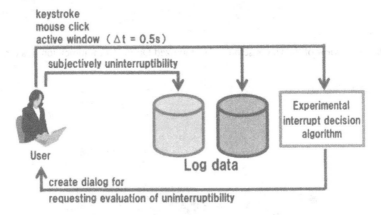

Fig. 3. Experimental Logging Tool

3.1.1 Log Data Analysis: AS vs. NAS

Table 1 shows the uninterruptibility comparison between AS and NAS. The experimental results suggested that the interrupts at AS are significantly acceptable for the users than the interrupts during continuous work ($p < 0.01$).

However, there are some high uninterruptible evaluations in AS. It means there are some kinds of AS that has less uninterruptibility reduction effect. So, we analyzed relation the uninterruptibility and the AS frequency. From this analysis, the interrupts at less frequent AS were more acceptable than the more frequent AS ($p < 0.05$).

The result revealed the interrupts at AS are significantly acceptable for the users than the interrupts during continuous work. Therefore, the AS expression to interaction partner by avatar motion is useful for assisting pleasantly-acceptable dialogue start.

Table 1. Subjective evaluation of system interrupt at AS and NAS

	Subjective score of uninterruptibiliy					
	1	2	3	4	5	Ave.
Application Switch	51	80	67	45	36	**2.8**
Not Application Switch	7	14	22	20	12	**3.2**

3.1.2 Log Data Analysis: Activity and Uninterruptibility During NAS

From the analysis, AS is suitable timing for starting dialogue than during continuous work. However, there are some situations that the user can't wait for AS because of some reasons; emergency, important information and so on. Therefore, the uninterruptibility estimation during NAS is needed for encouraging / discouraging to start dialogue too. We analyzed the uninterruptibility and activity, keystroke and mouse click for the estimation during NAS.

In this study, the activity A(t) is calculated using equation (1). Kt is the keystroke count, Ct is the mouse click count and Ht is the amount of mouse wheel use. The keystroke is given larger weighting factor because it better reflects the busyness [1].

$$A(t) = 2 Kt + Ct + Ht \qquad (1)$$

Fig. 4 shows the relationship between the 30 seconds accumulated activity and the subjective score of the uninterruptibility score. We expected that the uninterruptibility corresponding to the lower activity would be low. However, the subjects answered higher uninterruptibility numbers of times, even if the activity is zero.

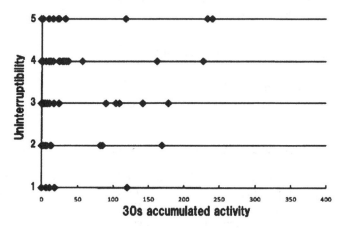

Fig. 4. 30 seconds accumulated activity and uninterruptibility

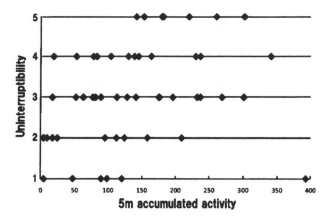

Fig. 5. 5 minutes accumulated activity and uninterruptibility

Fig. 5 shows the 5 minutes accumulated activity and the uninterruptibility score. There is no data that has zero activity. That suggests that at least 5 minutes of activity accumulation is needed to distinguish the working and the resting status. The correlation between the uninterruptibility and the 5 minutes accumulated activity was also observed. That suggests that the 5 minutes accumulated activity reflects the uninterruptibility during NAS.

3.2 Estimation of Two User Uninterruptibility Components

Based on the experimental analysis, we defined two user uninterruptibility components. One is the activity component; another is the task break component. The activity component is calculated as the weighted summation of the keystroke and mouse click counts for 5 minutes. The task break component is an instantaneous negative value generated at AS, that represents the uninterruptibility reduction effect of AS. The AS with shorter interval is given smaller value because the frequent AS may mean busyness not termination of a task. The system sends the activity component to the server every second. When the user switches his/her application, the system sends the task break component immediately.

4   Expression of User Uninterruptibility

The system awares the uninterruptibility of interaction partner using CG Avatar's posture and motion based on two components, activity component and task break component.

4.1   Two Mode of Expressions for Two Components

The posture and the motion of the avatar are controlled to allow the user naturally recognize the uninterruptibility of the partner. Fig.6 shows a relationship between two components and two expressions of uninterruptibility. The posture reflects the gradual change of the activity component that is sent every second. The dynamic motions such as "drinking coffee" are used to express task break component.

4.2   Control the Uninterruptible Impressions

In order to adequately control the intensities of uninterruptible impression, the uninterruptible impressions of various postures and motions of human in daily life were subjectively evaluated prior to the expression design. According to the trends of the evaluation, the following factors were utilized for the uninterruptibility intensity expression.

(1) Distance between body and workspace (PC, desk etc): bend forward / neutral / lean against the chair
(2) Body direction relative to workspace: face to workspace / face to other place
(3) Head direction relative to workspace: face to workspace / face to other place
(4) Hand position: on the keyboard / on the desk / under the desk

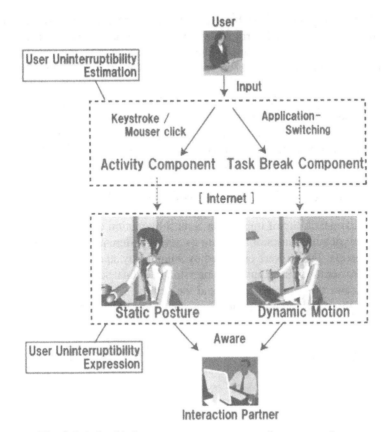

Fig. 6. Relationship between two components and two expressions

Fig. 7. Examples of postures and motions for uninterruptibility expression

These factors are found useful for expressing uninterruptibility. However, the individual difference in the uninterruptible impression for a posture makes it difficult to control the strength of the uninterruptible impression. For example, the more uninterruptible motion between "bend forward" and "keystroke" is different among individuals.

In this research, we overlapped the avatar motions to express the higher uninterruptibility intensity instead of changing the motions. It allows us to avoid identifying which motions have stronger uninterruptibility impression. Fig.7 shows the examples of the postures and motions that express the activity and the task break components using the overlap.

4.3 Evaluation of Uninterruptibility Impression Control

To examine the possibility of impression control by motion overlapping, the uninterruptible impression intensities of the postures having different body direction distance and face direction (Fig. 8) were evaluated by 9 university students. The subjects were required to answer the uninterruptible impression in ordinal scale.

Table 2 shows the expected orders and the results. The results demonstrated the possibility of the uninterruptible impression control by the posture overlapping.

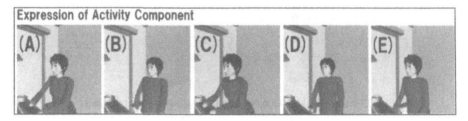

Fig. 8. Examples of the postures and the motions for uninterruptibility expression

Table 2. Evaluation of uninterruptible impression control

	A	B	C	D	E
Expected Score	2	4	1	5	3
Average Score	2.0	4.1	1.1	4.9	2.9

5 Conclusion

We proposed an overview of the unconsciously harmonized online communication system and a method for estimating user uninterruptibility based on operation activity and application-switching. The avatar animation is also proposed to expresses the intensity of the partner uninterruptibility by using postures and motions. The experimental evaluation of the effect of the uninterruptibility expression is remained.

References

1. Honda, S., et al.: A Home Office Environment Based on the Concentration Degrees of Wokers: A Virtual Office SystemValentine. Trans. Info. Processing Society of Japan 39(5), 1472–1483 (1998) (in Japanese)
2. Hudson, S.E., et al.: Predicting Human Interruptibility with Sensors: A Wizard of Oz Feasibility Study. In: SIGCHI conf. on Human Factors in Computing Systems, pp. 257–264 (2003)
3. Lester, J., et al.: A Hybrid Discriminative/Generative Approach for Modeling Human Activities. In: IJCAI 2005, pp. 766–772 (2005)
4. Vertegaal, R.: The GAZE Groupware System: Mediating Joint Attention in Multiparty Communication and Collaboration. In: CHI 1999, pp. 15–20 (1999)
5. Lee, J., Marsella, S.: Nonverbal Behavior Generator for Embodied Conversational Agent. In: 6th International Conference on Intelligent Virtual Agents, pp. 243–255. Springer, Heidelberg (2006)
6. Lance, B., Marsella, S.C.: Emotionally Expressive Head and Body Movement During Gaze Shifts. In: 7th International Conference on Intelligent Virtual Agents, pp. 72–85. Springer, Heidelberg (2007)
7. Kobayashi, K., Yamada, S.: Informing a User of Robot's Mind by Motion. In: The third International Conference on Computational Intelligence, Robotics and Autonomous Systems (CIRAS 2005), SS4B-3 (2005)
8. Second Life, Linden Research, Inc. http://secondlife.com/

A Novel Web Page Analysis Method for Efficient Reasoning of User Preference

Seunghwa Lee, Minchul Jung, and Eunseok Lee

School of Information and Communication Engineering
Sungkyunkwan University
Suwon 440-746, South Korea
{shlee,mcjung,eslee}@ece.skku.ac.kr

Abstract. The amount of information on the Web is rapidly increasing. Recommender systems can help users selectively filter this information based on their preferences. One way to obtain user preferences is to analyze characteristics of content that is accessed by the user. Unfortunately, web pages may contain elements irrelevant to user interests (e.g., navigation bar, advertisements, and links.). Hence, existing analysis approaches using the TF-IDF method may not be suitable. This paper proposes a novel user preference analysis system that eliminates elements that repeatedly appear in web pages. It extracts user interest keywords in the identified primary content. Also, the system has features that collect the anchor tag, and track the user's search route, in order to identify keywords that are of core interest to the user. This paper compares the proposed system with pure TF-IDF analysis method. The analysis confirms its effectiveness in terms of the accuracy of the analyzed user profiles.

Keywords: Recommendation system, User preference, User profile, TF-IDF.

1 Introduction

The amount of information on the Web is explosively growing. Research relating to recommender systems, which aims to offer suitable information based on user preference, has become an important subject. Traditional recommender methods consist of content-based and collaborative filtering approaches. Content-based method computes the similarity between the current user preference and content, and collaborative filtering computes the similarity between users. These methods generate recommendations based on user preference. Hence, acquisition of an accurate user preference is very important.

Representative methods for generation of the user preference are explicit and implicit approaches. The explicit approach obtains user preference by direct inquiry of the user [1][2]. Thus, this approach compels the user onerously, and it is hard to get an accurate response from the user. Conversely, the implicit approach deduces user preference based on behavior [3][4]. Hence, the implicit approach may be more propitious.

One way to implicitly obtain user preference is to analyze characteristics of content used by each user. Most existing information systems identify frequently appearing terms as user interest keywords using the TF-IDF method [5][6]. However, using only

S. Lee et al. (Eds.): APCHI 2008, LNCS 5068, pp. 86–93, 2008.
© Springer-Verlag Berlin Heidelberg 2008

the TF-IDF method may be unsuitable, because these pages contain elements irrelevant to user interest (e.g., navigation bar, advertisements, and copyright notices). These elements commonly appear on dynamically generated documents. These elements are defined as *noncontent blocks* [7]. S. Debnath et al.,'s algorithm offers web page to users with mobile devices of limited resources.

Unimportant words may be identified by Inverse Document Frequency (IDF) computation. IDF lowers the weight of common terms in an overall document set. However, analyzing a document that includes all non-content blocks leads to inefficient utilization of time and inaccurate results.

This paper proposes a novel user preference analysis system that eliminates noncontent blocks that are repeated in web pages. It extracts keywords to the user interest in the primary content identified. Moreover, the proposed system features include collecting anchor tags, and tracking the user's search route, in order to identify keywords of core interest to the user. This paper compares the proposed system with the pure TF-IDF analysis method. It confirms the effectiveness in terms of the accuracy of the user profiles analyzed.

The paper is organized as follows: Section 2 introduces work related to profile analysis. Section 3 describes the overall structure and behavior of the proposed system, designed in order to cope with the weaknesses identified in the previous work. Section 4 evaluates the results of using our approach. Finally, Section 5 concludes the paper and identifies possible future work.

2   Related Work

The advent of ubiquitous computing has promulgated the desire for information with varied format and content. For instance, even TV program guides and movie clips may include textual information [8]. Hence, methods that analyze textual information to derive characteristics of the content may be useful in recommender systems.

$$w_{ij} = tf_{ij} \times (\log \frac{N}{df_i}) \tag{1}$$

* where, tf_{ij} : the frequency of word i on document j

   N : the number of sample documents

   df_i : the number of documents including word i

In general, user preference is obtained by analyzing the terms of web documents accessed by the user. To do this, the Term Frequency * Inverse Documents Frequency (TF*IDF) approach is commonly utilized. TF represents how frequently each word appears. IDF reduces the weight of terms commonly appearing in the overall document set.

This method is applied in a number of studies [9][10][11][12]. The weight value for each term is computed in formula (1). Terms that appear frequently in the documents are regarded as interest keywords. If the terms are commonly appear in the overall document set, the weight of the terms is reduced.

However, current web documents are generated dynamically, and they may include elements irrelevant to the user's interests. Hence, analyzing such terms may reduce the accuracy of the user's profile, as well as delaying the processing time.

Researchers have been investigating how to eliminate meaningless parts of web documents and how to identify the informative blocks [7][13][14]. These are carried out in order to convert web pages, which are created for a desktop PC, to information more useful for mobile devices with a limited display.

Fig. 1. Example of informative blocks

Examples of the principal informative blocks are marked as a dotted line in Figure 1. The figure on the left side is general news content. The right side item is information pertaining to the shopping mall site.

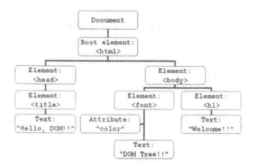

Fig. 2. Example DOM tree

In this paper we apply a method similar to that of related work in order to more efficiently analyze the user profile. This method converts the web document, composed by HTML, to the DOM Tree [15]. It then identifies repeatedly appearing parts as non-content blocks by comparing each node of the web pages obtained from a given web server. An example DOM tree is shown in Figure 2.

An alternative method extracted the keywords of interest to users by analyzing the hyperlink and content of the linked document [16]. This approach has some inefficiency. For instance, it analyzes all terms included in the linked documents. However, it has one aspect similar to that of our proposed system. It observes the user's search route, by using the hyperlink information in the web document, and then considering it as clue to more efficiently extract the user's interests.

Information on the Web is being continuously renewed. Information is presented through email or Web site links to the user. Generally, a hyperlink sentence about new information is composed of an expression full of overtones of the linked document. This is applied to various areas such as internet news, community notices, and new items appearing at the e-commerce site. A user refers to the textual reference to the link, and decides whether or not to move to the other web page by clicking on the link representing the url (uniform resource locator). Thus, we consider that the text associated with the link includes an important clue to analyze user preference.

3 Proposed System

The objective of the proposed system is to more accurately extract the keywords representing the user's interest from recently visited web pages, in order to deduce the user's preferences. The proposed system is located on the client device, and performs eliminating the stop word, stemming, and indexing phase for the web pages.

The overall system structure is shown in Figure 3.

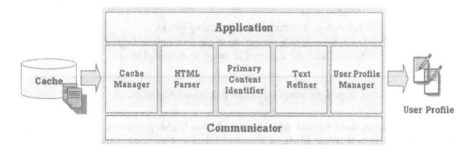

Fig. 3. Overall structure of the proposed system

The role of each module and overall behavior are as follows:

1) *Cache Manager (CM)*: manages the user's web usage log and web pages stored in the cache. It also examines web pages sent from the same web server, and forwards the page or page set to the *HTML Parser*.
2) *HTML Parser (HP)*: loads the page in sequence, and generates a HTML DOM tree by analyzing the HTML structure. In the case of the *anchor* tag, the *HP* stores the URL and link text included in the tag as a mapping table.
3) *Primary Content Identifier (PCI)*: compares the DOM tree structure for all pages in the page set. If the same node is detected, the *PCI* examines the sub-leaf node. When the all nodes are checked, elements with the same structure and text are regarded as non-content blocks, and these are eliminated.
4) *Text Refiner (TR)*: handles the identified primary content. A stop word list is used to remove common words. In addition, terms that appear in only one web page are removed, and Porter stemmer [17] is also applied to each term.
5) *User Profile Manager (UPM)*: computes the weight value for the each term based on the TF-IDF method. The *UPM* also ranks the terms in descending order of weight value, and renews the user profile. If any page among the page set received from the *CM* is present in the mapping table generated in phase 2, an additional weight value is applied to the terms of the text linked with the anchor tag.

The algorithm identifying informative blocks is similar to the research of S. Debnath et al., [7]. In this paper the algorithm is applied to more efficiently analyze the user profile. The basic process is to identify parts that repeatedly appear in documents obtained from same web server as the non-content blocks. In the proposed system, the algorithm is performed by *PCI*. The algorithm is as follows:

Informative-blocks Extraction Algorithm

Input: document set stored in the cache
Output: user profile extracted from the informative blocks of the each document
Method:
Begin
　Step 1. *CM*: identify the document set whose first words in the URL are identical
　Step 2. *HP*: extract the tag and text information
　　　Step 2.1. *HP*: generate the HTML DOM tree
　Step 3. *TR*: refine the document (eliminating the stop words, stemming, etc)
　Step 4. *PCI*: examines all nodes(tag)
　　　Step 4.1. *PCI*: identify the non-content blocks that have the same structure
　　　　　　and content
　　Step 5. *UPM*: extracts the terms in the remaining blocks
　　　Step 5.1. *UPM*: computes the weight of the terms using TF-IDF
　　Step 6. *UPM*: generates the user profile based on extracted terms
　End

Fig. 4. Informative-blocks Extraction Algorithm

After the non-content blocks are identified, the USM generates the user profile based on the extracted terms in the remaining blocks. The system then examines the hyperlink sentences to identify the keywords of core interest to the user. The algorithm is shown in Figure 5.

Core-interest keyword Extraction Algorithm

Input: document set whose first words in the URL are identical
Output: user profile that applies the weights for the keywords of core-interest
Method:
Begin
　Step 1. *HP*: extracts the hyperlink information (i.e., anchor tag block, link sentence, url info.)
　　　Step 1.1. *HP*: generate a mapping table
　　　Step 1.2. *HP*: examines correspondence between url of another document and url information in the table
　(if correspondence == true){
　　　　Step 1.2.1 *HP*: extracts the hyperlink information in the table
　　　　Step 1.2.2 *TR*: refines the keywords included in the hyperlink
　　　　　　　　(eliminating the stop words, stemming, etc)
　　　　Step 1.2.3 *UPM*: re-computes the weight value of refined keywords
　　Step 2. *HP*: deletes the table in memory
　End

Fig. 5. Core-interest keyword Extraction Algorithm

Figure 6 shows an example of extracting the keywords of interest to the user from the anchor tag. In the example, additional weight is applied to the terms clicked by user (i.e., samsung, q1, ultra, mobile, tablet, etc). In this paper, the weight value only doubles.

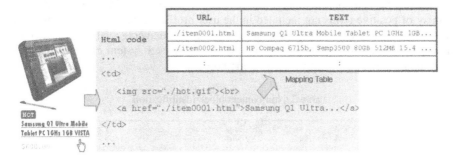

Fig. 6. An example of extracting the keywords of interest to the user from the anchor tag

The user profile is represented by the vector space representation that is commonly used in the information filtering area [10][12][18].

$$User\_profile_{id} = (term_1, w_1), (term_2, w_2)...(term_n, w_n) \tag{2}$$

* where, w : weight value for the each term

4 System Evaluation

The performance of the proposed system is measured in terms of accuracy of the generated user profile. For this, we performed two types of experiments as follows:

The first test was to evaluate the accuracy in the identification of the non-content blocks. 10 users participated in the test. First, we selected web pages randomly from each user's cache, and split each of the pages as section units based on the principal leaf nodes of the DOM tree. Then, we showed these section lists to the users. The primary content sections and non-content blocks are checked by the users. This survey is repeated 10 times, each time using a different web page.

We analyzed the web pages using the pure TF-IDF method against the proposed system, and generated user profiles. The precision is used as the evaluation metric. The type of the each factor is shown in Table 1.

Table 1. Metric factors

	Primary content	Non-content block
Positive	PP	NP
Negative	PN	NN

$$Precision = \frac{PP}{PP + NP} \tag{3}$$

Where, PP is the number of cases where positive terms included in the primary content are collected in the user profile. NP is the number of cases where useless terms, included in the non-content blocks, are collected in the user profile. PN represents the number of positive terms not included in the user profile, and NN represents the number of useless terms not included in the user profile. The average values evaluated are shown in Table 2. The result confirms that the proposed system can identify more meaningful terms than the pure TF-IDF method.

Table 2. Non-content block identification

	User1	User2	User3	User4	User5	User6	User7	User8	User9	User10
Pure TF-IDF	0.613	0.548	0.642	0.435	0.534	0.613	0.642	0.528	0.617	0.624
Proposed System	0.818	0.751	0.768	0.761	0.615	0.738	0.724	0.646	0.728	0.732

The second test was to evaluate the effectiveness of the generated user profile. We showed the 50 highest ranked terms in the generated user profile. The users checked those that were irrelevant. The experiment was performed using the user profile generated after the identification of the non-content block, the user profile generated after identification of the core interest keywords by analyzing hyperlinks, and the user profile generated by the pure TF-IDF method, respectively. The results shown in Table 3 demonstrate that the proposed system is more efficient.

Table 3. Accuracy of the user profile generated

	User1	User2	User3	User4	User5	User6	User7	User8	User9	User10
Pure TF-IDF	0.261	0.343	0.252	0.443	0.364	0.514	0.231	0.344	0.275	0.352
Proposed System 1	0.521	0.487	0.532	0.577	0.452	0.513	0.431	0.565	0.437	0.632
Proposed System 2	0.521	0.51	0.542	0.584	0.452	0.513	0.446	0.571	0.439	0.632

5 Conclusion

In this paper, we proposed a novel method for user preference analysis, an essential phase in recommender systems. The proposed system improved analysis accuracy by eliminating useless elements, in the web pages, unrelated to the user's preference. The system extracted the keywords of core interest to the user by analyzing the hyperlink elements. The experiment confirmed that the system can solve some of the limitations of existing TF-IDF method that are inadequate in reviewing recently visited web pages. We expect that the proposed system can be applied in various recommender applications.

Subsequent work will further investigate the proposed analysis method and will apply it to efficient web recommender systems.

Acknowledgments. This work was supported by the Ministry of Knowledge Economy 21st Century Frontier R&D Program in Korea and a result of subproject UCN 08B3-B1-10M, ITRC IITA-2008-(C1090-080-0046), Grant No. R01-2006-000-10954-0, Basic Research Program of the Korea Science & Engineering Foundation.

References

1. Melamed, D., Shapira, B., Elovici, Y.: MarCol: A Market-Based Recommender System. IEEE Intelligent Systems 22(3), 74–78 (2007)
2. Aciar, S., Zhang, D., Simoff, S., Debenham, J.: Informed Recommender: Basing Recommendations on Consumer Product Reviews. IEEE Intelligent Systems 22(3), 39–47 (2007)
3. Balabanovic, M., Shoham, Y.: Fab: Content-based, Collaborative Recommendation. Communication of the ACM, 66–72 (March 1997)
4. Linden, G., Smith, B., York, J.: Amazon.com Recommendations Item-to-Item Collaborative Filtering. IEEE Internet Computing, 76–80 (January 2003)
5. Robertson, S.: Understanding Inverse Document Frequency: on theoretical arguments for IDF. Journal of documentation 60(5), 503–520 (2005)
6. Salton, G.: Introduction to Modern Information Retrieval. Mcgraw Hill, New York (1983)
7. Debnath, S., Mitra, P., Pal, N., Giles, C.: Automatic Identification of Informative Sections of Web Pages. IEEE Transactions on Knowledge and Data Engineering 17(9), 1233–1246 (2005)
8. Chang, S., Sikora, T., Puri, A.: Overview of the MPEG-7 Standard. IEEE Transactions on Circuits and Systems for Video Technology 11(6) (June 2001)
9. Beil, F., Ester, M., Xu, X.: Frequent Term-Based Text Clustering. In: Proceedings of the eighth ACM SIGKDD international conference on Knowledge Discovery and Data Mining, pp. 436–442 (2002)
10. Pazzani, M., Muramatsu, J., Billsus, D.: Syskill & Webert: Identifying interesting web sites. In: Proceedings of the 13th national conference on Artificial Intelligence (1996)
11. Chen, L., Sycara, K.: WebMate: A Personal Agent for Browsing and Searching. In: Proceedings of the 2nd international conference on Autonomous Agent, pp. 132–139 (1998)
12. Pierre, S., Kacan, C., Probst, W.: An agent –based approach for integrating user profile into a knowledge management process. Elsevier Knowledge-Based Systems 13, 307–314 (2000)
13. Lin, S., Ho, J.: Discovering Informative Content blocks from Web Documents. In: Proceedings of the eighth ACM SIGKDD international conference on Knowledge Discovery and Data Mining, July 2002, pp. 588–593 (2002)
14. Ramaswamy, L., Lyengar, A., Liu, L., Douglis, F.: Automatic Fragment Detection in Dynamic Web Pages and Its Impact on Caching. IEEE Transactions on Knowledge and Data Engineering 17(6), 859–874 (2005)
15. http://www.w3.org/dom/
16. Armstrong, R., Freitag, D., Joachims, T., Mitchell, T.: WebWatcher: A Learning Apprentice for the World Wide Web (February 1995)
17. Frakes, W.B., Baeza-Yates, R.: Information Retrieval: Data Structures and Algorithms. Prentice-Hall, Englewood Cliffs (1992)
18. Yu, Z., Zhou, X.: TV3P: An Adaptive Assistant for Personalized TV. IEEE Transaction on Consumer Electronics 50(1), 393–399 (2004)

Mood and Recommendations: On Non-cognitive Mood Inducers for High Quality Recommendation

Tiffany Y. Tang[1] and Pinata Winoto[2]

[1] Department of Computing, Hong Kong Polytechnic University,
Hung Hom, Hong Kong SAR
cstiffany@comp.polyu.edu.hk
[2] Department of Computer Science, Konkuk University,
Chungju-Si, 380-701, Korea
pinata@kku.ac.kr

Abstract. Watching a comedy can help a user escape from the negative mood, which in turn affect the user's feedback over the movie. In other words, a non-cognitive mood inducer (the movie) can affect a user's post-consumption evaluation over the inducer (the rating the user give) which is directly associated with users' assessment over consumed goods. If these goods are generated from a recommender system, they will then directly affect the performance of the system. As such, our study attempts to enrich our understanding of the inducers and their effects in the recommendation performance. In addition, this paper provides a preliminary exploration of a mood-based filter to enhance the interaction between human and the system.

Keywords: Mood, Recommendation system.

1 Introduction

Recommender Systems (RSs) make suggestions of an item (or a set of items) to a target user based on the content of the item and those items the user likes before (known as content-based recommendation [1]), observing the like-mindness of similar users with the target users (known as collaborative-filtering approach or CF [2][3][4]), or a series of interactive user-specified critiques (known as the knowledge-based approach [5]). It has been studied extensive in the literature and adopted in a variety of commercial systems including Amazon.com[TM], Netflix[TM], and many others [2][3][4]. The early years of RS research have seen numerous research outputs on designing and evaluating more efficient and accurate algorithms. Recently, thanks to the great potential of RS in commercial systems, researchers have shifted their attention to the human aspects of a RS from its algorithmic design: that is, how to improve the quality of human-recommender interactions [4][6][7][8]. Fundamental to this research direction is the way RS should be judged by its end-users, which determines how the system should be evaluated accordingly. As such, from this perspective, we see a shift toward human-centered design of RSs.

In this paper, we discuss a human-centered design of a RS that considers user mood before making recommendation, in which the term *mood* refers to '*constantly*

S. Lee et al. (Eds.): APCHI 2008, LNCS 5068, pp. 94–103, 2008.

evolving general affective states felt by individuals' (p.166 [9]). The underlying consideration is that users are capable of dynamically updating their mood during and following various activities such as listening to a light music, watching a comedy or playing a strategy game [9][10]. That is, users can make conscious and unconscious selection over entertainment content that serves to maintain positive mood and repair or diminish pain in terms of both intensity and duration [11][12], which have been pointed out under the label of mood management [13]. The following example shows a situation in which user mood is relevant and important to the recommendation.

Example. Suppose a sales manager is on a train heading home after a hectic and frustrated Friday, and he is browsing an entertainment portal using his PDA with a plan to download and watch a movie. Suppose the portal, which maintains his past records and user model, has predicted that he will like *Will Smith*'s drama *'The Pursuit of Happiness[1]'* that is based on a true story and vividly portraits how a single father overcomes the so many sad moments during his life-changing professional endeavor. It is an inspiring movie and is preferred by many people (with an average rating of 7.7 out of 10 from 41,960 votes in IMDB.com, as of the writing of this paper). However, due to the plots of the movie that characterized by keywords *homelessness, unhappy marriage, homeless shelter, financial problems*, and *single father*, the sad manager with high job pressure may not like to watch it at that night, because it will 'down-grade' his mood, and makes him unhappy. Hence, it is necessary for the portal to detect his mood, either by questioning him or other means, and then recommends appropriate movies or other entertainment items that are more suitable for the manager. For instance, the system can cross-recommend a simulation game such as *SimSociety* to fulfill the short-term well-being of the manager so as to increase the efficacy of the manager, which in turn increase his enjoyment or repair his mood [10].   ■

This example highlights the importance of designing RSs that can *recognize* a user's current mood and attempts to recommend more appropriate item(s) in order to repair the user's mood. We believe that by incorporating user emotional and other contextual information in the recommendation framework, users are expected to be more satisfied with the recommended items. Unfortunately, very few RSs consider it during recommendation, which motivates our study here. Hence, in this paper we will provide a brief literature review on user mood and discuss the RS model that incorporated user mood. Our research draws upon previous research from three main areas: human computer interaction, consumer psychology and the psychology of entertainment, and recommender systems. We propose a mood-filter on top of a cross-domain RS that can make recommendation on games and movies. Our proposed mood-filtered recommendation works in between a cross-domain RS and the user, and suggests more appropriate items based on current user mood. Note that a cross-domain RS differentiates itself from a typical one in that it is capable of making recommendation on items from more than one domain/category [4]. The potential application is on mobile RSs that can detect user mood either through a dialog system or other means.

We consider several possible mood-inducing factors that include user's current location, recommendation time, and user's current mood. For instance, a user might feel

---

[1] See the movie's plot keywords and other information at its IMDB site at
http://www.imdb.com/title/tt0454921/

more stressful in the office than at home; conversely, s/he feels better on sunny days [14]. In addition, we want to prolong or maintain our happy mood, but try to improve our situation (in the short-term) when we are in negative mood, e.g. by not focusing on the negative parts [9][15][16]. Note that we will follow most studies in the community that prefer broad indication of either positive or negative moods, and will not attempt to assess specific moods.

The rest of this article is organized as follows. In the next section, we will discuss previous works that have been done in consumer psychology and human-recommender interaction. The system architecture and framework will be presented in Section 3, followed by the future work in Section 4.

2   User Mood and Its Implications to Recommendation

In this section we will discuss related research on three areas: consumer psychology, the psychology of entertainment, and human recommender interaction. At the end, we will discuss some implications of them to the design of better RSs.

2.1   The Role of Emotions in Consumer Behaviors

Individual mood is known to be quite easily influenced by little things [17], and is known to play a key role in customer purchase decisions and a variety of future consumption behaviours (e.g. [18], [19]). Since some RSs are intended to faciliate purchasing decisions, it is important for us to understand how user mood affects the purchasing behavior.

Individuals try to escape from negative moods by focusing on positive memories or engaging in future consumptions [20][21]. Compensatory consumer consumption is regularly found to fight negative mood; for instance, listening to light music [9], hearing good news [22], watching a comedy, etc. Ryan et al [10] empirically confirmed that the attractiveness or '*pull*' of games, regardless of specific genre, can fulfil player psychological needs, thus, in turn increase his/her enjoyment, although they assume that different genres of games can bring different degree of satisfaction and enjoyment. For instance, they pointed out that '*a life-simulation game like 'The Sims''... no double satisfies different needs than 'first-person shooter' games such as 'Halo', puzzle games 'such as "Tetris" or action games such as "GrandTheft Auto"* (p. 361).

Furthermore, Bloemer and de Ruyter [23] found out that positive consumption emotion can lead to customer satisfaction and strengthen positive '*word-of-mouth*' intentions. In addition, individuals in positive mood levels tend to demonstrate better abilities in interpreting and integrating information, and at finding creative solutions [17], which might in turn trigger more future mood-related consumptions. Moreover, consumers might bias the consumed goods or service encounters (including the user interface in the system) in mood-congruent directions; that is, those in positive/negative moods after consumptions tend to rate the goods/service more positively/negatively [15]. The observation is interesting and can be used as a psychological foundation to encourage the interaction between users and a service counter (i.e. the RS in our case).

2.2 The Psychology of Entertainment

Zillmann [12] recognized that a wide range of information consumption from news, documents, sport to comedies, dramas, music are affected by user's mood. The idea has been further explored in the mood management research community [13]. In particular, entertainment selection is characterized by hedonistic motivations to either maintain their positive mood or repair their negative mood in terms of both intensity and duration. In this regard, a user's affective state serves as a crucially useful predictor of their entertainment decisions. Although a variety of genres can potentially drive entertainment selection, sad or tragic contents are arguably more likely to be avoided by the majority of users; while light-hearted or funny entertainment is mostly sought after [11][24].

As for movie-goers, Tesser et al [25] identified three major motivations triggering users' movie-going behaviours: *self-escape, entertainment* and *self-development*. The first two seems to be consistent with *hedonic* considerations for users to repair or maintain positive mood; while self-development appears to be the least related to hedonic considerations, in contrast, it reflects users' *eudaimonic* motivations in seeking greater insight and meaningfulness towards life for self-reflection [26]. As such, a wider range of movies have been tested to establish the relationships between users' tender states and entertainment preferences [11].

2.3 Human-Recommender Interaction

In the human computer interaction community, emotion and affect have been recognized as important [27][28]; however, the majority of the work has focused on the design and evaluation of various *emoticons* (emotional icons) in a mobile application [29], an instant messenger [30], a health-care system [31], as well as how to construct evaluation framework for affective user interface systems [32][33][34].

In the human recommender interaction, to the best of our knowledge, making recommendation based on user mood remains inadequately studied, which is not surprising, since only recently did researchers switch from the extensively explored algorithmic design to the human-centred design of RSs (referred to as human-recommender interaction [8]). Existing human-centred RS has been focusing on the human computer interaction aspect of RS, such as the usability of the system and transparency of the recommendations made [35][36][37], or the social tagging [4][7]. For instance, both [36] and [35] examine the role of transparency (inform users of why a particular recommendation was made) and the latter further examines several approach of visually presenting recommended items to users, and both agreed that designing user-friendly user interface can strengthen user trust over the perceived quality of the recommender. These studies set another research direction focusing on user acceptance of the recommendations by constructing an appropriate evaluation framework to assess recommendation quality [4][7][37].

2.4 Implications

There are many implications to the development of future RSs that can be derived from previous work. However, we will only enumerate four here.

Firstly, depending on the user mood, the most effective item to repair or retain user mood could be a movie, song, game, news, or others. Hence, the RSs should not only recommend a single category (e.g. movie), but be able to process information from multiple categories or domains and recommend an appropriate item(s) according to user mood. This requires multi-domain RSs [4].

Secondly, since user ratings are affected by the user's mood when consuming the items [15], it may pose a threat to the performance of collaborative-filtering (CF) based RSs. The reason is that the accuracy of the CF-based recommendation depends on the *truthfulness* of ratings given by users, that is, they should be invariant from environmental factor such as user mood. Hence, it will be interesting to study the effect of users' mood toward the truthfulness of their ratings and the accuracy of CF-based RSs in the future.

Thirdly, we need an integrated method to collect the contextual information that can be used to predict the user mood. The information may include the location, time, weather, how the item(s) will be consumed, self-report by the user, etc. Hence, we need a more integrated method than merely asking the user his/her mood; for example, through pervasive technology or a sensor network.

Lastly, new recommendation methods that can effectively and efficiently incorporating user mood should be studied in the future. In the next section, we will describe our attempt toward the development of such method.

3 Dual-Layer Recommendation System

Unlike typical RSs which make recommendation on items from only one category (i.e. movie or music RS), we will include items from more than one category as the candidates, i.e. movies, music and games. The reasons of designing RSs for multiple domains are threefold: (i) many current mobile devices (e.g. pocket PCs) are capable of delivering multi-domain items to users (e.g. music, movies, and games), (ii) we believe that the future RSs should satisfy the need of user in various situation or activities (e.g. listening to music during driving or watching movies during relaxing, etc.), and (iii) different negative mood may be remedied using item from different domains; hence, by including more candidate items the RSs have a higher chance of recommending a "correct" item to remedy or improve user mood.

In the context of this paper, strategy or action games, romantic comedies, happy news, good weather, etc., are referred to as non-cognitive mood inducers. A mood inducer, say, a movie, can affect a user's *post-consumption mood* as well his/her *post-consumption evaluation* to the inducer (e.g, the rating given by the user). Since the latter is directly associated with users' assessment over consumed goods, and if these goods are generated from a RS, it will then affect the performance of the system. However, we will not pursue whether the user's post-consumption mood can either be altered or maintained as it is beyond the scope of this paper. In addition, we do not intend to draw a complete picture in discerning users' various tender state covering a wider range degree of sadness and happiness from gloomy, blue, low, fine, upbeat, cheerful etc; instead, we calibrate users' perceptions of movies as a dichotomous decision (like to watch the movie or not like to watch) relative to their three broad mood (i.e. happy, sad, neutral).

Information about the possible emotional status of a movie (i.e. a user in positive mood will remain in the state after watching it) can be elicited from the plot keywords (as shown in the motivational example), as well as from its genre (i.e. comedy, romantic comedy, etc). Since current studies only conclude that playing games can help users preserve their mood, we will treat games as a neutral element; however, we will differentiate a game which is suitable for family or not in order to help a player preserve his mood. For instance, a player might want to fight his unhappiness by playing '*Halo*' at a weekday night, while the same player intends to play a family game such as '*How to be a Millionnaire*' with his family members during a family day. In both cases, playing the game can either help the player escape from the negative mood or prolong the positive one. As for the news and weather information, they can easily be Googled. At our current stage, we will only consider movies and games and show how the mood-filter can work effectively by guiding the system to make appropriate recommendations. Fig. 1 illustrates the theme of the system.

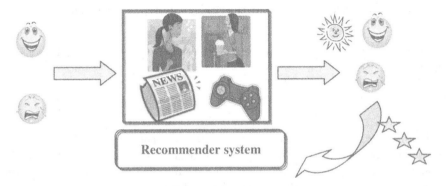

Fig. 1. Depending on the pre-consumption mood of users, the mood-inducers can affect their after-consumption mood as well as their evaluation over the consumed goods

The proposed system consists of multiple layers with at least one to filter items that degrade the user mood. Fig. 2 shows an example of dual-layer RSs in which the first layer is a traditional collaborative filtering module (CF) and the second layer is the heuristic-based filtering module (HF). CF utilizes ratings given by a target user (Ru) and other users (Rt) on a set of items to find his/her 'neighbors' who are believed of having similar preferences to him/her (a kind of data clustering process). The common method to determine the neighborhood is by calculating the Pearson correlation between Ru and Rt. Then, CF recommends items that have not been consumed by the target user and are preferred most by the neighbors (S_1).

In most study, Ru and Rt are provided in a mood-independent condition, that is, without considering the mood of the target or other users. As a result, items S_1 are mood-independent too. Thus, HF will filter out those items that do not fit the situation or are not appropriate in relation to user mood at the time of recommendation; resulting in items S_2. The input information comes from user model (Cx_1) such as user input of his/her mood, his/her activity patterns, human-body sensors, etc. and

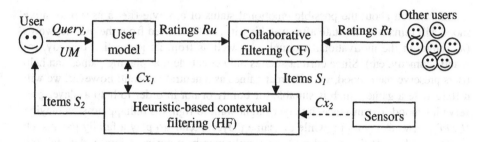

Fig. 2. A dual-layer recommendation system consisting of a collaborative filtering module and a heuristic-based filtering module

environmental sensors (Cx_2), e.g. current time, location, weather, etc. Here, we consider several possible mood-inducing factors. For instance, a user might feel more stressful in the office than at home; conversely, s/he feels better on sunny days [14]. Since the mood-related information is stochastic, our proposed heuristics on the HF will be in the form of probabilistic rules, such as:

Time(Weekday_nighttime) & Location(Home) & PhysicState(Tired) $\rightarrow_{0.9}$ *¬Games(Action)*
Time(Weekend_daytime) & Location(Beach) & Weather(Sunny) $\rightarrow_{0.6}$ *¬Games(All)*
Time(Holiday_daytime) & WithKids(Yes) $\rightarrow_{0.9}$ *¬Movie(X-rated)*
MoodState(Sad) $\rightarrow_{0.8}$ *¬Movie(Sad)*
... etc.

The first rule excludes action games to be recommended by probability 0.9 to a user who is physically tired and staying at home on a weekday night. The second rule excludes all kind of games by probability 0.6 to be recommended to a user who is on the beach at a sunny weekend morning. The third and fourth rules exclude X-rated (for adults/mature audiences) and sad movies under different conditions. Here, the probability parameters are adjusted according to user model and his/her previous experience. The following attributes are considered in our current design: {{Weekday, Weekend, Holiday},{nighttime, daytime}} for CurrTime, {Home, Beach, Office, ShoppingMall, TrainOrBus, Street} for Location, {Sunny, Rainy, Stormy, Snowy} for Weather, {Tired, Fit} for PhysicState, {Sad, Happy} for MoodState, {Yes} for WithKids, WithPartner, WithParent and InPublic, {Action, Strategy, Puzzle, Simulation, FPS, MPRG, X-rated, All} for Games, and {Action, Thriller, Mytery, Comedy, Wars, Cartoon, Sad, X-rated, All} for Movies.

Since a user requesting a movie(s) may also be recommended with a game(s), and vice versa, a rule to select the appropriate category is needed. The algorithm shown in Fig. 3 returns S_2 when S_1 consists of both movie(s) and game(s), and when the user requests a movie. Movies have a higher priority being recommended unless all of them are filtered out. In this case, the system may return a game. The output is guaranteed because when all candidate movies and games are filtered out after several repetitions, the unfiltered movies will be recommended.

Algorithm. *SelectCategory*
Precondition: *CandidateGame, CandidateMovie* ∈ *S₁* are non-empty
Output: *S₂*

FilteredMovie ← Filter(CandidateMovie)   // Filter( ) is the heuristic function to
FilteredGame ← Filter(CandidateGame)   // filter out unfit movies/games
If *FilteredMovie* ≠ ∅ **Then**
  Return *FilteredMovie*
Else
  If *FilteredGame* ≠ ∅ **Then**
    Return *FilteredGame*
  Else
      For *i = 1* **to** *N*   *// repeat the filtering N times due to stochastic rules*
        FilteredMovie ← Filter(CandidateMovie)
        If *FilteredMovie* ≠ ∅ **Then**
          Return *FilteredMovie*
      End For
      Return *CandidateMovie*   *// when we fail to get filtered item, we*
  End If   *// return the unfiltered CandidateMovie* ∈ *S₁*
End If

Fig. 3. Algorithm to select an item when both categories are returned by CF

4   Current Stage and Future Work

We have performed a series of study on multi-domain recommendation using collaborative filtering (CF) in order to validate the possibility of developing such RSs. The results showed that cross- or multi-domain CF produce higher recommendation errors (calculated in the mean absolute errors or MAE) compared to that of single-domain CF [4]. However, the results convince us that using CF in multi-domain RSs will not severely degrade the accuracy of the candidate items (items S_1 in Fig. 2) as the cost to increase the opportunity to remedy or prolong user mood or happiness, which increases user acceptance of the system.

At the current stage, the HF module is under development with more than 20 probabilistic rules have been included. As the next step, we will test the performance of HF in our proposed RS. In order to determine the initial probability values in the rules, we will collect opinion from our students through a questionnaire. Later, these values can be adjusted and personalized by the user of our RS. Another potentially interesting study will be to measure the effect of a user's mood on the rating given by him/her. Also, we believe that various environmental conditions (e.g. with kids, in the office, etc.) when the user enjoys the movie/game may affect his/her rating. We will address these issues in the future.

References

1. Shardanand, U., Maes, P.: Social Information Filtering: Algorithms for Automating 'Word of Mouth'. In: Proc. ACM CHI 1995, pp. 210–217 (1995)
2. Konstan, J., Miller, B.N., Maltz, D., Herlocker, J., Gordon, L.R., Riedl, J.: GroupLens: Applying Collaborative Filtering to Usenet News. CACM 40(3), 77–87 (1997)
3. Tang, T., Winoto, W., Chan, K.C.C.: Scaling Down Candidate Sets Based on the Temporal Feature of Items for Improved Hybrid Recommendations. In: Mobasher, B., Anand, S.S. (eds.) ITWP 2003. LNCS (LNAI), vol. 3169, pp. 169–186. Springer, Heidelberg (2005)
4. Winoto, P., Tang, T.Y.: If You Like the Devil Wears Prada the Book, Will You Also Enjoy the Devil Wears Prada the Movie? A Study of Cross-domain Recommendations. New Generation Computing 36(3) (2008)
5. Smyth, B., McGinty, L., Reilly, J., McCarthy, K.: Compound Critiques for Conversational Recommender Systems. In: Proc. 2004 IEEE/WIC/ACM Int. Conf. Web Intelligence, pp. 141–151 (2004)
6. Riedl, J., Dourish, P.: Introduction to the Special Section on Recommender Systems. ACM TOCHI 12(3), 371–373 (2005)
7. Herlocker, J., Konstan, J., Terveen, L., Riedl, J.: Evaluating Collaborative Filtering Recommender Systems. ACM T. Info. Systems 22(1), 5–53 (2004)
8. McNee, S., Riedl, J., Konstan, J.A.: Making Recommendations Better: An Analytic Model for Human-recommender Interaction. In: Proc. CHI 2006 Extended Abstracts on Human Factors in Comp. Sys., pp. 1103–1108 (2006)
9. Holbrook, M.B., Gardner, M.P.: Illustrating a Dynamic Model of the Mood-updating Process in Consumer Behavior. Psychology and Marketing 17(3), 165–194 (2000)
10. Ryan, R., Rigby, C.S., Przybylski: The Motivational Pull of Video Games: A Self-determination Theory Approach. Motivation and Emotion 30(4), 347–363 (2006)
11. Oliver, M.B.: Tender Affective States as Predictors of Entertainment Preference. J. Communication 58, 40–61 (2008)
12. Zillmann, D.: Mood Management: Using Entertainment to Full Advantage. In: Donohew, L., Sypher, H.E., Higgins, E.T. (eds.) Communication, Social Cognition, and Affect, pp. 147–171. Lawrence Erlbaum, Hillsdale (1988)
13. Knobloch-Westerwick, S.: Mood Management: Theory, Evidence, and Advancements. In: Bryant, J., Vorderer, P. (eds.) Psychology of Entertainment, pp. 239–254. Erlbaum, Mahwah (2006)
14. Schwarz, N., Clore, G.L.: Mood, Misatribution, and Judgments of Well-being: Informative and Directive Functions of Affective States. J. Personality & Social Psychology 45(3), 513–523 (1983)
15. Gardner, M.P.: Mood States and Consumer Behavior: A Critical Review. J. Consumer Research 12(3), 281–300 (1985)
16. Isen, A.M.: Toward Understanding the Role of Affect in Cognition. In: Wyer, W., Srull, T., Isen, A. (eds.) Handbook of Social Cognition, vol. 3, pp. 179–236. Lawrence Erlbaum, Mahwah (1984)
17. Isen, A.M., Daubman, K., Nowicki, G.: Positive Affect Facilitates Creative Problem Solving. J. Personality and Social Psychology 52(6), 1122–1131 (1987)
18. Babin, B.J., Darden, W.R., Griffin, M.: Work and/or Fun: Measuring Hedonic and Utilitarian Shopping Value. J. Consumer Research 20, 644–656 (1994)
19. Weinberg, P., Gothwald, W.: Impulsive Consumer Buying as a Result of Emotions. J. Business Marketing 10, 43–57 (1982)
20. Hess, J.D., Kacen, J.J., Kim, J.: Mood Management Dynamics: the Interrelationships between Moods and Behaviors. British J. Math. and Stat. Psychol. 59(2), 347–378 (2006)
21. Kacen, J.J.: Retail Therapy: Consumers' Shopping Cures for Negative Moods. Working paper. University of Michigan, School of Management (1998)

22. Veitch, R., Griffitt, W.: Good News-Bad News: Affective and Interpersonal Effects. J. Applied Social Psychology 6(1), 69–75 (1976)
23. Bloemer, J., de Ruyter, K.: Customer Loyalty in High and Low Involvement Service Settings Moderating Impact of Positive Emotions. J. Marketing Management 15(4), 315–330 (1999)
24. Schaefer, A., Nils, F., Sanchez, X., Philippot, P.: A Multi-criteria Assessment of Emotional Films (2005) (unpublished manuscript)
25. Tesser, A., Millar, K., Wu, C.H.: On the Perceived Functions of Movies. J. Psychology 122, 441–449 (1998)
26. Waterman, A.S.: Two Conceptions of Happiness: Contrasts of Personal Expressiveness (eudaimonia) and Hedonic Enjoyment. J. Personality and Social Psychology 64, 678–691 (1993)
27. Brave, S., Nass, C.: Emotions in Human-Computer Interaction. In: Jacko, J., Sears, A. (eds.) Handbook of Human-Computer Interaction, pp. 82–96. Lawrence Assoc. (2003)
28. Picard, R.W., Vyzas, E., Healey, J.: Toward Machine Emotional Intelligence: Analysis of Affective Physiological State. IEEE T. Pattern Analysis and Machince Intelligence 23(10), 1175–1191 (2001)
29. Fagerberg, P., Ståhl, A., Höök, K.: eMoto: Emotionally Engaging Interaction. Personal and Ubiquitous Computing 8(5), 377–381 (2004)
30. Sánchez, J.A., Kirschning, I., Palacio, J.C., Ostróvskaya, Y.: Towards Mood-oriented Interfaces for Synchronous Interaction. In: Proc. Latin American Conference on Human-Computer Interaction (CLIHC 2005), pp. 1–7 (2005)
31. Lisetti, C.L., Nasoz, F., Lerouge, C., Ozyer, O., Alvarez, K.: Developing Multimodal Intelligent Affective Interfaces for Tele-home Health Care. Int. J. Human-Computer Studies 59(1-2), 245–255 (2003)
32. Boehner, K., DePaula, R., Dourish, P., Sengers, P.: How Emotion is Made and Measured. Int. J. Human-Computer Studies 65(4), 275–291 (2007)
33. Isbister, K., Höök, K.: Evaluating Affective Interactions. Int. J. Human-Computer Studies 65(4), 273–274 (2007)
34. Isomursu, M., Tähti, M., Väinämö, S., Kuutti, K.: Experimental Evaluation of Five Methods for Collecting Emotions in Field Settings with Mobile Applications. Int. J. Human-Computer Studies 65(4), 404–418 (2007)
35. Herlocker, J., Konstan, J., Riedl, J.: Explaining Collaborative Filtering Recommendations. In: Proc. CSCW 2000, pp. 241–250 (2000)
36. Sinha, R., Swearingen, K.: The Role of Transparency in Recommender Systems. In: Proc. CHI 2002 Extended Abstracts on Human Factors in Comp. Sys., pp. 830–831 (2002)
37. McNee, S., Riedl, J., Konstan, J.A.: Being Accurate is Not Enough: How Accuracy Metrics Have Hurt Recommender Systems. In: Proc. CHI 2006 Extended Abstracts on Human Factors in Comp. Sys., pp. 1097–1101 (2006)

Intelligent Information System Based on a Speech Web Using Fuzzy Association Rule Mining

Hyeong-Joon Kwon and Kwang-Seok Hong

School of Information and Communication Engineering,
Sungkyunkwan University, Suwon 440-746, South Korea
katsyuki@skku.edu, kshong@yurim.skku.ac.kr

Abstract. In this paper, we propose and implement an intelligent information system that is based on both a wired and a wireless telephone network-based speech Web using fuzzy association rule mining, and we present a session management method in a VXML-based speech Web. The proposed system collects voice content that is requested by the user, and it considers the user's listening time, which is an important data in speech applications. The system uses a reasoning process to identify the related contents from the collected transaction database by using fuzzy association rule mining, and then the system recommends it to the user. This method considers the user's listening time and it can explore the database with an accuracy that is made possible by the dynamic generation of the fuzzy membership function. The experimental results confirm that we are obtaining more accurate reasoning result than the speech Web applications that use the existing generic data mining algorithm.

1 Introduction

The speech Web provides an environment in which a user is available to navigate the Web using a voice interface. To implement the speech Web application, the application developer uses the voice extensible markup language (VXML), which is a XML-based document format. It was proposed by the World Wide Web Consortium (W3C) for defining voice dialogs [1].

Because the speech Web that is based on VXML has many potential merits, VXML was used for the construction of the interactive voice response system and the automatic response system [2]. This is because a pure VXML application is classified into a mixed-initiative form dialog and a machine-controlled form dialog, and both dialogs have one characteristic in common—both contain a fixed scenario and static voice-anchors, and these recognition candidates are defined by the application developer [1][3]. It is difficult to develop applications that appear dynamic and intelligent by creating only pure VXML documents. Because of this structural defect of VXML, methods using a server-side-script and relational databases have been proposed to construct a more useful and efficient system. Combining VXML with existing Web-based technology, it provides various voice scenarios to the user by using dynamic control of the recognition candidates. A survey of trends in a recent study showed that by means of these studies, a speech Web was improved by substituting IVR and ARS to create a better e-Commerce solution, and this solution

S. Lee et al. (Eds.): APCHI 2008, LNCS 5068, pp. 104–113, 2008.
© Springer-Verlag Berlin Heidelberg 2008

was applied to the syndication of information using the next generation Web [4][5][6][7]. It also uses a voice-enabled multimodal interface, a real time news service, e-Education, and a term dictionary using regular expressions [8][9][10][11]. Among these studies, there was one remarkable study that showed a trend in information systems toward making the speech Web intelligent and personal [12]. Though the basic structure for running a speech Web is similar to the existing visual Web, the method can be distinguished according to the differences in the interfaces. An existing study analyzes the user's input pattern using the apriori algorithm-based intelligent agent that recommends the related contents about the user's input according to a mining result [12][13]. However, this study can exclude noise data that is generated by incorrect speech recognition or implausible titles of contents, because the system considers only the user's input pattern, which provides a recognition result from only one connection.

In this paper, we propose and implement a speech Web-based information system that considers the user's listening time together with the user's input pattern. Our proposal includes this hypothesis: "if the listening time of a person is long, then the person has a great deal of interest in the content". Because all of the contents have a maximum listening time according to performance of the text to speech (TTS) engine, the user's degree of interest in any content is calculated as the ratio of the user's listening time to the maximum listening time. To appropriately assess the listening time in speech applications, we apply fuzzy association rule mining. This algorithm can consider the amount of data in one of the various data mining algorithms [14][15][16] and discriminate an ambiguous element from the amount of data. For example, if any person listens to any content for 27 seconds, we will not be able to determine that the listening time is long. Exactly, it's not clear to determine whether long or short. Fuzzy association rules are useful in such a context, and we tune the fuzzy association rule algorithm to the existing speech Web.

The structure of this paper is as follows. In Section 2, we explain the structural weak point of VXML and the limitations of the speech Web applications that are based only on VXML. We also discuss the related existing research. In Section 3, we propose a method that applies a fuzzy association rule algorithm to the speech Web, and then we discuss a proposed system and we provide the results of an experiment using this system in Section 4. Finally, we conclude in Section 5.

2   Related Works

2.1   Speech Web

A speech Web application using pure VXML mainly comprises fixed scenarios. In order to accommodate various scenarios a speech Web-based information system must contain a great deal of dialog or many VXML files [4][6]. Before discussing various scenarios in the VXML-based speech Web, we must particularly consider the importance of the <grammar> element of a VXML document. This element implies that the recognition candidates are described by the developer. A word that does not exist in the <grammar> element will not be recognized. Namely, the user is provided a service based on the scenario developed by the developer, so the application is an initiative solely of the developer. By using such a feature, VXML was used in the novel computer-telephony integration (CTI) because the VXML-based CTI system allows simpler, more flexible and effective constructions than the existing CTI platform, which requires hard coding and low-level work [2].

In order to improve the VXML application comprising the fixed scenario and the static recognition candidates, R. R. Vankayala et al. proposed a prototype of a VXML application using DBMS and the active server pages (ASP), which is one of the server-side script programming languages [4]. With dynamic control of the recognition candidates, they implemented a speech application that was an improvement over a pure VXML application. It changes the recognition candidates according to the user's speech input. H. Reddy et al. proposed the concept of a dynamic voice-anchor [6]. The anchor in the visual Web is linked to other HTML documents, and their proposal operates in a similar manner; the voice-anchor is linked to other VXML documents. They have successfully designed, implemented, and demonstrated the dynamic voice interface for an existing e-Commerce speech Web application. To manage the voice-anchors, they used a server-side script and DBMS. This dynamic voice system has a fully functional voice interface and contains functionalities similar to those of existing Web applications. It provides a prototype for the creation of a dynamic voice interface as an alternative or supplement to any existing browser-based application. This study presents the construction of a speech-domain hyperlink structure. In addition, a user-controlled structure that uses simple natural processing is proposed [7]. As a result of these studies, the speech Web was improved from an information service system to an information retrieval system. We has also proposed a real time news service using really simple syndication (RSS), which is a document exchange format in the semantic Web [8]. This system delivers contents to the user without the user having to navigate using speech-domain hyperlinks. In other words, this system assists the user's acquisition of information.

2.2   Data Mining in the Speech Web

The research area of VXML-based speech information systems is becoming large, but the study of intelligence in the speech Web is insufficient. One of the recent studies of the speech Web applies a data mining technique to the speech Web and explains its efficiency [12]. This system accumulates the user's input pattern and discovers association rules for accumulated transaction data according to the apriori algorithm [13]. By exploration of the association rule, the system can recommend related contents to the user. This system searches for frequently occurring patterns from the user's input transaction database. Figure 1 shows the concept of this system.

Connetion ID	List of requested contents	Itemset	Support	Itemset	Support	Itemset	Support
		1	0.5	1, 2	0.25	1, 3, 5	0.25
100	1, 3, 4	2	0.75	1, 3	0.5	2, 3, 5	0.75
101	2, 3, 5	3	0.75	1, 5	0.25		
102	1, 2, 3, 5	4	0.25	2, 3	0.5		
103	2, 5	5	0.75	2, 5	0.75		
				3, 5	0.5		

Fig. 1. An example of processing a speech Web application using the apriori algorithm

Figure 1 shows an example of processing in which the apriori algorithm explores the frequently occurring patterns from four transactions. This system collects the number of requested contents from one connection, and then the system explores the frequently occurring itemsets that appear in the collected transaction. In Figure 2, it discovered one pattern consisting of 2, 3 and 5. The threshold of support in this case is 0.49, and it is calculated with the support of a calculating formula that is the itemset count in a transaction divided by the total transaction count. Next, it calculates a confidence value using the discovered frequently occurring patterns. The confidence is calculated using the pattern 2, 3 and 5, and the calculating method is $\text{conf}(x \rightarrow y) = ((\sum_i \min (\mu_x(t_i), \mu_y(t_i))) / ((\sum_i \mu_x(t_i)))$. For example, in Figure 1, the calculated confidence result is 0.66 (0.5 / 0.75) for the rule that 'if a user requests content 2, then the user will request contents 3 and 5 as well (R: 2 to 3 and 5)'. The system can recommend contents 3 and 5 according to the threshold of confidence for a user who requests content 2. The merit of this study is that it can reduce the navigation time according to the type of user, but this system contains a weak point; a transaction that includes only data from a short listening time appears as noise. Only patterns that occur frequently are suitable for forming rules that help users in transactions in the speech Web.

2.3 Fuzzy Association Rule Mining

Fuzzy association rule mining is proposed to discover other knowledge from a large database. It is especially useful to consider the quantities involved in the user's request [14][15][16]. If generic association rules mining can discover *R1: Beer* → *Potato*, a fuzzy association rule can discover *R2: (Beer, 1 bottle)* → *(Potato, 150 gram)*. Such merit presents more detail and a more reliable exploration of the association rules than a generic association rule. This algorithm is composed of three steps.

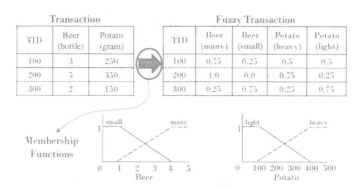

Fig. 2. A method of converting a generic transaction into a fuzzy transaction

In first step, it converts a generic transaction into fuzzy transaction [16]. We show this method in Figure 2. In the second step, it calculates supp ($Beer_m$) using the following formula with the fuzzy transaction to discover the frequently occurring item. D is the total count in the transaction. As a result of calculating the support value, if threshold is 0.5, the discovered frequently occurring itemset is $Beer_m$. Also, it calculates the support value with the subsets, so the formula and calculated result are as follows:

$$\text{supp}\left(Beer_{many}\right) = \frac{\left(\sum_i \mu_{Beer_{many}}(t_i)\right)}{D} = 0.66$$

$$\text{supp}\left(Beer_{many}, Potato_{heavy}\right) = \frac{\left(\sum_i \min\left(\mu_{Beer_{many}}(t_i), \mu_{Potato_{heavy}}(t_i)\right)\right)}{D} = 0.5$$

It can discover $Beer_m$, $Potato_{hs}$, and $Potato_{li}$ as frequent with minimum support threshold is 0.5. In the last step, it calculates a confidence value with the all subsets of discovered frequently itemset according to:

$$\text{conf}(item1 \rightarrow item2) = \frac{\text{supp}(item1, item2)}{\text{supp}(item1)}$$

If it considers $R1$: $Beer_{many} \rightarrow Potato_{li}$, the result will be as follows:

$$\text{conf}\left(Beer_{many} \rightarrow Potato_{light}\right) - \frac{\frac{\left(\sum_i \min\left(\mu_{Beer_{many}}(t_i), \mu_{Potato_{light}}(t_i)\right)\right)}{D}}{\frac{\left(\sum_i \mu_{Beer_{many}}(t_i)\right)}{D}} - 0.5$$

Namely, the rule 'if a person purchases many bottles of Beer, he will also purchase light Potatos' is obtainable. We improve the existing speech Web with this algorithm, and use this method to exclude noise that is not trusted data from the transaction database.

3 Proposed the Speech Web-Based Intelligent Information System

3.1 System Architecture

In this Section, we describe a method of implementing the proposed system. It includes the whole system architecture and an optimization method of fuzzy association rule mining in the speech Web with our application for algorithm simulation. Figure 3 shows a simplified illustration of the proposed information system. The proposed system is composed of a Web server container, a VXML context interpreter, and a CTI server. A user's speech input is converted into a digital signal via the CTI device. The ASR recognizes a speech signal and forwards the recognized result to the VXML interpreter. According to the recognition result, in the Web server container, the VXML-based speech application carries out the following steps: 1) form a mining association rule, 2) measure the listening time, 3) collect the contents that were requested by the user, 4) generate a dynamic VXML document with templates. In this paper, we focus on the speech application in the Web server container.

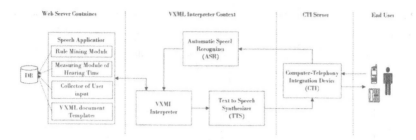

Fig. 3. Architecture of the proposed information system

3.2 Session ID Management in the Speech Web

To collect the user's input list and measure the listening time, we use a session ID, which is a proper number associated with the Web connection. A client is connected to the Web, and then the server provides a session ID to the user in the Web server container software.

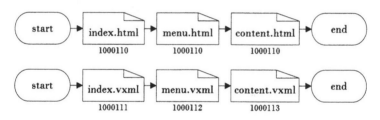

Fig. 4. Monitoring result of the session ID with page movements in the speech and visual Web

A generic visual Web application identifies each connection with a session ID. The session ID becomes extinct when the connection with the client is lost, for example, when a user closes the Internet Explorer, so it can catch the start and end points of the connection. Because the basic structure of the speech Web is the same as the generic visual Web, we experience it the same way, but we discovered that the speech Web is somewhat different from the generic visual Web. This difference is shown in Figure 3 through a comparison with the generic visual Web. As Figure 4 indicates, the session ID in the visual Web is maintained, but the session ID in the speech Web is renewed each time the user moves within the VXML document. Then, we collect the user's input list and measure the listening time using the first session ID. The proposed system delivers the session ID received from the Server container to the global variable of the VXML. We could obtain a result that is formatted as in Table 1. The session ID 1027036835 shows that four contents were provided and the contents were heard for 14, 3, 9 and 7 seconds, and total connection count was 6. We actually use the format in Table 1 as a transaction for fuzzy association rule mining.

Table 1. A collection result from the list of contents requested by the user and its session ID

Session ID	List of requested content (content number, listening time)
1027036835	5,14 I 1,3 I 3,9 I 2,7
1027036839	5,9 I 3,11 I 2,9
1027036842	1,9 I 3,7 I 4,13
1027036845	4,12 I 1,16 I 2,17
1027036848	1,12 I 3,14 I 2,16 I 5,12
1027036852	1,9 I 2,7 I 5,15I 4,4

3.3 The Proposed Method Considers the Listening Time

In fuzzy system, a membership function is defined by the system designer. The proposed system automatic generates a membership function according to the maximum running time of the content.

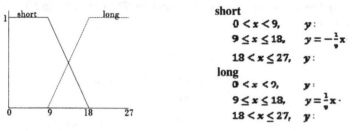

Fig. 5. An example of the automatic generation of a membership function

Because each of the contents is different in maximum running time according to the size of the content, it cannot be effective in one fixed membership function. Therefore, the proposed system flexibly defines a fuzzy membership function for each maximum running time. For example, in any content, if the maximum running time is 27 seconds and the scale is 3, then the proposed system will generate a membership function like the one shown in Figure 5.

Table 2. A generation result of the fuzzy transaction using the proposed method

1 (short)	1 (long)	2 (short)	2 (long)	3 (short)	3 (long)	4 (short)	4 (long)	5 (short)	5 (long)
1	0	1	0	0.714	0.285	empty	empty	0	1
empty	empty	1	0	0.428	0.571	empty	empty	0.5	0.5
1	0	empty	empty	1	0	0.375	0.625	empty	empty
0.222	0.777	0.3	0.7	empty	empty	0.5	0.5	empty	empty
0.666	0.333	0.4	0.6	0	1	empty	empty	0	1
1	0	1	0	empty	empty	1	0	0	1
Max 27 seconds		Max 30 seconds		Max 21 seconds		Max 24 seconds		Max 18 seconds	

By using the proposed method of generating an adaptive membership function, Table 1 is converted into Table 2 by the method of generating a membership function with a total of five contents. According to the Fuzzy association rule mining in Section 2.3, it uses the total count of the transaction to calculate the support value, but 'empty' cannot be considered when calculating the support, so we improved it. If we calculate supp (1_{sh}), the existing algorithm calculates it as (1+empty+1+ 0.222+0.666+1) / 6, but the improved method is (1+1+0.222+0.666+1) / 5 and supp (4_{sh}) is calculated as (0.375+0.5+1) / 3, so the proposed method chooses the right transactions from the database transaction. An example of calculated result from all of the support values when the threshold is 0.7 is as follows:

$$\text{supp}(5_{long}) = \frac{1 + 0.5 + 1 + 1}{4} = 0.875$$

In addition, $\text{supp}(2_{shc}$ is 0.74 and $\text{supp}(1_{shc}$ is 0.777. This is to discover the frequency of the itemsets, which means that the user hears content 5 for a long time and hears contents 2 and 1 for a short time. With this result, a confidence value is calculated to discover the frequency of the pattern, which is new knowledge. When a confidence value is calculated, the denominator is the difference between the new method and the existing calculation method, which does not consider transactions that include 'empty' as well as the proposed method does when calculating the support value. The result obtained when using a threshold of 0.85 is as follows:

$$\text{conf}(5_{long} \rightarrow 1_{short}) = \frac{\frac{1 + 0.666 + 1}{3}}{\frac{1 + 1 + 1}{3}} = 0.888$$

In addition, $\text{conf}(2_{short} \rightarrow 1_{shc}$ is 0.971, $\text{conf}(1_{short} \rightarrow 5_{lo}$ is 1 and $\text{conf}(1_{short} \rightarrow 2_{shc}$ is 0.907. We formed a hypothesis in Section 1: "if the listening time of a person is long, then the person has a great deal of interest in the content". Therefore, the discovered frequently occurring pattern is $R: 1_{short} \rightarrow 5_{lc}$. Namely, if is lo in $R: x \rightarrow$, it is association rule in the proposed system. The system recommends content 5 as related content to the user who requests content 1.

4   Experimental Results

We performed experiments on the proposed system using the proposed method. To evaluate the performance, the apriori algorithm was used and we compared the proposed system with the apriori algorithm that is based on the same database transaction in Table 1. The minimum support threshold is each 0.3 (1), 0.5 (2) and 0.7 (3) and the minimum confidence threshold ranges from 0.1 to 0.9. As a result, the proposed system discovers many more association rules then the apriori algorithm. This fact shows that the proposed system explorers the association rules accurately. In addition, because the proposed system considers the listening time, it is effective in excluding noise data, y is short in Section 3.2. They are ambiguous because the selection cannot be used to judge the user's interest.

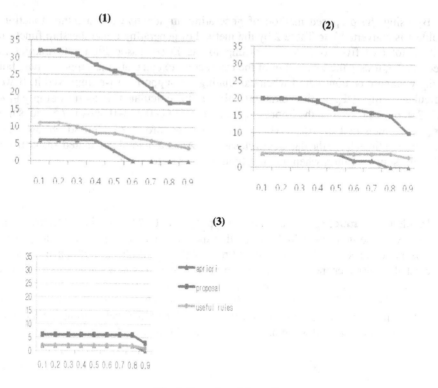

Fig. 6. Experimental results

5   Conclusions

We applied and implemented fuzzy association rule mining to the speech Web in order to discover related content. To make the rule mining applicable to the speech Web, we tuned the existing fuzzy association rules for a speech application and also proposed a session management method in the VXML-based speech Web. As a result, the proposed system successfully discovers association rules from transactions while taking into consideration the user's listening time.

Proposed system can filter out noise data in transaction for mining association rule to consider user's listening time and voice content's maximum playing time. Comparison to existing intelligent speech Web-based information system, the system which capacitates to explore much strong association rule; throughout expansion of association rule to subdivide and extract the result qualifying for system administrator's satisfaction. In this paper, proposed system assumes the long listener to be the interesting information and aimed to recommend related contents to both current and future users. Other technical issue will be studied in the future, such as the 'empty' transaction in Section 3.

Acknowledgment. This research was supported by MKE, Korea under ITRC IITA-2008-(C1090-0801-0046).

References

1. McGlashan, S., et al.: Voice Extensible Markup Language Version 2.0 Specification (2004)
2. Shin, J.-H., et al.: Implementation of New CTI Service Platform Using Voice XML. In: Laganá, A., Gavrilova, M.L., Kumar, V., Mun, Y., Tan, C.J.K., Gervasi, O. (eds.) ICCSA 2004. LNCS, vol. 3046, pp. 754–762. Springer, Heidelberg (2004)
3. Miller, M.: VoiceXML. Wiley Publishing INC, Chichester (2002)
4. Vankayala, R.R., et al.: Dynamic Voice User Interface Using VoiceXML and Active Server Pages. In: Zhou, X., Li, J., Shen, H.T., Kitsuregawa, M., Zhang, Y. (eds.) APWeb 2006. LNCS, vol. 3841, pp. 1181–1184. Springer, Heidelberg (2006)
5. Chugh, J., Jagannathan, V.: Voice-Enabling Enterprise Applications. In: Proceeding of the Eleventh IEEE International Workshops on Enabling Technologies, pp. 188–189. IEEE Press, Los Alamitos (2002)
6. Reddy, H., et al.: Listener-Controlled Dynamic Navigation of VoiceXML Documents. In: Miesenberger, K., Klaus, J., Zagler, W., Burger, D. (eds.) ICCHP 2004. LNCS, vol. 3118, pp. 347–354. Springer, Heidelberg (2004)
7. Kwon, H.-J., et al.: A User-Controlled VoiceXML Application Based on Dynamic Anchor and Node. In: Thulasiraman, P., He, X., Xu, T.L., Denko, M.K., Thulasiram, R.K., Yang, L.T. (eds.) ISPA Workshops 2007. LNCS, vol. 4743, pp. 265–272. Springer, Heidelberg (2007)
8. Kwon, H.-J., et al.: Design and Implementation of Enhanced Real Time News Service Using RSS and VoiceXML. In: Smith, M.J., Salvendy, G. (eds.) HCII 2007. LNCS, vol. 4557, pp. 677–686. Springer, Heidelberg (2007)
9. Kim, J.-H., et al.: MMSDS: Ubiquitous Computing and WWW-Based Multi-modal Sentential Dialog System. In: Sha, E., Han, S.-K., Xu, C.-Z., Kim, M.-H., Yang, L.T., Xiao, B. (eds.) EUC 2006. LNCS, vol. 4096, pp. 539–548. Springer, Heidelberg (2006)
10. Kim, J.-H., et al.: Intelligent Multi-Modal Recognition Interface Using Voice-XML and Embedded KSSL Recognizer. In: Gabrys, B., Howlett, R.J., Jain, L.C. (eds.) KES 2006. LNCS (LNAI), vol. 4251, pp. 798–807. Springer, Heidelberg (2006)
11. Shin, J.-H., et al.: Simple and Powerful Interactive E-Learning System Using VXML: Design and Implementation of Web and PSTN Linked Efficient Learning System. In: Gavrilova, M.L., Gervasi, O., Kumar, V., Tan, C.J.K., Taniar, D., Laganá, A., Mun, Y., Choo, H. (eds.) ICCSA 2006. LNCS, vol. 3980, pp. 354–363. Springer, Heidelberg (2006)
12. Kwon, H.-J., et al.: SpeechWeb Application with Information Selection Agent. In: Proceedings of the International Conference on New Exploratory Technologies. IEEE Press, Los Alamitos (2007)
13. Agrawal, R., et al.: Mining association rules between sets of items in large databases. In: Proceedings of the 1993 ACM SIGMOD International Conference on Management of Data. ACM Press, New York (1993)
14. Dubois, D., et al.: Fuzzy rules in knowledge-based systems modeling gradedness, uncertainty and preference. In: Yager, R.R., Zadeh, L.A. (eds.) An Introduction to Fuzzy Logic Applications in Intelligent Systems. Kluwer, Dordrecht (1992)
15. Au, W.H., et al.: Mining fuzzy association rules. In: Proceedings on 6th International Conference on Information Knowledge Management, Las Vegas, NV, pp. 209–215 (1997)
16. Delgado, M., et al.: Fuzzy Association Rules: General Model and Applications. IEEE Transactions on Fuzzy Systems 11(2), 214–225 (2003)

Restaurant Recommendation for Group of People in Mobile Environments Using Probabilistic Multi-criteria Decision Making

Moon-Hee Park, Han-Saem Park, and Sung-Bae Cho

Department of Computer Science, Yonsei University
134 Shinchon-Dong Seudaemun-Gu Seoul 120-749, Korea
{moony,sammy}@sclab.yonsei.ac.kr, sbcho@cs.yonsei.ac.kr

Abstract. Since 1990s, with an advancement of network technology and the popularization of the Internet, information that people can access has proliferated, thus information recommendation has been investigated as an important issue. Because preference to information recommendation can be different as context that the users are related to, we should consider this context to provide a good service. This paper proposes the recommendation system that considers the preferences of group users in mobile environment and applied the system to recommendation of restaurants. Since mobile environment has plenty of uncertainty, our system have used Bayesian network which showed reliable performance with uncertain input to model individual user's preference. Also, restaurant recommendation mostly considers the preference of group users, so we have used AHP (Analytic Hierarchy Process) of multi-criteria decision making method to get the preference of group users from individual users' preferences. For experiments, we have assumed 10 different situations and compared the proposed method with random recommendation and simple rule-based recommendation. Finally, we have confirmed that the proposed system provides high usability with SUS (System Usability Scale).

Keywords: Information recommendation, Bayesian network, AHP, Multi-criteria decision making.

1 Introduction

With the advancement of high-speed network technology and the popularization of the Internet, the amount of data accessible is growing exponentially. Accordingly, information recommendation is an important issue for research [1]. Recently, as 'personalization' became a keyword for various services, many companies investigate it and provide the functionalities for it. Many web portals including Google and Yahoo provided services considering personalization such as personalized layout, and most online shopping malls such as Amazon started to provide item recommendation service for individual customers. Because the amount of digital contents will be expected to increase exponentially, it will be more important job for information recommendation service to help individual users find the information they need.

Mostly, recommendation services target the individual users, but services such as restaurant or movie recommendation should consider the preference of several

S. Lee et al. (Eds.): APCHI 2008, LNCS 5068, pp. 114–122, 2008.

persons because they are in the same group and want to get the service together. Recommendation for group users is another issue in information recommendation, and the target domain includes recommendation of traveling sites, movies, and music. Lieberman *et al.* proposed 'Let's Browse' which recommends a group of people with common interest based on the single user web browsing agent Letizia [2], and O'Connor *et al.* presented a new collaborative filtering recommender system designed to recommend items for group users [3].

This paper uses Bayesian network to model the preference of each user and AHP of multi-criteria decision making to integrate the preference of individual users, so that can be used to recommend information to group users. Implemented system has been applied to restaurant recommendation in mobile environment, and its' evaluation has been conducted successfully with recommendation experiment and usability test.

2 Mobile Context and Information Recommendation

Preference of user to a certain service is easy to change as the context, and context often changes in mobile environment. Thus, information recommendation in mobile environment requires context inference first. Dey defined context as any information that can be used to characterize the situation of an entity such as a person, place, or object that is considered relevant to the interaction between a user and an application, including the user and the application themselves [4]. Tewari *et al.* used user location, ID, time as context [5], and Kim *et al.* classified the context into private one and environment context and used for the mobile web [6].

Mobile context includes uncertainty because people use mobile devices while they are moving. Therefore, Bayesian networks, which provide reliable inference, have been used frequently [7]. Korpiaa *et al.* in VTT used naïve Bayes model to learn and classify mobile user context [8], and Horvitz et al. in MS Research proposed the system that infers what a person is focusing in uncertain environment [9].

3 Proposed System

Figure 1 summarizes the proposed recommendation method using multi-criteria decision making. Whole process divides into four steps: context-log collection, preference modeling of individual users using Bayesian network, their integration using multi-criteria decision making, and recommendation.

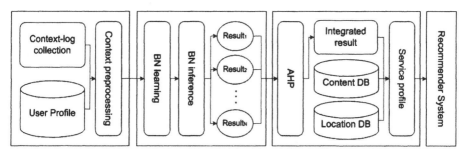

Fig. 1. An overview of information recommendation using AHP (Analytical Hierarchy Process) and Bayesian network

3.1 Context-Log Collection in Moblie Environment

Mobile context used in this paper includes temperature and weather from Web, season and period information from operating system, latitude and longitude from GPS receiver, and various user input from application program. Figure 2 shows context logs explained above. This context information is preprocessed to be used as input of Bayesian network model.

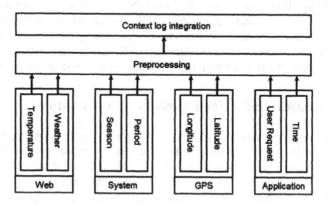

Fig. 2. Context log collected in mobile environment

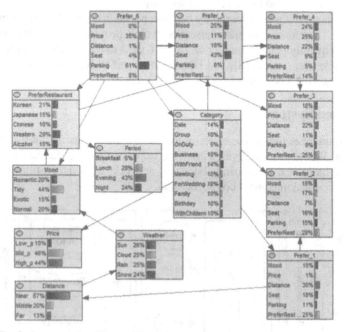

Fig. 3. An example of learned Bayesian network model for individual user

Preprocess is to discretize each input because Bayesian network requires one. For example, season data are discretized into four states: spring (from March to May), summer (from June to August), fall (from September to November), and winter (from December to February), and restaurant type are discretized into five: Korean, Japanese, Chinese, western, and alcohol.

3.2 Modeling Preference of Individual User with Bayesian Network

Bayesian network to model preference of individual user is learned from collected data based on the scenario, and the K2 algorithm and maximum likelihood estimation are used to learn BN structure and parameter [7]. Figure 3 illustrates learned Bayesian network model.

In Figure 3, six nodes of Prefer_1 through Prefer_6 are query nodes. Here, node Prefer_1 is the most important one, and Prefer_6 is the least. Thus, this user prefers the distance to the restaurant than other factors.

3.3 Multi-criteria Decision Making Using Analytical Hierarchy Process

Inferred result in Bayesian network model let us know which restaurant each user prefers, but the decision will be difficult if more than two persons want to go to the restaurant together. AHP (Analytic Hierarchy Process) is a multi-criteria decision making method that makes conclusion considering the preferences of several users [10].

We assumed that the inferred probability set containing the probabilities that each type of restaurant is selected is Type = $\{t_1, t_2, \dots, t_l\}$, the probabilities that each restaurant of a certain range of price is selected is Price = $\{p_1, p_2, \dots, p_m\}$, the probabilities that each restaurant of a certain mood is selected is Mood = $\{m_1, m_2, \dots, m_n\}$, and the probabilities that each restaurant of a certain range of distance is selected is Distance = $\{d_1, d_2, \dots, d_o\}$, and called each attributes t_i^{name}, p_j^{name}, m_k^{name}, d_l^{name}, respectively. After that, we have decided the weights for each attributes with AHP. Figure 4 depicts the proposed AHP hierarchy. The criteria to decide restaurant for n persons are restaurant type, price, mood and the distance to the restaurant, and the alternatives are n users. Final goal is to select the preferred restaurants for n users.

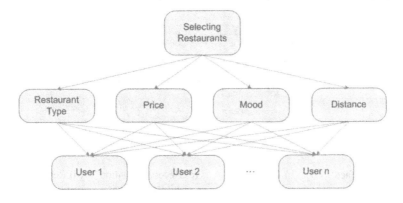

Fig. 4. Proposed AHP hierarchy

Based on AHP hierarchy in Figure 4, the pair-wise comparison matrix shown in Equation (1) is generated. Each value in matrix is set with the following pair-wise comparison criteria. An importance value in matrix is 1 if A and B are equally important, and the value in matrix is 9 if A is much more important than B. Values inbetween have importance between A and B as those. After adding each column in the matrix using Equation (2), Equation (3) divides each value by the sum of column and gets the average from each row. Computed averages are used as weights.

$$A = \begin{pmatrix} a_{11} & a_{12} & \cdots & a_{1n} \\ a_{21} & a_{22} & \cdots & a_{2n} \\ \vdots & \vdots & \cdots & \vdots \\ a_{n1} & a_{n2} & \cdots & a_{nn} \end{pmatrix} \tag{1}$$

$$S_i = \sum_{k=1}^{n} a_{ki} \tag{2}$$

$$w_i = \frac{\sum_{k=1}^{n} \dfrac{a_{ki}}{S_k}}{N} \tag{3}$$

In Equation (2) and (3), w_i and N represent the weight of ith criterion and the number of all criteria for selecting restaurants. Weight = $\{w_{type}, w_{price}, w_{mood}, w_{distance}\}$ is a set of weights obtained by Equation (3), and the value for recommendation with this weight is computed with Equation (4).

$$X_{ijk} = (t_i \times w_{type}) + (p_j \times w_{price}) + (m_k \times w_{mood}) + (d_t \times w_{distance}) \tag{4}$$

$$Recommended\ value = \max_{i=1\ \ldots\ l,\ j=1\ldots\ m,\ k=1\ \ldots\ n}(X_{ijk}) \tag{5}$$

Among all combination of attributes, we assigned the maximum value of X_{ijk} as a recommendation value and selected the corresponding restaurant.

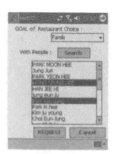

(a) Log in interface   (b) User input   (c) Recommendation result (text viewer)   (d) Recommendation result (image viewer)

Fig. 5. Recommender system implemented in mobile device

3.4 Implementation of the Recommender System

Figure 5 shows the recommender system implemented in a mobile device. In (a), the system load the learned preference model of a user. In (b), user sends information of the group and a goal of the meal. (c) and (d) provide the recommendation result in test view and image view, respectively.

4 Experiments

4.1 Experimental Data and Scenario

For experiments, we have collected the information of 90 restaurants in area of $870 \times 500m^2$ in Shinchon (Located in Seoul, Korea). User data consist of questionnaire surveys of 20 men and women.

10 situations were presented to subjects, and then we conducted evaluation of the recommended results and usability of the system. For example, situation #1 is "A date with a boy (or girl) friend in front of the Hyundai department store in snowy evening in December." Experiments were performed with 50 groups and 153 people.

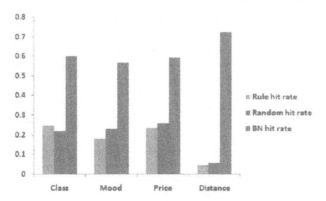

Fig. 6. Accuracy of individual user's preference model

4.2 Recommendation Result of Individual User's Preference Model

First, we attempt to evaluate the recommendation using individual user's preference model. Figure 6 provides accuracy comparison of a simple rule-based recommendation, random recommendation, and the recommendation with Bayesian network model. Comparing with other two methods, Bayesian network model provides much better accuracy. To compute the accuracy, we regarded the user answer in a given situation as a correct one.

4.3 Recommendation Result as Scenario and Group

In this section, we have analyzed the results of one user who experienced all situations. Table 1 summarizes the changes of situations and groups and the recommendation results according to them.

Situation ID, group ID, and restaurant ID represent 10 different situations presented in Section 4.1, the ID of made groups for experiments, and each restaurants, respectively. As shown in Table 3, the proposed multi-criteria decision making recommends restaurants according as the situation and the group changes while other two models recommend restaurants according to the situation only. Rules used in a rule-based recommendation model are simple ones based on the common sense like "Select the restaurant A, which usually serves warm foods, if it is rainy and cold day."

Table 1. Recommendation results considering changes of situations and groups

Person ID	Situation #	Group ID	Restaurant #		
			Individual's preference model	Multi-criteria decision making	Rule-based recommendation
1	S1	G6	16	**16**	11
	S2	G6	58	**88**	88
	S3	G1	89	**49**	49
		G4	89	**49**	49
		G5	89	**83**	49
	S4	G1	71	**2**	88
		G4	71	**6**	88
		G5	71	**71**	88
	S5	G1	44	**2**	71
		G4	44	**44**	71
		G5	44	**44**	71
	S6	G1	36	**42**	44
		G4	36	**6**	44
		G5	36	**88**	44
	S7	G1	50	**50**	38
		G4	50	**50**	38
		G5	50	**49**	38
	S8	G1	36	**46**	89
		G4	36	**58**	89
		G5	36	**46**	89
	S9	G1	36	**88**	71
		G4	36	**88**	71
		G5	36	**88**	71
	S10	G1	16	**46**	48
		G4	16	**11**	48
		G5	16	**30**	48

4.4 Usability Test of the System

To evaluate the usability of the proposed system, we have requested the answers after we have let users experience the system. For questionnaire, 10 questions in SUS (System Usability Scale) have been used. SUS test measures three aspects of the system: effectiveness (can users successfully achieve their objectives), efficiency (how much effort and resource is expended in achieving those objectives), and satisfaction (was the experience satisfactory) [11]. Subjects should answer of five degrees from "strongly disagree" to "strongly agree." The result is a single score on a scale of 0 to 100, and our result shows a range of 60 ~ 82.5 (average of 70.58).

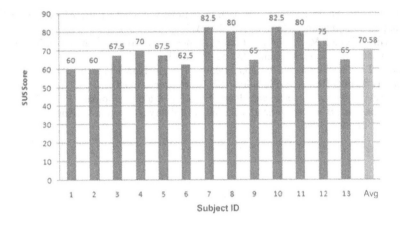

Fig. 7. SUS score by subject and average score

5 Conclusion

This paper exploited Bayesian network to model the preference of individual user and integrated the results of group users using AHP of multi-criteria decision making process to apply it to restaurant recommendation for group users. In experiments, we confirmed the proposed recommender system provides better performance than a random recommendation and a simple rule-based recommendation. The result of usability test also shows our system is usable. For future works, we will attempt to apply the proposed recommendation model to other services like movies.

Acknowledgment. This research was supported by MKE, Korea under ITRC IITA-2008-(C1090-0801-0046).

References

1. Adomavicius, G., Tuzhilin, A.: Toward the next generation of recommender systems: A survey of the state-of-the-art and possible extensions. IEEE T Knowl Data EN 17(6), 734–749 (2005)
2. Lieberman, H., et al.: Let's browse: A collaborative web browsing agent. In: Proc. of the Int. Conf. on Intelligent User Interfaces, pp. 65–68 (1998)
3. O'Connor, M., et al.: PolyLens: A recommender system for groups of users. In: Proc. of the European Conf. on Computer-Supported Cooperative Work, pp. 199–218 (2000)
4. Dey, A.K.: Understanding and using context. Personal and Ubiquitous Computing 5, 20–24 (2001)
5. Tewari, G., et al.: Personalized location-based brokering using an agent-based intermediary architecture. Decis Support Syst. 34(2), 127–137 (2003)
6. Kim, C.Y., et al.: Viscors: A visual-content recommender for the mobile web. IEEE Intell Syst. 19(6), 32–39 (2004)
7. Cooper, G., Herskovits, E.A.: A Bayesian method for the induction of probabilistic networks from data. Lach Learn 9(4), 109–347 (1992)

8. Korpipaa, P., et al.: Bayesian approach to sensor-based context awareness. Personal and Ubiquitous Computing 7(2), 113–124 (2003)
9. Horvitz, E., et al.: Models of attention in computing and communications: From principles to applications. Commun. Acm 46(3), 52–59 (2003)
10. Saaty, T.L.: Multicriteria Decision Making: The Analytic Hierarchy Process, Planning, Priority Setting, Resource Allocation. RWS Publications (1990)
11. Brooke, J.: SUS: A "quick and dirty" Usability Scale. In: Jordan, P.W., Thomas, B., Weerdmeester, B.A., McClelland, A.L. (eds.) Usability Evaluation in INdustry. Taylor and Francis, London (1996)

Augmented Reality Based Vision System for Network Based Mobile Robot

Ho-Dong Lee[1], Dongwon Kim[2], Min-Chul Park[3], and Gwi-Tae Park[1]

[1] School of Electrical Engineering, Korea University, Seoul, Korea
{juragic, gtpark}@korea.ac.kr
[2] Dept. Of Electrical Engineering and Computer Sciences, University of California Berkeley
dkim@eecs.berkeley.edu
[3] Korea Institute of Science and Technology, Seoul, Korea
minchul@kist.re.kr

Abstract. The human machine interface is an essential part of intelligent robotic system. Through the human machine interface, human user can interact with the robot. Especially, in tele-robotic environment, the human machine interface can be developed with remarkable extended functionality. In this paper, we introduce a tele-presence vision system for monitoring of a network based mobile robot. The vision system is a vision part of human machine interface with augmented reality for the network based mobile robot. We synchronize head motion of human user and the camera motion of the mobile robot using visual information. So user of the mobile robot can monitor environment of the mobile robot as eyesight of mobile robot. Also, the system partially creates a panoramic image to solve a pose latency problem. In this paper, we evaluate and compare panoramic images from two different methods. One is pattern matching method which is simple and fast, the other is Scale Invariant Feature Transform (SIFT) which is complex and slow. Finally, proposed vision system provides high resolution and wide Field Of View (FOV) to user who is wearing a Head Mounted Display (HMD).

Keywords: Tele-operation, Tele-presence, Augmented reality, Human Machine Interface, Head Mounted Display.

1 Introduction

Many researchers have been tried to make a robot more intelligent and serviceable. Consequently, robot system will be used widely in various fields and become more important in our daily life. But, up to now, most robotic systems are not fully intelligence and these are leading the necessity of human machine interface(HMI) which are conducted by many researchers. As a result, human machine interface forms an essential part of successful robotic system.

Owing to advent of computer network and internet, environment of industry and human's lifestyle are extensively changed. Robot system is also affected by these trends. Many robot developers are carrying out research on network based robot which is combined computer network and robot system into one methodology. Especially they have paid much attention to the human machine interface.

S. Lee et al. (Eds.): APCHI 2008, LNCS 5068, pp. 123–130, 2008.

We can check the essential role and importance of the human machine interface in the field of tele-presence technique. Tele-presence is the paradigm that user who is in a certain place will feel as if he/she is at another place and receives environment stimuli.

For tele-presence, panoramic images are used frequently[2][3]. To create panoramic images, there are various techniques such as omni-directional camera, multiple-camera, and revolving single camera. However, low resolution and narrow field of view(FOV) are problem[2][3][5] to be solved in the methods stated above.

In this paper, we propose a vision system which is an essential part of human machine interface with augmented reality for the network based mobile robot[1]. This system synchronizes human and mobile robot using visual information. In other words, motions from user's head and camera in mobile robot are identical. So user can monitor surroundings of the mobile robot as eyesight of the robot. In addition, the proposed system creates a partial panoramic image to solve a pose latency problem[2][3] and provides high resolution and wide field of view(FOV) to the user wearing a head mounted display(HMD).

In section 2, we introduce proposed network framework for network based mobile robot. Vision system to be targeted will be followed in Section 3. Finally we made conclusions in Section 4.

2   Network Framework for Network Based Mobile Robot

Figure 1 shows interaction between human and a mobile robot through the network and human machine interface.

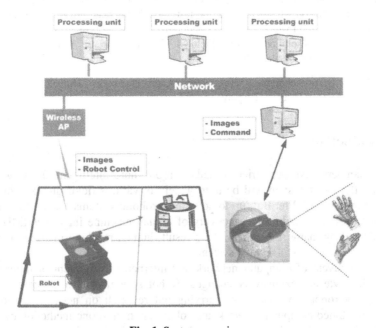

Fig. 1. System overview

In this system, all resource such as vision system, the mobile robot and processing units are connected via network. A low performance PC which has main roles of sensory data collection and control of mobile robot is equipped in the mobile robot. User can interact with the mobile robot more easily and intelligently displaying all information from HMD in Fig. 1.

To manage network connection, The Common Object Request Broker Architecture(CORBA) is used as middleware in our system. The Common Object Request Broker Architecture(CORBA) is a widely recognized middleware standard for heterogeneous and distributed systems. We used the public domain implementation of CORBA, called The Adaptive Communication Environment / The Ace Orb (ACE/TAO), as a middleware for the proposed system[6].

3   Vision System

We propose a synchronization scheme for pan and tilt positions between camera in mobile robot and HMD to ensure wide range of field of view.

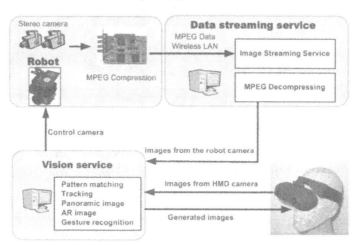

Fig. 2. Vision system

Figure 2 shows proposed vision system. In this system, captured images from camera in the mobile robot and HMD are sending to data streaming service region and vision service region, respectively.

Two images from robot camera and HMD camera are gathered into vision service region. In addition, panoramic images and augmented reality(AR) images for user who is wearing the HMD are created in the service region. Using the augmented reality and gesture recognition system, user can control the mobile robot more intelligently.

3.1   Augmented Reality and Synchronization of Mobile Robot and HMD

The vision system in Fig. 2 receives images from a robot camera and a HMD camera. Then it calculates each motion factor of the HMD and the robot camera. If the motion factor calculated is different from each other, the vision system tries to synchronize these motion factors by controlling pan, tilt position of robot camera.

We simply applied pattern matching technique. An image is divided as several blocks in the vision system and each block is comparing and matching with previous images. If the vision system found the most matched block, then it will be a base block. Using the base block the motion factor will be calculated from vision system. Example of the pattern matching method is shown in Fig. 3. The vision system calculates motion factor based on the base block.

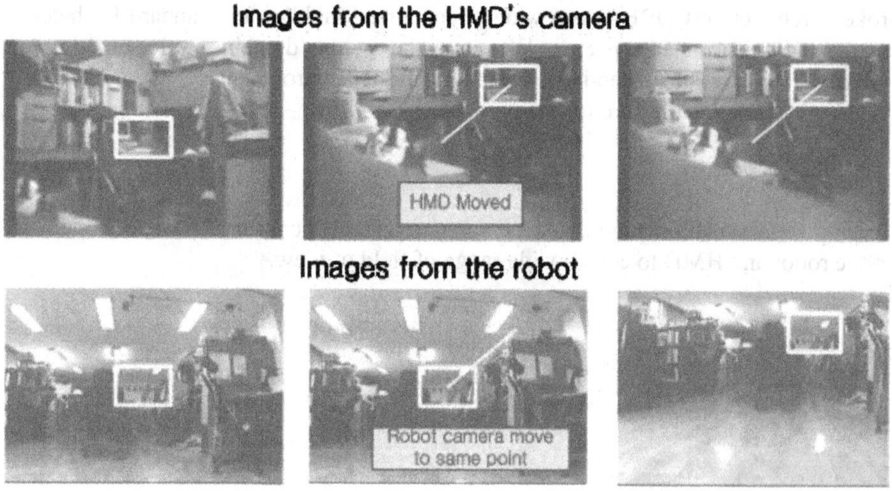

Images from the HMD's camera

HMD Moved

Images from the robot

Robot camera move to same point

Fig. 3. Calculation of motion factor using pattern matching and tracking

As augmented reality, if the user's gesture or environments are recognized, then virtual interfaces on the HMD will be generated like in Fig. 4.

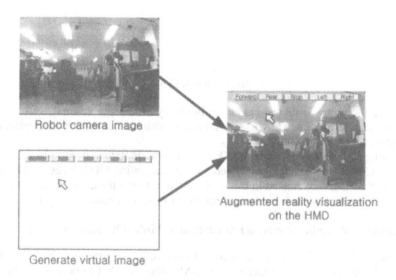

Robot camera image

Generate virtual image

Forward   Rear   Stop   Left   Right

Augmented reality visualization on the HMD

Fig. 4. Augmented reality

3.2 Generation of Panoramic Images

For a virtual absorption in an augmented reality environment, pose latency problem must be solved[2][3][5]. To handle the problem, researchers use panoramic images. However, it is difficult to create panoramic image with high resolution at real time.

In proposed system, panoramic image will be used to find the base block when the vision system fails to contact the position of the HMD camera. Considering pose latency problem, already calculated motion factor will be employed and position of the robot camera will be displayed into the HMD before the camera of the robot synchronizes that of the HMD.

After synchronization is completed between cameras of the HMD and the robot, the panoramic image used is useless any more. This is why we don't need whole panoramic image. Therefore, the vision system partially creates panoramic image. Fig. 5 shows partially generated panoramic image.

Fig. 5. Partially generated panoramic image

Using the revolving robot camera, panoramic image is generated partially and changed its displaying area slowly. In this paper, two methods, pattern matching and scale invariant feature transform(SIFT), are employed to generate panoramic images.

To generate a panoramic image, already calculated motion factor of each image block is used in Fig. 6(a). Using the calculated motion factors stated before, current image blocks are attached to the corresponding positions in the panoramic image plane directly. This method is very fast and easy to create panoramic image, but it has low precision than another method. This method takes the average of 10 ms at the Pentium IV 3Ghz computer.

When the scale invariant feature transform(SIFT) method is used, the result is shown in Fig. 6(b). After calibrating received images, matching point of current image and already generated panoramic image are found using SIFT algorithm. After finding matched points, homographies and warping parameters are found and current image are projected to the panoramic image plane using these parameters.

This method can make highly accurate panoramic image but it takes too much time to generate a panoramic image. This method takes the average of 15 seconds at the same computer.

(a) Panoramic image from pattern matching

(b) Panoramic image from SIFT

Fig. 6. Panoramic image from pattern matching and SIFT method

3.4 Vision System Flow

Using the current poison of the HMD, position of the panoramic image in which an image is displaying on the HMD is calculating. At the same time, images from a robot camera and current position of the panoramic image are updating continuously. Based on the above process, every new image is checked for motion factor and synchronization.

When a center position of the HMD goes out of the base block region, view point is expanded and new panoramic image is generated using information from current panoramic image and current received image from robot camera and HMD camera. Proposed algorithm flow for vision system is as follows.

    a. Set initial position. Create panoramic image plane for images from a HMD camera, and panoramic image plane for images from a robot camera.
    b. Receive images from the HMD camera and the robot camera.
    c. Calculate motion factors from the HMD image and the robot image. If those motion factors are different, send control signals to the robot to synchronize those motion factors(Fig. 3).

   d.   During vision system try to synchronize positions of the HMD camera and the robot camera,

      1. Check both motion factors. If those factor over a threshold, following statement execution. Otherwise, go to step 5.

      2. Create panoramic images.

      3. Calculate position of panoramic image plane of the robot using current position of panoramic image plane of the HMD.

      4. Get an image that calculated position of panoramic image plane of the robot.

      5. Receive augmented images from augmented reality service(Fig 4).

      6. Merge and display the image on the HMD.

      7. Update current image to panoramic image plane.

      8. Loop. Go to step b.

4 Conclusion and Future Work

Designing a good human machine interface(HMI) is the key to the successful robot system. In addition, Building an infrastructure and a base framework for augmented reality are very complex task. However, it is essential technique for HMI.

In this paper, we have attempted to build an augmented reality based vision system for the network based mobile robot. Proposed vision system uses revolving single camera to generate a panoramic image instead of an omni-directional camera or multiple cameras configuration. We implemented a very fast and simple method to create partially the panoramic image using revolving single camera and simple pattern matching method. This method can generate the panoramic image at real time. In addition, we implemented another method using SIFT to create high quality panoramic image. Both algorithms can be used without time constraint on our vision system. The vision system uses the panoramic image to synchronize a HMD camera position and the robot camera position. Also, the vision system uses the panoramic image to solve pose latency problem. Proposed vision system provides wide range of FOV and high resolution images.

In our future work, we will update our HMI system. Especially, we intend to project the panoramic image plane to a cylindrical and a spherical projection plane for a virtual absorption in an augmented reality environment.

Acknowledgments. This work was supported by the Korea Research Foundation Grant funded by the Korean Government(MOEHRD): KRF-2007-357-H00006.

References

1. Lee, H.-D., et al.: Human Machine Interface with Augmented Reality for the Network Based Mobile Robot. In: Apolloni, B., Howlett, R.J., Jain, L. (eds.) KES 2007, Part III. LNCS (LNAI), vol. 4694, pp. 57–64. Springer, Heidelberg (2007)
2. Fiala, M.: Pano-presence for teleoperation. In: 2005 IEEE/RSJ International Conference on Intelligent Robots and Systems, August 2-6, 2005, pp. 3798–3802 (2005)

3. Dasqupta, S., Banerjee, A.: An augmented-reality-based real-time panoramic vision system for autonomous navigation. Systems, Man and Cybernetics, Part A, IEEE Trans. 36(1), 154–161 (2006)
4. Azume, R.: A survey of augmented reality. In: Presence, vol. 6(4), pp. 355–385. MIT Press, Cambridge, MA (1997)
5. Fiala, M.: Immersive panoramic imagery. In: Computer and Robot Vision 2005. Proceedings. The 2nd Canadian conference on, May 9-11, 2005, pp. 386–391 (2005)
6. http://www.cs.wustl.edu/schmidt/TAO.html
7. Lowe, D.G.: Object recognition from local scale-invariant features. In: Proceedings of International Conference on Computer Vision, pp. 1150–1157 (1999)
8. Lowe, D.G.: Distinctive Image Features from Scale-Invariant Keypoints. International Journal of Computer Vision 60(2), 91–110 (2004)
9. Lee, K.-S.: Viewpoint Adaptive Object Recognition Algorithm and Comparison Experiments. Department of Mechatronics Engineering Graduate School, Korea University, a thesis of MS degree (2007)

Embedded Robot Operating Systems
for Human-Robot Interaction

Taehoun Song[1], Jihwan Park[1], Soonmook Jung[1],
Keyho Kwon[2], and Jaewook Jeon[2]

[1] School of Information and Communication Engineering,
Sungkyunkwan University, Suwon, Korea
{thsong,fellens,kuni80}@ece.skku.ac.kr
[2] School of Information and Communication Engineering,
Sungkyunkwan University, Suwon, Korea
{khkwon,jwjeon}@yurim.skku.ac.kr

Abstract. This paper focuses on the framework of the interface program that contains the controls and communication architectures to realize embedded robot operating systems for multi sensor system. The application builds the embedded operating system by using Mid Level Functions Layer for the robot's peripherals, and deploying a Low Level Functions Layer. The research proposes a hierarchical architecture for the user interface in order to realize an effective control command and status menu using an embedded sensor interface board. The operating system contained by an Ultrasonic and a Position sensing detector (PSD) and the operation of the Embedded Robot Operating System is implementation by Follow-Wall function. The proposed interface architecture gives easy and intuitive control of interaction with the robot and can be easily build to user interface program with multi sensor system.

Keywords: Robot operating system, User interface architecture, Human-Robot Interaction, Mobile robot.

1 Introduction

Currently, service robots research field is very growing up [1]. Design of service robot paradigm is very different of manufactured robots. The manufactured robots perform the same motion and repeated simple works in terms of user command. The other side, service robots is being many kinds of special tasks in human life space. Human and robot needs interaction while human is transmit order to robot and teach them. Also service robot has ability of communication method for interaction with human. Therefore Human-Robot Interaction method and a framework of robot operating system technology has been developed.

Human-robot interaction consists of four types of techniques. First, the interaction method contains an input device and an input method. The basic input mechanism uses a keyboard and mouse [2. 3]. A haptic interface device is more sensitive and accurate than either a keyboard or a mouse. Haptic devices and wearable input devices may be specially designed for robot control of, for instance, mobile or

S. Lee et al. (Eds.): APCHI 2008, LNCS 5068, pp. 131–140, 2008.

humanoid robots [4. 5. 6. 7]. Second, the technology is configured to build maps of and display unknown environments. Cognition can be built into the robot to sense and estimate the environment using ultrasonic detectors, position sensing detectors, cameras, and laser range finders. A robot can simultaneously build 2D or 3D environment maps and it can remotely monitor the area around the robot [8. 9]. The third technology of human-robot interaction is cognition: sensitivity to user's commands and reactions. The commands for interaction between a human and a robot consist of voice, gestures, emotions, touch, and force, etc [10. 11. 12. 13]. Last of all, the technique for efficient control of the interaction method is the framework for the user interface program [14. 15]. The newest interface framework or robot middleware architecture method is the semantic web and multimodal sensor interface [16. 17].

The human and robot interaction operating system [18] provides a structured software framework for building human-robot teams and robots to engage in task-oriented dialogue, and facilitates integration of robots through an extensible API. This research was contained Peer-to-Peer human-robot interaction technology and a novel infrastructure, and implement welding and inspector task in tack welds field. But this research's framework contained many kinds of components and very complex context. Therefore, this research's framework needs very powerful computing system.

In this paper, the focus is on the user interface program framework with the aim to develop the simple user interface program architecture for interaction with a robot. The special components for the interactive framework solution are the function of sensor interface and the function of the self-diagnosis component. These proposed functions of the user interface framework can improve the ease and efficiency of robotic control applications as the error ratio of the robot is decreased by using the self-diagnosis function when the robot sensor is non operational. The paper is organized as follows: Section 2 presents the system architecture. Section 3 describes the components of the Embedded Robot Operating System and, Section 4 presents the Embedded Robot Operating Menu. The implementation Embedded Robot Operating System for Human-Robot Interaction is shown in Section 5 and the paper concludes with the main contributions of the paper in Section 6.

2 System Architecture

2.1 Embedded Robot Operating System Architecture

The robot's embedded operating system contains three levels of function (Fig. 1). Each levels are separated and can't accessible directly, except Function Call mechanism. Low level functions contain sensor controller and sensors. This low level function is provides information to user what around robot environments. Sensor controller is control PSD and Sonar sensors by microprocessor general I/O ports. Mid level function is managing sensor controllers located in low level function by Low Level Function Call command. We called Low Level Function Call Manager (LLFCM). LLFCM communicate with low level's sensor controllers through SPI

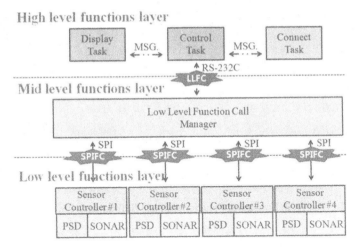

Fig. 1. Robot Operating Systems Architecture

protocol (SPIFC). Finally, LLFCM transmit command from high level to low level. High level functions consist of Tasks: Display Task; Control Task; and Connect Task. Each task will be present in section 2.4.

2.2 Low Level Functions Layer

This low level functions layer is provides information where around robot environments. Sensor controller communicates with PSD or Ultrasonic sensor. Each sensor controller contains eight PSD sensors and eight Ultrasonic sensors. PSD sensor's output value is analog. Sensor controller I/O controlled for PSD operation and convert PSD analog value to digital using 8bits analog to digital converter. Ultrasonic sensor's interface protocol is I2C bus. Sensor controller can control Ultrasonic through I2C bus in sensor controller internal function. Each Ultrasonic sensor own by different sensor IDs. Sensor controller is 8bit microcontroller with 128K Bytes in-core programmable flash. Low level function, PSD and Ultrasonic interface, is transmit to Low Level Function Call Manager in Mid Level Function Layer through SPIFC. SPI function call return length is two types: One byte data length format; and Eight bytes data length format (Fig. 2).

Sensor read SPI function call return format

Fig. 2. SPI Function Call Return Format

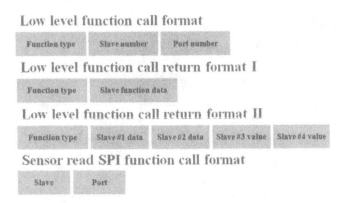

Fig. 3. Low Level Function Call and SPI Function Call

2.3 Mid Level Functions Layer

Mid level functions layer is communication layer, between high level function layer and low level functions layer, using Low Level Function Call format and SPI Function Call format. LLFCM handling four sensor controllers in low level functions layer. LLFCM contain two communication protocols. First is LLFC and the other is SPIFC. If that is user can be request command to low level functions layer through LLFC format. Then LLFCM received LLFC format from high level functions layer and parsing user command and seek type of sensor, slave number and port number. Slave number is sensor controller number, and port number is sensor number contained sensor controller in low level functions layer. After parse of user command, and generate SPIFC format and transmit user requested sensor controller through SPI. If LLFCM received acknowledge form sensor controller then delivery sensor value to high level functions layer through Low Level Function Call return format (Fig. 3).

2.4 High Level Functions Layer

High level functions layer in Embedded Robot Operating System consists of three main tasks. The first is the Robot Connect Task. This task communicates with Multi Sensor Interface Board for autonomous vehicles through LLFC format. The second Control Task has been linked with a human-interface device. The human-interface device that we use is the Microsoft XBox360 and the Logitech Extreme 3D PRO joystick. The third task of the Multi Robot Operating System User Interface is the Display Task. The Display Task consists of monitoring for autonomous vehicles in a remote area. This monitor task uses Visual Studio 2005 and the Simple Direct-media Layer library. Simple Direct-media Layer (SDL) is a cross-platform multimedia library designed to provide low level access to hardware. This supports Linux, Windows, BeOS, Mac OS etc. The display task shows the sensor status and the robot position. Each task, the Display Task, the Control Task, and the Connect Task, use the window message driven method.

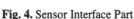

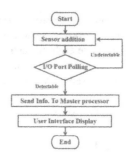

Fig. 4. Sensor Interface Part   **Fig. 5.** Sensor Polling Interface

3 Components of Embedded Robot Operating System

3.1 The Robot Sensors

The robot's operating system sensor interface consists of ultrasonic, and position sensing detectors. The position sensitivity detector (GP2D120) has a viewing angle that is cone shape in characteristic with an angle of about 15 degrees; this is able to detect nearby obstacles within a range of approximately 4cm ~ 30cm from the robot. The ultrasonic sensor (SRF08) also has a cone type viewing angle of about 60 degrees and its detection range is approximately 4 ~ 100 cm. As a result, the position sensitive detector is used to measures obstacles in close proximity whereas, the ultrasonic sensor is used to measure obstacles at longer distances from the robot (Fig. 4).

This sensor interface can utilize a low cost processor and use a polling input port in the processor which is efficient in continuously checking the signal. Although this method gives better results than the alternative of using an interrupt function, the polling period cannot be very fast. If the polling period is too fast then the processor's performance decreases making it less efficient. If the slave processor detects a signal from the plug-in sensor, then the slave processor transfers the sensor information to the master processor through the Serial Peripheral Interface (SPI) protocol (Fig. 5).

3.2 Sensor Self-diagnosis

The self-diagnosis system for the robot consists of three parameters as follows:

1. a check parameter to measure how faithfully the robot executes the required user commands, the user can order the robot to move or to perform a task. The movement command controls the robot's navigation and, the task command performs the required service. The self-diagnosis only checks the move command. The fault check procedure for the robot measures the difference between the intent of the user's command and actual repositioning of the robot. If the difference is above the POSITION_FAULT_VALUE threshold then the FAULT_POSITION_COUNT is incremented.
2. the time taken to perform the user command. If the robot does not respond within the expected time then the FAULT_PENDING_COUNT is incremented.

3. whether or not the sensor is operating normally. The sensor check is complex, however, the proposed system of sensor checking is defined by sensor type and number. There are eight ultrasonic sensors and eight position-sensing detectors. The fault check mechanism for the ultrasonic and position sensing detector can be detected by the sensor's setting in the robot. The ultrasonic and position sensing detectors are cross-checked against distance data. If a sensor fault is detected then the FAULT_SONAR_COUNT or FAULT_PSD_COUNT is incremented (Table 1).

Table 1. PENDING_FAULT_VALUE by user commands

USER COMMAND	PENDING_FAULT_VALUE
MOVE GO	5 sec
MOVE BACK	5 sec
TURN LEFT	5 sec
TURN RIGHT	5 sec
REQUEST SENSOR DATA	3 sec
REQUEST ROBOT STATUS	3 sec
MOVE POINT TO POINT	30 sec

4 The Embedded Robot Operating System Menu

4.1 Low Level Function Call Manager (LLFCM) Menu

The Embedded Robot Operating System Menu consists of nine menu items as follows:

- The robot direction control menu: MOVE FORWARD; MOVE BACKWARD; TURN LEFT; and TURN RIGHT.
- The sensor interface
- Sensor status display
- Sensor self-diagnosis menu: SPI TEST; SONAR; PSD; and MOTOR

These are shown in Fig. 6.

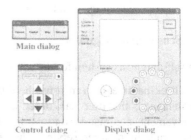

Fig. 6. Embedded Robot Operating system Menu   **Fig. 7.** High Level User Interface Program

4.2 High Level User Interface Dialog

High level user interface program is control the mobile robot and display sensor status. Main dialog is handing tasks: Display task; Control task; and Connect Task. Connect task is connected with Low Level Function Call Manager in mid level functions layer. Control task is contained Wall-Follow algorithm and input device driver. This task will be developing continuously for human-robot interaction algorithm (e.g. gesture recognition, voice recognition, robot control interface device, and haptic generation mechanism). Display task show robot status. This task support visualization PSD sensor and Ultrasonic sensor status. And also display sensor diagnosis status (Fig. 7).

5 Implementation of the Embedded Robot Operating System

5.1 Robot Operating System Hardware Specification

The experiment evaluating the proposed Embedded Robot Operating System for Human-Robot Interaction is as follows. The robot used in the experiment consists of motorized and sensory systems, and a control strategy. The motors are powered by DC 12V and have a maximum torque of 2kg/cm, and normal toque of 102rpm. The motorized system consists of four motors in total and includes two encoders. The encoders are fitted on the front of the robot on the left and right motors. There are two types of sensor namely, eight ultrasonic sensors (SRF08), and eight position sensing devices (GP2D120). All of the sensors and motors are controlled by low cost microcontrollers in the Robot Operating System Board which can communicate between the robot server and the robot through RS-232C protocol (Fig. 8, Fig. 9).

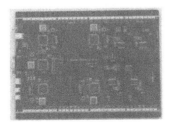

Fig. 8. Robot Operating System Board   **Fig. 9.** Implementation Mobile Robot

5.2 Wall Follow Algorithm

The Embedded Robot Operating System test environment is a 2.2m x 28m corridor. Our test implements the Wall-Following algorithm using our Embedded Robot Operating System architecture. Our mobile robot follows the left wall from the start position to the target position (Fig. 10, Fig. 11). The wall following controller has two kinds of input variables. The first are the Front Wall Distance Input Variables: ZF, SF, MF, BF, and NF (Fig. 12). ZF is the nearest distance (smaller than 5cm) in front of the robot and BF is farthest distance (larger than 25cm) from the robot. The Front

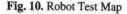

Fig. 10. Robot Test Map   **Fig. 11.** Robot Test Environment

Wall Distance Input Variables are shown in Table 2. The second input variables are the Left Wall Distance Input Variables: ZL, SL, ML, BL, and NL (Fig. 13). ZL is the nearest distance (smaller than 5cm) to the left of the robot and BL is farthest distance (larger than 25cm) to the left of the robot. The Left Wall Distance Input Variables are shown in Table 3.

Table 2. Front wall distance input variables

Variable	Means
ZF	Front wall distance is larger than 5cm and less than 10cm.
SF	Front wall distance is larger than 10cm and less than 18cm.
MF	Front wall distance is larger than 18cm and less than 25cm.
BF	Front wall distance is larger than 25cm.
NF	Do not exist front wall in front of robot.

Table 3. Left wall distance input variables

Variable	Means
ZL	Left wall distance is larger than 5cm and less than 10cm.
SL	Left wall distance is larger than 10cm and less than 18cm.
ML	Left wall distance is larger than 18cm and less than 25cm.
BL	Left wall distance is larger than 25cm.
NL	Do not exist left wall beside robot.

The wall following operation is based on the control table (Fig. 14). The wall following controller has seven output variables: NB, NM, NS, ZO, PS, PM, and PB. NB means to turn left by 90 degrees; ZO means that the robot is to move forward, and PS means to turn right by 90 degrees. The meaning of each variable is shown in Table 4.

Table 4. Wall follow controller's output variables   **Table 5.** Wall follow direction control table

Variable	Means
NB	Turn left 90 degrees.
NM	Turn left 60 degrees.
NS	Turn left 30 degrees.
ZO	Move forward.
PS	Turn right 30 degrees.
PM	Turn right 60 degrees.
PS	Turn right 90 degrees.

Input variables		Distance of left side wall				
		ZL	SL	ML	BL	NL
Distance of front wall	ZF	NB	NB	NB	NB	NB
	SF	NB	NB	NB	NB	NM
	MF	NB	NB	NM	NM	NS
	BF	NM	NM	NS	NS	ZO
	NF	NS	NS	ZO	ZO	PS or PB

Table 5 shows the wall following control table. This table generates the robot control dir ection for following the wall. The wall following control speeds are as follows:

- ZO : the left and right wheel speeds are 200 millimeters per second
- NS : the left wheel speed is 100 and the right wheel speed is 200 millimeters per second
- NM : the left wheel speed is 100 and the right wheel speed is 300 millimeters per second
- NB : the left wheel speed is -300 and the right wheel speed is 300 millimeters per second
- PS : the left wheel speed is 200 and the right wheel speed is 100 millimeters per second
- PM : the left wheel speed is 300 and the right wheel speed is 100 millimeters per second
- PB : the left wheel speed is 300 and the right wheel speed is -300 millimeters per second

The proposed function of the Embedded Robot Operating System architecture provides an easy and intuitive control mechanism using low cost sensors and an embedded sensor interface board. The useful functions of Low Level Function Call, SPI Function Call, and self-diagnosis have been shown to help upgrade the robot operating system. The features are embedded in the software of the functionally operating robot.

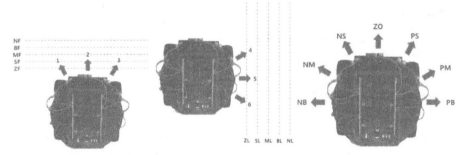

Fig. 12. Front Wall Distance Input Variables   **Fig. 13.** Left Wall Distance Input Variables   **Fig. 14.** Wall Following Controller Direction Output Variables

Acknowledgments. This research was supported by the MKE (Ministry of Knowledge Economy), Korea, under the ITRC (Information Technology Research Center) support program supervised by the IITA (Institute of Information Technology Advancement) (IITA-2008-(C1090-0801-0046)).

References

1. IFR UN-ECE, World Robotics 2000 (2000)
2. Yanco, H., Drury, J., Scholtz, J.: Analysis of Human-Robot Interaction at a Major Robotics Competition. Journal of Human-Computer Interaction (2004)
3. Maxwell, B., Ward, N., Heckel, F.: Game-Based Design of Human-Robot Interfaces for Urban Search and Rescue. In: CHI 2004 Fringe (2004)
4. Zhai, S.: User performance in Relation to 3D Input Device Design. Computer Graphics 32(4), 50–54 (1998)
5. Zhai, S., Kandogan, E., Barton, S.A., Selker, T.: Design and Experimentation of a Bimanual 3D Navigation Interface. Journal of Visual Languages and Computing, 3–17 (October 1999)
6. Lapointe, J., Vinson, N.: Effects of joystick mapping and field-of-view on human performance in virtual walkthroughs. In: Proceeding of the 1st International Symposium on 3D Data Processing Visualization and Transmission, Padova, Italia, June 18-21 (2002)
7. Hasunuma, H., Kobayashi, M., Moriyama, H., Itoko, T., Yanagihara, Y., Ueno, T., Ohya, K., Yokoi, K.: A Tele-operated Humanoid Robot Drives a Lift Truck. In: IEEE International Conference on Robotics and Automation, Washington, D.C, pp. 2246–2252 (May 2002)
8. Park, J., Lee, Y., Song, J.: Intelligent Update of a Visual Map Based on Pose Reliability of Visual Features. In: International Conference on Advanced Robotics, Jeju, Korea, August 21-24 (2007)
9. Ahn, H., Sa, I., Choi, J.: 3D Remote Home Viewer for Home Automation Using Intelligent Mobile Robot. In: International Joint Conference 2006, Busan, Korea, October 18-21, 2006, pp. 3011–3016 (2006)
10. Trafton, J., Cassimatis, N., Bugajska, M., Brock, D., Mintz, F., Schultz, A.: Enabling Effective Human-Robot Interaction Using Perspective-Tacking in Robot. IEEE Transactions on Systems, Man, And Cybernetics-Part A, Systems and Humans 35(4), 460–470 (2005)
11. Kim, K., Kwak, K., Chi, S.: Gesture Analysis for Human-Robot Interaction. In: ICACT, pp. 1824–1827 (February 2006)
12. Mourant, R., Sadhu, P.: Evaluation of Force Feedback Steering in a Fixed Based Driving Simulator. In: Proceedings of the Human Factors and Ergonomics Society 46th Annual Meeting, pp. 2202–2205 (2002)
13. Scheutz, M., Schermerhorn, P., Middendorff, C., Kramer, J., Anderson, D., Dingler, A.: Toward Affective Cognitive Robots for Human-Robot Interaction. Amerian Association for Artificial Intelligence (2006), http://www.aaai.org
14. Ha, Y., Sohn, J., Cho, Y., Yoon, H.: Design and Implementation of Ubiquitous Robotics Service Framework. ETRI Journal 27(6), 666–676 (2005)
15. Yanco, H., Drury, J.: A Taxonomy for Human-Robot Interaction. AAAI Technical Report FS-02-03, pp. 111–119 (November 2002)
16. Ryu, D., Kang, S., Kim, M.: Multi-modal User Interface for Teleoperation of ROBHAZ-DT2 Field Robot System. In: Proceedings of 2004 IEEE/RSJ International Conference on intelligent Robots and Systems, Sendai, Japan, September– October 2, 2004, pp. 168–173 (2004)
17. Sharma, R., Pavlovic, V., Haung, T.: Toward multimodal human-computer interface. Proc. IEEE 86, 853–869 (1998)
18. Fong, T., Kunz, C., Hiatt, L.M., Bugajska, M.: The Human-Robot Interaction Operating System. In: Proc. The 1st ACM SIGCHI/SIGART conference on Human-robot interaction, Salt Lake City, March 02-03, 2006, pp. 41–48 (2006)

A User Interface Transmission System for Public Robots

Jihwan Park[1], Taehoun Song[1], Soonmook Jung[1],
Keyho Kwon[2], and Jaewook Jeon[2]

[1] School of Information and Communication Engineering,
Sungkyunkwan University, Suwon, Korea
{fellens,thsong,kuni80}@ece.skku.ac.kr
[2] School of Information and Communication Engineering,
Sungkyunkwan University, Suwon, Korea
{khkwon,jwjeon}@yurim.skku.ac.kr

Abstract. This paper discusses the development of a control system for public robots. When a user requests a user interface for a public robot, the public robot sends this robot's user interface to the user's PDA, and then the robot can be efficiently controlled from this user interface on the PDA. This control system is highly efficient because one high performance robot can serve many users. This paper's purpose is not to present another method for one person to control one robot. Instead, when the user needs any service, the user connects to a p2p server and requests the service, and then the robot server will connect the user to the robot that supports the service.

Keywords: User interface, Public robot, UI, Robot interface.

1 Introduction

When a robot is controlled by using a specific immobile controller, the mobility and expandability of the robot can be limited. When a user installs an application program for robot control from a PC, the resource of the PC is wasted. A PC is not mobile whereas a PDA is. The user interface programs used for robots are not necessarily similar for each robot, so a user must study several new user interfaces when robots change. In previous work, the robot control method via the internet showed good performance [1-2].

Most robots operate and think independently of other robots. However, robot technology and computer networks are developing rapidly, and many research organizations have attempted to integrate robot technology and communication networks. This research assumes that robots interact with each other or with a computer network, and that they can perform a large number of functions [3].

When a public robot is connected to a p2p robot server, the user can connect to the robot and control it. If a robot incorporates a traveling support function, then the robot can guide the user, explain destinations, navigate to the destination, and notify the user when the destination is reached. The user can control any service of any robots that are connected and registered to the p2p robot server from anywhere. Existing

S. Lee et al. (Eds.): APCHI 2008, LNCS 5068, pp. 141–148, 2008.

technologies require the robot to be connected to a home server, and the user can use the robot within the home, but it is difficult for the user to control public robots. Low-priced robots have limited functions and they are not as efficient as public robots because the high performance and expense of a public robot can be justified when the services of the robot are offered to many users. This paper's purpose is not to present a method of letting users directly control any particular robot. When the user needs any service, the user connects to a p2p server and requests the service, and then the robot server will connect the user to the robot that supports the service.

Section 2 describes the interface transmission system, Section 3 presents the results of this paper, and Section 4 provides the conclusion.

2 Interface Transmission System

2.1 Service List

In the work described in this paper, an interface is in the user's client. This user interface is divided into two parts. The standard interface module is a common part of

Table 1. The common function of robots

	Movement	Voice Output	Camera Output	Range sensor
Patrol robot(5)	5	3	5	5
Cleaning robot(6)	6	1	1	3
Housework robot(5)	5	4	5	5
Toy robot(14)	12	3	3	6
Military robot(10)	10	3	8	7
Total(40)	38	14	22	26

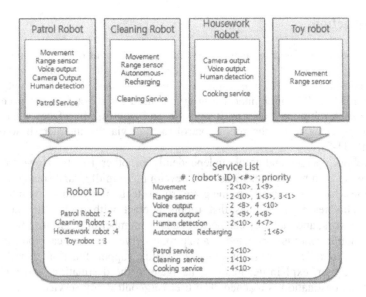

Fig. 1. The architecture of the Service List in a P2P Server

the interface. The service interface module is a module that is transferred to a service robot. Table 1 shows that many robots may have common services. A large number of robots have movement, rotation, camera output, and a range sensor service [5-14].

According to our research, movement, rotation, voice output, camera output, and a range sensor service constitute parts of the standard interface module. Other services are constituted in the service interface module. Each robot has a service list. The service interface module and the standard interface module are managed using the service list.

Service lists are stored in service robots and servers. A service list of a robot is stored only if it is a service of that robot, but a service list of the server represents the service lists of all connected robots. Figure 3 is the architecture of the home server's service list. The service list of the server is the stored service robots' lists and the priority list of the robots. If another user controls any robot, the robot is marked as being down and then other users cannot control the service robot when requests for service overlap.

Example of the service list which was produced with XML

```
<server>
    <service>
        <robot name="Patrol robot">
            <ID>2</ID>
        <robot name="Cleaning robot">
            <ID>1</ID>
        <service_list>
            <service_rot name= "movement">
                <ID="2" priority="10">
                <ID="1" priority="9">
            </service_rot>
            <service_rot name= "range sensor">
                <ID="2" priority="10">
                <ID="1" priority="3">
            </service_rot>
        </service_list>
    </service>
</server>
```

An example is the service list that constitutes XML. The service list of the service robot is different from the service list of the home server. The service list of the server is stored as a command protocol of all functions of the robot and the supported service. For example, we have camera output, navigation, and patrol service.

2.2 P2P Robot Server

Fig. 2 shows that this paper's system consists of the user's client, a p2p robot server, a network, and any robot that supports any service. The user's client is connected to the p2p robot server to request any service. The p2p robot server is divided into the robot's ID list and the user's ID list. The robot's ID list contains the robot's information and this information is available when the robot is connected to the p2p robot server. When the users request any service, the p2p robot server sends the Robot ID list of the robot that can support the requested service. The robot's ID list contains the robots' IP, so the user can connect to the robot directly. The service robot consists

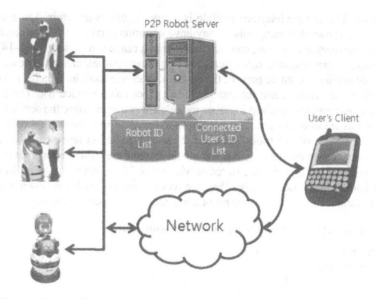

Fig. 2. The constitution of the user interface transmission system using network for public robot

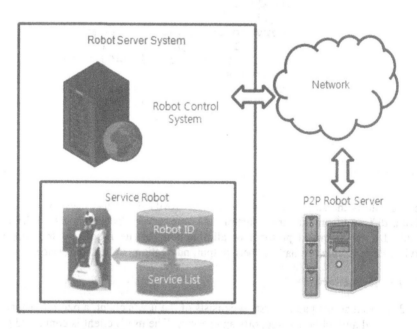

Fig. 3. The architecture of the robot server system

of the real robot and the Robot Server System. The Robot Server System can be used to connect to the robot, so it is possible for the user to control the robot using the network without the p2p robot server.

2.3 Robot Server System

Fig. 3 shows the architecture of robot server system. The p2p robot server system consists of two parts: the control servers of the robots and service robots. The service robot is the robot that can offer the service that is requested by the user. It contains the ID list, which is retrieved from the p2p robot server, and the service list of the robots. There is also a Robot Control System for the robots. This is not necessary when the robot's intelligence is sufficiently high, in which case the robot can connect to the network directly.

When the robot's intelligence is low, the Robot Control System controls the robot and the user connects to the Robot Control System. The user connects to the p2p robot server using a client program. When the user requests a service, the client program sends the service name to the p2p robot server. When the p2p robot server receives the service that is requested by the user, the p2p robot server searches for the service and the results of the search are sent to the client program. The user will then select any service robot that supports the service.

2.4 Interface Transmission

Fig. 4 is a flow chart that shows how the user controls the robot. First, the user connects to the p2p robot server using a client program. The user requests any service

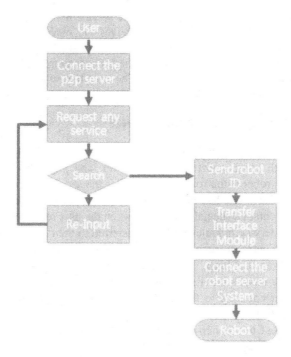

Fig. 4. A flow chart that shows how the user controls the robot

using this client program, and then the client program sends the service name to the p2p robot server. The p2p robot server searches for the service robot that can support the service. If there is no service robot that can support the requested service, the p2p robot server requests a re-input to the client program. If there is an appropriate service robot, the p2p robot server sends the service robot' ID list to the client program. The client program is shown the service robot' ID list in the result list window, and then the user selects a robot that is shown in the result list window. The client program then tries to connect to the robot using the information and the IP of the service robot's ID list, and the service robot transfers the interface modules. The user's client program and the service robot are operated without a p2p robot server.

3 Result

In this paper, the system needs five parts. These are the service robot, the robot server system for the service robot, a network that can connect to a p2p robot server, a p2p robot server for the public robot, and a client program that can connect to the robot and control it.

3.1 The Client Program

The client program consists of an input window and a result window. The users enter the service into the input window, and then the service name will be sent to the p2p robot server. When the p2p robot server receives the service name, the p2p robot server will search for the service in the robot ID list and the search results will be transferred from the p2p robot server to the user's client program. The client program is shown the result in the result window. The search results contain a location, a name, and the major service.

3.2 The Service Robot, The P2P Robot Server

The user cannot show the service robot, the robot server system for a service robot, the network which can connect p2p robot server, and p2p robot server for public robot. The service robot is the robot that can offer the service that is requested by the user and the service robot has both the service list and the service modules. The service modules contain a special service, so when the user requests the service of the service robot, the service modules will be transferred to the client program of the user where the Robot Control System for the robot is located. This is not necessary when the robot's intelligence is high, in which case the robot can connect to the network directly. When the robot's intelligence is low, the Robot Control System controls the robot and the user connects to the Robot Control System. The robot server system needs a network that can connect to the p2p robot server. When the robot server system is connected to the p2p robot server, the server list of the service robot is registered in the service list of the p2p robot server. The p2p robot server gives the robot server system the robot's ID, and then the user can request the robot's service. When the robot's intelligence is low, the Robot Control System controls the robot and the user connects to the Robot Control System. The user connects to the p2p robot server using a client program. When the user requests a service, the client program sends the service name to the p2p robot server. When the p2p robot server receives the service that is requested by the user, the p2p robot server searches for the service and the results of the search are sent to the client program. The user will then select any service robot that supports the service.

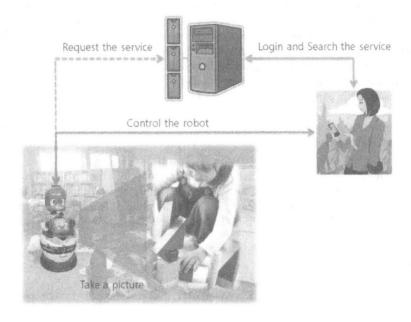

Fig. 5. A User Interface Transmission System in the kindergarten

3.3   The Service Robot in the Kindergarten

When the user wants to watch his child in the kindergarten, the user runs the client program. The client program tries to connect to the p2p robot server, and then the p2p robot server requests approvals for the access permission from a security service and the user searches for the camera service of a robot. The p2p robot server then searches the service list for the camera service and the search result is sent to the client program. The user then selects the service that is available in the robot in the kindergarten and the client program receives the service modules from the service robot. The service robot is then connected and the user can control the robot using its client program and the network without the p2p robot server, so the user does not need to remember the IP address of the robot, and there is no need to have the interface program beforehand. Only the user needs the client program that can connect to the p2p robot server and the user can reduce the resources of the user's client because the client program receives the interface program from the service robot. This system is shown in Fig. 5.

4 Conclusion

This paper proposed the p2p robot server system. When the information about a public robot resides in a p2p robot server, the user can connect to the robot and control it. If the robot has traveling support capabilities, then the robot can guide the user and explain destinations, so the user can navigate at will. The user can control any service of any robots that are connected and registered in the p2p robot server from any location. Existing technologies require the robot to be connected to a home server and the user can use the robot within the home, but it is difficult for the user to control public robots. Low-priced robots have limited functions and their efficiency is limited also. A public robot has high performance, more capability, and it is offered to many users. This paper's purpose is not to provide a mechanism for users to directly control any robot. When the user needs any service, the user connects to a p2p server and requests the service, and then the robot server will connect the user to the robot that supports the service.

Acknowledgments. This research was supported by the MKE(Ministry of Knowledge Economy), Korea, under the ITRC(Information Technology Research Center) support program supervised by the IITA(Institute of Information Technology Advancement) (IITA-2008-(C1090-0801-0046)).

References

1. Suzuki, T., Fujii, T., Yokota, K., Asama, H., Kaetsu, H., Endo, I.: Teleoperation of Multiple Robots through the Internet. In: Proc. of IEEE Int. Workshop on Robot and Human Communication, pp. 84–89 (1996)
2. Taylor, K., Dalton, B., Trevelyan, J.: Web-Based Telerobotics. Robotica 17, 49–57 (1999)
3. Jung, B.-c., Park, J.-h., Choi, D.-s., Kim, H.-m.: A study on intelligent robot based on home network. The Korea Society of Mechanical Engineers autumn collected papers, 792–798 (2003)
4. Luo, R.C., Hsu, T.Y., Lin, T.Y., Su, K.L.: The development of intelligent home security robot. Mechatronics. In: IEEE International Conference on ICM 2005, July 10-12, pp. 422–427 (2005)
5. http://www.cybermotion.com/datasheets/sr3esp.pdf
6. http://www.joymecha.com
7. http://imoyo.com/
8. http://www.roombavac.com
9. Robobolck, http://www.roboblock.co.kr
10. http://www.aibotown.co.kr
11. http://www.airobot.com
12. http://irobot.com
13. http://packbot.com
14. http://www.honda.co.jp/ASIMO/

Development of a WS-ECA Rule Management System for a Healthcare Robot

Jaeil Park[1], Haining Lee[1], Peom Park[1], and Dongmin Shin[2]

[1] Industrial & Information System Engineering, Ajou University,
San 5, Woncheon-dong, Yeongtong-gu, Suwon, 443-749, Korea
{leehaining,jipark,ppark}@ajou.ac.kr
[2] Department of Information and Industrial Engineering, Hanyang University,
Ansan. 1217, Kyunggi-do, Korea
dmshin@hanyang.ac.kr

Abstract. Providing healthcare services to patients and elderly people has been an emerging application domain in ubiquitous computing technologies. The current trend toward long-term healthcare is accessing healthcare services in the ubiquitous environment instead of in care centers, hospitals or convalescent homes. The Web Service Event-Condition-Action (WS-ECA) rule management system is designed to enable the heterogeneous communication devices in ubiquitous computing environments to achieve inter-operability via event-driven coordination. This paper presents developing a WS-ECA rule management system for a healthcare robot to provide ubiquitous healthcare services for elderly people.

Keywords: Ubiquitous service system, Healthcare services, WS-ECA rule management system.

1 Introduction

Providing healthcare services to patients and elderly people has been an emerging application domain [1-3]. The current trend toward long-term healthcare is accessing healthcare services in the ubiquitous environment instead of in care centers, hospitals or convalescent homes. Most research is related to a basic platform design of a teleoperated home healthcare system via healthcare robot platform via the Internet [4]. The mobile robotics techniques involved in the robot platform are sensing, task planning, navigating, and human-robot interacting [5]. To be a successful healthcare application of mobile robots for healthcare, ubiquitous computing techniques needs to be integrated with the mobile robotics techniques.

Web Services-ECA (WS-ECA) rules are designed to provide a general mechanism that can integrate a wide variety of reactive behaviours of various ubiquitous web services as well as service interactions [6]. It is to facilitate event-driven coordination among various distributed devices in ubiquitous computing environments [7]. WS-ECA) rules are an XML based rule description language for defining various web services and their interactions throughout distributed devices. WS-ECA language

S. Lee et al. (Eds.): APCHI 2008, LNCS 5068, pp. 149–156, 2008.

embedded into the devices is triggered by internal events or external devices provided corresponding guarding conditions are satisfied [8].

This paper presents development efforts of a WS-ECA rule management system for a healthcare robot, which is a mobile robot system designed to provide ubiquitous healthcare services for elderly people. In addition, we construct a test bed to demonstrate the usability of the healthcare robot. In Section 2, the WS-ECA management system is presented, and Section 3 shows how the WS-ECA framework is developed for ubiquitous healthcare service including implementation of a Healthcare Robot. Section 4 concludes the paper with future work.

2   WS-ECA Rule Management System

The WS-ECA rule management system is a XML based rule management system designed to facilitate seamless inter-operation among ubiquitous computing devices. A WS-ECA rule consists of event, condition, and action: 1) the event is notification messages from services or users, 2) the condition is a Boolean expression that must be satisfied in order to activate devices and that is defined by use of event variables contained in an event message or device variables maintained by a device, and 3) the action includes instructions that can invoke services or generate events [9].

A service device is surrounded by various event sources and service providers that, respectively, offer event notifications and web services. An ECA rule triggered by an event associated with a device results in the invocation of its corresponding service in a ubiquitous system. For effective interoperation of ubiquitous service devices, subsequently, the WS-ECA rule management system includes an effective algorithm that can detect and resolve potential inconsistencies among the rules [10].

The WS-ECA rule management system consists of three modes: 1) registration mode, 2) rule making mode, and 3) rule managing mode as shown in Fig. 1. Events, conditions, and actions are the basic components of WS-ECA rules. The registration mode has three type registrations: 1) event, variable, and 3) action registration. Events that are used to notify event occurrences are registered in the event registration. The variables that are used to express conditions are registered in the variable registration. The actions that invoke services, external events, and internal events are registered in the action registration. The registration mode provides all the information of events, variables, and actions to be able to design WS-ECA rules in the rule making mode. With the variables and actions provided by the registration mode, healthcare providers can design WS-ECA care rules with various distributed sensors and devices according to care guidelines The rule managing mode processes internal and external events in a such way that it senses events by acquiring sensory data from external sensors and sends out action commands to the ubiquitous computing devices such as PDA, cellular phone, etc. In addition, it handles conflict detecting and resolving and manages activated services.

The WS-ECA rule management system can be integrated into a mobile robot platform in which it processes WS-ECA care rules through communicating with sensor networks and executing ubiquitous computing devices.

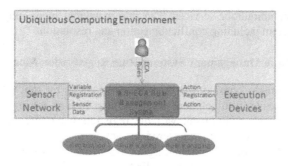

Fig. 1. WS-ECA rule management system

3 WS-ECA Rule Management System for a Healthcare Robot

To apply the WS-ECA rule management system for ubiquitous healthcare services, we are developing a healthcare robot which is composed of a mobile robot and various healthcare perception sensors. The initial goal of developing the robot is to provide a doctor or a nurse with useful patient information.

3.1 Healthcare Robot Configuration

As illustrated in Fig. 2, the robot platform is equipped with various sensors such as ultrasonic sensors for distance measurement, human detection sensor for human detection, battery sensors and IR sensors for navigation. Besides, it can collect vital signals, such as heart rate, blood pressure, breath rate, through bio-sensors which are detachable from the robot platform. These sensor data are transferred to WS-ECA rule management system.

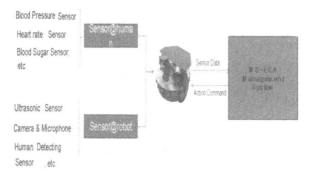

Fig. 2. Healthcare robot configuration

The WS-ECA management system comprises registration, rule making, and rule managing modes. The registration mode is to collect all the information of devices, environments, and services surrounding users. The rule making mode is to generate working rules for ubiquitous services. The rule managing mode plays a key role in managing the system including conflict detection and resolution.

3.2 WS-ECA Rule Management System: Rule Registration Mode

The registration mode consists of 1) events registered by the event registration module, 2) variables used to compose condition expressions are registered by device registration mode and environment variable registration module, and 3) actions to provide ubiquitous services are registered by action registration module. When an event occurs in the ubiquitous computing environment, WS-ECA rule management system generates action commands according to ECA rules registered. Fig. 3 shows the example of event, device variable, environmental variable, action registration. In this example, weight_messurement event, variables of weight sensor and temperature of bedroom, and alarm action are registered. The information is used to compose ECA rule in the following ECA Rule Making Mode.

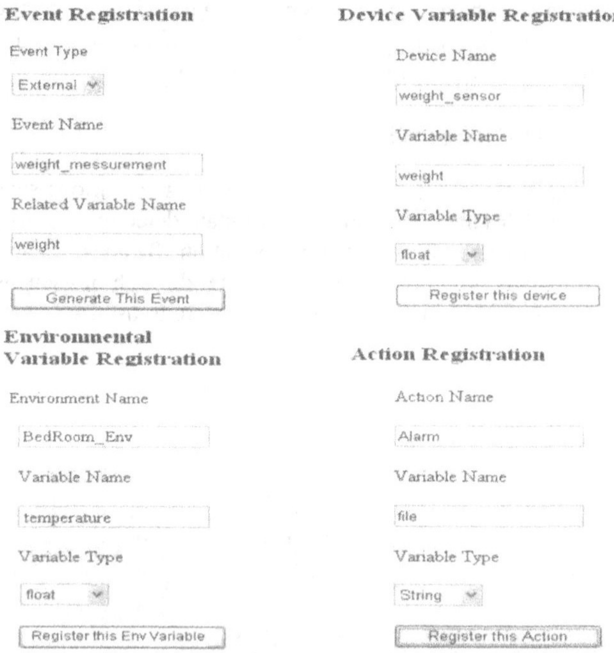

Event Registration

Event Type

External

Event Name

weight_messurement

Related Variable Name

weight

Generate This Event

**Environmental
Variable Registration**

Environment Name

BedRoom_Env

Variable Name

temperature

Variable Type

float

Register this Env Variable

Device Variable Registration

Device Name

weight_sensor

Variable Name

weight

Variable Type

float

Register this device

Action Registration

Action Name

Alarm

Variable Name

file

Variable Type

String

Register this Action

Fig. 3. An example of Event, Device, and Action Registration Mode

3.3 WS-ECA Rule Management System: Rule Making Mode

The rule making mode is to provide interfaces for healthcare providers who plan healthcare services. Healthcare providers prepare for a care guideline, which is a what-if scenario comprising: 1) emergency-related guideline, 2) time-related guideline, and 3) behavior-related guideline. The emergency-related guideline dictates what to do when emergency events happen. The time-related guideline dictates when to do when scheduling events happen. The behavior-related guideline dictates what to do when certain behavior events happen. These care guidelines are translated into WS-ECA care rules, which are processed by WS-ECA rule management system.

When an event triggers a WS-ECA care rule, the WS-ECA rule management system generates action commands. For example, a healthcare designer can register a heart rate sensor to the WS-ECA rule management system with such a rule description that if the heart rate of a patient is over 150/min, send heart rate information to a doctor. Fig. 4 shows the rule making mode with following ECA rule description:

Heart_Rate_Over_Speed Rule:
Event: Heart_Rate_Overspeed (150)
Condition: Doctor.position.inOffice=False
Action: SMS(healthcare_doctor, heart_rate)
         Video Call(healthcare_doctor)

ECA Rule Making Module

Please input a new ECA rule

ECA Rule Name

over_weight_rule

Event

Event Type External ∨

Event Name

weight_messurement

Condition Expression (Use the available variables below only!)

(weight>70)&&(speakerOr

Action

Action Name Alarm   Argument file   Argument's Value c:\over_weight_alarm.mp3

Register this ECA rule

Available Device Variable Information

device name: weight_sensor

variable name: weight

variable type: float

device name: AudioSystem

Fig. 4. An ECA Rule Making Example of Over_Weight_Rule

If patient's heart rate is over 150 when a patient's heart rate is checked by the WS-ECA rule management system, Heart_Rate_Overspeed event occurs. Heart_Rate_Overspeed triggers a Heart_ Rate_Over_Speed rule. The WS-ECA rule management system processes the corresponding action command such as sending Heart_Rate information to doctor. The patient's heart rate information is sent to a doctor immediately, which enables a doctor to monitor the patient by video call in real time.

3.4 WS-ECA Rule Management System: Rule Managing Mode

When an event occurs, the rule managing mode updates the status of related device and environmental variables, search for the corresponding ECA rules, and activates the rule whose guarding conditions are satisfied. An example is shown in Fig. 5. Weight_Messurement Event occurs, the rule managing mode search for the corresponding ECA rule and check whether the specific rule's condition is satisfied by updating the status of related variables.

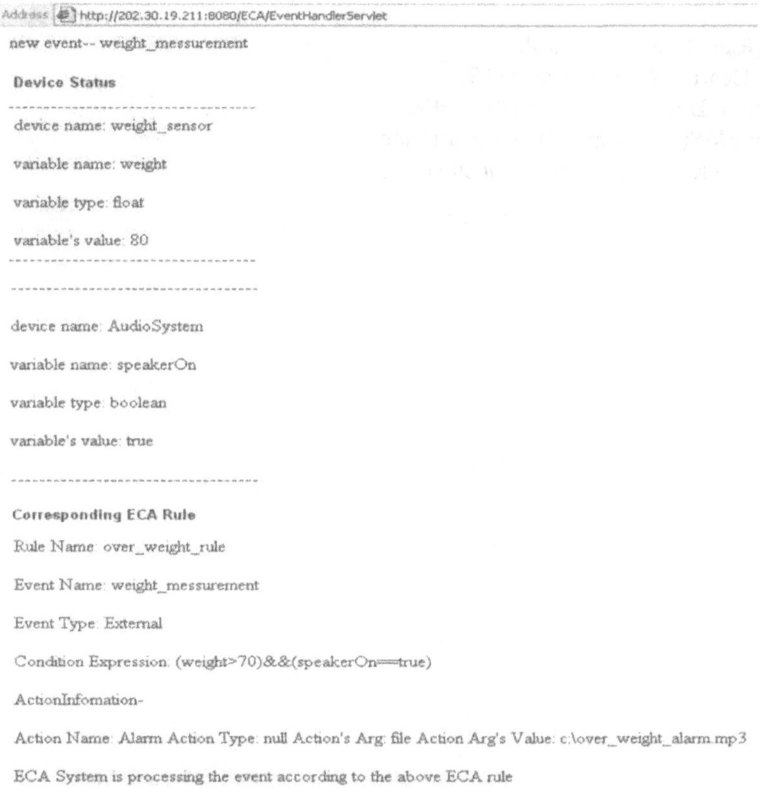

```
Address  http://202.30.19.211:8080/ECA/EventHandlerServlet

new event-- weight_messurement

Device Status
-----------------------------------
device name: weight_sensor

variable name: weight

variable type: float

variable's value: 80
-----------------------------------

-----------------------------------
device name: AudioSystem

variable name: speakerOn

variable type: boolean

variable's value: true
-----------------------------------

Corresponding ECA Rule
Rule Name: over_weight_rule

Event Name: weight_messurement

Event Type: External

Condition Expression: (weight>70)&&(speakerOn==true)

ActionInfomation-

Action Name: Alarm Action Type: null Action's Arg: file Action Arg's Value: c:\over_weight_alarm.mp3

ECA System is processing the event according to the above ECA rule
```

Fig. 5. Rule Managing Mode handles event

3.5 Healthcare Robot Test Bed

• Normal Health Checking

Fig. 6 shows a under developing a healthcare robot test bed for normal health checking service for the elderly people. The robot collects and analyzes sensory data by approaching a care receiver. The care guideline for this care service is as follow:

1. The robot carries the sensors to the care receiver
2. The care receiver uses the sensors to measure weight, blood pressure, etc

3. Health data is displayed on the robot
4. The health data is sent to the healthcare centre database
5. Healthcare centre analyses the health data and provides health cares;
6. The health cares are displayed on the robot.

According to the care guideline, WS-ECA care rules are created. The WS-ECA management system processes the rules.

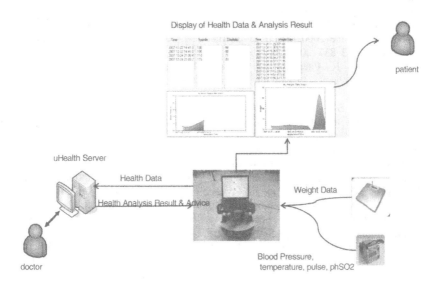

Fig. 6. Normal Health Checking Service

4 Conclusion and Future Work

This paper presents developing a WS-ECA rule management system for a healthcare robot to provide ubiquitous healthcare services while the robot are approaching elderly people. Our current work is developing the next level of the WS-ECA management system for a healthcare robot to provide monitoring, medication, emergency, and regular check-up services by collaborating with a regional hospital. Besides, care providers have certain care guidelines to take good care of their care receivers. The care guidelines need to be described in a XML-based description language so that they are automatically translated into WS-ECA care rules. The future work includes this subject.

Acknowledgments. This research is supported by Humintec and the Ubiquitous Computing and Network (UCN) Project, the Ministry of Information and Communication (MIC) 21st Century Frontier R&D Program in Korea

References

1. Yamamoto, H., Endo, H., Kitajima, K., Ohashi, S., Kondoh, I., Kuwahara, M.: A health care robot for patients. In: IEEE International Workshop on Intelligent Robots and Systems 1990, 3-6, Ibaraki, Japan (July 1990)
2. Evans, J.M.: HelpMate: a Service Robot Success Story. International Journal of Service Robot 1(1), 19–21 (1995)
3. Engelberger, J.F.: Health-care Robotics Goes Commercial: The 'HelpMate' experience. Robotica 11(6), 517–523 (1993)
4. Meng, M., Chen, C., Liu, P.X., Rao, M.: E-Service Robot in Home Healthcare. In: Proceedings of the 2000 IEEE/RSJ International Conference on Intelligent Robots and Systems, pp. 832–837 (2000)
5. Matia, F., Sam, R., Puente, E.A.: Increasing Intelligence in Autonomous Wheelchairs. Journal of Intelligent and Robotic Systems: Theory and Applications 22(3-4), 211–232 (1998)
6. Lee, W., Lee, S., Lee, K.: Conflict Detection and Resolution Method in WS-ECA Framework. In: 9th International Conference on Advanced Communication Technology, Gangwon-Do, Republic of Korea (ICACT 2007) (2007)
7. Bailey, J., Poulovassilis, A., Wood, P.: An Event-Condition-Action Language for XML. In: Proceedings of the 11th Int. Conf. on the World Wide Web (2002)
8. Jung, J., Han, S., Park, J., Lee, K.: WS-ECA: An ECA Rule Description Language for Ubiquitous Services Computing. In: Proceedings of the Workshop on Empowering the Mobile Web (MobEA IV) in conjunction with WWW 2006 (2006)
9. Jung, J., Park, J., Han, S., Lee, K.: An ECA-based Framework for decentralized Coordination. Information and Software Technology (in press, 2006)
10. Lee, H., Park, J., Park, P., Jung, M., Shin, D.: Dynamic Conflict Detection and Resolution in a Human-Centered Ubiquitous Environment. In: Stephanidis, C. (ed.) UAHCI 2007 (Part II). LNCS, vol. 4555, pp. 132–140. Springer, Heidelberg (2007)

Making Reading Experience Rich with Augmented Book Cover and Bookmark

Nobuhiro Inagawa and Kaori Fujinami

Department of Computer, Information and Communication Sciences,
Tokyo University of Agriculture and Technology,
2-24-16 Naka-cho, Koganei, Tokyo, Japan
samotanoshigena@gmail.com, fujinami@cc.tuat.ac.jp

Abstract. In this paper, we describe the design and the prototype implementation of a virtual illustration system. An ordinal book is augmented to provide a reader with value added experiences while keeping the original sense of utilization intact, e.g. a texture of paper. Multimedia information is automatically presented based on the page s/he is reading. The electronic version of a book is not needed. Anyone can create and share contents like posting a book review on a blog. Two types of add-on devices for page-flipping detection have been investigated, where a book cover and a bookmark with two 3-axes accelerometers have been augmented. A preliminary usability test shows the concept mostly preferred. The accuracy of flipping detection for a book cover and a bookmark version is 88.1% and 92.5%, respectively.

Keywords: Virtual illustration, Augmented book, Page-Flipping detection, Embedded interaction.

1 Introduction

Today, digitally enhanced books for entertainment are getting available. A typical functionality includes providing multimedia information, e.g. a music, a picture, and/or a video clip matched with a scene that a user is reading then [5, 2]. This is regarded as a *virtual illustration* in a sense that it realizes the role of a traditional (printed) illustration by digital contents. For example, one can imagine more about the Gion Festival, a festival of Kyoto, if the pictures and the festival music are presented and played according to the corresponding description. This allows a reader who has no idea of the festival to imagine it, that supports the understanding of the description. The functionality provides a reader with more exciting experience than a traditional paper-based book reading. However, such a digital book is not so popular now, and the functionality is not working enough due to the lack of contents.

From the technical points of view, the reasons come from the difficulty in reading a text through Liquid Crystal Display (LCD) for a long period of time and the lack of the texture of paper. The electronic paper and flexible display technologies would improve the readability and the sense of turning a page, respectively [6]. However, a very advanced Virtual Reality technology is required to provide the sense of the weight of the remaining pages. When we read a mystery book, we implicitly predict

S. Lee et al. (Eds.): APCHI 2008, LNCS 5068, pp. 157–166, 2008.
© Springer-Verlag Berlin Heidelberg 2008

the change of the suspect or the conclusion according to the current position in the book, that is obtained by the weight perception as well as a visual feedback. This is very important and interesting perspective for the interaction with a book.

The complexity of the right to publish the electronic version is a problem from the non-technical aspect. It is not clear who owns the right: the author or the publisher. Furthermore, in case of a book based on an animation film, the organization that holds the copyright of the characters owns the right. This prevents the digital version from being created and widely distributed in the market, that is the fundamental issue in a digital book. To address these issues, we propose an extension of an ordinal book. The system provides a reader with multimedia information on a home A/V system according to the page that he/she is reading then. There is an external mapping of one or a range of pages to the information. This does not make an electronic version. Everyone can publish the contents like a book review in a blog. Also, it keeps the texture of a paper-based book intact. In this paper, we describe the design and implementation of a prototype version of the virtual illustration system. Also, preliminary evaluation of the performance and the usability of the systems have been conducted. The rest of the paper is organized as follows. We examine related work in section 2. In section 3, the proposed system is outlined. Then, the evaluation of the proposed system is presented in section 4. Finally, section 5 concludes the paper.

2   Related Work

In terms of the interaction with a paper-based document, the DigitalDesk [11] is a pioneering work. EnhancedDesk [7] also seeks the smooth integration of paper and digital information on a desk. They allow automatic retrieval and display of digital information by recognizing the contents [11] or the tag [7] printed on a page, and direct manipulation of digital information by gesture recognition. They are basically augmenting a desk operation, and thus constrained to the place of the desk. On the contrary, our augmentation is done on the book side, that provides mobility.

Regarding contents identification, detecting the reading page is a relative approach [3, 9], where content is linked to one or a range of pages. On the other hand, tagging content to a page allows direct identification using an appropriate detector [4, 8]. Back et al. augmented a book with RFID tags and a receiver to provide additional information based on a page [3]. Also, a reader of the Magic Book [4] sees 3D characters related to the page through a head mounted display. The Interactive Textbook system [8], an application of EnhancedDesk, literally provides an interactive experience with the electronic contents linked to a page. They are realized by visual tags. Furthermore, a completely new material of a paper is investigated to detect the bending action when it is turned by polymer conductive ink [9]. However, they need specially manufactured pages, i.e. *redesigning*, that makes the cost of a book high. It also prevents an existing book from adopting to an augmented service.

An extra device is also required in case of the Magic Book, where a reader need to adapt to the new style of reading a book. In contrast, our system aims to realize the page detection in a cost effective manner and provide a reader with almost the same way of reading an ordinal book. This is enabled by attaching a device to a common part of a book, i.e. book cover and bookmark, rather than on each page or requiring a reader to wear special glasses.

WikiTUI [12] is designed to provide bi-directional interaction with digital contents using Wiki infrastructure. A reader can add and obtain digital annotations based on the page he/she is reading. To determine the page, a reader must specify the number projected on the table by pointing gesture. This means he/she *turns* both the actual page and the virtual page. The page number is correct so far as a reader follows the turning rule, however it requires a reader's attention. We consider it is inadequate for a book like a novel since a reader concentrates more on reading a text.

3 Virtual Illustration System

3.1 Design Background

The basic concept is to add an add-on device to an existing book or an object related to a book, that solves the digitization issue and remains the tangibility of a book. Anyone can participate to the process of producing an augmented reading experience like posting a review of a book onto his/her blog. This does not need to take into account of the copyright issues so far as a contents creator follows the traditional copyright rules. On the other hand, a reader can select his/her preferred one from multiple contents for a book. Once he/she purchases the device, it is utilized for any contents. We consider this is an evolutional form of a traditional web system. A web browser provides a user with an experience on a digital document, while our device is for a paper-based document, book.

Two models of providing multimedia information have been considered: pull and push. In the pull model, a reader explicitly retrieves contents by pointing gesture [12], for example. In contrast, the push model provides contents when a system detects the triggering event. The event includes the detection of a visual tag [4, 8], an RFID tag [3], etc. We have taken the push-based approach since we have considered that the approach is less interruptive to a reader due to its automatic provision. This is important for a class of a book like a novel that a reader concentrates more on reading compared with a textbook, for example. Furthermore, we have considered that multimedia information is absolutely supplemental one. So, it would be better to provide in an implicit manner. A textual description added for detailed explanation seems appropriate for explicit acquisition, that, however, we do not intend to support so far. Finally, we have determined to utilize the page flipping event for the implicit contents retrieval. It is common in reading and does not need any specially manufactured page.

3.2 Architectural Overview

The system consists of an augmented book with a page flipping capability, a book contents description, multimedia contents, ContentsServer, BookServer, and a multimedia system. The core of the proposed system is the *contents description* that consists of the mapping of pages to corresponding multimedia information. Fig. 1 illustrates the overall system architecture. Reading experience is designed by the contents description. They are created by anyone who wishes to produce an enhanced book reading experience and uploaded to a ContentsServer (marked (1) and (2) in Fig. 1, respectively). The contents, e.g. image and audio, can be stored anywhere. They are specified by unique URLs. We have developed a contents markup language, *eBookML* that we will describe in more detail in section 3.3. A controlling entity, *BookServer*, downloads the contents description that corresponds to a book when a person starts reading (3). BookServer interprets the description (5), and a multimedia system is controlled (6) when the condition is satisfied on the detection of page flipping (4). This is very similar to the web contents distribution system, where clicking a mouse is analogous to a page flipping. Here, the number of the page flipping event is counted to represent the current page.

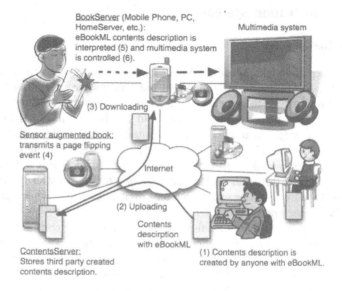

Fig. 1. Overall System Architecture

3.3   Contents Description with eBookML

We have defined an SMIL [10]-like original and simple language, *eBookML*, for the contents description. The description consists of a set of contents file locators and their controlling information for each event. An event corresponds to one or more (a range of pages, e.g. page 1 to 3) pages. More than one multimedia files can be processed in a sequential manner and repeatedly. Fig. 2 illustrates a snippet of an eBookML description, that corresponds to the page flipping of the first page, i.e. P.1, and continues until the next event matches. Currently, image and audio contents are supported; however it is extensible to any medium, e.g. smell, tactile, etc. Here, the definition of appropriate tags is needed as well as the development of their processing components.

WikiTUI [12] utilizes the Wiki infrastructure as a medium of annotation and sharing, while our system relies on a file generated per contents creator. The fundamental difference is *pre-selection by a creator*, that provides a reader with consist view on the book by a single creator. A reader can select contents creator based on his/her preference. This is the analogy to a *favorite blogger* from whom one likes to get information.

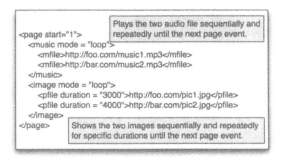

Fig. 2. A Snippet of eBookML File

3.4 Add-on Devices for Page Flipping Detection

Page flipping detection is realized in two ways: a book cover and a bookmark versions. An accelerometer has been utilized to detect the movements of a book cover and a bookmark every time a page is flipped. Two accelerometers have been attached for each device. One of them is utilized as a reference to avoid confusing the movement of a book itself. The flipping detection algorithm is described in the next section. Fig. 3 shows the devices and their usage scenes. Note that, in the figure, the page is flipped from left to right that is traditional reading way of a Japanese book (reading in vertical way from top to bottom, and from the right side to the left).

We have developed more than 20 prototypes of the two versions to find suitable design in the usability and the performance of the detection, where the size and the sensing position as well as the material are subject to test.

As shown in a), the book cover type is utilized by (1) picking up the inside part partially covering the reading surface when a reader flips the finished page (2). The inside part of the cover is translucent so that it avoid interrupting the reader's view. Every time a page is flipped, the part is flipped accordingly to hold the page.

Thus, a 3-axes accelerometer is attached there to detect the movement of the inside cover (marked as Sensor-1). Also on the front cover side, the other 3-axes accelerometer (Sensor-2) is attached. The material of the cover is polyethylene terephthalate (PET) with 0.3 mm thickness, and the "reverse gamma shape" of the inside part was finally determined to balance the usability (the readability of a text and the ease of manipulation) and the detection performance.

The flipping detection by the bookmark type is realized by the movement of a withy prop that holds the pages to read. We have augmented a product called *SwanTouch* [1]. Whenever a reader flips a new page, the page pushes the *beak* of swan forward, and soon the beak goes behind the page due to its withy material. So, the movement of the beak represents flipping of a page. One accelerometer is attached on the beak (Sensor-1), while the other is on the back cover (Sensor-2). SwanTouch is made of polypropylene. We have also tested other materials, i.e. an acrylic sheet with 0.5 mm thickness and a 0.3 mm PET one. Among them, the polypropylene one performed best.

In the two implementations, the sensor readings are collected on a PIC16F88 microcontroller. Then, they are wirelessly transmitted every 50 msec to a BookServer PC, where the detection is actually done. Our future implementation will detect the flipping locally (on PIC side), and only the event will be sent.

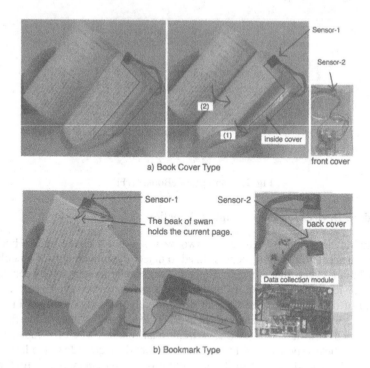

a) Book Cover Type

b) Bookmark Type

Fig. 3. Devices for Page Flipping Detection: a) Book Cover and b) Bookmark Type

3.5 Page Flipping Detection Algorithm

We have applied the same flipping detection technique for the two versions, which utilizes the ratio of Sensor-1 to Sensor-2. Fig. 4-(a) and (b) indicate the sensor readings from Sensor-1 and Sensor-2, respectively. Here, the page flipping with three styles of reading was recorded: horizontal, with a slope, and vertical. The average of the variances of the three axes (x, y, and z) within a certain window (20 samples, i.e. 1 second) is calculated (c) and then utilized to obtain the ratio (d). We have adopted the ratio since we found it difficult to distinguish the actual flipping from mere movement of a book itself when only one sensor (Sensor-1) is utilized. The two sensors show the same waveforms when a book is moved. However, only the inside and the beak parts are actually affected by page flipping in the book cover and bookmark versions, respectively (compare (a) and (b)). The body of a book moves independently. Therefore, we have considered the ratio performs well. Here, Sensor-2 acts as a baseline. To get the final answer, *the detection of flipping*, a threshold has been specified based on a preliminary experiment. Although the reading styles are changing continuously and they are apparent in the sensor readings (a), the ratio-graph becomes pretty clear (d). In next section, we evaluate the flipping detection performance and the usability.

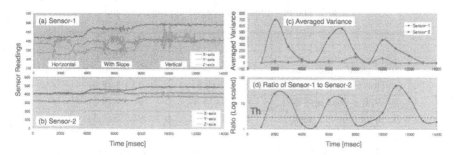

Fig. 4. Data Plotting of Sensor Readings (a) and (b), Averaged Variance (c), and Log-scaled Ratio of Sensor-1 to 2. "Th" in (d) indicates the threshold for flipping detection.

4 Evaluation

4.1 Methodology

Twelve people (10 people are undergraduates and the two are an adult couple in their 50's) were recruited to evaluate the detection performance and the acceptance of the system. To assess the intuitiveness of the augmentation, we did not tell them the usage for the first trial (0). Then, they were instructed the correct usage and the principles of the page identification. Three types of usage have been tested to see the robustness of the algorithm: (1) horizontal on a desk, (2) with slope on a desk, and (3) in air without any immobile object. The subjects were told to flip 20 times (pages) for each type. The accuracy of the flipping detection is defined by the ratio of the number of the counted pages to the total number of the pages that the subjects flipped. Standard deviation is also calculated to see the variation in individuals.

4.2 Results and Discussion

Performance of Page Flipping Detection: Table 1 shows the detection accuracy. The number in the parenthetic area is the standard deviation among individuals. The averaged accuracy for the book cover and the bookmark version are 88.1% and 92.5% (standard deviation in individuals are 11.4% and 8.3%), respectively. This indicates that the bookmark version detects the page flipping totally well with small variation in individuals. We consider the reason for the difference is that the book cover has a wide range of motion, which could lead to the variation of utilization among individuals. Also, this makes it difficult to detect using the simple thresholding. Furthermore, the algorithm is robust in that the differences among the three styles are small.

The case without explanation shows low accuracy and large deviation. In case of the book cover version, seven subjects could not find out picking up the cover when they were not told anything. They just put the flipped pages *on the cover*. We consider the gesture *putting the flipped page under the inside part of the cover* was far from natural reading. On the contrary, in case of the bookmark version, the accuracy is enormously low. This is because none knew the way of flipping, but they continued to read the book anyway. However, once they were instructed, the accuracy and the deviation were improved. They are easy to learn due to the simplicity and the seamless integration into ordinal book reading.

Table 1. The Performance of Page Flipping Detection

	Book Cover (N=820)	Bookmark (N=960)
(0) Without explanation	84.4%(*) (20.3)	21.3% (18.5)
(1) Horizontal on a desk	88.7% (8.5)	92.1% (8.5)
(2) With a slope on a desk	85.2% (15.4)	91.3% (9.2)
(3) In air (above a desk)	90.4% (11.4)	94.2% (8.3)

The memorability was also tested. Two subjects were asked to have the test a week to ten days after. They are the subjects who could not find out the methods without the instructions in the first trial (0). The result shows the accuracies of the three cases were almost the same as before. We consider this is because they were told not only the way itself, but the principle of the flipping detection. Also, the physical appearance of the devices reminded them of the usage.

The mis-detection in the bookmark version generally comes from the case in which the flipped page goes through the beak part without large movement. By making the material of the bookmark harder, the part can firmly hold the page to be flipped next. Then, the detection might be more accurate due to the larger bouncing acceleration of the beak. However, at the same time, it would become difficult to flip and sometimes the page might be damaged.

The common limitation in both cases is that they do not support *random access* to the contents. This comes from the method of identifying the current page. The advantage of random access is that not only it allows a system to know the page number that a reader opens suddenly, but also it can eliminate the accumulative errors of the page flipping detection. Although the performance of the detection is high (Table 1) and still there is room for improvement, this becomes problem if the book has large number of pages, i.e. more likely to make mistakes. Recognizing a page number by a video camera might remove the barrier. However, the technology should be carefully utilized since it looks like a spy camera when it is utilized outside. We can also consider the extension of the current devices with the error correction or page number adjustment functionality. A visual feedback shows the current page number, and the page flipping sound might be useful as an ambient feedback. A proper input modality allows the correction or the adjustment to whatever pages the reader specifies. We will investigate such functionality while taking into account of the impact on a traditional reading style.

Usability and Preference: The subjects were shown the demo and asked the impression of the system after the performance evaluation. Fig. 5 indicates a) the perceived difference from an existing book (1: very obtrusive, 5: not obtrusive at all) , and b) preference of creating contents and utilizing the system (1: do not like to do it at all, 5: like to do it very much).

The proposed devices have been designed to keep the traditional reading style as much as possible. The subjects felt less obtrusive against the bookmark version than the book cover version. The bookmark version requests a user to pay attention to the beak part to some extent, however it has great advantage over the book cover version. The beak holds the page to read the next (Fig. 3-(b)), while the flipped page is hold by

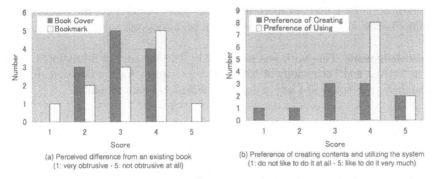

Fig. 5. User Survey on the Acceptability of the Devices and Preference of the System

the book cover (Fig. 3-a). This means a reader of the book cover version needs to open the cover when he/she wants to check the flipped pages again. This causes the mis-detection of the flipping since the movement of the inside cover is the same. In contrast, the bookmark version has no such limitation. The information is provided based on the incremented page by the movement of the beak. So, a reader would be presented different information while he/she is checking a page that he/she flipped before. We consider this is not so big problem in a novel book since the activity is basically *confirming* unclear point. However, the *pause* button can be added to the beak or somewhere to improve the usability.

Regarding the preference, all the subjects liked to utilize the system (score = 4 and 5). They agreed with the concept of *making reading experiences rich with an existing book*. Furthermore, some subjects requested additional functionalities: the improvement of the efficiency and the environment of reading, i.e. virtual bookmarking of preferred pages, finding the meaning of unknown words, automatic adjustment of ambient light, bad posture warning, etc. Currently, the eBookXML description is edited by a text editor basis. As can be seen in Fig. 5-(b), the subjects did not like to create contents so much as utilize them. To increase a creator in order to work the contents distribution system well, we will investigate a sophisticated authoring tool in the future.

5   Concluding Remark

In this paper, we have proposed a virtual illustration system. It is aware of the current page, and provides multimedia information based on the page currently read by a user. This is analogy to a printed illustration, with which a reader can have additional information on the text in a book. Accumulation of a page-flipping event is utilized to estimate the current page. Everyone can publish the contents written in *eBookML* like in HTML for a browser. Two types of add-on devices for the flipping detection have been investigated: *book cover* and *bookmark*. They were evaluated in the detection performance and the usability. The detection accuracy of the book cover and the bookmark versions are 88.1% and 92.5%, respectively. The concept of the augmentation was mostly accepted. We consider that a book with sequential access to the contents and the small number of the pages is appropriate in the current version, e.g. short novel. We are planning to investigate a mechanism to correct or adjust the page estimation by a user for more flexible service. Furthermore, the functionalities that improve the efficiency of reading will also be introduced.

Acknowledgments. This work was supported by The Ministry of Education, Culture, Sports, Science and Technology in Japan under a Grant-in-Aid for Division of Young Researchers. We would also like to thank the subjects of our evaluation.

References

1. SwanTouch, http://swanmark.hp.infoseek.co.jp/index.html
2. althi Inc. Image Novel, http://www.althi.co.jp/tat.html
3. Back, M.J., et al.: Page detection using embedded tags. In: 13th annual ACM symposium on User interface software and technology (UIST2000) (2000)
4. Billinghurst, M., et al.: MagicBook: transitioning between reality and virtuality. In: Extended abstract on Human factor in computing systems (CHI 2001) (2001)
5. CELSYS Inc. BookSurfing, http://www.celsys.co.jp/en/solution/booksurfing
6. E Ink Co. Electronic paper displays, http://www.eink.com
7. Koike, H., et al.: Integrating Paper and Digital Information on EnhancedDesk: A Method for Realtime Finger Tracking on an Augmented Desk System. ACM Trans. Comput.-Hum. Interact. 8(4), 307–322 (2001)
8. Koike, H., et al.: Interactive Textbook and Interactive Venn diagram: Natural and Intuitive Interfaces on Augmented Desk System. In: SIGCHI conference on Human factors in computing systems (CHI 2000), pp. 121–128 (2000)
9. May, K.W.: Conductive ink based page detection for linking digital and physical pages. In: CHI 2001 extended abstracts on Human factors in computing systems, pp. 275–276 (2001)
10. W3C. Synchronized Multimedia, http://www.w3.org/AudioVideo/
11. Wellner, P.: Interacting with paper on the DigitalDesk. Commun. ACM 36(7), 87–96 (1993)
12. Wu, C.-S., et al.: Turning a page on the digital annotation of physical books. In: Second International Conference on Tangible and Embedded Interaction (TEI 2008), pp. 109–116 (2008)

SPATIAL POEM:
A New Type of Experimental Visual Interaction in 3D Virtual Environment

Jinyoung Choi[1] and Sang Hyuk Hong[2]

[1] IDAS, Hongik University, Interaction Design Lab.,
110-770 Seoul, Korea
c.jinyoung@gmail.com,
www.concept-tree.co.kr/sp
[2] Sungkyunkwan University, School of Systems Management Engineering,
440-746 Suwon, Korea
spectra3@nate.com

Abstract. SPATIAL POEM is a new type of 'real-time visual interaction' expressing our own creative narrative as real-time visual by playing a musical instrument which is an emotional human behavior. There are sensors on each hole on the surface of the musical instrument. When you play it, sensors recognize that you have covered the holes. All sensors are connected to a keyboard, which means your playing behavior becomes a typing action on the keyboard. And it is programmed to spread out the visual of your words in a virtual 3D space when you play the musical instrument. The behavior when you blow the instrument, to make sounds, changes into the energy that makes you walk ahead continuously in a virtual space. It used a microphone sensor for this. After all by playing musical instrument, we get back the emotion we forgot so far, and your voice is expressed with your own visual language in virtual space.

Keywords: Tangible interaction, Physical computing, User interface, Game design and play, Interactive narrative.

1 Introduction

The more complicated society becomes, the more simple and clear way of thinking develops. Humans' wish a more emotional and personal behavior when interacting with tools they have made using high technology. Facing huge amounts of interfaces that quickly mushroom from industries and changes it causes us to not only succeed in communication with the proper target, but also fail in it by technical or cognitive errors. This brings us to live in a society that continuously forces us to look for a more proper interface with human emotions.

Humans deal with emotions on a continuous basis and emotion are intrinsically part of our intelligence, part of the social interaction and the ability to make decisions (Damasio, 1995).

S. Lee et al. (Eds.): APCHI 2008, LNCS 5068, pp. 167–174, 2008.
© Springer-Verlag Berlin Heidelberg 2008

Even with some basic interactions, several studies have shown that humans exhibit social behaviors when interacting with computers. (Reeves & Nass, 1996)

1.1 Computing and Tangible Emotions

Many studies of human-media interaction say that people exhibit their social-emotional responses when they interact with media. Even designers considered interface design as the tools for better performance of tasks during the last long period, but what is clear is that people do not respond to interactive interfaces putting aside their social-emotional concerns any more. [1]

In this point of view, user's rich and complex emotional aspects should be considered as a core value to improve our media environment with future interfaces. High-tech advances are needed for that but should be hidden behind the surface to make people interact with media naturally using their own emotion. It is not easy to define what emotion is, but when we interact with the digital environment we at least can let our abstract emotions become tangible like visuals to be seen or sounds to be heard.

1.2 Playful Human Communication

Meeting other people and sharing information is necessary to survive as a member of society, we call it a social activity which has been advanced in more playful ways. The same value with off-line communication has been expanded to on-line media and devices such as blog and trendy devices, and it is not a new aspect anymore. People like to create their own world where they can understand and can become a meaningful person in it by belonging to it. By that people always tend to make their own tribe with common sense based on social activity.

According to Friedrich Schiller a German poet and philosopher, human desire of pursuing fun is elemental impulse that is considerable to direct human behaviour. Humans tend to pursue fun through instinct without any instruction. Impulse wakens the desire of humans to meet the needs inside and encourage them to make it. Desire of humans for fun becomes the inherent power that makes people play. [2]

For that reason playful way of communication is the core thing that should be considered for a better human-like interaction. Humans do not respond to media by thinking of it as a mere machine or digital content.

1.3 Game: Experimental Digital Experience in Narrative Structure

Game that grew deeply in our daily life and became a culture has been developed as another giant industry. Types of game and tool for it have become various. That reflects exactly humans' needs for the culture variety. In this context, kinds of virtual reality and future input devices will be diverse and transformed in more exciting way.

Moreover the demand for more creative talent has driven game companies to bring in artists from outside of what one would traditionally call the video game industry. [3]

However, far from this variety and creativity, there exist a story driving through a game and narrative supporting it in the basis of all games. They are kinds of structures cause fun and immersion in a game. Narrative is a sort of total experience structure that can be made inside game story as a way of undergoing. Creation of a new type of narrative has potential to lead to a new game genre that shows different interaction than before.

Game generation has now become next adult generation that moves society. In consequence of this, insight into a game and suggesting future narrative based on that are very important job. [4]

1.4 Digilog: Digital+Analog

Digilog is the composite word of Digital and Analog which means the power made when the both components go together in the modern high-tech digital age. Digilog power has already been covering in all fields like industry, society, and culture by complementing digital products and services with analog emotion so that finds new opportunity in niche markets. It reflects, we can not pass the next digital generation with only IT power and advances in digital technology. People have been realizing that the best digital should be something more emotional which respect more human than technology. [5]

2 Playing Hangeul

Producing many kinds of sounds by playing musical instruments becomes the same behavior in which we express our emotions through speech. In this installation you can play your words by playing musical instrument and see your emotional rhythm through the real-time visual on a screen. I chose Hangeul as a visual component and Korean traditional musical instrument as a controller to play your words. When you voice your words by playing an instrument, the visual language is spread out in a 3D virtual environment.

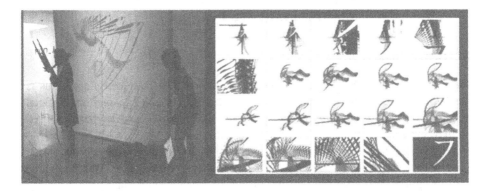

Fig. 1. Installation and performance. (Left) Visuals for virtual game environment made by Hangeul unit 'ㄱ'. (Right).

2.1 SCENARIO: Playing HANGEUL with Musical Instrument in 3D Virtual Space

There are several holes on the surface of a musical instrument to make sounds. I used some sensors to recognize specific Hangeul letters on each hole by connecting it with a mechanical keyboard so that it can produce Hangeul visual by playing. When I breathe through the entrance hole, that behavior becomes the energy for the game player to go ahead. Covering the holes during the play has the same function as a typing keyboard so that I can produce visuals planned to put on each. Controller can be any musical instrument that has holes in it, and visual can not only be letters but also letter combinations. By playing this musical instrument I can create my very own visual environment inside the game.

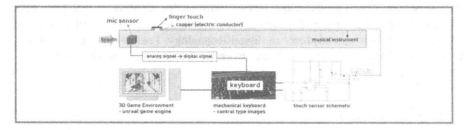

Fig. 2. Schematic

Fig. 3. Hardware and principle

2.2 Digilog Controller

Users play the game by playing a musical instrument and the electric apparatus is installed and hidden behind the instrument. This brings users to feel an artificial technology if compared to usual game devices like a mouse and keyboard. I used SangHwang as a controller.

SangHwang is an ideal instrument as a controller to express various visuals inside game with quite a lot of holes in it. When you start to play SangHwang, the game starts by going ahead on the screen. When you cover a hole during the play, the sensor being put on becomes active and sends the signal to the computer. That brings a dynamic visual processing in a 3D virtual environment.

Fig. 4. Playing game using SangHwang as a controller

Each hole of the instrument is connected to a Korean letter shape of images that are already made inside in an unreal game engine. When users touch each hole, the image coming under them spreads out in the game space at the same time. If users play a cord, which means covering more than two holes at the same time, related images spread out together. Through this principal, user themselves make their own visual experience that is unexpected with a random composition of images and screen conversion through their manipulation. That brings to users themselves to go through elevated visual experience by playing a musical instrument meaning emotional behavior and not by manipulating mechanical devices.

Unreal Game Engine. Visual and programming work for functional realization is accomplished like this: First, I register images made by 3D software 'MAYA' at section of Unreal game editor 'Static Meshes'. Then I make the root 'NewWeapon>classes' under program folder and save the 'uc' files inside. The 'uc' files are to import each image registered before. This 'uc' file has options to change characters like size and speed, etc.

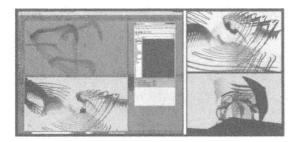

Fig. 5. Unreal game engine editor and environment visuals

After I delete the file 'newweapon.u' located under the system folder of game engine, add the script 'EditPackages=NewWeapon' in the file 'ut2004.ini'. Then I compile files modified by run 'ucc make'. For the last step I modify the key mapping in the file 'user.ini' inside system folder.

Sensors and system. Copper tape located around the hole of instrument is connected to each key of mechanical keyboard through the electrical apparatus with touch sensors. Through playing the musical instrument, users are able to manipulate the keyboard and control the game environment. Microphone sensor located inside the entrance of instrument is connected to ADC so that the analog signal is transferred to a digital signal. The digital signal is delivered to the key '↑' on the mechanical keyboard through the amplifier equipment. This camera view of the game starts to move ahead with user's breathing when they start to play the musical instrument.

Fig. 6. Connection between musical instrument and touch sensor. (Left) A use of mechanical keyboard by connecting to a circuit of touch sensor. (Right)

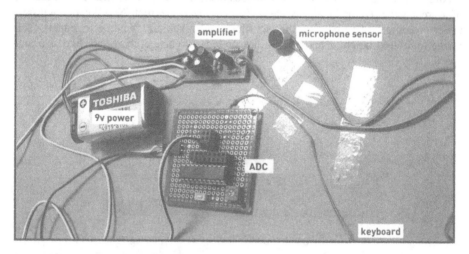

Fig. 7. A circuit to transform analog signal of microphone sensor into digital signal

The microphone is connected to simple amplifier (OP-AMP, LM386) and the gained signal is send the ADC converter (ADC0804). ADC converter transfer users breathe into digital signals to operate keyboard. The PhotoMOS relay is used to connect ADC converter to mechanical keyboard.

At first, CdS cells are used for touch sensor. But, that are needed adjusting threshold each time to use, because of CdS is sensitively affected by lighing around user. So, CdS cells are not suited for our system, and we need the perfectly signal for fast tapping during playing SangHwang. Finally, we choose the copper tape for touch sensor.

2.3 Experimental Visual Processing by User

In this paper, we will find an interesting interaction tools. Next SangHwang will make the dynamic word. If the system recognize the chording input signal by simultaneous tapping with multiple fingertips to the SangHwang, the system will show the word in korean or english. And, if the system divide into 3~4 digital signal from user's breathing, we will make different size or color for making word.

Fig. 8. Visual processing by inexperienced user's manipulating (Installation in public)

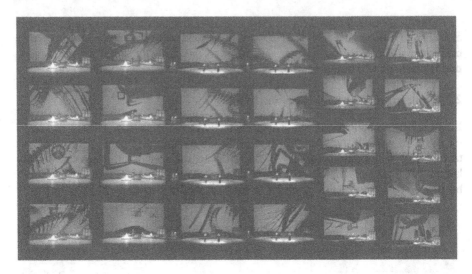

Fig. 9. Interactive concert in The National Center for Korean Traditional Performing Arts

3 Conclusion

The goal of my thesis is to create an experimental visual interaction in 3D a virtual environment. Through this work I wanted to show how an effective emotional communication may be realized into a human media communication. I studied many different design methods including technical issues in this project to create an interactive digital media space and visual with a physical and human-like experience. The required affective reasoning naturally breaks down into two areas: emotional communication through human-like interface and affective virtual game environment. The idea of SPATIAL POEM project can be adapted into game, play and concept architecture. If this is developed more with sound effects on its original sound, it definitely can be expanded into other areas like film and music video as well as any other genre.

References

1. Picard, R.W.: Future Interfaces: Social and Emotional. MIT Press, Cambridge (2002)
2. Hakjin Kim, et al.: Digital fun! Fun creates the value, Samsung Economic Research Institute, Seoul, pp. 21–22 (2007)
3. Crawford, C.: The Art of Computer Game Design (1982)
4. Hyeonjoo, R.: Computer game and narrative, Hyeonamsa, Seoul (2003)
5. Lee, O.: Digilog: Digital+Analog. Tree of thought Press, S.Korea (2006)

Human Genome Data Visualization
Using a Wall Type Display

Kunihiro Nishimura, Tomohiro Tanikawa, and Michitaka Hirose

Graduate School of Information Science and Technology, The University of Tokyo,
7-3-1, Hongo, Bunkyo-ku, Tokyo, 113-8656, Japan
{kuni,tani,hirose}@cyber.t.u-tokyo.ac.jp

Abstract. Information visualization is an effective method to grasp a complete
view of huge data. In the field of genome science, researchers are faced with a
large biological data set analysis. Large biological data set are accumulated in
public web sites. They want to grasp whole view of the data and extract biological meanings from the data. We have taken an information visualization approach for supporting genome data analysis. In addition, we have chosen a wide
viewing angle display, a wall type display which enables us to experiment virtual environment, as a display of visualized data. A wall type display has an
ability to present large amount of data in the broad view. It will help users to
see the data summary and to detect abnormal regions. In this paper, we discuss
human genome data visualization using a wall type display. We could present a
human chromosome data on the wall. This could help genome researchers to
browse the data.

Keywords: Information visualization, Interaction, Immersive projection Display, Genome science, Data visualization.

1 Introduction

Information visualization is a computer-supported, interactive, visual representation
of abstract data to amplify cognition [1]. With adequate information visualization, it is
easy to relay the information to the users. Information visualization is an effective
method to grasp a complete view of the data. The way to visualize information is a
key issue.

In the field of genome science, researchers are constantly faced with the challenges
of finding useful information from a huge amount of experimental information. Computer science can help these problems. A field between computer science and genome
science is called bioinformatics. Our focus for this paper is concerning visualization
of bioinformatics data.

Virtual reality technology has been developed for about 20 years. An immersive
projection technology, such as CAVE type display [2] or PowerWall type display[3],
is one of powerful technologies to present us large amount of information. General
usage of this technology is for implementation of virtual environments like city towns
or virtual car models. We believe that information visualization with immersive

S. Lee et al. (Eds.): APCHI 2008, LNCS 5068, pp. 175–182, 2008.

projection technology is an effective solution to present complex data. Thus we have chosen an immersive presenting visualized data.

We have studied virtual environments for genome science data using immersive projection display. We have used a five-screen CAVE type display, named CABIN, for the virtual environment. We have developed a virtual environment for supporting genome researchers' analysis [4]. The data are visualized in three-dimensional space. Researchers can manipulate the data by moving their hand or arms. They can refer the part of the data and conduct the analysis in the virtual environment. By constructing these virtual environments, we could know that these kinds of virtual environments are helpful for researchers' understandings of the analysis process [5]. And CAVE type display is useful for one-person usage. However, genome researchers sometimes discuss the data with their colleagues. They want to watch the same display, check the data, and extract biological meanings from them. For this purpose, a wall type display is more adapted for multiple users.

In this paper, we have applied information visualization methods with an immersive projection technology to the field of genome science. We have developed a genome viewer for supporting genome researchers' analysis. With the viewer, you can browse genes, gene annotations, and experimental results with a seamless zooming function, search, and detecting meaningful regions by calculating statistical evaluations. A user can analyze the data with the viewer. We present this viewer on a wall type display that provides us a broad view angle. The user can check the large data as a human body scale.

2   Genome Data Analysis

In the field of genome science, technology of sequencing and microarray enable us to get large biological data at a time. Using these high-throughput technologies, experimental data are accumulated rapidly in the public web sites, such as UCSC Genome Bioinformatics Group [6] and NCBI [7]. Genome researchers have to analyze and interpret them biologically and medically. They have to get the public data from the web sites, compare them with their experimental data, and extract features from them.

Genome data consists of patients, expression levels of genes, copy number of genomes, sequence of genomes, and many other variables. In addition, there are a lot of annotations for genome data. Some annotations were determined by biological experiments, some annotations were written by researchers who read a lot of journal papers, and others were estimated by computationally. Genome researchers can use these annotations by referring the public web sites.

In addition, genome data has a feature of multiple ranges. Genome researchers observe and check the data in whole chromosomes level, or in one chromosomal level, then zoom up into a chromosomal band level. Finally, they could also zoom up to a gene level and a genome sequence level. For example, human chromosome No.1 has 247M bp (sequence characters) and average gene size is 27K bp. Some meaningful regions are about from several bp to tens bp. Thus, the range of genome data is from 10^1 to 10^8 ranges.

Due to two features of genome data, researchers have to browse the data from whole view to focused view. They should extract biological meanings from the data.

In general, they can compare experimental data between normal samples and disease samples. By the comparison, they can detect abnormal regions that have more alternations in the disease samples. When they compare many samples, they can extract common abnormal regions in the disease samples. Consequently they will compare among different patients because they want to learn if the abnormal regions are isolated cases or common among many individuals. These regions sometimes relate to the disease.

To discover biological relationship, a novel integrated analysis viewer is needed. Requirements of the viewer are comparison of the data and full picture of the data. Sockeye is one example tool for visualization and analysis of comparative genomics [8].

There are many proposed genome viewers. However, current viewers have two big problems. The first problem is intermittent zooming. When you access to genome database web sites, there are web-based viewers. They provide you some pictures of the data. When you want to see the data more precisely, you can push a "zoom" button. After one or two second, you can get a zoomed picture. However, you sometimes forget the previous picture because of the interval. Thus, seamless zooming from large view to detailed view is required. The second problem is a window frames. When you use a normal personal computer display, you have a limit of window size that depends on a display size. In our dairy life, we can see much information by moving our eyes and heads. In addition, when we want to discuss the data with colleagues, we use large displays or projectors in order to provide a view to all persons. Thus, a broad view display that can share by multiple persons is required. A wall type display can solve both view and window size.

There is a report to visualize genome sequence data on a one screen three-dimensional display [9]. This report focused on the clustering and visualization algorithm of genome sequence and did not write much about the display. Another report is to visualize genome sequence data on an arch type display [10]. They collaborated with pharmacological company. This report indicates a possibility of genome data analysis on a large display.

3   Visualization of Genome Data

In this paper, we propose a visualization method with wall type display. Our method is for supporting genome data analysis to meets the requirements described above; continuous zoom from chromosome to gene, presented data with a wide field of view in order to refer the surrounding data.

We have developed a visualize tool for integrating various genome data. We have designed a viewer that has the following features; 1) a seamless zoom-in and zoom out function, 2) both whole genome view and detailed view to give users comprehensive information of the data, 3) simultaneous display of various types of data at a locus in order that users can see relationships between them. The viewer also can be selected both three-dimensional and two-dimensional mode.

Data are visualized according to the viewing levels; chromosomal band patterns are visualized in whole chromosomal level, gene structures are visualized in a gene level. Various genome data are integrated in the viewer. Gene expression, which indicates a gene working state, is visualized by color. Red color indicates high expression level and green color indicates low level. Gene modification data, such as methylation which inactivate genes, are visualized as color bars after pre-process. The data are measured by DNA chip that has several millions of sampling points in a genome. They are processed by statistical calculation. The significant regions that concentrate high signals compared to background are extracted by a certain p-value. Only significant meaningful regions are visualized.

Fig. 1 shows a whole view of all chromosomes and a whole view of one chromosome. Users can zoom up to the gene level. A gene named TFPI2 is shown in Fig. 1. There are some visualized signals on this area; this indicates this area should be a significant region. You can see whole chromosome view, zoom up to each chromosome view, and see a gene view. You can see the gene modification regions and its expression in a gene view.

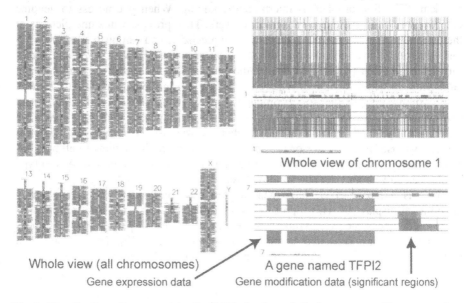

Whole view of chromosome 1

Whole view (all chromosomes)   A gene named TFPI2
Gene expression data   Gene modification data (significant regions)

Fig. 1. Visualization of genome data. (Left) Whole view of all chromosomes. Gene expression data is visualized by green-red color. (Upper Right) Whole view of chromosome 1. (Lower Right) A view of a gene named TFPI2. There are gene modification data near this area which indicates significant meanings.

The visualized data is shown in Fig.2. A seamless zooming function is visualized in Fig.2. In the midmost of the image, there is a chromosome bar that indicates the position of the chromosome. Near the chromosome bar, there is gene structure information. Gene structure has two components; exon (coding region) and intron (non-coding region). Above the chromosome bar, data from multiple diseased samples are presented. Under the chromosome bar, data from multiple normal samples are plotted. Expression data from multiple samples are visualized by color. User can know which part of the gene is worked and whether related gene modifications are activated or inactivated.

The viewer also provides continuous zooming from chromosomal level (about 10^8 bp; sequence characters) to gene level (10^2 or 10^3 bp). User can zoom up and zoom down the current view seamlessly. Seamless zooming enables users to think the data without breaks. Fig. 3 shows the seamless zoom-in and zoom-out images.

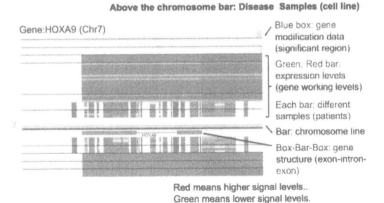

Fig. 2. Visualized data. In the middle of the data, there is a chromosome bar and gene structure. Above and under the chromosome bar, gene expression level data are visualized by color. Gene modification data is visualized by a box structure.

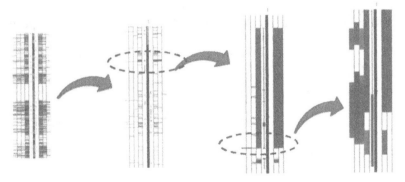

Fig. 3. A seamless zoom-in and zoom out function from chromosome level to gene level. The data is presented detailed view based on the focused point.

4   Visualization Using a Wall Type Display

On the basis of our proposal, we have implemented the genome viewer using C++ with the OpenGL library. We use a wall type display that has 9m width and 2.68m height. Fig.4. shows the system image. This display uses three projectors that provide stereoscopic view by the time division method. IR positioning sensors (VICON) are installed and enable us the head tracking. We use stereoscopic mode at the three dimensional mode. At the two dimensional mode, we use non-stereo display mode. A game controller (SONY PS2 controller) is used for the interface device. We use four computers. One computer takes charge of the management of the other computers. The interface controller is connected to this computer. The other three computers work on rendering for each projector's image.

The visualization result using this wall type display is shown in Fig.4. The data is visualized in a human body scale. Fig.4 shows the whole view of human chromosome 1 data. We could browse the data by moving our eyes and heads.

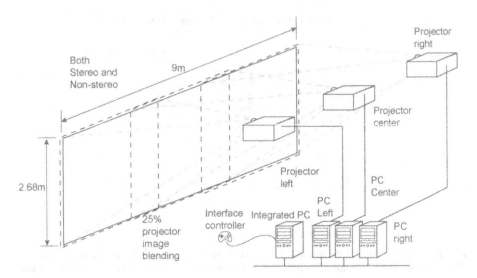

Fig. 4. A wall type display that has three projectors, 9 m width and 2.68m height screens. Each projector's image is rendered by a PC. There are 4 PC; one is for integration. The other three is for rendering the data. Interface controller is connected to the integrated PC. The integrated PC manages the visualized data positions for all PCs.

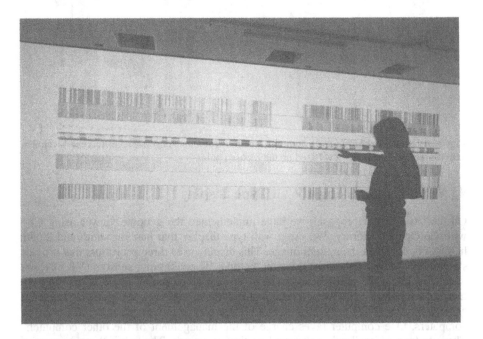

Fig. 5. Human genome data visualization on the wall type display. Data are visualized in the 9 m width screens. Users get 132 degrees wide view and watch the data as human scale.

When we look this screen from 2 m distance, we can get 132 degrees wide view angle. That is, we can look large data in the large screens. Compared to the ordinal PC monitors, we can easy to grasp the data size and remember the data positions. This solves the limit of window size written above.

Genome science researchers who are our collaborators use our proposed integrating interactive viewer. Seamless zooming is welcomed for many researchers. Some researchers have analyzed their experimental data. And they found known meaningful regions, which makes sure the correctness of this viewer. Their impression of this system on the wall type display is useful to check huge data. It was convenient to discuss the data with browsing them at the same time.

5 Conclusion

In this paper, we have proposed the genome viewer on the wall type display. Seamless zooming genome viewer with a broad view display indicates that it will enhance utility and convenience of the genome data analysis. Genome researchers who are our collaborators were welcome to this proposal. The seamless zooming genome viewer is also acceptable to genome researchers. Some researchers found novel meaningful regions with the genome viewer and now they are conducting biological experiments to support the data. Application of more genome data remains future tasks.

Evaluation of this system is a future task, especially for the interfaces. In this paper, we use the game controller. For the multiple users, we should think about a suitable interface. We also have a plan to support user's analysis by integrating the data and interfaces. Researchers have to detect abnormal regions from the data on a large display. Thus, when the system can navigate the user by navigation or attention, it will be helpful for users. The navigation or attention to the featured data position is our future task.

References

1. Card, S.K., Mackinlay, K., Shneiderman, B.: Readings in Information Visualization: Using Vision to Think. Morgan Kaufmann Pub, San Francisco (1999)
2. Cruz-Neira, C., Sandin, D.J., DeFanti, T.A.: Surround-screen projection-based virtual reality: the design and implementation of the CAVE. In: Proceedings of the 20th Annual Conference on Computer Graphics and interactive Techniques SIGGRAPH 1993, pp. 135–142. ACM, New York (1993)
3. The University of Minnesota, PowerWall projects, http://www.lcse.umn.edu/research/powerwall/powerwall.html
4. Nishimura, K., Abe, K., Ishikawa, S., Tsutsumi, S., Aburatani, H., Hirota, K., Hirose, M. :Virtual Environment Design Guidelines for Gene Expression Analysis: The Utility of a Lab Bench Metaphor and a Road Metaphor. In: IEEE Virtual Reality Conference 2004, pp.247–248 (2004)
5. Nishimura, K., Ishikawa, S., Abe, K., Tsutsumi, S., Aburatani, H., Hirota, K., Hirose, M.: Virtual Environment Design for Gene Selection Using Gene Expression Data. In: 10th International Conference on Human - Computer Interaction (HCI International 2003), vol. 1, pp. 1213–1217 (2003)

6. UCSC Genome Bioinformatics Group, University of California, Santa Cruz, USA, http://genome.ucsc.edu/
7. National Center for Biotechnology Information, National Library of Medicine, National Institute of Health, USA, http://www.ncbi.nlm.nih.gov/
8. Montgomery, S.B., Astakhova, T., Bilenky, M., Birney, E., Fu, T., Hassel, M., Melsopp, C., Rak, M., Robertson, A.G., Sleumer, M., Siddiqui, A.S., Jones, S.J.: Sockeye: a 3D environment for comparative genomics. Genome Research 14(5), 956–962 (2004)
9. Ruths, D.A., Chen, E.S., Ellis, L.: Arbor 3d: an interactive environment for examining phylogenetic and taxonomic trees in multiple dimensions. Bioinformatics 16(11), 1003–1009 (2000)
10. Stolk, B., Abdoelrahman, F., Koning, A.H.J., Wielinga, P., Neefs, J.M., Stubbs, A., Bondt, A., Leemans, P., Spek, P.: Mining the human genome using virtual reality. In: EGPGV 2002, pp. 17–21 (2002)

An Experience with Augmenting a Mirror as a Personal Ambient Display

Kaori Fujinami[1] and Fahim Kawsar[2]

[1] Department of Computer, Information and Communication Sciences,
Tokyo University of Agriculture and Technology,
2-24-16 Naka-cho, Koganei, Tokyo, Japan
[2] Department of Computer Science, Waseda University,
3-4-1 Ohkubo, Shinjuku, Tokyo, Japan
fujinami@cc.tuat.ac.jp, fahim.kawsar@gmail.com

Abstract. In this paper, we describe a case study on augmenting a daily object, *mirror*, for a personalized ambient display. The mirror displays information relevant to a person in front of it on the periphery of his/her sights. The interaction methods with the mirror were evaluated by a Wizard-of-Oz method and an in-situ experiment. The subjects preferred more controllability over the proactive functionalities and the understandability of information than the passive and the reflective nature of a mirror.

Keywords: Ambient display, Daily object, Embedded interaction, User study.

1 Introduction

Due to the advancement of technologies, our daily lives and environments are full of computational devices and a heavy amount of information. Not only traditional computers, but also small palm sized devices like cellular phones and personal digital assistants (PDA) have network connectivity and offer various types of information like weather forecasting, today's schedule, etc. This allows people to acquire information anytime anywhere. Also, a new variation of traditional displays like ambient displays [11] is installed into our daily living for showing information to a user. However, if these devices do not provide information in an appropriate way, i.e. considering proper timing, location, identity, and intuitiveness, then computation devices cannot offer comfortable services, because people feel inconvenient to their daily living, and the inconvenience makes them confused how to use the technologies. This means that a user needs to have some efforts to acquire useful information. Offering appropriate information in respective situations is a major research topic in ubiquitous/pervasive computing environments, and this is known as *context-awareness*.

A mirror has been utilized since ancient days [3]. It reflects physical objects appearing in front of it. Often we become inquisitive about our physical appearance by looking at a mirror. Moreover, while using a mirror we can also see and comprehend what is happening in the backgrounds, e.g. someone is passing, a kettle is boiling, etc. This reflective nature is essential for a mirror. We usually stay in front of a mirror for a period of time, which suggests the acceptability of presenting information on the

S. Lee et al. (Eds.): APCHI 2008, LNCS 5068, pp. 183–192, 2008.
© Springer-Verlag Berlin Heidelberg 2008

surface of the mirror. In our earlier study [2], an augmented mirror was realized by attaching a translucent mirror board on an ordinary computer monitor, where a bright color behind is seen through while an object in front of the board is reflected in the dark colored area. The mirror, *AwareMirror*, presents information relevant to a person in front of it. We can change our behavior once we notice some unwanted/unknown situation. Our initial design principle is to preserve the metaphor of a daily object intact while adding some values. We have considered that such seamless augmentation reduces the burden of accessing digital world. The primary user feedbacks on the contents and the user identification method were mostly positive. In this paper, we focus on the extensive evaluation of the interaction methods with the mirror. That aims to investigate a user's attitude towards the trade-off between active involvement with augmented functionalities and passive utilization of the traditional reflective nature, which has not been revealed by existing work and products that deal with such an augmented mirror [4, 7].

The following sections are organized as follows. Section 2 describes the overview of the AwareMirror system. In section 3, user studies by a Wizard-of-Oz (WoZ) method and an in-situ experiment are presented. Related work is examined in section 4, and finally section 5 concludes the paper.

2 AwareMirror System

In this section, the AwareMirror system is introduced. Then, a discriminative feature of the system, i.e. two modes of information rendering, is reviewed for later evaluation. The evaluation is the contribution of this paper. For more detail on the design rationale and initial evaluation of the system, please refer to [2].

2.1 Overview

AwareMirror displays information relevant to a person in front of it on the periphery of his/her sights. A *user* is implicitly identified in a privacy aware manner. This is an important aspect for augmenting a mirror since the place around a mirror is highly privacy sensitive. We have determined to integrate three types of low-level information, rather than utilizing a single and rich data source like a video camera. They are 1) the existence of a person in front of a mirror using an infra-red range finder, 2) the collocation of a personal (unshareable) artefact with a mirror, and 3) utilization of the personal artefact. Context information can be retrieved from a user's daily activities in a natural way. Such everyday artefacts include a safety razor (an electric shaver), a toothbrush, a comb, etc. We have decided to use a toothbrush for detecting a user because it is gender neutral and utilized by almost everyone.

We brush our teeth, make up, etc., that is normally done in situations where we are considering immediate events or something important over the day to come in the morning. We consider information related to immediate event is useful in such a case. We also often change our decision if someone tells us about weather forecasting, traffic accident, etc. Considering these facts, we have selected three types of information to be displayed that can affect our behavior and supports decision making: 1) weather forecasting (state and temperature) at the destination where he/she will go, 2) state of a public transportation system that the person is going to use, and 3) information about the next appointment. These types of information can remind us of taking something required, e.g. umbrella and documents, and offers us the opportunity to take an alternative route to go to the destination, or rush ourselves. So, we consider that it is appropriate for information presented on a mirror.

2.2 Two Modes of Information Rendering

Although the above listed information is useful, it might disturb a user's primary task if all information appears on the surface of a mirror. Also, privacy sensitive information can be revealed. Therefore, we have decided to apply two types of information rendering and interaction methods with the mirror. We have designed the mirror to start presenting information with abstract images so that a user could perceive the contents at a glance (Fig. 1-(a)). On the other hand, Fig. 1-(b) shows textual messages for clear understanding, where the message describes the image. The numbers in Fig. 1-(a) correspond to the three types of information introduced in the previous section.

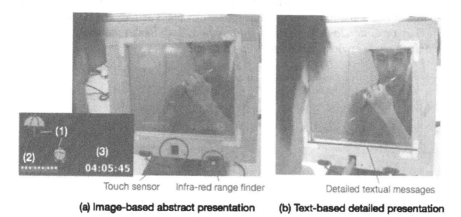

| | | | |
| Touch sensor | Infra-red range finder | | Detailed textual messages |

(a) Image-based abstract presentation   **(b) Text-based detailed presentation**

Fig. 1. Using AwareMirror: (a) abstract and (b) detailed mode of presentation. Three types of decision supportive information are presented: (1) weather forecasting (state and temperature) at his next destination, (2) state of a public transportation system to be used, and 3) information about the next appointment (time to the event). A user can change the level of abstraction by touching an area on the bottom (b).

There are three presentation modes including the default one. Fig. 2 illustrates the modes, where the solid and dotted lines indicate automatic and manual transition, respectively. In the default mode, the mirror does not display anything, so it just looks like a mirror. However, when a person appears in front of AwareMirror and a toothbrush is utilized, AwareMirror enters into the abstract mode. In the abstract mode, it plays a role of an ambient display, which shows abstract information on the periphery of a user's line of sight. So, in this mode, people use AwareMirror as an ordinary mirror. Abstract information can be represented using images and colors we are familiar with and therefore easy to understand at a glance. This is also a solution that takes into account of the characteristic of the place, *in front of a mirror*, since some people often take their glasses off while brushing their teeth and washing their faces. Therefore, we consider that it is useful for them to be just notified of some important events.

In the detailed mode, they explicitly use it as a display rather than a mirror. It shows information in more detail using text information. Offering detailed information automatically might break our design philosophy, i.e. *keeping the original usage of a mirror intact*. It could interrupt a user's current task with sudden appearance of text message. So, we provide the flexibility to change the mode of the usage by him/herself. On entering into the detailed mode, the role of AwareMirror turns into an information display, not an ordinary mirror. The person causes this explicitly. Hence, we consider that a feeling of disturbance does not come up in his/her mind. Although the mode is more detailed than the image-based one, we do not intend to complete the information acquisition process of a user within the AwareMirror system. There have already been many media for detailed information like a TV and a website. A user who has more interests in the information presented by the mirror should access them with more efforts. Too much information by the mirror would make the system complex and thus unusable. Role sharing with other media is crucial. We also consider our approach meets the requirements for ambient displays introduced by Mankoff et al. [8]: *Easy transition to more in-depth information*. Both modes automatically return to the default mode on detecting a user's leaving.

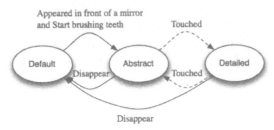

Fig. 2. Transition among default (left), abstract (middle), and detailed mode (right): The solid and dashed lines indicate automatic and manual transition, respectively

2.3 Prototype Implementation

Fig. 3 illustrates the relationship among the functional components (rectangle) and their implementation (cloud form). The system consists of a *sensing system, Aware-Mirror Controller, personalized contents acquisition, contents rendering*, and the *presentation mode controlling* components. The core functionality is *AwareMirror Controller* that accepts events from three sources to identify a person who is in front of the target mirror. The existence of a possible user is detected by the change of the distance to a mirror. To identify the person, the detection of a used toothbrush around the mirror is utilized. An RFID tag of an active type is attached to each toothbrush, where the owner ID is identical to the tag ID. A tag reader that is placed near the mirror is responsible for the detection of collocation of the mirror and a toothbrush. A toothbrush is also augmented with an accelerometer to detect the state-of-use, i.e. *start brushing* or *not*. As described in section 2.1, three types of information are utilized, that is based on a user's schedule. We have *mashed up* existing contents to provide real experiences in in-situ experiments. The *Contents Rendering* component draws the two modes as well as the default one based on the transition shown in Fig. 2. In the experiments, different policies for the contents rendering and presentation mode controlling were implemented for each comparative functionality.

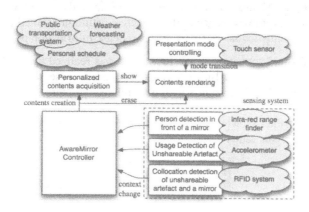

Fig. 3. Functional components and implementation of AwareMirror system

A touch sensor embedded into the bottom frame allows the explicit transition to the detailed mode (see Fig. 1-(a)). In our initial prototype, a "zipper" metaphor was utilized, where a variable resistance-based slider was attached to provide a user with tangible interaction to get information, i.e. *opening* for *getting detailed information*. However, it was not supported by the subjects because of 1) multiple roles and 2) statefulness. A zipper is utilized not only to extract something from inside (digital value), but also to fasten something at a proper position like a zip-up jacket (analog value). This made the subjects confused. Instead, they liked to utilize a touch sensor. Although the duality might be overcome by learning, the statefulness is problematic. AwareMirror turns to the black screen (default mode) when it detects a user's absence in the both abstract and detailed modes. Here, we assume that the zipper remains opened. When a new user comes in front of AwareMirror, it displays abstract information. So, he/she needs to close the zipper first, and then opens the zipper to change into the detailed mode, which makes them confused. Considering these two issues, we have changed to a touch-based interaction. People have already had a mental model for a (stateless) touch button since it is often utilized in controlling electronic appliances, e.g. a TV remote and a PC.

3 Evaluation

In this section, the interaction method with the mirror is evaluated with a WoZ method [1] and in-situ experiments.

3.1 Methodology

Contrastive functionalities were implemented, and tested together with the original ones described in section 2. The points of the comparison are as follows.

1.   Automatic vs. Manual activation of the first (abstract) presentation
2.   Automatic vs. Manual transition between abstract and detailed presentation
3.   Existence vs. Little-existence of the reflective nature in detailed presentation
4.   One phase (only textual message) vs. Two phase information provision

Note that the manual activation of the first scene was realized by touching the same area as the mode transition. Also, in automatic transition case, the second scene appeared after 10 seconds. The version with little reflective nature can be seen in Fig. 4. The message is drawn in black on white background, which reduces the reflection on the surface due to the characteristic of a magic mirror. Therefore, it looks like a traditional computer screen, rather than a mirror.

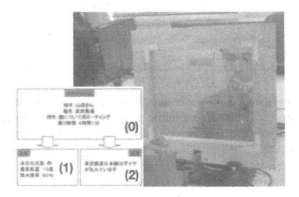

Fig. 4. The contrastive rendering of the detailed presentation, where static textual messages are written in black on white background. The number (1) and (2) correspond to the ones in Fig. 1-(a), while (0) indicates the details of the next appointment rather than the down counter (3) in the previous figure.

A WoZ method was applied to obtain comprehensive view while an in-situ experiment was conducted for intimate findings. Fourteen subjects (12 students from outside the authors' laboratories and 2 company employees) were recruited for the WoZ experiment. Each subject was directed to use the system, e.g. start brushing teeth, pressing the touch sensor. An observer actually controlled the system. Then, he/she had an interview session based on a filled survey form.

The in-situ experiments were conducted with totally four persons, i.e. one family (parents and an adult daughter) and a company employee living alone. A working prototype was installed in the living room at each home for 17 and 22 days, respectively. The subjects were asked to change the properties for the different experimental conditions by themselves through a simple GUI and a manual. They were also told to change the comparative functionalities just after the previous utilization. We consider the subjects should focus on performing the primary task or utilizing the functionality that is subject to evaluate. So, preparing for the experiment needs to be completed beforehand. Finally, they were interviewed based on a survey form and sheets of paper on which they had written any comments throughout the experiment. In the following discussion, the results of the above two experiments are combined.

3.2 Results and Discussions

Activation of Abstract Information Mode: The half of the subjects (7 people) preferred the automatic activation that does not require any explicit direction. The comments are that even simple touching was messy in a busy morning, and sometimes forgettable. This indicates that they preferred to confront the system as an ordinary mirror. Notably, all the four subjects from the in-situ experiments liked this version.

On the other hand, the subjects who liked manual activation needed the rendered information only when they wanted to see it. This comes from their situations where they usually had no specific plan that requires decision-making provided by Aware-Mirror. In that case, the presented information became obtrusive even if it is image-based abstract information. We consider that filtering out only relevant situation for a person by his/her preference or the system's intelligence is needed. For example, an accidental situation of a train to take can be shown while the normal case does not render any information. These facts suggest that preserving a mirror's original functionality is important for all the subjects.

The other interesting reason is that the unreliable behavior of the system due to a sensing subsystem made them refuse proactive information provision. A subject complained that he had been surprised at sudden activation of the system at midnight, i.e. the abstract mode was presented, since he had been looking his face into the mirror at that time. People may feel *monitored*.

Transition to Detailed Information Mode: Manual transition was supported by 68.8% of the subjects (11 persons). The major reason for the preference is the feeling of controlling a system. They could not wait for the automatic transition (in 10 seconds) when they had something to know the detail. Also, they did not always wish to see the detailed information. Such user experiences are what we have designed. The subjects who liked automatic transition gave their negative impression on the manual one, i.e. touching with a wet hand and bothering with changing the mode. We consider this is not an affirmative preference in the automatic way. This indicates the request for a new (manual) controlling method that takes into account of the constraint in the lavatory.

Detailed Information Rendering: The full screen version (Fig. 4) was preferred by 68.8% of the subjects due to readability of presented information. It is realized by static textual messages in black color on the white background. It shows all the information in a screen at a glance, although it has little reflective nature. In contrast, the scrolling text version (Fig. 1) requires a user to follow the message to the end, and thus he/she needs to pay more attention. The reflective nature of the mirror would rather obstacle. The subjects pointed that they noticed the mirror was not functioning during the full screen. But they did not mind it since the time to check the detailed information was short because of the readability. This suggests that the full screen version contributes to reduce the interruption into the primary task consequently. On the contrary, a subject who had negative impression on the full screen version requested to see her face in the whole period of brushing teeth. This indicates the desire to keep the original function intact at any time, which is supportive of our design principle.

Two Phase Information Presentation: Ten subjects (66.7%) wanted the two-phase information presentation, i.e. the detailed information with textual message is presented after the graphical abstract information. The major reasons are that 1) they do not always need detailed information and 2) it is difficult to read the textual message from the beginning in case that they do not wear glasses. The subjects who participated to the in-situ experiment turned to the textual expression mode when they actually wanted to know the detail. Two of the subjects changed their behavior twice based on the information (one for low temperature and one for an accident of public transportation). Such a decision making support during ordinal task is what the mirror is aiming at. Four of the ten subjects actually thought that only the first scene was needed. We consider it is very difficult to render detailed information like the time, location, and estimated recovering time of a train accident. So, finally, we have classified them into the group who preferred two-phase information presentation as potential members. Furthermore, a subject looked forward to seeing a change in the image. We could say this is interesting and important aspect in a daily life computing paradigm. Such an aspect is basically ignored by a traditional "efficiency-based" computing paradigm. Also in this point, the two-phase presentation proved useful.

4   Related Work

Regarding the application and the interaction method with an augmented mirror, information that supports decision making like ours has also proposed in [7], where gesture and touching is utilized for the manipulation of presented information. Also, Miragraphy [4] provides more active involvement. Information about clothes and their coordination is shown by the detection of an RFID tag, and the history of daily clothes captured by a video camera is presented. To the best of our knowledge, a user explicitly *utilizes* the functionalities provided by these systems, which could make a gap between a user and a system. Our interaction method described in section 2.2 would provide very small gap since the involvement is designed to be the extension of the activities in front of an ordinal mirror.

In terms of information representation, an ambient display [11] in the context of tangible user interfaces [6] offers information using human's peripheral awareness capabilities. Our AwareMirror is also an ambient display in a sense because it allows a person to focus on his/her main tasks while offering information in his/her line of sights. The work of Rodenstein [9] can also be categorized into an ambient display. It applies the opposite notion of a mirror and the biggest characteristic of a window, *transparency*, to overlap information in cyber space, i.e. short-term weather forecast, onto a view of outside. Information visualization with artistic impression like Informative Art [5] and InfoCanvas [10] suggests an "augmented paintings", which can naturally fit into daily living. Their roles are presenting information from the beginning, while AwareMirror has more strict constraints that it should not change its original usage as a mirror while offering additional values, *personalized information.*

5 Concluding Remarks

A mirror was augmented to present information relevant to a person in front of it. Our initial design principle was to keep the original metaphor of a mirror intact, where 1) presentation starts with an abstract image on identifying a user, 2) detailed information appears/disappears at his/her request, and 3) even the detailed information is rendered in a form that keeps a mirror's reflective feature.

The design principle was evaluated by comparative functionalities. That aimed at investigating a user's attitude towards the trade-off between a) active involvement with the augmentation and b) passive utilization as a traditional mirror. The result shows that the majority of the subjects preferred the *two-phase information provision*, the *automatic activation* and the *manual transition*. However, *realizing the second phase with a mirror's reflective feature* was not the majority. These findings suggest that a user likes to confront AwareMirror as an ordinary mirror at the beginning, but once he/she has interests in the information, it should be *useful* as an information display. Here, a designer of an augmented artefact needs to take care of the controllability of a system and the efficiency of understanding information, rather than adhering to keeping an artefact's original functionality intact. This may sound trivial in a context-aware system design. However, we believe the findings would contribute to update the design principle of a new type of a display that provides information through its original usage.

References

1. Bernsen, N., Dybkjaer, H., Dybkjaer, L.: Designing Interactive Speech Systems – From First Ideas to User Testing. Springer, Heidelberg (1998)
2. Fujinami, K., Kawsar, F., Nakajima, T.: AwareMirror: A Personalized Display using a Mirror. In: Gellersen, H.-W., Want, R., Schmidt, A. (eds.) PERVASIVE 2005. LNCS, vol. 3468, pp. 315–332. Springer, Heidelberg (2005)
3. Gregory, R.L.: Mirrors in Mind. W.H. Freeman and Company, New York (1997)
4. HITACH, Human Interaction Laboratory. Miragraphy (in Japanese), http://hhil.hitachi.co.jp/products/miragraphy.html
5. Holmquist, L.E., Skog, T.: Informative art: Information visualization in everyday environments. In: GRAPHITE 2003: the 1st international conference on Computer graphics and interactive techniques in Australasia and South East Asia, pp. 229–235 (2003)
6. Ishii, H., Ullmer, B.: Tangible Bits: Towards Seamless Interfaces between People, Bits and Atoms. In: conference on Human Factors in Computing systems (CHI 1997), pp. 234–241 (1997)
7. Lashina, T.: Intelligent bathroom. In: Ambient Intelligence technologies for wellbeing at home, a workshop on European Symposium on Ambient Intelligence (EUSAI 2004) (2004)
8. Mankoff, J., Dey, A.K., Hsieh, G., Kientz, J., Lederer, S., Ames, M.: Heuristic evaluation of ambient displays. In: Conference on Human factors in computing systems (CHI 2003), pp. 169–176 (2003)

9. Rodenstein, R.: Employing the Periphery: The Window as Interface. In: Extended abstract of International Conference on Human Factors in Computing Systems (CHI 1999), pp. 204—205 (1999)

10. Stasko, J., Miller, T., Pousman, Z., Plaue, C., Ullah, O.: Personalized Peripheral Information Awareness through Informative Art. In: Davies, N., Mynatt, E.D., Siio, I. (eds.) UbiComp 2004. LNCS, vol. 3205, pp. 18–35. Springer, Heidelberg (2004)

11. Wisneski, C., Ishii, H., Dahley, A., Gorbet, M., Brave, S., Ullmer, B., Yarin, P.: Ambient Displays: Turning Architectural Space into an Interface between People and Digital Information. In: Streitz, N.A., Konomi, S., Burkhardt, H.-J. (eds.) CoBuild 1998. LNCS, vol. 1370, pp. 22–32. Springer, Heidelberg (1998)

Universal Video Adaptation Model for Contents Delivery in Ubiquitous Computing

Yongik Yoon, Svetlana Kim, and Jongwoo Lee

Department of Multimedia Science, Sookmyung Women's University
Chungpa-Dong 2-Ga, Yongsan-Gu, 140-742, Seoul, Korea
{yiyoon,xatyna,jwlee}@sookmyung.ac.kr

Abstract. A video personalization system is designed and implemented an incorporating usage environment to dynamically generate a personalized video summary. The personalization systems adopt and deliver media contents to each user. The video content delivery chain poses today many challenges. There are an increasing terminal diversity, a network heterogeneity and a pressure to satisfy the user preferences. The situation encourages the need for the customized contents in order to provide the user in the best possible experience. In this paper, we address the problem of video customization. For the customized content, we suggest the UVA(Universal Video Adaptation) model that uses the video content description in MPEG-7 standard and MPEG-21 multimedia framework.

1 Introduction

In ubiquitous computing, users are not concerned about time and place. They expect to be provided with services that grant access to information. The service might be due to the increased accessibility of technologies on a broad level. It confronts service providers with the need to customize the services according to the user's receiving device which could be from a handheld to a widescreen terminal. The access to multimedia information by any terminal through any network is a new concept referred in the Universal Video Adaptation (UVA) [1, 2]. The objective of UVA technology makes available different presentations of the same information, more or less complex in terms of media types or bandwidth, suiting different terminals, networks and user preferences.

In UVA scenarios, it is essential to customize more easily and efficiently for the desired content. The contents have available descriptions of the parts that fit to be matched/bridged—the content and the usage environment. The major objective of this paper designs a video customization system in heterogeneous usage environments and provides a new notion on their associated issues in MPEG-7 and MPEG-21. The server maintains the content sources, the MPEG-7 metadata descriptions, the MPEG-21 rights expressions, and the content adaptability declarations. The client communicates the MPEG-7 user preference, MPEG-21 usage environments, and user query to retrieve and display the personalized content. The middleware for video delivery is powered by the personalization engine and the adaptation engine.

S. Lee et al. (Eds.): APCHI 2008, LNCS 5068, pp. 193–202, 2008.

2 UVA Model for Video Delivery

Universal Video Adaptation (UVA) refers to the ability to access by any user to any video contents over any type of network with any device from anywhere and anytime. To support the adaptation, the application is required to directly execute an adaptation mechanism when the lower level informs about an occurred change. Even if an application is able to catch the change of the running environment, it is more efficient if the middleware manages such adaptation mechanisms. The middleware for ubiquitous computing has to be recognizable, and the applications executed on middleware have to be adapted to the changed context by using diverse logics [4, 5]. UVA allows application developers to build a large and complex distributed system that can transform physical spaces into computationally active and intelligent environments. UVA applications need a middleware that can detect and act upon any context changes created by the result of any interactions between users, applications, and surrounding computing environment for applications without users' interventions.

MPEG standardization culminates with the MPEG-21 multimedia framework which offers a wrapper to allow all the pieces in a multimedia customization chain to integrate and interact with each other [17, 19]. The UVA adaptation engine at the center of in Fig. 1 is responsible for matching the user query and the Digital Item(DI), either by selecting the most adequate available variation or by performing some adaptation. As processing a user query, the customizing application creates an adapted variation of the Digital Item to be sent to the user—the new variation and its corresponding description may also be added to the DI resources available at the server.

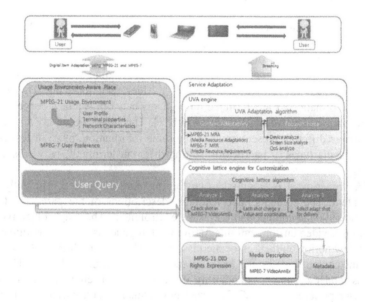

Fig. 1. UVA model

The user query response may be delivered through a network, eventually using a real-time connection. In this case, the streaming module will deliver the scalable or non-scalable content to the user; in the case, real-time transcoding is been performed. It may happen that real time adjustments to the transcoding process are implemented using measures which characterize, for example, the network fluctuations.

3 UVA Customization Engine

The UVA customization consists of the Cognitive lattice engine for customization and Cognitive lattice algorithm as illustrated in the system overview of Fig 1. In the Cognitive lattice engine the user query and usage environment are matched with the media descriptions and right expression to generate the customized content.

3.1 Cognitive Lattice Algorithm

The objective of our system is to show a shortened video summary that maintains as much semantic content within the desired time constraint. The Cognitive lattice algorithm performs this process by three different matching analyzes and is described next in Fig 2.

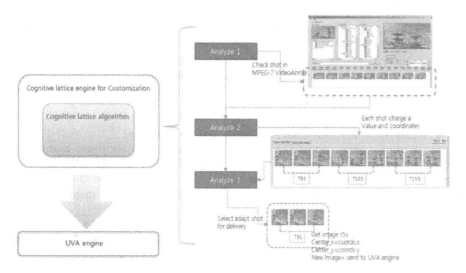

Fig. 2. UVA Customization engine

3.1.1 Analyze 1 Check Shot in MPEG-7 VideoAnnEx

This analyze takes MPEG-7 metadata descriptions from our content sources along with the MPEG-7/MPEG-21 user preference declarations and user time constraint to output an optimized set of selected video segments, which will generate the desired customized video summary[6][7]. Using shot segments as the basic video unit, there are multiple methods of video summarization based on spatial and temporal compression of the original video sequence [13][14]. In our work, we **focus** on the insertion or deletion of each video shot depending on user preference. Each video shot is either included or excluded from the final video summary. In each shot, MPEG-7 metadata describes the semantic content and corresponding scores. Assume there are a total of N attribute categories. Let $\bar{P} = [P_1, P_2, ..., P_n]^1$ be the user preference vector, where p_i denotes the preference weighting for attribute i, $1 \le i \le N$. Assume there are a total of M shots. Let $\bar{S} = [S_1, S_2, ..., S_M]^T$ be the shot segments that comprise the original video sequence, where s_i denotes shot number i, $1 \le i \le M$. Subsequently, the attribute score $cor_{i,j}$ is defined as the relevance of attribute i in shot j, $1 \le i \le M$ and $1 \le i \le N$. It then follows that the weighted attribute w_i for shot i given the user preference $\bar{P}$ is calculated as the dot product of the attribute matrix A and the user preference vector $\bar{P}$:

$$\bar{W} = \begin{bmatrix} w_1 \\ w_2 \\ ... \\ w_m \end{bmatrix} = \begin{bmatrix} cor_{1,1} & cor_{1,2} & ... & cor_{1,n} \\ cor_{2,1} & ... & ... & ... \\ ... & ... & cor_{i,j} & ... \\ cor_{m,1} & ... & ... & cor_{m,n} \end{bmatrix} * \begin{bmatrix} p_1 \\ p_2 \\ p_n \end{bmatrix} ;$$

w_i specifies the relative weighted importance of shot i with respect to the other shots. Assume shot s_i spans a durations of t_i, $1 \le i \le M$. Consequently, shot s_i is included in the summary if the importance weighting w_i of this shot is greater than some threshold, $w_i > \theta$, and excluded otherwise. θ is determined such that the sum of the shot durations t_i is less than the user specified time constraint. Consequently, each shot is initially ranked according to its weighted importance and either included or excluded in the final personalized video summary according to the time constraint. Furthermore, the *VideoSue* engine generates the optimal set of selected video shots for one video as well as across multiple video sources.

3.1.2 Analyze 2 Each Shot Charge a Value and Coordinates

Video summaries are composed of a set of independent shots or frame a unit that optimally matches the user preferences while limited by the total time constraint. The resulting video summaries do not take value and coordination for UVA. In this section, we examine a cognitive lattice algorithm analyze 2, where using cognitive lattice each shot charge a value and coordinates.

First, we divide the shot into lattices $v\_num[k] = \sum (x_1) V_i[k]$, and divide the shot vertically and horizontally $h\_num[k] = \sum (x_2) H_i[k]$. Next, we have to number each lattice. Vertical lattice is assign the value i, horizontal lattice the value j.

$$\text{For shot } s_i = \sum_h^w k_i \sum_{v \in (i,j)} w_1, h_i[k_{i,j}] ;$$

Since there could be several objects in each lattice, we must analyze them one by one.

Coords.x = get x (Object [found_y][foung_x]), Coords.y = get y (Object [found_y][foung_x])

Here, *Coords* indicates the value of each shot. Find the value and coordinates by analyzing each lattice we send the *value* and *Coords* to UVA engine and display it on the viewer's device through UVA adaptation algorithm. Finally, in analyze 3 select adapt shot for customization delivery.

3.2 Media Descriptions and Right Expression

Media descriptions identify and describe the multimedia content from different abstraction levels of low-level features to various interpretations of semantic concepts. MPEG-7 provides description schemes (DS) to describe content in XML to facilitate search, index, and filtering of audio-visual data. The DSs are designed to describe both the audio-visual data management and the specific concepts and features. The data management descriptions include metadata about creation, production, usage, and management. The concepts and features metadata may include what the scene is about in a video clip, what objects are present in the scene, who is talking in the conversation, and what is the color distribution of an image[16, 18].

MPEG-7 standardizes the description structure; however, technical challenges remain. The generation of these descriptions is not part of the MPEG-7 standard and the technologies for generating them are variable, competitive, and some—nonexistent. As such we have developed an annotation tool to describe the semantic meaning of video clips to capture the underlying semantic meaning by a human. These annotators are assisted in their annotation task through the use of a finite vocabulary set. This set can be readily represented by the *MPEG-7 Controlled Term List*, which can be customized for the different domains and applications.

Right expression is another subcomponent of *MPEG-21 Digital Item Declaration* and describes the rights associated with multimedia content. They include the rights and permissions for an individual or designated group to view, modify, copy or distribute the content. Among these expressions that are relevant to personalization is *adaptation rights*. For example, the owner of an image may allow cropping of the image to fit the desired display size, but not scaling

4   UVA Adaptation Engine

The objective of the adaptation engine is to perform the optimal set of transformations on the selected content in accordance with the adaptability declarations and the inherent usage environment. The adaptation engine must be equipped to perform transcoding, filtering, and scaling such that the user can play the final adapted personalized content Fig 3.

4.1   Content Adaptability

Content adaptability refers to the multiple variations that a media can be transformed into, either through changes in format, scale, rate, and/or quality. Format transcoding may be required to accommodate the user's terminal devices. Scale conversion can represent image size resizing, video frame rate extrapolation, or audio channel enhancement. Rate control corresponds to the data rate for transferring the media content, and may allow variable or constant rates. Quality of service can be guaranteed to the user based on any criteria including SNR or distortion quality measures. These adaptation operations transform the original content to efficiently fit the usage environment.

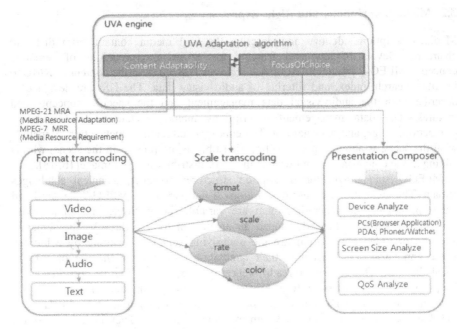

Fig. 3. UVA engine architecture

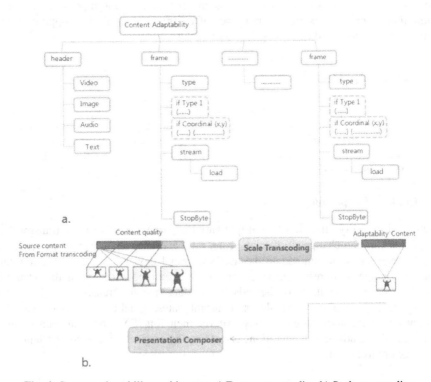

Fig. 4. Content adaptability architecture a) Format transcoding b) Scale transcoding

The *MPEG-7 media resource requirement* and the *MPEG-21 media resource adaptability* both provide descriptions for allowing certain types of adaptations. These adaptation descriptions contain information for a single adaptation or a set of adaptations. The descriptions may possibly include required conditions for the adaptation, permissions for the adaptation, and configurations for the adaptation operation Fig 4(a,b)[11, 12, 16, 20].

4.2 Presentation Composer

The UVA adaptation engine performs the optimal set of transformation on the selected content in according with the adaptability declarations and the inherent usage environment [21]. The adaptation engine must be equipped to perform transcoding, filtering and scaling. Today, it does not provide the quantified measure of perceptibility indicating the degree of allowable transcoding. For example, it is difficult to measure the loss of perceptibility when a video is transcoded to a set of cropped and scaled ones. To overcome this problem, UVA adaptation engine uses a content value function V for any transcoding configuration C: C={I, r}, where $I \subset \{1,2...,n\}$ represent a class of video and r is the resolution reduction factor of the transcoding video. The content value function V can be defined as:

$$V = C(I, r) = \sum_{i \in I} V_i(r) = \sum_{i \in I} (s_i \cdot u(r - r_i)),$$

$$\text{where,} \quad u(x) = \begin{cases} 1, & \text{if} \quad x \geq 0 \\ 0, & \text{elsewhere} \end{cases}$$

Denoting the width and height of the client display size by W and H, respectively, the content adaptation is modeled as the following resource allocation problem:

$$\text{Maximize} \quad C(I, r), \text{ such that} \begin{cases} r|x_u - x_I| \leq W \\ r|y_u - y_I| \leq H \end{cases} \text{and},$$

where the transcoding $C(I, r)$ is represented by a rectangle bounding box whose lower and upper bound point are (x_I, y_I) and (x_u, y_u) respectively. For any I, the maximum resolution factor is given by

$$r_{max}^i = \frac{\min r_{ij}}{i, j \in I},$$

$$\text{where,} \quad r_{i,j} = \min\left(\frac{W}{|x_i - x_j|}, \frac{H}{|y_i - y_j|}\right).$$

Only those configuration $(C=\{I,r\}$ with $r \leq r_{max}^I)$ are feasible. This implies that for a given I, the maximum value is attainable when $C = \{I, r_{max}^I\}$. Therefore other possibility configurations is $C = \{I, r\}, r < r_{max}^i$, do not need to be searched.

5 Usage Environment-Aware Place

The usage environment holds the profiles about the user, device, network, delivery, and other environments. This information is used to determine the optimal content selection and the most appropriate form for the user. Other than MPEGs, several standards have been proposed. HTTP/1.1 uses the composite capabilities/preference profile (CC/PP) to communicate the client profiles. The forthcoming wireless access protocol (WAP) proposes the user agent profile (UAProf) includes the device profiles, which covers the hardware platform, software platform, network characteristics, and browser [9, 10].

The MPEG-7 *UserPreferences DS* allows users to specify their preferences (likes and dislikes) for certain types of content and for ways of browsing [8]. To describe the types of desired content, the Filtering And Search Preferences DS is used that consists of the creation of the content, the classification of the content (Classification Preferences DS), and the source of the content (Source Preferences DS). To describe the ways of browsing the selected content requested by the user, the Browsing Preferences DS is used along with the Summary Preferences DS. Furthermore, each user preference component is associated with a preference value indicating its relative importance with respect to that of other components. For instance, we can have a user preference description to encapsulate the preference ranking among several genre categories (Classification Preferences DS) that are produced in the United States in the last decade (Creation Preferences DS) in wide screen with Dolby AC-3 audio format (Source Preferences DS). And, the user is also interested in nonlinear navigation and access of the retrieved summarization content by specifying the preferred duration and preference ranking.

The MPEG-7 *User Preferences Descriptions* specifically declares the user's preference for filtering, search, and browsing of the requested multimedia content. But, other descriptions may be required to account for the terminal, network, delivery, and other environment parameters. The MPEG-21 *Usage Environment Descriptions* cover exactly these extended requirements even thought the specific requirements are still currently being defined and refined [10]. The descriptions on terminal capabilities include the device types, display characteristics, output properties, hardware properties, software properties, and system configurations. This allows the personalized content to be appropriately adapted to fit the terminal. For instance, videos can be delivered to wireless devices in smaller image sizes in a format that the device decoders can handle. The descriptions on the physical network capability allow content to be dynamically adapted to the limitation of the network. The descriptions on the delivery layer capabilities include the types of transport protocols and connections. These descriptions allow users to access location-specific applications and services [15].

The MPEG-21 *Usage Environment Descriptions* also include *User Characteristics* that describe service capabilities, interactions and relations among users, conditional usage environment, and dynamic updating.

6   Conclusion and Future Work

Content description shows a different situation, since the MPEG-7 standard is available and provides a vast variety of description tools. The great technical challenge is now associated to the automatic low-level to high-level mapping. On other fronts, the standard is still missing licensing conditions and may be because of that the industry did not yet take this powerful and still very much unexplored standard with full heart. In this paper we present a Universal Video Access system for multimedia customization, concluding adaptation content so that any information can be delivered to different terminals and networks. The content delivery in heterogeneous environments, notably through terminal and network driven customization, will take great benefit of scalable audiovisual coding techniques.

A Universal Video Access system is presented matching media descriptions with usage environment in a server-middleware-Mpeg-21 framework in order to deliver customized media content to user. The three-tier architecture provides a standards-compliant infrastructure using our tools and engines to select, adapt, and deliver customized video summaries to the users effectively. The *Video-AnnEx* MPEG-7 Video Annotation Tool to describe video segment using semantic concept. The *VideoSue* Summarization on Usage Environment Engine determines the optimal selection of media contents according to user preferences and time constraint. The *VideoEd* Editing and Composition Tool and *Universal Tuner* Tool gather the selected contents and generates one customized video for the user.

In the future, we will add the functionalities that allow users to input any query keywords, and then let *VideoSue* to match them with the existing ones according their semantic distance. We will also test the performance of other possible fusion methods, in addition to the weighting method that is current used. We will also work on increasing the coverage and accuracy of the concept models in *VideoAl*, and conduct more experiments on the subjective user satisfaction studies.

Acknowledgment. "This research was supported by the Ministry of Knowledge Economy, Korea, under the ITRC(Information Technology Research Center) support program supervised by the IITA(Institute of Information Technology Assessment)" (IITA-2008-C1090-0801-0020)

References

1. Special Issue on Universal Multimedia Access, IEEE Signal Processing Magazine 20(2) (2003)
2. Special Issue on Multimedia Adaptation, Signal Processing: Image Communication 18(8) (2003)
3. MPEG Requirement Group, MPEG-21 Multimedia framework, Part 1: Vision, technologies and strategy, Proposed Draft Technocal Report, 2nd edn., Doc. ISO/MPEG N6269, MPEG Waikaloa Meeting, USA (2003)
4. Adams, W.H., Iyengart, G., Lin, C.Y., Naphade, M.R., Neti, C., Nock, H.J., Smith, J.R.: Semantic indexing of multimedia content using visual, audio and text cues. EURASIP J.Appl. Signal Process. 2003(2) (2003)

5. Joyce, D.W., Lewis, P.H., Tansley, R.H., Dobie, M.R.: Semiotics and agents for integrating and navigating through multimedia representations. In: Proc. Storage Retrieval Media Databases 3972 (2000)
6. Tseng, B.L., Lim, C.-Y., Smith, J.R.: Video personalization system for usage environment. Multimedia Database Management System 15 (2004)
7. Tseng, B.L., Lin, C.-Y., Smith, J.R.: Video summarization and personalization for pervasive mobile devices. In: SPIE Electronic Imaging 2002—Storage and Retrieval for Media Databases, San Jose (2002)
8. ISO/IEC JTC 1/SC 29/WG 11/N 4242, Text of 15938-5 FDIS, Information Technology—Multimedia Content Description Interface—Part 5 Multimedia Description Schemes, Final Document International Standard (FDIS) edition (2001)
9. Butler, M.H.: Implementing content negotiation using CC/PP and WAP UAProf, Technical Report HPL-2001-190 (2001)
10. Tseng, B.L., Lin, C.-Y.: Personalized video summary using visual semantic annotations and automatic speech transcriptions. In: IEEE Multimedia Signal Processing MMSP 2002, St. Thomas (2002)
11. ISO/IEC JTC1/SC29/WG11/M8321, MPEG-7 Tools for MPEG-21 Digital Item Adaptation, Fairfax, VA (2002)
12. ISO/IEC JTC1/SC29/WG11/N5354, MPEG-21 Digital Item Adaptation, Awaji Island, Japan (2002)
13. Lin, C.-Y., Tseng, B.L., Smith, J.R.: VideoAnnEx: IBM MPEG-7 annotation tool. In: IEEE International Conference on Multimedia and Expo, Baltimore (2003)
14. Lin, C.-Y., Tseng, B.L., Naphade, M., Natsev, A., Smith, J.R.: VideoAL: a novel end-to-end MPEG-7 video automatic labeling system. In: IEEE International Conference on Image Processing, Barcelona (2003)
15. Manjunath, B.S., Salembier, P., Sikora, T.: Introduction to MPEG-7: Multimedia Content Description Language. Wiley, New York (2002)
16. Pereira, F.: MPEG Multimedia Standard: Evolution and Future Developments,MM 2007, Augsburg, Bavaria, Germeny (September 2007)
17. Burnett, L.S., Pereira, F., Van de Walle, R., Koenen, R. (eds.): The MPEG-21 book. John Wiley & Sons Ltd, Chichester (2006)
18. Tian, D., Hannuksela, M., Gabbouj, M.: Sub-sequence video coding for improved temporal scalability. In: Proc. of IEEE Int. Symposium on Circuits and Systems (ISCAS), Kobe, Japan (2005)
19. ISO/IEC JTC 1, Dynamic and distributed adaptation, ISO/IEC 21000-7:2004/Amd.2 (work in progress) (2006)
20. ISO/IEC JTC 1, Information Technology—MPEG systems technologies—Part 1: Binary MPEG format for XML, ISO/IEC 23001-1:2006 (2006)
21. De Neve, W., De Schrijver, D., Van Deursen, D., De Keukelaere, F., Van de Walle, R.: An MPEG-21 BS Schema for the first version of H.264/MPEG-4 AVC, MPEG-document ISO/IEC JTC1/SC29/WG11 m12823, Moving Picture Experts Group (MPEG), Bangkok, Thailand (2006)

Selective Visual Attention System
Based on Spatiotemporal Features

Min-Chul Park[1] and Kyungjoo Cheoi[2,*]

[1] Intelligent System Research Division, Korea Institute of Science and Technology
39-1 Hawolgok-dong, Wolsong-gil 5, Seongbuk-gu, Seoul, 136-791, Korea
minchul@kist.re.kr
[2] School of Electrical & Computer Engineering, Chungbuk National University
12 Gaeshin-dong, Heungduk-gu, Chungbuk, 361-763, Korea
kjcheoi@chungbuk.ac.kr

Abstract. In this paper, a selective visual attention system for motion pictures is proposed. The proposed attention system is new in that it utilizes motion information for the purpose of detecting Region Of Interest (ROI) or Focus Of Attention (FOA) in motion pictures. Typical feature integration model is expanded to incorporate motion stimulus in our suggested model. Suggested model is able to respond to motion stimulus by employing motion fields as one of temporal features to the feature integration model. Analysis of motion field maps and incorporation of the result are distinct from some of the previous studies on spatial feature integration. Comparative experiments with a human subjective evaluation show that correct detection rate of visual attention regions improves by utilizing temporal features compared to the case of using only spatial features.

Keywords: Visual attention, Spatiotemporal features, Integration.

1 Introduction

Humans generally pay attention to only a few areas of visual field selectively without completely scanning the whole images [1,2]. This performance has been emulated for the purpose of applications such as image compression, computer vision for automatic target detection, navigational aids, and image database [2]. Models of selective visual attention system have been suggested on the basis of psychology, psychophysics, physiology, neuroscience and etc. Visual attention is the capability of biological visual systems to rapidly reduce the amount of data for complex processing tasks such as feature binding and object recognition.

One of the biggest challenges in understanding perception is to understand how the nervous system manages to integrate the multiple codes it uses to represent features in multiple sensory modalities [3,4]. The early anatomists and neurologists considered the posterior parietal cortex a classic "association" area that combined information from different sensory modalities to form a unified representation of space [5]. A feature integration theory proposed by Treisman and Gelade [6] are one of the

---

* Corresponding author.

S. Lee et al. (Eds.): APCHI 2008, LNCS 5068, pp. 203–212, 2008.

representative models to integrate multiple sensory features and in some situations visual attention takes the form of inhibition of distractor locations [7,8,9].

Our models of bottom-up attention and saliency for selective visual attention are based on the "a feature-integration theory of attention" proposed by Treisman and Gelade. Visual input is first decomposed into a set of topographic feature maps. Different spatial locations then compete for saliency within each map where locations locally standing out from their surroundings can persist. All feature maps feed, in a purely bottom-up manner, into a master "saliency map", which topographically codes for local conspicuity over the entire visual scene. Koch and Ullman introduced the idea of a saliency map to accomplish preattentive selection. This is an explicit two-dimensional map that encodes the saliency of objects in the visual environment [1]. Competition among neurons in this map gives rise to a single saliency map.

In this paper, a selective visual attention system for motion pictures is proposed. The proposed attention system is new in that it utilizes motion information based on the feature integration theory in the bottom-up manner. Typical feature integration model is expanded to incorporate motion stimulus in our suggested model. Suggested model is able to respond to motion stimulus by employing motion fields as one of temporal features to the feature integration model. Motion field maps are explored by center-surround computations for motion analysis about its direction and velocity vector to obtain temporal visual conspicuity in addition to spatial visual conspicuity. Analysis of motion field maps and incorporation of the result are distinct from some of the previous studies on spatial feature integration[7,10,11].

A previous model in [12] is similar with our model in that it is able to respond to motion stimulus by employing motion fields as one of temporal features to the feature integration model. But the main difference between our model is in integration process of multiple maps. In [12], this could be done by weighted sum of all information in the map. However, the performance of the model highly relies on the appropriate choice of the weights. In case of the mode in [12] uses only temporal feature maps for motion pictures, and only spatial feature maps for still pictures. Unlike it, our model uses integration method that promoting those maps in which a small number of meaningful high activity areas are present while suppressing the others, using local competition relations and statistical information of pixels in pre-computed maps.

In Section 2, analysis and integration part of the proposed approach is described. In Section 3, experimental results of the proposed attention system are presented, followed by concluding statements in Section 4.

2   The Proposed System

The general operation of the proposed attention system is described in Fig. 1. The proposed system consists of two main parts: analysis part and integration part.

Starting with current frame (t) RGB image, four elementary spatial feature maps for color and intensity are generated. To generate elementary temporal feature map motion field map as motion stimulus is generated by two gray scale images of current frame (t) image and the previous frame (t-1) image using block matching algorithm, and base on motion field map two elementary temporal feature maps are generated which are modeled with the "Double-opponent" receptive fields and "Noise Filtera-tion" in MT(middle temporal cortex). Center-surround computations with orientations are performed on elementary spatial and temporal features maps. It is employed to imitate "ON-center and OFF-surround" effect in human receptive cells [13], as shown in Fig 2. After generating spatial and temporal feature maps, these maps are integrated into one single saliency map.

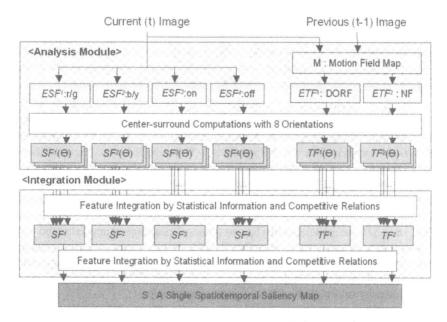

Fig. 1. Schematic diagram of the suggested attention system based on bottom-up approach. The model consists of two main parts, analysis and integration parts. Each part consists of feature extraction and/or integration process based on massive parallel processing.

2.1 Elementary Spatial Feature Maps

There are two types of photoreceptors in the human retina: rods and cones. Rods are responsible for vision at low light levels, scotopic vision. They do not mediate color vision, and have a low spatial acuity. Cones are active at high light levels, photopic vision. They are capable of color vision and are responsible for high spatial acuity and populate the central fovea exclusively [14,15]. The human visual system encodes the chromatic signals conveyed by the three types of retinal cone photoreceptors in an opponent fashion. This opponency is interpreted as an attempt to remove correlations in the signals from different cone types caused by the strong overlap of the cone spec-tral sensitivities [16].

In our system, four elementary spatial feature maps are represented by $ESF^k_{x,y}$ $k=1,....,4$, and a corresponding number of spatial feature maps $SF^k_{x,y}, k=1,....,4$ which separates regions of pixels largely different from their surroundings.

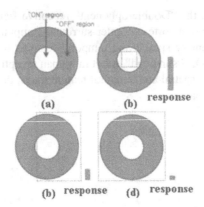

Fig. 2. ON-center and OFF-surround models of isotropic forms respond differently to the locations or sizes of the region of luminance. Dotted-line boxes describe the regions where luminance changes temporally. When the region of luminance changing is "on" from off the corresponding receptive field responds positive way, but when it is "off" from on it does not respond. When the region of luminance changing covers a whole receptive field it hardly generates the correspond response, as shown in (d). Shaded bars describe the corresponding responses between receptive fields and the regions of luminance changing.

ESF^1 and ESF^2 are modeled with the two types of color opponency exhibited by the cells with homogeneous type of receptive fields in visual cortex, which respond very strong to color contrast. ESF^1 is generated to account for 'red/green' color opponency and ESF^2 for 'blue/yellow' color opponency. ESF^3 and ESF^4 are generated by ON and OFF intensity information of input image, respectively.

2.2 Elementary Temporal Feature Maps

Motion field map(M) as motion stimulus is generated by two gray scale images of current frame (t) image and the previous frame (t-1) image using block matching algorithm. Base on motion field map, two elementary temporal feature maps(ETF^k, k=1,2) are generated which are modeled with the "Double-opponent" receptive fields(ETF^1) and "Noise Filteration"(ETF^2) in MT(middle temporal cortex) as shown in Fig 1.

A Model of Double Opponent Receptive Fields. The MT(middle temporal cortex) cell responds best to movement in its preferred direction within its receptive field [17]. This response gets stronger if the visual scene around the receptive field moves in the direction opposite to the cell's preferred direction. On the other hand, cell response to movement within its receptive field gets weaker by movement in the same direction in that part of the visual scene surrounding the receptive field. Movement in the non-moving surroundings within the receptive field does not modulate an MT neuron's response. Such "Double-opponent" receptive fields in MT would be useful for detecting motion borders and defining the extent of a surface based on them [18].

The designed analysis model responds best to the preferred direction of visual stimulus when a pair of surround motion directions is against it as shown in Fig 3. The cell's response is measured along 8 directions($\theta \in \{0, \pi/4, , \cdots, 7\pi/4\}$). Table 1 describes 8 directions θ, the positions of center and surround motion vectors related with preferred direction. The reponse of a pixel is computed by Equation (1). $V_c(\theta)$ presents the motion vector of an observation point. $V_{s1}(\theta+\pi)$ and $V_{s2}(\theta+\pi)$ descrbe surroundings motion vectors. $V_{s1}(\theta+\pi)$ and $V_{s2}(\theta+\pi)$ appear to the parallel direction of $V_c(\theta)$, but not on the direction of $V_c(\theta)$.

Table 1. Look up table for orientations and positions

θ	Surround1 (S1)	Center (C)	Surround2 (S2)
0 , $4\pi/4$	(x+0, y-1)	(x,y)	(x+0, y+1)
$\pi/4$, $5\pi/4$	(x-1, y-1)	(x,y)	(x+1, y+1)
$2\pi/4$, $6\pi/4$	(x-1, y+0)	(x,y)	(x+1, y+0)
$3\pi/4$, $7\pi/4$	(x-1, y+1)	(x,y)	(x+1, y-1)

$$\text{If } |V_C(\theta)| \neq 0, \text{ Set } |R(\theta)| = \left| -\frac{1}{2}V_{s1}(\theta+\pi) + V_C(\theta) - \frac{1}{2}V_{s2}(\theta+\pi) \right|$$

$$\text{else Set } |R(\theta)| = \left| -\frac{1}{4}\{V_{s1}(\theta+\pi) + V_{s2}(\theta+\pi)\} \right|$$

(1)

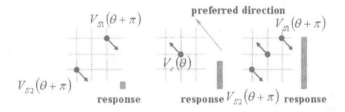

Fig. 3. Designed analysis model based on "Double Opponent Receptive Fields" is described. A yellow arrow describes the preferred direction and shaded bars describe the corresponding responses.

A Model of Noise Filteration. "Noise filtration" is designed using a pair of two surround motion vectors in our approach. The MT cell's response is very weak when one is moving in the cell's preferred direction and the other is moving against it diagonal direction, as shown in Fig 4. The suggested model responds to a pair of surround motion vectors at 4 directions ($\theta \in \{2\pi/4, \cdots, 5\pi/4\}$) when their directions are opposite to each other. Table 2 describes θ of 4 directions, the positions of center and surround motion vectors related with preferred direction. The reponse of a pixel is computed by Equation (2).

Table 2. Look up table for orientations and positions

θ	Surround1 (S1)	Center (C)	Surround2 (S2)
$2\pi/4$	(x+0, y-1)	(x,y)	(x+0, y-1)
$3\pi/4$	(x+1, y+1)	(x,y)	(x-1, y-1)
$4\pi/4$	(x-1, y+0)	(x,y)	(x-1, y+0)
$5\pi/4$	(x+1, y-1)	(x,y)	(x-1, y+1)

If $\left|V_c(\theta)\right| \neq 0$ and $\left|V_{S1}(\theta)-V_{S2}(\theta+\pi)\right| \geq 0$, Set $\left|R(\theta)\right|=\left|V_{S1}(\theta)-V_{S2}(\theta+\pi)\right|$

If $\left|V_c(\theta)\right| \neq 0$ and $\left|V_{S1}(\theta)-V_{S2}(\theta+\pi)\right| < 0$, Set $\left|R(\theta)\right|=0$　　　　(2)

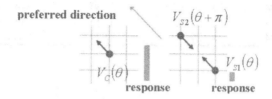

Fig. 4. Designed analysis model based on "Noise filtration" is described. A yellow arrow describes the preferred direction and shaded bars describe the corresponding responses.

2.3 Spatial and Temporal Feature Maps

After generating elementary feature maps, center-surround computations with 8 orientations based on the *DOOrG* (Difference-Of-Oriented-Gaussians) model [17] are performed on spatial and temporal elementary features maps to extract additional feature, orientation, and enhance the regions of pixels whose values are largely different from their surroundings'.

The resulting 32 spatial feature maps($SF^k(\theta)$, $k=1,..,4$) and 16 temporal feature maps($TF^k(\theta)$, $k=1,2$) are integrated into a single "saliency map(S)" which topographically codes for local conspicuity over the entire visual scene by a simple iterative nonlinear mechanism which uses statistical information and local competition relation of pixels in each maps.

2.4 Saliency Map

Each computed feature map is convolved with the large size of the *LoG*(*Laplacian of Gaussian*) filter and iterated. The result is added with the original one to obtain the effect of reducing noises, short-range cooperation and long-range competition among neighboring values in the map [18]. Therefore, the maximum value in the multiple feature maps to the average value over all pixels in the maps represents that how different the most active locations are from the average. The most active region stands out when the difference is large. Otherwise, the map contains nothing unique. Also, comparing a feature map with the other maps enables us to retain relative importance of the feature map with respect to the other ones. And irrelevant information extracted from ineffective feature map would be reduced. Finally, multiple feature maps are linearly summed into a single saliency map(S).

3 Experimental Results

Experiments were carried out for various real image sequences.

Some standard image sequences for video compression are tested known as Clair, Highway, Waterfall, and Paris have CIF(Common Intemediate Format) 352X288 resolution. Each image sequence consists of 150 frames and lasts 5 seconds (30 frames/sec). Some original images used in the test and the results are shown in Fig. 5.

Attention regions detected from the attention module are described in the gray scale image as shown in Fig 5(c). The intensity on the map represents saliency : the brighter the more conspicuous.

In our experiment, a human subjective evaluation is used by comparing its results with the output of the suggested attention module because no objective eavluation method is known yet. 40 people took part in the evaluation experiments. Three randomly chosen image sequences were shown to 20 men and 20 women aged from twenties to thirties. We asked subjects to mark the most attended region or object as soon as they found it during each trial.

In Claire image sequence, mouth and eye regions were markedd as the most conspicuous regions (62.5%) from human. If mouth and eye regions are included in the face region it takes up 70% of the most conspicuous regions of human evaluation. A woman's face region except eyes is detected as ROI when spatial features are simply used, however eyes are selected as ROI with the secondary priority when temporal features are applied. Eye regions take 25% of the most conspicous regions in the human experiment. The correct detection rate could be improved by applying temporal features to the previous visual attention system. In our proposed system no more than bottom-up approach is used while previous studies use spatial conspicuity in a bottom-up manner applying temporal conspicuity top-down approach[14]. The proposed system identifies mouth and eyes regions as ROIs when temporal features are applied, on the other hand the face region except eyes is detected as ROI when only spatial features are applied.

In Pairs image sequence, a ball region is marked as the most conspicuous one (60%) by human observers. When spatial features were simply applied, the proposed system detected small pink color note and yellow documents in the foreground with the highest priority, but the ball was detected with very low priority. As shown in the human experiments the ball was noticed with the higheset priority. When temporal features were applied, the ball was detected as ROI with the hightest priority as

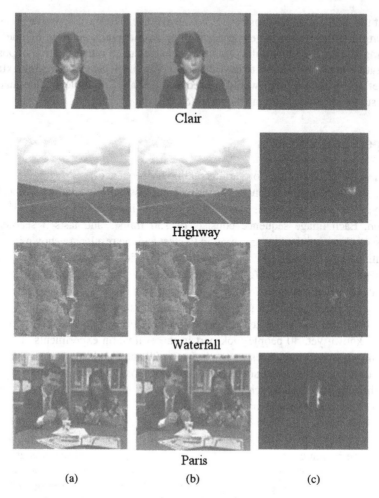

Clair

Highway

Waterfall

Paris

(a)   (b)   (c)

Fig. 5. Some examples of images used in the experiment and the results of them : (a) previous frame (t-1) image (b) current frame (t) image (c) attention region

desired. Consequently applying spatiotemporal features alternatively brings the selective visual attention system to obtain more generally accepted results. The ball is detected with highest conspicuity also from the proposed attention system using temporal features as shown in Fig. 5.

In Highway image sequence, 87.5% of human subjects marked traffic sign and highway, in waterfall image sequence, 95% marked waterfall.

Through the human evaluation tests, it is revealed that applying temporal features in addition to spatial ones improves the correct attention region detection.

We also tested another types of real image sequences and some results are shown in Fig. 6.

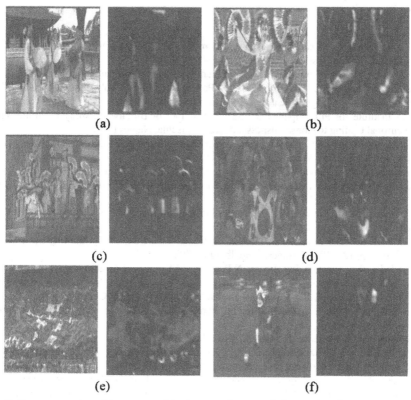

Fig. 6. Some examples of images used in the experiment and the results of them. Moving objects are (a)~(c) : dancers, (d) : People wearing red T-shirts and Taegeukgi, (e) : People wearing red cloth and the flag of Red Devils, (f) Football players and the white ball.

4   Conclusions

A selective visual attention system based on bottom-up approach using spatiotemporal features is proposed. A new analysis and integration techniques are proposed based on the facts known from former psychological studies. Previous analysis methods of the visual attention system used bottom-up approach for spatial features while top-down approach for temporal features accomplishing feedback system. On the other hand, we fully exploited the bottom-up approach for both spatiotemporal features to detect attention region. The proposed system responds to spatial and temporal stimulus by analyzing each feature. Though the suggested system reproduces certain aspects of human attention performance in a qualitative way, a more quantitative comparison is premature for several reasons. First of all, only a handful amount of knowledge about human cognitive mechanism is known to us. Correct attention region detection capability is expected to be improved further by some ways based on psychological studies. Further experiments will be carried out focusing on the integration relationship of spatial and temporal conspicuous maps for various image sequences hereafter. Base on these experiments more detailed comparison with previous study will be done.

References

1. Itti, L., Koch, C.: A saliency-based search mechanism for overt and covert shifts of visual attention. Vision Research 40(10-12), 1489–1506 (2000)
2. Osberger, W., Maeder, A.J.: Automatic identification of Perceptually important regions in an image. In: Proc. of 14th Intl. Conf. On Pattern Recognition, vol. 1, pp. 701–704 (1998)
3. Clark, A.: Some Logical Features of Feature Integration. In: Inaugural lecture for the Italian Institute for Philosophical Studies, Intl School of Biophysics Study Program "From Neuronal Coding to Consciousness", pp.12–17, Ischia, Naples (1998)
4. Clark, A.: Neuronal Coding of Perceptual Systems. Series on Biophysics and Biocybernetics, vol. 9, pp. 3–20. World Scientific, New Jersey (2001)
5. Anderson, R.A., Snyder, L.H., Bradley, D.C., Xing, J.: Multimodal Representation of Space in the Posterior Parietal Cortex and Its Use in Planning Movements. Annual Review Neuroscience 20, 303–330 (1997)
6. Treisman, A.M., Gelade, G.: A Feature-integration Theory of Attention. Cognitive Psychology 12(1), 97–136 (1980)
7. Cave, K.R.: The FeatureGate Model of Visual Selection. In: Psychological Research, vol. 62, pp. 182–194. Springer, Heidelberg (1999)
8. Cepeda, N.J., Cave, K.R., Bichot, N.P., Kim, M.S.: Spatial Selection via Feature-driven Inhibition of Distractor Locations. Perception and Psychophysics 60(5), 727–746 (1998)
9. Kim, M.S., Cave, K.R.: Top-down and Bottom-up Attentional Control: on the Nature of Interference from a Salient Distractor. Perception and Psychophysics 61(5), 1009–1023 (1999)
10. Milanese, R., Wechsler, H., Gil, S., Bost, J., Pun, T.: Integration of Bottom-up and Top-down Cues for Visual Attention Using Non-Linear Relaxation. In: Proc. of IEEE Conf. on Computer Vision and Pattern Recognition, pp. 781–785 (1994)
11. Cheoi, K.J., Lee, Y.: A Feature-driven Attention Module for an Active Vision System. In: Van Gool, L. (ed.) DAGM 2002. LNCS, vol. 2449, pp. 583–590. Springer, Heidelberg (2002)
12. Park, M.C., Cheoi, K.J.: An Adaptive ROI Detection System for Spatiotemporal Features. Journal of the Korea Contents Association 6(1) (2006)
13. Hanazawa, A.: Visual Psychophysics (2): Neural Mechanisms of Visual Information Processing. Journal of Image Information and Television Engineers 58(2), 199–204 (2004)
14. Boynton, R.M.: Human Color Vision. Holt, Rinehart and Winston, New York (1979)
15. Hecht, E.: Optics. 2nd edn., Sec.5.7. Addison Wesley, Reading (1987)
16. Lee, T.W., Wachtler, T., Sejnowski, T.J.: Color Opponency is an Efficient Representation of Spectral Properties in Natural Scenes. Vision Research 42, 2095–2103 (2002)
17. Hiroshi, A.: Visual Psychophysics (8): Visual Motion Perception and Motion Pictures. Journal of Image Information and Television Engineers 58(8), 1151–1156 (2004)
18. http://web.psych.ualberta.ca/~iwinship/vision/visualpathways.html

A Technique for Displaying Presence Information on a Live Camera Image Using 3-D Mask Objects

Jun Higuchi, Shin Takahashi, and Jiro Tanaka

Department of Computer Science
Graduate School of Systems and Information Engineering
University of Tsukuba
1-1-1 Ten-noudai, Tsukuba, Ibaraki 305-8573, Japan
{higuchi,shin,jiro}@iplab.cs.tsukuba.ac.jp

Abstract. Installing a live camera in an office or laboratory can provide reliable high-quality communication among collaborators who are physically separated, but may also lead to privacy concerns. We propose a technique for displaying presence information using a three-dimensional object as a mask that covers the image of people in the live camera system. Our technique enables information to be shared partially, enabling sufficient communication while alleviating the discomfort of feeling monitored by the camera. The system also clarifies less-visible activities such as typing text using a keyboard or moving a mouse of people in the camera image. We implemented the *Koka-ComeCam* system using our proposed technique.

Keywords: Live camera, Communication support, Privacy, 3-D, Visualization.

1 Introduction

Using a live camera to support communication among physically separated collaborators has become common [6, 8-10]. Live video provides more reliable and higher-quality communication to group members compared to text-based tools such as Instant Messenger [8]. For example, a live camera in an office or laboratory indicates at a glance who is there and what they are doing. Unlike video chat and video conferencing, which use Web cameras, a live camera provides continuous coverage of the daily routine in the room. Moreover, the image can be easily monitored from anywhere via the Internet. In addition, using a camera with a pan/tilt/zoom (PTZ) function enables video coverage of a wide area such as an entire room.

However, some people may feel uncomfortable about being recorded by a live camera. One common technique to alleviate such discomfort is to mask the video image (e.g., using a mosaic or blur), but this reduces the information provided by the camera and thus questions the merit of installing a live camera.

We propose using three-dimensional (3-D) virtual objects in the video image to partially mask images and therefore support live camera communication as well as privacy. The technique basically overlays an avatar on the images of people to mask

S. Lee et al. (Eds.): APCHI 2008, LNCS 5068, pp. 213–221, 2008.

their direct appearance but identify them individually. The level of detail of the mask can be changed according to the level of privacy desired, and this setting is controlled by the person represented by the avatar. This enables one to balance what information is shared with privacy. Moreover, the mask represents each person's current and past activities, thereby presenting information that would otherwise be hidden in traditional masking systems.

The rest of this paper is organized as follows. In Section 2, we summarize our previous work and introduce the basic 3-D mask object. In Section 3, we describe the *Koka-ComeCam* system as it relates to our proposed technique. In Section 4, we explain the architecture and implementation details of the system. Related work is provided in Section 5, and the conclusion is given in Section 6.

2 Previous Work: *ComeCam*

We previously developed the *ComeCam* system [5], which supports communication between two ends of a live camera connection. The user[1] can display a mask in the video output that covers his or her image. The mask is a 3-D virtual object, which we call a *3-D mask object*. Unlike a mosaic or blur, a 3-D mask object functions as an avatar chosen by the user as shown in Figure 1. A 3-D mask object covers the user, but enables others to identify him or her based on its unique character and displayed position. Because the system manages each user's position as a 3-D coordinate relative to the size of the room, the mask can cover the user's area even if the view of the camera is changed using PTZ operations. We propose a new technique for displaying users' presence information based on this 3-D mask object, and describe the *Koka-ComeCam*[2] system implemented with the new technique.

Panned, tilted, and zoomed images

Fig. 1. An example of a 3-D mask object displayed on a live camera image

---

[1] This indicates the observed person in this paper.
[2] "Koka" means "effect" in Japanese.

3 Displaying Presence Information with a 3-D Mask Object

A 3-D mask object in *ComeCam* works as an avatar and is displayed according to the camera movement via a PTZ operation, but it is basically a mask for the privacy problem. Compared to a mosaic or blur, overlaying a virtual 3-D object on the real camera image enables user presence information to be represented more naturally and more effectively. In this section, we introduce our new technique and use it to implement the *Koka-ComeCam* system.

3.1 Changing the Mask According to User Privacy Level

Masking the video image blocks some information from remote users. Because it is preferable to give users control over masking, our system links masking to privacy settings. The user selects a privacy level of [high], [middle], or [low], as shown in Figure 2(left), or [none] for no mask. As the privacy level is lowered, the mask's appearance becomes simpler, and finally becomes a simple cube. The size of the mask area also becomes smaller. At the same time, the transparency of the mask increases, so that the user's video image can be gradually seen through the mask (Figure 2(right), a snapshot of *Koka-ComeCam*). Initially, the mask at the [middle] level of privacy is automatically chosen by the system (just after starting the application on the user's own PC).

Because the mask plays the role of avatar, even if the privacy level is [high], the minimum presence information, such as whether the user is available, is always maintained in the output video image. In contrast, the [low] and [middle] levels of privacy lessen the masking of the object so that it does not perfectly cover the user, making the user's actions and state more visible. However, it still provides a sense of security to the observed person because it obscures the user's direct appearance.

Users can change the level of privacy to suit their situation. For example, if a user wants to sleep for a few hours, and determines that it would not be a good idea to broadcast this to colleagues or the boss, the user could temporarily raise the privacy level. If, however, a user wants to be seen working, he or she could lower the privacy level. However, in some cases, changing the privacy level manually might be difficult. For example, if a person decides to take control of the camera and zoom in on a specific user, the system will automatically increase (or decrease) the privacy level; each user sets the conditions of the zoom function and other specific operations.

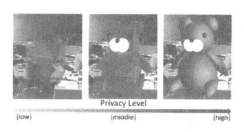

Fig. 2. Changing a mask according to user privacy level

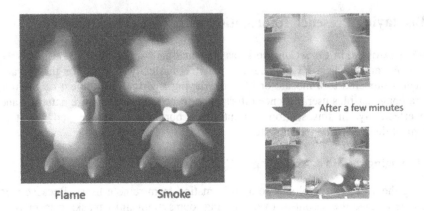

Fig. 3. Special effects represent user activities

From the standpoint of sharing information between research groups or laboratories, it is preferable to set the system at low privacy/high sharing and only occasionally switch to high privacy/low sharing. However, because users can control their own privacy settings, the potential exists for users to always use the high privacy/low sharing setting, thereby undermining the advantage of installing a live camera. To address this potential problem, the system assumes that live cameras are installed in two or more rooms and that users monitor the appearance of each others' rooms interactively. Thus, other room members are covered by the high-privacy mask as long as the viewing user does not decrease the privacy level. This maintains equality between groups.

3.2 Representing User Activities with a 3-D Mask Object

The technique of showing the mask described in Section 3.1 allows observers to access user information without compromising privacy, by masking and not completely blocking images of people. A live camera by itself can only display the current situation or activity. In addition, it remains unclear whether users are working or sleeping if they are facing a computer and not moving. To address this issue, we introduced graphical effects used in cartoon animations and computer games to provide additional information about users. Other systems have applied such effects to represent abstract information such as a person's feelings or atmosphere. We built on this to depict current and past activities of users graphically by overlaying additional information on the 3-D mask object. Figure 3(left) shows two examples. First, when the user starts working at his or her own computer, such as typing text using a keyboard or moving the mouse, a flame graphic is displayed around the mask. The flame grows or shrinks according to the level of keyboard or mouse operation. Second, when the user stops operating the computer and becomes inactive, a smoke graphic is displayed around the mask. The amount of smoke changes according to the amount of time spent inactive. In this way, the user's past activities can be inferred (Figure 3(right)). For example, smoke is displayed for some time after a user leaves the room (after the user logs out from the system). Thus, even if the user is no longer

Fig. 4. An example of a live camera image of Koka-ComeCam

displayed on the camera image, it can be inferred that the person was there working relatively recently. Because these effects are also represented as 3-D virtual objects, they can robustly follow any changes in the camera view made by a PTZ operation.

In addition, users can leave messages such as "I'll be back soon" near their mask. The message is displayed around the mask as a balloon. It is also possible to automatically show or hide messages according to the focus and the zoom level of the camera. For example, if a remote user zooms in on someone's image in the camera, the imaged user can set the system to display the message "Don't bother me! I'm busy now!"

A 3-D mask object masks users, but by overlaying additional information, our system enables the sharing of additional important information, such as activity status. Because these effects are displayed around each user's mask, user activities and status can be easily understood at a glance. In fact, when an effect is displayed, the mask moves as shown in Figure 3(left) to make it even easier to map between the mask and effect. Figure 4 shows an example of a live camera image using *Koka-ComeCam*. By simply viewing the overview of the room, observers can instantly know what people in the room are currently doing, thereby facilitating communication among group members.

Some users may be uncomfortable revealing this extra information to others, but these effects represent abstract information only, such as whether the keyboard and mouse are currently being operated, and thus our system strikes a better balance between information sharing and privacy than other existing systems.

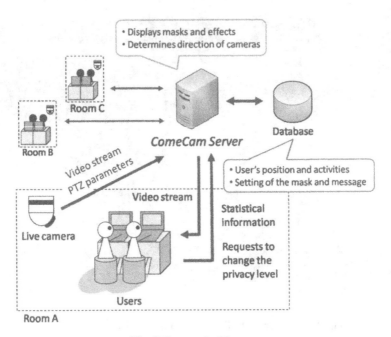

Fig. 5. System Architecture

4   Implementation

4.1   System Architecture

Figure 5 shows the architecture of *Koka-ComeCam*. The system consists of networked PTZ cameras, client PCs in each room, a database server that maintains information such as user positions and activities, and the central *ComeCam Server*, which connects all of the PCs. Each client PC runs the application with the interface to allow control over the mask and messages. Each client PC sends user statistics (e.g., keyboard activity) and requests (e.g., privacy level settings) to *ComeCam Server*. The server receives the video stream from each live camera, overlays masks and effects at each user's position according to the user's privacy level and activities, and then transmits the resulting animated video image to each user's PC. In this way, no raw images are transmitted directly to users.

Our system uses AXIS 214 PTZ[3] as a live camera. The parameters for this camera can be queried or set simply by referring to specific URLs. Each time the PTZ values of the camera change, *ComeCam Server* acquires the pan and tilt angle values (-180 - +180) to determine if the camera is pointing at the user. If the system decides that the camera is pointing at the user, it refers to his or her settings of the mask and messages from the database and overlays the mask according to this information. The paper [5] supplies more details about the algorithm that determines whether the camera is pointing at the user.

---

[3] AXIS 214 PTZ http://www.axiscom.co.jp/prod/214/

4.2 Displaying 3-D Mask Objects on a Live Camera Image

When the camera is moved using the PTZ operations, the two-dimensional area of the image to be masked changes considerably, and so it must be calculated in three dimensions. *Koka-ComeCam* uses 3-D graphical objects as masks, and places them virtually at the position of the user to cover them even if the camera is moved. For zooming, we match the horizontal angle of view in the perspective projection of the virtual camera and the real camera. The current angle of view of the real camera can be calculated by the zoom level (0 - 9999), which is acquired from the real camera. For panning and tilting, the current referenced coordinates of the real camera can be acquired by the pan and tilt angle value, so we match them to the referenced coordinates of the virtual camera. *Koka-ComeCam* acquires the PTZ parameters of the camera and redraws objects whenever the PTZ operation is executed. As a result, it synchronizes the display of objects with the movements in the real camera. We use OpenGL library to draw masks and effects.

To render 3-D mask objects and effects as if they exist in the real world, we display them after clipping according to the shape of real objects. To input the shape of real objects in the room, we put ARToolKit[4] markers on them (e.g., at the four corners of a desk) as shown in Figure 6(a) and capture their coordinates with the camera. ARToolKit is a library that determines the relative position of the marker to the camera in 3-D space. We create the 3-D virtual object of the real object (Figure 6(b)), clip the overlapping part of the 3-D virtual object (Figure 6(c)), and overlay it on the camera image (Figure 6(d)). In this way, the mask can be naturally integrated to the live camera image.

4.3 Setting up User Positions Using Markers

Those with the authority to use *Koka-ComeCam* are members of the workspace (e.g., office or laboratory) in which the system is being operated. Currently, users' positions are

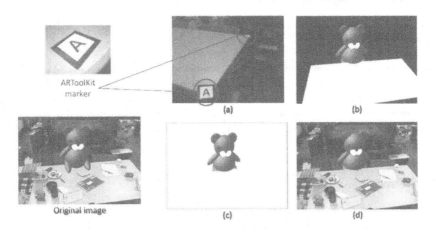

Fig. 6. Displaying the mask after clipping according to the shape of real objects

---

[4] ARToolKit http://www.hitl.washington.edu/artoolkit/

fixed based on their desk position, where most of their work is centered. The position of the user and the camera are handled as 3-D coordinates relative to the size of the room. Therefore, it is necessary to measure the absolute positions of the user and the camera at least once, but using ARToolKit and its markers can reduce the time to input these values. We capture the marker assigned to each user's position, convert it into coordinates relative to the size of the room, and store it in the database. In this way, we can update the user's position easily even if it changes by moving the position of the desk.

5 Related Work

Many systems use video to help provide the sense that distantly located collaborators are in the same room [2, 7, 4]. In particular, GestureCam [3] uses a moving camera mounted on an actuator to achieve high-quality results. These techniques aim to synchronize and improve collaborative work by sharing images for one-on-one communication, and thus require special devices. Our technique requires only a live camera to provide continuous coverage of the daily routine in the entire room.

Live video communication systems must balance information sharing and privacy. Hudson et al. [8] proposed the Shadow-View technique to address privacy, while Boyle et al. [6] used a mask-like mosaic and blur. Tansuriyavong et al. [9] used silhouettes to represent people, and other research [10] made images of people transparent to a certain degree depending on distance to the camera. Many techniques, however, do not support dynamic changes of the camera view via PTZ operations. Our technique uses a 3-D virtual object as a mask, and shares other information such as activity status using special effects.

A previous study [1] extended Instant Messenger so that users can recognize presence information visually from a 3-D display. The advantage of our technique is that because our display is based on a real video image, it can represent not only awareness information of remote users but also environmental information of remote places, and all the input unites naturally on the display.

6 Conclusion

We proposed a technique for displaying presence information using a 3-D object as a mask that covers the people in a live camera system. We applied the method to *ComeCam* and implemented *Koka-ComeCam* using the system. Our system provides much more awareness information of remote users while also protecting privacy. In future work, we will examine a new technique for representing user information, and discuss the balance between it and privacy.

References

1. Neustaedter, C., Greenberg, S.: Supporting Coherence with a 3D Instant Messenger Visualization. In: CHI 2002 Workshop on Discourse Architectures (2002)
2. Ishii, H., Kobayashi, M., Grudin, J.: Integration of Interpersonal Space and Shared Workspace: ClearBoard Design and Experiments. ACM Transactions on Information Systems 11(4), 349–375 (1993)

3. Kuzuoka, H., Kosuge, T., Tanaka, M.: GestureCam: a video communication system for sympathetic remote collaboration. In: 1994 ACM conference on Computer-Supported Cooperative Work, pp. 35–43 (1994)
4. Kuzuoka, H., Yamashita, J., Yamazaki, K., Yamazaki, A.: Agora: A Remote Collaboration System that Enables Mutual Monitoring. In: CHI 1999 extended abstracts on Human factors in computing systems, pp. 190–191 (1999)
5. Higuchi, J., Takahashi, S., Tanaka, J.: ComeCam: A Communication Support System Between Both Ends of The Live Camera Connection. In: Third International Conference on Collaboration Technologies, pp. 33–38 (2007)
6. Boyle, M., Edwards, C., Greenberg, S.: The Effects of Filtered Video on Awareness and Privacy. In: 2000 ACM Conference on Computer-Supported Cooperative Work, pp. 1–10 (2000)
7. Morikawa, O., Maesako, T.: HyperMirror: Toward Pleasant-to-use Video-Mediated Communication System. In: 1998 ACM Conference on Computer-Supported Cooperative Work, pp. 149–158 (1998)
8. Hudson, S.E., Smith, I.: Techniques for addressing Fundamental Privacy and Disruption Tradeoffs in Awareness Support System. In: 1996 ACM Conference on Computer-Supported Cooperative Work, pp. 248–257 (1996)
9. Tansuriyavong, S., Hanaki, S.: Privacy protection by concealing persons in circumstantial video image. In: Workshops on Perceptual/Perceptive User Interfaces 2001, pp. 1–4 (2001)
10. Tansuriyavong, S., Susuki, T., Chokchaitam, S., Iwahashi, M.: Privacy Conscious Video Communication System Based on JPEG 2000. In: International Workshop on Antenna Technology 2007, pp. 50–55 (2007)

Background Subtraction Based on Local Orientation Histogram

DongHeon Jang, XiangHua Jin, YongJun Choi, and TaeYong Kim

Department of Image Engineering, Graduate School of Advanced Imaging Science
Multimedia, and Film, Chung-Ang Univ., 221 Heukseok-Dong Dongjak-Gu,
156-756 Seoul, South Korea
tellamon@gmail.com, hyanghwa_kim@naver.com, yongjc0602@yahoo.com
kimty@cau.ac.kr

Abstract. Background Subtraction is an important preprocessing step for extracting the features of tracking objects in the vision-based HCI system. In this paper, the orientation histogram between the foreground image and the background image is compared to extract the foreground probability in the local area. The orientation histogram-based method is partially robust against illumination change and small moving objects in background. There are two major drawbacks of using histograms which are quantization errors in histogram binning and slow computation speed. With Gaussian binning and integral histogram, we present the recursive partitioning method that gives false detection suppression and fast computation speed.

Keywords: Background subtraction, Orientation histogram, Integral histogram, Vision–based game interface.

1 Introduction

The detection of foreground region is a primary object of the vision-based HCI system [1]. It is always desirable to achieve very high sensitivity in the detection of foreground objects with the lowest possible false alarm rates. Background subtraction is a method typically used to segment moving regions in images sequences taken from a static camera by comparing each new frame to a model of the scene background. The normal distribution model $N(\mu, \sigma^2)$ for the intensity value of a pixel is the underlying model for many per-pixel background subtraction techniques. For example, one of the simplest background subtraction techniques is to calculate an average image of the scene with no foreground objects, subtract each new frame from this image, and threshold the result. In [9] a mixture of three Normal distributions was used to model the pixel value for traffic surveillance applications. Stauer and Grimson [8] used the mixture of Gaussian on changes of pixel intensity taking several frames to converge each Gaussian. Pfinder [12] uses a multi-class statistical model for the tracked object and single Gaussian per pixel for the background. Updating of background was conducted with linear prediction using the in [10]. However, those methods require several frames to build a background model properly. Furthermore,

S. Lee et al. (Eds.): APCHI 2008, LNCS 5068, pp. 222–231, 2008.

the number of Gaussian distribution is taken account of performance since there is a trade-off between accuracy and detection rates.

The histogram-based object tracking technique or background subtraction has been practiced in many previous researches [1], [2], [3], [4], [5]. The histogram basis comparison suppresses the false detection of foreground rather than the per-pixel comparison. A color or intensity histogram is easy to compute and is partially robust against small perturbations since it represents color distribution of the area while lacking of its spatial information. In spite of the lacks of its spatial information, [1] successfully used the local color histograms as reduced features for HCI vision system. However, in many natural images, the color or intensity histogram-based approach fails since they are tightly associated with intensity values which are sensitive to self-shadows or illumination changes.

Orientation histogram has been identified as a potential technique of using histogram-based descriptors for visual tracking [11]. Especially, it keeps the probability density function of local gradients which is strong against illumination changes and easy to compute. However, histogram-based approaches have some inherent drawbacks. First, they are sensitive to quantization errors that may cause bin changes even though an image variation is small. The second drawback occurs when we try to access multiple regions in a number of local regions. Since histogram computation speed depends on its size and location, it costs the computation load and prevents the real-time system. The goal of this paper is to deal with these drawbacks while keeping the advantages of orientation histograms.

The local histograms model the background and the foreground by dividing each frame into small local regions. The local region has the foreground probability given by comparing local orientation histograms between background and foreground image. In this paper, we have adopted the multi-scaled approach [1] and proposed a new algorithm that dynamically partition and compare regions in a recursive manner to achieve both fast computation speed and suppression of local false detection.

The following section explains how to calculate the local histograms with Gaussian kernel. Section 3 introduces the advantage of integral histogram and the recursive partitioning method. Section 4 is the experimental results and the final section concludes the paper.

2 Local Orientation Histogram with Gaussian Kernel

For the real-time application, it is necessary to reduce the amount of data by grouping neighboring pixels to the local region (hereby *cell*) and by quantizing the feature space before histogram computations. We divided a $V \times H$ sized high-resolution image into $v \times h$ number of cells. At each cell in an image, an N-bin histogram of its neighborhood is computed. In discrete histogram, each bin covers $180/N$ degree of gradient, so we need to choose proper N to trade off quantization error against memory usages. The first step to compute any gradient orientation histogram in cell is as follows.

$$dx = I(x+1, y) - I(x-1, y)$$
$$dy = I(x, y+1) - I(x, y-1)$$
$$m(x, y) = sqrt(dx^2 + dy^2)$$
$$\theta(x, y) = arctan(dy / dx)$$

(1)

dx and dy are gradients of axis and $m(x, y)$ $\theta(x, y)$ are its magnitude and orientation respectively. Secondly, θ is quantized into N bins. Determining the number of histogram bins is an important yet unresolved problem in the histogram-based method, so the bin number is empirically set($N=8$ in our case) and the selection of the bin number accounting for environment changes is left for future works. In order to reduce the effect of noise, the contribution of each point in $\theta(x, y)$ to the corresponding bin is weighted by its magnitude $m(x, y)$.

Limiting the corresponding histogram bin of pixel (x, y) to a single bin is a major reason of quantization errors. The corresponding bin of (x, y) tends to change the bin position at each frame because of noise in the coarse quantization process which produce many false positives/negatives in histogram-based comparison. For this reason, we applied Gaussian kernel to 1D histogram for the $\theta(x, y)$ to contribute many bins according to Gaussian weights.

$$d_\theta = \theta_k - \theta_j,$$

$$G_j(\theta_k) = \frac{1}{2\pi\sigma_c} \exp(-\frac{d_\theta^2}{2\sigma_c^2})$$

(2)

where θ_k is a orientation value of the (x, y).

Given the local histograms of the background and the foreground, we can determine which areas of the current frame contain foreground objects by computing the distance of two histograms using the Bhattacharyya distance measurement. Note that the orientation histogram is not normalized because of the gradient magnitude weighting. Furthermore, in our experiment, the false detection using orientation histogram occurs in a flat region in which the weak magnitude-weighted histogram looses discriminating features. So we marked the cell as *undefined* by applying the following rule before the distance measurement

$$P_l = \begin{cases} undefined, & if\ M(H^{ref}) < T_m\ and\ M(H^{cur}) < T_m \\ \sum_{j=1}^{N} \sqrt{h_j^{ref} h_j^{cur}}, & otherwise \end{cases}$$

(3)

where P_l is the foreground probability of the cell and $M(H)$ is the running sum of magnitudes in the histogram. The thresholding technique above with T_m to the background local histogram H_{ref} and the foreground histogram H_{cur} prevents the false detection in single-colored regions. In this paper, the filtered cells with *undefined* mark are processed later by applying morphological processing in a cell level. However, with excessive computing resources, the average intensity or color-histogram can be applied for more accurate results. The example of local histogram comparison is given in Figure 1. Note that the background image contains both the flat region and edge-intensive region. The results show that the shadow cast by the stretched arm over flat region is successfully classified as the background region. Although the illumination invariance of orientation histogram gives satisfied results for coarse feature extraction, we have introduced the more robust method that suppresses local false detection shown in Figure 3.

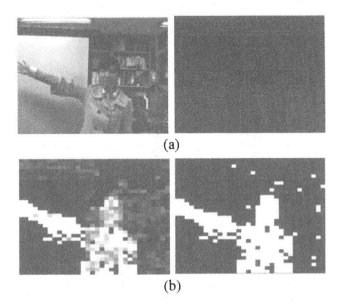

(a)

(b)

Fig. 1. (a) The foreground image (left) and its local orientation histogram plot (right) with $v=h=32$, $T_m = 330$. The direction of line represents its angle and its length is magnitude. (b) The extracted foreground probability (left) and the threshold ($P_l > 0.18$) applied to the image (right).

3   Integral Histogram Based Recursive Comparison

3.1   Integral Histogram

The recursive partitioning algorithm requires multiple extractions of histograms from multiple rectangular cells. The tool enabling this to be done in real time is the integral histogram described in [3].

The integral histogram method is an extension of the integral image data structure [7]. The integral histogram holds the sum of all the bins contained in the rectangular region at the point (x,y) in the image as the following formula.

$$I_{(x,y)}[j] = \sum_{x' \le x, y' \le y} h_j(x, y), \; j = 1, ..., N \cdot \qquad (4)$$

This image allows to compute the sum for the pixels on arbitrary rectangular regions by considering the 4 integral image values at the corners of the region i.e it is computed in constant time independent of the size of the region. The integral histogram at each position (x, y) is calculated with a wavefront scan propagation that 3 neighbor integral histograms and the current orientation value are used. It is done at each frame and consumes the most of computation time. The Figure 2 gives the calculated integral histogram data with N bins.

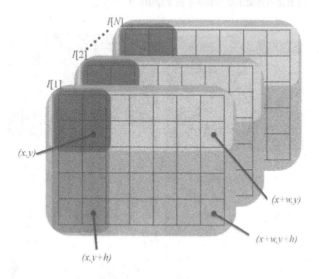

Fig. 2. The integral histogram data. Each corner *(x,y)*, *(x+w,y)*, *(x,y+h)*, *(x+w,y+h)* contains its integral data within overlapped colored regions. The histogram data in rectangle region *(x,y,w,h)* can be computed with equation (4).

Once the scanning process is done, we can immediately compute the local histogram in a given region with integral data at four corners as follows.

$$H_l = I(x+w, y+h) - I(x+w, y) - I(x, y+h) + I(x, y).$$ (5)

3.2 Recursive Partitioning

If we use fixed $v \times h$ sized cells, it requires $v \times h$ number of histogram comparison and each computation cost depends on histogram quantization size N. Rather than subtracting cell by cell, we have adopted the multi-scale search algorithm to skip large regions where no foreground objects come in [1]. The key algorithm is that it recursively checks the histogram distance between foreground and background until the search level reaches to the maximum level considering the local variations in foreground affects the global distribution. Note that there is no additional histogram quantization process for searching at each level. With the help of the pre-scanned integral histogram, multiple extractions of histogram over different scaled regions are done in constant time. The search level starts from the global cell to the local cells. We set the whole image region to the target region with level 0 and start comparing the histogram to the corresponding background region. If a foreground object comes in screen, the changes in global level are detected and then sub-divide the target region into 4 local regions and recursively do the same process at each target region until the given maximum search level is reached.

The number of cell counts with the proposed approach depends on the maximum search level s, as given by $v \times h = 2^s$, that for the 320×240 sized image, 32×32 number of cells having 10×7 size(16 horizontal pixels are padded to the last cell) where s is 5. The algorithm first initializes the $v \times h$ foreground probability cells with 0 values. Since the search process starts from lager regions, there is no need to do the cell by cell processing if the test at the prior level produces a value under threshold T_l/Lev^2 in histogram comparison.

This approach mainly has two advantages. The first benefit of using the recursive partitioning is that it suppresses the false positives due to small changes in the background. Another one is the superior computation speed. It automatically skips the large background area and goes to the deeper level to find foreground cells while cell by cell comparison always consumes $v \times h$ computation time. The below is the pseudo code for the proposed algorithm.

Pseudo Code for comparing local histograms recursively

```
program RecursiveCompare (x,y,w,h,lev)
  Href = GetIntegHist(x,y,w,h);
  Hcur = GetIntegHist(x,y,w,h);
  Mref = Sum(Href);
  Mcur = Sum(Hcur);
  if(Mref < Th_m && Mcur < Th_m)
    FgProbability[x1,y1,x1,y2] = undefined;
    return;
  endif
  Normalize(Href);
  Normalize(Hcur);
  dist = Bhattacharyya(Href,Hcur);
  if( lev == maxlevel)
    FgProbability[x1,y1,x1,y2] = dist;
    return;
  else
    if(Th_lev/lev² > dist)
      RecursiveCompare (x      ,y       ,w/2,h/2,lev+1);
      RecursiveCompare (x+w/2,y       ,w/2,h/2,lev+1);
      RecursiveCompare (x      ,y+h/2 ,w/2,h/2,lev+1);
      RecursiveCompare (x+w/2,y+h/2 ,w/2,h/2,lev+1);
    endif
  endif
end.
```

Figure 3 shows the efficiency of the recursive partitioning method. Note that the searched level is highlighted in red rectangles. The large local area implies that it skips the sub-region searches which results in suppression of the false detection and computation advantage compared to the cell by cell comparison method.

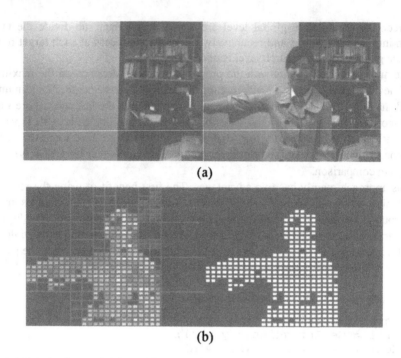

(a)

(b)

Fig. 3. (a) The background (left) and foreground image (right). The result of recursive partitioning method. (b)The result of recursive partitioning image (left) and the threshold ($P_l > 0.18$) applied to the image (right).

4 Experiment

We first captured the background image and initialized the integral histogram data. Then we captured 100 test images with a color CCD camera using 320x240 pixels

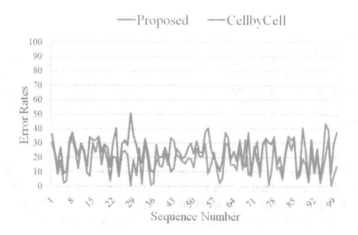

Fig. 4. The error rates comparison graph

resolution. We built ground truth data of 100 test images by manually marking at the cell level. Figure 4 is the error rate of the proposed method comparing to the cell by cell approach. The average error of the cell by cell approach was 24.33 and the recursive partitioning was 17.78 where the proposed method shows the robust extraction of a foreground object by suppressing local false detections.

Each 20 images of 100 test images contains the different sized foreground object that covers about 10% to 50% of total image size. With the recursive partitioning method, the number of integral histogram extraction depends on the foreground object size. If the foreground object is small, then most of regions are filtered out and the computational performance is increased. Table 1 shows the histogram extraction count including overhead in which all of the searching process conducted before the maximum level are counted. Note that the extraction time is fixed to 1024 with $v=h=32$ for all cases in the cell by cell approach.

Table 1. The number of histogram extraction

Foreground object size	Overhead	Cells in maximum level	Total
50%	157	511	668
40%	80	402	482
30%	54	305	359
20%	32	199	231
10%	13	95	108

The overall computation time of the proposed method was 15ms in Intel Dualcore 2.0G processor, 1G memory. The main computational load is the scanning process of integral histogram. If the foreground object size is 10% of total image size, we achieve 5ms of performance increase rather than 50% of that.

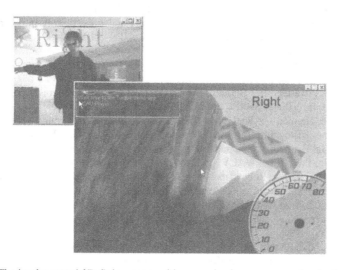

Fig. 5. The implemented 3D flying game with recognized pose on complex background

We have developed a simple game using 3D game engine to show the usability of the proposed algorithm in the real-time processing situation. The game application built by us is free flying simulation over a simple terrain map with first person view. When foreground objects are detected, the position of both arms produces one of four keyboard inputs and transmitted to the game system. With the classified input, the user can turn left/right or accel/stop. Figure 5 shows the both recognized pose and its keyboard input in the game scene.

5 Conclusion

This paper has demonstrated the illumination invariant extraction of foreground cells using the local orientation histogram. To reduce the quantization error in computing histogram we applied Gaussian kernel to 1D orientation histogram. Integral histogram was exploited to provide fast extraction of histogram over multiple overlapped cells. The proposed recursive partitioning method is proved to suppress to local false detection and increases performance rather than cell by cell comparison. Combining color histograms to resolve the flat region issue will be addressed for future works.

Acknowledgments. This research was supported by the ITRC (Information Technology Research Center, MIC) program and Seoul R&BD program, Korea.

References

1. Jang, D.H., Chai, Y.J., Jin, X.H., Kim, T.Y.: Realtime Coarse Pose Recognition using a Local Integral Histogram. In: International Conference on Convergence Information Technology, November 21-23, 2007, pp. 1982–1987 (2007)
2. Mason, M., Duric, Z.: Using histograms to detect and track objects in color video. In: Applied Imagery Pattern Recognition Workshop, AIPR 2001 30th, October 10-12, 2001, pp. 154–159. IEEE, Los Alamitos (2001)
3. Porkili, F.: Integral histogram: A fast way to extract histograms in cartesian spaces. In: Proc. IEEE Conf. on Computer Vision and Pattern Recognition (CVPR) (2005)
4. Noriega, P., Bascle, B., Bernier, O.: Local kernel color histograms for background subtraction. In: VISAPP, vol. 1, pp. 213–219. INSTICC Press (2006)
5. Noriega, P., Bernier, O.: Real Time Illumination Invariant Background Subtraction Using Local Kernel Histograms. In: British Machine Vision Association (BMVC) (2006)
6. Bradski, G.: Real time face and object tracking as a component of a perceptual user interface. In: Proc. IEEE WACV, pp. 214–219 (1998)
7. Viola, P., Jones, M.: Robust real time object detection. In: IEEE ICCV Workshop on Statistical and Computational Theories of Vision (2001)
8. Stauer, C., Grimson, W.E.L.: Adaptive background mixture models for real-time tracking. In: Computer Vision and Pattern Recognition Fort Collins, Colorado, June 1999, pp. 246–252 (1999)
9. Friedman, N., Russell, S.: Image segmentation in video sequences: A probabilistic approach. In: Uncertainty in Artificial Inteligence (1997)

10. Toyama, K., Krumm, J., Brummit, B., Meyers, B.: Wallflower: Principles and practice of background maintenance. In: International Conference on Computer Vision, Corfu, Greece (September 1999)
11. Marimon, D., Ebrahimi, T.: Orientation histogram-based matching for region tracking. In: IEEE Eight International Workshop on Image Analysis for Multimedia Interactive Services(WIAMIS 2007) (2007)
12. Wren, C., Azarbayejani, A., Darrell, T., Pentland, A.: Pfinder: Real-time tracking of the human body. In: Photonics East, vol. 2615, SPIE, Bellingham, WA (1995)

Relationship between Viewing Distance and Visual Fatigue in Relation to Feeling of Involvement

Kiyomi Sakamoto[1], Shoichi Aoyama[1], Shigeo Asahara[1],
Kuniko Yamashita[2], and Akira Okada[2]

[1] Corporate R&D Strategy Office, Matsushita Electric Industrial Co., Ltd., 3-1-1 Yagumo-naka-machi, Moriguchi City, Osaka 570-8501, Japan
{sakamoto.kiyomi,aoyama.shoichi,asahara.shigeo}@jp.panasonic.com
[2] Osaka City University, 3-3-138, Sugimotocho, Sumiyoshi-ku, Osaka 558-8585, Japan
{yamasita,okada}@life.osaka-cu.ac.jp

Abstract. In this study, we carried out experiments to measure the effect of viewing distance on visual fatigue using two kinds of visual content. Both experiments showed that visual fatigue reached a minimum at a distance of 3 to 4 times the height of the display (3–4H) and that sympathetic nerve activity peaked at around 3H. These results indicate that the viewing distance for less visual fatigue and a closer feeling of involvement might be in between the two distances. These indices, which we adopt in this study, have the potential to be effective evaluation indices for measuring visual fatigue taking feeling of involvement into consideration.

Keywords: Viewing distance, Visual fatigue, Feeling of involvement, TV, Physiological and psychological measurements.

1 Introduction

Technological progress and shifting lifestyles have led to significant changes in the everyday TV viewing environment. On the technical side, the replacement of CRT TVs with widescreen PDPs and LCDs has progressed rapidly. Bigger screens and longer TV viewing times make it increasingly necessary to consider the effects of these changes on visual fatigue and health. To develop TVs that do not cause visual fatigue and to propose optimum TV viewing conditions, these factors need to be investigated in addition to image quality and presence.

Numerous studies have been carried out on visual fatigue experienced during VDT work, particularly in the field of ergonomics [1].

Conventional VDT work is mainly text input tasks. However, TV viewing comprises mainly video material and animations, and TV viewing styles are becoming more diversified due to broadening content, such as video games and web pages in addition to conventional TV programs. For these reasons, more studies need to be carried out on visual fatigue caused by viewing video and animations.

Methods for measuring visual fatigue include CFF (critical flicker fusion frequency), blinking rate (the number of blinks per minute), and pupil accommodation [2].

S. Lee et al. (Eds.): APCHI 2008, LNCS 5068, pp. 232–239, 2008.
© Springer-Verlag Berlin Heidelberg 2008

However, it is not possible to evaluate visual fatigue using single and direct measurements of the type employed for evaluating fatigue in other parts of the body. Moreover, highly sensitive measurements are needed to detect and measure visual fatigue.

With regard to viewing distance, nowadays, the recommended distance for high definition TV is 2 or 3 times the display's height [3]. However, this recommended value appears to be based on the distance needed to experience a feeling of involvement, rather than the visibility of individual pixels. The evaluation methods for the current distance recommendations are mainly arrived at by subjective evaluation, and thus are not based on objective physiological data.

In this study, to measure visual fatigue objectively and obtain information about optimum viewing distance, the authors investigated both the physiological and the psychological angles [4][5][6]. In our physiological evaluation, CFF, blinking rates, and a sympathetic nerve activity index are used; and in the psychological evaluation, we employed questionnaires and interviews. We attempted to build an objective index of visual fatigue and feeling of involvement from a combination of two or more indices.

2 Experiment 1: Acute Fatigue Test

The first experiment was an acute fatigue test. This was an animation task that caused rapid visual fatigue. The subject had to steadily stare at the screen and count the number of horses running around in a pasture, without succumbing to boredom.

2.1 Methods

Subjects: The subjects were ten women in their 50s. Each worked on the task under four sets of experimental conditions: 2H, 3H, 4H, and 6H.

Display device: 42-inch plasma TV (PDP)

Measured items: The following items, verified by prior study to yield effective results, were adopted: subjective assessment of fatigue (SAF) by interview, blinking rate, heart rate variability (level of sympathetic nerve activity, LF/HF). LF/HF is defined by the ratio of the low frequency band (LF) and high frequency band (HF) which is calculated employing FFT analysis using the R-R interval based on heart rate variability obtained from an electrocardiogram [7] [8]), and critical flicker fusion frequency (CFF) [4] [5].

Viewing distances: 2H (110 cm), 3H (165 cm), 4H (220 cm) and 6H (330 cm). Viewing distance was defined by screen-to-eye distance based on the height (H) of the screen.

Test room environment: Test room conditions were maintained at constant levels: ambient temperature of 23 °C, relative humidity of 50% RH, and illumination of 150 lx. Humidity, which affects blinking rates, was strictly controlled. Illumination was set at 150 lx to simulate the light level of the average Japanese living room.

234   K. Sakamoto et al.

Procedure: In 2H, 3H, 4H and 6H, to eliminate the order effect, 3 minutes' rest was imposed before, between and after the two 10-minute animation tasks. (The task time totaled 20 minutes). The tests were performed under two sets of conditions on two consecutive days, and under the two remaining sets of conditions on two consecutive days one week later. (It took 4 days in all for each person to perform the tests under the 4 sets of conditions). To eliminate the effect of habituation, the target horses for the animation task were changed every 2 sets of conditions. The results of a statistical analysis (2-factor analysis of variance: two-sided Tukey-Kramer test: among viewing distances and among subjects) for subjective assessment and physiological evaluation (blinking rates, heart rate variability (LF/HF), CFF) and task performance as measured by number of correct answers, were as follows. In addition, a *post hoc* test was performed to identify significant difference between the indices among these distances. The level of significance was set at $p = 0.05$.

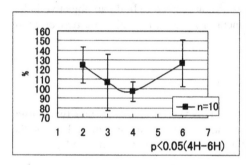

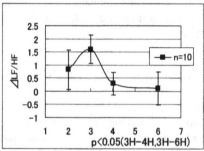

Fig.1. Relation between viewing distance and blinking rates (Experiment 1)

X Axis: Viewing distance (×H)
Y Axis: Relative blinking rates during rest after the test

Fig. 2. Relation between viewing distance and LF/HF (Experiment 1)

X Axis: Viewing distance (×H)
Y Axis: Relative level of LF/HF during rest after the test

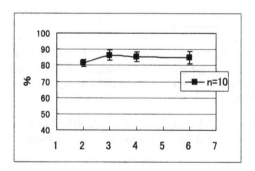

Fig. 3. Relation between viewing distance and task performance rates (Experiment 1)
X Axis: Viewing distance (×H)
Y Axis: Task performance rates of correct answers

2.2 Results

The results of a statistical analysis (2-factor analysis of variance: two-sided Tukey-Kramer test: among the viewing distances and among subjects) for Subjective assessment and physiological evaluation (blinking rates, heart rate variability (level of sympathetic nerve activity: LF/HF), CFF) and task performance as measured by number of correct answers, were as follows.

Subjective Assessment of Fatigue (SAF)
There was no significant difference in SAF among 2H, 3H, 4H or 6H.

Blinking rates: A significant difference was observed between the rate at 4H and that at 6H ($p < 0.05$)

LF/HF: A significant difference was observed between LF/HF in 3H and that in 4H ($p < 0.05$) and between LF/HF in 3H and that in 6H ($p < 0.05$) (Fig. 2).

Task performance rates of correct answers: There was no significant difference among the task performances in 2H, 3H, 4H and 6H (Fig. 3).

CFF: No significant difference was observed among CFF in 2H, 3H, 4H or 6H.

3 Experiment 2: Ordinary Viewing Test

The next experiment was an ordinary viewing test with content that was similar to everyday TV programs. The program comprised scenery, sport, drama, etc., with commercials sandwiched in between. For the purpose of not only evaluating character-reading ability but also inhibiting depression of arousal level due to sleep, on-screen text was included for 1 minute after each commercial. The task was to count the number of target characters in the on-screen text. However, to eliminate the effect of boredom caused by watching the same program several times, four different programs were prepared, with the same structure and pattern but with different scenes.

3.1 Methods

Subjects: Eight women in their 50s. Each person viewed the material under four sets of experimental conditions: 2H, 3H, 4H, and 6H.

Display Device: 42-inch plasma TV (PDP)

Measured items: same as Experiment 1.

Viewing distances: 2H (110 cm), (165 cm), 4H (220 cm) and 6H (330 cm)

Test room environment: same as Experiment 1.

Procedure: In 2H, 3H, 4H and 6H, 3 minutes' rest was imposed before, between and after the two 30-minute video films. (The task time totaled 60 minutes). The tests were performed under the two sets of conditions on two consecutive days, and under the two remaining sets of conditions on two consecutive days one week later. (It took each person 4 days in all to perform the tests under the 4 sets of conditions).

3.2 Results

The same statistical analysis was used same as for Experiment 1.

Subjective assessment of fatigue (SAF): There was no significant difference among SAF for 2H, 3H, 4H or 6H.

Blinking rates: A significant difference was observed between the rate in 2H and that in 3H ($p < 0.05$) and between the rate in 2H and that in 4H ($p < 0.05$) (Fig. 4).

LF/HF: A significant difference was observed between LF/HF in 3H and that in 6H ($p < 0.01$) and between LF/HF in 2H and that in 6H ($p < 0.05$) (Fig. 5).

Task performance rates of correct answers: Task performance rates of correct answers which peaked at 2H then decreased with increasing viewing distance. A

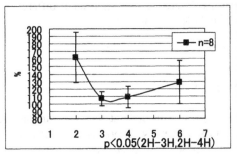

Fig.4. Relation between viewing distance and LF/HF (Experiment 2)
X Axis: Viewing distance (×H)
Y Axis: Relative blinking rates during rest after the test

Fig. 5. Relation between viewing distance and blinking rates (Experiment 2)
X Axis: Viewing distance (×H)
Y Axis: Relative level of LF/HF during rest after the test

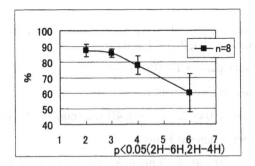

Fig. 6. Relation between viewing distance and task performance rates (Experiment 2)
X Axis: Viewing distance (×H)
Y Axis: Task performance rates of correct answers

significant difference was observed between task performances at 2H and those at 6H ($p < 0.05$) and between those in 2H and in 4H ($p < 0.05$) (Fig. 6).

CFF: No significant difference was observed among CFF for 2H, 3H, 4H or 6H.

4 Discussion

Experiment 1 investigated the relationship between viewing distance and blinking rate (relative to blinking rate while resting after the test) and the relationship between the viewing distance and level of sympathetic nerve activity (relative level of sympathetic nerve activity while resting after the test) in each subject. The curves for blinking rate formed a U-shaped curve that bottomed out at 3H or 4H in eight of the ten subjects, indicating that visual fatigue was lowest at a viewing distance of around 3H or 4H. However, the curves for LF/HF were convex U-shaped curves peaking at 3H in six of the ten subjects, indicating that 3H was the optimum viewing distance for causing a feeling of excitement or mental stress.

In Experiment 2, the curves for blinking rate formed a U-shaped curve that bottomed out at 3H or 4H in five of the eight subjects; and the curves for LF/HF were convex U-shaped curves peaking at 3H in four of the eight subjects. The results for the average curves obtained from these indices showed almost the same pattern as the results of those in Experiment 1.

In Experiments 1 and 2, the level of sympathetic nerve activity (LF/HF) at 3H was significantly greater than that at 4H or 6H, suggesting that the mental stress caused by a feeling of involvement and excitement at 3H is greater than at 4H and 6H. However, it is possible that the visual workload also influences the level of sympathetic nerve activity (LF/HF), since a significant difference was indicated in an earlier investigation [4] of the influence of residual images and luminosity. However, in this case, the results for blinking rates, which were lowest at 3H and 4H in Experiment 1 and Experiment 2, suggest that visual workload adds little to sympathetic nerve activity (LF/HF).

However, the correlation between the curve for blinking rates and the curve of sympathetic nerve activity varies according to the individual. Some participants whose curves for blinking rate were U shaped but whose sympathetic nerve activity curves were convex, and other participants had curves for blinking rate and sympathetic nerve activity that were both U-shaped. The source of these variations in individuals may be due to differences in visual acuity, preferred viewing distance and degree of involvement in the visual content or task. It will be necessary to investigate a control method for feeling of involvement and carry out additional experiments; and furthermore, to verify in detail the relationship between viewing distance and blinking rates and the relationship between the viewing distance and sympathetic nerve activity.

On the other hand, different results were obtained between the task performance rates of correct answers rates in Experiment 1 and Experiment 2. In Experiment 1, where the task was to count the number of target horses, the rates were almost the same among the four conditions, indicating that the targets could be seen equally well at any viewing distance. However, in Experiment 2, where the task was to count the number of target characters, there were significant differences between the rates in 2H and 4H, and in 2H and 6H, although the rates in 2H and 3H were almost the same. It would appear that a viewing distance of between 2H and 3H is the optimum distance for reading on-screen text.

In Experiment 1, the TV screen size in each participant's home varied from 26-inch to 42-inch types, with 9 persons using a CRT and 1 person using a PDP. It was found that the subjective optimum viewing distance, obtained by interview after the tests, was close to the daily usual viewing distance at home by eight of the ten subjects, and the subjective optimum viewing distance for 9 persons was between 3H and 4H.

In Experiment 2, the TV screen size in each participant's home varied from 20-inch to 42-inch types, with 5 persons using a CRT, 2 persons using a PDP and 1 person using an LCD display. It was found that the subjective optimum viewing distance, as obtained by the interview after the tests, was close to the daily habitual viewing distance at home by seven of eight subjects, with the subjective optimum viewing distance for 7 persons being between 3H and 4H: the same as in Experiment 1.

Concerning the subjective optimum viewing distance in Experiment 2 (ordinary viewing test), some participants felt the optimum viewing distance depended on content and viewing mood, although the subjective optimum viewing distance was clustered at 3H and 4H.

For example, the following comments were made by the subjects:

(1) When watching scenery, 2H and 3H are good, but it is hard to watch at 2H if there is a lot of motion in the video.
(2) Although 2H gave a strong feeling of involvement, this also resulted in visual fatigue like when watching movie in a theater.
(3) As for on-screen text, it is easy to read the characters at 2H and 3H, but it is hard to read them at 6H.
(4) The viewing distance that gives the greatest feeling of involvement is between 2H and 3H; however, the viewing distance that gives the most relaxed feeling is 4H.

Although it was shown, through the acute fatigue test and the ordinary viewing test, that blinking rates can be an effective index of visual fatigue, the results of the subjective assessment of fatigue showed wide variation. It appears that it is necessary to examine methods to improve the accuracy of the subjective evaluations.

Furthermore, considering both the graph of the relationship between viewing distance and blinking rates and the relationship between the viewing distance and the level of sympathetic nerve activity, there was a discrepancy between the viewing distance that gave less visual fatigue but a feeling of involvement and the viewing distance that gave less visual fatigue but a relaxed feeling.

We thus conclude that the optimum viewing distance may depend on the viewing style and content, since it was confirmed in Experiment 2 that the subjective optimum viewing distance also depends on content (ordinary viewing test).

Although the display size was fixed at 42 inches, and in this study only the viewing distance was varied, it will be necessary to investigate the effects of various display sizes and viewing distances on visual fatigue, as well as the relationship between feeling of involvement (which might increase with increasing TV screen size) and visual fatigue under different types of viewing styles, exemplified by the trend towards larger displays and the use of TVs as PC display devices.

5 Conclusions

Both experiments showed that at a certain distance, three to four times the display height, visual fatigue reached a minimum and that sympathetic nerve activity was highest at a distance of around 3H. These results indicate that a viewing distance characterized by less visual fatigue and a greater feeling of involvement may fall between those two distances. The indices adopted in this study have the potential to be effective evaluation indices for measuring visual fatigue, while taking into account the feeling of involvement with the action on the screen.

Acknowledgments. Thanks are due to the subjects who took part in these experiments for their many valuable comments.

References

1. Takahashi, M.: Subjective Visual Fatigue Symptoms of Visual Display Terminal Workers. J. Science of Labour 69(5), 193–203 (1993)
2. Mitsuhashi, T.: S Study of Measurement and Analysis Methods for CFF, and Observer Fatigue Caused by TV Watching. The Journal of Institute of Electronics, Information and Communication Engineers J77-A, 1768–1776 (1994)
3. Narita, N., Kanazawa, M., Okano, F.: Optimum Screen Size and Viewing Distance Ultra High Definition and Wide-Screen Images. The Journal of Institute of Image Information and Television Engineers 55(5), 773–780 (2001)
4. Okada, A., Yamashita, K.: Physiological Measurement of Visual Fatigue in the Viewers of Liquid Crystal Display and Plasma Display Panel. The Japanese Journal of Ergonomics society Kansai branch, 85–88 (2005)
5. Sakamoto, K., Aoyama, S., Matsuoka, M., Asahara, S., Ishihara, H., Yamashita, K., Okada, A.: A Relation between the Viewing Distance and the Visual Fatigue in the Watching Environment in a House. In: FIT 2007(Forum on Information Technology), pp. 291–294 (2007)
6. Sakamoto, K., Aoyama, S., Matsuoka, M., Asahara, S., Yamashita, K., Okada, A.: Effect of the Viewing Distance on Visual Fatigue for TV in a House. In: IDW 2007 Proceedings of The 14th International Display Workshops, vol. 3, pp. 2279–2282 (2007)
7. Ishibashi, K., Kitamura, S., Kozaki, T., Yasukouchi, A.: Inhibition of Heart Rate Variability during Sleep in Humans By 6700 K Pre-sleep Light Exposure. Journal of Physiological Anthropology 26(1), 39–43 (2007)
8. Ishibashi, K., Ueda, S., Yasukouchi, A.: Effects of Mental Task on Heart Rate Variability during Graded Head-Up Tilt. Journal of Physiological Anthropology. 18(6), 225–231 (1999)

Tactile Icon Design Using a Vibration Actuator in Mobile Devices

Meng-Dar Shieh and Zheng-Bin Wu

Department of Industrial Design, National Cheng Kung University
No. 1, University Rd., 701 Tainan City, Taiwan (R.O.C.)
mdshieh@hotmail.com, amouro@gmail.com

Abstract. This study presents three attributes for composing vibration patterns: *Rhythm*, *intensity difference*, and *continuous variation in intensity*. The intervals and the duration of the vibrations offer the elements of rhythm; intensity difference, and continuous variation in intensity, which add a second dimension to encoding the vibration pattern. Based on the attributes, fourteen vibration patterns were encoded according to four rhythm and four different intensity types. Rhythms are composed of two vibration durations and one interval. Intensity types are *High intensity*, *Low intensity*, *Strengthening*, and *Weakening*. The results achieve 78.57% accuracy for the overall vibration patterns. *Intensity differences* have a correct rate of 80.89%. The results for recognition of *rhythm types* are 90.97%. The result shows that people can really differentiate rhythms and intensity by using their tactile senses, but this has limitations. This research provides guidelines for vibration pattern design, and a third scenario for non-visual interaction.

Keywords: Vibration pattern, Tactile sense, Non-visual interaction.

1 Introduction

1.1 Background

In the past, tactile displays were either shape displays or relied on distributed vibration stimulation [1]. The sense of touch has been used very well by the blind from the Traditional Braille Display to the Virtual Braille Display [2].

The sense of touch offers the lay-user a third way to communicate with handheld devices. For instance, users cannot see their devices in some situations, e.g. when they are driving, in the theater or on the phone. However, once users become proficient, they would be able to use a tactile interface instead of GUI.

Recently, several tactile displays have been presented: Virtual Braille Display (VBD)[3] uses Lateral Skin Deformation; Audio-Haptic[4] synchronizes sound and vibration; while Tactons [5] improves interaction in a range of different areas.

1.2 Scope

This research tries to apply vibration patterns of general events to handheld devices. The actuator generates vibration patterns that can transmit unique messages and

S. Lee et al. (Eds.): APCHI 2008, LNCS 5068, pp. 240–247, 2008.

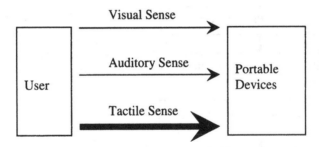

Fig. 1. A third way of communicating with handheld devices

interact with the user. Based on user's cognition of vibration limitations, the research have created a set of initial vibration patterns, to see if the patterns make sense, really transmit information, and whether the user can differentiate the patterns appropriately.

2 The Present Study

In the field of human computer interaction, researches on tactile user interfaces have been attracting increasing attention. Tactile user interfaces, both hardware and software, provide access to computer-based graphical information, taking advantage of humans' inherent tactile sense provided by the fingers and hands, as well as head or body movements.

In the past, tactile displays were either shape displays or relied on distributed vibration stimulation [1]. The Braille system is one kind of tactile display, which is an invaluable communication tool for the blind. Just as Louis Braille's reading method gave the blind access to the written word, refreshable Braille displays provide a way for the blind to interact with a computer interface.

The tactile sense has been applied very well to help the blind from the Traditional Braille Display to the Virtual Braille Display. It also offers many potential benefits for people in general when using handheld devices, such as PDAs, mobile phones, GPSes, or portable media players.

3 Method

This research explores the initial vibration pattern for a unique event like the ring tone of an ID. The authors have developed a set of initial patterns through a survey of users' requirements and relevant emotional reactions to specific events. After determining the users' cognition parameters, usability engineering methods are applied to concept generation to evaluate the prototype before user testing. They are also applied to the experiment period to analyze and compare the performance between basic vibration and vibration patterns.

3.1 Usability Engineering Methods

Depending on each stage of the product design, usability engineering methods can be divided into six parts: from the definition of requirements, through the concept,

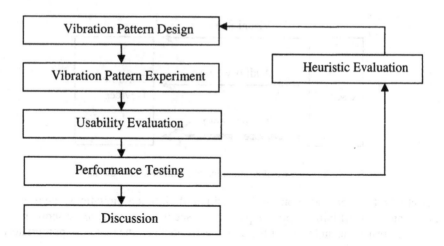

Fig. 2. Flowchart of Vibration Pattern Design

Fig. 3. Experimental equipment

design and implementation, to the end of testing and subsequent measurements. Each phase uses several methods in which different objectives can be estimated. Therefore, during the iterative design circle, multiple methods are often integrated to evaluate the system as a whole.

This research will adopt "heuristic evaluation" to evaluate the initial prototype. It uses "Performance Testing" to obtain the specific value of various fields, and for further statistical analysis.

3.2 Prototype

Nineteen Experimental mobile phones were chosen by specialists who evaluated 38 commercially available phones during the last two years. The experimental size is 106x47x18(mm).

The tangible vibration is produced by vibration actuator, and the actuator is activated by an USB experiment board (VM110) which is controlled by PC program (Fig 3).

3.3 Guideline for Designing Vibration Patterns

According to the results of previous research [6] and other studies in the literature, guidelines have been drawn up to follow when creating vibration patterns. These guidelines form part of the structural method used to add vibrations to mobile devices. There are three attributes required for making vibration patterns:

3.3.1 Rhythm
The results of experiments of preliminary study suggest three attributes of Rhythm. The shortest interval is at least 50 milliseconds, the shortest vibration duration is 100 milliseconds, and the minimum difference in the duration of the vibration, which can be recognized by most people, is no less than 100 milliseconds.

Make rhythms as different as possible. Putting different numbers of notes in each rhythm is very effective [7]. In this case, vibrations can be drawn on a vibration chart as different as possible. The length of each vibration pattern should also be different to make it more effective.

3.3.2 Intensity
Higher intensity makes it easier for the user to be aware of the vibrations. Differences in vibration intensity, which is generated by 1.3 volts and higher in this research, are difficult to recognize. This research easily separates the intensity into two parts to use in the vibration pattern: low intensity, which operates at less than 1.0 volts; and, high intensity, which operates at more than 1.3 volts.

3.3.3 Continuous Variation in Intensity
Music not only has rhythm separated by each note. Sometimes, it has to strengthen or weaken gradually (crescendo, decrescendo). Continuous variations in intensity can make people aware of the gradual changing intensity. We suggest that this kind of vibration is operated from a lower voltage level (e.g. 0.5 or 0.9 volts) and that minimum difference between the beginning and the ending voltages should be greater than 1.1 volts.

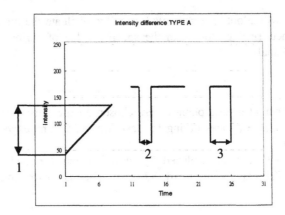

Fig. 4. Sample of vibration pattern. 1: Intensity; 2: Interval; 3: Duration. x-axis presents duration of vibration; y-axis presents intensity.

3.4 Initial Vibration Pattern Generation

Initial vibration patterns are generated based on the guideline. Four patterns are assembled by two levels of duration, which are 100 and 400 milliseconds and broken up into 50 milliseconds intervals. Each pattern has four different kinds of intensities except for the combination with two short durations. All fourteen initial vibration patterns are shown in Table 1.

This experiment provides initial results of the subjects' cognition for different vibration patterns. Surely, using a different number of beats for each rhythm should help to make the rhythms more distinguishable [8]. But this research focuses on whether the principle of vibration combination works. If it does, this guideline should help to determine the effective vibration patterns.

Table 1. Combination of fourteen vibration patterns

Durations	100,400	400,400	100,100	400,100
Low intensity				
High intensity				
Strengthening				
Weakening				

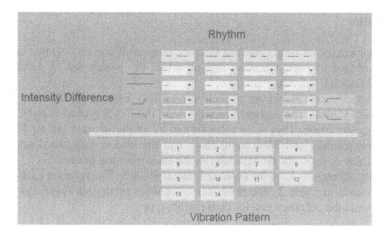

Fig. 5. Experimental interface

Fourteen vibration patterns, which have both the attributes of rhythm and intensity difference, are randomized in an experimental program interface (Fig 5).

Nine subjects participated and were requested to carry out this experiment in two stages. The first stage was to divide fourteen vibration patterns into four groups of rhythms. In the second stage, the vibration patterns have to be switched into the correct row of the corresponding intensity difference. Participants needed to wear an earphone to avoid the influence of the vibration sound because they may have recognized the vibration attributes by the sound. After filling out the form for each stage, the results were kept for analysis.

Fig. 6. Experimental environment

4 Results

The experimental data were collected from the number of correct cognition responses to the attributes of each vibration pattern, while the percentage of accuracy was calculated for each individual attribute.

The overall result shows an average recognition rate of 78.57% (the standard deviation is 26.24%). The best performances were those of Rhythms B and C while in a Low Intensity mode. They were recognizable by all participants but the Rhythm A in the Strengthening and Weakening mode had the lowest recognition rate at only 55.56%. Table 3 shows the recognition rate for each vibration pattern.

Intensity differences have the corrected rate of 80.09%. The rates for each Intensity type are shown in Table 3. The result for recognition of rhythm types was 90.97%. Table 2 shows the accuracy rate for each rhythm type.

Table 2. Accuracy of intensity and rhythm difference with standard deviations

Intensity			Rhythm		
Attribute	Mean(%)	Std. Deviation	Attribute	Mean(%)	Std. Deviation
Low intensity	88.89	22.05	100,400	91.67	12.50
High intensity	83.33	25.00	400,400	91.67	12.50
Strengthening	74.07	32.39	100,100	88.89	22.05
Weakening	74.07	32.39	400,100	91.67	17.68

Table 3. Overall recognition rate

	Rhythm A	Rhythm B	Rhythm C	Rhythm D
Low intensity	77.78%	100.00%	100.00%	77.78%
High intensity	77.78%	88.89%	77.78%	88.89%
Strengthening	55.56%	77.78%		66.67%
Weakening	55.56%	66.67%		88.89%

5 Discussion

When calculating individual attributes, the accuracy of the rhythm type had a higher recognition than the intensity difference. The accuracy of strengthening and weakening, which had continuous variations in intensity, was lower than that achieved by those composed only by low intensity (88.89%) and high intensity (83.33%).

According to the results, the intensity difference is the main factor for determining the vibration pattern. In this experiment, vibration patterns had only one vibration after the oscillating (strengthening and weakening) vibration, as little as one vibration in 100 milliseconds. Adding further vibrations of high intensity after strengthening, and vibrations of low intensity after weakening may provide an obvious clue to continuous variation in intensity.

References

1. Hayward, V., Cruz-Hernandez, J.M.: Tactile Display Device Using Distributed Lateral Skin Stretch. In: ASME International Mechanical Engineering Congress & Exposition (2000)
2. Lévesque, V., Pasqueror, J., Hayward, V., Legault, M.: Display of Virtual Braille Dots by Lateral Skin Deformation: Feasibility Study, vol. 2, pp. 132–149. ACM Press, New York (2005)
3. Luk, J., Pasquero, J., Little, S., MacLean, K., Lévesque, V., Hayward, V.: A role for Haptics in Mobile Interaction: Initial Design Using a Handheld Tactile Display prototype. In: SIGCHI conference on Human Factors in computing systems, ACM Press, Montréal, Québec, Canada (2006)
4. Chang, A., O'Sullivan, C.: Audio-haptic Feedback in Mobile Phones. In: CHI 2005 extended abstracts on Human factors in computing systems, ACM Press, Portland, OR, USA (2005)
5. Brewster, S., Brown, L.M.: Tactons: Structured Tactile Messages for Non-Visual Information Display. In: 5th Conference on Australasian user interface, Australian Computer Society, Dunedin, New Zealand (2004)
6. Wu, Z.B.: Novel Design of Tactile Icon Using Vibration Actuator in Mobile Devices. Thesis (2007)
7. Brewster, S.A.: Providing a Structured Method for Integrating Non-Speech Audio Into Human-Computer Interfaces, University of York, UK. PhD. (1994)
8. Brown, L.M., Brewster, S.A., Purchase, H.C.: Multidimensional Tactons for Non-Visual Information Display in Mobile Devices. In: MobileHCI 2006, ACM Press, Espoo, Finland (2006)

Design of 3D Mobile Phones and Application for Visual Communication

Min-Chul Park[1] and Jung-Young Son[2]

[1] Intelligent System Research Division, Korea Institute of Science and Technology,
39-1 Hawolgok-dong, Seongbuk-gu, Seoul, 136-791, Korea
`minchul@kist.re.kr`
[2] School of Computer and Communication Eng., Daegu University,
Jillyang, Gyeongsan, Gyeongbuk, 712-714, Korea
`sjy@daegu.ac.kr`

Abstract. This paper discusses realization of 3D mobile phones in respect of acquiring stereo images and displaying them. The parallel and radial types as 3D imaging layouts and autostereoscopic 3D displays are realized and their experimental results are compared. This paper proposes that when a mobile is equipped with a single camera the radial type has an advantage for taking stereo images satisfying fusible 3D images in a short distance because it has a permissible disparity in a arm length specially only. However, when a mobile phone is equipped with a pair of cameras the parallel-type has more advantage in that it offers a large fusible area in providing 3D depth cue to viewers relatively. A slanted parallax barrier generates viewing zone to the viewer without Moiré effect, but the complexity of the structure causes computational burden for image display. To testify 3D mobile visual communication stereo images are transmitted over CDMA mobile networks and the experiment is successfully accomplished keeping an acceptable image quality and 3D effects.

Keywords: 3D, Imaging, Displaying, Mobile, Phone, Communication.

1 Introduction

There is growing interests of displaying 3D images on the mobile phone for the purpose of gaming, visual communication and new service development. A mobile phone has strength in the networking capability and portability. Now it is becoming a personal mobile multimedia center for communication, broadcasting and internet use. Wired communication networks have been evolving into wireless ones. Simultaneously the typical telecommunication is changing in a way of using a monotone voice to multimedia. There has been much attention to 3D multimedia because it makes people experience similar environment where they belong to. However, the incompleteness of 3D imaging and displaying technology had been an obstacle to popularization.

Recent technological development is making another breakthrough. Some of 3D technology research groups or companies already presented few types of 3D mobile phones. Most of them are developed based on the parallel type in 3D imaging layouts and a parallax barrier or lenticular lens in 3D displaying method. Autostereoscopic

S. Lee et al. (Eds.): APCHI 2008, LNCS 5068, pp. 248–257, 2008.
© Springer-Verlag Berlin Heidelberg 2008

displays are realized for portability and convenience in use. Up to now the radial type layout is hardly realized though they have some strength in satisfying fusible 3D images taken in a short distance. The strength and weakness of each layout is discussed through the experimental results in Section 2.

3D mobile visual communication system requires to integrating technologies of 3D image display, processing and mobile networking. A slanted parallax barrier generates 3D viewing zone to the viewer without Moiré effect, but the complexity of the structure causes computational burden for image display. An autostereoscopic 3D display for mobile visual communication using the typical parallax barrier strip is exploited in our experiment considering computational capability of mobile phones and electric power consumption. To testify 3D mobile visual communication stereo images are transmitted over CDMA networks. This will be discussed in Section 3 and conclusion is followed in Section 4.

2   Comparison of 3D Imaging Systems for Mobile Phone Use

The parallel and radial types are two typical camera arrangements for taking multiview images in 3D imaging systems. In the parallel-type layout, cameras are aligned with a constant interval to have their optical axes parallel to each other in a camera array, but in the radial-type layout, they are aligned with a constant angle interval on an arc with a certain radius of curvature. In an aligning point of view, the radial type layout is relatively easier than the parallel type because it has a reference point as its center of the radius curvature. In the distortion point of view, both types are suffering from nonlinearity distortions caused by geometrical mismatches between left and right eye images in the stereo image pair. In case of the radial type layout, it is suffering from keystone distortion that caused by the size between a pair of stereo images projected on the screen. In case of the parallel type layout it is difficult to align cameras keeping their axes parallel to each other [1-5].

In our experiments, two types of camera arrangements are realized and the results are compared. In case of the radial type a mobile phone is supposed to have a single camera regarding typical mobile phones are equipped with a single camera. The radial type is appropriate for a single camera case because it provides the reference point when taking pictures. The parallel arrangement is somewhat immune to geometrical distortions such as nonlinearity and keystone if optical axes of stereo cameras are well aligned. The parallel type is more suitable for mobile phone use than the radial one because it offers relatively large fusible area in providing 3D depth cue to the viewers.

2.1   The Radial Arrangement

For the experiment of the radial arrangement HP iPAQ rw6100 series pocket PC as a mobile phone is used. The optimum distance of camera shifting in horizontal direction in the radial arrangement is approximated by the experiment. It turns about $1/30^{th}$ of the photographic distance for the case of the mobile phone. Fig. 1 shows the effect of the base distance between camera positions for left and right images for the case when the distance between camera and object is 21cm. When the base distance is 5mm, the parallax difference is too small to provide a perceivable depth, except a handle part. As shown in Fig. 1 (b) the entire cup provides a perceivable depth when the base distance is 10mm. The parallaxes in the handle part are too big to fuse when it is longer than 15mm as shown in Fig. (c) and (d). The same result is obtained with other objects.

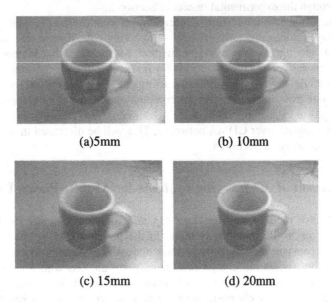

(a)5mm   (b) 10mm

(c) 15mm   (d) 20mm

Fig. 1. The effect of the base distance

In radial arrangement the object plane difference causes mainly the keystone distortion. It is caused by the differences in the vertical direction, y -axis between corresponding points in stereo images, and nonlinear magnification of images in the horizontal direction, x -axis. They make the images have a trapezoidal shape and mathematical fusing of stereo images impossible. Though a perspective distortion affects to the 3-D image human visual system can fuse the images as a 3-D image until the differences are within a certain limit. To restrict the distortion to a fusible limit by modifying the images requires satisfying the following relationships in Eq.1. It concludes that the image projected to viewers' eyes in radial photographic and projecting geometry becomes the same as that in parallel photographic and projecting geometry.

$$\frac{\sin \varphi_C}{\sin \varphi_P} = m\frac{z_C}{z_P} \text{ and } z_P^2 = mpz_C^2 / c \tag{1}$$

where, φ_C (φ_P), z_C (z_P), m , c and p are the half of left and right camera (projector) crossing angle, the camera (projector) distance from the focused plane parallel to the plane containing aperture centers of left and right cameras (projectors)screen, the size ratio of projected image to photographed image, and base distance between left and right cameras (projectors), respectively.

The permissible magnification difference is 5% [1]. It indicates that the image size differences of 8 pixels (320 X 0.05/2 for top and bottom) in vertical and 6 in horizontal direction are allowed for the mobile phone camera, in the display point of view. When object distance is far great than the focal length of the objective of a camera, the image of the object is appeared in the focal plane of the camera, i.e., the image magnification becomes inversely proportional to the object distance. This is the case for the camera employed because it has a very short focal length.When the object distance for left eye image is a, the permissible distance range for right eye image is calculated as $20a/21 \sim 20a/19$. If a equals to 1m the range becomes 952 ~ 105mm. It allows about 10cm room to move around. But when a becomes 10cm, the room is reduced to 1cm. This room will be too small to keep the range. Therefore, it would be better to choose a as big as possible in stereo photography with the mobile phone camera.

The allowable vertical direction shift between left and right images turned out to be 3 pixels of LCD display in the mobile phone, which has a pixel pitch of $180\ \mu m$. Fig. 2 shows the synthesized images by shifting left image 2, 3 and 4 pixels vertically. When the shift is 4 pixels, two images are hardly fused. It means that 3 pixels are the fusing limit. The pixel number is less than a half of the number from the magnification difference. This indicates that when the 5% magnification can be permissible only when the centers of two images are matched. When they are not matched the allowable magnification difference will be reduced.

Fig. 3 shows the synthesized stereo images for the case when left image is rotated 4, 5 and 6 degrees by pivoting its center. 5-degree is observed as the fusible limit. This

| (a) 2 pixels | (b) 3 pixels | (c) 4 pixels |

Fig. 2. Synthesized images of stereo images by shifting the center of left image vertically 2, 3 and 4 pixels

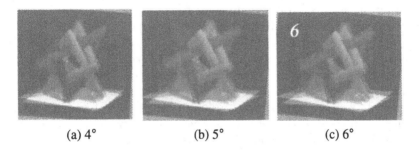

| (a) 4° | (b) 5° | (c) 6° |

Fig. 3. Synthesized images of stereo images when left image is rotated 4°, 5° and 6° in CCW direction

angle is equivalent to 9 pixels shift of left image to the vertical direction at the left and right ends of the image. Since the synthesized image is extended only 2/3 of the image area, the actual image shift is approximated as 6 pixels. This result is consistent with the previous results and it also informs that matching the image centers of left and right images is very important to extend the fusion range of the images.

In the case of the mobile phone with a single camera the radial type is more convenient for realizing stereo photography than the parallel type. Centering of the images by the view finder in the mobile phone in the radial type is easier than the aligning the optical axes in the parallel type.

The resolvable depth in stereo photography can be calculated by the following relationship [7];

$$N = \frac{2t\sqrt{s^2 - (\frac{2.44\lambda F}{D})^2}}{sD} \tag{2}$$

where N, t, s, D, λ and F are a number of resolvable depth, camera distance, pixel size of a camera, objective aperture diameter and focal length of the camera, and wavelength, respectively. In our experiment, when $t = 3cm$ (the photographic distance is assumed as 1m), $s = 4.5\mu m$, $D = 3.2mm$ and $F = 8mm$, N is calculated as 15.8, 12.5 and 2.5 for $\lambda = 0.4$, 0.55 and 0.7 μm, respectively. Since the N numbers cover almost entire distance range in the mobile phone, the depth resolution of the mobile phone photography will be very poor. The depth resolution will be further reduced as the resolution of the camera increases. The increasing resolution will reduce each pixel size and consequently the value in the root of Eq. 2 becomes smaller. As a result, the camera's depth resolution is reduced and sensible spectral range can be reduced due to the diffraction effect [6].

2.2 The Parallel Arrangement

The parallel arrangement has an advantage over geometrical distortions relatively if optical axes of stereo cameras are aligned in parallel. The parallel type is more suitable for the small sized display than the radial one because it offers relatively large fusible area in providing 3D depth cue to the viewers.

Taking a pair of stereo image with a single camera requires a shifting according to the horizontal axis in the parallel arrangement. The parallel translation shifts the object image position in the view finder accordingly. This makes the visual comparison of the object image position difficult. Furthermore, small changes in photographing distance and camera position in the process of shifting can result unacceptable differences between left and right images. Therefore, the parallel type has weakness when a single camera is used. Fig. 4 shows schematic diagram for aligning optical axes and realized a pair of stereo camera in our experiment. Table 1 compares 3D imaging systems through the obtained experimental results.

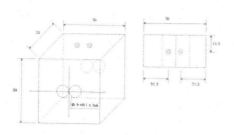

(a) Schematic diagram for aligning optical axes   (b) Realized stereo camera

Fig. 4. Schematic diagram and Realization of a pair of stereo cameras

Table 1. 3D imaging systems and comparison for mobile phone use

3D imaging system	Comparison	
	Strength	Weakness
Radial - type layout	1. No need to align optical axes 2. Relatively easy to take stereo images with an acceptable difference in case of a single camera	1. Provides relatively small 3D fusible area than the parallel type 2. Relatively suffers from keystone distortion than the parallel type
Parallel - type layout	1. Provides relatively large 3D fusible area offers 3D depth cue than the radial type 2. Relatively somewhat immune to geometrical distortions than the radial type	1. Requires aligning of optical axes of a pair of cameras 2. Relatively difficult to take stereo images with an acceptable difference in case of a single camera

3 Comparison of 3D Display Systems for Mobile Phone Use

A parallax barrier strip autostereoscopic 3D displays is constructed by placing a barrier of lines in front or back of an LCD display device. Parallax barrier method provides mobile phone viewers with an acceptable 3D sense at a low cost. However, this typical method suffers from Moiré effect. A slanted parallax barrier generates viewing zone to the viewer without Moiré effect, but the complexity of the structure causes computational burden for image display. Autostereoscopic display is the most preferred one as a 3D display for its convenience because it does not wear any glasses. Users of the mobile phone with a 3D display and imaging system can go through autostereoscopic effect by changing the position of the phone to find out viewing zone, instead of using a tracking system.

In our experiment, two types of 3D display systems are realized to testify 3D mobile applications. Software programs for supporting 3D display system are developed using Embedded Visual C++ 4.0 (VCCE) and VCCE IDE(Integrated Development Environment). The VCCE can create and debug application software for devices running Windows CE and is compatible with Pocket PC. In our experiment PDA type mobile phone is used and it is working under the Windows CE environment.

3.1 Realization Based on Typical Parallax Barrier

An autostereoscopic effect is achieved by making stereo images to interleave portions of left and right eye images in appropriate positions on the display. In our experiments, a 3D image display system is realized using the parallax barrier method on the mobile phone with QVGA (320 by 240) resolution. Generation of an acceptable 3D sense is tested by human subject evaluation through the realized 3D image display for still and moving images. The mobile phone is equipped with touch panel. In our experiment, parallax barrier is formed on the transparent film and it is put on the touch panel. The approach has an advantage over reducing a gap between TFT-LCD panel and the barrier. The gap affects image brightness and separation of left and right images to the viewer's eye. The short gap provides the brighter and clear 3D effect. 2-D/3-D switchable parallax barrier is a good solution for displaying 2-D and 3-D images in the requirement.

3.2 Realization Based on Slanted Parallax Barrier

To display the stereoscopic image pair taken by the mobile phone without Moirés, the image pair has to go through step-wise shifting each image line of each view image, combining the pair and stretching the combined image for display. After taking left and right images, the software creates a combined image of left and right images with images created at each step of the image processing. To view the stereoscopic image, it is only necessary to attach a viewing zone forming optics.

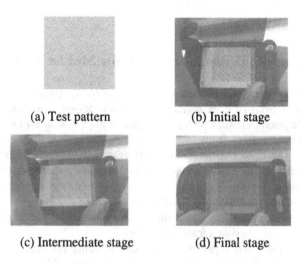

(a) Test pattern   (b) Initial stage

(c) Intermediate stage   (d) Final stage

Fig.5. Aligning Procedure of Optical Plate

Fig. 5 shows the process of taking stereo photograph, image processing and displaying. For the display, a detachable parallax barrier is put on the mobile phone. The barrier is attached only when displaying 3-D image. Since some of mobile phones are equipped with touch panel, a firmly attached viewing zone forming optics on the top of the display panel will reduce the sensitivity of touch panel. The detachable structure allows 2-D/3-D switchable screen without interfering the sensitivity. Table 2 compares features of 3D display systems through the obtained experimental results. Typical type has strength in structural simplicity but it induces Moiré effect, but the slanted type has structural complexity without Moiré effect [5].

Table 2. 3D Display systems and comparison for mobile phone use

3D display	Parallax barrier type	Comparison	
		Strength	Weakness
Autostereo-scpic	Typical	Structural simplicity	Moiré effect exists
	Slanted	No Moiré effect	Structural complexity

3.3 Application for 3D Mobile Visual Communication

To testify 3D mobile visual communication stereo images are captured and transmitted to a server terminal in real time as shown in Fig. 6. External stereo cameras are used in our experiment because mobile phones in daily use are not equipped with stereo cameras up to now. Transmitted images are compressed using JPEG Codec module and the optimized condition of compression ratio is determined by QoS(Quality of Service) function. Allowable transmission bandwidth of CDMA network is 128kbps and compression ratio is determined by perception of 3D effect and image brightness by subject evaluation. General description of the process is

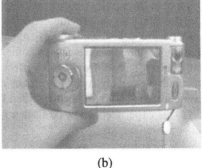

(a)   (b)

Fig. 6. (a) shows image processing at the sever terminal, and (b) shows stereo images are successfully transmitted to the mobile phone. Parallax barrier film is put on the screen and some Moiré effect is observed on the screen because it adopted a typical parallax barrier type.

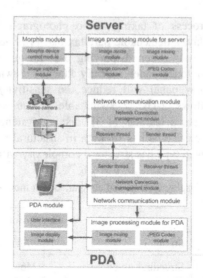

Fig. 7. General description of 3D mobile visual communication

described in Fig. 7. In our case the compression ratio is determined around 20%, and left and right images are transmitted separately to avoid image deterioration. Combining the images for 3D display is processed at the mobile phone.

4 Conclusion

This paper presented the design of imaging and displaying of 3D mobile phones.

Visual communication is tested for the CDMA networks making use of 3D mobile phones. In the design of imaging of 3D mobile phones the parallel and radial types realized and experimental results are compared. The radial type has an advantage for taking stereo images satisfying fusible 3D images in a short distance with the condition that the mobile is equipped with a single camera. The parallel-type provides a large fusible area in providing 3D depth cue to viewers relatively. The slanted parallax barrier generates viewing zone to the viewer without Moiré effect, but the complexity of the structure causes computational burden for image display. Typical parallax barrier suffers from Moiré effect, but the structure is relatively simpler than the slanted type. Stereo images are transmitted over CDMA mobile networks and the experiment is successfully accomplished keeping an acceptable image quality and 3D effects. This experiment shows a further application of 3D mobile phones beyond 2D visual communication.

References

1. Takehiro, I. (ed.) : Fundamentals of 3D Images :NHK Broadcasting Technology Research Center. pp. 72–73 (1995)
2. Woods, A., Docherty, T., Koch, R.: Image Distortions in Stereoscopic Video Systems. In: Proc. of SPIE, vol. 1915, pp. 36–48 (1993)

3. Rule, J.T.: The Shape of Stereoscopic Images. J.Opt. Soc. Am. 31, 124–129 (1941)
4. Saunders, B.G.: Stereoscopic Drawing by Computer-is It Orthoscopic? Appl. Opt. 7, 1459–1504 (1968)
5. Son, J.Y., Gruts, Y.N., Kwack, K.D., Cha, K.H., Kim, S.K.: Stereoscopic Image Distortion in Radial Camera and Projector Configurations. OSA 24(3), 643–650 (2007)
6. Son, J.Y., Saveljev, V.V., Cha, K.H., Kim, S.K., Park, M.C., Jang, S.H.: Stereo-Photography with Hand Phone: SPIE Optics East, vol. 6392(05), pp.1–8, (2006)

A Comparative Evaluation of User Preferences for Mobile Chat Usable Interface

Daniel Kuen Seong Su[1] and Victoria Siew Yen Yee[2]

[1] The University of Nottingham, Malaysia
daniel.su@nottingham.edu.my
[2] Financial Services, Accenture, Malaysia
victoria.yee@accenture.com

Abstract. This paper aims to investigate user preferences for mobile chat usable interfaces. We have designed graphical-based usable interfaces for mobile chat to ease the navigation control for efficient tracking of specific messages in a long chat archive We have conducted a comparative evaluation between text-based and graphical-based usable interfaces for mobile chat systems. The statistical research outcomes exemplified that there were significant differences on user preferences between text-based and graphical-based systems with regards to gender, education level, and usage frequency of one-to-one mobile chat systems. Additionally, the experimental evaluation results have highlighted the potential use of graphical-based usable interfaces for mobile chat systems that have significantly gained user preferences and were well perceived as usable interfaces among the test subjects.

Keywords: User interface design, Mobile chat, Evaluation.

1 Introduction

User interface defined in [1] embodied both physical and communicative aspects of input and output, or interactive activity. Hence, a good user interface should be grounded on usability issues discussed in [2], [3] to possess usable interfaces that are attributed to user friendliness, ease of navigation, learnability, well integration of functions, consistency and simplicity of design. Usability has become one of the main issues when designing usable interfaces that meet diversify users' requirements. Nevertheless, usability has come a realisation that usability may no longer be the only, or the even the main determinant of user satisfaction [4], [5]. User interfaces have been given to "look and feel", and its capability to engage the users in fulfilling interaction and generating affective responses [6]. In addition, aesthetic design on user interfaces influences user preferences [7]. The aesthetic quality design affects user attitude, and plays an important role in its marketplace success [8]. User interfaces that demonstrate its beauty attributes potentially attract more positive dimensions to individual and to other users [9], [10]. Moreover, initial research suggested a correlation between aesthetic quality of user interfaces, its perceived usability, and increased user preferences, and directly promoted user satisfaction [5].

S. Lee et al. (Eds.): APCHI 2008, LNCS 5068, pp. 258–265, 2008.

2 Related Work

Principally, communication in mobile chat is carried out in turns. Turns are lines(s) of text sent by a particular participant to be viewed by others [11]. Linear progression of turns forms an archive of conversation or chat history. The primitive user interface of these designs suffers from incoherent conversation due to poor arrangement of turns. The simultaneous participation of multiple conversations in one chat room leads to confusion and high repetition rate of misapprehension [11]. Graphical chat systems have been proposed to rectify these shortcomings. Chat Circle [12], [13] manipulated basic geometry and unique colour to represent each participant, and as a result it reduced the disorder of turns. Geyer et al. [14] and Vronay et al. [11], on the other hand, rearranged conversational layout to maximise screen display and to form comprehensible archive of turns. Despite their effort, none are widely adopted in the commercial arena. An evaluation of the interface reveals that these new designs do not resemble the conservative interface that users are accustomed to. This observation reveals the resistance to learn and familiarise with the new interface. This can be one reason why graphical-based mobile chat systems are poorly received. Furthermore, chat system that depends on text as the sole communicative element lacks in the ability to convey non-verbal cues presented in face-to-face communication. Thus, this paper aims to enrich the chatting experience by reducing keypad navigation to improve user satisfaction and assisting messages tracking. We incorporate avatars and emoticon in user identification and human embodiment to facilitate ease of understanding of the messages' contents. Finally, we have conducted an initial pilot study to evaluate user preferences between text-based and graphical-based for mobile chat systems.

3 Mobile Chat Usable Interfaces

In the effort to constantly maintain awareness of current spatial location in the chat archive, the display screen is divided into two halves. The first half displays the chat archive and the second half exhibits the specific message from a particular chatter corresponding to the node defined. Fig. 1a depicts the chat archives and turns. Chatters are assigned a horizontal bar which is labelled with the chatters' pseudo name and contains node(s) that signified the turns send in a chronological order. When chatters send a turn, the new message is represented as a black rectangular drawn after the last node in the horizontal bar assigned to the sender, and the yellow vertical bar is moved to highlight the last node. The blue bar that is controllable by the chatters can traverse the chat archive in bi-directional and select a specific node. The messages are corresponding to the node displays at the second half of the screen. Each turn displays begin with a label of the senders' avatar, pseudo name and the sending date-time in the message. For a long turn that exceeds the space allocated for the display, a scroll bar is automatically inserted to render the space for the incorporation of long turn such as in Fig. 1b.

The strategic placement of frequently used functionalities organised in menus facilitates chatters to access and utilise these commands with ease as shown in Fig. 2a. Functions related to chatting such as "Send Message," "Pause Chat," "End Chat," "Join Chat" and initiates a "New Chat" are classified under a menu labelled as "Chat." The options to view the selected chatter profile include "View User Profile," "View

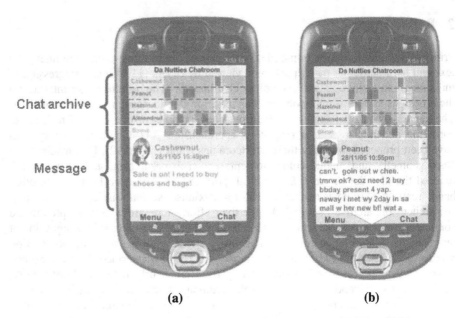

Chat archive

Message

(a)   (b)

Fig. 1a. 5 chatters with non-scrollable turn   **Fig. 1b.** 5 Chatters with scrollable turn

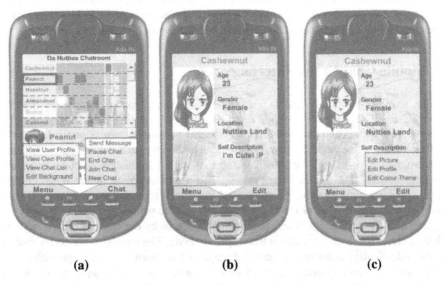

(a)   (b)   (c)

Fig. 2a. Menu   **Fig. 2b.** Chatter's profile   **Fig. 2c.** Edit chatter's profile

Own Profile," "View Chat List" and "Edit Background" images are categorised as "Menu." By constructing the menu with the consideration of usage frequency, highly utilised commands can be made apparent and easily accessible to the chatters. Consequently, usability of the system is considerably enhanced by filtering the higher priority from the list of lower priority information. This design proposed to support complex human expressions, specifically behavioural cues which add values to the interpretation of the messages as the chatters' mood can be evidently perceived through the use of expressive avatars as illustrated in Fig. 2b. We designed a "profile" feature to allow chatters to specify the details about their age, gender, location and brief self description to be viewed by the other participants as shown in Fig. 2c.

4 Pilot Study

Mobile Chat Prototypes. The chosen local mobile chat service was Maxis SMS Chat which uses Short Messaging Service (SMS) as the underlying communication protocol for messages exchange. Maxis SMS Chat is referred as a text-based mobile chat system (TMC), and our proposed system as a graphical-based mobile chat system (GMC). The notable difference between TMC and GMC was that the user interface design of TMC utilised text as the sole element; whereas GMC employed a myriad of text and graphics, background images and appropriate avatars, emoticons and colours in the interface design.

Demography of Test Subjects. Teenagers were chosen as the target sample for this study, and it has been noted as the forerunners in the use of mobile chat systems. Four similar surveys have been carried out in different times and locations to take into account the availability of the test subjects. The experiment involved 53 test subjects with ages ranging from 15 to 21, including 25 females and 28 males. To distinguish participants in the sample based on the education level, 27 test subjects were selected from The University of Nottingham, Malaysia, and 26 from a local secondary school in the district of Klang Valley, Malaysia.

Experiments' Procedures. The procedures began with a briefing, highlighting the aims of the experiment, followed by testing and evaluation of TMC and GMC. Test subjects were required to explore the user interfaces and functionalities of TMC and GMC prototypes for an hour, and filled in the questionnaires at the end. The questionnaire used was adapted and modified from [15] in order to enhance the validity of this study.

5 Findings, Results, and Discussions

Hypothesis Evaluation. There were three hypotheses formulated as initial presumptions on the sample's preferences and demography profile between TMC and GMC as documented in Table 1. The hypotheses were formulated to test and assess at 95% (0.05) significance level as to fulfil the research objectives. Hence, hypotheses H_1, H_2, and H_3 were analysed via independent sample t-test to assess. The variable set to examine the acceptability of H_3 was a mean of both SMS and Multimedia Messaging Service (MMS) usage frequency scores which logically represented the value for of one-to-one mobile chat (OMC) usage frequency.

User Preferences with Regards to Gender. The research results tabulated from the data analysis highlighted three significant differences related to preferences on both TMC and GMC based on gender. The need for technical support in the usage of

Table 1. Research hypothesis statements

H#	Narration
H₁	There is a significant difference on user preferences between TMC and GMC among test subjects with regards to gender.
H₂	There is a significant difference on user preferences between TMC and GMC among test subjects in secondary and tertiary education.
H₃	There is a significant difference on user preferences between TMC and GMC with regards to usage frequency of one-to-one mobile chat (OMC) services among test subjects.

GMC was significantly different (p< 0.05) between both gender, with males ($\bar{x}$ =4.57) needing less support as compared to females ($\bar{x}$ =4.08). This finding can be justified by overall computing literacy of male inclusive of mobile systems was self-perceived to be higher than female which aligned to the study reported by Alshare et al., [16]. Another plausible explanation is the actual computer literacy between both sexes differs with males being more knowledgeable in computing [17]. Nonetheless, results based on the highly scored mean with both rated above four, it can be safely concluded that both sexes discovered GMC was easy to use and needless of technical support. Perception on various functionality in GMC was well integrated differed significantly (p=0.013) between female ($\bar{x}$ =4.20) and male ($\bar{x}$ =4.61). Although the overall rating on the integration of functions for GMC was high (above 4.20), females rated the integration lower in comparison with males. This may be attributed to the general less positive attitudes in computing among females as reported by Scott [18]. The final significant difference (p =0.013) in the light of gender was perceived aesthetical value of GMC user interface with the females ($\bar{x}$ =4.60) scored higher than males ($\bar{x}$ =4.11). The research outcome was consistent with the findings and results from [17] which reported on the user preferences of same gender user interface design, specifically, female respondents are in favour of the user interface which is designed by the same gender. The opinions from both sexes to the aesthetical value of GMC were very encouraging. In short, H₁ experienced rejection of null hypothesis as there were significant differences in the preferences between TMC and GMC with regards to gender in terms of necessitate of technical support, functions integration and aesthetical assessment on the user interface of GMC.

User Preferences with Regards to Education Level. The analysis result underlined a significant difference (p=0.012) between the secondary and tertiary students on the effect of TMC user interfaces on usage desire with secondary school students ($\bar{x}$ =1.35) scored lower than tertiary students ($\bar{x}$ =1.81). The differences highlighted that text-based mobile chat systems did not promote usage in the less computer savvy students who have less computing access and knowledge as compared to the tertiary students who mostly major in computer science and information technology. The significant difference (p=0.015) was regarded to education level stressed that secondary students ($\bar{x}$=4.58) preferred to use GMC to tertiary students ($\bar{x}$=4.15). The encouragement of usage among secondary students can be contributed to the graphical design and coding of GMC which simplified the understanding of the chat systems. This argument can be further proven by a significant difference (p=0.028) that explained secondary students ($\bar{x}$=4.65) found GMC was easier to learn than tertiary students ($\bar{x}$=4.22). Hence, H_2 manifested rejection of null hypothesis on user preferences with regarded to the usage frequency based on user interfaces of TMC, usage frequency of GMC, and learnability of GMC. The initial findings suggested that graphical-based mobile chat systems promote ease of learning and increase usage frequency among the less computer literate students.

User Preferences with Regards to OMC Usage Frequency. The statistical research outcomes shed lights in significant differences on user preferences for OMC usage frequency. The significant difference (p=0.055) between the less frequent ($\bar{x}$=1.48) and frequent ($\bar{x}$=1.88) on TMC was being not very cumbersome to use. These findings revealed that frequent interaction with accustomed interface although in different platform increased the comfortability in usage. The significant difference (p=0.001) between the less frequent ($\bar{x}$=1.14) and frequent ($\bar{x}$=1.66) test subjects on the impact of TMC user interfaces to the ease of navigation has been detected with less frequent test subjects reported that TMC was harder to navigate. In particularly, user interface that has been familiarised by the test subjects enhanced the ease of navigation. The mean difference between the less frequent ($\bar{x}$=4.14) and frequent ($\bar{x}$=4.53) was significant (p=0.010) on GMC. The frequent test subjects agreed that GMC was less complex, perhaps due to the higher exposure on mobile chat systems that offered them an advantage in comprehending the logic of the interface design. The result patterns indicated that a significant difference (p=0.034) between the frequent ($\bar{x}$=4.53) and less frequent ($\bar{x}$=4.14) on the consistency of GMC. While both groups were in the opinion that GMC was highly consistent, the frequent test subjects scored higher, which may be attributed to the richer experience with OMC that led to sufficient understanding and knowledge for the features and functionalities on GMC systems. Although the significant difference (p=0.044) between less frequent ($\bar{x}$=4.43) and frequent ($\bar{x}$=3.97) on the learnability of GMC was expected, the outcomes that underscored the less frequents found GMC easier to learn was unforeseen. A possible justification may be due to the stronger resistant from the frequent test subjects to relearn the well accustomed text-based user interfaces and adjust themselves to the novel concept of graphical-based usable interfaces for mobile chat systems. Similarly to the significant difference on TMC was graded being easy to navigate, the frequent test subjects ($\bar{x}$=4.59) found GMC were significant (p=0.028) easier to navigate as compared to the less frequent ($\bar{x}$=4.29). The importance of establishing understanding on the user interfaces of mobile chat systems that enhances the users experience is the ease of navigation. Initial findings suggested that knowledge of user interfaces for OMC relatively increases the navigation ease in both text-based and graphical-based mobile chat systems. Concisely, H_0 is rejected as the user preferences between TMC and GMC based on the usage frequency of OMC were differed. Higher interaction and exposure of OMC promote ease of use and ease of navigation on mobile chat systems that implement accustomed user interfaces. Frequent usage of OMC ensued in better comprehension on the design logic of the novel applications which facilitates ease of navigation. Nonetheless, frequent OMC test subjects were not as flexible as the less frequent counterpart in relearning the new user interface design due to resistant of change.

6 Implications and Conclusions

Statistical research outcomes have evidently exemplified the pivotal aspects and benefits gained by employing graphical-based usable interface design for mobile chat systems. The hypotheses evaluations have manifested rejection of the null hypotheses in H_1, H_2 and H_3. Specifically in the aspect of gender, female chatters should receive higher attention in being briefed about the technical issues of GMC as they may not be as computer savvy as compared to the males [16], [19]. Furthermore, thorough understanding of the benefits and functionalities of GMC alters the less positive attitude of female chatters to that of confident [19]. In the light of the same gender designers' preferences, the user interface of GMC should be reviewed by male designers to avoid interface that is biased to female [19]. In opposition, computer literacy of chatters plays a vital role in promoting or limiting the usage of both TMC and GMC. The findings and results patterns indicated that teenagers with lesser exposure to computing prefer usage of the graphical-based to text-based as they found GMC was easier to learn. Hence, graphical coding of information to enhance simplicity of design should be given sufficient consideration in the design of mobile chat systems which target less computer literate chatters. Higher exposure on OMC applications that subsequently sharpen the knowledge in mobile usage domain affects the perception and experience in the interaction with other similar or novel mobile chat systems. Text-based mobile chat systems that packed messages onto the small screen display in chronological order as long chat archive was perceived to be cumbersome to use and hinder navigation by less experienced OMC test subjects. As a result, text-based designers should focus on the navigation of the long chat archive and ease of use to appeal to less experience chatters. As for the graphical-based designers, the focal point is to educate the less experience chatters by means of system walkthrough to improve the understanding of the systems and to erase the usage of doubts.

References

1. Marcus, A.: Dare we define user-interface design? Interaction COLUMN: Fast forward 9(5), 19–24 (2002)
2. ISO/IEC, 9241-11 Ergonomic Requirements for Office Work with Visual Display Terminals (VDT)s – Part 11 Guidance on Usability 1998: ISO/IEC 9241-11: 1998 (E) (1998)
3. Nielsen, J.: Usability Engineering. Morgan Kaufman Publisher, Academic Press (1993)

4. De Angeli, A., Lynch, P., Johnson, G.I.: Pleasure versus efficiency in user interfaces: Towards an involvement framework. In: Green, W.S., Jordan, P.W. (eds.) Pleasure with products: Beyond usability, pp. 97–111. Taylor & Francis, London (2002)
5. Tractinsky, N., Shoval-Katz, A., Ikar, D.: What is beautiful is usable. Interacting with Computers 13(2), 127–145 (2000)
6. De Angeli, A., Sutcliffe, A., Hartmann, J.: Interaction, Usability and Aesthetics: What Influences Users' Preferences? In: Proceedings of the 6th Conference on Designing Interactive Systems, University Park, Pennsylvania, USA, June 26-28, pp. 271–280. ACM Press, New York (2006)
7. Norman, D.A.: Emotional Design: Why We Love (or Hate) Everyday Things. Basic Books, New York (2004)
8. Bloch, P.: Seeking the ideal form: Product design and consumer response. Journal of Marketing 59, 16–29 (1995)
9. Dion, K., Berscheid, E., Walster, E.: What is beautiful is good. Journal of Personality and Social Psychology 24, 285–290 (1972)
10. Meiners, M.L., Sheposh, J.P.: Beauty or brains: Which image for your mate? Personality and Social Psychology 3, 262–265 (1977)
11. Vronay, D., Smith, M., Drucker, S.: Alternative interfaces for chat. In: Proceedings of the 12th Annual ACM Symposium on User Interface Software and Technology, North Carolina, USA, pp. 19–26 (1999)
12. Viegas, F., Donath, J.: Chat circles series: Explorations in designing abstract graphical communication interfaces. In: Proceedings of the Conference on Designing Interactive Systems (DIS): Processes, Practices, Methods, and Techniques, London, England, pp. 359–369 (2002)
13. Viegas, F., Donath, J.: Chat circles. In: Proceedings of SIGCHI Conference on Human Factors in Computing Systems: The CHI is the Limit, Pennsylvania, USA, pp. 9–16 (1999)
14. Geyer, W., Witt, A.J., Wilcox, E., Muller, M., Kerr, B., Brownholtz, B., Millen, D.R.: Chat spaces. In: Proceedings of the Conference on Designing Interactive Systems (DIS): Processes, Practices, Methods, and Technique, Cambridge, USA, pp. 333–336 (2004)
15. Brooke, J.: SUS: A Quick and Dirty Usability Scale. In: Jordan, P.W., Thomas, B., Weerdmeester, B.A., McClelland, A.L. (eds.) Usability Evaluation in Industry. Taylor and Francis, London (1996)
16. Alshare, K., Grandon, E., Miller, D.: Antecedents of computer technology usage: Considerations of the technology acceptance model in the academic environment. Journal of Computing Sciences in Colleges 19(4), 164–180 (2004)
17. ISO/IEC JTC1 SC36.: Abstract collaborative workplace conceptual architecture contribution. [Online] (2004) (accessed on November 18, 2005), WWW URL: http://collab-tech.jtc1sc36.org/doc/SC36_WG2_N0077.pdf
18. Scott, V.A.: Why are girls under represented? Ten years on. Journal of the Australian Educational Computing 11(1) (1999)
19. Straub, K.: Much ado about sex and web sites (2005) (accessed on 27th March 2006), WWW URL https://www.humanfactors.com/downloads/aug05.asp

The Impact of Multimedia Extensions for Multimedia Applications on Mobile Computing Systems

Jong-Myon Kim

School of Computer Engineering and Information Technology,
University of Ulsan, Ulsan, Korea, 680-749
jongmyon.kim@gmail.com

Abstract. Multimedia is a key element in human-computer interaction systems. Multimedia applications, however, are among the most dominant computing workloads driving innovations in high performance and low power imaging systems. Parallel implementations of multimedia applications mostly focus on the use of parallel computers. Modern general-purpose processors, however, have employed multimedia extensions (e.g., MMX, VIS, MAX, AltiVec) or subword parallel instructions to their instruction set architectures to improve the performance of multimedia. This paper quantitatively evaluates the impact of multimedia extensions on multiprocessor systems to exploit subword level parallelism (SLP) in addition to data level parallelism (DLP). Experimental results for a set of multimedia applications on a representative multiprocessor array shows that MMX (a representative Intel's multimedia extension) achieve an average speedup ranging from 3x to 5x over the same baseline multiprocessor array. MMX also outperforms baseline in both area efficiency (a 13% increase) and energy consumption (a 73% decrease), resulting in better component utilization and sustainable battery life. These results demonstrate that MMX is a suitable candidate for mobile multimedia computing systems.

Keywords: Mobile multimedia computing systems, Multimedia extensions, Multiprocessor arrays, Parallel processing.

1 Introduction

Advances in low cost, high resolution imagers and displays have enabled a new generation of mobile electronic products. Yet strict size, weight, power, and cost constraints of this market segment are reshaping the processing requirements for these new devices. Reductions in power requirements are as important as improved performance. Architectural departures from existing embedded processors can be explored, as long as significant performance and efficiency improvements can be delivered across a reasonable set of applications (e.g., graphics generation, video compression, and speech processing) [1].

The increasing availability of parallel computers makes parallelizing these tasks an attractive option. Modern general-purpose microprocessors (GPPs), however, have included multimedia extensions (MMX [2], SSE [3], MAX-2 [4], VIS [5], AltiVec [6]) or subword parallel instructions to their instruction set architectures (ISAs) to

S. Lee et al. (Eds.): APCHI 2008, LNCS 5068, pp. 266–275, 2008.

improve the performance for multimedia applications with little added cost to the processors. These extensions exploit subword parallelism by packing several small data elements (e.g., 8-bit pixels) into a single wide register (e.g., 32-, 64-, and 128-bit) while processing these separate elements in parallel, shown in Fig. 1.

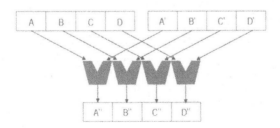

Fig. 1. An example of multimedia extensions (or subword parallel instructions)

Researchers have explored these multimedia extensions on a single general-purpose microprocessor whereas this paper quantitatively evaluates the impact of the multimedia extensions on multiprocessor systems. Since chip size and battery life are as critical for mobile multimedia systems as performance, this paper evaluates and contrasts MMX (a representative Intel multimedia extension) and baseline in terms of system area efficiency and energy consumption in addition to processing performance. The evaluation using application simulation and technology modeling shows that MMX on a representative multiprocessor array achieves a speedup ranging from 3x to 5x (an average of 3.7x) over the same baseline performance. MMX also decreases energy consumption from 67% to 80% while improving area efficiency from 6% to 22% over the baseline version. These result in better component utilization and sustainable battery life, respectively, for mobile multimedia computing systems.

2   Related Research

Numerous research groups and individuals have addressed the effectiveness of multimedia extensions for imaging applications on general-purpose processors. For example, Ranganathan *et al.* [7] analyzed the performance of image- and video-processing applications on an UltraSPARC processor with and without the VIS media extensions. They observed that the conventional superscalar instruction-level parallel (ILP) techniques provided 2.3x to 4.5x performance improvement, and the VIS extensions provided an additional 1.1x to 4.2x performance improvement. Bhargava *et al.* evaluated the MMX extensions for a set of DSP and multimedia applications on the X86 architectures [8]. In their study, the image applications were the best suited for MMX because the images were stored in a large array of eight-bit data and properly aligned on eight-byte boundaries, showing an average 5.5x speedup and an 81% reduction in dynamic instruction count. Unlike these research approaches, this paper quantitatively evaluates the impact of multimedia extensions on multiprocessor systems to exploit subword level parallelism (SLP) in addition to data level parallelism (DLP).

3 Methodology Infrastructure

This section presents the selected imaging applications and methodology infrastructure for the evaluation of the MMX-type instructions on a specified multiprocessor array.

3.1 Imaging Applications

To capture a range of image and video processing, five imaging applications have been selected: a chroma-keying program (CHROMA), edge detection (ED), the vector median filtering (VMF), vector quantization (VQ), and motion estimation (ME) within the MPEG standard. These applications, briefly summarized in Table 1, form significant components of many current and future real-world workloads such as streaming video across the internet, real-time video enhancement and analysis, and scene-visualization. All the applications are executed with QCIF resolution (176x144 pixels) 3-band (i.e., channel) input image sequences.

Table 1. Summary of imaging applications used in this study

Application	Description
Chroma-Keying	Combines foreground and/or background frames into a final image (e.g., everyday on television weather channel).
Edge Detection	Extracts edge information from an image through a Sobel operator which accounts for local changes.
Vector Median Filter	Suppresses impulse noise from an image.
Vector Quantization	Compresses and quantizes collections of input data by mapping k-dimensional vectors on vector space $\mathbf{R}^k$ into a finite set of vectors.
Motion Estimation	Removes temporal redundancies between video frames in MPEG/H.26L video applications.

3.2 Methodology Infrastructure

Fig. 2 shows an overall methodology infrastructure which is divided into three levels: application, architecture, and technology. At the application level, an instruction-level single instruction, multiple data (SIMD) array simulator [9] is used to profile execution statistics such as issued instruction frequency, PE utilization, and PE memory usage for the two different versions of the programs: (1) baseline ISA without subword parallelism (Base-SIMD) and (2) baseline plus MDMX ISA (MMX-SIMD). At the architecture level, the HAM tool [10] is used to calculate the design parameters of these architecture models. The design parameters are then passed to the technology level. At the technology level, the GENESYS tool [11] is used to calculate technology parameters (e.g., latency, area, power, and clock frequency) for each configuration. Finally, the database (e.g., cycle times, instruction latencies, instruction counts, area, and power of the functional units) is combined to determine execution times, sustained throughput, area efficiency, and energy efficiency for each case.

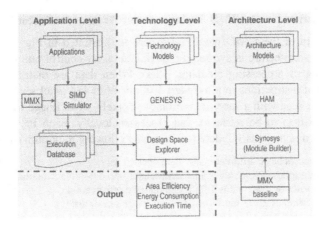

Fig. 2. An overall methodology infrastructure for exploring the design space

3.2.1 Application Level: Instruction Level Simulation Environment

The SIMD multiprocessor array simulator tool is an instruction level simulator which allows editing, assembling, executing, and debugging parallel applications in a single integrated workbench for the SIMD multiprocessor array architecture [9]. This software tool provides important execution parameters, such as cycle count, dynamic instruction frequency, and PE utilization for the two different versions of the programs: (1) baseline ISA without subword parallelism and (2) baseline plus MMX ISA. A screenshot of the simulator is given in Fig. 3.

Fig. 3. A screenshot of the SIMD simulator during execution of chroma keying

3.2.2 Architecture Level: SIMD Multiprocessor Array Architecture

A block diagram of the SIMD model used here is illustrated in Fig. 4. This SIMD multiprocessor architecture is symmetric, having an array control unit (ACU) and an array consisting of processing elements (PEs). When data are distributed, the PEs executes a set of instructions in a lockstep fashion. With 4x4 pixel sensor sub-arrays, each PE is associated with a specific portion (4x4 pixels) of an image frame, allowing streaming pixel data to be retrieved and processed locally. Each PE has a reduced instruction set computer (RISC) datapath with the following minimum characteristics:

- ALU – computes basic arithmetic and logic operations,
- MACC – multiplies 32-bit values and accumulates into a 64-bit accumulator,
- Sleep – activates or deactivates a PE based on local information,
- Pixel unit – samples pixel data from the local image sensor array,
- ADC unit – converts light intensities into digital values,
- Three-ported general-purpose registers (16 32-bit words),
- Small amount of local storage (64 32-bit words),
- Nearest neighbor communications through a NEWS (north-east-west-south) network and serial I/O unit.

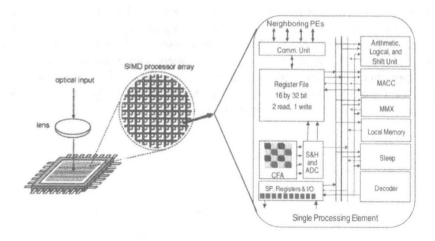

Fig. 4. A block diagram of a SIMD multiprocessor array

3.2.3 Technology Level: Generic System Simulation Environment

To evaluate the system area and power of the two modeled architectures: (1) baseline SIMD and (2) MMX-SIMD, an analytical technology modeling tool with macro cell capability (GENESYS) [11] is used. GENESYS integrates a hierarchical set of models that capture key limits such as fundamental, material, device, circuit, and system, shown in Fig. 5. The first three levels capture the physical effects of material properties and switching device behaviors. The circuit level estimates all components of the signal propagation delay through gate. The system level contains architecture, interconnect, and packing details of a single chip.

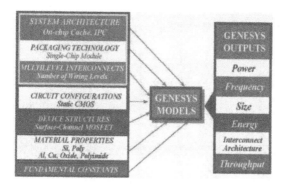

Fig. 5. GENESYS system hierarchy

4   Experimental Results

Cycle accurate simulation and technology modeling have been used to determine the performance and efficiency characteristics of the MMX-SIMD architecture. Moreover, the selected imaging applications have been developed in their respective assembly languages for the SIMD array, in which all two versions for each program have the same parameters, data sets, and calling sequences. The metrics of the execution cycle count, energy consumption, sustained throughput, and energy and area efficiency of each case form the basis of the study comparison, defined in Table 2.

Table 2. Summary of evaluation metrics

execution time	sustained throughput	energy efficiency	area efficiency
$t_{exec} = \dfrac{C}{f_{ck}}$	$Th_{sust} = \dfrac{O_{exec} \cdot U \cdot N_{PE}}{t_{exec}}$	$\eta_E = \dfrac{O_{exec} \cdot U \cdot N_{PE}}{Energy} [\dfrac{Gops}{Joule}]$	$\eta_A = \dfrac{Th_{sust}}{Area} [\dfrac{Gops}{s \cdot mm^2}]$

C is the cycle count, f_{ck} is the clock frequency, O_{exec} is the number of executed operations, and N_{PE} is the number of processing elements. Note that since an MMX instruction executes more operations (typically four times) than a baseline instruction, this paper assumes that each MMX and baseline instruction executes four and one operation, respectively, for the sustained throughput calculation.

4.1   Performance Evaluation Results

This section evaluates the impact of MMX on processing performance for the selected imaging applications on the SIMD array. Fig. 6 illustrates execution performance (speedups in executed cycles) attained by MMX when compared with the baseline performance without subword parallelism. MMX achieves a speedup ranging from 3x to 5x (an average of 3.7x) over the baseline performance.

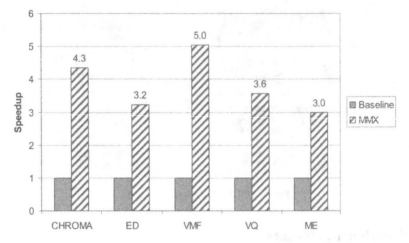

Fig. 6. Speedups of MMX-SIMD, normalized to the baseline performance

MMX also achieves higher sustained throughput than the baseline version across all the application tasks. Table 3 summarizes the execution parameters for each case in the SIMD array.

Table 3. Application performance on a 1,584 PE system running at 80 MHz

Application	ISA	Execution Time [us]	Vector Instruction	System Utilization [%]	Sustained Throughput [Gops/sec]
CHROMA	Baseline	15	1,227	88	122
	MMX	4	283	100	155
ED	Baseline	90	7,177	100	122
	MMX	26	2,117	100	160
VMF	Baseline	467	37,397	93	118
	MMX	93	7,430	97	158
VQ	Baseline	2,257	180,551	91	115
	MMX	631	50,503	97	133
ME	Baseline	1,215	97,229	95	120
	MMX	406	32,502	98	140

4.2 Energy Evaluation Results

Fig. 7 shows energy consumption for the SIMD multiprocessor array with MMX, normalized to the baseline version. Each bar divides the energy consumption into the functional unit (FU, combines ALUs, Barrel Shifter, and MACC), storage (combines Register file and Memory), and others (combines Comm., Sleep, Serial, and Decoder) categories. The use of MMX significantly reduces energy consumption for all the programs because of a large reduction in the vector instruction count, in which all the implementation have been examined at the same 80 MHz clock frequency and 100nm

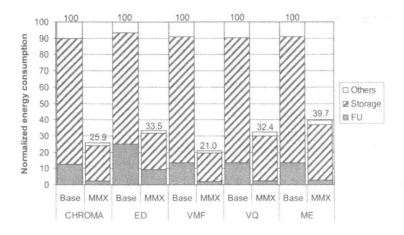

Fig. 7. Energy consumption of MMX-SIMD, normalized to the baseline version

technology. MMX reduces energy consumption from 60% (ME) to 79% (VMF) over the baseline version. Since MMX reduces a significant number of ALU and memory instructions, less energy is spent on the ALU and storage units. Decreasing energy consumption improves sustainable battery life for given system capabilities.

4.3 Area Efficiency Results

Area efficiency is the task throughput achieved per unit of area. Fig. 8 show the area efficiency for the SIMD array with MMX, normalized to the baseline version. MMX outperforms baseline across all the programs in the area efficiency metric, indicating a 13% increase with MMX. This is because MMX achieves higher sustained throughput with smaller area overhead. Increasing area efficiency improves component utilization for given system capabilities.

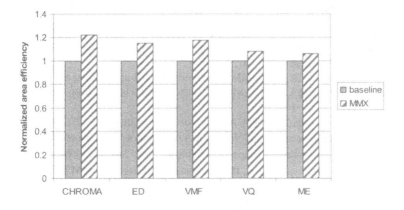

Fig. 8. Area efficiency of MMX-SIMD, normalized to the baseline version

5 Conclusions

As emerging portable multimedia applications demand more and more tremendous computational throughput with limited area and power, the need for high efficiency, high throughput embedded processing is becoming an important challenge in computer architecture. To meet the requirements, this paper has quantitatively evaluated the impact of MMX on multiprocessor systems to exploit subword level parallelism (SLP) in addition to data level parallelism (DLP). Moreover, this paper addressed application-, architecture-, and technology-level issues in an existing processing system to provide efficient processing of image sequences. MMX outperforms the baseline version in terms of execution time, energy consumption, and area efficiency. These results indicate that MMX is a suitable candidate for energy- and performance-hungry mobile systems. Moreover, these evaluation techniques composed of performance simulation and technology modeling can provide solutions to the design challenges in a new class of mobile multimedia computing systems.

Acknowledgments. This research was supported by the Ministry of Knowledge Economy, Korea, under the ITRC(Information Technology Research Center) support program supervised by the IITA(Institute of Information Technology Assessment) (IITA-2008-(C1090-0801-0039)). The author would like to thank the PICA Group at Georgia Tech and its director, Prof. D. Scott Wills for developing the SIMD array and its simulation environment.

References

1. Jennings, M.D., Conte, T.M.: Subword Extensions for Video Processing on Mobile Systems. Concurrency, IEEE 6(3), 13–16 (1998)
2. Peleg, A., Weiser, M.: MMX Technology Extension to the Intel Architecture. IEEE Micro 16(4), 42–50 (1996)
3. Raman, S.K., Pentkovski, V., Keshava, J.: Implementing Streaming SIMD Extensions on the Pentium III Processor. IEEE Micro 20(4), 28–39 (2000)
4. Lee, R.B.: Subword Parallelism with MAX-2. IEEE Micro 16(4), 51–59 (1996)
5. Tremblay, M., O'Connor, J.M., Narayanan, V., He, L.: VIS Speeds New Media Processing. IEEE Micro 16(4), 10–20 (1996)
6. Nguyen, H., John, L.: Exploiting SIMD Parallelism in DSP and Multimedia Algorithms using the AltiVec Technology. In: Proceedings of International Conference on Supercomputer, pp. 11–20 (1999)
7. Ranganathan, P., Adve, S., Jouppi, N.P.: Performance of Image and Video Processing with General-Purpose Processors and Media ISA Extensions. In: Proceedings of the 26th International Symposium on Computer Architecture, pp. 124–135 (1999)
8. Bhargava, R., John, L., Evans, B., Radhakrishnan, R.: Evaluating MMX Technology using DSP and Multimedia applications. In: Proceedings of the IEEE/ACM Symposium on Microarchitecture, pp. 37–46 (1998)

9. Kim, J., Wills, D.S., Wills, L.M.: Implementing and Evaluating Color-Aware Instruction Set for Low-Memory, Embedded Video Processing in Data Parallel Architectures. In: Yang, L.T., Amamiya, M., Liu, Z., Guo, M., Rammig, F.J. (eds.) EUC 2005. LNCS, vol. 3824, pp. 4–16. Springer, Heidelberg (2005)

10. Chai, S.M.: Real Time Image Processing on Parallel Arrays for Gigascale Integration. PhD dissertation, Georgia Inst. of Technology (1999)

11. Eble, J.C., De, V.K., Wills, D.S., Meindl, J.D.: A Generic System Simulator (GENESYS) for ASIC Technology and Architecture beyond 2001. In: Proceedings of the Ninth Annual IEEE International ASIC Conference, pp. 193–196 (1996)

The Use of Photo Retrieval for EEG-Based Personal Identification

Hideaki Touyama and Michitaka Hirose

Graduate School of Information Science and Technology,
The University of Tokyo, Japan
tou@cyber.rcast.u-tokyo.ac.jp

Abstract. A research on biometry based on human brain activities has lately become attracted and emerging. In this study, we investigate the feasibility of personal identification based on photo retrieval using three-channel electroencephalogram. Nine photo images were randomly presented one after another to five subjects without training. The Principal Component Analysis and the Linear Discriminant Analysis were applied to perform the simulation of the personal identification. The algorithm correctly identified 82.5, 93.0, and 100.0 % of the subject using EEG activities with 5, 10, and 20-times averaging, respectively. This study reveals a future possibility of photo retrieval tasks to realize the personal identification system using human brain activities, which will yield rich controls of machine for the users of brain-computer interface.

Keywords: Personal identification, Electroencephalogram, Photo retrieval.

1 Introduction

In recent years, there have been many discussions about a new interaction technique which directly connects a human brain and a machine. A brain-computer interface (BCI) is a communication channel which enables us to send commands to external devices only by using brain activities [1]. As one of the candidates for noninvasive and compact BCI systems, an electroencephalography (EEG) has been investigated. A variety of brain activities has been reported in the context of the BCI based on EEG; for instance, motor imageries [2,3], visual evoked potentials (VEP) [4,5], P300 evoked potentials [6,7], etc. With these brain activities, many applications have been developed in laboratories such as a virtual keyboard or computer mouse.

The research field of the BCI developments has driven a new research paradigm; the EEG-based biometry. The concept of the biometry has lately become more and more attracted. For example, face, fingerprint etc. have been considered and the part of those has been in practical use. By using human brain activities as a new modality, we have several advantages as mentioned in the previous work [8]. It is confidential, very difficult to mimic, and almost impossible to steal, and furthermore it is easy for the users to change the 'password' according to the users mental tasks.

In spite of the expected use, there has been little work on the EEG-based biometry [8]. Paranjape et al. [9] studied on the EEG signals recorded from the subjects with eyes open and closed. They examined the EEG trials from 40 subjects, and the classification accuracy of about 80 percent was achieved. Poulos et al. [10] investigated one-channel EEG on occipital site to extract the four major EEG rhythms (alpha, beta, delta and theta) during closed eyes, where the classification performance of 95 percent was obtained involving four subjects. Palaniappan et al. [11] reported the VEP-based biometry. Thorpe et al. [12] proposed the concept of 'pass-thought' using P300 evoked potentials based on oddball paradigm with flashing letters on a computer monitor. Marcel et al. [8] studied the person authentication based on motor imageries and word generation tasks. These works revealed the feasibility of the EEG-based biometry. However, it would be difficult to change the EEG signals, except for the method using P300 responses.

In this paper, we reveal the feasibility of EEG activities during photo retrieval to perform the personal identification extracting the P300 evoked potentials. There are several advantages in our approach; the photo retrieval is very familiar with people and easy to achieve without subject training, it would be easy to change the pass-thought based on the scheme of the oddball paradigm, and the number of electrodes is only three, which contributes to reduce the stress of the users in preparing the EEG electrodes.

This paper is structures as follows: In section 2, the experimental methods are explained. The analysis protocols and the results of the personal identification will be shown in section 3 and 4, respectively. The identification performances will be examined by using Principal Component Analysis (PCA) with a variety of conditions of EEG averaging. Finally, the discussions and conclusions will be mentioned.

2   Experimental Methods

Five normal volunteers (s1-s5) with normal vision participated in the experiments as subjects (males, 23, 25, 36, 24 and 21 yr, respectively). The subjects were naïve for the EEG measurement in this study and comfortably sitting on an arm-chair facing a screen.

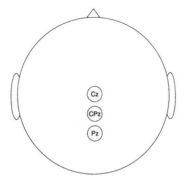

Fig. 1. The location of electrodes on the scalp. Three electrodes were attached using a modular EEG cap system according to the international 10/10 system.

2.1 EEG Recordings

To address the performance of the personal identification, a modular EEG cap system was applied for scalp recordings. Three-channel EEG signals were recorded from Cz, CPz, and Pz according to the international 10/10 system (Fig.1). The analogue EEG signals were amplified at a multi-channel bio-signal amplifier (MEG-6116, Nihon Kohden Inc., Japan). The amplified signals were band-pass filtered between 0.5 and 30 Hz and sampled at 128 Hz by using a standard A/D converter. The digitized EEG data was stored in a personal computer.

2.2 Experimental Tasks

The experimental task sequence was shown in Fig.2. Nine photo images were randomly projected one by one from backside every 0.5 sec on the screen with about 11.4 degrees of visual angle. Earlier 2.0 sec was for eye-fixation and the following 4.5 sec included one-time presentation of each photo. The 20 times repetitions were performed to construct 1 session (for 130 sec = 6.5 sec x 20 times). The session was repeated at most 5 times to collect the datasets for each subject.

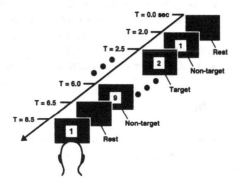

Fig. 2. An example of the experimental task sequence. The subject focused attention on the centre of the interested photo images silently counting the number of times the photos were presented.

Table 1. The contents of photo images used in this study. These photo images were selected before the experiments by the author.

Photo number	Photo images
1	Face of a man
2	Female bust with a bikini
3	Face of a baby
4	Face of a puppy
5	Girl's COSPLAY
6	Kiss of men
7	Broken buildings
8	Corpse of a bird
9	Dolls buried in mud

The task was to focus attention on one or more specified photos in which the subject was interested and silently count the number of times that the target photos were presented (oddball tasks). These interested photos were selected before the experiments by subjects themselves and were keys for the personal identification. The photo image sets were sampled by the author from a public photo archive of the web site flickr.com [13]. The contents of the photos are shown in Table 1.

3 Analysis Protocols

3.1 Questionnaire

After the EEG recordings, the subjects received a brief questionnaire. A question was *"Which were your target (interested) photos?"* The result was used in the following analyses.

3.2 Averaging

The uniqueness of the recorded EEG activities is one of the important keys to achieve the personal identification. To check this, the features of the brain signals were extracted by averaging the EEG data in time domain. The average waveforms for both target (interested) and non-target (non-interested) photos were investigated for each subject (Fig.3).

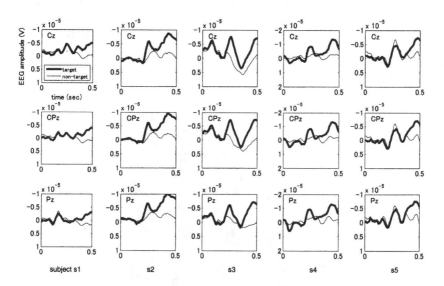

Fig. 3. Average EEG waveforms during target retrieval (thick line) and non-target retrieval (thin line) for three electrode sites (Cz, CPz, and Pz). According to the convention, the positive potentials were expressed in down directions (y-axis). Left to right columns denotes the subject s1 to s5, respectively.

3.3 The identification Algorithm

For the personal identification, the EEG data only during target photo retrieval were extracted for each subject. The datasets were categorized into five according to the number of the subjects. There were 300, 100, 200, 100, and 300 single-trial EEG datasets for the subject s1, s2, s3, s4, and s5, respectively. The datasets were divided into N segments to have N-times averaging datasets. In this study, N was taken to be 0, 5, 10, or 20, where 0 denotes the single-trial (non-average) EEG.

For future applications, only three-channel EEG was investigated in the identification. From the three electrode sites (Cz, CPz and Pz), the N-times average EEG potential values were considered to have 192-dimensional feature vectors. The number of the feature dimension was reduced to 24 by applying PCA. Linear Discriminant Analysis (LDA) was used for the classification.

Using the N-times average EEG datasets, a leave-one-out method was adopted to simulate the performance of the identification, where only one data is used for the testing and the others are for the training.

4 Results

In the questionnaire, it was found that the number of the selected photos were three, one, two, one, and three among nine photo images for the subject s1, s2, s3, s4, and s5, respectively.

In Fig.3, it was clearly found that the waveforms of each subject were very unique, which would be responsible for the personal identification. The tendency of the enhancements of the EEG amplitudes was observed with target photo images for all subjects. The P300 evoked potentials were clearly observed for several subjects, which would be responsible for the high performance of the oddball-based BCI controls [14].

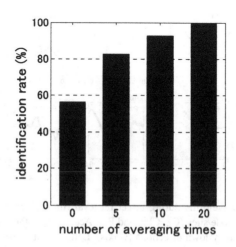

Fig. 4. The dependence of the number of EEG averaging times on personal identification rate. The 0-times average corresponds to non-average (single trial) EEG datasets.

With non-average EEG data, the PCA-LDA algorithm correctly identified 56.2 % of the subject. It was found that the performances were successfully improved with average data (Fig.4). The performances could be 82.5, 93.0 % for 5, and 10 times of averaging, respectively. Note that the 20-times averaging resulted in the complete (100.0 %) personal identification. As an example of the visualization of the performance, three of the most significant components of the PCA space were shown in Fig.5. It could be seen that the plotted data was successfully localized in the PCA space reflecting the subject's personality.

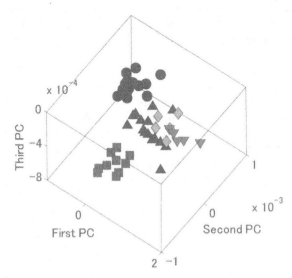

Fig. 5. Three of the most significant components (principal component: PC) in the PCA space. This result is shown for 20-times average EEG. In this case, the identification was complete. The markers of circle, diamond, square, inverted triangle, and normal triangle denotes the subject s1-s5, respectively.

5 Discussions

In this study, the performance of the personal identification based on human brain activities was simulated and the feasibility was suggested. It was found that the personal identification was possible with high identification rate involving five subjects. The rate could be 93.0 % with 10-times and be complete with 20-times averaging EEG.

There were several advantages in our approach. The first one was the photo retrieval tasks which was familiar with people and required no subject training. The second was the number of EEG electrodes, which was only three in our experiments. In the scheme based on photo retrieval, the user would change the interested photos to have another 'password', which will be discussed elsewhere. Note that in other modalities of the biometry such as face, fingerprint, iris etc., the changing of the 'password' cannot be achieved.

On the other hand, there are several points to be improved for future applications. The first one to be considered is to shorten the time during photo retrieval. The response time can be one of the performance indices. In general, using EEG signals, it is thought that there is a trade off between the response time and the system performance, which is explained by the information transfer rate in the BCI controls [1]. According to the experimental results and protocols in this study, the time to obtain complete identifications was 30.0 sec (= 4.5 sec x 20 times / 3 times), if the subject selected three among nine photo images. The increase of the target photo images would be one of the solutions, although the decrease of the P300 amplitudes might be accompanied by more often presentations of the target photo images. The second is the number of the subjects. There is still a possibility to reduce the identification performance with many subjects. More sophisticated feature extractions and the classification algorithm would be required in future works. The third is the authentication. In our study, only the identification was addressed. But, for the practical use, the authentication is very required. In the authentication, the system should confirm and deny the identity claimed by a person [8]. It was found in the previous studies that the P300 evoked potentials were detected also using the auditory or other possible stimuli. In future applications, a variety of stimuli would be used in this paradigm. Furthermore, the VEP and the brain activities during motor imagery would be combined to improve the system performances.

The EEG-based personal identification and authentication was motivated and driven by the novel studies on the EEG-based interfacing systems. The personal identification system would serve rich controls of the BCI systems.

6 Conclusions

In this study, we investigated the feasibility of personal identification based on photo retrieval using only three-channel EEG. Nine photo images were randomly presented one after another to five subjects without training. The PCA and the LDA were applied to perform the simulation of the personal identification. With non-average EEG data, the algorithm identified only 56.2 % of the subject. However, the performances of the identification with 5, 10, and 20-times averaging were remarkably improved to be 82.5, 93.0, and 100.0 %, respectively. In our approach, the metal tasks of the photo retrieval were very familiar with people and the changing of the 'password' would be easily achieved in the oddball paradigm. Our study revealed a future possibility of photo retrieval tasks to realize the personal identification system using human brain activities, which will yield rich controls of machine for the users of brain-computer interface.

References

1. Wolpaw, J.R., Birbaumer, N., McFarland, D.J., Pfurtscheller, G., Vaughan, T.M.: Brain computer interfaces for communication and control. Clinical Neurophysiology 113(6), 767–791 (2002)
2. Pfurtscheller, G., Neuper, C.: Motor imagery activates primary sensorimotor area in humans. Neurosci. Lett. 239(2-3), 65–68 (1997)

3. Blankertz, B., Dornhege, G., Krauledat, M., Muller, K.R., Kunzmann, V., Losch, F., Curio, G.: The Berlin Brain-Computer Interface: EEG-based communication without subject training. IEEE Trans Neural Syst. Rehabil. Eng. 14(2), 147–152 (2006)
4. Middendorf, M., McMillan, G., Calhoun, G., Jones, K.S.: Brain-Computer Interfaces Based on the Steady-State Visual-Evoked Response. IEEE Transactions on Rehabilitation Engineering 8(2), 211–214 (2000)
5. Cheng, M., Gao, X., Gao, S., Xu, D.: Design and Implementation of a Brain-Computer Interface With High Transfer Rates. IEEE Transactions on Biomedical Engineering 49(10), 1181–1186 (2002)
6. Farwell, L.A., Donchin, E.: Taking off the top of your head: toward a mental prosthesis utilizing event-related brain potentials. Electroencephalogr. Clin. Neurophysiol. 70(6), 510–523 (1988)
7. Bayliss, J.D.: The use of the evoked potential P3 component for control in a virtual apartment. IEEE Transaction on Neural Systems and Rehabilitation Engineering 11(2), 113–116 (2003)
8. Marcel, S., Millan, J.R.: Person authentication using brainwaves (EEG) and maximum a posteriori model adaptation. IEEE Transaction on pattern analysis and machine intelligence 29(4), 743–752 (2007)
9. Paranjape, R.B., Mahovsky, J., Benedicenti, L., Koles, Z.: The Electroencephalogram as a Biometric. In: Proc. of Canadian Conf. on Electrical and Computer Eng., vol. 2, pp. 1363–1366 (2001)
10. Poulos, M., Rangoussi, M.: Parametric person identification from the EEG using computational geometry. In: Proc. of the Sixth Int'l Conf. on Electronics, Circuits, and Systems, vol. 2, pp. 1005–1012 (1999)
11. Palaniappan, R., Mandic, D.P.: Biometrics from brain electrical activity: a machine learning approach. IEEE Transaction on pattern analysis and machine intelligence 29(4), 738–742 (2007)
12. Thorpe, J., van Oorschot, P.C., Somayaji, A.: Pass-thoughts: Authenticating With Our Minds. In: Proc. of ACSA 2005 New Security Paradigms Workshop (2005)
13. (The photo images in this study were downloaded only for the research purpose), See the website, http://www.flickr.com/
14. Krusienski, D.J., Sellers, E.W., McFarland, D.J., Vaughan, T.M., Wolpaw, J.R.: Toward enhanced P300 speller performance. J. Neurosci. Methods 167(1), 15–21 (2007)

Music Wall: A Tangible User Interface Using Tapping as an Interactive Technique

Catherine Hu, Kinsun Tung, and Lawrence Lau

Interaction Design Lab, School of Design,
The Hong Kong Polytechnic University
Hung Hom, Kowloon, Hong Kong, China
{sdcathhu,sdkinsun,sdlau}@polyu.edu.hk

Abstract. This paper describes a tangible user interface that uses taps on a hard surface as the mode of interaction between the user and the information device. The surface is constructed by a matrix of small acoustic sensing modules that work together to track both the location of taps on the surface and the rhythm of tap sequences. Each module is also embedded with LEDs to provide visual feedback and novel lighting effects. The system is a generic input/output system and could be used to interface with digital devices. The present prototype of a music wall is one embodiment of the system, implemented as a digital music player. A function set using position-based tap sequence recognition has also been designed to work with music enjoyment on the system.

Keywords: Acoustic sensing modules, Interactive surfaces, Tangible user interface, Interaction method, Input/output device.

1 Introduction

Taps, or knocks, is one form of informal communication. Tapping or knocking can share universal meaning in different cultures. For instance, both in Eastern or Western countries, it is polite for one to tap on the door to seek approval before entering a room. The taps signify the person's intention of entering the room and also arouse attention amongst those inside the room to address this intent. In Chinese culture, there is a convention to gently tap on the table with one's knuckles to express gratitude to the person who is filing one's cup with tea.

In addition to common causal communication, tapping could also be used to communicate more specific information. Much like Morse code, a tapping sequence at a particular rhythm (i.e., with specific time intervals in between taps) could be used to represent or encode a particular piece of information or message. Finally, tapping is also one form of physical externalization of thoughts and emotions. While listening to music, we sometimes tap along to the rhythm with our fingers or feet. Taps, being a natural physical action and an informal form of communication, offers good potentials as an interaction method to communicate with digital devices.

2 Taps as Input Method

In recent years, research in Tangible Interaction (TI) has explored varied technology and paradigms. The goal is to offer direct manipulation to digital information through

S. Lee et al. (Eds.): APCHI 2008, LNCS 5068, pp. 284–291, 2008.
© Springer-Verlag Berlin Heidelberg 2008

the physicality of our environment [1]. Of particular interest to most researchers in this area is the exploration of haptic interfaces and techniques: interaction using the touch sense. A great amount of exciting work is centered around explorations in interactive multi-touch surfaces that respond to different touch movements on a sensitive surface [2]. Other projects explored gestures and motion as interactions, allowing a user to control a device by making gestures like tilting or shaking, or drawing circles while holding the device [3].

While multi-touch systems are currently in the spotlight with a growing number of commercial applications, researchers continue to explore other possibilities of freeing humans from the desktop keyboard and computer mouse. One such direction is to explore the use of gentle taps as interaction method. Research in this area includes the use of acceleration sensors to detect taps on a mobile phone and mapping these to instructions like muting the ring tone of an incoming call or turning the volume up or down [4]. The Responsive Environments Group at the Media Lab investigated the use of taps atop a large projected surface to drive the display of digital information on the surface by analyzing sound waves coming from a tap [5, 6]. Such acoustics-based remote sensing technology is also pursued by the TAI-CHI project (Tangible Acoustic Interfaces for Computer Human Interaction) with the goal to augment ordinary objects and surfaces with such sensing technology thereby turning any solid surfaces or objects into tangible interfaces [7]. Apart from multi-touch systems, tapping offers another form of natural interaction with application potentials awaiting to be further explored.

In this paper, we discuss the development of a modular approach in constructing an acoustic-sensitive system and its application as a digital music player. The approach is more from an interaction design perspective to explore application possibilities rather than a scientific approach to innovate the underlying acoustic-sensing technologies.

2.1 The Proposed Tap Recognition System

This paper proposes a scalable interactive surface constructed by modular units of acoustic sensitive blocks arranged in a matrix. Each module is individually embedded with a tap sensing unit to pick up tap signals and relative positions, and an RGB LED unit to provide visual feedback. These are housed inside a vibration-proof silicone shell to prevent tap vibrations from affecting adjacent modules.

The modules are designed to work at a minimal configuration of a 3x3 matrix, but expandable to any configuration the controlling processing unit could support. The matrix of modules is in communication with an encoder, a decoder, a networking device, and a processor.

One of the goals associated with this modular approach in building a tap recognition surface is that the system could locate precisely where a tap has occurred. From the user's point of view, the visual grid also encourages experimentation with different tap patterns on the surface and association of meanings with such patterns. These patterns could be capitalized on by the system to map to different instructions or information. Another advantage is the scalability of the interactive surface. The modular system could be built to wall size and installed in public spaces like a shopping mall as an integrated interactive surface in the built environment.

In addition to tracking relative positions of a tap sequence, the proposed system could also recognize the time intervals in between taps at a particular location. We applied the system into the context of music enjoyment and built a prototype called the 'Music Wall', which is described in greater detail in the following section.

2.2 The Music Wall

Since rhythm in music is time-based, music naturally becomes a potential domain to try out the capabilities of the proposed tap recognition system. We also observed that people generally remember songs by a particular tune in the song. This led us to imagine that the tap recognition system could become the controlling interface for a music player, the basic premise being the tune of a song that a person remembers will be used to retrieve the song instead of having to search through a regular text-based song list.

To achieve the above, a necessary first step is for the system to understand which tune represents which song. This is carried out through a Web-based 'Song Profile Creation' software developed to run on regular personal computers. The user first selects a song from his music archive on the computer. Then he taps on the spacebar, the short rhythm that comes to mind as he remembers the song. The software records, encodes and maps this tap sequence to the selected song. Figure 1 shows the main interface of this software, with the input tap sequence represented as a line of white dots in the middle of the screen. The user then chooses a lighting effect for the playback of the selected song later on the Music Wall. Other songs could be defined by their corresponding tap sequences in similar fashion.

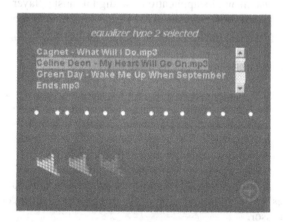

Fig. 1. Main interface of the Song Profile Creation software

In order to unify tap sequences for efficient matching, time intervals of each pair of white dots (i.e., taps) in a tap sequence must be converted into percentages relative to the total time span of the complete sequence. Finally the information is encoded as a *string* and stored in a Web database accessible via the Internet. Figure 2 shows an example of the encoding procedure using one phrase which the user remembers from the song "My Heart Will Go On".

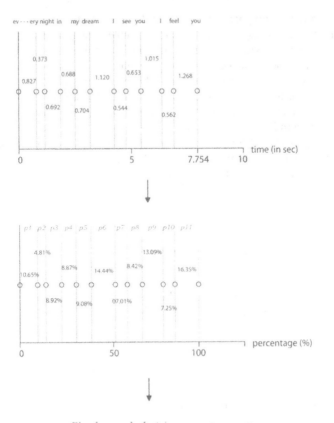

Fig. 2. The encoding procedure converts absolute time intervals in a tap sequence into relative percentages

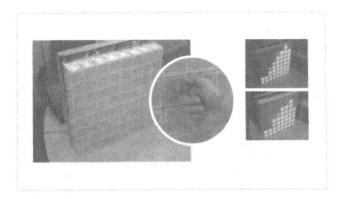

Fig. 3. The Music Wall prototype: user plays a song by tapping the rhythm of a tune that comes to mind on any block. Lighting effects accompany music playback to add visual pleasure.

After this initial set up phase, the user could begin to interact with the Music Wall as a regular audio playback system. The current implementation uses an 8x8 matrix of the tap recognition blocks. To begin playing his favorite song, the user recalls the familiar tune which he associates with the song and taps this out on any block on the music wall. This tap sequence is recorded and encoded by the tap sensing unit of the system and sent back to the Web database to search for a matching sequence. If a match is found, the corresponding song will begin to play with the previously selected lighting pattern on the music wall.

The matching process is divided into two steps: step one compares the length of the encoded strings while step two compares the percentages of each pair of taps, allowing certain degrees of tolerance, t. Figure 4 shows the algorithm for the matching process.

step 1:

    if (encoded string newly input).length == (encoded string database).length then step 2
    else MATCHING FAILED

step 2:

    if (p1 newly input - p1 database)<t AND (p2 newly input - p2 database)<t AND ... AND (pn newly input - pn database)<t then MATCHING SCCESSFUL
    else MATCHING FAILED

t - percentage tolerance

Fig. 4. Algorithm for the matching process of recorded tap sequences

2.3 Interaction Method Using Position-Based Tap Sequences

The position-recognition capability of the tap recognition system is implemented as a set of playback controls on the Music Wall to support regular functions such as play, stop, step forward, step backward, looping a song, as well as volume control. This set of position-based tap patterns replaces knobs and buttons on the home hi-fi system or an MP3 player. They are highly intuitive to understand and its novelty offers an added level of pleasure to the interaction. This function set is malleable and could be adapted to mean different functions when the interactive system was used in another context connecting with other devices.

In addition to the above mentioned basic playback controls, we also explored the possibility of implementing some of the more advanced operations on the Music Wall system. One such operation is the creation of a play list. On the current Music Wall system, this is accomplished by tapping on the four corner blocks of the Music Wall to signify the setting up of a virtual 'container'. The system acknowledges the intent by lighting up the four sides of the Music Wall and then waits for song input. At this point, tapping the familiar tune of a song on the Music Wall will not only cause the system to search for the song from the database, but once found, will also assign it into the play list automatically. One after another, songs are added into the play list. Tapping on the four corner blocks again completes the play list and the Music Wall begins to play the songs on the virtual list one after another.

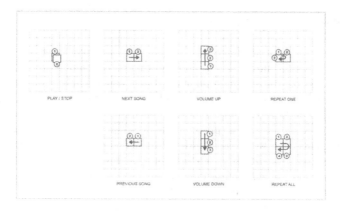

Fig. 5. Function set using position-based tap sequence recognition

3 Application, Relevance and Context

The Music Wall prototype is an attempt to explore the application of acoustic-sensitive system from an interaction design perspective. It proposes a combination of position-based and time-based recognition for greater utility, and explores application areas other than recognizing taps as mouse clicks for information display. In this regard, it is suggested that a function set of tap patterns should be developed to expand the functionality of the interactive surface.

Music Wall is proposed as a domestic appliance suitable as a wall fitting in the home environment. Since the tap recognition system is a generic input/output system, a more holistic concept for this wall-mounted interactive panel is that it could be used as a central controlling unit whereby tapping on different blocks will launch the panel as a control interface for different appliances like the television set, the home lighting system or the air conditioning system. With its network and display capabilities, the system could also be used to display real-time weather or traffic conditions with different lighting effects in an emotive manner. The modules could also work together to form custom-made static or animated pictograms, offering yet another form of display of intended information.

Outside of domestic setting, the Music Wall system could be implemented as a digital juke box in restaurants or pubs. There could be a fun factor involved in guessing which tune from a song is used to command its playback. We also envisioned application of the proposed interactive system in a public setting like a shopping mall. The networked nature of the system means that any person could upload his personal pictograms, visual messages or lighting patterns remotely, and then while physically present at the public installation, tap his pre-defined tap sequence on the interactive surface to cause the download and display of the personal visual messages. This ability to affect public spaces with personal 'messages', and the blurring of boundary between public and private spaces is an interesting notion to explore. In this context, the tap interaction surface seems particularly suitable as it offers a simple and elegant way of manipulating digital contents when having a regular computer screen and keyboard and computer mouse is deemed inappropriate.

4 Conclusion

In this paper, we have described a modular tap-sensitive system, its practical application as a digital music player, and the kind of interaction the system affords. The system is capable of tracking time interval data and absolute and relative position data of a tap sequence. We proposed to employ a combination of position-based and time-based tap sequence tracking to expand the utility of the interactive surface. In terms of usability of the music player system, initial user test had involved over twenty participants who were asked to input their favorite songs with respective tap sequences into a remote computer, and then interacted with the tap-sensitive system to playback their songs. Results showed that around 40% of the participants successfully retrieved their songs through tapping on the interactive surface within the first and second trials. 55% of all participants managed to retrieve their songs within four trials while the remaining 5% experienced difficulty and did not retrieve their songs until after the fifth or sixth trials. All participants however, found the use of tapping a familiar tune (rhythm) to playback a song, a delightful and fun experience. Although void of a textual display, participants valued the emotive experience over precision and efficiency. More vigorous tests are intended to be carried out to test the robustness of the system both as a personal music player as well as a public system. For future work, we intend to explore other application contexts. We feel this tangible interaction system also has application potentials in fields such as education and rehabilitation, possibly supporting people with learning disabilities or impairment of the senses. The modular nature of the system enables flexibility of the interactive surface such that it could be in many different sizes and shapes. Its networked nature also implies that these systems could interact with each other. This inter-system communication is another aspect which future work could continue to explore. A final direction will be to further shrink the system to handheld sizes and explore its application as a portable interface. We feel this would have potentials in areas where using the visual sense to interact with digital information is not as suitable compared with using the haptic sense or auditory sense.

References

1. Ishii, H., Ullmer, B.: Tangible Bits: Towards Seamless Interfaces between People, Bits and Atoms. In: Proceedings, SIGCHI Conference on Human Factors in Computing Systems, pp. 234–241. ACM Press, New York (1997)
2. Han, J.Y.: Multi-touch Sensing Through Frustrated Total Internal Reflection. In: Proceedings, International Conference on Computer Graphics and Interactive Techniques, ACM SIGGRAPH 2005 Sketches, SESSION: Interfaces, p. 145. ACM Press, New York (2005)
3. Jacucci, G., Kela, J., Plomp, J.: Configuring Gestures as Expressive Interactions to Navigate Multimedia Recordings from Visits on Multiple Projections. In: 3rd International Conference on Mobile and Ubiquitous Multimedia. ACM International Conference Proceeding Series, vol. 83, pp. 157–164. ACM Press, New York (2004)
4. Ronkainen, S., Häkkilä, J., Kaleva, S., Colley, A., Linjama, J.: Tap Input as an Embedded Interaction Method for Mobile Devices. In: Proceedings, 1st International Conference on Tangible and Embedded Interaction, SESSION: Body Movements, pp. 263–270. ACM Press, New York (2007)

5. Paradiso, J.A., Che, K.L., Checka, N., Hsiao, K.: Passive Acoustic Sensing for Tracking Knocks Atop Large Interactive Displays. In: Proceedings, The 2002 IEEE International Conference on Sensors, vol. 1, pp. 521–527. IEEE Press, New York (2002)
6. Checka, N.: A System for Tracking and Characterizing Acoustic Impacts on Large Interactive Surfaces. MS Thesis, MIT Dept of EECS and MIT Media Lab (2001)
7. Phama, D.T., Wang, Z., Ji, Z., Yang, M., Al-Kutubi, M., Catheline, S.: Acoustic Pattern Registration for a new type of Human-Computer Interface. In: Proceedings of the IPROMs 2005 Virtual Conference (2005)

Double-Crossing: A New Interaction Technique for Hand Gesture Interfaces

Takashi Nakamura, Shin Takahashi, and Jiro Tanaka

Department of Computer Science
Graduate School of Systems and Information Engineering
University of Tsukuba
1-1-1 Ten-noudai, Tskuba, Ibaraki 305-8573, Japan
{takashi,shin,jiro}@iplab.cs.tsukuba.ac.jp

Abstract. We propose double-crossing, a technique for interacting with large displays using hand gestures. This technique extends crossing, which was developed for a pen-based interface, and enables the ease of use by incorporating easy hand gestures such as finger movements.

Keywords: Crossing, Hand gesture, Large display.

1 Introduction

Hand gesture recognition is a promising approach for remote interaction with large displays. Several existing interaction techniques are based on hand gestures [9, 10]; Fig. 1 shows one such method. Complex hand gestures, however, are often difficult to recognize, are prone to errors, and tend to require expensive devices such as the dataglove. Even the problem of using hand movements to control a simple pointer presents difficulties because of unavoidable hand tremors.

Fig. 1. Example of remote interaction with large display

To cope with this problem, we propose a simple new interaction technique, called double-crossing, which extends to hand gestures the crossing technique that was originally developed for pen-based interfaces[1, 2]. Double-crossing can be implemented using an ordinary web camera and an LED placed on the user's fingertip. The system

S. Lee et al. (Eds.): APCHI 2008, LNCS 5068, pp. 292–300, 2008.

tracks the position of the user's hand accurately enough to create a robust interface. We additionally designed a set of widgets for double-crossing interaction. By combining these widgets, we can easily implement customized hand gesture interfaces for different applications.

The rest of this paper is organized as follows: In section 2, we introduce the double-crossing interaction. In section 3, we describe the Hand-Bin prototype system. In section 4, we discuss the evaluation of the technique. In section 6, we summarize the paper.

Fig. 2. (single) crossing   **Fig. 3.** (left)Hand Movement for double-crossing (right)Movement of pointer and double-crossing

2 Double-Crossing

One problem encountered in hand gesture interfaces is that it is difficult to stabilize the user's hand at a fixed position. It is therefore hard to move a pointer to follow the hand's position and to select or click at the intended location accurately. To solve this problem, a pen stroke is used instead of clicking [7, 11]. In particular, we focus on the crossing technique, in which a crossing bar motion is made to trigger a command (see Fig. 2).

In our hand gesture interface, the hand movement of crossing is recognized by the camera so that it can be used to press a button or select a menu item in the GUI. To implement this idea, however, we must cope with unintentional hand movements that may be recognized as crossing. We hence propose to use a double-crossing action, which is a crossing bar motion that occurs twice during a short time interval. Since unintended double-crossing occurs much less frequently than unintended crossing, we will show that double-crossing is effective as a basic interaction primitive for hand gesture-based graphical user interfaces. Double-crossing is a local finger gesture that moves a finger up-and-down, left-and-right; this action is simple enough that the user does not need to train the system (see Fig. 3).

3 Hand-Bin

We developed a prototype interface based on double-crossing, called Hand-Bin. Hand-Bin is a widget overlayed onto the Windows GUI (see Fig. 4). It consists of three types of components: click icon at the center of Fig. 5 (see Fig. 7 for details), menu icons around the click icon (see Fig. 8 for details), and toggling bars (two bars at the top-left of Fig. 5). The Hand-Bin widget always follows the pointer.

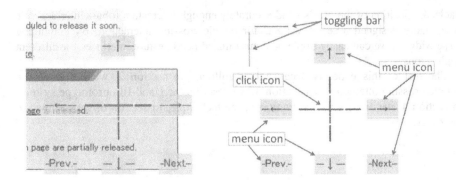

Fig. 4. Hand-Bin overlayed on Windows GUI

Fig. 5. Detail of Hand-Bin

The widget shown in Fig. 5 is an example of Hand-Bin interface designed for Internet browsing. We can easily design other widgets for other applications by arranging menu icons and the click icon for specific applications.

Fig. 6 shows an implementation of the Hand-Bin interface. The user has an LED placed on a fingertip, and the system detects the position of the LED by using images captured from the web camera. The system moves the pointer and detects double-crossing using the captured movements.

3.1 Click Icon

As shown in Fig. 7, the click icon consists of two parts: the cross hairs at the center and four click bars around the cross hairs. The Hand-Bin click event emulates a mouse left-button click occurring at the center of the cross hairs when the user double-crosses one of the click bars. The cross hairs can be moved by pushing them with the pointer. Because of hand tremors, it is difficult to fix the pointer at a single position, so the cross hairs do not move directly with the pointer; this allows the user more precisely to move the cross hairs to an intended location.

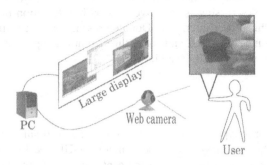

Fig. 6. System setting

3.2 Menu Icons

Menu icons are buttons in the Hand-Bin interface that trigger commands such as scrolling a page and switching tabs. Fig. 5 shows the Hand-Bin interface for Internet browsing. The up and down arrow buttons are scrolling buttons, the left and right arrow buttons are used for switching tabs, and the remaining two are the "previous page" and "next page" buttons in the web browser.

By double-crossing the invoking bar at the middle of the button, the user can execute the command assigned to the button. Although an invoking bar appears to be divided into two parts by the label, it is in fact one horizontal bar at the middle of the button. When invoking one command repeatedly, the second and following executions are invoked each by only one crossing of the invoking bar. The user can thereby quickly repeat commands. One double-crossing of the scrolling button, for example, scrolls the web page slightly, but the repeated up-and-down finger gesture enacted on the scroll button executes the scroll command repeatedly so the user can scroll the web page to the intended position. This repeated mode of action ends when the crossing does not occur for some time period.

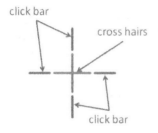

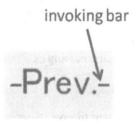

Fig. 7. Click icon   **Fig. 8.** Menu icon

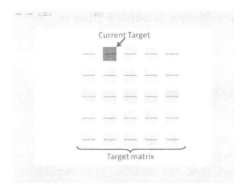

Fig. 9. The screen of the experiment

3.3 Toggling the Display of the Widget

The display of the click icon and the menu icons is toggled by double-crossing one of two toggling bars at the top-left of the Hand-Bin widget. The upper horizontal bar is used to toggle the display of the click icon, and the lower vertical bar is used to toggle the display of the menu icons. The click icon and the menu icons are not normally displayed, leaving only the two toggling bars at the top-left.

3.4 Movement of the Hand-Bin Interface

The Hand-Bin widget is always displayed near the pointer; when the pointer moves away from the Hand-Bin widget, the widget moves to follow. In addition, we developed two methods by which the user can finely adjust the position of the cross hairs. One method uses the boundary region and the other uses the cross hairs click icon.

3.4.1 Movement Using the Boundary Region

The boundary region in the Hand-Bin widget is implemented to follow the pointer, so that the pointer always occupies a boundary region. When the pointer crosses over the boundary region, the Hand-Bin widget moves according to new coordinate with respect to direction. This method could look like pulling the boundary region and the Hand-Bin widget.

3.4.2 Movement Using the Cross Hairs

The Hand-Bin widget can be moved by placing the cross hairs of the click icon in the boundary region, with the intent being to move the cross hairs to a place where a user wants to click. In this method, the Hand-Bin widget is moved when the pointer meets the cross hairs, moving as if the cross hairs were pushed by the pointer.

3.5 Feedback

It is important to give the user feedback to register which operation is being carried out, and Hand-Bin uses sound for feedback. Because allocating a different sound to each possible operation might cause confusion when the number of sounds being emitted increases, we use only one kind of sound for all operations. The issue of proper feedback generally deserves further consideration.

4 Evaluation

4.1 Double-Crossing Experiment

4.1.1 Methods

We prepared 5 x 5 targets such as in Fig. 9. The sizes of the targets were 100 pixels by 100 pixels, with 50 pixels between targets. The experiment was performed with 10 users. Nine of the users were not familiar with interaction using hand gestures, whereas one user was well versed in hand gesture interfaces because he had conducted research in this area.

In the experiment, users selected specified targets using crossing. The specified target was the red target in Fig. 9. We used two crossing techniques: the existing single-crossing technique and the proposed double-crossing technique.

For each crossing technique, we proceeded as follows. First, users practiced 10 times before attempting five sets. In each set, they were given 20 targets. We measured the time taken and the error rate of object selection.

When a target that was not the specified target was selected, we labeled it as an error. The error rate was calculated as (number of trials in which a wrong target was selected)/(total number of trials), and ranged from zero to one. If a user crossed once over a wrong target, it was counted as an error in single-crossing, but was not counted as an error in double-crossing.

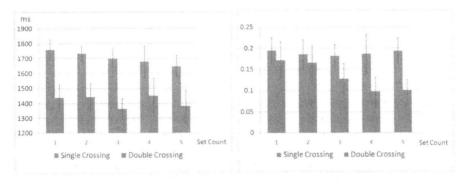

Fig. 10. Averages of selection time   **Fig. 11.** Averages of error rate

4.1.2 Results
Fig. 10 and Fig. 11 show the selection time and the error rate for each set, both averaged over the 10 users.

Selection time: When we compared selection time, double-crossing was faster than single-crossing, with a difference of more than 150 ms. The average selection times for the 10 users were approximately 1702 ms in single-crossing and approximately 1414 ms in double-crossing. With single-crossing, the selection time became shorter as the number of sets increased, whereas double-crossing did not yield any such difference in selection times as the number of sets increased.

Error rate: The error rate of double-crossing was lower than that of single-crossing in all sets. The average error rates over the 10 users were approximately 0.188 for single-crossing and approximately 0.132 for double-crossing. With single-crossing, the error rate did not change substantially as the number of sets increased. In contrast, the error rate for double-crossing decreased greatly as the number of sets increased: the error rate on the first set was approximately 0.171, whereas that on the fifth set was approximately 0.099.

4.1.3 Discussion
The selection time and error rate for double crossing were better than those for single-crossing. It was possible for users to move the pointer to the specified target in a straight line in the case of double-crossing, as in Fig. 12(a). In contrast, with single-crossing, the users often had to make a detour so as not to select other targets, as in Fig. 12(b) (c). These likely accounts for the higher selection time for single-crossing than for double-crossing.

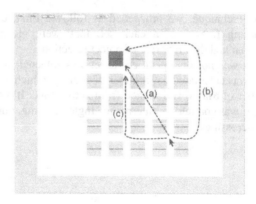

Fig. 12. How to move the pointer to the specified target

Moreover, movements such as those in Fig. 12(c) require users to execute fine motions. As compared to a mouse, however, the pointer wobbles easily when moving by hand gestures, so users often crossed unintended targets. As a result, the error rate of single-crossing was higher than that of double-crossing.

In double-crossing, the selection time did not change substantially although the error rate decreased greatly as the number of sets increased. We observed that users did not change the way in which they moved the pointer to the specified target. Some users, however, changed the manner of double-crossing as the number of sets increased. They moved their fingers too little at first and crossed the same target multiple times, often generating an error. However, they learned how to move the pointer for double-crossing as the number of sets increased and ceased to do erroneous crossing. This caused the error rate for double-crossing to decrease gradually.

4.2 Realistic Hand-Bin Evaluation

In addition to the evaluation experiment, we allowed various people to use a prototype Hand-Bin interface with double-crossing. We found that people who used the Hand-Bin interface for the first time were able to use it without discomfort.

We discovered one problem in particular: many users felt that the click operation using the click icon was odd. This might possibly be explained by the fact that users had to complete two steps to click: first, to move the cross hairs to the place where they wanted to click; and second, to execute the click operation by using the click bar. It was difficult for users to move the pointer precisely by hand when moving the cross hairs to the desired location. It will therefore be necessary to devise a clicking method that does not use the click icon. We propose several possible solutions here.

4.2.1 Improvement of the Click Operation
A simple improvement to the click operation would be to execute the click at the location of the pointer whenever it stays in one place for a fixed duration (see Fig. 13(a)). With hand movements, however, it is difficult for users to fix the pointer in one location. Moreover, because this technique is slow to execute, it will not be an effective method.

A click could also be executed at a target when it is enclosed by the pointer. If, for example, a user wants to click some targets or links, he or she can enclose them as in Fig. 13(b) by moving the pointer with hand gestures. The click operation is executed at the center of the enclosed place (marked by an 'x' in Fig. 13(b))

Another option is to execute a click wherever the user draws an 'x', for example, moving the pointer as in Fig. 13(c). The click operation is executed at the intersection generated by the trajectory of the pointer (given by the 'x' in Fig. 13(c)).

In both of these techniques, the click execution and the specification of the click location are accomplished simultaneously. The influence of the user's unintentional hand movements will be small because these techniques use moving gestures as opposed to still hand poses.

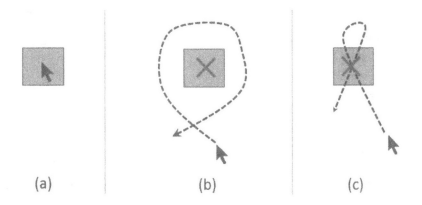

(a)   (b)   (c)

Fig. 13. A variety of click techniques: (a) immobilizing the pointer on the target, (b) enclosing the target using the pointer, (c) making an 'x' over the target

5 Related Work

Sören et al. [8] proposed an interaction technique that used hand gestures and FlowMenu [5, 4] to operate consumer electronics remotely. They used the direction of the finger for interactions and to operate FlowMenu. This method, however, takes a substantial amount of time, and it is difficult to use a continuous direction of one's finger to interact.

Dhawale[3] devised a technique for interacting with displays using only hand gestures. In this system, interaction with the display was accomplished by detecting the movement and inclination of the hand in three dimensions. Although the user can easily figure out the positional relation between the pointer and the hand, i.e., the position of the hand is projected on the display, operation becomes complex because gestures are tracked in three dimensions. Moreover, this technique requires a large horizontal space, which makes interaction difficult in the presence of obstacles such as a desk. This technique is not well suited to operation at a distance.

Hisamatsu et al.[6] used a laser pointer, crossing, and encircling to enable interaction. This technique executes a specific operation when the trajectory of the laser pointer crosses the edge of the screen or encircles an object. We have drawn upon these techniques in our work. When using hand gestures, however, it is very difficult to move the pointer to a distant location instantaneously and directly as when using laser pointer, which has an on/off switch. We have designed the crossing technique with this problem in mind.

6 Summary

We proposed a hand gesture interface based on double-crossing for remote interaction with large display systems. We also described a prototype system called Hand-Bin. A Hand-Bin widget consists of a click icon and menu icons that can be tailored to specific applications. Hand-Bin works with the common Windows GUI and can be implemented with only a low-cost web camera and an LED, yet it works robustly in a real usage environment. We plan to conduct further formal evaluation of the usability of the Hand-Bin system and to improve the Hand-Bin system with intelligent cross hairs that recognize web pages.

References

1. Accot, J., Zhai, S.: More than dotting the i's - foundation for crossing-based interfaces. In: CHI 2002, pp. 73–80 (2002)
2. Apitz, G., Guimbretiere, F.: CrossY: A Crossing-Based Drawing Application. In: UIST 2004, pp. 3–12 (2004)
3. Dhawale, P., Masoodian, M., Rogers, B.: Bare-Hand 3D Gesture Input to Interactive Systems. In: Chinz 2006, pp. 25–32 (2006)
4. Guimbretiere, F., Martin, A., Winograd, T.: Benefits of merging command selection and direct manipulation. ACM Trans. Comput.-Hum. Interact. 12(3), 460–476 (2005)
5. Guimbretiere, F., Winograd, T.: FlowMenu: Combining command,text, and data entry. In: UIST2000, pp. 213–216 (2000)
6. Hisamatsu, T., Shizuki, B., Takahashi, S., Tanaka, J.: A novel click-free interaction technique for large-screen interfaces. In: APCHI 2006 (2006)
7. Kurtenbach, G., Buxton, W.: The limits of expert performance using hierarchic marking menus, CHI 1993, pp. 482–487 (1993).
8. Lenman, S., Bretzner, L., Thuresson, B.: Using Marking Menus to Develop Command Sets for Computer Vision Based Hand Gesture Interfaces. In: NordiCHI, pp. 239–242 (2002)
9. Malik, S., Ranjan, A., Balakrishnan, R.: Interacting with Large Displays from a Distance with Vision-Tracked Multi-Finger Gestural Input. In: UIST 2005, pp. 43–52 (2005)
10. Vogel, D., Balakrishnan, R.: Distant Freehand Pointing and Clicking on Very Large, High Resolution Displays. In: UIST 2005, pp. 33–42 (2005)
11. Zhao, S., Agrawala, M., Hinckley, K.: Zone and Polygon Menus: Using Relative Position to Increase the Breadth of Multi-Stroke Marking Menus. In: CHI 2006, pp. 1077–1086 (2006)

Acquisition of Off-Screen Object by Predictive Jumping

Kazuki Takashima[1], Sriram Subramanian[2], Takayuki Tsukitani[1],
Yoshifumi Kitamura[1], and Fumio Kishino[1]

[1] Human Interface Eng. Lab, Osaka University
{takashima.kazuki,takayuki.tsukitani,kitamura,
kishino}@ist.osaka-u.ac.jp
[2] University of Bristol
sriram@cs.brs.ac.uk

Abstract. We propose predictive jumping (PJ), a fast and efficient algorithm that enables user navigation to off-screen targets. The algorithm is inspired by Delphian Desktop [1] and the off-screen visualization technique–Halo [2]. The Halos represented at the edge of the viewport help users estimate off-screen target distance and encourage them to make a single fluid mouse movement toward the target. Halfway through the user's motion, the system predicts the user's intended target and quickly moves the cursor towards that predicted off-screen location. In a pilot study we examine the user's ability to select off-screen targets with predictive models based on user's pointing kinematics for off-screen pointing with Halo. We establish a linear relationship between peak velocity and target distance for PJ. We then conducted a controlled experiment to evaluate PJ against other Halo-based techniques, Hop [8] and Pan with Halo. The results of the study highlight the effectiveness of PJ.

Keywords: Mouse, Scroll interaction technique, Prediction, Kinematics.

1 Introduction

The ready availability of GPS systems and the increasing popularity of map applications such as Google Earth have heightened the need for map navigation techniques. When examining a map, users often look for off-screen content by relocating the view-port to examine various regions of the map and identifying interesting locations. Researchers have started exploring various navigation and visualization aids to support navigating to off-screen targets. Halo [2] is one such visualization technique that uses rings around objects to provide information, at the screen edge, about targets placed in off-screen areas. Irani et. al. [8] extended Halos by combining it with Drag-and-pop [3] to create Hop - a technique that gathers proxies of off-screen targets by sweeping a laser beam using circular mouse movements and teleports to the target by clicking on the proxy. Hop adapts a well-understood large-display pointing technique like Drag-and-pop with an off-screen visualization technique that requires the users to adopt different input strategies for general browsing and for navigating to specific off-screen targets.

S. Lee et al. (Eds.): APCHI 2008, LNCS 5068, pp. 301–310, 2008.

Navigating to off-screen locations is fundamentally a pointing task with two unique challenges: lack of target visibility and limited areas for cursor movement. We believe a technique which can leverage the benefits of goal-directed pointing by combining a suitable large-display pointing technique with an appropriate visualization of off-screen targets, will yield better performance with off-screen navigation while simultaneously allowing users to browse through the map without navigating to a specific target.

Here we present predictive jumping (PJ) a novel technique that allows navigation to off-screen targets with a pointing movement. The algorithm combined the benefits of Delphian Desktop [1] and Halo [2]. We describe the overview of PJ and several design implications derived from the results of the user study.

2   Related Work

2.1   Pointing Interaction and Kinematics

Pointing and goal-directed movement have been analyzed since 1900 to understand human perceptual-motor process and proposed a two component model to explain the movement [4]. In the model, a pointing movement consists of an initial feed-forward movement based on the target distance and a final error-corrective feedback movement based on real time control by visual feedback [9]. Many studies on the model agree with that peak velocity is the most important kinematics feature that includes information of a user's spatial recognition of the target distance [4].

Delphian Desktop [1] exploits this observation by using the peak velocity of the initial feed-forward movement to estimate target distances and jump the cursor to the target's vicinity to reduce pointing time. Prediction is based on a linear relationship between peak velocity during pointing and the target distance. Several other enhancements to pointing techniques, such as Drag-and-pop [3], have been proposed to improve pointing in desktop environments. Drag-and-pop brings proxies of potential targets near the current cursor position as the dragging movement is started.

2.2   Map Navigation and Visualization Technique of Off-Screen Contents

When the viewed document is larger than the system's display, users rely on assorted navigation techniques to examine various regions. Several enhanced navigation techniques have been proposed to facilitate traditional methods like pan, scrollbar.

To overcome the limitation of 'motion blurs' when scanning documents at a high speeds, Igarashi [7] proposed SDAZ, which automatically couples the document's zoom-level with scroll-speed based on the simple algorithm: scale X speed = constant.

Proposed by Baudisch [2], Halo is a technique that enables users to visualize the distance and location of targets placed in the off-screen area. In Halo, the off-screen object has a large ring around the object point, and users can infer target location from the curvature on the screen's edge. Hop [8] is an interaction technique for off-screen navigation that combines Halo [2], proxies, and teleporting. Users gather targets or object proxies (duplicates of the object) around the cursor using a laser beam that can be swept using circular movements to find the proxies. Users can teleport to the target location by clicking the proxy placed near the cursor point. In a controlled study they compared hop with traditional pan and zoom techniques and showed that Hop is faster.

3 Predictive Jumping

Goal-directed movement is an intuitive operation performed by hand in the real world. The movement relies on controlled and subconscious human perceptual-motor coordination skills. We believe that applying this simple movement for navigation to off-screen locations can be valuable when users want to rapidly obtain a target.

In designing our technique we wanted to overcome two challenges. First, the interaction technique should allow users to maintain the same movement gesture for casual browsing and seeking specific off-screen targets. Second, when using a goal-directed movement for off-screen targets, users typically cannot see the targets. Thus, the interaction technique should allow user to estimate the distance of the target located off-screen prior to initiation of the pointing task.

For the first challenge, while traditional pointing methods to augment off-screen navigation requires explicit mode switching to move between specific off-screen targets and general browsing, the PJ eliminates the need for an explicit mode switch by dynamically distinguishing between movements made to select targets (both on and off-screen) or for general browsing. The proposed PJ uses the prediction algorithm described in Delphian Desktop [1] to estimate the user's goal of a natural pointing movement. PJ relies on the user's peak movement velocity to determine if the object of interest is within or beyond the current viewport. If the object is beyond the current viewport the algorithm predicts the target distance and moves the cursor to the specified object with a smooth animation. This cursor movement complements the user's natural pointing movement, whether for an on- or off-screen target or for general browsing. Users can use familiar pointing movements to reach for targets and still benefit from reduced movement time.

For the second challenge we use large elliptical rings around the object point that resemble the Halo visualization (See Figure 1(b)). The curvature of ring represented at the edge of the viewport allows users to estimate the distance to the off-screen object and plan their goal-directed movement.

4 Calibration Study: Establishing Prediction Model

4.1 Overview and Apparatus

To investigate if users can plan the initiation of goal-directed movements based on estimated target distances with Halo and to determine if Halos can be used to aid PJ we carried out a calibration study. In this study, we examined the difference if any in relationship of the peak velocity during a pointing movement with the target distance of a normal pointing task and a pointing task with object distance estimated by Halo.

We used a 50 inch display. The graphical environment was controlled by an optical mouse (Microsoft IntelliMouse 1.1A) with an extra large 408 x 306 mm mouse pad (Power Support's AirPad Pro III AK-07) to enable users to easily perform a set of continuous mouse movements. The C-D ratio was set to a constant value of 0.3.

We wanted to simulate the off-screen navigation environment with large maps about three times the current viewport window size. In the experimental setup shown in Figure 1(a), the white square on the display is the user's viewport (on-screen area), while the gray region is the off-screen area.

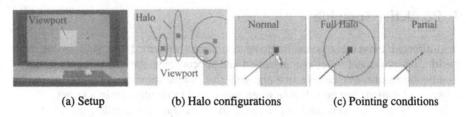

(a) Setup   (b) Halo configurations   (c) Pointing conditions

Fig. 1. Experimental conditions

4.2 Task and Experimental Design

The experiment used a simple pointing task. Subjects moved the cursor to the target from the center of their viewport as rapidly and accurately as possible. Depending on the condition, targets were not always visible, and instead they received visualization cues for the target location. If subjects correctly clicked the target, or if the distance between the clicked and target points was less than 100 pixels, the system played an audio signal to indicate success or almost success. If the subject missed, a failure sound was played. The purpose of this task is to measure kinematics features such as peak velocity rather than measuring all pointing features, such as error and pointing time. Therefore, instead of high precision, natural initial movement was required. So feedback signals that did not produce rewards were used to discourage subjects from only concentrating on precision even if the target was not visible.

We used a within-subject design of pointing condition (Normal, Full Halo, Partial Halo), target distance (500, 700, 900, 1100 pixels), and target direction (0, 45, 90, 135, 180, 225, 270, 315°) with 10 repetitions per condition. The experiment conditions were presented in random order. Subjects were given about 100 practice trials before starting the experiments. The study was conducted with eight subjects (six males) from ages 22 to 36. All subjects were right handed.

4.3 Pointing Conditions and Halo Configurations

Figure 1(c) shows the three types of pointing conditions: Normal, Full Halo, and Partial Halo. In this figure, gray area means off-screen while white means on-screen are. So the dashed and solid lines indicate invisible and visible cursor movements, respectively. The viewport (white squire) is always visible. The details of the pointing conditions are listed below.

Normal: The target is visible, and Halo is not displayed. Users have to move the cursor to the target and click on it.

Full Halo: Users see the target and a circle around it. Users move the cursor to the target and click on it without visual feedback. The cursor disappears when it reaches the edge of the viewport. This condition helps users understand the relationship between the target and the circle drawn around the target.

Partial Halo: The target is not visible, but the Halo curvature at the edge of the screen is visible. Users have to estimate the target position based on this curvature, move the cursor to the estimated target location, and click on the target with the invisible cursor. The cursor disappears when it reaches the edge of the viewport.

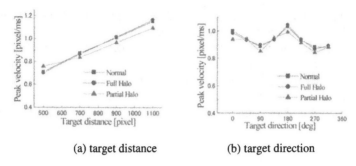

(a) target distance   (b) target direction

Fig. 2. Peak velocity relative to target distance and direction

For targets at the top, left, or right sides of the viewport, we use an ellipse-shaped Halo at the edge of screen. For diagonal targets, the Halo is shaped as a circle. We used the same Halo configuration described by Irani et al. [8]. The Halo's line width becomes thin with target distance, which resembles a rubber band (See Figure 1(b)).

4.4 Results and Discussion

We found a main effect of target distance ($F_{(3, 21)} = 37.6$, $p < .001$) and target direction ($F_{(7, 49)} = 9.61$, $p < .001$). However the main effect of the pointing condition was not significant ($F_{(2, 14)} = 1.02$, $p > .05$). Multiple comparisons of target distance show significant differences among all distance conditions ($p < .05$). Figure 2(a) shows peak velocity and target distance for each pointing condition. The result indicates that the relationship between peak velocity and target distance is linear whether the target is visible or only the Halo curvature is visible. There is no significant difference among pointing conditions ($p > .05$). The r^2 values range of the linear regression analysis is from 0.883 to 0.996. There are individual differences among subjects. Figure 2(b) and multiple comparisons of target direction show significant differences among horizontal movement directions of 0 and 180, vertical movement directions of 90 and 270, and diagonal movement tasks ($p < .05$).

The results suggest that this method is effective to calibrate and establish the prediction model of the linear relationship between peak velocity and the distance of the off-screen target. It leads users to estimate target distances and plan them with goal-directed movements. From Figure 2(a) we see that target distance predictions can be applied to off-screen target acquisition tasks by considering pointing direction. However, some practice with reference conditions, i.e., Full Halo conditions, is necessary to learn the Halo effect well and estimate the absolute target distance.

5 Specifying Predictive Jumping

PJ estimates a user's spatial intention and rapidly moves the cursor to the target location in a smooth animation. By applying Delphian Desktop's prediction and jump algorithm to scrolling, users can use familiar pointing movements to reach for the target and simultaneously benefit from the automatic jump.

PJ uses the relationship between target distance and peak velocity obtained by the Partial Halo condition in the calibration (regression model). The system tracks user cursor movements toward the off-screen region. Once it detects peak velocity and cursor direction, it selects a regression model based on the cursor direction from a set of eight prepared regression models for each direction (see Figure 2(b)). Then it predicts target distance by using the selected model and scrolls with smooth animation to the target location. Figure 3 shows PJ behavior used in the experiment.

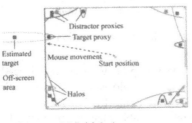

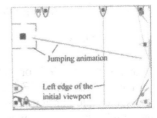

(a) Initial view   (b) Jump animation with view transition

Fig. 3. Behavior of Predictive jumping

Analysis of calibration data shows that peak velocity was detected when the cursor reached about half the distance between start and target locations for all distances. This leads to a limitation in PJ imposed by the viewport-size. When the system cannot detect peak velocity within the current viewport (since the map is much larger than the viewport), the velocity at the edge of the viewport is regarded as peak velocity.

6   User Study: Comparison of Off-Screen Navigation Techniques

We carried out a user study to compare PJ with other Halo-based interaction techniques-Hop and Pan with Halo. Pan with Halo is a combination of Pan widely used for commercial map systems and Halo as a visualization aide for off-screen objects. We are primarily interested in determining if users can quickly reach their target and improve their spatial comprehension of the map. The experimental task consisted of a target search and selection task, followed by a spatial recognition test.

6.1   Experimental Design

A repeated measures within-subject design of interaction technique (predictive jumping, Hop, Pan with Halo) x target distance (700, 900, and 1100 pixels) x object density (16, 32, and 48 objects) was used. We used an all crossed design that resulted in 27 combinations with 16 repetitions (8 directions x 2 repeats) per condition. The experiment was divided into three blocks and inserted subjects' relaxed time. The task orders were counterbalanced to reduce order effects. Object density is an important factor in both searching a target and recalling the specified target. The map was divided into nine regions, and eight direction areas were defined from the center of the viewport. When object density was set to 16, two distracter objects were randomly placed in each region. A target was not selected from these distracters. Subjects were given enough practice trials before starting the actual experimental loops. The entire experiment took around 110 minutes with additional time to calibrate PJ.

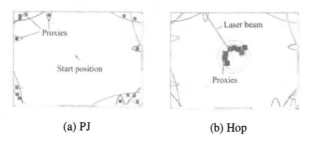

(a) PJ   (b) Hop

Fig. 4. Initial view and proxies for PJ and Hop

6.2 Interaction Techniques

Predictive jumping: An initial view of the display screen for the target selection using PJ is shown in Figure 4(a). The user first has to search for a target location shown in blue. Then the user moves the cursor towards the object and the system performs a predictive jump. The technique works as described in the previous section. If the predicted point is contained within 300 x 300 pixels (tolerance area) of an object, the cursor snaps to the object location. If the predicted point is not near an object, the cursor moves to the predicted point without adjustment. When the target appears on-screen, users can move the cursor to the target and click on it. In case the target is still off-screen, users can continue to use PJ to get to the target. The pointing *ID* is in the range of 1.72 to 2.20 bits calculated using tolerance area and target distance according to Hinckley's model [6]. The duration of automatic scrolling for PJ (and Hop) is a constant value of 1000 ms.

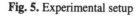

Fig. 5. Experimental setup   **Fig. 6.** View of spatial recognition test

Hop: Here in the initial view of the display, only Halos are visible at the edge of the viewport, not proxies. In the first step, users gather proxies by sweeping a laser beam with a circular mouse movement. During this movement, they simultaneously gather and search for targets (see Figure 4(b)). The positions of the proxies around the movement arc are calculated from the regions and the points where the laser and Halos interact. If the target proxy is found in the set of visible proxies, the user can teleport it to the target by clicking on the proxy. The cursor is then automatically set on the target. The pointing *ID* ranges from 1.8 to 2.20 bits calculated by the proxies layouts based on Fitts' law [5].

Pan with Halo (PwH): Here the initial view and first step are identical to PJ. Users then pan several times to obtain the target in the center of the viewport using the mouse in a drag-and-shift-and-release operation. A tolerance area is displayed by dotted lines at the center of viewport, and the user is asked to position the target within this square and to click on it. Pointing *ID* in this technique is the same as PJ.

6.3 Apparatus, Subject and Procedure

We used the same desk, chair, PC, mouse, C-D ratio, and mouse pad as in the calibration study described at previous section. A 15 inch display (1024 x 768 pixels) and tablet PC for the spatial recognition test were used (See Figure 5).

12 subjects (8 males) from ages 22 to 36 participated in our study. All were experienced in map navigation interfaces. All went through a short calibration procedure for the system to learn their regression model

The procedure consisted of two tasks, selection task, and spatial recognition test to determine if users were able to recall the location on the map. In task 1, subjects had to select the target shown as a blue proxy using the specified interaction technique. The color of other distracters was set to either green or red. After task 1, subjects indicated the target which they selected in task 1 from the entire map displayed with all the same color objects on a tablet PC using the stylus (See Figure 6). After completing this task, next trial began following the experimental order.

6.4 Results

A repeated measures ANOVA was conducted on the task completion time. We found that a main effect of the interaction technique ($F_{(2, 22)}$ = 5.86, p < .001), target distance ($F_{(2, 22)}$ = 74.7, p < .001), target density ($F_{(2, 22)}$ = 8.77, p < .05), and interaction between interaction technique and target distance.

Figure 7(a) shows target distance and task completion time for each interaction technique. Multiple comparisons showed that PJ was significantly faster than Hop for 700 and 900 pixel target distances. But there was no significant difference between PJ

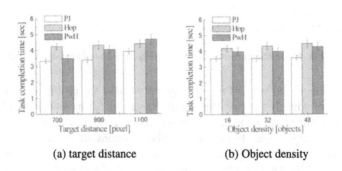

(a) target distance   (b) Object density

Fig. 7. Task completion time of interaction techniques

and Hop for distances of 1100 pixels. PJ was significantly faster than PwH except for the 700 pixel target distance. PwH strongly depended on target distance. The performance of PJ dropped at the 1100 pixel distance condition. Figure 7(b) shows the effect of object density on interaction techniques and PJ was significantly faster than the others. In Hop and PwH, task time increases as object density slightly.

From the analysis of the spatial recognition accuracy rate we found no significant difference of interaction techniques ($F_{(2,22)}$ = 1.87, p >.05), and an interaction between interaction technique x object density ($F_{(6, 66)}$ = 2.93, p < .05). For high object densities, PJ's spatial recognition accuracy was worse than other techniques.

7 Discussion

Our results show that PJ effectively reduced task completion time for off-screen target selection. Users felt as if they were a using simple and familiar method, an attitude also reflected in their subjective preferences for this technique. If the prediction was correct, the task was completed very rapidly.

For PJ, the effect of object density was lower than others for task completion time because when using PJ, subjects only needed to attend to the planning of goal-directed movements from current position to estimated location. This meant that they did not attend and interact with other distracters while the others interacted with distracters in the stage of gathering proxies or panning operations. Thus, when users need to rapidly access off-screen targets, PJ is an effective navigation tool.

PJ's performance dropped slightly at the condition of maximum target distance. In this condition, sometimes the system could not correctly detect peak velocity within the initial viewport. Thus, we are planning to improve the tracking method during the pointing tasks by detecting the actual mouse position instead of the cursor position so that detecting precision does not depend on display size or C-D ratio.

Another reason for dropped performance reflects current Halo setting's ineffectiveness as a target distance cue for large distances. For smaller target distances, Halos offered subjects a strong distance cue to start with a strong planned movement. For the largest distance condition, the cue becomes weak, and users' planned movements are weakened (see Figure 2(a)). Halo settings such as line width and ring size need to be explored to improve users' ability to plan pointing movements.

The following design implications emerged from our study.

– PJ is a powerful navigation technique that can be used for off-screen navigation and casual browsing.
– Designers can harvest goal-directed pointing techniques to improve performance in off-screen navigation tasks.
– Halos can be used as strong cues for the distances of off-screen objects for planning the pointing movement for short to medium range distances.

8 Conclusion

We proposed predictive jumping (PJ), which allows users to effectively navigate off-screen targets using a goal-directed movement. Predictions of user intentions and jumping are used to reach off-screen objects with a fluid pointing movement. Halos are used to estimate off-screen target distance and plan the intuition of goal-directed movements. We established a calibration method to make a prediction model based on the linear relationship between off-screen target distance and peak velocity.

A user study by comparing PJ with Hop and Pan with Halo showed that PJ effectively shortened task completion time for quick off-screen target acquisition tasks. In the future, we are planning to explore representation of Halo and extend PJ's ability by improving the cursor tracking method.

Acknowledgments. This research was supported in part by "Global COE (Centers of Excellence) Program" of the Ministry of Education, Culture, Sports, Science and Technology, Japan and Microsoft Institute for Japanese Academic Research Collaboration.

References

1. Asano, T., Sharlin, E., Kitamura, Y., Takashima, K., Kishino, F.: Predictive interaction using the Delphian Desktop. In: ACM UIST 2005, pp. 133–141 (2005)
2. Baudisch, P., Rosenholtz, R.: Halo: a technique for visualizing off-screen objects. In: ACM CHI 2003, pp. 481–488 (2003)
3. Baudisch, P., Cutrell, E., Robbins, D., Czerwinski, M., Tandler, P., Bederson, B., Zierlinger, A.: Drag-and-pop and drag-and-pick: techniques for accessing remote screen content on touch- and pen-operated systems. In: INTERACT 2003, pp. 57–64 (2003)
4. Elliott, D., Helsen, W.F., Chua, R.: A century later: Woodworth's (1899) two-component model of goal-directed aiming. Psychological Bulletin 127(3), 342–357 (2001)
5. Fitts, P.M.: The information capacity of the human motor system in controlling the amplitude of movement. J. Exp. Psychology 47(6), 381–391 (1954)
6. Hinckley, K., Cutrell, E., Bathiche, S., Muss, T.: Quantitative analysis of scrolling techniques. In: ACM CHI 2002, pp. 65–72 (2002)
7. Igarashi, T., Hinckley, K.: Speed-dependent automatic zooming for browsing large documents. In: ACM UIST 2000, pp. 139–148 (2000)
8. Irani, P., Gutwin, C., Yang, X. D.: Improving selection of off-screen targets with hopping. In: ACM CHI 2006, pp. 299–308 (2006)
9. MacKenzie, C.L., Marteniuk, R.G., Dugas, C., Liske, D., Eickmeier, B.: Three-dimensional movement trajectories in Fitts' task: implications for control. The Quarterly J. Exp. Psychology 39A(4), 629–647 (1987)

Hands-Free Input Interface Using Mimetic Muscle Movements for Wearable Computer

Atsushi Hiyama, Tomohiro Tanikawa, and Michitaka Hirose

Graduate School of Information Science and Technology, The University of Tokyo,
7-3-1, Hongo, Bunkyo-ku, Tokyo, Japan
{atsushi,tani,hirose}@cyber.t.u-tokyo.ac.jp

Abstract. In recent years, we have many chances to operate cellular phone to browse e-mails or web sites. However, operating cellular phone in transit may cause dangerous conditions. This paper describes the ergonomic evaluation of hands-free input interface for wearable computing. The Interface is designed to operate the computer by mimetic muscle movements, which are detected by piezo films attached to the surface of the skin. In order to evaluate the input interface using facial actions, we measured user's behavior and mental state by wearable measuring device. The user's behavior is observed by the CCD camera and pedometer, and user's mental workload is measured by the RRV (variance of R-R intervals of ECG). We evaluated the efficiency of the developed interface by comparing with cellular phone, which can connect to the Internet. We proved that the input interface using mimetic muscle movements has high compatibility between computer operation and daily activities.

Keywords: Wearable computing, Input interface, Facial muscles.

1 Introduction

In order to achieve true wearable computing, it is essential to lighten the overhead when manipulating interface and make compatibility between computer operation and daily activities at the same time. The highest overhead is that users of mobile terminals are not able to pay enough attention to their surrounding circumstances during manipulation of input interfaces. In this research, we developed hands-free input interface that can reduce such overhead. We also evaluated the developed interface by setting a task to users' and measured their behavior and mental workload and compared with users' doing the same task by using cellular phone.

2 Input Interface for Wearable Computer

Input interface for wearable computer can be classified into two categories. The conscious type input interface and the unconscious type. The unconscious type of input interface has well researched in the field of context awareness. Wearable computer provides appropriate services to users by sensing the user's situation, location or mental workload [1].

S. Lee et al. (Eds.): APCHI 2008, LNCS 5068, pp. 311–320, 2008.

On the contrary, conscious type of input interfaces is required when user wants to get a service in a proactive manner. Typical input interface for wearable computer is Twidller (Handykey Inc.) [2]. Twidller can act as a full-sized keyboard that can operate with one hand but user must grip the device to operate the computer. Finge Ring is ring type input device and it can also act as a keyboard, but it is impossible to operate computer while walking or carrying a baggage [3]. The most widely used hands-free input method is a speech recognition system [4]. Speech recognition can be a strong support for workers in plant, hospital or other professional work. But using speech recognition system during daily activities, it is difficult to distinguish background noise or utterance that is not an input operation. Also, we feel anxious about using speech recognition in public space.

Therefore, we propose a conscious type input interface using mimetic muscle movements. It is known that mimetic muscle can match the expressions of hands. Figure 1 illustrates the division of labor in primary motor area and somatosensory area of cerebral cortex of man [5]. Both face and hand dominate particularly large area in cerebral cortex. It is obvious that face has high degree of freedoms in movement, since face can make various types of expressions. From the studies of Facial Action Coding System (FACS), mimetic muscle movements are classified in 44 action units [6]. From these bases, we chose mimetic muscle movement for input method.

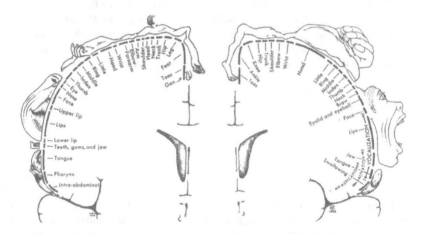

Fig. 1. Sensory Homunculus (left) and Motor Homunculus (right) [5]

Examples mentioned as conscious type input interface are designed to carry the function of PC keyboard and its application does not assume the particular work under wearable or mobile computing environment. As a supposed application we chose to realize the task that we often handle with cellular phone while walking. Cellular phones that can connect to Internet are very common in Japan nowadays, so we decided to equip the capability to bear a task of browsing web sites for cellular phones or e-mails. For browsing web sites or e-mails we use four kinds of input operations. Scrolling up and down the browser, and selecting an item or cancel and back to the previous menu. Developed interface has these four input functions.

2 Sensor for Mimetic Muscle Movements

For sensing mimetic muscle movements, sensor has to detect subtle change of the surface of the face, such as tension or relaxation of mimetic muscle. Besides, face is the best part that draws others' eyes, and also it has the best variety of aesthesia, we must be careful not to block those functions. The requirements for sensor are summarized as follows.

(1) The sensor must be sensitive enough to catch the mimetic muscle movements arise in a second under various conditions.
(2) The sensor must be compact and light enough to be low profile and low burden.
(3) The sensor must not interrupt the movement of mimetic muscle.
(4) The sensor must not block the senses of visual, auditory, tactile, olfactory and gustatory.

This time we selected piezo electric polymer film for sensor (LDT1, Measurement Specialties Inc.) that meets those requirements (Figure 2). Specification of LDT1 is 16[mm] wide, 41[mm] long and 205[μm] thick. It is thin and compact that can reflect the movements of surface of the skin. Moreover, it can attach to the skin just like an adhesive tape.

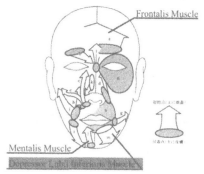

Fig. 2. Piezo Film LDT1

Fig. 3. Mimetic Muscles and its Direction of Contraction[7]

The characteristic of LDT1 is that it gives the output of change in electrical potential according to the time derivative of curvature factor of its surface. For example, In case of attaching the sensor above the eyebrow, if subject blink her/his eyes, the sensor generates electropositive potential while the movement of closing the eyes and the sensor generates electronegative potential while the movement of opening the eyes. If subject starts to open her/his eyes wide, the sensor generates electronegative potential while the movement of opening up the eyes and the sensor generates electropositive potential while the movement of becoming normal position of eyelids (Figure 4). Additionally, momentary movement of muscle generates high and instantaneous potential change and slow movement of muscle generates low and prolonged potential change even if subject moves her/his face widely.

Considering above-mentioned characteristic of the sensor, we studied the applicable region of face to attach the sensor. As a result, we decide to attach the sensor and allocated four operations to following two regions (Figure 3).

(A) Cursor up and down: Region between mentalis muscle and depressor labii inferioris muscle

(B) Selection and Cancelation: Upper region of frontalis muscle

Cursor up and down are respectively homologize to the movement of up and down of mentalis muscle (Figure 4(a)(b)). And selection and cancelation operations are respectively homologized to the movement to opening the eyes wide and blinking the eyes strong (Figure 4(c)(d)). Two sensors are attached to the region which involuntary movements are not likely to detect. The sensors detect only relatively large voluntary movemets.

There is approximately no individual difference in the sensor output for the movement of frontalis muscle that is used for unpeeling and blinking. Thus, we decided to treat the signal from the sensor attached above the eyebrow as a binary signal. And for the cursor inputs, detected from the movement of mentalis muscle, are treated the as an analog signal, in order to make the flexibility for the adjustment of individual difference and the expandability to two-dimensional cursor input.

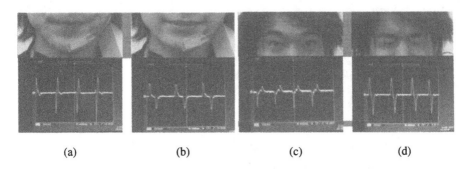

(a)   (b)   (c)   (d)

Fig. 4. Input "Up"(a), "Down"(b), "Select"(c) and "Cancel"(d)

3   Configuration of Wearable Device

Figure 5 shows the developed wearable computer using mimetic muscle input. Signals from the sensors are processed as follows. Signal from the sensor attached above eyebrow is amplified and have threshold processing. Then interpreted to selection or cancellation input by Z80 processor and sent to PC (Libretto70, Toshiba Inc.) via RS232C. A signal from the sensor attached to the jaw tip is amplified and has analog-digital conversion at Z80, then sent to PC via RS232C. PC distinguishes operation of cursor up or down by threshold processing. We used QVGA HMD (MicroOptical corp.) for the display, in order to keep hands-free condition.

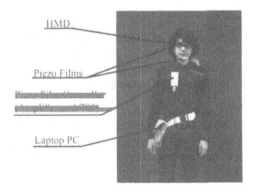

Fig. 5. Developed Wearable Computer

4 Proficiency Test

We tested if users can perfect themselves with the developed interface using mimetic muscle movement. As an experiment, we instructed to make the four input operations randomly on PC display for 50 times continuously to five subjects. The experiment is repeated for three times for each subject. From the result, the average percentage of correctness were under 60% for the first trial, but in the third trial, the average percentage has increased nearly 90%(Table 1). Therefore, the developed interface can be utilized as wearable computer interface.

Table 1. Result of Proficiency Test

	First	Second	Third
Subject1	34	44	70
Subject2	44	62	80
Subject3	60	66	92
Subject4	64	82	96
Subject5	78	78	94
Average	56	66	86

(%)

5 Wearable Computing Experiment

We applied the developed interface for wearable computing experiment. The experiment is designed to browse web pages during walking along the ordered course. Subjects are force to go up and down the stairs and open the door during experimental route. We also asked subjects to take the same experiment by using existing cellular phone. Evaluation is made by comparing above two different interfaces by measuring several kinds of biological reactions and the performance of web browsing during the experiment. We had three subjects for this experiment. The evaluation items for this experiment are as follows.

(1) RRV (R-R interval)

RRV is variance of R-R intervals of electrocardiograph (EGC). RRV is used as an indicator of metal workload in fields of physiology and psychology. RRV value becomes lower when subject is suffering high mental workload. We measured RRV as an autonomic nerve response for workload.

(2) Cadence

Human being is using entire body to maintain a balance while walking. But we may lose this balance when we are operating computer while walking. We measured cadence as a response of motor nervous system for workload.

(3) Movement of the head

The field of vision has an important role in perceiving the surrounding environment. We measured movement of the head also as a response of motor nervous system for workload.

(4) Performance of web browsing

Browsing web pages or e-mails are possible work as we walking down the street. For the experiment, we asked subjects to read the text of our laboratory's text based web pages. Evaluation has made by the number of research projects she/he read. We measured this as a cognition performance under workload.

Figure 7 shows the developed wearable device that measures biological performance of the subjects. This wearable device has a DV camera for recording the experiment data. Movement of the head is captured by a CCD (0.26 mega pixels and its field of view is 40[°] vertical and 52[°] horizontal) attached to the glasses. We used pedometer for the measurement of the cadence and used photo interrupter as a heart rate meter.

RRV officially indicates the variance of R-R interval in ECG. However, it is a heavy burden for subject to measure ECG, since it requires them to attach electrodes on their breast. Therefore, though it is indirect way of measuring R-R interval, we detected a blood stream of the fingertip that corresponds to R-R interval.

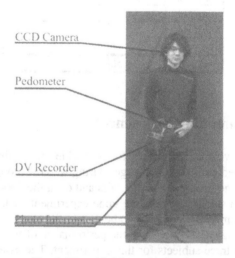

Fig. 6. Wearable Measuring Device

Fig. 7. Field of View of Cellular Phone(left) and Wearable Computer(right)

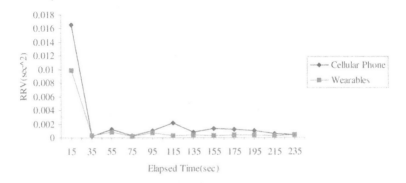

Fig. 8. RRV of Subject 1

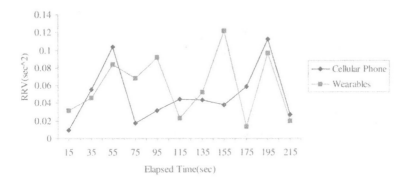

Fig. 9. RRV of Subject 2

In order to synchronize the captured image of head mounted camera, cadence and R-R intervals precisely, we recorded signals of cadence and R-R intervals as audio signals to DV recorder. Cadence data is recorded in right channel of audio and R-R interval data in recorded in left channel of audio.

From results of this experiment, it can be said that adopting developed wearable computer using mimetic muscle movement and HMD made subjects to assure the field of view that is necessary to look around the surrounding circumstances than cellular phone (Figure 7). Mental workload was generally high in using wearable computer since it is burdensome to wear, but significant rise of mental workload is observed when subjects could not combine interaction with computer and surround environment in the trial using cellular phone (Figure 8, 9, 10). Furthermore, the cadence is stable and subjects were able to open the door smoothly when using the developed wearable computer (Figure 11, 12, 13). Additionally, all the subjects could walk faster and had higher performance of web browsing (Table 2).

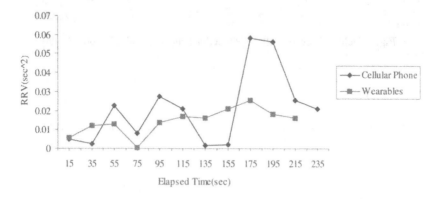

Fig. 10. RRV of Subject 3

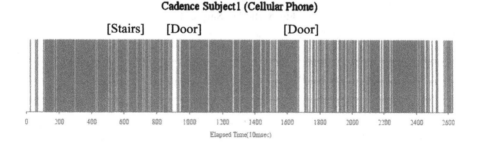

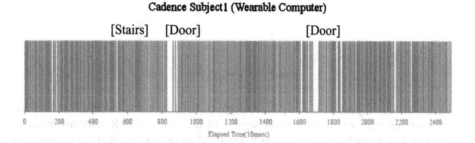

Fig. 11. Cadence of Subject 1

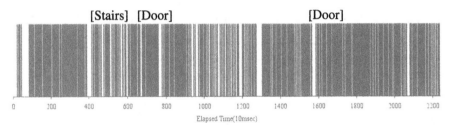

Fig. 12. Cadence of Subject 2

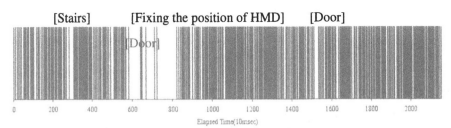

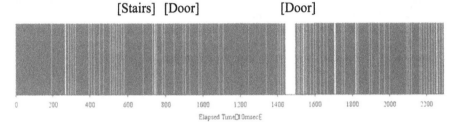

Fig. 13. Cadence of Subject 3

Table 2. Performance of web Browsing

	Topics Read	Total Time
Cellular Phone	3	260sec
Wearable Computer	6	250sec

	Topics Read	Total Time
Cellular Phone	3	220sec
Wearable Computer	5	215sec

	Topics Read	Total Time
Cellular Phone	3	300sec
Wearable Computer	5	230sec

6   Conclusion

We have developed a wearable computer that has high compatibility between computer operation and daily activities. Input interface using mimetic muscle movement made it possible to continuously operate the computer even if users faces situations that their hands are filled. Although, we still have to redesign the wearable computer to reduce the burden of wearing it. Also, we would like to add more input variation to the system without adding extra sensors and make the system advance to provide information services according to the users' circumstances by sensing the users' state.

References

1. Picard, R., Healey, J.: Affective Wearables. Personal Technologies 1, 231–240 (1997)
2. Handykey Corporation, http://www.handykey.com/
3. Fukumoto, M.: Body Coupling FingeRing Wireless Wearable Keyboard. In: CHI 1997, pp. 147–154 (1997)
4. Nuance – The Leading Supplier of Speech Recognition, Imaging, PDF and OCR Solutions, http://www.nuance.com/
5. Penfield, W., Rasmussen, T.: The cerebral cortex of a man: a clinical study of localization of function. Macmillan, New York (1952)
6. Ekman, P., Friesen, W.V.: Facial Action Coding System. Consulting Psychologists Press (1978)
7. Kurokawa, T.: Nonverbal Interface (In Japanese): Ohmsha, Ltd. (1994)

Muscle Loadings While Using Finger as Input Device

Yung-Hui Lee, Wei-Yow Chen, and Yi-Cherng Su

Department of Industrial Management,
National Taiwan University of Science and Technology,
No. 43 Kee-lung Road, Section 4, Taipei, Taiwan, ROC
yhlee@im.ntust.edu.tw

Abstract. Finger-operated input device (FOID) might provide effective pointing and dragging control. However, it was suspected that the repetitive nature of the pointing and dragging tasks while operating the FOID would induce finger muscle fatigue. This study examined the finger strain by collecting electromyographic (EMG) data from 10 subjects while playing "computer solitaire" using the FOID or a trackball mouse for 40 minutes each. Pair-wise comparisons of electrical activity and median frequency showed no significant differences in these fatigue measurements between the new FOID and the trackball mouse. On the other hand, results of JASA indicted less finger muscle loading for the new FOID than that of the trackball. These results are of heuristic value and provide a promising basis for future development of the concept of FOIDs.

Keywords: Finger-operated input device, Trackball, Mouse, Electromyography, JASA.

1 Introduction

Mouse use increases the muscular burden in the hand and forearm, especially in the extensor carpi ulnaris and extensor digitorum communis, when the device is held with ulnar/radial deviation [1]. Rredesign efforts are encouraged to provide ergonomic input into future design of these ubiquitous devices. Zhai et al., [2] investigated the controllability of a six degrees-of-freedom input device and found that incorporating fingers in the operation of this device resulted in improved performance. Brown, et al. [3] demonstrated their design of new input device, controlled by thumb movements, could be used within the same realm of accuracy as commercial devices, while imposing a lesser degree of postural stress. These suggest that finger-operated input devices (FOIDs) provide effective pointing and dragging control.

To allow fuller examination of this notion, a finger-operated input device (FOID) was designed by the authors [4]. However, we suspected that the repetitive nature of the pointing and dragging tasks while operating the FOID would induce finger muscle fatigue. Thus, electromyographical (EMG) examinations were performed, with the aim of examining the influence of various control movements on the muscular strain of the fingers while using either the new FOID or a trackball mouse (Figure 1).

S. Lee et al. (Eds.): APCHI 2008, LNCS 5068, pp. 321–327, 2008.
© Springer-Verlag Berlin Heidelberg 2008

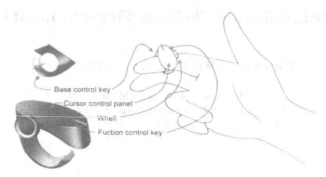

Fig. 1. Prototype of the finger operated input device (FOID)

2 Methods

2.1 Subjects

Ten participants, who had given informed consent to participate, were paid study volunteers. None of the participants had previously had any musculoskeletal injuries of hands and arms. The mean (SD) age of the participants was 25.4 (1.7) years.

2.2 Finger-Operated Input Device

The main body of the FOID was placed on the user's forearm and connected to the control keys through cables. The cursor movement key, the base control key and the function control key were placed on the lateral side of the index finger. The thumb activated the keys to move the cursor, or to point or select. The wheel and the base control key were placed on the lateral side of middle finger. The wheel and the base control key were pressed using the index finger to drag the cursor. The index finger or thumb was used to move the page up or down using the wheel, and to activate the laser pointer.

2.3 Muscle Loading Comparison Task

Participants played the game "solitaire" continuously for 40 minutes on the computer. Either the new FOID or the trackball mouse was selected as the first input device for half of the participants. The game required subject to use the pointing and dragging functions of the device with little cognitive demands. A resting period of 20 min was provided between each test once the input device had been selected to ensure that no cumulative local muscle fatigue occurred between tests. Each subject completed the experimental tasks within a two-hour session.

2.4 Electromyography

EMG activities of the target muscle groups were recorded by means of bipolar direct measurements (Noraxon MyoSystem XP). Pairs of Ag/AgCl surface electrodes separated by 2 cm were placed on bellies of the right adductor pollicis, abductor

Table 1. Mean activation level of finger's muscles in %RVC (N=10)

Finger muscles	Logitech TrackMan Wheel	FOID	Paired-t p
M. Adductor Pollicis	3.60 (1.35)	5.74 (2.24)	0.012*
M. Abductor Pollicis longus	3.81 (2.31)	3.88 (2.31)	0.804
M. Oponens Pollicis	3.61 (1.28)	3.58 (1.53)	0.797

* Significant at 0.05 level

pollicis longus and opponens pollicis muscles after the skin was prepared in the standard manner. These muscles were selected as activators for thumb adduction, thumb abduction, and thumb and finger oppositions. The sample rate was 1500 Hz. EMG data evaluation was performed off-line, in three parts: time-related changes in EMG amplitude, time-related changes in spectra throughout the test, and JASA comparisons were evaluated using the NORXON MyoResearch XP Master. The scientific basis and applications of JASA methods are found in Luttmann, et al. [5].

2.5 Subjective Rating

Participants subjectively rated the use of each device at the end of each experiment by rating the comfort levels in the neck, shoulders, forearm, wrist, hand, and lower and upper back. They also rated the ease with which they could perform precision tasks, limitations of space and posture during manipulation and overall preference. A 5-point rating scale was used: 5 represented 'very comfortable' or 'very easy to use' and 1 indicated 'very uncomfortable' or 'not easy to use.'

2.6 Statistical Analysis

Means and standard deviations (SDs) of all measurements were calculated by standard methods. Student's paired t tests were used to study the effects of inter-subject variability and the differences between input devices and task variables. The Wilcoxon matched-pairs signed-rank test was used to detect the differences between subjective ratings. An alpha of 0.05 was selected as the minimum level of significance.

3 Results

Mean activation levels of the adductor pollicis, abductor pollicis longus and opponens pollicis muscles while playing "Solitare" using the trackball mouse and new FOID are compared in Table 1. The new FOID resulted in significantly ($p < 0.05$) higher adductor pollicis EMG (5.74 (2.24) %RVC) compared to that of the trackball mouse (3.60 (1.35) %RVC).

3.1 Time-Related Changes in EMG Amplitude and Frequency

Table 2 shows the comparison of regression line slopes for time-related changes of electrical activity and median frequency for the three muscles while using the new

FOID or the trackball mouse. Taking the data for the adductor pollicis muscle as an example, the regression line slope for electrical activity for the new FOID was -0.035 (0.093) and it was 0.013 (0.052) for the trackball mouse. A negative slope represents a time-dependent decrease in EMG amplitude during the course of the test (Table 3). Regression line slopes for electrical activity and mean frequency did not differ significantly in comparisons with zero or between devices ($p < 0.05$) (Table 2). We failed to identify any significantly fatigued muscle using either of these two input devices based on electrical activity and median frequency.

Table 2. Slope of the time-related changes of EMG amplitude and mean frequency of the three muscles (N=10)

Finger muscles	Logitech Trackman Wheel	Paired-t FOID	p
Electrical activity (EA)			
M. Adductor Pollicis	0.013 (0.051)	-0.035 (0.093)	0.128
M. Abductor Pollicis longus	0.023 (0.082)	-0.040 (0.171)	0.382
M. Oponens Pollicis	0.098 (0.166)	0.005 (0.103)	0.260
Mean frequency (MF)			
M. Adductor Pollicis	0.610 (0.571)	-0.038 (0.941)	0.101
M. Abductor Pollicis longus	-0.027 (0.405)	0.070 (0.086)	0.469
M. Oponens Pollicis	-0.202 (0.505)	0.148 (0.698)	0.313

* significant at 0.05 level

3.2 Application of JASA

Figure 2 illustrates the joint analyses of time-related changes in electrical activity and median frequency for the adductor pollicis, abductor pollicis longus and opponens pollicis muscles. The summary of the joint analyses of the slopes of the regression lines for electrical activity and median frequency are shown in Table 3. Of the 10 participants with three muscles each in the JASA analysis (total of 30 cases), 7/30 cases fell into the lower right quadrant when using the new FOID. This means that in the corresponding EMG recording of electrical activity and median frequency, both showed muscular fatigue. The corresponding number of cases for the trackball mouse was 9 of 30 cases.

An increase in the muscular force used in the course of tests occurred for the 6 cases located in the upper right quadrant for the new-FOID as compared to 11 cases for trackball mouse. Electrical activity and median frequency indicated recovery from early fatigue for the relevant muscles for 12 cases located in the upper left quadrant when the new FOID was used. The corresponding number for the trackball was 5 cases.

3.3 Subjective Ratings

Subjects rated the new FOID and trackball mouse for ease of pointing on a 5-point scale (5 being the most and 1 being the least easy and comfortable to use). The subjective mean rating for the new FOID was 3.9 (0.6), and for the trackball mouse, it was also 3.9 (0.9). The overall mean preference for the new FOID (3.8) was the same as that of the trackball (3.8). Wilcoxon matched-pairs signed-rank analysis showed no significant differences among the entries ($p < 0.05$).

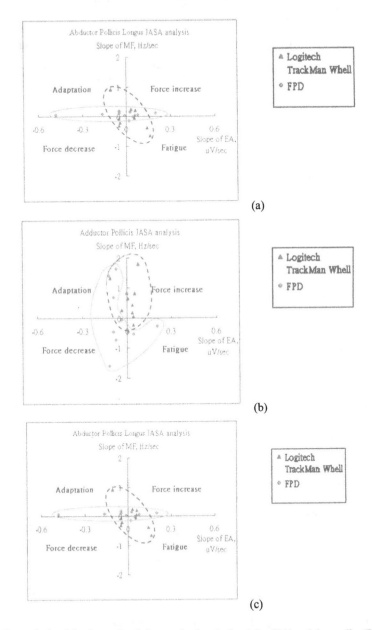

(a)

(b)

(c)

Fig. 2. Joint analysis of the time-related changes in electrical activity (EA) and the median Frequency (MF) of EMG of the right Adductor Pollicis (a), Abductor Pollicis Longus (b), and Opponens Pollicis(c) when using the new-FOID (in grey color) and the trackball mouse (in blue color)

Table 3. Joint analysis of the slopes of the regression lines of electrical activity (EA) and mean frequency (MF) of EMG derived from all three muscles under test

Interpretation	force increase	adaptation	force decrease	fatigue	
		Number of cases with:			
	Positive EA Positive MF	Negative EA+ Positive MF	NegativeEA + Negative MF	Positive EA+ Negative MF	
Trackball mouse					
M. Adductor Pollicis	6	3	0	1	
M. Abductor Pollicis longus	3	1	3	3	
M. Oponens Pollicis	2	1	2	5	
Total	11	5	5	9	30
New FOID					
M. Adductor Pollicis	0	3	4	3	
M. Abductor Pollicis longus	4	5	0	1	
M. Oponens Pollicis	2	4	1	3	
Total	6	12	5	7	30

4 Discussion

The FOID is held between the flexed fingers (index and middle fingers) and the thumb [5]. These fingers form a prehensile tripod that is used for precision activity, thus, the user is able delicately to adjust his/her posture in response to the activity of the skin receptors on each finger tip. Results of paired-t tests showed there was a significantly higher adductor pollicis EMG (5.74 %RVC) for the new FOID compared to 3.60%RVC for the trackball mouse ($p < 0.05$). The main operation of the new FOID is to "move" the cursor and to "activate" the "key." These two operations were conducted separately in the pointing tasks, whereas it required simultaneous downward pressing of the thumb and adduction of the middle finger to work against the index finger in the dragging tasks. Perceptions of usability may also be influenced by familiarity. Unfamiliarity with the three fingers operation for dragging tasks affected the usability and could explain why there was a higher adductor pollicis EMG.

Examining separate fatigue indicators (Table 2) showed that there was no electrical activity increase or median frequency spectral shift toward lower frequencies in the 40-minute tests using the new FOID or the trackball. However, joint considerations of the two fatigue indicators (Table 3) revealed there were seven cases (out of 30) of fatigue for the new FOID (three for adductor pollicis, one for the abductor pollicis longus and three for the opponens pollicis muscles). This is less than the nine fatigue cases for the trackball mouse. In addition, with the new FOID, there were 12 cases (out of 30) of recovering from earlier fatigue (three for the adductor pollicis, five for the abductor pollicis longus, and four for the opponens pollicis muscles). This is far more than the five cases for the trackball mouse. There were 6 occurrences of EMG increasing as a direct result of an increase in muscle contraction strength when using the new FOID (two for the abductor pollicis longus and four for the opponens pollicis muscles), which is far less than the 11 cases for the trackball mouse (six for the adductor pollicis, three for the abductor pollicis longus and two for the opponens pollicis muscles). Results of JASA indicted there was less finger muscle loading with the new FOID than with the trackball mouse. This can be explained by the alternative interactivities of the thumb, index and middle fingers for the new FOID. The user is able to delicately adjust his/her posture in response to the activity of the skin receptors on each finger tip while using the FOID rather than solely repetitive flexions of the MCP joint of the thumb, as in the use of the trackball mouse.

Examining the fatigue indicator of electrical activity and median frequency showed no evidence for development of fatigue with the new FOID. Pair-wise comparisons of electrical activity and median frequency showed no significant differences in these fatigue measurements between the new FOID and the trackball mouse. On the other hand, results of JASA indicted less finger muscle loading for the new FOID than that of the trackball. These results are of heuristic value and provide a promising basis for future development of the concept of FOIDs.

Acknowledgments. We gratefully acknowledge that this study was supported by a grant from the National Science Council, Taiwan ROC (project no. NSC 95-2221-E-011-075).

References

1. Fernström, E., Ericson, M.O.: Computer Mouse or Trackpoint–effects on Muscular Load and Operator Experience. Applied Ergonomics 28, 347–354 (1997)
2. Zhai, S., Milgram, P., Buxton, W.: The Influence of Muscle Groups on Performance of Multiple Degree-of-freedom Input. In: Proceedings of the CHI 1996 Conference on Human Factors in Computing Systems, pp. 308–315. ACM, New York (2006)
3. Brown, J.N.A., Albert, W.J., Croll, J.: A New Input Device: Comparison to Three Commercially Available Mousse. Ergonomics 50(2), 208–227 (2007)
4. Lee, Y.H., Su, M.C.: Design and Validation of a Desk-free and Posture- Independent Input Device. Applied Ergonomics 39, 399–406 (2008)
5. Luttmann, A., Jager, M., Sokeland, J.: Electromyographical Study on Surgeons in Urology. II. Determination of Muscular Fatigue. Ergonomics 39, 298–313 (1996)

Design and Analysis of Conceptual Sketches Based on Context Awareness

Cuixia Ma[1], Hongan Wang[1,2], Dongxing Teng[1], and Guozhong Dai[1,2]

[1] Intelligence Engineering Lab, Insititute of Software, Chinese Academy of Sciences,
Beijing, China
[2] State Key Lab of Computer Science, Chinese Academy of Sciences, Beijing, China
{cuixia,tengdongxing}@ios.cn, {wha,dgz}@iel.iscas.ac.cn

Abstract. This paper presents a framework of sketch editing environment for conceptual design process based on context. It analyzes the characteristics of design process and presents sketch description model for sketch based interface. Furthermore, it discusses the context fusion methodologies and algorithms to infer design context to understand designers' intent and communicate with designers intuitively. The context mainly is related to user, environment, and machine. A sample application is given to conduct the process planning drawings by sketching, exploring and modifying their ideas interactively, with immediate and continuous visual feedback. In the paper, we aims to study designing a sketch based interface enabling both computer and designer aware of underlying design contexts and providing intelligent operations.

Keywords: Sketch based Interface, Conceptual sketches, Context awareness.

1 Introduction

Sketch-based interface is the new generation natural user interface, which can break the bottleneck of current WIMP interface and adopt the nature and efficiency of pencil and paper based interface. Freehand sketching is a natural and crucial part of everyday human interaction, especially in early design processing. Currently there exists a very limited computer aided design support for conceptual design because various CAD systems usually require complete, concrete and precise design information input, which is only available at the end of the design process. Thus, designers often use paper and pencil based sketches for design and communication [1,2,3].

In recent years, the development of pervasive computing provides deep insight and wide prospects for conducting research on context-awareness computing, which are spreading into many kinds of application domains. The sketch-based interface is one of them. It mimics the traditional pencil and paper to provide a natural and effective communication and design tool. It also integrates the flexibility of the traditional pencil and paper tool with the high performance of a computer to understand what is being drawn and to improve human machine interaction. Designers can express their ideas with flexible pen and paper drawings, without any burden of learning how to operate computers with a mouse and keyboard as in many computer aided design (CAD)

S. Lee et al. (Eds.): APCHI 2008, LNCS 5068, pp. 328–335, 2008.

systems. Meanwhile, they can maintain their train of thought without being interrupted by excessive selections of menus, operations on buttons and keyboard input.

Context-awareness is a good method for performing the intelligence in sketch-based interface. Systems can automatically capture the context, the history and environment information to adjust their behaviors [4,5]. By improving the computer's access to context of sketch process, the richness of communication and intelligence in human-computer interaction would be increased and make it possible to produce more intelligent computational services based on sketch interface. By providing context awareness that integrates a wide range of context related to user, environment and machine, the user can enter information more easily meanwhile keeping a natural style of interaction and leveraging the power of computation.

The main idea behind sketch-based interfaces is to mimic pencil and paper that represents a natural way of thinking about ideas and communication. However, design with sketching provides much rich design contexts and experiences. During design sketching, as designers view a drawing, thoughts come to mind, which can alter their perceptions and suggest new possibilities. These activities are guided by sketching out ideas. The emerging representation allows them to explore avenues that could not be foreseen. In other words, the design is developed with context awareness of interface, presentation and interaction. Meanwhile, intelligence in sketch-based interface is important to give aid to exploring ideas and better communication. The paper is organized as follows. After the literature review in Section 2, the overview of sketch edit environment is detailed in Section 3, followed by system structure and illustration Section 4. Then the conclusion is given in Section 5.

2 Related Work

Sketching is a rapid and nature way to capture those creative points, which support designers to explore new ideas on sketch, compare them and capture inspirations [6,7,8]. After many years development, sketch-based interface again becomes the very interesting research topic. It can be used in many application domains, such as animation [9,10], garment design, mathematical sketching, botanical modeling [14], floral modeling [15], hairstyle modeling [16,17] and so forth. Turquin [11, 12] presented a method for interactively creating basic garments for dressing up virtual characters. The user draws an outline of the front or back of the garment, and the system makes reasonable geometric inferences about the shape of the garment. Igarashi [13] presented interaction techniques for putting clothes on a 3D character and manipulating them. The user can paint freeform marks on the clothes as well as on the 3D character; the system then puts the clothes around the body so that corresponding marks match. In these systems, sketching is used to create the prototype of the design quickly and efficiently. Recognizing and understanding of sketches is performed based on domain knowledge.

There are also many definitions of context [18]. Some refer context as the environment or situation, which are quite general but provide little guidance to analyze the constituent elements of context. Others define context by example [19], which are difficult to apply. Toolkits and frameworks, such as the Context Toolkit that addresses the integration of context in programming applications are already available [18]. The integration of context in the design of interactive applications has, received less attention until recently [20]. Some are intended to model context-sensitive user interface. Although much work on context-awareness has been conducted in the pervasive computing area, there is less work existing in sketch-based interface and modeling research field.

On sketch-based interface, we present the new methods to input and organize sketches based on context-awareness (underlying knowledge and constraints) and to support requirements for flexible interaction. Our goal is to develop easy-to-use conceptual design tools.

3 Sketch Editing Environment

3.1 Analysis of Sketch Design Process

Most ideas in conceptual design stage are sketchy and short of detailed geometric information. The main characteristics of sketch process include natural, continuous interaction and ambiguity. Figure 1 shows its important role.

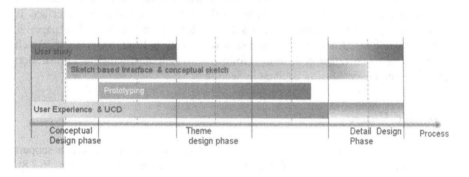

Fig. 1. Design process

The continuum of design process reflects the fluency of ideas record and visual thinking, as is better than that by WIMP interaction. Even if people can concentrate on changing their operating patterns, such as keeping in mind that they should switch to the menus and icons to make sure that they are doing job in the right viewpoint, this imposes an extra cognitive load that interferes with the creative process. For example, when creating a graphical shape, after they finish drawing a line, they have to click the circle button before they can draw a circle. Meanwhile, rough and recognized sketches both are important during the process.

3.2 Sketch Description Model

In order to facilitate the design process, modeling the sketching process can improve the human computer interaction. There are some characteristics for sketching which are different with those of WIMP interface. First, sketching using a pen is still more natural than using keyboard and mouse with frequent interruption. And continuous sketching provides continuous experience of input and feedback for better communication and working through the problems. Designers often work with freehand sketches to quickly communicate since free form sketching is more intuitive than the formal shapes to lead to more design alternatives. Second, most systems cited sketch to be kind of interaction without unified model and description about sketch and context. Iterative operations on sketch and context are in redundancy. Sketch Description model is presented by the multi-layered structure tree which includes sketch, grouping stroke context(constraints as well), stroke, point, from high to low level.

We define a basic unit of a sketch as a drawing stroke with different context involving constraints, operation history, user context or interaction context. A drawing stroke (line) is a set of sequent points captured (sensed) from an input device during a time period between a pair of pen-down and pen-up events. Each point has a time stamp. Grouping stroke integrates annotation and accessional attributes with related strokes, like shading drawing.

Strokes should be operated in the vector format under the model. For an instance, instead of that in WIMP, for a straight line user may draw several strokes, continuously or overlapping, we need to groups some strokes into different edges in sketch level. Edge is a high level geometrical concept. Modifications in either sketch can cause corresponding changes in another, which makes datum correlated.

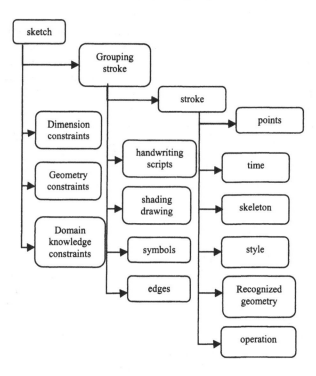

Fig. 2. Sketch model

3.3 Context-Awareness in Sketching

Context-awareness needs to obtain information from history, environment and the user interaction and synchronize them together to infer users' intention. The context based on gestures in pen interaction is an instance of general context in pen interface [21]. Context fusion involves the understanding of various design contexts from environment, history and interaction, and capturing proper design information such as geometric properties and constraints. An example can be given in Figure 3.

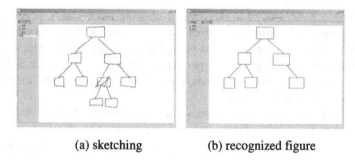

(a) sketching   (b) recognized figure

Fig. 3. (*a*) sketchy figure, with one deletion operation by pen gesture (zigzag) (*b*) corresponding recognized one, synchronous editing between them are done with context

The context can be divided into static and dynamic ones according to their states. The contexts such as object, constraint, gesture are static. The contexts, such as user, location, scope which are related with specific operation, are dynamic. Different context can be interpreted by the related algorithm. Generally, it is difficult to provide the clear interpretation based on the limited information from a sole context. The fusion of different context can provide more information.

Contexts will involve understanding of various design contexts from environment, history and interaction, and capturing proper design information such as geometric properties and constraints. The appropriate view of context contained in a designing process depends on the process that context needs to support and on whether that process will be carried out by a user or by a software tool.2.

4 System Structure

We have developed a sketch-based interactive process planning system. Its hierarchical structure is given in Fig 4. Typical design input for process planning is a set of geometric and annotation information such as graphics, forms, texts, and formulas. The user can draw graphics representing parts of the garment with some degree of fuzziness.

The hierarchy structure is given to describe the system structure for process planning design based on sketch interface, which includes four levels: data level, calculation level, application level and interaction level. Data level presents the knowledge and experience during the process planning, as well as the original input data. It provides general data access for the external application. Calculation level

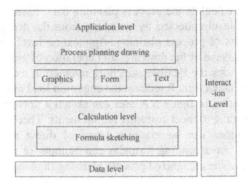

Fig. 4. Hierarchy structure

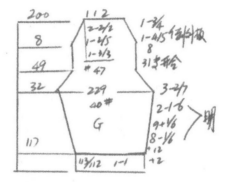

(a) Process planning drawing of knitting garment part

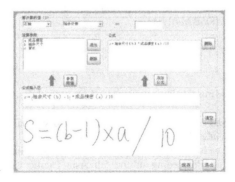

(b) Formula sketching

Fig. 5. *(a)* the recognized process planning drawing. The drawing can be transferred to workers for knitting the garment on the machines. *(b)* the formula can be inputted by sketching out symbols in it, and the semantic representation is also given in the window .

provides functions to calculate the process planning data, based on the formulas and values from the data level collected by sketching from the designers themselves, as leading to personalities of process planning. Application level provides functions of creation, modification, save of the drawings and operation of graphics, forms and text. Interaction level provides the flexible sketching interaction technologies to improve the human-computer interaction. It reduces the cognition load of users.

We give an illustration in figure 5.A user can sketch a drawing of a garment part, as he/she wants according to meet customer requirements. There is more than one size drawn and modifications can be made in terms of direct manipulation and pen gestures. Meanwhile, corresponding formulas can be input or reused to calculate the process planning data. The recognized process planning drawings are generated. They can be transferred to workers for knitting the garment on the machines.

5 Conclusion

Sketch-based interface, kind of natural user interface, has the potential to alter the way that designers conduct ideas. With the emergence and development of sketch-based interface and context-awareness technologies, ideas of new design methods and interactive technologies are incited to aid the design and communication, especially by incorporating both into conceptual design tool to work intelligently with designers to quickly and effectively transform dynamic design context into a design model for improving intelligence in conceptual design and modeling. By creating interfaces that mimic pencil and paper and providing context awareness that integrates a wide range of contexts from machine–based and user-based, users can enter information more easily meanwhile keeping a natural style of interaction and leveraging the power of computation.

Acknowledgments. *This work was* supported by National Natural Science Foundation of China under Grant No.60703079 and by the National Science and Technology Supporting Program under Grant No. 2006BAF01A44.

References

1. van Dijk, C.G.C.: New insights in computer-aided conceptual design. Design Studies 16(1), 62–80 (1995)
2. Hsu, W., woon, L.M.Y.: Current Research in the Conceptual Design of Mechanical Products. Computer- Aided Design 30(5), 377–389 (1998)
3. Ma, C., Dai, G.: An Infrastructure Approach to Gesture interaction Computing in Conceptual Design. In: Proceeding of the 5th Asia Pacific Conference on Computer Human Interaction (APCHI 2002), Beijing, November 1-4 (2002)
4. Henricksena, K., Indulska, J.: Developing context-aware pervasive computing applications: Models and approach. Pervasive and Mobile Computing 2(1), 37–64 (2006)
5. Dey, A.K., Abowd, G.D., Salber, D.: A Context-based Infrastructure for Smart Environments. In: Proceedings of the 1st International Workshop on Managing Interactions in Smart Environments (MANSE 1999), pp. 114–128 (1999)
6. Davis, R.: Magic Paper: Sketch-Understanding Research. Computer 40(9), 34–41 (2007)
7. LaViola, J.J.: An introduction to sketch based interface. ACM SIGGRAPH Course (2006)

8. LaViola, J.J.: Sketch-Based Interfaces: Techniques and Applications. ACM SIGGRAPH Course (2007)
9. Thorne, M., Burke, D., van de Panne, M.: Motion Doodles: An Interface for Sketching Character Motion. ACM Transactions on Graphics 23(3), 424–431 (2004)
10. Igarashi, T., Moscovich, T., Hughes, J.F.: Spatial Keyframing for Performance-Driven Animation. In: SCA 2005: Proceedings of the 2005 ACM SIGGRAPH/Eurographics symposium on Computer animation, pp. 107–115. ACM Press, New York (2005)
11. Turquin, E., Wither, J., Boissieux, L., Cani, M.-P., Hughes, J.F.: A sketch-based interface for clothing virtual characters. IEEE Computer Graphics & Applications, 72–81 (2007)
12. Turquin, E., Cani, M.-P., Hughes, J.F.: Sketching garments for virtual characters. In: Eurographics Workshop on Sketch-Based Interfaces and Modeling (2004)
13. Igarashi, T., Hughes, J.F.: Clothing Manipulation. ACM Trans. Graph 22(3), 697 (2003)
14. Okabe, M., Owada, S., Igarashi, T.: Interactive Design of Botanical Trees Using Freehand Sketches and Example-based Editing. In: Eurographics (2005)
15. Ijiri, Takashi, Owada, S., Okabe, M., Igarashi, T.: Floral Diagrams and Inflorescences: Interactive Flower Modeling Using Botanical Structural Constraints. ACM Trans. Graph 24(3), 720–726 (2005)
16. Mao, X., Kato, H., Imamiya, A., Anjyo, K.: Sketch Interface Based Expressive Hairstyle Modeling and Rendering. In: Proceedings of IEEE Computer Graphics. International (CGI), pp. 608–611 (2004)
17. Malik, S.: A Sketching Interface for Modeling and Editing Hairstyles. In: EUROGRAPHICS Workshop on Sketch-Based Interfaces and Modeling (2005)
18. Deya, K., Salber, D., Abowd, G.D.: A conceptual framework and a toolkit for supporting the rapid prototyping of context-aware applications. Hum.-Comput. Interac. J., 97–166 (2001)
19. Schilit, B., Theimer, M.: Disseminating active map information to mobile hosts. IEEE Network 8(5), 22–32 (1994)
20. Den Bergh, J.V., Coninx, K.: Towards modeling context-sensitive interactive applications: the context-sensitive user interface profile (CUP). In: Proceedings of the 2005 ACM symposium on Software visualization, pp. 87–94 (2005)
21. Sun, Z.X., Feng, G.H., Zhou, R.H.: Techniques for Sketch-Based User Interface: Review and Research. Journal of Computer-Aided Design & Computer Graphics 17(9) (2005)

Accuracy of Velocity Perception Generated by Tactile Apparent Motion

Kentaro Kotani, Yuki Imae, Takafumi Asao, and Ken Horii

Faculty of Engineering Science, Kansai University,
3-3-35 Yamate-cho, Suita, Osaka 564-8680, Japan
kotani@iecs.kansai-u.ac.jp

Abstract. The objective of this study is to empirically compare the accuracy of velocity perception generated by visual apparent motion with that generated by tactile apparent motion. From the results, the subjects were able to perceive velocity information through tactile stimulus presentation more accurately than through visual stimulus presentation. When tactile stimuli were presented, the effect of apparent motion enhanced the accuracy of velocity perception; however, this was not the case when the stimulus sets were visually presented.

Keywords: Tactile interface, Apparent motion, Tactile perception, Virtual reality.

1 Introduction

Tactile interface, a user interface that employs tactile perception for input/output, has been the focus of an increasing number of studies [1][2]. The objectives of these studies include an effective representation of the patterns and enhancement of reality with regard to texture sensation using a tactile interface. According to Hayashi, et al. [3], a design guideline that maximizes the characteristics of human tactile perception has not yet been fully developed for the tactile interface. They indicated a lack of understanding about the fundamental characteristics required for tactile interface design including studies associated with the mechanics of velocity perception in order to establish such a guideline. Thus, the accuracy with which a human can perceive the velocity of a stimulus presented as tactile information remains to be elucidated. An accurate presentation of velocity information using a tactile interface can be a potential use for transmitting such information to users; further, interface designers may be able to use this to apply multi-modal interface techniques to allocate information to different sensory modalities [4].

The present study focuses on tactile apparent motion, as a medium for transmitting velocity information. Tactile apparent motion is a perceptual phenomenon. It invokes a feeling in which the continuous motion from the initial stimulus to the subsequent stimulus is perceived when a series of discrete stimuli is presented with a certain time lag at different locations on the skin. Shimizu, et al. [5] explored the ability to transmit information presented by characters using tactile displays by applying these characters to the palm with three presentation modes: stationary, moving, and tracing. They concluded that the tracing mode using apparent motion displayed the highest percentage

S. Lee et al. (Eds.): APCHI 2008, LNCS 5068, pp. 336–343, 2008.
© Springer-Verlag Berlin Heidelberg 2008

of correct responses. Sakai, et al. [6] studied the effectiveness of the transmission of Braille characters using tactile displays and demonstrated that recognition rates improve when the Braille characters are presented with the tracing mode such that the subjects perceive apparent motion on their palmar surface of fingers. As a result of the evident improvement in information transmission by using apparent motion, their results suggested that the tactile interface may not only have the possibility for an effective transmission of pattern information but also have the possibility to transmit velocity information by using apparent motion through the interface.

With regard to studies related to apparent motion, the visual presentation of apparent motion has been considerably more researched than its tactile presentation. The outcome of such research has been applied in many areas such as movie technology and flashing ad-boards. Thus, to some extent, humans have been encountering opportunities to perceive velocity that is generated by visual apparent motion on a daily basis, regardless of their conscious efforts to obtain such information. Current applications related to visual apparent motion do not possess such situations that require people to acquire velocity perception in an accurate manner. If a tactile interface can transmit velocity information more accurately than visual presentation technologies, the usability of such an interface will certainly increase. Akabane and Sato [7] indicated that in comparison with the temporal resolutions of visual perception, which have values that are typically in the range of tens of hertz, temporal resolutions of tactile perception are much higher in that their values are typically about hundreds of hertz. This suggests that tactile displays possess the potential technology to effectively transmit velocity information. Thus far, there have been no studies that directly compare visual and tactile modalities in terms of both accuracy and transmission rates with regard to velocity information.

Therefore, the objective of this study is to empirically compare the accuracy of velocity perception generated by visual apparent motion with that generated by tactile apparent motion, and to discuss the effectiveness of using a tactile interface to present velocity information.

2 Presentation of Tactile Apparent Motion Using an Air Jet

It has been reported that tactile apparent motion was clearly perceived when it was presented in the form of vibrotactile bursts [8]. In comparison with other stimulation mediums, vibrotactile devices have been extensively used in recent years to study tactile apparent motion [9]. However, presenting vibratory stimuli for a certain period of time entails certain problems: it increases stresses that plague the users of tactile display [10], and it causes instability in couplings between the vibrotactile probes and the skin [11]. These problems result in an incomplete transmission of information through the vibratory stimuli.

In this study, an air jet was used to present tactile apparent motion. In a system in which an air jet is used to present tactile apparent motion, there is no physical contact between the skin and the presentation equipment. Therefore, the skin indentation approach using an air jet potentially makes up for the problems that arise when using vibrotactile displays. Major advantages in using an air-based tactile interface [12] were (1) the ease with which the presentation areas could be expanded, (2) the minimum body restriction, and (3) the considerably safe nature of this approach.

3 Methods

For the purpose of comparison, the following two sets of experiments were performed based on the difference of modalities: (1) a tactile experiment using tactile apparent motion and (2) a visual experiment using visual apparent motion. These experiments were identical in nature, with the exception of the characteristics of the stimuli and a part of the apparatus that was used to present the stimuli.

3.1 Subjects

A total of 12 subjects, aged between 21 and 25, participated in the study. All subjects performed both the experiments. Further, all subjects were students at Kansai University, and consent was obtained from each of them.

3.2 Stimuli

A set of 10 different stimuli was used for each modality, characterized by the differences in the duration and ISOI (inter-stimulus onset interval). The stimulus sets were divided into two groups. The one comprising eight stimulus sets was the group of stimuli with clear apparent motion, and the other consisting of two stimulus sets was the one with unclear apparent motion. These groupings were determined based on the results of our pilot experiment on the clarity of apparent motion perception [13]. The reason why we used two groups in our experiment was to examine whether or not the clarity of apparent motion perception was a factor that contributed to the accuracy of velocity perception. The stimulus set used in our study is presented in Table 1. Each experiment has a marginally different combination of stimulus sets; this is because the clarity of apparent motion, determined by the duration and ISOI, is dependant on the modality of perception.

Table 1. Stimulus set used in the experiment

	Tactile stimulus set	Visual stimulus set
Clear apparent motion	50 * 50	50 * 50
	50 * 70	50 * 70
	100 * 70	50 * 100
	100 * 100	100 * 50
	150 * 100	100 * 70
	150 * 130	100 * 100
	200 * 100	150 * 70
	200 * 130	150 * 100
Unclear apparent motion	250 * 50	50 * 200
	150 * 200	150 * 200

3.3 Apparatus

The system configuration of the air jet tactile display is presented in Figure 1. An air compressor (Hitachi Koki, EC1430H2) was used to generate compressed air; the amount of air produced was controlled by a digital electro-pneumatic regulator (CKD, EVD-1900-P08 SN) and a precision regulator (CKD, RP2000-8-08-G49PBE). Subsequently, the air jet was produced by the operation of the solenoid valve (CKD, FAB11-M5-1-12C-3). The system was capable of producing an air jet with a resolution of 1.0 kPa.

3.4 Procedure

The subjects were seated with their non-dominant hands on a partially top-opened box. Inside the box, two air nozzles, 3 cm apart from each other, were located under their index fingers' distal and medial parts such that the subjects were able to receive the stimuli produced by the air jet directly from underneath the box. Subjects were required to look down at the target LED, which was at a vertical visual angle of 40 degrees. The target LED was located at a distance of 45 cm from each subject's body on a sagittal plane, as illustrated in Figure 1. After a three-second auditory signal, a set of two consecutive stimuli was presented to the subjects. These stimuli, based on a predetermined duration and ISOI, resulted in a flow that was directed toward the target LED with a certain velocity. After receiving the stimuli, the subjects estimated the speed at which the velocity of the stimuli moved away from them and estimated when the flow of stimuli would reach the target LED. Their dominant hands were placed on the computer mouse, clicking on the left button indicated when the flow of stimuli reached the target LED. The time from the start of the stimuli presentation to its completion, indicated by the pressing of the mouse button, which represented the estimated time interval based on the perceived velocity, was recorded.

3.5 Data Analysis

The subjects completed the velocity estimation tasks across 10 different combinations of stimuli conditions. Each condition consisted of 12 trials, yielding total of 120 trials. The order of the trials was fully randomized. Table 2 summarizes the experimental conditions. The estimated time at which the flow of stimuli reached the target LED was compared with the theoretical arrival time of the same; subsequently, the relative contribution of apparent motion to the accuracy of the perceived velocity, expressed as an absolute error, was evaluated by the effect of the apparent motion and by the differences in the modalities. The theoretical arrival time was calculated by the following equation.

$$\text{Theoretical arrival time} = \text{ISOI} * \frac{Dt}{Ds} + \frac{\text{Duration}}{2} \tag{1}$$

where Dt is the distance between the first stimulus and the target LED (45cm), and Ds is the distance between two stimuli (3cm).

Since the absolute errors were not normally distributed, the Mann-Whitney U test was conducted to examine the significance of the absolute errors.

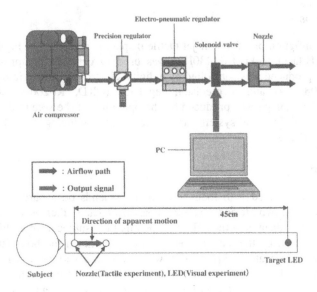

Fig. 1. Experimental setup (top) and location of stimulus presentation and target LED (bottom)

Table 2. Experimental conditions

	Tactile experiment	Visual experiment
Subject	Twelve healthy males	
Number of stimulus sets	10	
Number of trials in a block	12	
Distance between stimuli	30 mm	
Order of presentation	Random	
Distance between the skin and the nozzle	5 mm	–
Nozzle diameter	1.0 mm	–
Force generated by the air jet	7 gf	–

4   Results

Figure 2 presents the estimated and theoretical arrival times in different stimuli conditions for both experiments. The estimated arrival time appeared to be the same as the theoretical arrival time. The average absolute errors resulting from each stimulus condition have been compared in Figure 2. In this figure, only the values where the stimuli conditions were common for both experiments have been selected and presented. In all the combinations, the tactile stimulus presentations had significantly lesser absolute errors than did the visual stimulus presentations. In figure 2, the absolute errors obtained in the conditions with clear and unclear apparent motion presentations have been compared with respect to tactile and visual modalities.

There was a significant difference in the absolute errors for clear and unclear apparent motion presentations when tactile stimuli were presented; however, there were no significant differences in the visual stimulus presentations.

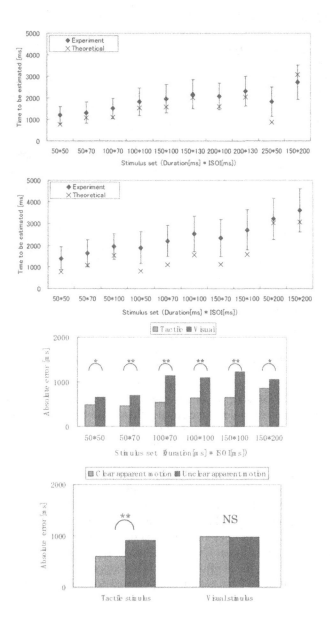

Fig. 2. Estimated arrival time overlapped with the theoretical arrival time for different stimulus sets in two experiments (the first from the top: tactile stimulus presentation, the second from the top: visual stimulus presentation), comparison of the absolute errors obtained in tactile and visual stimulus presentations (the third from the top) and in clear and unclear apparent motion presentations (the fourth from the top). (**: p < .01, *: p < .05, based on the Mann-Whitney U test).

5 Discussion

5.1 Comparison between the Two Experiments

As illustrated in figures, there was a certain similarity in the arrival times obtained experimentally and theoretically for both modalities, indicating that the subjects were, to some extent, able to estimate the arrival time based on their perceived information of the presented stimulus pairs. When studied in detail, however, relatively smaller differences as well as variances between the estimated and theoretical arrival times were found when the tactile stimulus sets were presented. In comparison with the absolute errors for the two modalities, as presented in figure 2, the tactile stimulus sets generated smaller errors than the visual stimulus sets did. The results of the Mann-Whitney U tests showed significant differences in the absolute errors for the two modalities. Therefore, velocity information was perceived more accurately when the tactile stimuli were presented than when the visual stimuli were presented.

This may be because of the difference in the temporal resolution rates of tactile and visual perceptions. The temporal resolution rates of tactile perception are considerably superior to those of visual temporal perception, as Akabane and Sato [7] indicated. Hence, this advantage of the tactile temporal resolution rates enhances perception with regard to the element information associated with time, such as duration and ISOI in this study.

5.2 Contribution of Apparent Motion to Velocity Perception

The stimuli groups with/without clear apparent motion perception were compared. The results implied that with regard to tactile presentation, the absolute errors for clear apparent motion perception were smaller than those for unclear apparent motion, whereas no significant differences were found in absolute errors resulting from the visual presentation. According to the responses from the subjects, 75% of them agreed that it was easier to feel the velocity of the stimuli when the clear apparent motions were presented. On the other hand, when the subjects received the stimulus set with unclear apparent motion, 150 ms of duration and 200 ms of ISOI for instance, they reported that the arrival time was not estimated by referring to the perceived velocity generated by the stimulus pairs. Instead, the discrete intervals between the offset time for the initial stimulus and the onset time for the subsequent stimulus were used to estimate the arrival time. Thus, even though apparent motions were presented, they had no influence on the absolute errors. This suggests that the advantages of the spatial resolution of visual perception compensated for the incomplete information with regard to velocity perception.

6 Conclusion

This study examined the accuracy of perceived velocity when the stimulus was presented in the form of a tactile sensation with the perception of apparent motion. We conclude the following. The subjects were able to perceive velocity information through tactile stimulus presentation more accurately than through visual stimulus presentation. When tactile stimuli were presented, the effect of apparent motion enhanced the accuracy of velocity perception; however, this was not the case when the stimulus sets were visually presented. Future study on this subject should incorporate the effect of the intensity of apparent motion on velocity perception and the relationship between tactile presentation on different locations on the body and the accuracy of velocity perception.

References

1. Benali-Khoudja, M., Hafez, M., Alexandre, J.-M., Kheddar, A.: Tactile Interfaces: A State-of-the-Art Survey. In: Proc. ISR 2004, pp. 721–726 (2004)
2. Hafez, M., Benali-Khoudja, M.: Tactile interfaces: Technologies, applications and challenges. In: REM 2005, Annecy, France (2005)
3. Hayashi, S., Watanabe, J., Kajimoto, H., Tachi, S.: Study on motion after effect in tactile sensation. Trans. VR Soc. Japan 11(1), 69–75 (2006) (in Japanese with English abstract)
4. Van Erp, J.B.F., Verschoor, M.H.: Cross-modal visual and vibrotactile tracking. Applied Ergonomics 35(2), 105–112 (2004)
5. Shimizu, Y., Saida, S., Wake, T., Nakamura, A., Ohzu, H.: Optimum design of tactile display for a reading aid. In: Uses of Computers in Aiding the Disabled, pp. 383–391. North-Holland publishing, Amsterdam (1982)
6. Sakai, T., Tazaki, M., Ito, T.: An evaluation of an optimum stimulus presentation method considering tactile sensation on passive 6-finger Braille. The IEICE Trans. Info. and Syst. 90(3), 742–753 (2007)
7. Akabane, A., Sato, M.: Structure of tactile senses. J. Instit. Image Info. Telev. Engin. 57(11), 1417–1418 (2003) (in Japanese)
8. Kirman, J.H.: Tactile apparent movement: The effects of interstimulus onset interval and stimulus duration. Percep. Psychophysics 15, 1–6 (1974)
9. Wall, S.A., Brewster, S.: Sensory substitution using pin array: Human factors, technology and applications. Sign.Process. 86(12), 3674–3695 (2006)
10. Asonuma, M., Matsumoto, M., Wada, C.: Direction indicating method by presenting tactile stimulation to the face. J. Hum. Interf. Soc. 8(4), 545–554 (2006) (in Japanese)
11. Cohen, J.C., Makous, J.C., Bolanowski, S.J.: Under which conditions do the skin and probe decouple during sinusoidal vibrations? Exp. Bra. Res. 129, 211–217 (1999)
12. Suzuki, Y., Kobayashi, M.: Air jet driven force feedback in virtual reality. IEEE Comp.Graph. Appli. 25(1), 44–47 (2006)
13. Imae, Y., Kotani, K., Horii, K.: Characteristics of apparent motion induced by tactile stimuli using air-jet. Res. Rep. Hum. Interf. Soc. 9(2), 53–56 (2007) (in Japanese)

A New Framework on Measuring Customer Perceived Value in Service Interface Design

Chang K. Cho[1], Minjoo Jung[2], Chai-Woo Lee[2], Sangwoo Bahn[2], and Myung Hwan Yun[2]

[1] CIRCLEONE Consulting Inc., Seoul, Korea
[2] Department of Industrial Engineering, Seoul National University
Seoul, 151-744 Korea
mhy@snu.ac.kr

Abstract. This paper explored the possible ways to apply various principles of NPD, NSP and UCD, and combined them appropriately in context of mobile internet service development in order to provide a high customer value via useful and usable service design. We investigated the characteristics of mobile internet and usability problems, and identified the benefits and limitations of previous UCD principles applied to mobile internet service development. Then applicability of CPV in mobile service design has been investigated in phases of divergent and convergent thinking. During the scenario-based ideation, potential customer values can be used as ideation stimuli in the process of structured brainstorming. In divergent thinking, CPV can be applied as evaluation criteria in comparing new ideas with alternative services. For the efficient implementation, work templates for accelerated front-end UCD are developed in co-operation with mobile service staffs in Korean mobile operator. This paper could be helpful for mobile industry and practitioners to develop and evaluate new mobile internet service which reflects users' implicit needs and CPV concept in the efficient and effective way.

Keywords: Mobile service, User centered design, New service design, Customer Perceived Value (CPV).

1 Introduction

Phone-based mobile internet has a poor capability compared to the traditional PC-based internet in terms of usability and cost of access. However, characteristics of mobile internet such as ubiquity, personalization, localization and instant accessibility can be utilized to enhance the value of mobile internet. According to Miller & Swaddling (2002) [1], most mobile internet service users perceive cost more critical than benefit. Therefore, it is required to make mobile service more valuable by maximizing its benefit factors utilizing the characteristic features of mobility and minimizing cost factors of mobile usability, capability and expense.

To overcome the usability and performance constraints, academic researches emphasized the importance of balancing the trade-off between benefits and costs in terms of user perception during the early phase of mobile service development. Many

S. Lee et al. (Eds.): APCHI 2008, LNCS 5068, pp. 344–353, 2008.
© Springer-Verlag Berlin Heidelberg 2008

researches on new product development (NPD) have emphasized user focus as an important aspect of successful product or service innovation [2, 3, 4] According to the result of CPAS (Comparative Performance Assessment Study) carried out by PDMA (Product Development and Management Associate), strong voice of customer input was identified as one of the key success factors of outstanding corporate innovators along with well-defined process, strong commitment to cross functional team, strong linkage of NPD to strategy[3]. Cooper (2005)[4] also considered user centeredness as one of key success factors of product innovation that separate the winners and the losers.

In this study, customer perceived value (CPV) is suggested as a helpful concept in explaining the gap between high expectation on the contents of mobile service by advertisement or hype, and low acceptance of mobile internet service. Applicability of CPV in mobile service design has been investigated with divergent and convergent thinking.

2 Literature Survey

2.1 Usability in Mobile Internet Service

Mobile internet has its own unique strengths and weaknesses that are different from PC-based internet. Thus issues considering usability problems, NPD and user-centered design (UCD) principles on mobile internet have been considered very important recently. Mobile internet can be characterized by mobility from wireless internet, with its definition being internet access via mobile devices [5, 6]. Mobile internet has some critical problems that act as barriers, including the fact that it is a very highly penetrated service, but its usage rate is very low. This symptom acts as a big challenge for mobile service industry. Another problem is aroused by the limitedness and biasedness of use, which means that the usage of mobile internet usage is very limited and biased even in countries with high acceptance, although there are a lot of potential application areas [7, 8]. Also, it is known that users prefer one time download, which indicates that the high expense for mobile internet connection is one of the critical barriers.

The concept of mobility is essential in mobile internet. A broad definition of mobility encompasses dimensions of device, user and service. Other than mobility, characteristics such as localization, instant connectivity and personalization are emerging with advance in technologies. These concepts are expected to help in development of usability of mobile internet, and new wireless devices will eventually become the preferred way to access information. Mobile internet service can be described as technology-based self-service in terms of technology infusion and value creation process [9]. However, inventing applications on such environment is difficult due to the novelty and openness that are inherent in the nature of service [10]. In such situation, some opportunities have be found in mobile service development, and five principal developments including increase of bandwidth, unbundling of industry, convergence, new business model, and new service have been outlined [11].

Usability problems of mobile internet arise from its unique characteristics such as small display, limited input functionality, poor system capabilities and distracting environments of use. To overcome such problems, many researches have provided usability guidelines [12 13, 14]. Also, more guidelines and UI style guides have been made in related industrial areas. Usability requirements for mobile internet have been identified as portability, adaptability, availability, learnability, security, reliability, attractiveness and interoperability [15]. Thus usability is recognized as an important concept in NPD, and therefore the consideration on usability is done early in the process efficiently to save both time and money [16, 17, 18].

2.2 New Product and Service Development

Since mobile internet is composed of tangible product and intangible service, the difference between NPD and new service development (NSD) should be commented. NPD aims to improve the effectiveness of people engaged in developing and managing new product. The process of NPD includes opportunity identification, concept generation, concept evaluation, development and launch [2]. Also, stage-gate model which breaks the new product into discrete stages is widely accepted [4]. However, because of the diversity in the market and organizations, NPD process is varied and customized in many ways. NSD is mostly based on NPD processes, with more informality and reproducibility [19, 20]. In NSD, user expectation to service should be carefully considered. Since applying NPD models to services might nit suffice, a specific model for NSD is needed. An example of NSD process includes innovation strategy, problem identification, idea generation, concept development, business analysis, service development, testing, and commercial operations [21]. Mobile internet has characteristics of two major trends in NSD; development and utilization of technology and blurring of lines between products and services [21]. Thus the approach of NSD should be different from NPD.

In the early stages of NPD, the concept of CPV plays an important role, because it is useful in predicting customer loyalty, purchase behavior and achieving sustained competitive advantage [22]. CPV is a consumer's overall assessment of the utility of a product or service based on perceptions of what is received and what is given [23]. Other definitions and components of CPV have been suggested by many researches. CPV should be distinguished from customer satisfaction, since they differ in terms of the target, orientation, benefits, etc [1]. The research on CPV can be approached in three steps; exploratory, secondary and confirmatory. Also, the measurement of CPV can be done with an additive model, where benefit and sacrifice are considered in same dimension (CPV=benefit-sacrifice), or a ratio model, where benefit and sacrifice are compared relatively (CPV=benefit/sacrifice) [9]. CPV is now considered as the concept that can provide a means to effectively understand and solve many problems in mobile internet service.

2.3 Considerations on User-Centered Design

UCD, a concept which aims to make products easy to use, is another important principle to consider in development of mobile internet service. The approach adopted by UCD is different from the traditional product design in many significant aspects, which include the source of requirements, the main focus area, the range of cooperation, the view or orientation on user experience and measurements, the range of target customers, etc. However, it is undoubtedly beneficial to integrate it with product development cycle.

There have been efforts to provide principles and guidelines on applying UCD. International standards on UCD have been established for computer-based systems. The standards define the principles of UCD; active user involvement, appropriate function allocation, iteration of design solutions, and multi-disciplinary design. They also define the design activities considering UCD; understanding and specifying the context of use, specifying user requirements, producing designs and prototypes, and evaluating such designs [17].

In accordance with the standards, a research had tried to find the user requirements, technologies, application methods, and usability experiment methods for future mobile service development, and emphasized adaptivity in mobile internet service [24]. Another research had proposed an UCD framework and a process for e-commerce service, which include steps such as opportunity analysis, context of use build-up, creation of user experience, and continuous improvement [25]. Several studies tried to tighten the relationship between software engineering and HCI, but most have focused mostly on analysis and evaluation. Thus, most have failed to pay enough attention on the actual design process, even though usability is never separable from the software development process. To overcome such limits, a design model has been suggested to integrate usability into the software development cycle [26]. Another study has proposed early user involvement in design [27]. Also, a checklist on UCD process in software development has been published.

Mobile internet service is concerned with UCD because of its problems caused by the ever-changing context of use [29]. Context of use is considered as an essential concept in UCD [17, 18, 29, 30]. Thus scenario-based approach is becoming more popular in mobile NPD process, because it is a tool that can effectively and efficiently identify the mobile context.

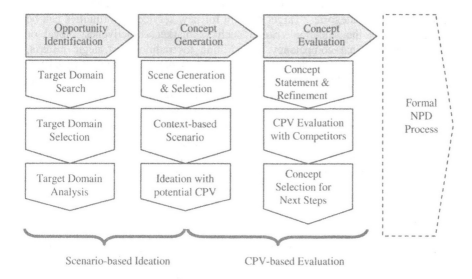

Fig 1. An accelerated front-end UCD process for mobile service development

3   Framework for Generating New Mobile Services

As discussed in literature survey, previous principles and standards of UCD tend to be so general and focused on post-development phase of new product process. Furthermore, mobile internet services need to be considered with their specific characteristics especially in front-end activities. Based on these needs, new framework for generating and evaluating a concept of mobile service is build up and the overall process is shown in fig. 1. Similar with general process of new product development, the proposed framework begins with opportunity identification. With the consideration of mobile characteristics, 3 sub-processes are proposed in each of the precedent processes such as opportunity identification, concept generation and concept evaluation. Although they are often considered to be carried out in iterative way, for the acceleration of the process sequential flow is suggested considering repetitive short iteration cycle for each process.

3.1   Opportunity Identification

Opportunity is a business or technology gap that exists between the current situation and an envisioned future that suggests one to capture competitive advantage, respond to threats, and solve difficulties. Mobile service opportunity can be either a new business model or a new service opportunity in this context. In general, opportunity identification involves environment analysis for target domain industry. Environment analysis includes customer, competitor and company. Technical trend and user trend are also reviewed in the opportunity identification phase.

Based on the assumption that target business domain for new mobile service can be found from existing internet services, internet services can be a good source for new business model or new mobile service. Internet service statistics or internet ranking sites provide service categories. Target domain for new service opportunities can be identified by using the selection criteria such as market attractiveness, level of competition and internal competency. In addition to traditional strategic criteria, mobile applicability considers the balance of trade-off between cost and benefit in mobile internet service for maximizing benefit and minimizing cost. During the research on new mobile service opportunity analysis, 77 business domains originated from 663 internet services as potential opportunities were selected by the use of secondary source of internet service statistics and mobile applicability criteria. Strategic and maximizing benefit criteria are used for selection criteria, and minimizing cost criteria are used for cut-off criteria for the services of which usability problems are too critical to be provided in mobile internet channel.

3.2   Concept Generation

Analyzing context of use is the key to identify the service requirement. By the utilization of user, task and environmental contexts, service concepts can be derived. Such concepts should be tested by users iteratively. There are general set of attributes on context of use in ISO 9241-11. Contextual attributes on users, tasks, equipment and environment should be customized as mobile context for the application of mobile service development.

There are many ways to get a better understanding of users. Indirect methods such as surveys, log files, contact history and billing data and direct methods such as observations or interviews can be used. Basic user profiles and usage history can be used as a valuable input to user profiling. This is one of the most advantageous characteristic of mobile internet from the viewpoint of service providers. When someone buys a new phone, needs for new service such as screensavers, ring-tones or downloadable games will increase. Based on a subscriber's information and usage history, more customized services can be developed.

When various scenarios are prepared for idea generation, a structured ideation technique incorporating the concept of potential value components is suggested. Using the concept of CPV for divergent thinking, potential customer values in mobile services are investigated for enhancing the effectiveness of scenario-based ideation. From the literature survey, basic value components are selected in hierarchical structure including hedonic and utilitarian dichotomy [31], functional, emotional, social, and epistemic value components in [32, 33], and conditional or contextual value [9, 32]. From the successful mobile services in terms of high user acceptance which are supposed to deliver relatively high customer value, potential value components and entities are derived by an expert group composed of 5 mobile service staffs in Korean mobile operator companies and 3 mobile service consultants. To reflect the market perception, a review on the results of market surveys is needed before and during the discussion. After mapping the generic set of value components with the present successful mobile services, potential mobile value components were grouped together and coupled with their representative example, respectively, for efficient association during idea generation. Seventeen values were selected and their descriptions and examples are in table 1. Although validity and reliability of these potential mobile values are not verified, techniques such as Osborn's checklist, Small's checklist [2] and TRIZ [34] will be helpful to accelerate the scenario analysis when considering structured creative ideation. Comparing characteristics of mobility with potential mobile values, and analyzing relationships between them can be helpful to find out some potential value drivers that enhance potential customer value with the characteristics of mobility.

3.3 Concept Evaluation

CPV and usability concept can be used as criteria in the evaluation of ideated concepts. In this study, CPV measurement methods were used in concept evaluation. In the concept generating level, several ideas were generated from the result of previous research or interview. With the ideas clustered for evaluation, alternatives were selected to be compared against the concept of CPV. CPV measurement method consists of two parts; additive methods and ratio methods. With comparable services, breaking down the sub-entities of cost and benefit of services is executed to calculate their value and relative importance. When using ratio methods, the ratio of benefit to cost is used to compare generated services. However, it can be difficult to find comparable services. In this case, additive method can be useful to investigate components of value and to summarize them in terms of CPV.

Table 1. Potential value components in mobile contexts

Potential value in mobile service		Descriptions in mobile context	Mobile service example
Cost	Economic	cost-saving	Membership discount
Quality	Available	urgent use, anytime, anywhere	Camera phone
	Effective	goal achievement, multi-purposed	CNID
	Efficient	time reduction, minimal efforts	SMS P2P
	Convenient	ease of use	SMS W2P
Social	Superior	superior to others	New phone
	Different	different from others, unique	Ring-tone
	Homogeneous	empathy, sympathy	Screensaver
	Isolated	private, with no interaction with others	Adults contents
	Etiquette	considering others	Ring-back-tone
Emotional	Fun	fun, exciting	Mobile Game
	Relief	peaceful, trustworthy, reliable	Kids phone
	Preferable	preference, taste, esthetic,	Ring-tone, Screensaver
Epistemic	Educational	knowledge, useful	Mobile news
	Curious	newness, curiosity	Mosquito repellant
Contextual	Magnifying	situation increasing value	CNID for salesperson
	Minifying	undesirable situation decreasing value	Stalking block

In this study, CPV was used as a representative measure of user acceptance. Therefore, market attractive was considered and evaluated with market volume by opinions of potential customers and result of scenario frequency analysis. It showed that service ideas that are related to the present situation and potential users are considered as promising value. By combining the series of considerations on CPV, market volume, scenario frequency, and the most promising concepts were selected to go on to the next step of NPD.

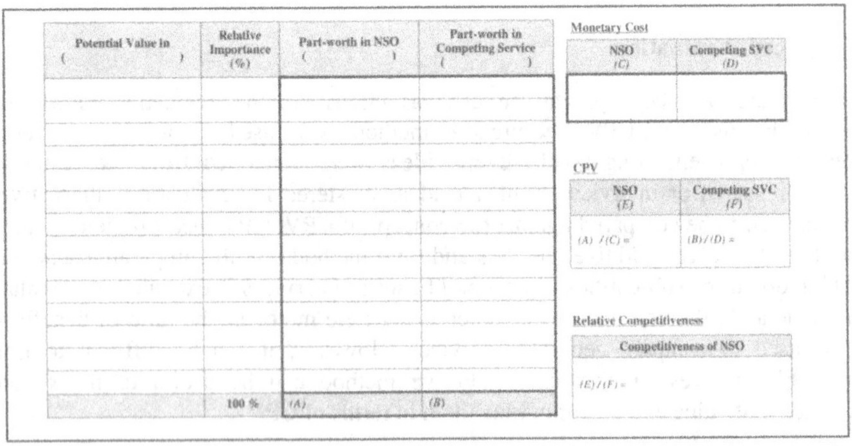

Fig. 2. An example of template for evaluation of competing service concepts

In ISO 9241-11 [35], measures of usability are defined as effectiveness, efficiency and satisfaction. Considering the measures of usability during the evaluation stage is important, because of its implication on the measures. Most benefit components involve effectiveness, efficiency and satisfaction attributes. Effectiveness can be defined as the accuracy and completeness with which customers achieve specified goals. Efficiency is the accuracy and completeness of goals achieved in relation to resources. Satisfaction is the freedom from discomforts, and having positive attitudes towards the use of mobile service. Attributes of key performance indicators can be expressed in adjectives such as useful, usable, unique, fun, efficient, attractive, simple, quick to learn, etc. This attributes can be quantified by measurement of CPV and fig.2 shows the proposed template which can evaluate the competing services from the point of CPV.

4 Conclusion

In this study, a new framework is proposed to generate and evaluate a concept of new mobile service with CPV and user-based design. The framework consists of three parts, as opportunity identification, concept generation and concept evaluation. In the first part, opportunity identification, target domain search is precedent to analyze the market and customers' needs. During the second part of the proposed framework, concept generation, customer based-research and generating context based-scenario is executed. The last part of the framework, concept evaluation is conducted with concepts of CPV. With these three processes, new mobile service can be generated and validated with new concept as CPV. And to apply the proposed framework efficiently, work template was developed.

Previous researches about NPD and UCD, the quantitative concept to evaluate proposed concept of service or product didn't exist. In this study, a new concept as CPV is proposed to evaluate the generated concept during the previous part of framework. CPV is the quantitative measure which is an effective way of understanding and indicating users' perception about value of the service or product. This paper could be helpful for mobile industry and practitioners to develop and evaluate new mobile internet service which reflects users' implicit needs and CPV concept in the efficient and effective way.

Acknowledgment. This work was supported in part by the Seoul R&BD program at Seoul National University.

References

1. Miller, C., Swaddling, D.C.: Focusing NPD research on customer perceived value. In: Belliveau, P., Griffin, A., Somermeyer, S.M. (eds.) PDMA toolbook for new product development, pp. 87–114. John Wiley & Sons, Inc., Chichester (2002)
2. Crawford, M., Benedetto, A.: New products management. McGraw Hill, Boston (2003)
3. Boike, D., Hustad, T., Jankowski, S., Kay, S.E., Moran, J., Page, A., Parker, N.: Lessons learned from outstanding corporate innovators. In: Kahn, K.B. (ed.) PDMA handbook of new product development, pp. 527–545. John Wiley & Sons, Inc., Chichester (2005)

4. Cooper, R.G.: New products- what separates the winners from losers and what drives success. In: Kahn, K.B. (ed.) PDMA handbook of new product development, pp. 3–28. John Wiley & Sons, Inc, Chichester (2005)
5. Mobile Commerce Report (2000), http://www.durlacher.com
6. Koh, J., Kim Y.: Mobile internet application primer. UBS Warburg (2000)
7. Cho, C., Ji, Y., Yun, M.: User-centered design framework for the development of mobile internet service. In: Proceedings of 7th International Conference on Work with Computing Systems, Kuala Lumpur, Malaysia, June 29 - July 2 (2004)
8. Lee, I., Kim, J., Kim, J.: Use Contexts for the Mobile Internet: A Longitudinal Study Monitoring Actual Use of Mobile Internet Services. International Journal of Human-Computer Interaction 18(3), 269–292 (2005)
9. Heinonen, K.: Reconceptualizing customer perceived value: the value of time and place. Managing Service Quality 14(3), 205–215 (2004)
10. Kuutti, K., Iacucci, G., Iacucci, C.: Acting to know: Improving creativity in the design of mobile services by using performances. In: Proceedings of the 5th conference on Creativity & cognition, Loughborough, United Kingdom, pp. 95–102 (2002)
11. Berkhout, G., van der Duin, P.: Mobile data innovation: Lucio and the cyclic innovation model. In: Janssen, M., Sol, H.G., Wagenaar, R.W. (eds.) Proceedings of Sixth International Conference on Electronic Commerce, pp. 603–608 (2004)
12. Buchanan, G., Farrant, S., Jones, M., Thimbleby, H., Marsden, G., Pazzani, M.: Improving mobile internet usability. In: Proceedings of the 10th International Conference on World Wide Web, pp. 673–680 (2001)
13. Duda, S., Schießl, M., Hess, J.M. : Mobile usability. Eye Square GmbH. Schlesische Str. 29-30, D-10997 Berlin (2001), http://www.eye-square.de
14. Uther, M.: Mobile Internet usability: What can 'mobile learning' learn from the past? In: Proceedings of the IEEE international workshop on wireless andmMobile technologies in education (2002)
15. Terrenghi, L., Kronen, M., Valle, C.: Usability requirements for mobile service scenarios. In: IHCI 2005. IADIS Virtual Multi Conference on Computer Science and Information Systems (MCCSIS 2005) (2005)
16. Nielsen, J.: Usability Engineering. Academic Press, New York (1993)
17. ISO 13407: Human-Centered Design Processes for Interactive Systems. Geneva, Switzerland: International Standards Organization (1999)
18. Bevan, N.: International standards for HCI and usability. International Journal of Human computer Studies 55, 533–552 (2001)
19. Fitzsimmons, J.A., Fitzsimmons, M.J.: New service development: creating memorable experiences. Sage Publications, Inc., London (2000)
20. Lovelock, C.H., Wright, L.: Principles of Service Marketing and Management, 2nd edn. Prentice Hall, Englewood Cliffs (2002)
21. Kuczmarski, T., Johnston, Z.: Service development. In: Kahn, K.B. (ed.) PDMA handbook of new product development, pp. 92–108. John Wiley & Sons, Inc., New York
22. Ulaga, W., Chacour, S.: Measuring Customer-Perceived Value in Business Markets. Industrial Marketing Management 30, 525–540 (2005)
23. Zeithaml, V.A.: Consumer perceptions of price, quality, and value: A means–end model and synthesis of evidence. Journal of Marketing 52, 2–22 (1998)
24. EURESCOM 2001. The third dimension – human centered aroach to designing new mobile services for different terminal equipment. European institute for research and strategic studies in telecommunication (2001)
25. Travis, D.: E-commerce usability: tools and techniques to perfect the on-line experience. Talor & Francis, London (2003)

26. Göransson, B., Gulliksen, J., Boivie, I.: The usability design process – Integrating user-centered systems design in the software development process. Software process improvement and practice 8, 111–131 (2003)

27. Kankainen, A.: UCPCD: User-centered product concept design. In: Proceedings of the conference on designing for user experiences, San Francisco, CA (June 2003)

28. Tamminen, S., Oulasvirta, A., Toiskallio, K.: Understanding mobile contexts. Personal and ubiquitous computing 8, 135–143 (2004)

29. Beyer, H., Holtzblatt,: Contextual design: defining customer-centered systems. Morgan Kaufmann publishers, San Francisco (1998)

30. Conley, C.V.: Contextual research for new product development. In: Kahn, K.B. (ed.) PDMA handbook of new product development, pp. 228–248 (2005)

31. Batra, R., Ahtola, O.T.: Measuring the hedonic and utilitarian sources of consumer attitude. Marketing Letters 2(2), 159–170 (1990)

32. Sheth, J.N., Newman, B.I., Gross, B.L.: Why we buy what we buy: A theory of consumption values. Journal of Business Research 22, 159–170 (1991)

33. Sweeney, J.C., Soutar, G.N.: Consumer perceived value: The development of a multiple item scale. Journal of Retailing 77, 203–220 (2001)

34. Altshuller, G.: The innovative algorithm: TRIZ, systematic innovation and technical creativity. Worchester, MA. Technical innovation center (2002)

35. ISO 9241-11: Ergonomic Requirements for Office Work with Visual Display Terminals (VDTs) – part 11. Geneva, Switzerland: International Standards Organization (1998)

Novice Word Processor User Performance with Pictorial and Text Icons

Tanya René Beelders, Pieter Blignaut, Theo McDonald, and Engela Dednam

Department of Computer Science and Informatics, University of the Free State, Bloemfontein,
Republic of South Africa
{beelderstr,pieterb,theo,dednameh}.sci@ufs.ac.za

Abstract. The word processor has evolved since its inception to become a valuable and integral part of modern life. Novice users, as potential users possessing little to no knowledge of either the interface or domain, justifiably encounter a learning curve when commencing to use a word processor. The question arises as to whether this learning curve can be lessened through adaptation of the interface which has been accepted as the industry standard. Usability was measured when users completed tasks using pictorial icons and when completing the same tasks using text buttons. Analysis detected no difference in either effectiveness or efficiency, leading to the conclusion that all novice users require is extensive training and practice.

Keywords: Word processor, Icons, Text, Usability.

1 Introduction

The word processor has become an integral part of everyday life [14] and possesses the capability of evolving to exploit increased capabilities provided by advances in technology. This ensures that it provides a rich environment for research purposes. This research study exploited these properties of the word processor in an intensive usability study concentrated on the style of the interface icons. As a dominant feature of the word processor, the pictorial icons were replaced with text buttons to gauge whether that could ease the learning curve experienced by novice users and increase the overall usability of a word processor. Since images are processed at a higher speed than text, it could be assumed that the pictorial icons would promote a higher degree of efficiency than text buttons. However, the advantages associated with the use of icons are all applicable to the use of text buttons and could provide sufficient countermeasures to neutralise the negative effects of verbal processing when comparing with nonverbal processing. Furthermore, the text buttons would not require any interpretation of meaning of an image, such as would be required with the pictorial icons. Since there are both arguments for and against the use of text in place of images the effect on usability could not be predicted and subsequently had to be tested to provide empirical evidence of the superiority of one icon type over the other.

To lay the foundation for the research undertaking, it was important to determine what difference, if any, existed between the mental processing of images and texts,

S. Lee et al. (Eds.): APCHI 2008, LNCS 5068, pp. 354–361, 2008.

and to study the reasoning behind the popular use of icons in software applications today. Following is a discussion on the topics which assisted in the formulation of the research hypotheses. The methodology used to achieve the research aims is also discussed, as well as the analysis of the collected data and the conclusions drawn from the collected data.

2 Background

2.1 Usability

The definition of usability that was accepted for the purposes of this study was derived from a combination of two ISO definitions [6] and is as follows:

The capability of the software product to be not only understood and learned but also to be used by specific users to achieve specified goals with effectiveness and efficiency. Furthermore, a usable system must incorporate the capacity to be attractive to the user and provide satisfaction during and after use.

From this definition, four distinct components of usability can be identified, namely effectiveness, efficiency, satisfaction and learnability each of which can be gauged according to a set of measurable objectives [1].

2.2 Verbal and Nonverbal Processing

Information is received, processed, stored in short-term memory, and eventually transferred to long-term memory [11], from where it is retrieved when needed [8]. The way in which this information is stored and processed differs between verbal and nonverbal information [12] as information is stored in memory according to the format of the external stimulus [16]. Generally, the difference can be explained in broad terms as the difference between processing in the left and right hemispheres of the brain. While the left hemisphere is responsible for the processing of language, which is done in a linear fashion, the right hemisphere uses parallel processing to absorb visual information [12]. Thus, images can be processed at a much higher speed than what text or language can.

2.3 Icons

Icons are common interface components that employ images [13] to represent an object or an action that can be carried out by the user [2]. Icons have replaced commands and menus as the format by which communication is achieved with the user [5] as they reduce the complexity of the system while increasing the ease of use and learnability [13] and reducing the number of errors made by the user [10] thereby increasing the overall productivity of the user [7]. Icons do, however, possess a distinct and overwhelming disadvantage in that they are open to misinterpretation by users if the chosen image invokes unintended or multiple associations [2] – the picture that "speaks a thousand words may say a thousand different words to different viewers" [18]. While misinterpretation of icons has been revealed in numerous studies (for example, [4]) it is unlikely to occur with words when used in a menu or text-based interface.

2.4 Icons or Text – Which is Better?

Any attention that is devoted to the interface detracts from the concentration of the user and constitutes interference with the primary task [2]. For this reason Shneiderman [17] surmises that word processor applications should generally make use of textual menus to save the user from having to switch between differing cognitive styles [3]. Conversely, it has been proposed that more interference will be caused when using a text-based interface as it draws on the same cognitive resources as those required during completion of a task [2]. Both theories have been disproved as no performance difference was found between users of pictorial and users of text icons [2]. Similarly, performance of word processor users was not affected by the type of menus used but icons were found to be more memorable than the name-based menus [15], findings which do not extend to an information retrieval task [9]. However, in a study similar to the current undertaking, users of a word processing application performed faster, although not significantly so, when using an iconic interface but they also had a higher error rate, albeit not significantly higher than the other users [3].

3 Methodology

3.1 Word Processor Application

A scaled down word processor (Figure 1), representative of an advanced text editor, was developed in order to conduct the usability tests. The application was capable of capturing user demographics and displaying the tasks individually and sequentially in a separate pane below the working area of the word processor. The word processor application also captured certain measurements while users completed the tasks.

3.2 Participants

Participants for the study were sourced from the maintenance department of a South African university and consisted of employees who were responsible for the cleaning of buildings. Potential users were classified into categories based on the depth of their interface knowledge paired with the extent of their domain knowledge [17]. The task knowledge of these participants was considered to be minimal, if they possessed any at all, since they had a limited educational background and the nature of their work does not demand a working knowledge of any tasks normally associated with word processing. Since they had never before used a computer they were assumed to have no knowledge of the interface domain. Therefore, these users were considered to be novice users.

Of the total of 45 users in this study, 40 were female. The vast majority of the users (31 users or 69%) spoke either Sesotho or Setswana as their first language. 20% of the users were native Afrikaans speakers, 1 participant was English speaking and the remainder (4 users) spoke an African language other than Sesotho and Setswana. Regarding education and socio-economic standing, these users all belonged to the same ranges.

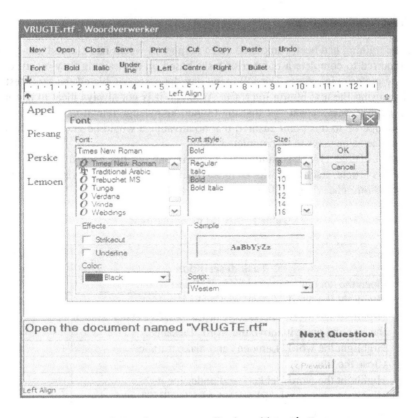

Fig. 1. Word processor application with text buttons

3.3 Interfaces

The interfaces developed for the study could be used interchangeably with the developed application and either had pictorial icons or text buttons. The text buttons contained no imagery associated with the depicted function (Figure 1); instead, the button contained only the text equivalent of the function name.

3.4 Training

Since these participants had no previous experience with a computer, they were provided with limited training with the aim that they would eventually be able to complete simple tasks. As the only language to be fully understood by both the participants and the facilitators, Afrikaans was chosen as the instruction medium. Users were however, taught the English and Sesotho terminology so that they could interact with the application to the greatest potential that it offered. The training course was divided into a series of one-hour training sessions which were spread out over a two-week period. Training was only provided on the pictorial icon interface.

3.5 Test Administration

Once the training had been completed and a number of weeks had elapsed, these users were required to complete a number of tasks based on the training they received and using the pictorial interface. The following day the users completed the same test but this time using the text button interface. Although it is not always ideal to test users on consecutive days, it was felt that the limited knowledge retention that these users had exhibited up to this point ensured that no advantage would be granted to them by requiring the same tasks to be completed again.

The test (Table 1) was administered in Afrikaans but has been translated for the sake of this article. Each task was assigned a difficulty index based on the number of actions and inferences required to complete the task.

Table 1. Task list for novice users

Task no	Task description	Difficulty index
1	Open the document named "VRUGTE.rtf"	5
2	Highlight the word "Appel" and make it bold.	4
3	Highlight the word "Perske". Cut the word "Perske" out of the text and paste it above the word "Piesang".	8
4	Highlight the word "Lemoen" and make it italic.	4
5	Close the file.	3
6	Highlight the word "lekker" and underline it.	4
7	Highlight the word "REKENAARKURSUS" and change the font size to 28.	5
8	Highlight the word "REKENAARKURSUS", if it is not already highlighted, and change the font type to Impact.	5
9	Highlight the word "REKENAARKURSUS", if it is not already highlighted, and change the colour of the word to green.	5
10	Highlight the word "REKENAARKURSUS", if it is not already highlighted, and centre align the word.	4
TEST TOTAL		**47**

4 Analysis

The overall score, calculated as the sum of the difficulty indices of the correctly completed tasks, was calculated for each individual user and provided a measure of user effectiveness. Efficiency measures of (i) time taken to complete a task, (ii) the number of actions required and (iii) errors made during completion of a task were also analysed. Due to time constraints the subjective satisfaction of the users was not measured. Only those tests that had been completed on both interfaces were included. This resulted in only a total of 14 tests being available for comparison.

4.1 Analysis of Effectiveness Measure

If there is a significant difference between the scores obtained using the different interfaces, then the interface that allowed for a higher average score (Table 2) would logically be the more effective interface. Since the data was normal a paired t-test was used to evaluate the following hypothesis:

H_0: The text buttons are not easier to use than the pictorial icons.

Table 2. Mean and standard deviation of test scores

	Score	
	Pictorial icons	**Text buttons**
n	14	14
Mean score	14.143	18.286
Std. dev	10.791	12.060

No significant difference could not be proven as H_0 could not be rejected t(13) = 1.190, p = 0.128 > 0.05. This result indicates that neither interface facilitates easier completion of the tasks at hand, or leads to significantly higher scores, and therefore, neither interface was significantly easier to use.

4.2 Analysis of Efficiency Measures

Following an established evaluation method [3] each task was analysed separately. Furthermore, only those tasks where attempts were made to complete the task were included in the analysis. The completion times were captured in seconds and then converted into 1/time in order to increase the possibility of obtaining a normal distribution. The number of actions for each task was calculated as the sum of the number of mouse clicks and key presses and the user was judged to have made an error if they clicked on an incorrect icon during completion of the task.

The measurements from the two tests were compared by means of a paired t-test or a Wilcoxon one-tailed paired test depending on whether the distribution was normal. Statistical analysis results are shown in Table 3 (tasks not shown did not have sufficient observations to complete a meaningful statistical analysis) for the following null hypotheses:

$H_{0,1}$: Text buttons do not decrease the amount of time needed to complete a task.

$H_{0,2}$: Text buttons do not decrease the number of actions needed to complete a task.

1. $H_{0,3}$: Text buttons do not decrease the number of errors made during completion of a task.

$H_{0,1}$ could only be rejected for the first task (p = 0.037) which required users to open a document. The test 2 task was completed in a significantly shorter time than the test 1 task. As this was the first task, and no other task showed a significant difference between the completion rates, a possible explanation for this observance could be that users were hesitant at the start of the first test and took some time to familiarise themselves with the workings of the application again, thus contributing to a longer completion time for that task.

$H_{0,2}$ could not be rejected for any of the tasks, thereby showing that the text buttons did not facilitate fewer actions for the users to complete the tasks. Similarly, $H_{0,3}$ could not be rejected for any of the tasks, leading to the conclusion that the text buttons did not assist the users any more than the pictorial icons, and that the use of text buttons did not lower the error rate of the users.

Table 3. Analysis results of the efficiency measurements

Task no	n	Completion time		No. of actions		No. of errors	
		t-test	Wilcoxon paired test	t-test	Wilcoxon paired test	t-test	Wilcoxon paired test
1	6	0.037*			0.855		0.678
2	5		0.094	0.418			0.968
4	8		0.371		0.611		0.052
5	7	0.185			0.364		0.086
6	5	0.203			0.392		Sample had no variance

* $p < 0.05$

5 Conclusion

No difference was detected between the performances of the users in terms of score, time to complete each task, the number of actions required or the number of errors made during completion of the task. The only exception was the significant time difference detected for the first task, where the task was completed faster using the text buttons. Since this can be explained by the fact that users had to familiarise themselves with the way the tests worked during the first test, it can be concluded that the text buttons did not facilitate increased user performance. These findings confirm those of previous studies ([2], [3]) in finding no significant difference in user performance between pictorial and text icons.

However, the fact that the second interface was text-based and users simply had to identify the icon with the correct function word could have played a role in the easy adaptability of these users between the two interfaces. This is an area which should be explored to test comprehensively the ease with which these users adapt to changes in the interfaces.

These results show that these users were able to adapt easily to a slightly changed interface once they had become comfortable using the original interface. All that is required by novice users is training and exposure to the product in order to familiarise themselves with the usage and workings of the application.

References

1. Abran, A., Suryn, W., Khelifi, A., Rilling, J., Seffah, A.: Consolidating the ISO usability models. In: Proceedings of 11th International Software Quality Management Conference (2003a)
2. Benbasat, I., Todd, P.: An experimental investigation of interface design alternatives: Icon vs. text and direct manipulation vs. menus. International Journal of Man-Machine Studies 38, 369–402 (1993)
3. Ellis, J., Tran, C., Roo, J., Shneiderman, B.: Buttons vs. menus: An exploratory study of pull-down menu selection as compared to button bars. Technical report CAR-TR-764/CS-TR-3452, University of Maryland (1995)
4. Ferreira, J., Noble, J., Biddle, R.: A case for iconic icons. In: Proceedings of the 7th Australian User Interface Conference (2006)
5. Gittins, D.: Icon-based human-computer interaction. International Journal of Man-Machine Studies 24, 519–543 (1986)
6. ISO9241.: ISO 9241-11: Ergonomic requirements for office work with visual display terminals. Beuth, Berlin (1998)
7. Kacmar, C.J., Carey, J.M.: Assessing the usability of icons in user interfaces. Behaviour and Information Technology 10(6), 443–457 (1991)
8. Kent, E.W.: The brains of men and machines. McGraw-Hill, New York (1981)
9. Lansdale, M.W., Simpson, M., Stroud, T.R.M.: A comparison of words and icons as external memory aids in an information retrieval task. Behaviour and Information Technology 9(2), 111–131 (1990)
10. Lodding, K.N.: Iconic interfacing. IEEE Computer Graphics and Applications 24, 11–20 (1983)
11. Norman, D.A., Bobrow, D.G.: Active memory processes in perception and cognition. In: Cofer, C.N. (ed.) The structure of human memory, pp. 114–132. Freeman, San Francisco (1976)
12. Paivio, A.: Imagery and verbal processes. Holt, Rinehart and Winston, New York (1971)
13. Preece, J., Rogers, Y., Sharp, H., Benyon, D., Holland, S., Carey, T.: Human-computer interaction. Addison-Wesley, England (1994)
14. Roberts, T.L., Moran, T.P.: The evaluation of text editors: Methodology and empirical results. Communications of the ACM 26(4), 265–283 (1983)
15. Rogers, Y.: Icons at the interface: Their usefulness. Interacting with Computers 1(1), 105–117 (1989)
16. Sadoski, M., Paivio, A.: A dual coding theoretical model of reading. In: Ruddell, R.B., Unrau, N.J. (eds.) Theoretical models and processes of reading, 5th edn., pp. 1329–1362. International Reading Association, Newark (2004)
17. Shneiderman, B.: Designing the user interface: Strategies for effective human-computer interaction, 3rd edn. Addison-Wesley, Massachusetts (1998)
18. Zammit, K.: Computer icons: A picture says a thousand words, or does it? Journal of Educational Computing Research 23(2), 217–231 (2000)

Exploring Factors That Make Online Interactive Games Successful: A Heuristic Approach

Yin-Leng Theng, Agnes Kit-Ying Ho, and Esther Shir-Wei Wee

Wee Kim Wee School of Communication and Information
Nanyang Technological University, Singapore
{tyltheng,agnes,esther}@ntu.edu.sg

Abstract. Game design is challenging and expensive. It is challenging in that it is difficult to create games that are easy to learn as well as enjoyable to play. It is also expensive as only a small number of games, having spent millions in creating the games, eventually becomes successfully in the market yearly. While technologies have been improving swiftly, game design guidelines have evolved slowly, and developers have to rely on limited theoretical findings, experiences and foreknowledge to create innovative and successful games. Using a theoretical model underlying game heuristics, this paper describes a study to investigate factors that might make online interactive games successful. The findings identified that usability and aesthetic appeal of the game interface are the two most important factors governing gamers' decisions to purchase a particular game. The paper concludes with implications for the design of online interactive games.

1 Introduction

Online games enable multiple gamers to interact with one another within the online game environment. In the early days, these games began as turn-based games where gamers took turns to make a move. Today, online games have already evolved to a stage where multiple gamers can access and play concurrently, assisted by Web-based and ubiquitous technologies.

But, the first multi-player online game, developed as early as in 1960 by Rick Blomme, was a dual-player game. In 1979, Rich Bartle and Roy Trubshaw designed the first multiple-user dungeon (MUD) interactive game. MUDs are role-playing computer games (RPGs) that operate on an Internet server or a bulletin board system. Through MUDs, players get to see the textual descriptions of objects, rooms and computer-controlled characters in a virtual game world. The introduction of MUDs boosted online games in the late 80's to early 90's. With the release of a four-player game called Doom and the emergence of the World Wide Web, we witness the beginning of an era of online games in 1994.

According to a research report provided by DFC Intelligence (see http://www.dfcint.com/index.php; retrieved 4 April 2008), it is forecasted that 120 million people worldwide played online games in the 2007. This report also suggests that leading top online games rake in revenues in excess of millions of dollars.

S. Lee et al. (Eds.): APCHI 2008, LNCS 5068, pp. 362–371, 2008.

Over the last couple of years, the importance of gaming has increased significantly being one of the main entertainment media, comparable in profit, customers and employees to the film and music industries. Online gaming is becoming more popular and the usage increases rapidly. Take for example, Lineage (see http://en.wikipedia.org/wiki/Lineage_(computer_game); retrieved 4 April 2008), a subscription-based online game has around 10 million of subscribers with simultaneous access by over 100 thousand gamers worldwide.

Although the gaming industry may be booming, not every game attracted a big flock of gamers. System lag is one of the main reasons. Lagging means the server that hosted the game application is not reacting fast enough to obtain the necessary information, or performing fast enough for the gamers to access. Online games are operated from servers that contain all of the game codes determining the gaming strategies, storing gamers' profiles and the players' games data. These game servers could be housed across town, on the other side of the country or even another continent, thus causing different accessing speeds for different users. Game design is challenging and expensive. It is challenging in that it is difficult to create games that are easy to learn as well as enjoyable to play. It is also expensive as only a small number of games, having spent millions in creating the games, eventually becomes successfully in the market yearly. While technologies have been improving swiftly, game design guidelines have evolved slowly, and developers have to rely on limited theoretical findings, experiences and foreknowledge to create innovative and successful games.

2 Understanding Game Usability

In recent years, there is a growing body of literature written on online games specifically from a design perspective (Desurvire, Caplan, Toth, 2004). The studies discuss the evolution of online games and discuss various design factors and considerations. A number of research papers also focus on factors that make online games enjoyable, challenging as well as easy to play (for example, Aycock, 1992; Grice, 2000; Shelley, 2001; etc.). Other studies, for example by Frokjaer, Hertzum and Horbaek (2000), claimed that the ISO's (ISO 9241-11) usability components of effectiveness, efficiency and satisfaction should be considered as individual and distinct aspects of usability. ISO's definition of usability (ISO 9241-11) identifies three measures: effectiveness (the accuracy of users completing their target goals); efficiency (the time and effort needed to achieve goals); and satisfaction (the amount of happiness derived from the completion of user's goal).

It is advocated that similar to other kinds of application software, games need to have a user-friendly interface to provide an efficient and effective way for gamers to play the games. The critical issue is what game developers should do to design exciting, immersive, and compelling games (for example, Jørgensen, 2004; Malone, 1982; etc.). However, looking beyond the interface to the playability of the game, which is vital to a game's usability, it is envisaged that the effectiveness and efficiency measures are not evenly significant or appropriate and may be different from conventional interactive systems:

- *Efficiency* is normally associated with utilizing the least amount of resources to accomplish an end goal. Gamers play games to attain a goal. If the gamer does not find it challenging while achieving the goal, the game is considered unexciting and dull. When a game is too efficient and that little effort is required from the player, the objective of providing entertainment to gamer while playing is not achieved.
- If there is an optimal route to complete a game, *effectiveness* could possibly be computed for the game, however, there is usually neither best route nor single completion path for games. Therefore, the measurement of effectiveness will be nearly impossible to constitute or relate to the overall game usability. Since the objective of the game developer is to ensure the player stays engaged in gaming as long as possible, then a game is never genuinely complete (Bickford, 1997). Every individual has a different definition of goal accomplishment and even if there is a specific end-point to a game, there may be numerous ways to attain it. The player may continue to participate in the game to uncover more, which eventually clouds the determination of what path is correct in attaining the goal.

The remaining sections of this paper are structured as follows. Section 3 reports the aim, objectives and protocol of the study conducted to investigate game usability based on users' perceptions of satisfaction of compliance/violation of design heuristics. Results and analyses are described in Section 4. Finally, Section 5 concludes with a discussion on factors that make online games successful.

3   The Study

Since efficiency and effectiveness measures that are normally applied to assess the productivity of software may not apply in the context of games, perhaps we should examine more critically, *satisfaction*, the third component. Quantifying satisfaction is important to understand game's usability evaluation and that game satisfaction is a multi-dimensional concept relating to experiences such as enjoyment, amusement and excitement. Since gaming is for entertainment purposes, the measure of satisfaction could also be directly related to a gamer's yearning for long playing hours, and indirectly related to a game's interface, playability and aesthetics (Myers, 1990).

3.1   Research Questions and Model

Hence, the study aimed to on gamers' satisfaction leading to playability and repeated playing. The two questions investigate factors that may contribute to success in online games, focusing (RQs) were:

- RQ1: To what extent are players' perceptions of the success of an online game influenced by the game usability and playability?
- RQ1: To what extent are players' perceptions of the success of an online game influenced by the subscription of the online game based on game review and game demo, and hence lead to repeated playing?

From previous studies ((Desurvire, Caplan, Toth, 2004; Jørgensen, 2004; etc.), several factors that may affect success of online games were elicited, and the associated questions asked in the survey instrument (see Tables 1 and 2 for questions asked).

Table 1. Factors on Satisfaction While Playing

Factors for Successful Games	Indicate the extent of your agreement or disagreement with each statement, using a 7-point scale

A. Playability	1. To what extent do the following issues result in players' frustrations?
	    ▪ Poor graphics
	    ▪ Poor music/sound effects
	    ▪ Poor user interface
	    ▪ Difficulty level of the game too high
	    ▪ Difficulty level of the game too low
	    ▪ Limited number of stages
	    ▪ Poor plot

Table 2. Factors on Satisfaction Leading to Repeated Playing

Factors for Successful Games	Indicate the extent of your agreement or disagreement with each statement using a 7-point scale

B. Repeated Playing	2. To what extent do these reviews affect your decisions in subscribing to an online game?
	    ▪ Game review on TV
	    ▪ Game review in computer magazines
	    ▪ Game review from other players
	    ▪ Personal review from trying the demo of the game
	3. To what extent do these aspects of the reviews affect your decisions in subscribing to an online game?
	    ▪ Overall rating of the game
	    ▪ Rating on the game graphics
	    ▪ Rating on the sound/music of the game
	    ▪ Rating on the user interface of the game
	    ▪ Difficulty level of the game
	    ▪ Screenshots and video clips in the review
	    ▪ Plot of the game
	4. To what extent do game demos affect your decisions in subscribing to an online game?
	    ▪ Graphics of the game
	    ▪ Sound/music of the game
	    ▪ User interface of the game
	    ▪ Difficulty level of the game
	    ▪ Plot of the game

3.2 Survey Instrument

The survey instrument was a questionnaire. Respondents indicated the extent of their agreement with the survey questions using a seven-point Likert-type scale. The items were modified to make them relevant to the context of online gaming. There are three different sections in the questionnaire: (i) Section I looks at the demographic details such as gender, age, and educational level of the players; (ii) Section II includes questions asking players' experiences and preferences; and (iii) Section III consists of questions on online game playability, usability and repeated playing. Tables 1 and 2 tabulate questions asked on game usability with regard to playability and subscription respectively, addressing satisfaction while playing and satisfaction leading to repeated playing.

Several versions of the questionnaire were prepared successively. Five students were selected for pre-testing as a means of obtaining feedback on the questions. Participants in the pre-testing were requested to review the questionnaire for ambiguity, repetition, inconsistency, incorrect grammar and any other problems there might be in providing responses to the questions. They were also asked to evaluate the visual appearance of the questionnaire. Pre-testers provide invaluable to feedback and necessary changes were therefore made to improve the questionnaire.

3.3 Protocol and Data Analysis

The study was focused on the intentions of online gaming with young adults. Undergraduate and postgraduate students of a local university were selected to participate in the study. The survey instrument was sent via email to course mates and students from the postgraduate programmes. Responses were collected over a period of three weeks from 26 February 2007 to 12 March 2007.

A total of 100 students participated in the study. Based on the data collected, a 1-D analysis was performed to summarize the data and the players' with common traits were grouped together. A 2-D analysis was used to analyze the relationship between the variables. Cluster analysis was also used to determine the different profiles of the players and Pearson's chi square test was used to determine the significance of the relationships between variables.

4   Findings and Analyses

4.1 Demographics and Profiles

A total of 100 responses were collected for the purpose of this study. Most respondents were aged between 21 and 30 years old. 74% of the respondents were males and aged between 24 to 27 years old. 61% of the respondents had more than 3 years of gaming experience. Only 1 % of the respondents had less than a year of gaming experience. An average of 53% of the respondents spent at around 1 to 5 hours daily on online games, with 2% of the respondents spending more than 15 hours daily on online game. 65% of the respondents played only one game during the past month. Only 1% of the respondents played more than 5 online games a month. 48% of the respondents played online games at home. Only 1% of respondents played in other places. 76% of the respondents expressed their interests in strategy online games.

We also conducted cluster analysis on the respondents to group them based on their attributes. Clustering variables such as gaming experience, time spent on online gaming daily and numbers of subscribed online games are used. Using 2-D analysis on the cluster variables, there is no relatedness between experience in online gaming and the time spent on online gaming daily. However, chi square test shows strong relationships between the two variables: time spent and experience.

After performing several tests by using different hierarchical clustering algorithms with different distance measures, the optimal solution was to group the respondents in 6 clusters. K-means clustering algorithm was used to initialize the different clustering centroids obtained using hierarchical clustering. Using squared Euclidean distance, different solutions were derived and the one with the best in terms of the mean of the silhouette values was chosen.

Table 3 shows a detailed breakdown of the various background attributes and profile attributes. Background attributes refers to the gender, education and age of the respondents. Profile attributes refer to the gaming experience, type of online games, time spent on gaming and the platform. A good clustering solution will reassert the relationships that resulted after performing 2-D analysis. Based on the clusters' centroids composition, the six groups of clusters were formed:

- *Cluster 1.* This group of players belongs to the hard core gaming group. They had long gaming experience and spent most of their time daily on online games (between 1 hour and 5 hours). They had a high subscription rate of various online games. These were mostly young male players (aged 20 - 25 years old) with tertiary education.

- *Cluster 2.* This group of players has long gaming experience. They engaged in online gaming ranging from 15 minutes to 5 hours daily. The cluster for this group of players is not homogenous. It can be seen that this cluster has less number of online games compared to cluster 1 and there is a mixture of players with different gender. There are 14% of the female players with tertiary education.

- *Cluster 3.* This group of players has more than 3 years of experience in online game playing. They play less than an hour daily, and 79% of them had subscribed to less than 10 games. Both males (69%) and females (31%), with tertiary education are in this group.

- *Cluster 4.* This group of players has only 1 to 3 years of online gaming experience and they spent a relatively small amount of time on online games daily. 63% of them played online games for less than 1 hour. They subscribed to 3 to 4 online games monthly and this group comprises both men and women with tertiary education.

- *Cluster 5.* This group of players has more than 3 years of online gaming experience. They played for less than an hour daily but subscribed to more than 5 gaming communities monthly. There were mostly males with tertiary education in this group.

- *Cluster 6.* This group of players has short gaming experience. 89% of them played online games less than a year. They are also known as novices in online gaming. They played for less than an hour daily and subscribed to only a few games. 67% of the players in this group are females with low level of education.

All these 6 groups display similar characteristics. They rated usability and user interface as the most critical factors in affecting their decision to get a game. We did not manage to validate these findings against any known literature we know. Previous empirical studies did not support the view that usability and quality of the user interface play an important role in online gaming or is a determining factor in buying a game. Based on the findings of the survey, it seems that usability is very important for game design and evaluation.

Table 3. Cluster Analyses of the Variables

		Cluster 1 N1=12	Cluster 2 N2-14	Cluster 3 N3=38	Cluster 4 N4=8	Cluster 5 N5=20	Cluster 6 N6=9
Gender	Male	100%	86%	61%	62.50%	90%	33%
	Female	0%	14%	39%	37.50%	10%	67%
Age	21 to 23 yrs old	21%	14%	12%	23%	14%	22%
	24 to 27 yrs old	68%	74%	78%	49%	66%	56%
	28 to 30 yrs old	11%	12%	10%	28%	20%	22%
Academic Level	O/N/A Levels	0%	12%	13%	25%	0%	27%
	Diploma	87%	88%	64%	75%	85%	45%
	Bachelor	12%	0%	13%	0%	15%	11%
	Masters	1%	0%	10%	0%	0%	8%
	Others	0%	0%	0%	0%	0%	9%
Experience	< 1 year	0%	0%	18%	21%	12%	12%
	1 to 5 years	68%	85%	64%	76%	78%	80%
	> 5 years	32%	15%	18%	3%	10%	8%
Time	< 1 hr	0%	0%	92%	63%	0%	0%
	1 to 5 hrs	0%	0%	8%	37%	55%	100%
	6 to10 hrs	0%	36%	0%	0%	44%	0%
	11 to 15hrs	83%	50%	0%	0%	1%	0%
	>15hrs	17%	14%	0%	0%	0%	0%
Quantity	1 game	0%	0%	52%	13%	0%	0%
	2 games	0%	12%	0%	44%	45%	100%
	3 games	50%	45%	44%	22%	45%	0%
	4 games	50%	13%	4%	10%	10%	0%
	>= 5 games	0%	30%	0%	11%	0%	0%
Platform	Home	57%	50%	63%	88%	70%	67%
	School	14%	7%	18%	0%	5%	11%
	Gaming shops	29%	43%	8%	12%	20%	22%
	Workplace	0%	0%	1%	0%	2%	0%
	Others	0%	0%	10%	0%	3%	0%
Type of online games	Action	85%	44%	46%	67%	89%	78%
	Strategy	15%	34%	28%	13%	11%	12%
	Sports	0%	22%	26%	20%	0%	10%

4.2 Summary of the Findings

Due to space constraints, we were not able to report detailed findings. Here, we summarise our findings into factors leading to satisfaction and playability, and repeated playing.

a.   Factors Leading to Satisfaction and Playability

Table 4 shows a list of factors that may affect players' satisfaction and game playability. In answering the question on playability (see Table 1), the respondents were asked what factors would cause them to feel "frustrated". Top of the list is poor user interface with 82% agreeing, followed closely by poor plot (72%). Poor music/sound effect is the least factor in affecting the respondents' frustrations.

Table 4. Factors affecting players while playing online gaming

Factors affecting players while playing	Disagree	Neutral	Agree
Poor user interface	13%	5%	82%
Poor plot	17%	11%	72%
Poor graphics	32%	16%	52%
Difficulty level of the game too high	32%	27%	41%
Limited number of stages	53%	19%	28%
Difficulty level of the game too low	54%	19%	27%
Poor music/sound effects	57%	18%	25%

b.   Factors on Satisfaction Leading to Repeated Playing

For satisfaction leading to repeated playing, we examined the following factors influencing purchase of online games: (i) game reviews; (ii) ratings of reviews; and (iii) game demo. These questions aimed to examine the ways respondents evaluate games and the issues that they would contemplate when making decisions to subscribe to an online game. Tables 5 to 7 show respondents' feedback on these issues. In Table 5, it seems apparent that respondents' onw assessment of the game via the demo set is an important factor affecting the decision to subscribe to an online game with 57% of the respondents agreeing that this is the most important criteria. Reviews from other players next affected the respondents' decision to purchase or subscribe to an online game account, with 25% of the respondents citing this as the second most important criteria. The games reviews on TV have an influence on only 3% of the respondents but 25% regarded the review as one of the factors that will influence their decision to get an online game. Game review in computer magazine was rated least important in affecting their decision to purchase online games.

   Going into the contents of the game reviews, the three critical factors that most influence respondents' decision in subscribing to an online game are (see Table 6): (i) user interface (73%); (ii) the plot of the game (71%); and (iii) overall ratings of the game (63%).

   When trying out an online game demo, 87% respondents felt that the user interface was the main determining factor in their decision to subscribe to an online game (see Table 7). This was then followed by plot of the game, which accounted for 66% of the respondents. Having great sound or music seems least important as agreed by 75% of the respondents.

In summary, good user interface had been cited as the most important factors affecting respondents' decisions to get an online game. In contrast, previous empirical studies did not support the view that usability and quality of the user interface play an important role in online games or is a determining factor in buying an online game. Based on the findings of the survey, it seems that usability is very important for game design, and perhaps contributing to the success of online games.

Table 5. Factors Influencing Purchase of Online Games

Factors	Most Important	Affect Decision
Personal review of demo of game	57%	35%
Game review on TV	3%	25%
Game review from other players	25%	25%
Game review in computer magazines	15%	15%

Table 6. Factors Influenced by Game Reviews

Factors affecting players while playing	Disagree	Neutral	Agree
Rating on the user interface of the game	17%	10%	73%
Plot of the game	17%	12%	71%
Overall rating of the game	22%	15%	63%
Difficulty level of the game	31%	18%	51%
Rating on the game graphics	36%	28%	36%
Rating on the sound/music of the game	65%	12%	23%
Screenshots and video clips in the review	78%	5%	17%

Table 7. Factors Influencing Purchase Based on Game Demo

Factors affecting players while playing	Disagree	Neutral	Agree
User interface of the game	8%	5%	87%
Graphics of the game	22%	12%	66%
Plot of the game	25%	10%	65%
Difficulty level of the game	53%	14%	33%
Sound/music of the game	75%	8%	17%

5   Discussion and Conclusion

The main purpose of this study was to investigate factors that might make online gaming successful in these two main areas by examining: (i) factors affecting players' decisions to get a particular online game; and (ii) factors affecting usability of the online games. From this pilot study, game usability (as identified mainly with good user interface) plays an important role in influencing a decision to purchase/subscribe to a game. In addition, players often rely on other players or game reviews when evaluating a particular online game. In this pilot study, the respondents were young, working adults. It would be interesting to explore other categories of players in future studies, for example, players from different countries or cultures. Designing a successful online game requires much resources and creativity. Our findings in understanding factors in satisfaction, playability, and repeated playing may be useful to game designers when online games. Other interesting issues also surface that warrant further studies and larger sample size with diverse experiences and backgrounds:

- Advertising is a powerful tool that is capable of reaching and motivating large audience, and potential players subscribing to a particular online game may be influenced by game aggressive advertising (Wernick, 1991). It seems apparent that advertising plays a role in affecting players' decisions to subscribe to a game.
- There may be different interpretations of usability due to different experiences, backgrounds and cultures of the development team. Hence, it is important that the development team is multi-disciplinary and multi-cultural.
- Perception that the game is easy does not significantly affect the decisions to subscribe to an online game. This pilot study seems to concur with other studies that players are motivated to play online games because of the presence of fun and challenges (Malone, 1982).

Acknowledgements. The authors would like to thank the respondents for their feedback, and NTU-MOE for funding the pilot study (RG8/03).

References

1. Aycock, H.: Principles of good game design. Compute! 14(1), 94–96 (1992)
2. Bickford, P.: Interface design: the art of developing easy-to-use software. Academic Press, Chestnut Hill (1997)
3. Desurvire, H., Caplan, M., Toth, J.A.: Using Heuristics to Evaluate the Playability of Games. In: CHI 2004 extended abstracts on Human factors in computing systems, pp. 1509–1512 (2004)
4. Frojkaer, E., Hertzum, M., Hornbaek, K.: Measuring Usability: Are Effectiveness, Efficiency, and Satisfaction Really Correlated. In: CHI 2000, pp. 345–352. ACM Press, New York (2000)
5. Grice, R.: I'd Rather Play Computer Games Than Do Real Work! (Wouldn't you?): The Appeal and Usability of Games Interfaces. In: Make It Easy 2000 Conference, IBM (2000) (retrieved on October 2, 2001), http://www-3.ibm.com/ibm/easy/eou_ext.nsf/Publish/1217
6. Jørgensen, A.H.: Marrying HCI/Usability and Computer Games: A Preliminary Look. In: Proc. NordiCHI 2004, Tampere, October 2004, pp. 393–396 (2004)
7. Malone, T.W.: Heuristics for designing enjoyable user interfaces: Lessons from computer games. In: Thomas, J.C., Schneider, M.L. (eds.) Human Factors in Computing Systems, Ablex Publishing Corporation. Norwood (1982)
8. Myers, D.: A Q-Study of Game Player Aesthetics. Simulation & Gaming 21(4), 375–396 (1990)
9. Shelley, B.: Guidelines for Developing Successful Games. Gamasutra (August 15, 2001), http://www.gamasutra.com/features/20010815/shelley_01.htm
10. Wernick, A.: Promotional Culture: Advertising, Ideology and Symbolic Expression (Theory, Culture & Society S.). Sage Publications Ltd., London (1991)

Users' Perception and Usability Study of a Parser for Headings

Safiriyu A. Elegbede[1], Mukaila A. Rahman[2,3], and Imran A. Adeleke[3]

[1] Department of Management Science, University of Strathclyde, Glasgow
[2] NUST School of Electrical Engineering and Computer Science, Pakistan
[3] Department of Computer Sciences, University of Lagos, Nigeria
safiriyu.elegbede@strath.ac.uk, rahmalade@niit.edu.pk,
ade1424@yahoo.com

Abstract. Headings as used in many research articles play a significant role in helping readers to easily understand the organization of documents as well as the relative importance of sections. These headings are usually words or word-sequences which do not constitute full sentences. Despite the available text and speech parsing applications, none is designed towards parsing of such fragmentary word-sequences. We tackle this challenge by designing an application which implements active chart parser (ACP) using java technology. The system is designed to parse headings using context free phrase structure grammar. We present in this paper the study of the evaluators' perception and usability of the system. The result shows that most of the users rated the system very efficient, easy to use, and satisfactory. Apart from the system's heading parsing ability, the available text and speech processing systems can benefit immensely from integration with the application.

Keywords: Computer Human Interaction, Headings, Natural language Processing, Active chart parser.

1 Introduction

There is substantial ongoing research and development in many aspects of Natural Language Processing (NLP) such as text processing, machine translation and spoken dialogue. Also, significant commercial systems in this domain are in widespread use. Prior research literatures on language processing generally and in particular on parsing paradigms are very extensive and could be traced to the work of Chomsky [1] using two approaches - traditional and statistical. The traditional approach tries to cope with the enormous lexical and structural ambiguities of unrestricted text in their parsing process by relying heavily on hand-coded grammar rules. A simple parsing algorithm makes use of such context-free grammars. Quantitative or Statistical linguistic, the second approach, either augment the traditional grammar rule paradigm or replace it with statistical and machine learning techniques which automatically derive parse grammars and the frequencies of various words, word combinations, and constructions from previously gathered statistics. A parser is a programming code that computes text input sequence and transforms them into a data structure represented in the form of

S. Lee et al. (Eds.): APCHI 2008, LNCS 5068, pp. 372–379, 2008.

parse tree or nested structure (syntactic analyses output) which in turn becomes the input for the semantic processing. In order words, parsing process verifies that the input tokens form valid syntax with respect to a given formal grammar and derives semantic structure from the syntactic structure of the input tokens.

The Earley parsing algorithm [2] is well known for its great efficiency in producing all possible parses of a sentence in relatively little time, without back-tracking, and while handling left recursive rules correctly. It is also known for being considerably slower than most other parsing algorithms [3]. This type of parser is referred to as active chart parser. A chart is a data structure that stores completed constituents (inactive constituents) and constituents being parsed (partial/active constituents). Moreover, *active* chart parsing, that is, parsing where the chart itself drives the parsing process, provides a general framework in which alternative parsing and search strategies can be compared.

There have been many improvements on the Earley's parser taking care of the observed shortcoming. These include work as discussed in [3,4,5,6]. However, none of this work is considered for parsing headings. Heading parser paradigm may find its greatest application in applied linguistic systems which are widely used in scientific, technical and business domains for many purposes. For instance, it could be beneficial for text preparation or text editing. Furthermore, such algorithm could be useful in sophisticated internet search engines and several other information retrieval systems (IRS) in scientific, technical and business document databases. It is well known that headings contribute to better search engine optimization (SEO) as well as semantic HTML [7]. Consequently, NLP systems that will incorporate parsing of headings are highly indispensable.

This work seeks to tackle this open problem in natural language processing by designing an application for parsing headings. An ACP algorithm highlighted in [6] was implemented to parse headings using context free phrase structured grammar. Java technology was use for coding the parser. We thereafter evaluate users' perception of the system to determine whether the system meets performance and usability criteria such as learnability, efficiency, memorability, error handling, and satisfaction. The application was rated excellent in performance and usability by majority of the evaluators. Elimination of ambiguity in headings, automatic correction of misspellings and morphological analysis are not within the scope of the work. The outline of the paper is as follows. First we make a survey of related work in section 2. In section 3, we describe the system architecture. The test and evaluation of the system is presented in section 4. The results of the system's evaluation is highlighted and discussed in section 5, while we draw conclusions and future direction of the work in section 6.

2 Related Work

Existing text processing tools significant to this study include the Classifier [8] and TextAnalyst [9]. The TextAnalyst, based on proprietary neural net technology, performs semantic analysis of texts in an arbitrary application domain. Its major strength lies in the determination of the main topics of a document and the relationships between words in the document. However, the system is not dictionary-based and words that ordinarily should not have been processed as meaningful words such as 'de' are regarded as main topic of any document. The Classifier is designed for topics in documents. When a set document is considered, it automatically determines the topics mentioned in a specified document and further determines similar documents ID_By Document pageto the chosen one with respect to the topics that has been mentioned. In 'Auto-Presentation' [10], the system builds a presentation automatically by parsing, summarizing and correlating information collected from the Internet based knowledge sources after receiving the presentation topic from the user. The agent characters used in the application presents the retrieved according to different outline referred to as heading in the work.

3   System Architecture

The model comprises codes for its ACP parser, grammar rules and lexicon to go through the parsing process. Its graphical user interface has reset button designed for repeated parsing of different headings, customization features to support the robustness of the parser as well as error handling mechanism to minimize possible errors in the parsing and interaction processes. This is illustrated in Fig. 1.

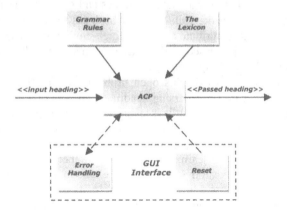

Fig. 1. Architecture of the system

During user interaction with the system while parsing a heading, the ACP invokes the grammar rules and the lexicon. The error handling module of the system likewise resolve errors emanating from user's input.

4   Test and Evaluation

The Lexicon (*electronic dictionary*), which is made up of collection of words with their syntactic classes and semantic fields containing exactly 104 lexemes, was designed and used. We also used an *electronic grammar*, a set of rules based on common properties of large groups of words which make the grammar rules equally applicable to many words. There are 15 such grammar rules for this Parser but more rules could still be added. The basic rules totaling 12 are permanent. The user can neither change nor add more of such rules to the application. Every effort has been taken to make this Parser as robust as possible which means that users may not actually have any need for additional rules with terminal constituents. However, the coding can still be changed for a greater robustness. Data from the publications of the ACM (Association of Computing Machinery) and IET (Institution of Engineering and Technology) were used for the study.

Every effort has been made to ensure error free interaction with the users. For example, the system yields an error message "Rule already exists", as shown in Fig. 2 when a user tries to add an existing rule. There is also a Checker to test whether input word(s) exists in Lexicon or not. If not, the message: "Please add the following words into the lexicon" is generated requiring that user add new word(s) before continuing.

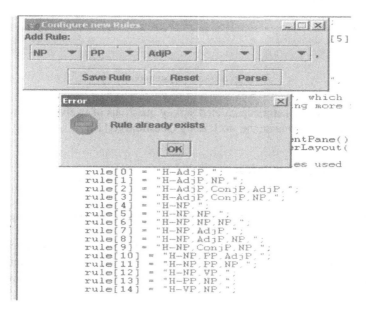

Fig. 2. Sample system error output, when a user tries to add an existing rule

Fig. 3 depicts sample output of the application, having parsed the heading, 'Contract Strategic Agenda'. The input is firstly syntactically analyzed using the grammar rules. Thereafter, in conjunction with the lexicon, the semantic analysis is done, and subsequently, the heading is parsed. The 'Contract Strategic Agenda' was parsed as shown below.

The performance measurement usability testing [11] method was employed in evaluating this system. Five sample of MSc Computer Science students were asked to test the system on the usability issues. They were requested to interact with the system by performing series of tasks expected of potential users of the application. The 'Test Tasks' instruction list that serves as guide for effective use of the system, consist of 13 items. These instructions were simplified even to be easily followed by non-java programming expert. Likewise, evaluators were asked to answer 'End-of-tasks Questions' of nine items. This was aimed at getting a heuristic evaluation of the system performance.

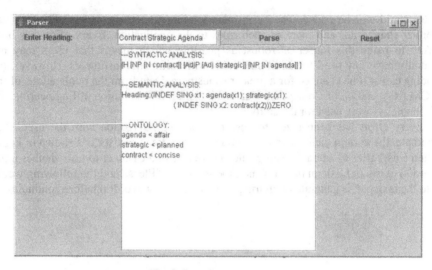

Fig. 3. Sample system output

Thereafter, the evaluators completed survey questions of twelve items which were used to statistically evaluate the work using QuestionPro [12].

5   Results and Discussion

In order to test the hypothesis

H_1: A user does not derive any satisfaction as a result of system ease of use, against the alternative (null),

H_0: there is significant relationship between ease of use and system's satisfaction, we cross-tabulate the survey results of item 1 and 12 on the questionnaire (see appendix 1). The Chi-square analysis to measure this relationship is illustrated in Table 1.

Table 1. The Pearson's Chi-square statistics for cross tabulation analysis between the system's ease of use and satisfaction derived

Pearson's Chi-Square Statistics	
Total Chi-Square	0.0
p Value	1.000
Degrees of Freedom	16
Critical Value for (p = .01 [1%])	32.0
Critical Value for (p = .05 [5%])	26.296
Critical Value for (p = .10 [10%])	23.542

Since the calculated chi-square value is lesser than the critical value (0.05), the null hypothesis is accepted. Thus, there is significant relationship between the system's ease of use and the satisfaction derived by users.

5.1 Overall Ratings

80% of the survey participants rated the design as *excellent* in performance and usability. While nobody rated it as *poor,* only one participant rated the design as *good.* Moreover, the simplicity of the use of the application, makes the evaluators derived much satisfaction from its use.

5.2 Other Measurements

Learnability. All participants (100%) strongly agreed it was very easy for them to have accomplished basic tasks the first time they interacted with the design.

Familiarity. 80% of the participants say they strongly agree it would be very possible for users to apply their real world experience and knowledge when interacting with the design. They believe the design has employed the usability standards to the core in properly placing and sizing of its interface objects. Only one participant says although she agrees to this possibility but not strongly because after using the 'Reset' button, one would need to place the cursor back into the parser textbox before another input to be parsed can be entered.

Consistency. 60% of the participants rated the application as excellently maintaining consistency while 40% believe the design is not per excellence in consistency but maintain a very good stand on it.

Predictability. Provision of support for users to be able to predict the next action is very high for the design as 80% said the application is highly predictable while 20% agreed it is very predictable.

Generalisability. In relation to support for users' ability to extend their knowledge of specific interaction within and across the design to other similar situations, 60% give the application 4 out of 5.

Synthesizability. Findings relating to users' ability to assess the effect of the past operations on the current state for the application show that 60% of participants found this very easy to do.

Satisfaction. 80% have expressed high satisfaction in using the application and are very much happy, comfortable and would welcome repeat interactions.

Efficiency. Again, 60% of those surveyed indicated that they were able to perform same tasks highly quickly after repeated tasks during interaction with the design.

Errors. One surveyed participant says he made two non-severe mistakes but that he was able to painlessly recover from these errors pretty quickly. No other participant indicated error commission.

6 Conclusions and Future Work

In this paper, we presented users' evaluation of a robust ACP application used in parsing headings as found in professional publications and e-mails. The application was used by five evaluators and their observations were elicited with the help of a structured end of tasks questions for heuristic evaluation of the system. The answer to a survey questions were use to statistically evaluate the work using QuestionPro [12]. The statistical evaluation shows that our application is very easy to use and contributed significantly to the satisfaction derived by the users.

A scalable and efficient active chart parser with full maintainability considerations was achieved. For example, new rules and words can be added and the system remains efficiently usable. These rules are quite simple even for non-computer expert to construct. Our aim is to integrate this application with existing text and speech processing systems.

Our future work shall consider the use of an electronic database such as mySQL for the grammar rules and the Lexicon. This further improvement will have to cater for the elimination of ambiguity in headings, automatic correction of misspellings, morphological analysis and aspects such as -*ing* and conjunctions.

Acknowledgements. M. A. Rahman from the University of Lagos, Nigeria thanks the Academy of Sciences for the Developing World (TWAS) Italy, and the National University of Sciences and Technology (NUST) Pakistan, for the ongoing one-year research fellowship sponsorship at NUST School of Electrical Engineering and Computer Science (SEECS), Pakistan.

References

1. Chomsky, N.A.: Syntactic Structures. The Hague: Mouton (1957) Reprint, Berlin and New York (1985)
2. Earley, J.: An Efficient Context-free Parsing Algorithm. Communications of the ACM 13, 94–102 (1970)
3. Voss, M.: Improving Upon Earley's Parsing Algorithm in Prolog, http://www.ai.uga.edu/mc/ProNTo/Voss.pdf
4. Mellish, C.S.: Some Chart-Based Techniques for Parsing Ill-Formed Input. In: 27th Annual Meeting of the Association for Computational Linguistics, pp. 102–109. University of British Columbia, Vancouver, Canada (1989)
5. Kato, T.: Robust Parsing: Yet Another Chart-Based Techniques for Parsing Ill-Formed Input. In: Proceedings of the 4th Conference on Applied Natural Language Processing, pp. 107–112. Morgan Kaufmann, California (1994)
6. Kaplan, R.M.: A General Syntactic Processor. In: Rustin, R. (ed.) Natural Language Processing. Algorithmics Press, New York (1973)
7. Nadgouda, A.: Importance of Heading Structure, http://ifacethoughts.net/2007/01/27/importance-of-heading-structure/
8. National Polytechnic Institute, Center for Computing Research. Natural Language Processing (NLP) Laboratory, http://www.gelbukh.com/classifier/
9. TextAnalyst. Microsystems Ltd., http://www.megaputer.com/php/eval.php3

10. Shaikh, M.A.M., Mitsuru, I., Tawhidul, I.: Creating Topic-Specific Automatic Multimodal Presentation Mining the World Wide Web Information. In: Proceedings of 8th International Conference on Computer and Information Technology (ICCIT 2005), Dhaka, Bangladesh, pp. 267–272 (2005)
11. Molich, R., Nielsen, J.: Improving a Human Computer Dialogue. Communications of the ACM 33(3), 338–348 (1990)
12. QuestionPro, http://www.questionpro.com/

Appendix 1: Survey Questionnaire

1. It was very easy to accomplish the basic tasks the first time interacting with the model.
   ○Strongly Agree   ○Agree   ○Neutral   ○Disagree   ○Strongly Disagree

2. It was very possible to apply my knowledge and real world experience when interacting with model.
   ○Strongly Agree   ○Agree   ○Neutral   ○Disagree   ○Strongly Disagree

3. How would you rate the model's consistency (likeness in input and output behavior arising from similar tasks)?
   ○Excellent   ○Very Good   ○Good   ○Fair   ○Inconsistent

4. How predictable is the model in determining the effect of future actions?
   ○Very Highly   ○Highly   ○Fairly   ○Not Predictable   ○Don't Know

5. Please rate degree to which you are able to extend your knowledge of specific interaction within and across the model to other similar situations (5 = Highly Able and 1 = Not Able).
   ○5   ○4   ○3   ○2   ○1

6. How easy are you able to assess the effect of the earlier operations on the current state?
   ○Very Easy   ○Fairly Easy   ○Easy   ○Not Easy   ○Don't know

7. How quickly can you perform same tasks after repeated interaction with the model?
   ○Highly Quickly   ○Very Quickly   ○Fairly Quickly   ○Quickly   ○Slowly

8. It was very easy to establish proficiency or to recall functions when you return to repeat a task you have performed earlier.
   ○Strongly Agree   ○Agree   ○Neutral   ○Disagree   ○Strongly Disagree

9. How many errors all together did you make during all your interactions with the model for the purpose of this study?
   ○More than 10   ○10 - 6   ○5 -2   ○Less than 2   ○No Error

10. How severe were these errors, if any?
    ○Very Severe   ○Severe   ○Not Severe   ○Don't Know   ○No Error

11. How easy were you able to recover from these errors?
    ○Very Easily   ○Easily   ○Slowly   ○Very Slowly   ○No Error

12. How satisfied are you having to interact with the model?
    ○highly Satisfied   ○Very Satisfied   ○Satisfied   ○Not Satisfied   ○Don't know

Development of Interactive Map-Based Tour Information System for Busan

Y. Batu Salman, Kyong-Hee Lee, Yoonjung Kim, Hong-In Cheng,
and Hyunjeong Kim

Graduate School of Digital Design, Kyungsung University, Busan, Republic of Korea
{batu,beyondlee,yjkim00,hicheng,kimhj}@ks.ac.kr

Abstract. The Internet is the most efficient modern media providing the tourists with the information for organizing many traveling activities. It is time consuming and difficult work to organize transportation, accommodation, restaurants, adventures etc. for effective and memorable trip. Although there are many tourist sites containing a great amount of information, it is not easy to find proper and tailored information satisfying various tourists. In this study, a development process to build the web-based tour information system for Busan, Korea, and the final prototype was introduced. Current tour information websites and online maps were inspected first for the information, contents, services, and functions provided on the web sites. The user study was conducted by employing six participants to investigate the users' preferences and needs. Design principles and final contents were determined based on the user requirements analysis. A design prototype for the map-based interactive tourist information system was finally developed and suggested.

Keywords: Tourism, Map-Based Tourist Information System, Information Architecture.

1 Introduction

Tourism is a business providing leisure, cultural, and recreational activities for traveling people when they are out of their everyday life. It is regarded as an important business because it is major financial source for many countries [1]. It is also one of the major financial sources for several countries Governments support management strategies to increase their benefits from tourism industry.

Recently the Internet has been developed significantly and become the most easily accessible and effective medium for tourists to search the information and perform related tasks freely. IT infrastructure was also improved world widely due to the technological investments. Tourism information systems are widely studied since tourism is a service business and information service to the customers is very significant [1]. Most tourists are using the Internet to search the tour information and make online reservations [2]. There are abundant web sites containing a great amount of tour information, however, it is not easy to navigate the most proper web sites. It is most crucial to understand the user's preferences and needs clearly in order to provide them with tailored information.

S. Lee et al. (Eds.): APCHI 2008, LNCS 5068, pp. 380–388, 2008.
© Springer-Verlag Berlin Heidelberg 2008

Bell and Tang (1998) investigated the effectiveness of some tourist information web-sites from the perspectives of users. Countryman (1999) evaluated the official USA tourism web-sites by the content analysis [4]. Understanding the characteristics of the tourists will help developers establish a more usable and effective information system [5].

The purpose of this study was to develop a usable and efficient web-based information system for tourists traveling around Busan, Republic of Korea. The system development process is introduced in detail and the screenshots of the developed prototype was also illustrated.

2 Development Process

There were four main phases in the development procedure. 1) Existing tourist web-sites were analyzed to examine their information architecture and content to understand the sorts of information and the technologies. 2) The requirements and interaction problems were investigated for the current Busan tourist information website. 3) Specific design elements were decided such as design guidelines, content types, information presentation methods, and so forth were examined. 4) After evaluation of the final content and design principle, the prototype was finally designed. Figure 1 shows the development process briefly.

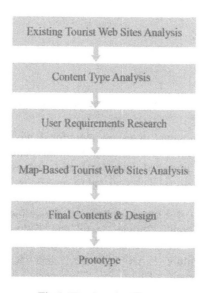

Fig 1. Development Process

3 Analysis of Current Tourist Information Systems

Currently existing tourist information web-sites were examined in the initial phase of the development process. The purpose of the examination was to know what kind of information was provided and how they were presented. Four tourists information web sites were investigated focusing on their homepage, navigation, information scheme and content: 1) Korean website of Seoul (www.visitseoul.net/visit2006), 2) Korean website of Busan (www.visit.busan.kr), 3) English website of Busan (www.tour.busan.go.kr/eng), 4) English website of Istanbul (www.istanbul.com). The information structure, navigation, design, and content of the websites were analyzed to develop the prototype.

The information structure of the Busan, Korea tourist web site is shown in Figure 2.

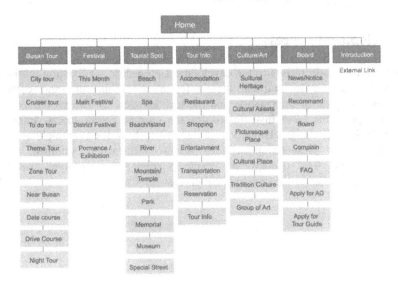

Fig 2. Information scheme of Busan, Korean tourist website

There are seven main menu items on the global navigation of Busan tourist information website. All choices have their own sub-menus except "Introduction". Information is generally provided with texts and images. Also board, map and panorama are used to help users. Pages related to specific information have contextual internal and external links.

The global navigation of Korean website of Seoul includes "Culture! Seoul", "Tour! Seoul", "Theme! Seoul", "Movie! Seoul" and "Culture Organization". Korean website of Busan has the menu items, "Busan Tour", "Festival", "Tourist Spot", "Tour Information", "Culture / Art", "Board", and "Introduction" as a global navigation on the homepage. There are "Transportation", "Busan City Tour", "Festivity Tour", "To Do Tour", "Entertainment", "Food", "Shopping", "Lodging", "Tour of Neighboring Attractions", and "Necessary Information" in the global navigation of English website of Busan.

The main navigation of Istanbul tourist information website consists of "News", "Transportation", "Going Out", "Accommodation", "Shopping", "Explore Istanbul", "Tours", "Business Life", "Events", and "Photo Gallery". There is additionally navigation on the site as "Istanbul Guide". It includes "Tourism - Travel", "Hotels", "Going Out", "Restaurants", "Shopping", "Health & Fitness", "Education", "Business

& Finance", "Art & Culture", "Community & Government", and "Local Services & Emergency". The Istanbul web site was providing two different menus containing same menu items resulting in users' confusion. The information presented on each website was investigated and analyzed in detail for the next step of the development procedure.

4 User Study

The purpose of the user study was to identify the needs and the interaction problems for the users when they are searching information on the Busan tourist website. Users searching behavior and their preferences were also observed. The experiment was performed in the Usability Laboratories of Graduate School of Digital Design, Kyungsung University. As a result of the experiment, an affinity diagram was generated considering the preferences, needs and interaction problems.

4.1 Participants

Six subjects participated from the faculty and students of the Graduate School of Digital Design, Kyungsung University. Four of them were female and two were male. Three participants were foreigners living in Busan, and other three participants were Koreans living out of Busan. The average age of the participants was thirty-one. All participants reported the they were familiar with searching information on the web sites.

4.2 Methods

Participants were explained briefly about the aim of the study before the experiment. Foreign and Korean participants were asked to explore English and Korean Busan tourist website respectively.

An interview was conducted first about their experiences in searching tourist information. Participants were then asked to organize their imaginary three-day trip in Busan by using the website with no limit and specific mission.

They were asked to think aloud their intentions, needs and interaction problems while planning the three-day trip. Each session took approximately one hour and was recorded by the video camera. Every selected menu item and navigation on the web site was also recorded with Camtasia software for each participant.

4.3 Results

The requirements and preferences of users were analyzed and summarized to generate the design ideas for the final prototype (Table 1).

The results showed that tourists want to know the location of the tourist spots, restaurants, hotels, etc. and way to get the place from where they are, which is not available on most tourist websites.

Brief textual information with pictures, search engine, familiar labels, logical navigation and graphical visualization were believed as useful content type. Required contents were most famous spots, recommended tours, price, review and comments, etc.

Table 1. Analysis of User Requirements by Affinity Diagrams

1. Map-Based Information	2. Content Type Requirements	3. Content Requirements
1.1. Different Layers by Category of tourist spots	2.1. Clear Categorization	3.1. Information about How to get there
1.2. Information of Near Attractions from a tourist spot	2.2. Need for Pictures	3.2. Most Famous Spots
1.3. Location of Place	2.3. Brief Text	3.3. Recommended Tour
1.4. Distance and Time	2.4. More than just Business Name List	3.4. Price
1.5. Geographical Information	2.5. Search feature	3.5. Review and Comments by other tourists
1.6. Tour Path	2.6. Consistency on Linked Information	3.6. Special Dishes
1.7. Access Final Content Page through Map	2.7. Familiar Labeling	3.7. Reservation
1.8. Less Amount of Information	2.8. Clear and logical Navigation and Links	3.8. Events and Festivals
	2.9. Graphical User Interface	3.9. Personalization features
		3.10. Culture and Tradition

4.3.1 Map-Based Information

Participants selected places to visit and then arranged the accommodations when they organized the imaginary three-day trip to Busan by using the website. All participants insisted on the importance of presenting information on easy-to-understand map. In addition to the big city map, the detailed district maps showing the locations of hotels, tourist spots, and restaurants were desirable. Participants also recommended some features such as finding their current position on the map, informing the distance, traveling time, and the most efficient route between two selected places, zooming in and out the map, etc. Participants also reported that the colorful drawing / graphical map is more attractive.

4.3.2 Content Type Requirements

Participants suggested that food and tourists spot information need to be classified into subcategories. Tourist spot can be categorized according to the attraction such as river, temple, beach, shopping, museum, park, etc. To search the information about the spots on the current Busan tourist website, users looked for short texts which were accompanied with photos. They were not observed to read the long textual information.

Another recommendation was to provide a hyperlinked list of the most famous restaurants and tourist spots. Users preferred looking the list over to find a interesting information and referring to linked web page showing the detailed information.

Participants complained about the ambiguous labels: 'Eating Town Busan', 'Specialty Dishes', 'Other Entertainment Facilities', and 'Gaya Culture Tour'. Even though Gaya is familiar term for Korean, foreign tourists did not understand the term without additional explanation.

Search engine was believed necessary to offer the information when tourists try to look for specific information with keywords. Primarily, search output should be directly related to the keywords entered by the user. System could help users by recommending terms and correcting the syntax when the keywords typed in. Participants reported that using the search feature on the Busan website is sometimes confusing.

4.3.3 Content Requirements

It is not easy to satisfy all tourists because their experiences, preferences, languages, cultures, educational backgrounds are different. The main contents that participants most looked for were transportation, accommodation, traveling, food, entertainment, and shopping.

Information about the shortest and efficient route between two locations is essential for everyone especially first time tourists to the city. Participants suggested detailed information should be described about bus, subway, railway, rent car, ship or taxi.

Sometimes users can not decide where to go easily. Displaying the list of the most famous "must go" places with various recommended tours on the website are also beneficial. Participants wanted to know more information than we expected. They also wanted information for the traditional and cultural activities and shopping.

Participants also indicated the importance of forums or comments written by other tourists. It seemed more useful and objective than the officially presented information on the website.

5   Analysis of Map-Based Tourist Web-Sites

A map-based interactive tourist information system was decided to be redesigned after the analysis of user requirements. Map is efficient graphical user interface (GUIs) to show the traveling information [6]. Participants answered their priorities, preferences related to the type and presenting method for the tour information.

The common need of all users was to show the information on the map for the convenience. The design principles, content types, presentation methods, and the information scheme for five online tourist maps were examined. Maps analyzed in the study were (1) Onion Map – in English, (2) Busan Map – in Korean, (3) Seoul Map – in Korean, (4) Jeju Map – in Korean, and (5) Beatle Map – in Korean.

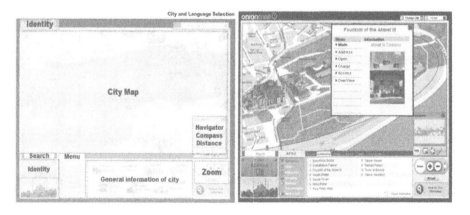

Fig 3. Main screen for Istanbul city on Onion Map (left: the screen layout, right: information presentation)

Onion map presents simple information about the city such as population, language, currency, phone codes, the Mayor and the oldest historical building (Figure 3). The application identity is shown on the upper-left corner of the screen and contains useful features like search, zoom, help, compass and navigator.

When a specific spot was clicked, a pop-up screen appears to show the simple information. The information was divided into several sub links to avoid displaying long texts.

6   Prototype Design

A web-based interactive map was developed as a final prototype reflecting the results of the analysis. 'Tour Spot' and 'Tour Course' were decided as two main navigation categories.

'Tour Spot' provides information about the famous tourist spots in Busan and has nine sub-menus; 'Zone Tour', 'Beach', 'Sea', 'Famous Street', 'Exhibition', 'Place of History', 'Mountain – Temple', 'River' and 'Park'. The information of the tourist spots was designed to be displayed and accessed through illustrated map which demonstrates the nature and geography of the region.

'Tour Course' is also main navigation menu showing the information organized by the city government and contains three sub-menus; "City Tour", "Cruiser Tour" and "Theme Tour".

Accommodations, restaurants, shopping and entertainment information was planned to be presented by highlighting the locations on the map (Figure 4) and they are grouped by a link named 'Related Information'.

Fig 4. Main screen shot of the prototype

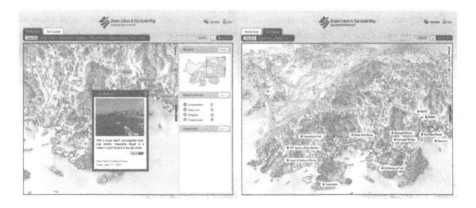

Fig 5. Snapshots of the prototype (left: Tour Course user interface, right: information display for the selected spot on mini-map with 'Related Information')

Final prototype has some other features: 1) 'Search' to search information by entering keywords, 2) 'Where am I' to show the location of the user on the map, 3) 'Mini-Map' to navigate easily on the whole map, (4) 'Transportation' to display the route from the starting point to the destination entered by the users (Figure 5).

7 Conclusion

Tourism is an important and valuable business and better tour information system plays an important role for the business. Developed internet technologies are being used to design better and more usable web based tour information system. It is expected more information system will be required and available in the future.

A design prototype for the map-based interactive tour information system was developed to suggest more satisfactory and effective online system by employing users study and the overall development process for the prototype was introduced.

More tourists need to be studied to know their requirements and behavior. Despite the small number of participants, basic information scheme and presentation methods were suggested for better web based information system.

References

1. Watson, R., Akselsen, S., Monod, E., Pitt, L.: The Open Tourism Consortium: Laying The Foundations for Future of Tourism. European Management Journal 22(3), 315–326 (2004)
2. Shi, Y.: The accessibility of Queensland visitor information centres, websites. Tourism Management 27, 829–841 (2006)
3. Bell, H., Tang, N.K.H.: The effectiveness of commercial Internet web sites: A users perspective. Internet Research: Electronic Networking Applications and Policy 8(3), 219–228 (1998)

4. Countryman, C.C.: Content analysis of state tourism web sites and the application of marketing concepts. In: Proceedings of the fourth annual conference on graduate education / graduate student research in hospitality and tourism, Las Vegas, NV, USA, pp. 210–218 (1999)
5. Alvarez, M., Asugman, G.: Explorers versus planners: a study of Turkish tourists. Annals of Tourism Research 33(2), 319–338 (2006)
6. Nivala, A., Sarjakoski, L.T., Sarjakovski, T.: Usability methods, familiarity among map application developers. Int. Journal of Human – Computer Studies 65, 784–795 (2007)

Development of Image and Color Evaluation Algorithm for the Web Accessibility Evaluation Tools

Seong Je Park, Young Moo Kang, Hyung Rim Choi, Soon Goo Hong, and Yang Suk Kang

840, Hadan-dong, Saha-gu, Pusan 604-714, Korea
Dong-A UNIVERSITY Division of Management Information Systems
{psjmis,ymkang,hrchoi,shong}@dau.ac.kr, kangyangsuk@naver.com

Abstract. In the web accessibility evaluation, many studies have been carried out on the evaluation methods related to the content types and features, and in particular, some problems have been raised in relation to the automatic evaluation tools from the aspect of image and color. Thus, this study has attempted to analyze the problems of typical automatic evaluation tools based on WCAG and KWCAG, to suggest improvements for the images and colors, and to prove validity of new algorithms suggested in this study.

Keywords: Web accessibility, Accessibility evaluation, Automatic evaluation tool.

1 Introduction

Nowadays we are living amid a flood of information, and because of the development of information technology and Internet, numerous kinds of web- and IT- related devices are widely spread[5]. For this reason, the importance and necessity of information accessibility as well as its convenience have been emphasized. Accordingly, many studies and discussions have been carried out on web accessibility evaluation[7]. Web accessibility can be divided into two categories: automatic evaluation by a program and manual evaluation by the human expert. Some problems in the automatic evaluation tools have been raised that program's feature either predisposes the evaluation on content to use a different method or makes an automatic evaluation impossible, and eventually being compelled to conduct a manual evaluation by source code analysis[7]. In particular, objects of images and colors can not be evaluated by the automotive evaluation tools such as A-Prompt and Bobby.

The objective of this study is to suggest the algorithm of images and colors for the automotive accessibility tools. Particularly, this study takes an in-depth look at the issues of automatic evaluation tools in terms of both the images using an "img tag" and the colors using a "bgcolor attribute."

To this end, this study first has summarized the features of well-known web accessibility evaluation tools included in the W3C (World Wide Web Consortium), analyzing the problems of the images using an "img tag" and the colors using a "bgcolor attribute" of both A-Prompt based on WCAG (Web Content Accessibility Guideline) and Kado-Wah based on KWCAG (Korean Web Content Accessibility Guideline), suggesting improvements, and proving its validity.

S. Lee et al. (Eds.): APCHI 2008, LNCS 5068, pp. 389–395, 2008.
© Springer-Verlag Berlin Heidelberg 2008

2 Web Accessibility Evaluation Tools

Since the W3C legislated its WCAG in 1997, a lot of automatic tools for web accessibility evaluation have been developed, and especially, the "Bobby" and "A-Prompt" are most well known among them. The Bobby checks the source codes that are liable to cause an accessibility problem based on WCAG, while testing the compatibility of a page. The A-Prompt developed by Toronto University, Canada also confirms and evaluates the accessibility based on WCAG 1.0, and provides the function of correcting an error. The "LIFT" developed by UsableNet has the strong point of simultaneously evaluating both web accessibility and web convenience.

Also in case of "Kado-Wah" developed KADO (Korea Agency for Digital Opportunity and Promotion), its web accessibility evaluation is not only in compliance with the above mentioned WCAG but also the Section 508-1194.22 of the U.S. Rehabilitation Act and KWCAG, checking an error, issuing a warning, and showing manual check items. The following [Table 1] has summarized the guideline of 50 automatic evaluation tools i.ntroduced in the W3C website[5].

Table 1. List of typical web accessibility evaluation tools

Used Standards	Evaluation Tools
only WCAG1.0	Acc - an Accessibility Evaluator, Colorfield Insight, Colour Blindness Check, CSS Analyser, EvalAccess, EveryEye, Hera, Hi-Caption Studio, IBM Rule-based Accessibility Validation Environment (RAVEn), Illinois Accessible Web Publishing Wizard, Lynx Simulator, Lynx viewer, Media Access Generator (MAGpie), NetMechanic, NIST WebMetrics Tool Suite, Ocawa, Page Valet, PEAT - Photosensitive Epilepsy Analysis Tool, Readability Test, Silvinha - Accessibility Validator and Repair Tool, Style and DictionTAW Standalone, Uaw, Visolve, Visual Impairment Simulator for Microsoft Windows, W3C CSS Validation Service, W3C Markup Validation Service, Web Accessibility Inspector, Web Accessibility Self-Evaluation Tool etc
WCAG1.0 & Section508	Bobby, Deque Ramp Ascend, Deque Ramp Personal Edition, Mozilla/Firefox Accessibility Extension, Readability index calculator, SWAP, Truwex 2.0, WebXACT, WebXM etc
WCAG1.0 & BITV	Visolve etc
WCAG1.0, Section508 & JIS	Colour Blindness Check, ColorDoctor etc
WCAG1.0, Section508, & BITV	A-Prompt etc
WCAG1.0, Section508, Stanca Act, & BITV	A-Checker etc

3 Problems of Evaluation on Images and Color

The patterns of the images and colors provided in the web are so diversified that their evaluation guidelines or methods can be overlapped. For example, in case of an image, the image evaluation guideline or method to be used for content can be different from that to be used for an image map. Likewise, in case of a color, the color evaluation guideline or method to be used for content can be different from that to be used for foreground and background color.

In particular, when taking into consideration the functional aspect of evaluation tools that can be conducted by the existence or non-existence of specific source code based on the WCAG and KWCAG, a certain tag or attribute alone such as img, background, color, and bgcolor cannot allow us to judge how the corresponding content has been used.

3.1 Analysis of Image and Color-Related Guidelines and Evaluation Methods

The generally accepted criteria in the web accessibility evaluation is the W3C's WCAG, and this has been modified and supplemented for KWCAG by KADO so that it can fully be qualified for Korean web environments. For this reason, in analyzing the problems of the image factor using an img tag and the color factor using a bgcolor attribute, we have used both WCAP and KWCAP, and the guidelines for image and color of WCAP and KWCAP have been summarized in the following [Table 2].

Table 2. Image and color related guidelines in the WCAG and KWCAG

Section	Image using an img tag	Color using a bgcolor attribute
WCAG	Item 1.1: Provide all non-text contents with substitutional text. [Importance 1]	Item 2.2: In case of the combination of both foreground color and background color, enough preparations have to be made not only for the color-blind and color-deficient but also for viewers using a black and white display. [In case of image color: importance 2, and in case of text color: importance 3]
KWCAG	Item 1.1: (Perception of non-text contents): All the contents that can be expressed in the language among the non-text contents must also be presented in the text which carries the same meaning or function as their corresponding contents.	Item 1.3 (Perception without using a color): All the information provided by the contents has to be able to be perceived without using a color.

Also in the A-Prompt based on WCAG and Kado-Wah based on KWCAG, the evaluation methods for "the image using an img tag" and for "the color using a bgcolor attribute" are illustrated in the below [Figure 1].

	A-Prompt (WCAG)	Kado-Wah (KWCAG)
Used 'img' tag image	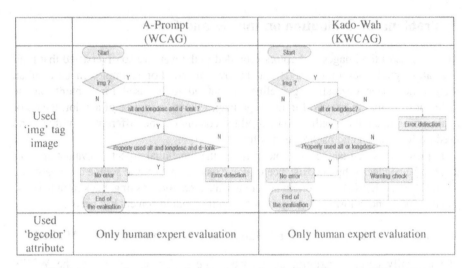	
Used 'bgcolor' attribute	Only human expert evaluation	Only human expert evaluation

Fig. 1. Image and color related evaluation method in the A-Prompt and Kado-Wah

3.2   Problems in the Image and Color Related Evaluation

As shown in the above [Figure 1], in case of image evaluation, the A-Prompt based on WCAG and the Kado-Wah based on KWCAG are different from each other. Also in case of color evaluation using a bgcolor attribute, both A-Prompt and Kado-Wah are depending on manual confirmation.

In case of inserting an image content by using an img tag, an appropriate additional explanation can be given by using "alt attribute," "longdesc attribute," and "d-links." However, the use of each attribute can be decided only in case of necessity. Therefore, there is no need to use all attributes. Also in case of "d-link," its support can be changed according to the kind of web browsers, consequently proving that this attribute has no absolute necessity.

Therefore, in the image content accessibility evaluation using an img tag, both activities of confirming the existence of every attribute by means of "AND Logic" and of confirming the existence of a specific attribute by means of "OR Logic" are inefficient. In particular, in the color evaluation using a bgcolor attribute, both A-Prompt and Kado-Wah are not available for automatic evaluation. Because of this, we have to confirm the corresponding code by using a source code. Considering that the "hexadecimal values" or "RGB color values" are being used for the expression of both background color and foreground color in the web, automatic evaluation can be made possible to some degree. As a result, we can find out that both A-Prompt and Kado-Wah are not good enough to evaluate the colors using a bgcolor attribute.

4   Image and Color Evaluation Improvement and Test

4.1   Image and Color Evaluation Improvement

As shown in the [Figure 1], we have found out that WCAG-based A-Prompt and KWCAG-based Kado-Wah are showing difference and inefficiency in terms of image

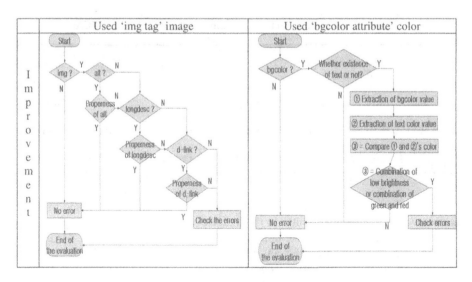

Fig. 2. Image and color accessibility evaluation improvement

and color evaluation. As a solution for these problems, this study provides the following suggestion for the image using an img tag and the color using a bgcolor in the web accessibility evaluation.

In the image evaluation using an img tag, we, first, have to check the existence of an "alt attribute" that is to be attached to an img tag, and if there is an alt attribute, the proper usage of its value (letter length, whether it has extension and any specific words or not, etc.) has to be confirmed. In accordance with its result, the existence of a "longdesc attribute" and the proper usage of attribute values have to be confirmed, and then finally the existence of "d-links" is to be confirmed. All these steps are required for the image accessibility evaluation using an img tag.

In case of the color using a bgcolor attribute, first of all, the existence of "bgcolor attribute" has to be confirmed, and then whether the text for its corresponding part exists or not has to be checked. And in accordance with its result, the color value of "bgcolor attribute" and the color value of the text are to be computed. And next, the comparison of each computed color value is to be made. If it is in the "combination of low brightness and contrast" or in the combination of "red and green," it is liable to cause an error. As all the text in the web and all color values from a "bgcolor attribute" are represented by a 6-digit hexadecimal number or RGB color values, it is possible to appoint the combination of color values that is liable to include errors.

4.2 Test of Improvement

To prove the validity of the newly improved accessibility evaluation method for the image using an img tag and the color using a bgcolor attribute, this study has prepared a simple test page (This includes each one of both the images using an img tag and the colors using a bgcolor attribute). The below [Table 3] shows the results of the tests for A-Prompt, Kado-Wah, and the improvement.

Table 3. Image and color related guidelines in the WCAG and KWCAG

	Used 'img tag' image					Used 'bgc olor attrib ute' color
	alt	alt, longdesc	alt, d-links	longdesc, d-links	alt, longdesc, d-links	
A-Prompt	Error 1	Error 0	Error 1	Error 1	Error 0	Unknown
Kado-Wah	Error 0	Error 0	Error 0	Error 0	Error 0	Unknown
Suggested Method	Error 0	Error 0	Error 0	Error 0	Error 0	Error 0

As mentioned above, in case of A-Prompt, by using an "AND Logic" for "alt attribute" and "longdesc attribute" in the image evaluation using an img tag, we have found out that it makes a mistake in judging whether it is an error or not. Meanwhile, in case of Kado-Wah, by using an "OR Logic" for "alt attribute" and "longdesc attribute" in the image evaluation using an img tag, we have fount out that it conducts an ineffective evaluation of checking the existence of necessary attributes.

However, instead of using an "AND Logic" and "OR Logic" for the "alt attribute" and "longdesc attribute," the way of checking sequentially the existence of each attribute and the proper usage of attribute values is far more effective. Furthermore, in case of the color evaluation using a "bgcolor attribute" both A-Prompt and Kado-Wah are not available for evaluation. But the way of comparing the color values of the "bgcolor attribute" and the text color value suggested in this study, has brought a better result.

5   Conclusions and Suggestions

Along with an increasing necessity and demand on web accessibility, the importance of efficient web accessibility evaluation has also increased. For this reason, we studied on typical web accessibility evaluations while analyzing the features of their evaluation tools.

Also, by taking an in-depth look at the two typical evaluation tools of WCAG and KWCAG, this study has found out the inefficiency in the image evaluation using an "img tag" and in the color evaluation using a "bgcolor attribute," suggesting an improvement, and proving its validity.

This study, however, has some limitations as mentioned in the following. Firstly, as this study has not yet made enough researches to cover all the existing evaluation tools, the problems discovered in the image evaluation using an img tag and the color evaluation using a bgcolor attribute cannot be applied to all the other evaluation tools. Secondly, in case of the color evaluation using the bgcolor attribute, the colors using a "background attribute" are not available for application.

However, we have high expectations that the image evaluation using an img tag and the color evaluation using the bgcolor will bring far more efficient and effective results for the web accessibility evaluation.

References

1. Andrew, P.: Accessibility of Alabama Government Web Sites. Journal of Government Information 29, 303–317 (2002)
2. Bowen, J.P.: Disabled Access for Museum Websites (2002)
3. Brian, S.: Achieving Web Accessibility. Indiana University School of Education, pp. 288–291 (2002)
4. Gregor, P.: Evaluating Web Resources for Disability Access (2000)
5. Seongje, P.: A Study on the Development of Web-based Education Service for the Blind. Journal of the Korean Society of IT Service 6(1) (2006)
6. Seongil, L.: A Study on Universal Design for Enhancing Information Accessibility of the Disabled. Journal of the Korean Institute of Industrial Engineers 20(4), 402–410 (2000)
7. Soongoo, H.: Government Website Accessibility: Comparison between Korea and the United States. Information System Review 7(1) (2005)
8. Sunkyo, K.: A Fault-Finding Website Analysis of Governmental Websites in the Republic of Korea and the USA. Sookmyung Women's University (2003)
9. Panayitos, Z.: Usability and Accessibility Comparison of Governmental, Organizational. Educational and Commercial Aging/Health Related Web Sites (2002)
10. Piotr, R., Michael, C., Jean, V.: Lessons Learned Internationalizing a Web Site Accessibility Evaluator (2002)
11. Sierkowski, B.: Achieving Web Accessibility. Indiana University School of Education, pp. 288–291 (2002)
12. Korea Agency Digital Opportunity & Promotion, http://www.kado.or.kr
13. Web Accessibility Initiative, http://www.w3.org/wai/

Longitudinal Study on Web Accessibility Compliance of Government Websites in Korea

Joonho Hyun, Junki Moon, and Kyungsoon Hong

Korea Agency for Digital Opportunity and Promotion, 645-11 Deung-chon Dong,
Gang-seo Gu, Seoul, Republic of Korea
jhyun22@kado.or.kr, jun1122@kado.or.kr, kshong@kado.or.kr

Abstract. The purpose of this paper investigates the status of web accessibility compliance of government websites in Korea. In order to look into the status of these, we used the "Annual web accessibility research" which was conducted by Korea Agency for Digital Opportunity and promotion (KADO) since 2005. Also, this paper introduces Korea web accessibility activities, such as relational laws, policies and guidelines. The result shows that compliance of web accessibility standards have increased by an annual, especially central government and provincial-level government.

Keywords: Web accessibility, People with disabilities, Digital divide, Government web sites.

1 Introduction

The dramatic development of information technology and internet penetration has brought information society forth. On information society, the source of wealth of the individual, the society and the nation is the ability to create and utilize information and knowledge. Also, internet access and use of it becomes an essential activity. However, people with disabilities cannot access and use the internet because of his/her physical defects [1, 2].

Governments around the world have been worried about unequal internet accessibility which deepens the social and economic discrimination individuals, communities, regions and nations. Global society increasingly depends on the internet deliver information, enhance communications, improve education and conduct business, so that equal internet access by the individual has become fundamental.

Therefore, web accessibility has become a main principle in many countries around the world. Developed countries such as U.S, U.K, and Australia already have recognized the importance of web accessibility. In order to promote accessibility to the internet and telecommunication devices, they have enacted laws and regulations such as Section 508 of the Rehabilitation Act, DDA (Disability Discrimination Act) and have supported development of assistive technologies [3].

This paper presents policies and standardization of Korea government for web accessibility, as well as a survey of web accessibility on government web sites in Korea. The web sites for the government agencies were examined using KADO-WAH

S. Lee et al. (Eds.): APCHI 2008, LNCS 5068, pp. 396–404, 2008.
© Springer-Verlag Berlin Heidelberg 2008

and subsequent manual tests for 13 Korean web accessibility checkpoints to determine their compliance of web accessibility [Table 5].

2 Overview of Korea Web Accessibility Status and Legislations

2.1 Status of Digital Divide in Korea

Korea is considered the fastest aging population in the world. According to the Korea national statistical office's report, 9.9 percent of the entire population is elderly, or older than 65 years old in 2007 [4]. Such rapid aging of the society will undoubtedly affect future socio-economic and IT usage. So, government and private companies which manufacture and performs service through IT should concern about accessibility issues.

Table 1. Number of over 65 years old in Korea (October, 2007)

				(Unit: Thousand, %)
Classification	1997	2000	2006	2007
Total population	45,954	47,008	48,297	48,456
# of over 65 years old	2,929	3,395	4,586	4,810
Ratio of the over 65 years old population	6.4%	7.2%	9.5%	9.9%

* Source: Korea National Statistical Office, *2007 Statistics on Aging*, 2007.10

Like aging population, number of registered people with disabilities has increased annually. In 2007, number of registered people with disabilities was 2,087,701 persons [5]. Physically handicapped people were 1,109,450, visually handicapped people were 216,407, hearing and speech handicapped people were 214,420, mentally handicapped people were 210,309, and other handicapped people were 337,115.

Table 2. Number of registered people with disabilities by types of disability in Korea(Sep, 2007)

						(Unit: Person)
Classification	Total	Physically handicapped	Visually handicapped	Hearing/Speech handicapped	Mentally Handicapped	Others
# of registered PWD	2,087,701	1,109,450	216,407	214,420	210,309	337,115

* Source: Ministry of Health, Welfare and Family Affairs, Statistics on registered people with disabilities, 2007.9

Korea is one of fastest growing countries regarding the use of broadband and Internet. The statistic in December 2007 showed that 34.8 million (76.3% of the Korean population) Korean who were older than 7 years old used the Internet more than once a month a average. According to the ITU's DOI (Digital Opportunity Index), Korea has ranked the top since 2005 [6].

In spite of the rapid growth of Internet usage, there are still marginalized groups that have difficulty in using Internet. According to the survey, the rate of Internet usage depended on disability, age, income and job. Internet usage of the underprivileged has increased since 2003. But, only 49.9% of the people with disabilities and 33.4% farmers and fishermen used the Internet in 2007 [7].

Table 3. Internet usage of the underprivileged in Korea (2003-2007)

Classification	2003	2004	2005	2006	2007
People with disabilities	27.6	34,8	41.0	46.6	49.9
The elderly (Over 50 years old)	13.0	19.3	22.5	28.3	34.1
Low-income	31.7	38.4	44.2	48.4	52.8
Farmers & Fishermen	16.2	16.9	23.0	29.4	33.4
Total Population	65.5	70.2	72.8	74.8	76.3

* Source: Ministry of Public Administration and Security & Korea Agency for Digital Opportunity and promotion, *2007 Digital Divide Survey*

2.2 Web Accessibility Legislations in Korea

Korean government has already recognized the problem caused from the digital divide. Korea government has taken active steps toward solving the digital divide for the disabled. Polices for improving IT usage of the disabled are classified into 6 groups : developing assistive technology for disabled people, providing IT learning opportunities, developing and distributing online contents, enacting laws and regulations for the disabled, constructing community access center, and distributing recycled personal computers.

In order to improve the web accessibility for the disabled, the government has formulated three important policies. Firstly, the government enacted laws and regulations. In 2001, the National Assembly of Korea enacted 'The Digital Divide Act' and implemented "Master Plan for Closing the Digital Divide (2001~2005)". In this initiative, the following four action plans were suggested: to provide at least one free internet accessible site in each local administration office, to train all the people who wish to learn the advanced as well as basic IT skills, to spread high-speed internet services throughout the nation including the remote areas, to assist the development of valuable online information for the disabled and the elderly [1. 2].

Also, the National Assembly of Korea enacted 'the Disability Discrimination Act" such as American with Disability Act (ADA), UK Disability Discrimination Act on March 2007. The aim of this Act is to end the discrimination that many disabled people face. It gives disabled people rights in the areas of employment, education, access to goods, facilities and services including IT, etc. Disability Discrimination Act will be come into force on April, 2008.

Second government policy is to support operation of the Information and Telecommunication Accessibility Promotion Standard Forum (http://www.iabf.or.kr)

which is founded in 2002. The purpose of the forum is to promote accessibility to telecommunication devices and telecommunications services through the sharing of relevant information among developers and scholars in this field. IABF forum developed web accessibility evaluation tools such as Korean version of 'A-Prompt' in 2003 and "KADO-WAH" in 2005.

Third government policy is to support for the disabled people to buy assistive technologies such as screen reader, braille display, and telephone for hearing-impaired people, etc. Also, government has supported to develop assistive technologies for disabled people.

2.3 Status of Web Accessibility in Korea

In order to examine the status of awareness on web accessibility in Korea, KADO conducted survey in 2003, 2006. The number of the total respondents was 300 people in 2003 and 600 people in 2006 who worked for web design and programming in Seoul. The survey was conducted by on-line with questionnaire which was made by ATRC (Adaptive Technology Research Center) and KADO together [8, 9].

The subjects of the survey were classified with five categories (Table 7): general, Web experience, the status of awareness on web accessibility, the usage of 11 checklists web accessibility standards and the policy direction which helps to promote web accessibility. According to the survey, only 26.0% of the web designers and programmers recognized web accessibility in 2003, but 84.3% recognized in 2006.

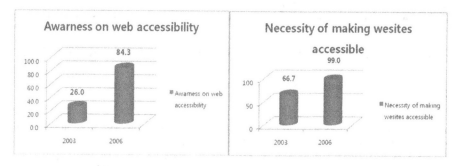

Fig. 1. The results of survey on awareness of web accessibility (2003, 2006)

* Source: Korea Agency for Digital Opportunity and promotion, *Survey on awareness of Web Accessibility Status,* 2003, 2006

Brown university has evaluated online government websites of around the globe since 2002. Subject of 2007's study were conducted 1,687 government websites in 198 countries during June and July 2007. Evaluation Criteria was consisted of 6 areas, such as disability access, the existence of publications and databases, the presence of privacy policies, security policies, contact information, and the number of online services. In order to evaluate disability access, the automated "Bobby 5.0" software was chosen. This commercial software tests websites against standards of compliance with the standards recommended by the Web Contents Accessibility Guidelines (WCAG) 1.0 of the World Wide Web Consortium (W3C) [10].

According to the survey, South Korea earned the top rank, followed by Singapore, Taiwan, but disability access scored zero. 23% of government websites have some form of disability access, meaning access for persons with disabilities, the same as last year. Most Asian countries government such as Bangladesh, Cambodia, China, Indonesia websites didn't meet W3C WCAG 1.0.

Table 4. Results of Brown University survey on web accessibility standard in 2007

(Unit: %)

Country	Online Services	Publications	DataBase	Privacy Policy	Security Policy	Disability Accessibility
Australia	53	97	57	100	97	73
Bangladesh	0	100	50	0	0	0
Cambodia	0	100	100	0	0	0
China	43	100	100	0	0	0
Germany	75	100	88	63	13	0
Great Britain	59	96	89	89	67	70
Hong Kong	28	100	100	22	0	67
Japan	5	100	95	45	45	55
Korea	100	100	100	100	100	0
Singapore	73	100	100	100	100	47
United States	59	100	98	84	80	54

3   Web Accessibility Compliance of Korea Government Web Sites

3.1   Korean Web Contents Accessibility Guidelines

The Internet Web Content Accessibility Guideline 1.0 (IWCAG 1.0) outlines design principles for creating accessible web content. Committee of web accessibility standardization had benchmarked W3C WCAG(Web Contents Accessibility Guidelines) 1.0 and Section 508 § 1194.22, a standard for accessible web-based intranet and internet information and applications, to establish IWCAG 1.0, we put minimum requirements that are similar to Priority 1 checkpoints of W3C WCAG 1.0 onto our guideline. Committee of web accessibility standardization also had referred to Core checkpoints of W3C WCAG 2.0 as of June 2003 that would be the minimum requirements. After efforts on these activities, IWCAG 1.0 accepted as TTAS Standard by TTA (Telecommunications and Technology Association) on December 2004, national standard as KICS (Korean Information and Communication Standards) standard by Ministry of Information and Communication on December 2005[1, 2, 12, 13, 14].

IWCAG 1.0 categorizes 14 checkpoints into 4 basic principles, such as perceivable, operable, understandable and robust. Perceivable web content implies that all content can be presented in forms that can be perceived by any user. Operable web content ensures that the interface elements in the content are operable by any user. Web content and controls that are easy to understand, they are known to be understandable. Robust web content is to use web technologies that maximize the ability of the content to work with current and future assistive technologies and user agents.

Korean government also closely observes the development of WCAG 2.0. We believe the government will start on revision of IWCAG 2.0 soon after WCAG 2.0 becomes an international guideline.

Table 5. 14 Checkpoints of IWCAG 1.0

#	Checkpoint
1	All non-text content that can be expressed in words has a text equivalent of the function or information that the non-text content was intended to convey
2	For any time-based multi- media presentation, synchronize equivalent alternatives with the presentation
3	Web pages shall be designed so that all information conveyed with color is also available without color, for example from context or markup
4	If image maps are used in the content, use client-side image map only or server-side image map with redundant text links
5	Use small number of frames of every web page, and title each frame to facilitate frame identification and navigation
6	Pages shall be designed to avoid causing the screen to flicker
7	All functionality is operable at a minimum through a keyboard or a keyboard interface
8	A method shall be provided that permits users to skip repetitive navigation links
9	When a timed response is required, the user shall be alerted and given sufficient time to indicate more time is required
10	Data table should be designed to provide enough information about corresponding cells
11	Structures and/or formats of documents shall be organized so they are understandable
12	When electronic forms are designed to be completed on-line, the form shall allow people using assistive technology to access the information, field elements, and functionality required for completion and submission of the form, including all directions and cues
13	Content elements, such as script, plug-ins, applets or other application can be used only when they can provide equivalent information using the current assistive technology
14	A text-only page, with equivalent information or functionality, shall be provided to make a web site comply with the provisions of this part, when compliance cannot be accomplished in any other way. The content of the text-only page shall be updated whenever the primary page change

3.2 Evaluation Methodology

In order to examine web accessibility compliance status of Korean government websites, we used the "Annual web accessibility research" which was conducted by Korea Agency for Digital Opportunity and promotion (KADO) since 2005. This research was conducted to improve web accessibility of government websites, increase awareness of web accessibility and develop policy for web accessibility in Korea [11].

Table 6. Overview of annual web accessibility research since 2005

Classification	2005	2006	2007
# of agencies of evaluation	77	79	326
Average score(Total : 100)	77.2	81.8	77.3

Annual web accessibility research conducted to use IWCAG 1.0 standard which has 14 checkpoints. Two processes have been accomplished: one is an automatic test by using an accessibility evaluation, and the other is a manual test to inspect undetected elements by the automatic test. In the automatic test, KADO-WAH, which was developed by Korea Agency for Digital Opportunity and promotion, was used to evaluate the existence of alternative text for non-text content, and to evaluate the existence of the title of the frame. Manual test was conducted to look at the source codes by web accessibility experts

3.3 Results

Figure 2 shows the results of our study. In 2005, 77 government agencies in Korea were evaluated. Average score of central government such as ministries, commission and services were 72.3 points, provincial government were 71.6 points out of 100

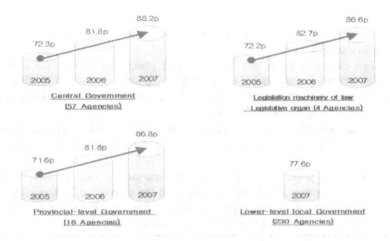

Fig. 2. Results on web accessibility on governmental websites in Korea since 2005

point scale. In 2006, 79 government agencies in Korea were evaluated. Average score of central government such as ministries, commission and services were 81.8 points, provincial government were 81.8 points out of 100 point scale. In 2007, 326 government agencies in Korea were evaluated. Average score of central government such as ministries, commission and services were 88.2 points, provincial government were 86.8 points out of 100 point scale.

Results of longitudinal study of web accessibility show that the rate of compliance of web accessibility standards has increased since 2005. But, government agencies in Korea have been violating at least one checklist of the IWCAG checkpoints since 2005.

4 Conclusions

In this paper, we examine web accessibility compliance of governmental websites in Korea since 2005. Results of longitudinal study of web accessibility show that the rate of compliance of web accessibility standards has increased since 2005. These results have occurred from government's various activities such as web accessibility education program for public servants, web accessibility quality mark, seminars, standardization, etc. But, web accessibility compliance of governmental websites in Korea is low.

Recently, disabled associations in Korea lift up their voice to enact a compulsory regulation for web content providers to make their web pages accessible. Such a movement would let IWCAG 1.0 be a mandatory regulation in government sectors. In 2007, the National Assembly of Korea enacted 'the Disability Discrimination Act" such as American with Disability Act (ADA), UK Disability Discrimination Act. Korea Disability Discrimination Act will be come into force on April, 2008. Therefore, many Korean governmental websites will be made accessible.

Therefore, Korea governments continue to increase web accessibility awareness, develop technologies related to web accessibility. In order to increase web accessibility, government needs to expand the various activities. First, government supports to make web accessibility standard, guidelines and handbooks how to make websites accessible. Second, government needs to operate the education programs for public servants and web developers. Third, government needs to increase public awareness such as campaign, competency test, seminars, award, etc. The last, government continues to support research and design for web accessibility such as developing assistive devices, conducting research of people with disabilities' accessibility and usability on web, and developing the ways how to increase accessibility using various new web technologies such as Ajax, Web 2.0.

References

1. Hyun, J., Choi, D., Kim, S.: An active step toward a web content accessible society. In: International Cross-Disciplinary Workshop on Web Accessibility (W4A Workshop) at WWW2005 Conference, Chiba, Japan (2005)
2. Lee, S., Choi, D., Hyun, J.: Public Awareness on Web Accessibility in Korea. In: 7th International conference of Human Services Information Technology Applications (HUSITA7), Hong Kong (2004)

3. Thatcher, J., Burks, M.R., Heilmann, C., Henry, S.I., Kipkpatrick, A., Lauke, P.H., Lawson, B., Regan, B., Rutter, R., Urban, M., Waddel, C.D.: Web Accessibility - Web Standards and Regulatory Compliance, Friends of ED (2006)
4. Korea National Statistical Office, 2007 Statistics on Aging (2007.10)
5. Ministry of Health, Welfare and Family Affairs, Statistics on registered people with disabilities (2007. 9)
6. International Telecommunication Union(ITU) & United Nations Conference on Trade and Development(UNCTAD), World Information Society Report 2007 : Beyond WSIS (2007)
7. Korea Agency for Digital Opportunity and promotion (KADO), 2007 Digital Divide Index in Korea (2008)
8. Korea Agency for Digital Opportunity and Promotion (KADO), 2003 Survey on awareness of Web Accessibility (2003)
9. Korea Agency for Digital Opportunity and Promotion (KADO), 2006 Survey on awareness of Web Accessibility (2006)
10. Brown University, Global E-Government, 2007, (2007. 8)
11. KADO, 2007 Web accessibility for government Website (2007)
12. Ministry of Information and Communication, Internet Web Contents Accessibility Guidelines 1.0 (2005.12)
13. Section 508 of Rehabilitation Act (2008.3.8), http://www.section508.gov
14. W3C, Web Content Accessibility Guidelines 1.0. (May 1999) (2008.3.8), http://wwww.w3c.org/TR/WCAG10/

Korean Web Site Usability for Disabled People

Seongeun Choi[1], Sejun Kim[2], and Sukil Kim[1]

[1] Chungbuk National University, Republic of Korea
sweetdream0921@gmail.com
[2] Jason R&D, Republic of Korea
monolese@gmail.com

Abstract. In this paper, we evaluated 10 Korean web sites whether these sites have enough usability for the disabled people. Theoretically, there must be no difference using web content to an ordinary user and to a user with disabilities. However, under practical manners, the difference cannot be overcome due to lack of sensory issues. We chose 10 most frequently accessing web sites in 5 categories. We also define the Disability Web Usability (DWU) that is the ratio between the web usability of the handicapped and the web usability of the ordinary. The experimental results show that DWUs of the web sites are between 0.49 and 0.76. This implies that the handicapped people are far more difficult to perform tasks navigating the given web sites.

Keywords: Web usability, Web sites, Disability web usability.

1 Introduction

Recently, activities to improve accessibility and/or usability of web contents have been wide spread around the world. The Web Accessibility Initiative (WAI) works with organizations around the world to develop strategies, guidelines, and resources to help make the web accessible to people with disabilities. WAI already published Web Content Accessibility Guidelines (WCAG) 1.0 [1] and WCAG 2.0 [2], User Agent Accessibility Guidelines (UAAG) 1.0 [1], and Authoring Tool Accessibility Guidelines (ATAG) 1.0 [3] and 2.0 [4]. These guidelines are widely adopted as a national standard in many countries.

In Korea, a working group was organized to prepare the Korean Web Content Accessibility Guidelines (KWCAG) 1.0 [5]. KWCAG 1.0 has been accepted as a TTS standard since Dec. 2003.

Recently, dramatic change has occurred. The Korean Disability Discrimination Act (KDDA) was legislated by the National Assembly in Mar. 2007. In Apr. 2008, an enforcement ordinance of the KDDA has been active. According to the enforcement ordinance, all the government and public web sites must provide web content accessibility for the handicapped after Apr. 2009.

Unfortunately, web content accessibility is a minimum requirement to access the contents of the web site. Theoretically, both the handicapped and ordinary people can complete given tasks on a very high usable web site almost at the same time. In the real world, this goal cannot be achieved. However, we can shorten the gap between

S. Lee et al. (Eds.): APCHI 2008, LNCS 5068, pp. 405–412, 2008.

the handicapped and ordinary people if we comply with well established web usability guidelines for the handicapped.

In this paper, we evaluated web sites that are frequently accessed in Korea. The results show that the disability web usability is very low. In section 2, we described related works on web accessibility and web usability. In section 3, we introduce the draft of the web usability guidelines for the handicapped. We perform evaluation in section 4. Finally, we draw a conclusion in section 5.

2 Relate Works

Jakob Nielsen has studied web usability for wide range of people [6]. According to his study, ordinary people can complete 78.2% of the given tasks, while the blind can complete 12.5% of the tasks and people with low vision can complete 21.4% of the tasks.

Concerning the task completion time, ordinary people require average 7min. 14sec., while the blind, low vision and senior citizens require 16min. 46sec., 15min. 26sec. and 12min. 33sec, respectively. Average completion time of the handicapped is 14min 55sec. It is 2.22 times more than the time required to ordinary people.

Jakob Nielsen also compares success rate of the tasks. He draws a conclusion wherein the success rate of the handicapped is 28.93% in average, while the success rate of ordinary people is 78.2%. This implies that handicap of disability draw back of the task completion. He also figures out that the usability of the elderly is 2.22 times lesser than that of ordinary people [7].

In Korea, no such intensive web usability studies have been achieved. In Dec. 2006, KADO reported 15 major web sites were not comply KWCAG 1.0 [8]. Web sites evaluated include portal sites, online news sites, and shopping sites. Especially, the blinds could not join as a member due to the lack of accessibilities. Besides the blind, overall task success rate was 26% in average.

3 Korean Disability Web Usability Guidelines

The Korean Disability Web Usability Guideline (KDWUG) consists of 56 requirements that are grouped into 14 categories [9]. The requirements are classified based on the 3 priorities as follow:

- P1: the requirement *must* comply to improve the web usability. Otherwise, one or more groups will find it impossible to use web site.
- P2: the requirement *should* comply to improve the web usability. Otherwise, one or more groups will find it difficult to use web site.
- P3: the requirement *may* comply to improve the web usability. Otherwise, one or more groups will find it somewhat difficult to use web site.

The number of requirements of which the priorities are P1, P2 and P3 are 26, 22 and 8, respectively. Total numbers of the requirements are 56. Table 1 shows 13 categories of the guidelines.

Table 1. Summary Korean web site usability guidelines for handicapped

Categories	# of Guidelines			
	P1	**P2**	**P3**	**total**
0. Precondition	2	0	0	2
1. Web page Structure	7	1	1	9
2. Table and Frame	3	1	0	4
3. Graphics and Multimedia	1	2	1	4
4. Content Structure	1	1	0	2
5. Content Expression	1	1	2	4
6. Dynamic Elements	0	3	0	3
7. Links and Buttons	2	4	0	6
8. Navigating Pages	1	0	1	2
9. Pop-up and New Windows	2	2	0	4
10. Online Forms	3	4	0	7
11. Task Group (Search)	2	1	0	3
12. Task Group (Payment)	1	0	3	4
13. Robustness	0	2	0	2

4 Usability Evaluation

Web sites classified into 5 fields, such as search engines, online new providers, online shopping malls, financial market and life-care sites as shown in Table 2. Two web sites of every area were chosen based on the click rates posted at the Rankey.com site in Sep, 2007.

Table 2. Web sites chosen for the experimentation

	Typical Feature	**Web Sites(URL)**
Portal site	Search	Naver (http://www.naver.com)
	E-mail	Daum (http://www.daum.net)
News site	Online news	Chosun.com (http://www.chosun.com)
	Broadcasting station	KBS (http://www.kbs.co.kr)
Shopping site	Online shopping	Shinsegaemall (http://mall.shinsegae.com)
	Prices comparison	Enuri.com (http://www.enuri.com)
Financial site	Online banking	Nonghyup(http://banking.nonghyup.com)
		Wooribank (http://www.wooribank.com)
Life-care site	Online hosp. reservation	Severance Hospital (http://www.severance.or.kr)
	Job portal	Worknet (http://www.worknet.go.kr)

We also prepared a typical task that can express the feature of a web site. For example, a task for *Nonghyup*, an online banking site, is to figure out the amount of deposit of a given bank account. Rest of tasks is also prepared similarly.

To perform the experimentation, we divided 50 participants into 40 experimental groups and 10 control groups. Also 40 experimental groups were divided into 7 small groups based on the difficulties of the participants as show in Table 3.

Table 3. Control and experimental groups

Control group	Experimental group							Total
Ord	Eld	H.I.	Phy	Bl	L.V	Spa	Enc	
10	5	5	5	10	5	5	5	50

Table 4. Success rate of the web sites (%)

Web sites	Ord	Experimental group							
		Eld	H.I	Phy	Enc	L.V	Spa	Bl	avg.
Naver	95.0	80.0	46.7	33.3	66.7	73.3	73.3	60.0	61.9
Daum	97.5	95.0	65.0	65.0	70.0	80.0	85.0	77.5	76.8
Chosun.com	100.0	100.0	40.0	40.0	40.0	80.0	80.0	80.0	65.7
KBS	100.0	100.0	50.0	60.0	100.0	90.0	80.0	40.0	74.3
Shinsegae mall	80.0	80.0	40.0	20.0	40.0	60.0	40.0	20.0	42.9
Enuri.com	100.0	100.0	80.0	60.0	100.0	80.0	80.0	90.0	84.3
Nonghyup	90.0	80.0	100.0	40.0	100.0	100.0	100.0	100.0	88.6
Woori bank	95.0	100.0	80.0	90.0	80.0	100.0	100.0	45.0	85.0
Severance hospital	100.0	100.0	80.0	90.0	50.0	90.0	100.0	25.0	76.4
Worknet	90.0	80.0	40.0	80.0	40.0	60.0	60.0	00.0	51.4
Average success rate	94.4	92.2	62.2	60.0	70.0	82.2	82.2	56.1	

We measured the following data from the 10 web sites.

- **Completion time** is how long a participant spent to accomplish given task on a given web site.

- **Success rate** is to show whether a participant accomplished the task within a time limit. In this paper, the time limit of all the experimental groups is given 3 times more time than the average time required by control groups.
- **Errors** are mistakes occur while participants had faced during the evaluation.

The disabilities with low vision and senior citizens require more times to complete tasks than other disability groups, while the success rate was very high. On the other hand, people with motor skill issues and cerebral palsy results requires more time to complete tasks, and also failed a lot more than other disability groups. We can also say that the blind group is the worst group that shows the poorest performance, the highest completion time and the lowest success rate.

Table 5. Completion time of the web sites (minutes: seconds)

Web sites	Ord.	Elderly and Handicapped People							
		Eld.	H.I.	Phy.	Enc.	LV.	Spa.	Bl.	Tot.
No Alt Text								112	112
Long Lists	20	7	12	8	23	8	6	22	86
Pop-up/New Windows	9		3	11	1	6	9	1	31
Uncertainty of Links	9	4	3	7	15	9	7		45
Too Small Links/Buttons	8	2	1	3	2		6		14
Ungrouping Option/Mand.	1	7	3	7	7	1	2	12	39
Lack of Instructions	7	11	3	11	14	8	3	20	70
Irregular Tab Movement				1		1		19	21
Difficulties in Color Ident.	6	6	2	6	1	5	6		26
Too small Text Fonts	14	12	7	11	1	4	16		51
Bad Layout of Search Result	7	4	2	6	2	10	1	6	31
Repeated Wrong Search	16		3	20	17	5	1	18	64
Complicated Tables		5	2	2	1	1		14	25
Table Order		2						8	10
Special Terminology	5	1	4	5	2	1	4	2	19
Total	102	61	45	98	86	59	61	234	

We define the disability web usability DWU factor that is to show how much the web site provides usability to the handicapped compared with while ordinary people use the same web site.

$$dwu \equiv \frac{rc + rsr + rsf + re}{4} \qquad (1)$$

where,

$$rc = \frac{Avg(Complete\ time\ of\ control\ group)}{Avg(Complete\ time\ of\ elderly\ and\ handicapped)} \qquad (2)$$

$$rsr = \frac{Avg(Success\ rate\ of\ elderly\ and\ handicapped)}{Avg(Success\ rate\ of\ control\ group)} \qquad (3)$$

$$rsf = \frac{Avg(Satisfactor\ rate\ of\ elderly\ and\ handicapped)}{Avg(Satisfactor\ rate\ of\ control\ group)} \qquad (4)$$

$$re = \frac{Avg(Error\ rate\ of\ control\ group)}{Avg(Error\ rate\ of\ elderly\ and\ handicapped)} \qquad (5)$$

Figure 1 shows the DWU of the web sites. As we can see in figure 1, *Chosun.com* (0.49) is the worst web site for the handicapped. *Shinsegae Mall* (0.54) is the next worst web site. The best web site for the handicapped is *Serverance Hospital* (0.76).

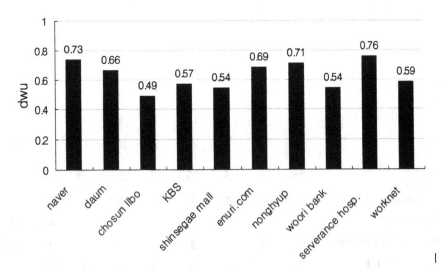

Fig. 1. Disability web usability (DWU) of the given web sites

Table 6. Numbers of Errors occur during the evaluation

Errors	Ord.	Elderly and Handicapped People							
		Eld.	H.I.	Phy.	Enc.	LV.	Spa.	Bl.	Total
No Alt Text								112	112
Long Lists	20	7	12	8	23	8	6	22	86
Pop-up/New Windows	9		3	11	1	6	9	1	31
Uncertainty of Links	9	4	3	7	15	9	7		45
Too Small Links/Buttons	8	2	1	3	2		6		14
Ungrouping Option/Mand.	1	7	3	7	7	1	2	12	39
Lack of Instructions	7	11	3	11	14	8	3	20	70
Irregular Tab Movement			1		1			19	21
Difficulties in Color Ident.	6	6	2	6	1	5	6		26
Too small Text Fonts	14	12	7	11	1	4	16		51
Bad Layout of Search Rslt	7	4	2	6	2	10	1	6	31
Repeated Wrong Search	16		3	20	17	5	1	18	64
Complicated Tables		5	2	2	1	1		14	25
Table Order		2						8	10
Special Terminology	5	1	4	5	2	1	4	2	19
Total	102	61	45	98	86	59	61	234	

We also make a collection of mistakes during the experimentation. The most frequently occurrence of errors is closely dependent upon the disability type. For example, senior citizen group has complained mostly on small text font size. Secondly, lack of color recognition follows. Following are the tow most frequently occurrence of errors for every type of disability. Numbers within ( ) implies the number of errors:

- Elder People - Small text (12), Lack of color recognition (6)
- Hearing Impaired - Professional terms (4)
- Physically Handicapped - Long lists and items (8), Pop-up/New Windows (11), Difficulties of recognizing search results (6)
- Encephalopathy - Long lists and items (23), Small links/button size (2)
- Low Visibility - Lack of color recognition (5), Small text (4), Difficulties of recognizing search results (10)
- Spastic - Professional terms (4)
- Blind - No alternate text (112), Dispart mandatory/optional items (12), Disordered tab control (19), Complicated table (14)

5 Conclusion

In this paper, we evaluated 10 Korean web sites that are widely accessed in 5 areas, based on the Korean Disability Web Usability Guidelines we made. For the evaluation, we invited 10 ordinary people as a control group, 5 elderly people, 10 blinds, 5 low vision, 5 physically impaired , 5 hearing impaired, 5 encephalopathy, and 5 spastic as experimental group.

We can figure out that 10 chosen web sites' usability is less than expected. Concerning the web accessibility, these web sites did not provide almost no accessibility to the handicapped. This implies we must do more effort to increase accessibility.

Acknowledgements. This research is supported by IITA, Korea, and BK 21 program, CBNU.

References

1. W3C: Web Content Accessibility Guidelines 1.0., http://www.w3c.org/TR/WAI-WEBCON TENT/
2. W3C: Web Content Accessibility Guidelines 2.0., http://www.w3c.org/TR/WCAG20/
3. W3C: Web Tool Accessibility Guidelines 1.0., http://www.w3c.org/TR/WAI-TOOLS/
4. W3C: Web Tool Accessibility Guidelines 1.0., http://www.w3c.org/TR/ATAG20/
5. TTA: Korean Web Contents Accessibility Guideline 1.0., http://www.tta.or.kr/
6. Nielsen, J.: Beyond accessibility: treating users with disabilities as people (2001), http://www.useit.com/alertbox/20011111.html
7. Coyne, K.P., Nielsen, J.: Web Usability for Senior Citizens, Nielsen Norman Group
8. Coyne, K.P., Nielsen, J.: Status of Disability Web-Usability: 15 web sites including portal, news and banking sites. Technical report, KADO (2006)
9. Coyne, K.P., Nielsen, J.: Development of Web-Contents Usability Evaluation Models and Guidelines for Disabilites. Technical report, IITA (2007)

A Proxy-Based System for Translation of Internet Content into Specific Form

Pavel Ocenasek

Brno University of Technology, FIT, Bozetechova 2, 612 66 Brno, Czech Republic
ocenaspa@fit.vutbr.cz

Abstract. The paper deals with the system based on proxy techniques for translation of Internet content into specific form. The first part of the paper presents the motivation for translation of internet content. The second part deals with the system concept. The system can be built-up either as a standard internet proxy-server or URL web-proxy. The right choice depends on the application (content security, web accessibility). The final part of the paper concludes with the features that will be developed in the system in future.

Keywords: Proxy server, URL web-proxy, Translation, Security, Accessibility.

1 Introduction

When the World Wide Web service was created and the markup language HTML became its main pillar of strength, only some people could foresee that it becomes one of the most valuable research or work instruments of wide society. Some of the best qualities that this service offers are availability and immediate diffusion of information published on the Internet. These characteristics are especially useful for users with some types of disability. Moreover, they have seen how their access to leisure, education, business or research activities has been improved.

2 Web Accessibility

To develop accessibility standards for Web sites and authoring tools, the W3C Consortium (www.w3.org) [2] [7] adopted the Web Accessibility Initiative (WAI). WAI guidelines group checkpoints into three levels of priority. Priority one includes checkpoints that Web site administrators "must" implement. For example, users must be able to avoid behavior that obscures the page content or disorients them. Flashing content can cause seizures in people with photosensitive epilepsy or distract cognitively impaired people. Distracting background images or sounds can affect those with visual or hearing problems. Priorities two and three are checkpoints that "should" or "may" be implemented [4] [6].

To avoid these problems, users must be able to filter WWW content or multimedia presentations. However, structure and meta information is hard to recognize and to filter.

The main problems are:

- to recognize and find titles
- to recognize and find links

S. Lee et al. (Eds.): APCHI 2008, LNCS 5068, pp. 413–419, 2008.

- to recognize and find non-textual elements (such as inline images)
- to navigate from title to title
- to navigate from link to link.
- to handle input elements (such as entry fields, radio-, check- and other buttons)

2.1 Web Content Accessibility Guidelines (WCAG)

The WCAG documents explain how to make web content accessible to people with disabilities.

WCAG is written for content developers as well as for the following:

- Authoring tool developers to create tools that generate accessible content
- User agent developers to create tools that render accessible content
- Evaluation tool developers to create tools that identify accessibility issues in content

WCAG 1.0 (www.w3.org/TR/WCAG10/) was published as a W3C Recommendation in May 1999. The WCAG 2.0 (www.w3.org/TR/WCAG20/) has been developed to apply to more advanced web technologies, be easier to use and understand, and be more precisely testable.

For more up-to-date information on WCAG, see "Web Content Accessibility Guidelines (WCAG) Overview" (www.w3.org/WAI/intro/wcag) and "Overview of WCAG 2.0 Documents" (www.w3.org/WAI/intro/wcag20).

2.2 Section 508

In the U.S.A., specifications for accessible design have been declared through legislation Congress enacted the Workforce Investment Act in 1998, which strengthened Section 508 of the Rehabilitation Act. Also known as the Rehabilitation Act Amendments of 1998, the legislation authorized the U.S. Access Board to enter into rule-making and the publication of the Electronic and Information Technology Accessibility Standards.

These standards became effective on June 21, 2001, and are broad in scope, covering technical standards in the following areas:

- Software applications and operating systems
- Web-based intranet and Internet information and applications
- Telecommunications products
- Video and multimedia products
- Self-contained, closed products
- Desktop and portable computers

3 Proxy Servers

Internet traffic is growing exponentially and increases the need for methods to minimize network latency. Proxy servers have been shown to be a well-suited approach to help improving the network performance. Their advantages start with reduced bandwidth consumption, a reduction in latency due to data dissemination and a reduction of the load for remote origin server

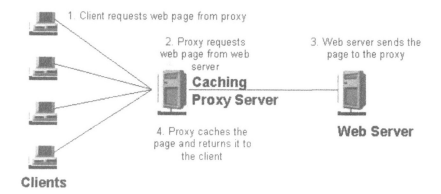

1. Client requests web page from proxy

2. Proxy requests web page from web server

3. Web server sends the page to the proxy

Caching Proxy Server

4. Proxy caches the page and returns it to the client

Web Server

Clients

Fig. 1. The basic principle of caching web proxy server

The proxy server model offers several advantages. For instance, the proxy may be combined with a firewall to provide added security to a local area network (LAN). This paper proposes a system that can maintain the modification and basic security of internet content without the need of using external firewalls.

4 System Concept

We have developed a new system, which will be useful for translation web pages into the form specified by a registered user. This system can be used for example for providing web pages accessibility [10]. It has been designed to make the web pages accessible independently [5] from the presentation devices and technologies used. The proxy can be also used for providing security, such as protect users from phishing, downloading dangerous content by checking the target URLs, removing the suspicious references or scripts, etc.

The main idea of the system can be seen from the figure below.

The system works as a proxy server for translating common internet pages into the specific form. The web accessibility is described by translation rules that are applied to the common pages.

The usage of our system is very easy. Before the first use, visually impaired user creates a profile where impairment-specific requirements for the translation are specified. Then the system is used via the standard web browser by specifying the URL to translate in the form: http://www.bezbarierovy.net/www.yahoo.com . The translation of the main page as well as all the linked pages that user visits from the starting page is done automatically.

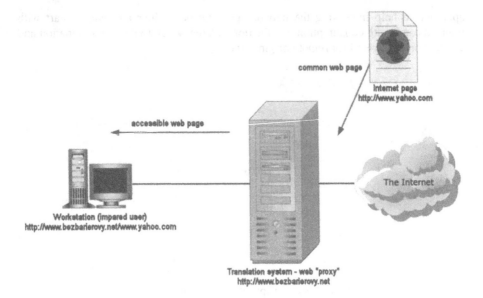

Fig. 1. The principle of automatic translation system. The system can be used either as a network proxy server (via proxy settings) or simple document proxy server (via URL prefix).

5 Accessibility for Users with Special Needs

In general, the accessibility is performed according to the following instructions:

1. IMAGES – images could be easily switched off, resized or the color depth/ contrast can be changed according to the user-specific requirements.
2. LINKS – visitors to the web pages are looking for information, and the more efficiently they can find it, the more valuable the site is to them. Most screen readers have a shortcut command that will give users a list of all the links on a page. This is a way to skim a page quickly.
3. COLOR – Consistent use of color can enhance the usability of your pages for many people. We have to be sure that no information is conveyed solely through the use of color.
4. TABLES – there are two simple things we can do to make tables more accessible without changing their appearance. One is to use the summary attribute. This attribute goes in the table tag along with the border, cell spacing and other attributes. The other thing we can do is to use the scope attribute in the first cell in each row and first cell in each column.
5. HEADINGS – those of us who are sighted use headings as a quick way to scan the organization of a page. To create headings, many people use the font tag to make larger text. However, most screen readers have a shortcut command that produces a list of all the headings on a page created with the heading tag. If the page is well organized and uses heading tags for headings, this can be a great way for visitors using screen readers to skim the page.

There are many rules and specific translations that belong to these (and other) categories. The detailed description is beyond the scope of this paper.

The proxy server can be used in two modes:

- Document proxy server, this mode is used when the impaired user enters the URL address in the standard browser in the following form: http://www.bezbarierovy. net/<URL_to_translate>. The system translates the starting page and automatically follows all links into the recursive translation.
- Network proxy server mode serves on a specified TCP port and translates all the content going through. The proxy server is activated by setting the proper address and port in the browser settings (the Connection/Proxy parameter). Then the common form of URL address is typed into the browser and the content is automatically translated.

In both modes of use the proxy server is transparent and browser independent. The translation is done according to the settings from the user profile.

6 Web Content Translation Examples

In the area of providing web content translation, results of the process can be seen from Figures 2a and 2b.

Fig. 2a. Original web page (http://www.bcc.co.uk) before translation

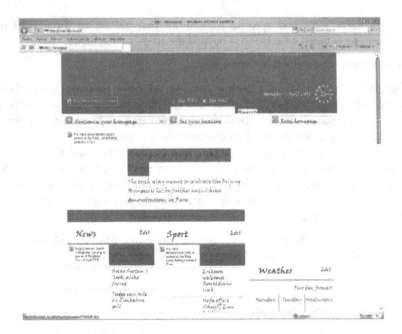

Fig. 2b. Previous web page after translation according to the user specified form. The pictures, background colors and selected tables were removed. The selected fonts and their colors were changed.

7 Conclusions and Future Work

In this paper we have presented several tools that help visually impaired users to solve problems they experience when accessing information published on the Internet. Some of these problems can be analyzed from the Web designer's standpoint and the others from the user's perspective.

The main contribution of this paper is the presentation of the system, which is based on document-proxy techniques and translates web pages into the accessible form upon specified translation rules. The main advantage of the presented system is the universality of use and browser independency. Therefore, visually impaired users can use this system from various places with access to the Internet, such as home computers, libraries, school laboratories etc. Additionally, users can use their own stored profiles to make the browsing and accessibility more specific to their requirements.

Our next plan is to improve the user interface, the user-specific profiles and to simplify the rules into regular expressions. In this way, we hope to improve the accuracy and utility of our transcoding system. We also plan to integrate other components, such as summarization, language translation and so on. Our final goal is to make the Web usefully available as a new information resource for the users with special needs. We hope that our approach will be a practical solution for accessing existing Web content and become an important milestone towards that goal.

Acknowledgement. The research has been supported by the Czech Ministry of Education in frame of the Research Intention MSM 0021630528: Security-Oriented Research in Information Technology, MSM 0021630503 MIKROSYN: New Trends in Microelectronic Systems and Nanotechnologies, and by the Grant Agency of the Czech Republic through the grant GACR 102/08/0429: Safety and security of networked embedded system applications.

References

1. Isaak, J.: Toward Equal Web Access for All. IT Pro 11-12 / 2000, IEEE 1520-9202/00, pp. 49–51 (2000)
2. Kirchner, M.: Evaluation, Repair, and Transformation of Web Pages for Web Content Accessibility. Review of Some Available Tools. In: Proceedings of the Fourth International Workshop on Web Site Evolution WSE 2002, 0-7695-1804-4/02 (2002)
3. Liu, S., Ma, W., Schalow, D., Spruill K.: Improving Web Access for Visually Impaired Users. IT Pro 7-8 / 2004, IEEE 1520-9202/04, pp. 28–33 (2004)
4. Macías, M., Sanchéz, F.: Improving Web Accessibility for Visually Handicapped People Using KAI. In: Proceedings of the 3rd International Workshop on Web Site Evolution WSE 2001 0-7695-1399-9/01 (2001)
5. Ocenasek, P., Toufarova, J.: Web Accessibility for Visually Handicapped People. In: INFORUM 2005: 11th Annual Conference on Professional Information Resources, Praha (2005) ISSN 1801-2213
6. Whitelaw, K.: Why Make Websites Accessibile? And How? In: SIGUCCS 2003, San Antonio, Texas, USA, pp. 259–261. ACM, New York (2003)
7. W3C World Wide Web Consortium. [online] Cited 2008-01-30 (2006), http://www.w3.org
8. Ocenasek, P.: Automatic System for Making Web Content Accessible for Visually Impaired Users. WSEAS Transactions on Computers Research 1(2), 325–328 (2006)
9. Ocenasek, P.: Automatic System for Making Web Content Accessible for Visually Impaired Users. In: Proceedings of the 6th International Conference on Applied Computer Science, Puerto De La Cruz, ES, 2006, pp. 430–433 (2006) ISBN 960-8457-57-2
10. Ocenasek, P.: Modification of Web Content According to the User Requirements. LNCS, vol. 2008(5093), pp. 324–327. Springer, Heidelberg (2008)

Extracting the Components of Elderly People's Capacity in Electrical Appliances and Grasping Relationship with the Components

Kanji Tanaka and Toshiki Yamaoka

Wakayama University, Faculty of system Engineering, Department of Design and
information science
s095027@sys.wakayama-u.ac.jp

Abstract. The purpose of this study is to extract the components of capacity
which elderly people have in electrical appliances and grasp the relationship
with the components. In this research, we interviewed elderly people for the
impression and experience of electrical appliances and conducted the tests, for
example, card sorting, tasks using digital video camera and so on. We used
Boolean algebra with tests data to simplify items. As a result, we found the
relationship with the components in electrical appliances.

Keywords: Elderly people, Capacity in electrical appliances, Components.

1 Introduction

Nowadays the population of elderly people has increased all over the world. In Japan,
it is said that 25% population will become elderly people in 2015[1, 2]. It is common
knowledge that information communication technology has developed rapidly and it
has changed our life and society considerably. Hence, it is essential to organize
universal society that elderly people and defective people can use electrical appliances
and information communication technology. There are a lot of researches about
elderly people. For example, some previous researches argued some factors to deal
with electrical appliances [3 - 5]. Therefore, it is important for elderly people to grasp
what factors are needed to use electrical appliances well.

1.1 Definition

We can define "Capacity" as the ability to operate with unknown electrical appliances
for oneself in this research.

2 The Test to Grasp Components (Test 1)

The purpose of this section is to grasp components of elderly people's capacity in
electrical appliances. Hence as an Test 1, we conducted card sorting about category
and some tasks with using PC. We also interviewed for the impression and experience
of electrical appliances.

S. Lee et al. (Eds.): APCHI 2008, LNCS 5068, pp. 420–426, 2008.

2.1 Participants

Subject: 30 (Men: 16 Women: 14)
Average age: 69, 2
SD: 2, 9

2.2 PC Tasks

The purpose of this test is to measure performance in electrical appliances for elderly people. This test was made by Micromedia Flash and showed on PC monitor. This test also copies digital camera because there are few elderly people having experience in digital camera. That's why we chose digital camera as a test not to bias. This test was evaluated by accomplishment time.

2.3 Interview

The purpose of this interview is to extract the impression and experience of electrical appliances. We interviewed for the impression or attitude to electrical appliances. As a result, we got many items of impression through this interview. These items were classified into interest, negative interest, body, anxiety and surrounding. In our understanding, anxiety for electrical appliances and surrounding influence elderly people's motivation to use. Moreover we interviewed the experience of electrical appliances including mobile phone and PC.

2.4 Card Sorting

Generally speaking, when we operate electrical appliances, firstly we understand categorized information and terms. Next we start to operate them. Moreover it is said that people having logical thinking can find common rule easily[6]. Therefore it needs the ability to understand the difference of concept to operate electrical appliances well. The purpose of this test is to examine whether elderly people have the ability to distinguish superordinate level, basic level and subordinate level. These levels were proposed by Rosch[7]. We conducted card sorting about category of terms.

2.5 Results

As a result of Test1, it was found that elderly people using mobile phone or PC have high possibility to use electrical appliances well. The main reason is that PC and mobile phone are most difficult to operate in electrical appliances. Elderly people using PC or mobile phone, in other words, are able to understand operating principle of other electrical appliances easily. Moreover Test1 revealed that some items of motivation have correlation with capacity in electrical appliances through the interview for impression.

3 Previous Work

3.1 Experience and Knowledge of Operation [3]

Okada conducted a questionnaire and description about procedure in electrical appliances to confirm whether age and experience, which are reached by Mental Model [8], affect knowledge about operation in electrical appliances.

In questionnaire, he surveyed experience in electrical appliances and conducted tests of air conditioner, copy machine, CD component, electronic dictionary, facsimile, TV game, massaging tools.

As a result, it was found that age and experience complete each other to create the knowledge about procedures for electrical appliances. Moreover it was found that age affect the knowledge about procedures more strongly than experience.

3.2 The Relationship between Capacity for Working Memory with Operation of Mobile Phone [4]

The purpose of this study is to grasp the relationship between capacity for working memory and the entry work of 5 touch type and QWERTY. It was measured capacity for working memory and entry work performance. As a result, it was found that 5 touch type was valid for even user who are not accustomed to dealing with electrical appliances and information communication technology. Also it was found the relationship between capacity for working memory and entry work performance.

3.3 Influence of Operation by Motivation [5]

In this research, Akatsu had the hypothesis. If elderly people have high motivation for electrical appliances, they may be able to use electrical appliances perfectly even if there are some usability problems in electrical appliances. As a test, it was used a game machine 'Nintendo DS'. But it was not found clear results.

4 Hypothesis

Regarding these previous works, they revealed that it is difficult to explain the elderly people's capacity for using electrical appliances by only one factor. Therefore it is clear that the capacity for using electrical appliances is composed of various factors. Then we proposed the following Hypothesis through previous works and Test 1.

The hypothesis describes that most elderly people's capacity in electrical appliances consists of motivation, experience, logical thinking and working memory. Generally speaking, it is difficult to operate all electrical appliances by only

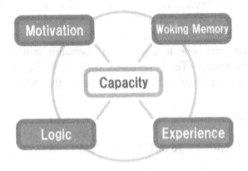

Fig. 1. Hypothesis

instinctive operation. Hence that means operating electrical appliances needs logical thinking. Furthermore it is said that Working memory is influenced with aging well [2]. It is reasonable to think that working memory relates with Capacity. As other items of components, there are an academic background and occupation as examples. In this research, logical thinking or working memory is estimated as an upper concept of an academic background and occupation.

5   The Test to Grasp the Relationship with the Components (Test 2)

We conducted 5 tests including questionnaire, card sorting about category, the task to measure working memory and "capacity" and 2 questionnaires about motivation and experience of electrical appliances, as Test 2. We used Boolean algebra to grasp features which elderly people having high capacity have. Furthermore we conducted the quantification 1. We described the results of 2 tests and the questionnaire about motivation of 5 tests.

5.1 Working Memory

There are commonly Reading span test and Tower of London, etc as a test to measure working memory [9]. Reading span test mainly deals with memory for sentence or letter. But it is likely that memory for sentence or letter doesn't relate with operation of electrical appliances. Hence we had subjects conduct Tower of London task to measure working memory [10]. Firstly we showed subjects the only pictures of "START" and"GOAL", then we had subjects think how to make "goal" from"start" without writing. As a rule, if subjects give up trying to think or run past the time limit (5 minutes), we permit subjects writing to think how to make "Goal".

This test was evaluated by accomplishment time.
Average time: 199 sec   SD: 103 sec
The following figure shows answer of Tower of London task.

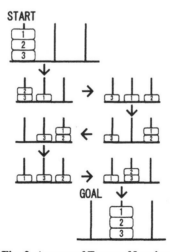

Fig. 2. Answer of Tower of London

As a result, it was found clearly that the difference between elderly people who accomplished the task or not is very large from SD.

If processing speed is slow, it takes a lot of time to process information. In other words, if working memory capacity is low, it is reasonable to think that performance is not good [11].

5.2 Motivation

The purpose of this questionnaire is to examine elderly people's motivation for electrical appliances and also grasp the items which influence motivation strongly. These questionnaire items are evaluated by 7-point scale.

The following items show questionnaire items, average point, SD.

Q1: You feel happy to operate electrical appliances well.
Average: 6.1   SD: 1.6
Q2: You are enjoyable to operate electrical appliances.
Average: 4.9   SD: 1.1
Q3: You are interested in electrical appliances generally.
Average: 5.1   SD: 1.2
Q4: You are interested in new electrical appliances.
Average: 4.6   SD: 1.7
Q5: You want to use many functions in electrical appliances.
Average: 3.9   SD: 1.6
Q6: You want to use electrical appliances as many as possible.
Average: 5.1   SD: 1.2
Q7: You have confidence to use electrical appliances perfectly if someone teaches you how to use them.
Average: 6.2   SD: 0.9
Q8: You are afraid of errors of operation.
Average: 4.1   SD: 2.7
Q9: You feel anxiety to vanish data or memory on electrical appliances.
Average: 4.9   SD: 2.4
Q10: You are discouraged if the way to operate seems to be difficult.
Average: 5.3   SD: 1.1
Q11: When you operate electrical appliances, you feel tiredness soon.
Average: 3.7   SD: 1.6
Q12: You are discouraged if there are no person who can teach you how to use electrical appliances around you.
Average: 4.1   SD: 1.9
Q13: You are discouraged if your friends or your family advise you to stop using electrical appliances.
Average: 2.1   SD: 1.3

As a result of this questionnaire, the highest average-point item is Q7. Judging from Q7, the fact suggests that elderly people generally have confidence in operating electrical appliances. But this result may not be valid because 'confidence for elderly people' varies from person to person.

High SD items also are Q8 and Q9. As for these items, elderly people who have much experience in electrical appliances don't have anxiety. Therefore they feel relief and reliance in electrical appliances. On the other hand, others have anxiety to operate electrical appliances.

5.3 Task to Measure "Capacity"

We provide subjects 9 tasks to measure "Capacity". In this test, we used a digital video camera as test task. Subjects have never operated a digital video camera before.
Rules are as follows.

① we don't advise subjects. Subjects have to accomplish the tasks for oneself.
② we distribute the instruction book.

This test was evaluated by 9 point-scale. For examples of tasks, there are "take a photograph" and "erase a picture"
As a result, average point: 4,5
The highest score: 7
The lowest score: 0

5.4 Boolean Algebra and the Quantification 1

We used Boolean algebra for the data through Test 2 to simplify items. Therefore it is possible to grasp relationship with four components. In using Boolean algebra, we dealt with high score of each test as "1" and low score of each test as "0". We further summed up the items.

Table 1. Karnaugh map

BA	00	01	11	10
00	0	0	1	0
01	0	0	1	1
11	0	0	1	0
10	0	0	1	1

A: Motivation
B: Experience
C: Logical thinking
D: Working Memory

We see the following formula from Table1.

$$=AB+Cd(AB+aB)+cD(AB+aB)$$

$$=AB+C(AB+aB)+D(AB+aB)$$

$$=AB+BC(A+a)+BD(A+a)$$

$$=AB+BC+BD$$

$$=B(A+C+D)$$

This formula shows elderly people having high ability to use electrical appliances have much experience of mobile phone or PC.

Moreover we conducted the quantification 1 to grasp the strength of influence related with capacity.

This result was expressed in percentage by partial correlation coefficient.

Logical thinking...31%
Working Memory...24%
Experience...39%
Motivation...6%

Consequently, it was found through the quantification 1 that the strongest influence on capacity is "experience of mobile phone or PC". On the other hand, it was found that "motivation" didn't influence capacity much. But it is necessary to interpret this result. The main reason is that elderly people who have the high ability to operate electrical appliances don't have high motivation for using electrical appliances. But it was found that they had high motivation to operate before using electrical appliances well.

6   Conclusion

It was found that elderly people who have high ability to use electrical appliances have at least 2 superior abilities including "experience" of four components. It follows from this that elderly people complete various abilities mutually to use electrical appliances well. On the other hand, elderly people having low ability have no more than one superior ability of four components. Finally it was found that the experience for PC or mobile phone is the most important components to operate electrical appliances perfectly of the four components.

References

1. Ito, K., Kuwano, S., Komatubara, A.: Ningenkougaku Handobuxtuku[Handbook of Ergonomics], pp. 594–603. Asakura-publisher (2003)
2. Park, D.C., Schwarz, N., Kuchinomati, Y., Sakata, Y., Kawaguchi, J.(ed.): Nintinoeijingu-nixyuumonhen[Cognitive Aging], pp. 305–307. Kitaouji-publisher (2004)
3. Okada, M.: Human Interface Society. Nitijoutekina denkiseihinno sousatejunnikansuru tisiki-nenreitokeikenno youin 9(4), 57–62 (2007)
4. Hosaka, R.: Conference of Japan Ergonomics Society, Keitaidenwakino sousaseito wakingumemori yoryou tono kanrensei nituite, vol. 43 special edn., pp. 354–355 (2007)
5. Akatu, Y.: Conference of Japan Ergonomics Society, Kadaitaxtuseidoukiga koureisha no kikisousataidoni ataeru eikyounituite, vol. 43, special edn., pp. 310–311 (2007)
6. Ikegaya, Y., Koudansha: Shinka shisugita nou, pp. 161–195 (2007)
7. Ichikawa, S., Ito, Y., Brainsha: Ninchi shinrigaku wo shiru, pp. 57–68 (1997)
8. Norman, D.A., Shinyousha: Dare no tameno dezain? [The psychology of Everyday Things], p. 25 (1990)
9. Nihon Ninchi Shinrigaxtukai, Kyouritu-publisher, Ninchi kagaku jiten, pp. 312–313 (2002)
10. http://www.pri.kyoto-u.ac.jp/brain/45-2/index-45-2.html
11. Osaka, M., Shinyousha: Nou no Memotixyou-working memory[working memory: The sketchpad in the brain], pp. 38–76 (2002)

The Choice of Communication Media and the Use of Mobile Phone among Senior Users and Young Users

Ayako Hashizume[1], Masaaki Kurosu[2], and Takao Kaneko[3]

[1] Graduate School of Comprehensive Human Science, University of Tsukuba, Japan
hashi-aya@kansei.tsukuba.ac.jp
[2] National Institute of Multimedia Education (NIME),
Research and Development Division, Japan
[3] School of Human Sciences, Waseda University, Japan

Abstract. The use of communication media including the land line, the cell phone, the letter, the telegram, the cell phone mail, the PC mail, asking somebody to convey the message, and the face-to-face meeting was analyzed in accordance with the situation comparing senior users and young users. Senior users showed the tendency to stick to the old media such as the land line.

Keywords: Communication, Media, Usability, Cellular phone, senior user, Young user, Artifact Development Theory (ADT).

1 Introduction

Generally, it is believed that high-tech devices are difficult to use for senior people. But it is observed some senior people are using the cell phone frequently that is one of the leading high-tech devices. It is not yet clear how much functionality they are using and how they are making the best use of the cell phone in their life.

Hence it is necessary to cast the light on the way senior people are using the cell phone by investigating how effectively and efficiently they are using it. If they are using the cell phone in the same/similar way and in the same/similar functions with the young people is one of the questions. The next question is how and why there are still many senior people who don't use the cell phone actively. And the third question is how the cell phone could be designed and be diffused senior people so that the quality of their social life could be improved. [1, 2, 3]

This paper deals with these questions by conducting the questionnaire research for senior people by comparing the result with those for young people. And the analysis was conducted from the viewpoint of Artifact Development Theory (ADT) [4, 5]. ADT is a new emerging field of user engineering that, in short, analyzes the use of artifact why "it" was selected for "that" purpose and why "others" were not selected for "that" purpose, thus clarify the reasonability of the artifact selection and the optimal design of artifact.

S. Lee et al. (Eds.): APCHI 2008, LNCS 5068, pp. 427–436, 2008.

2 Methods

Questionnaire researches were conducted for 70 senior people (35 male and 35 female) who already possess the cell phone and for 68 young people (42 male and 26 female) who, of course, possess the cell phone. Regarding the senior people, we defined them as of their age over 60, though WHO defines it for those over 65. It is because people retire from their job and their life environment changes drastically around 60 of age. The average age of senior people was 68.49 with the SD of 3.87, and the average age of young people was 22.31 with the SD of 2.08.

The research was conducted from October to December 2007. For senior people, the questionnaire was collected after 3 weeks from the delivery, and for young people, the questionnaire was collected after 2 weeks from the delivery.

2.1 Content of Questionnaire

The questionnaire contained total of 54 items that is shown below.

2.1.1 Question 1 : About 8 Types of Communication Medias (4 Items Each)
The informants were asked following questions on 8 types of communication media (Land line, Cell phone, Letter, Telegram, Cell phone mail, PC mail, Ask somebody to convey the message, Face-to-face meeting).

(a) How frequently do you use it? (Very often, Sometimes, Seldom, Almost none)
(b) Main Purpose - For what purpose do you use it mainly? (Free answer)
(c) Major Problems - What are major problems with it? (Free answer)
(d) If you can't use it, what would you use instead of it? (Free answer)

2.2.2 Question 2 : Select Which Communication Media to Use in Each of 11 Cases (2 Items Each)
Case 1: If you want to talk about everyday issue that is not urgent.
Case 2: If you want to tell family member(s) that you'll be late to return home.
Case 3: If you plan the party or something.
Case 4: If you want to tell that you are in a bad condition.
Case 5: If you want to know the schedule of the movie, the concert, etc.
Case 6: If you want to discuss about some critical issue.
Case 7: If you want to tell something quite interesting or funny to your friend.
Case 8: If you want to express thanks for the gift.
Case 9: If you want tell that you'll be late for the schedule.
Case10: If you want to borrow some money from your friend.
Case11: If you want to confirm if she/he is OK.

The informants were asked following questions in terms of above 11 cases.

(a) What kind of media do you use very often or sometimes? (Free choice from among: Land line, Cell phone, Letter, Telegram, Cell phone mail, PC mail, Ask somebody to convey the message, Face-to-face meeting, Do nothing, Other)
(b) Why would you choose it/them? (Free answer)

3   Results

3.1   Usage Frequency of Each of 8 Types of Communication Media

The result of Question 1 (a) is shown in Fig. 1. There was a significant difference for the use of the communication media between senior users (left) and young users (right).

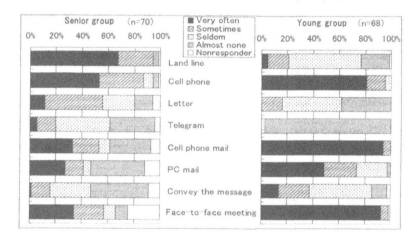

Fig. 1. Frequency of use of communication media among senior people (left) and young people (right)

Table 1. Result of the chi-square test comparing the proportion of each response between senior people and young people in Figure 1

Communication Medias	Chi-Square Value	
Land line phone	86.843	**
Cell phone	13.760	**
Letter	32.696	**
Telegram	60.100	**
Cell phone mail	57.861	**
PC mail	44.280	**
Ask somebody to convey the message	25.525	**
Meet directly	51.887	**

** P<.01

Result of the chi-square test and the residual analysis revealed differences of use at 5% level as follows.

(1) Land line – senior people use it very often, while young people use it seldom or for almost none (Tab.1).
(2) Cell phone – senior people use it for sometimes, while young people use it very often.

(3) Letter – senior people use it very often or for sometimes, while young people use it seldom or for almost none.
(4) Telegram – senior people use it very often or sometimes or seldom, while young people use it for almost none.
(5) Cell phone mail – senior people use it sometimes or seldom or almost none, while young people use it very often.
(6) PC mail – senior people use it for almost none, while young people use it very often or for sometimes.
(7) Ask somebody to convey the message – senior people use it for almost none, while young people use it very often of seldom.

Face-to-face meeting – senior people use it sometimes, seldom or for almost none, while young people use it very often.

3.2 Selection of Communication Media in 11 Situations

Results of Question 2 (a) are shown from Fig. 2 to Fig. 12. Applying the chi-square test, there were many different usage patterns between the senior people and the young people as shown in Tab. 2.

Table 2. Result of the chi-square test comparing the proportion of each response between senior people and young people for each case in 11 situations

Case		Land line phone	Cell phone	Letter	Telegram	Cell phone mail	PC mail	Ask somebody to convey the message	Meet directly	Doing nothing	Other
1	Want to talk about everyday issue that is not urgent	27.298 **	16.989 **	2.672	0.000	53.852 **	0.296	7.163 *	25.044 **	1.968	3.157
2	Want to tell family member(s) that you'll be late to return home	3.704	4.317	0.000	1.037	69.257 **	6.457 *	6.457 *	5.264	1.114	0.000
3	Plan a family party or something	15.717 **	5.562	0.979	2.089	77.722 **	8.429 *	1.568	11.668 **	1.779	2.089
4	Want to tell that you are in a bad condition	7.664 *	35.749 **	0.000	1.037	32.183 **	8.834 *	0.986	5.896	0.371	0.000
5	Want to know the schedule of the movie, the concert, etc.	7.569 *	24.373 **	0.000	0.979	13.412 **	6.921 *	0.371	8.814 *	6.595 *	33.311 **
6	Want to discuss about some critical issue	16.731 **	32.337 **	1.809	1.037	53.637 **	9.704 **	0.371	44.835 **	1.971	2.089
7	Want to tell something quite interesting	24.783 **	7.639 *	0.797	2.089	55.133 **	0.224	4.241	30.777 **	3.707	7.591 *
8	Want to express thanks for the gift	8.824 *	8.093 *	1.053	5.341	25.429 **	9.288 **	0.000	39.172 **	0.371	0.979
9	Want tell that you'll be late for the schedule	19.638 **	9.896 **	0.000	0.000	73.915 **	1.091	2.911	2.089	0.000	1.971
10	Want to borrow some money from your friend	3.063	2.997	2.288	1.037	6.600 *	0.312	1.037	15.812 **	3.209	0.000
11	Want to confirm if she/he is OK	7.786 *	32.829 **	4.358	0.179	15.941 **	1.049	4.893	13.487 **	1.292	0.979

** P<.01, * P<.05

3.2.1 Case 1: If You Want to Talk about Everyday Issue That is Not Urgent

For case 1, senior people selected the land line while young people selected the cell phone and the cell phone mail. It is significant at 5% level by Chi-square test. For the media that is used for sometime, senior people still selected land line, while young people selected the cell phone mail, convey the message and the face-to-face meeting.

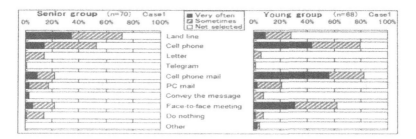

Fig. 2. Case1: media selection for the case "If you want to talk about everyday issue that is not urgent"

3.2.2 Case 2: If You Want to Tell Family Member(s) That You'll be Late to Return Home

For case 2, senior people selected the cell phone a bit, while young people selected the cell phone mail and the cell phone.

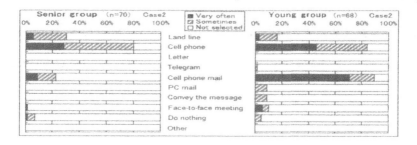

Fig. 3. Case2: media selection for the case "If you want to tell family member(s) that you'll be late to return home"

3.2.3 Case 3: If You Plan the Party or Something

For case 3, senior people selected the land line while young people selected the cell phone mail, the PC mail and the face-to-face meeting. Young people selected the face-to-face meeting as the communication media that is used for sometimes.

3.2.4 Case 4: If You Want to Tell that You are in a Bad Condition

For case 4, young people selected the cell phone and the cell phone mail. Senior people selected the cell phone while young people selected the cell phone mail and the PC mail as the communication media that are used for sometimes.

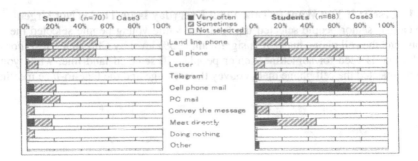

Fig. 4. Case3: media selection for the case "If you plan the party or something"

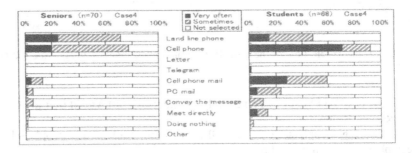

Fig. 5. Case4: media selection for the case "If you want to tell that you are in a bad condition"

3.2.5 Case 5: If You Want to Know the Schedule of the Movie, the Concert, etc

For case 5, young people selected the cell phone, the cell phone mail and the face-to-face meeting as the frequently used communication media. For the communication media that are used "sometimes", senior people selected the cell phone and doing nothing while young people selected the cell phone mail, the PC mail and others. "Other" response among young people includes the internet access via the cell phone (41.2%) or the PC.

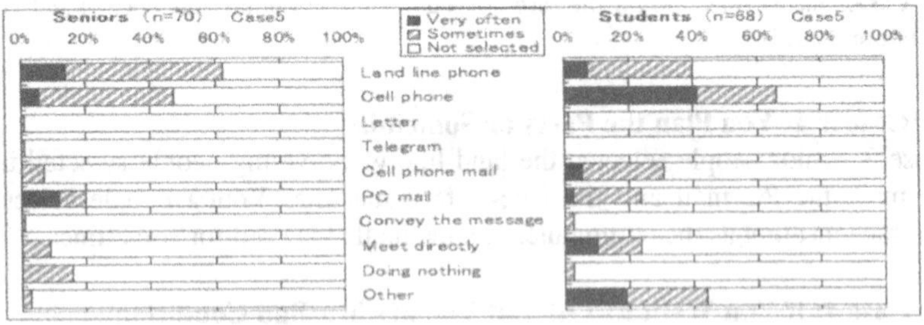

Fig. 6. Case5: media selection for the case "If you want to know the schedule of the movie, the concert, etc"

3.2.6 Case 6: If You Want to Discuss about Some Critical Issue

For case 6, young people selected the cell phone, the cell phone mail, the PC mail and the face-to-face meeting. For the communication media that are used for sometimes, senior people selected the land line while young people selected the cell phone mail.

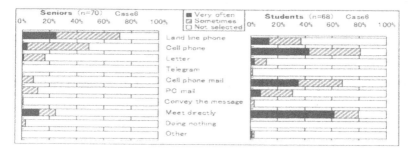

Fig. 7. Case6: media selection for the case "If you want to discuss about some critical issue"

3.2.7 Case 7: If You Want to Tell Something Quite Interesting or Funny to Your Friend

For case 7, senior people selected the land line while young people selected the cell phone, cell phone mail and the face-to-face meeting. For the communication media that are used for sometimes, senior people selected the land line while young people selected the face-to-face meeting and others. Other in young people included the SNS (7.4%), the messenger and the Skype.

Fig. 8. Case7: media selection for the case "If you want to tell something quite interesting or funny to your friend"

3.2.8 Case 8: If You Want to Express Thanks for the Gift

For case 8, young people selected the cell phone, the cell phone mail, the PC mail and the face-to-face meeting. For the communication media that are used for sometimes, senior people selected the land line while young people selected the cell phone mail.

3.2.9 Case 9: If You Want Tell That You'll be Late for the Schedule

For case 9, young people selected the cell phone and the cell phone mail. For the communication media that are used for sometimes, senior people selected the land line and the cell phone while young people selected the cell phone mail.

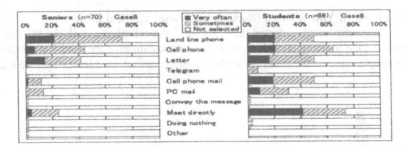

Fig. 9. Case8: media selection for the case "If you want to express thanks for the gift"

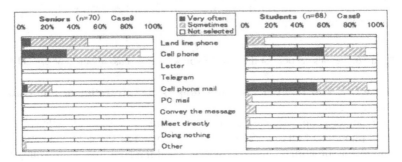

Fig. 10. Case9: media selection for the case "If you want tell that you'll be late for the schedule"

3.2.10 Case10: If You Want to Borrow Some Money From Your Friend
For case 10, young people selected the cell phone mail and the face-to-face meeting.

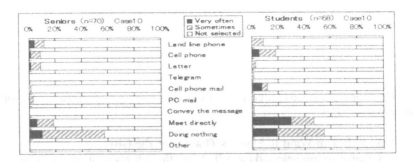

Fig. 11. Case10: media selection for the case "If you want to borrow some money from your friend"

3.2.11 Case11: If You Want to Confirm If She/He is OK
For case 11, young people selected the cell phone and the cell phone mail. For the communication media that are used for sometimes, senior people selected the cell phone while young people selected the cell phone mail and the face-to-face meeting.

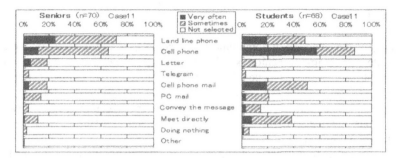

Fig. 12. Case11: media selection for the case "If you want to confirm if she/he is OK"

4 Discussion

General tendency found in this research is that senior people use "old media" such as the landline compared to young people as can bee seen in Fig. 1, but they also use the "new media" such as the cell phone and the cell phone mail depending on the situation. For such situations as case 1 (If you want to talk about everyday issue that is not urgent), case 6 (If you want to discuss about some critical issue), case 9 (If you want to express thanks for the gift) and case 11 (If you want to confirm if s/he is OK), the traditional land line is a frequently used media for senior people. While in such situations as case 2 (If you want to tell family member(s) that you'll be late to return home), and case 9 (If you want to tell that you'll be late for the schedule), senior people select the cell phone more than the land line and other media. And it is quite natural for them to select the cell phone for the purpose of communication from a remote place.

Young people showed a contrasting tendency to use the cell phone and the cell phone mail. It is striking that they tend to use the cell phone and the cell phone mail in such situations as case 1 (If you want to talk about everyday issue that is not urgent), case 2 (If you want to tell family member(s) that you'll be late to return home), case 3 (If you plan the party or something), case 4 (If you want to tell that you are in a bad condition), etc. But we should note that they are differentiating the use of media depending on the situation, i.e. in case 5 (If you want to know the schedule of the movie, the concert, etc) the cell phone call is more frequently selected while in case 3 and case 4 the cell phone mail are more frequently selected.

Another characteristic among young people is the high frequency of face-to-face meeting as can be seen in case 6 (If you want to discuss about some critical issue). It might be due to the fact that young people are more often to be outdoors compared to senior people.

The variety of alternatives to be selected has different tendencies among senior people and young people. As was pointed out, senior people select traditional communication media such as the land line and the letter but sometimes select the cell phone and the cell phone mail. It should also be noted that they seldom select the PC-based communication media. On the contrary, young people don't use the land line and letters and, instead, use the cell phone-based media and the PC-based media. Sometimes they use "other" media such as the SNS, Skype etc.

5 Conclusion

In this paper, the selection of communication media especially focusing on the use of the mobile phone among senior people and young people was discussed. It was evident that the cell phone has now become one of the popular communication media among senior people but the tendency to use the cell phone for the purpose of communication is somewhat different from young people. Young people differentiate using various new media depending on the situation and they show a tendency to use more ICT-based media.

In other words, the cell phone could be regarded as the communication media that is positioned at the logical "AND" for both senior people and young people.

References

1. Impress R&D: K-tai White Paper (in Japanese) (2007)
2. Impress R&D: Internet White Paper (in Japanese) (2007)
3. Dentsu: A Research for Information and Media Society (in Japanese) (2007)
4. Kurosu, M.: An Introduction to the Artifact Development Theory (in Japanese), HCD-Net 3(1), (2007)
5. Kurosu, M.: The Optimality of Design from the Viewpoint of the Artifact Development Theory (in Japanese), Human Interface Society SIGUSE (2007)

Prototyping and Evaluation for Smart Home Controller Based on Chinese Families Behavior Analysis

Fang You[1,2], HuiMin Luo[1], YingLei Liang[2], and JianMin Wang[2]

[1] School of communication and design, Sun Yat-sen university, Guangzhou, 510275, China
[2] Key Laboratory of Digital Life, Sun Yat-sen university, Ministry of Education, 510275, China
youfang@mail.sysu.edu.cn, anyluo@hotmail.com,
ivy_nameless@163.com, mcswjm@mail.sysu.edu.cn

Abstract. The fast development of Chinese architecture market and the smart home business have caused works on user research in smart home environment to be growing rapidly. Nonetheless, there are some problems related to product in use; and in this paper, we examine two problems that are present in smart home controllers from a user survey: one is the difficult in use for the Elderly; and the other is the complex operations for Nannies. Based on this we have examined and devised two prototypes designed for those two types of users; as well as the task sheet evaluation.

Keywords. User behavior analysis, Smart home controller, Prototyping, Functions grouping, Graphic interface.

1 Background

The Chinese architecture market has been prosperous since the end of 20th century, as has the following smart home and its controller business. Owning to the rapid growth of that, user research into the smart home environment has developped continuously. However, most research in the area does not focus on the typical Chinese families, which are actually target users of the smart home products.

For example, Tae Seung Ha, Ji Hong Jung, and Sung Yong Oh [1]; LEE J H and JUNG J H [2]; and Hyun-chul Cho, Ki-hoon Lee, Jin-sil Kim, Ji-hong Jung, and Young-hwan Pan [3] have proposed methods and models to analyze user behavior in the home environment [1,2,3]. Other research studies done in the smart home field include DimitarH.Stefanov, Zeungnam Bien, Won-ChulBang,[4];VictoriaHaines, ValMitchell, CatherineCooper,, and MartinMaguire, [5]; and George Demiris*, Marilyn J. Rantz, Myra A. Aud, Karen D. Marek, Harry W. Tyrer, Marjorie Skubic and Ali A. Hussam [6]. Some smart home products, for instance, Domotica Home Automation[7] and Philips Pronto[8], all adopt the hierarchical menu style which require the user to remember its logical layout. The previous work does not take into account family members behaviors done in the typical Chinese house. The works have some distance from the actual Chinese smart home target users. The aim of our work is to focus on the behaviors of users living in typically traditional Chinese house equipped with smart home appliances. This paper presents two remote controller prototypes of smart home to ameliorate the existing ones which have found some problems in user research.

S. Lee et al. (Eds.): APCHI 2008, LNCS 5068, pp. 437–445, 2008.

2 User Behavior Analysis

The nouveau riche is selected for study as one of the target users of smart homes in China. Generally, they do not possess a good technology background. The typical nouveau rich Chinese families include three generations of members: Co-owner, the parents and the children of the host, mostly with nannies employed. Their houses are usually either luxuriously decorated, or combined with Chinese classical and modern characteristics. (Figure1).

2.1 User Research

Before the personas were established, we investigated people living in penthouse or villa equipped with the smart home system in Figure2:

After analysis of the families with rapid growth in wealth, we found the following two main problems in existing smart home controllers: a). Difficulty in the use of the product for the Elderly.b).Nannies have to deal with a series of complex pages for a simple operation.

2.2 Personas

In order to figure out the significant behavior of our target users, we created four personas based in depth interviews, focus groups and relevant statistical data of Chinese Smart home. They are Fa Zhou (host), Fen Li (hostess), Xia Deng (grandma) and Mei Zhang(Nanny),all of them formed a typically nouveau riche family household. Due to 2.1, part of the research, we focused on analyzing two personas, grandma Xia Deng and Nanny Mei Zhang.(Figure3)

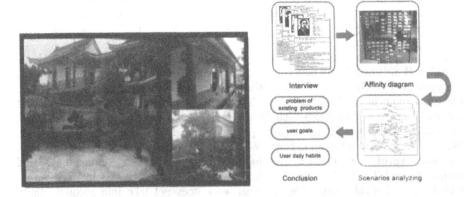

Fig. 1. A typical house of nouveau-riche family, combining Chinese classical and modern style

Fig. 2. The process of the user research

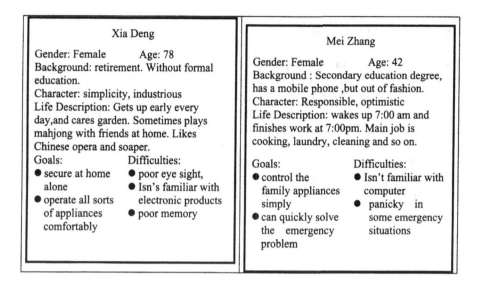

Xia Deng	Mei Zhang
Gender: Female Age: 78 Background: retirement. Without formal education. Character: simplicity, industrious Life Description: Gets up early every day,and cares garden. Sometimes plays mahjong with friends at home. Likes Chinese opera and soaper.	Gender: Female Age: 42 Background : Secondary education degree, has a mobile phone ,but out of fashion. Character: Responsible, optimistic Life Description: wakes up 7:00 am and finishes work at 7:00pm. Main job is cooking, laundry, cleaning and so on.

Xia Deng		Mei Zhang	
Goals:	Difficulties:	Goals:	Difficulties:
● secure at home alone ● operate all sorts of appliances comfortably	● poor eye sight, ● Isn's familiar with electronic products ● poor memory	● control the family appliances simply ● can quickly solve the emergency problem	● Isn't familiar with computer ● panicky in some emergency situations

Fig. 3. personas of grandma Xia Deng and Nanny Mei Zhang

2.3 User Behavior Analysis for Function Grouping

With the analysis of scenarios established for personas, we found out the reflects of the relations between the user behavior and the product function group, so as the interface feature division and logic design.

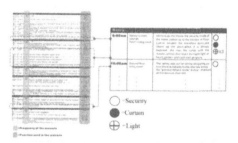

Fig. 4. User behavior analysis in user's one week based on personas and scenarios research. In combination of Mei Zhang and Xia Deng's scenarios ,we present the following function compositions and design elements based on the analysis of tasks reflecting the logical relationship among functions:

2.3.1 The Function Grouping

Function controls for lights, air conditioners, TV, and curtains are most frequently used by Mei Zhang and Xia Deng (Figure 5). Moreover, strong connection among these operations can be identified. For example, they often need to control the lights and air conditioners on different floors.

2.3.2 Independent Interface Especially for Elderly

Xia Deng (Grandma) needs to deal with the complex operations of the smart home controllers because of the frequent absence of Fa Zhou (host) during the the daytime. Xia Deng has to control the home electrical devices frequently in one week (Figure6) according to the analysis. An interface specifically designed for her is essential, with reduced functions consisting only of security, light, TV, curtain, air-condition control, and talk-backs specifically designed for her is essential. In short, the steps of the equipment that she often used will be simplified to emphasize the convenience of the smart home controllers.

3 Prototyping and Evaluation

3.1 Prototyping

With respect to these essentials and the analysis of scenarios, we designed the preliminaries of interface. The lighting, air-conditioning, TV operating and curtain drawing functions are implemented in the same page. Finally we have come up with a basic interface prototype which aims to satisfy the Nanny's requirements because she is the main user of the controller, and a special interface prototype for the Elderly.

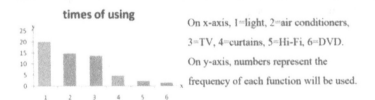

On x-axis, 1=light, 2=air conditioners, 3=TV, 4=curtains, 5=Hi-Fi, 6=DVD. On y-axis, numbers represent the frequency of each function will be used.

Fig. 5. Times of using each control function in everyday life

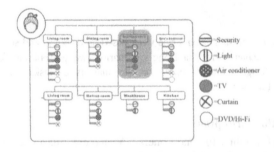

Fig. 6. Xia Deng utilizing remote control function in different rooms

The essentials for designing the prototype:

- User-friendly operation
- Smooth workflow of multiple appliance control(TV, light, curtain, air-condition)
- Easy access for the Elderly and the Nanny

3.1.1 Prototype1- Ordinary Interface

This prototype interface consists of a local enlarged map in the middle and a thumbnail on the upper right corner of the screen. The users can click on the thumbnail to select the specific place to be enlarged on the map. TV, light, curtain, air-condition control are placed on the large map, so the user (like Nanny) can easily control multiple functions at the same time (Figure 7).

3.1.2 Prototype2- Interface for Elderly

According to the function group design elements, lights air conditioners, TVs and curtains are the most often used appliances by Deng Xia. Her wish is for security and the easy control of these appliances when she is alone at home. Therefore the interface no longer adopts the function grouping based on a house map, but only her frequent use functions are shown in a single interface, enabling her to execute multiple controls without switching pages (Figure 8).The function control have been simplified. The Lighting function includes switching on/off and brightness control. The curtain function includes open/close and wideness of opening. The TV function includes switching on/off and channel switching. The air-conditioner function includes temperature control and basic model selection.

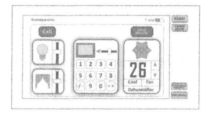

Fig. 7. Prototype1's interface consists of a local enlarged map and a thumbnail. When the user click on the icon, a pop up control panel appear.

Fig. 8. Prorotype2's interface

3.2 Evaluation of Prototypes

To test the usability of the design, two target user groups have been using the Prototypes 1 and 2, with four to five users in each group. They are given a task sheet which simulates the Nanny and the Elderly using the remote control in daily life.

The follow subsection provides the summary of   problems with Prototype 1 and 2 found in the testing

3.2.1 Evaluation Result of Prototype1

The main problems with Prototype1 are:

- The users are impatient when asked to switch off all the lighting simultaneously. The main reason is the repeated switch-off procedures.
- The user almost neglected the thumbnail view to navigate between different locations, but used the four-directional keys to roll the map more frequently. The reasons are raised as follows: firstly, the thumbnail is too small to be pressed accurately; secondly, it is troublesome to constantly switch one's attention between the map and the thumbnail; thirdly, it takes little time to roll the map by the four-directional key because the space of one floor is limited. (Figure 9)

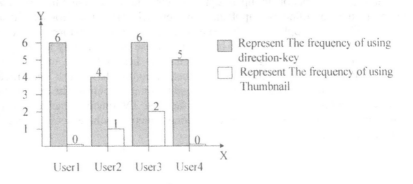

Fig. 9. The total frequency of using direction-key or thumbnail to navigate between different places in user evaluation

In response to the two main problems, we have revised the prototype by adding a key to switch all lights on/off simultaneously and we have removed the thumbnail view. Figures 10 and 11show the revised Prototype1.

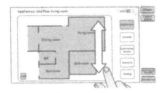
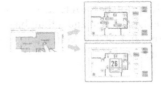

Fig. 10. The first page shows the global map of the present floor. The user can scroll up and down to reach different floors.

Fig. 11. Double clicking into an enlarged map and the four-directional key to roll the map to reach different rooms

3.2.2 Evaluation of the Prototype2 (for Elderly)

The main problems with Prototype 2 are:

● The caretaker call and local security control located on the top side under emergencies are not easy to reach or touch. Most of the users took a little time to find the way leading to such two buttons.

● The vertical layouts of the TV and air-conditioner control panels make it difficult for grandparents who have tight knuckle to control.

Figure 12 is the revised page of Prototype 2. The control panels of the TV and air-conditioner are changed into horizontal layouts to give grandparents more ease of use. The caretaker call and the local security buttons are placed lower and much easier to reach when the remote control device is placed on walls. Moreover, the caretaker call is located in the middle under emergencies for the convenience of grandparents during emergencies.

The testing of the prototype 2 with the same participants shows that the time to operate several functions is less than the previous one (Figure 13). For instance, one of the users moved her finger from curtain to light smoothly while doing an advanced task. She said that the prototype 2 is clearly understood, "At first sight I know what to do."

Fig. 12. The improved interface of prototype2 (for Elderly)

Fig. 13. Comparative prototype testing

3.2.3 Design Principles

Nannies equipped with the secondary education background, controlled a variety of multi-storey buildings household appliances in the nouveau riches family environment, have encountered difficulty. And so as do the Elderly, who also need to deal with the complex operations of the smart home controllers because of the frequent absence of the host.

Based on the data analysis of the two prototype evaluation, we can infer some guiding principles of the smart home remote controller interface design:

● Because of the screen size, design of a smart home remote controller should avoid using thumbnails. A direction key is a better navigation tool. The small screen with a local enlarged map and a thumbnail is too crowded so that the users neglect the use of the thumbnail. Using a direction key to navigate will concentrate the user's attention to the local enlarged map itself instead of identifying the details of the thumbnail.

- For the multi- floors control interface, a two-level menu with an overall view map first page and the local enlarged map with appliances in the second page is clear and easy to remember. Such a menu level is the coherent logic of an overall-partial situation in reality. It is easier to operate for Nannies to operate.
- The floor position controls and the location label should be placed close to each other, so that users can rapidly pay attention to the floor information feedback.
- Function zoning arrangements for the Elderly should be consistent with the Chinese people's reading habits where horizontal layouts are better than vertical ones.

Interface arrangement should suit the Elderly in the hands of activities, minimize the movement of cross-direction in functional operation.

4 Conclusion

In this paper, we examined the use of smart home remote controllers by certain targeted group. We have focused on the nouveau riche traditional family as our target group and we present the main problems in existing smart home controllers are the difficult in use for the Elderly and the complex operations for Nanny. Based on which, we design two remote controller prototypes for the Elderly and Nanny living with the traditional Chinese families with smart home equipment. In order to test the usability of the design, we invited two groups of users to have a task sheet evaluation. After that, we proposed some design principles for Chinese smart home controllers.

Acknowledgments. This paper is partially supported by the National Natural Science Fund (No.60776096, 60403039), the National High Technology Research and Development Program of China (863 Program) (No.2007AA01Z236), the Key Program of NSFC-Guangdong Joint Funds (No.U0735002).

Reference

1. Ha, T.S., Jung, J.H., Oh, S.Y.: Method to analyze user behavior in home environment. Pers. Ubiquit. Comput. 10, 110–121 (2006)
2. Lee, J.H., Jung, J.H.: A Context Visual ization Model for Smart-home. In: Proceedings of the Annual Conference of the JSSD, Kookmin Univ., Seoul, Kor, vol. 51, pp. 122–123 (2004)
3. Cho, H.-c., Lee, K.-h., Kim, J.-s., Jung, J.-h., Pan, Y.-h.: A concept model proposal study for Interactive Display set development. In: International Symposium on Ubiquitous VR (2007)
4. Stefanov, D.H., Bien, Z., Bang, W.-C.: The Smart House for Older Persons and Persons With Physical Disabilities: Structure, Technology Arrangements, and Perspectives, in Best Paper Selection for: IMIA Yearbook of Medical Informatics (2006); vol. 45 (suppl. 1), p. 56 (2006): Haux, R., Kulikowski, C. (eds.) Assessing Information Technologies for Health. Methods Inf. Med. (2006);

5. Haines, V., Mitchell, V., Cooper, C., Maguire, M.: Probing user values in the home environment with in A technology driven Smart Home project. Pers. Ubiquit. Comput. 11, 349–359 (2007)
6. Demiris, G., Rantz, M.J., Aud, M.A., Marek, K.D., Tyrer, H.W., Skubic, M., Hussam, A.A.: Older Adults attitudes towards and perceptions of ' smart home' technologies: a pilot study. Informatics for Health and Social Care Med. Inform. 29(2), 87–94 (2004)
7. Video (last visited: January 23,2008), http://www.domoelite.es.Coverpage.html
8. Video uploaded by MeitalGurman (last visited: January 23, 2008), http://tw.youtube.com/watch?v=lv2AKrK0pdg.Coverpage.html

Mapping User Accessibility Needs Systematically to Universal Design Principles

Kyohyun Song and Seongil Lee

Department of Industrial Engineering, Sungkyunkwan University
Suwon, 440-746, Korea
{ssong3588,silee}@skku.edu

Abstract. In a rapidly growing information-oriented society, people with disabilities and older people are faced with serious inconveniences in accessing IT products due to complicated use of technologies and poorly designed interfaces. To solve the problems, it is required for designers and engineers to find out and understand user needs, and then to figure out the functionalities and design characteristics to meet the needs. Figuring out the Engineering Characteristics (EC) of products from user needs for people with disabilities and older people who have problems using main stream products due to limited accessibility would take great efforts and time. We merged two important concepts of product design for people with disabilities and older people, accessibility and universal design, using an engineering design framework of QFD (Quality Function Deployment) to provide engineers and designers with a systematic methodology for universal product design. We adapted a technical report from the ISO/IEC JTC1 Special Working Group on Accessibility (SWG-A), the Information Technology – Accessibility Considerations for People with Disabilities – Part 1: User Needs Summary (ISO/IEC PDTR 99999-1), and mapped the detailed user accessibility needs to the guidelines of 7 universal design principles which are widely accepted. We explained how a process model was built for mapping relationship between the guidelines and user accessibility needs, and extracting the critical engineering characteristics for IT product design based on these two models. A model House of Quality(HOQ) was built for such procedures.

Keywords: Universal design process, User needs, Quality Function Deployment (QFD), design guidelines, ISO/IEC PDTR 99999-1.

1 Introduction

In product design, the most important procedure would be to figure out true user needs. User needs can be directly mapped to functionality or indirectly mapped to interface design of the intended product. It is required for designers and engineers to find out and understand user needs, and then to figure out the functionalities and design characteristics to meet the needs before starting to design a product. Figuring out the user needs, particularly of people with disabilities and older people who have problems using main stream products due to limited accessibility would take even greater efforts and longer time.

S. Lee et al. (Eds.): APCHI 2008, LNCS 5068, pp. 446–456, 2008.
© Springer-Verlag Berlin Heidelberg 2008

The concept of universal design plays an important role in this process of mapping user needs to products and services to provide variety of users with accessibility regardless of their age and individual capability. This concept has been summarized into guidelines by prominent researchers in this area. Ronald Mace (1991) defines universal design as "the design of all products and environments to be usable by people of all ages and abilities, to the greatest extent possible."[9] Vanderheiden argued that universal design is a process to seek combination of accessibility features for the requirements and abilities of all people including people with disabilities, and that this process means to include the characteristics of the people with disabilities in product design. [11, 12]

The design process for the commercial products, however, cannot always reflect the concept of universal design since those products were designed for making profits by sales. Even though designers want to make their products universally usable by people with disabilities or older people, it is very hard to develop or design such products since the existing guidelines and principles would not provide the concrete methods to reflect the concept. Without deeply understanding the concept of universal design, the principles and guidelines are not enough for product designers to make their products accessible and usable by all users. [14]

This paper proposes a model (1) to apply the seven principles of universal design to user needs, (2) to extract the engineering characteristics (EC) of the intended products by using Quality Function Deployment (QFD). We tried to utilize the House of Quality (HOQ), a tool for QFD, to examine the possibilities of using a systematic engineering design process in terms of universal design.

2 Background

In this section, the three methods to be used in our model for extracting the engineering characteristics from user needs would be examined in an engineering design framework: the 7 principles of universal design, user needs summary and quality function deployment.

2.1 The 7 Principles of Universal Design

Universal design means that the products need to be made in such a fashion that those products (i.e., devices, environment, system, or process) can be used by all people regardless of their capability or use context. [11, 12] It further requires that those products need to be commercial in general markets. The 7 principles of universal design are as follows: [15]

- Equitable Use: the design is useful and marketable to people with diverse abilities.
- Flexibility in Use: The design accommodates a wide range of individual preferences and abilities.
- Simple and Intuitive Use: Use of the design is easy to understand, regardless of the user's experience, knowledge, language skills, or current concentration level.

- · Perceptible Information: The design communicates necessary information effectively to the user, regardless of ambient conditions or the user's sensory abilities.
- · Tolerance for error: The design minimizes hazards and the adverse consequences of accidental or unintended actions.
- · Low Physical Effort: The design can be used efficiently and comfortably and with a minimum of fatigue.
- · Size and Space for Approach and Use: Appropriate size and space is provided for approach, reach, manipulation, and use regardless of user's body size, posture, or mobility.

2.2 Accessibility Considerations for People with Disabilities- Part 1: User Needs Summary (ISO/IEC PDTR 99999-1)

This technical report was reported open to public by the ISO/IEC JTC 1 - Special Working Group on Accessibility in 2005. It was originally developed by the TRACE R&D Center in University of Wisconsin-Madison as a "User Needs Summary". [6] The technical report categorizes 16 user accessibility needs of 13 types of disabilities and 134 specific user accessibility needs under the 16 categories. The 16 categories again are grouped into user perceive needs, user understand needs, user act needs, product needs, assistive technology needs, and environment needs. Figure 1 shows how the 16 categories were grouped into 6 types of user accessibility needs.

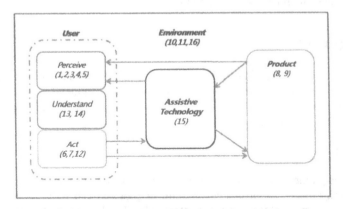

Fig. 1. The relationship between categories of user needs [6]

The categories consist of the following 6 groups: [6]

- · Perceive: User needs required to perceive all the outputs and capabilities of products (user needs categories 1-5)
- · Understand: User needs required to understand all the information (user needs categories 13-14)
- · Act: User needs required to act (user needs categories 6,7,12)
- · Assistive Technology: User needs to perceive, understand, and use the intuitive systems or safe assistive technology (user needs categories 15)

- Product: Product needs to support users (user need categories 8,9)
- Environment: All interactions need to be performed and protected within the overall environment (user needs categories 10, 11, 16)

User needs summary contains user needs derived from user problems of each disability type out of each category. Therefore, user needs have different relative importance for different disability types even though they are from the same category. Table 1 shows the user needs of "perceive" category derived from the user needs summary technical report for blind people and people with low vision as an example of its use. [6]

Table 1. User needs in perceive category in the user needs summary technical report

Category		User Needs in "Perceive" Category
1		**Perceive visual information**
1	1	Visual information also available in auditory form
1	2	Visual information also available in tactile form
1	3	Sufficient brightness for visually presented information
1	4	Sufficient contrast between all visual information and its background
1	5	Any information (other than the color itself) that is presented through color to be also presented in another way that does not rely on color.
1	6	Ability to change the colors of information.
1	7	Text readable with reduced visual acuity
1	9	Ability to avoid reflective glare
1	10	Ability to avoid glare from excessive brightness (of material or surrounding)
2		**Perceive auditory information**
2	5	When vibration is used as a substitute for different auditory events then some need vibration to have different vibration patterns (rather than vibration frequency or strength)
3		**Perceive existence and location of actionable component**
3	1	Locate and identify all keys and controls via non-visual means without activating them.
3	2	To have non-actionable elements (logos, decorative details) not look or feel like buttons or controls
3	3	Sufficient landmarks to be able to quickly re-find controls tactilely during use. Note: Nibs, groupings, spacing are examples of tactile landmarks.
3	4	Controls that visually contrast with their surroundings. Note: some benefit from ability to adjust colors of on screen controls
3	5	Controls be in places where they can be easily found with low vision and with no sight.
3	7	Focus and pointing indicators that are visible with low vision.
3	8	Information describing the layout of the operational parts.
4		**Perceive status of controls and indicators**
4	1	Non-visual equivalent to any visual indicators or operational cues, designed (power light) or intrinsic (e.g visual movements).
4	3	Non-tactile alternative to any subtle tactile feedback.
4	4	When different signals are used (e.g. different ring tones, or tactile or visual indicators) then some need alternatives that are different too.
4	5	Visual indicators (e.g. LEDs, on screen indicators, mouse cursors) that are visible with low vision.
4	6	Controls and indicators that are perceivable without relying on color
4	8	Tactile indicators (i.e. for those who need indicator to be both non-visual and non-auditory)
5		**Perceive feedback from operaton**
5	1	Feedback to be audio or tactile (i.e.non-visual).
5	2	Feedback to be tactile (i.e. both non-visual and non-auditory)
5	3	Visual or auditory alternative to any subtle tactile feedback.
5	5	Visual feedback that is obvious with low vision
5	6	Feedback perceivable without relying on color
5	8	Sufficient quality (e.g. volume, direction, clarity, frequency) for audio feedback.
5	10	Visual or tactile feedback to occur at the same location as the control
5	11	Clear feedback of connector engagement (e.g. power cord, PC card, USB connector, etc.)

User needs summary technical report presents the user accessibility needs derived from each category for 13 different disability types for using general IT products. It is possible, therefore, for product designers or engineers to selectively examine and derive user needs for the products they want to design.

2.3 Quality Function Deployment (QFD)

Quality function deployment (QFD) is a set of powerful product development tool. QFD is a method for developing a design quality aimed at satisfying users and translating the user's demand into design targets and major quality assurance points to be used throughout the production stage. [7, 8]

The House of Quality (HOQ) represents the user needs and characteristics of product design as a methodology for QFD. Hauser and Clausing describe that the house of quality is a kind of conceptual map that provides the means for inter-functional planning and communications. [5] HOQ's process starts with an interview, preview examination, or survey to qualitatively find out the Voice of Customer (VOC), the user needs. After that, a relationship between the Voice of Customer (VOC) and the Engineering Characteristics (EC), the product design requirements that are derived from the QFD team members is established. [10] There are nearly as many forms of the HOQ as there have been applications and it is this adaptability to the needs of a particular project or user group which is one of its strengths. [8] Demirbilek and Demirkan proposed the Usability, Safety, Attractiveness Participatory (USAP) model based on a quality function deployment design system. [3]

We adapted the use of QFD in our study since the qualitative user needs can still provide specific engineering characteristics for product design, and the HOQ can assure the consistency between the user needs and the measurable characteristics to be reflected in products. [4] Figure 2 shows how the HOQ's are developed to represent the relationship between VOC and EC.

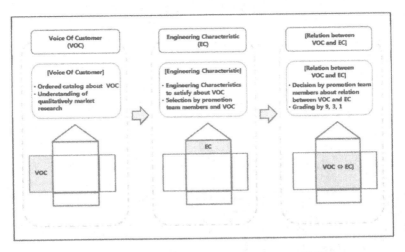

Fig. 2. House of Quality (HOQ) development [10]

3   Universal Design Process Using QFD

It is difficult to find out the user needs of the older people or people with disabilities. Companies are reluctant to pursue universally designed products due to the additional costs and time. The user needs summary technical report by the ISO/IEC JTC1

SWG-A can be a good tool to find out user needs of the people with disabilities and older people without actually performing user requirement study. We tried to utilize this tool in combination with the 7 principles of universal design and their design guidelines to systematically adopt the user accessibility needs in product design. The derived user accessibility needs would be put into as a VOC of a HOQ. By performing a series of such processes, the critical engineering characteristics would reflect the user needs according to the QFD's framework in product design.

To do that, the detailed guidelines of the 7 universal design principles are merged with a needed scope in user needs summary for target users with a certain disability in each of 6 user needs categories. Then, the user needs of particular target users with disabilities were applied to an HOQ to derive the engineering characteristics.

In 3.1, we will explain the process of merging the user needs and 7 universal design principles. In 3.2, we will explain the method of applying the HOQ to the user needs to derive the engineering characteristics. Figure 3 represents this procedure.

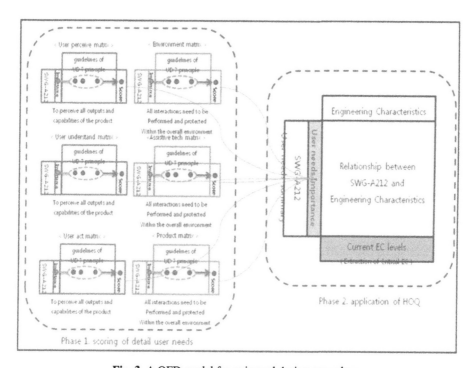

Fig. 3. A QFD model for universal design procedure

3.1   Comparison Matrix for Relationship between the User Needs Summary and the 7 UD Principles

In the user needs summary technical report of the ISO/IEC JTC1 SWG-A, the user accessibility needs are grouped into 4 categories - user, product, assistive technology, environment. The user category is further divided into the 'perceive', 'understand', and 'act' categories in more detail. We adapted the same notion of user needs - user-perceive, user-understand, user-act, product, the environment, and assistive technology to create a relationship matrix between the 7 UD principles and user needs. This matrix, which performs similar functions with the HOQ of the QFD procedures, maps the detailed items of user needs summary to the detailed guidelines of 7 UD principles by 1-to-1 comparison. This comparison matrix uses the weight in user needs summary technical report.

User needs summary technical report lists problems and user needs for 13 types of disabilities in using IT products in detail. Comparison matrix selects the disability type, category, and group from the user needs summary technical report, counts the number of listed user problems, and assigned the weight to each user needs item that is mapped to each user problem based upon this number of listed problems. Figure 4 shows the procedure to calculate the weight of user needs in the "User Perceive Needs" category for blind people and people with low vision

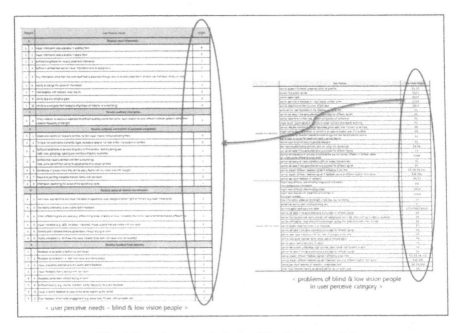

Fig. 4. Procedures to calculate weights for user needs items

The number of user problems counted for each disability type was used for importance weighting of user needs in this study. Figure 5 shows how the user needs and their weight are merged with 7 UD principles through a combination matrix to build a HOQ.

The relationship between the two methods, the user needs summary and the 7 UD principles, are compared using the comparison matrix. The relationship is checked only based on the existence of mutual relationship without considering the degree of relationship. In Figure 5, the 7 UD principles consist of the columns, and the user needs consist of the rows. The final score of each user needs (row) is calculated by multiplying the weight for each user needs with the number of checked items in UD principles (column) for relationship in the matrix, and is shown in the second rightmost column. This procedure of calculating the final score for each user needs is important to use the weight of user needs in the HOQ. We replaced these final scores with the weight value required to complete the HOQ.

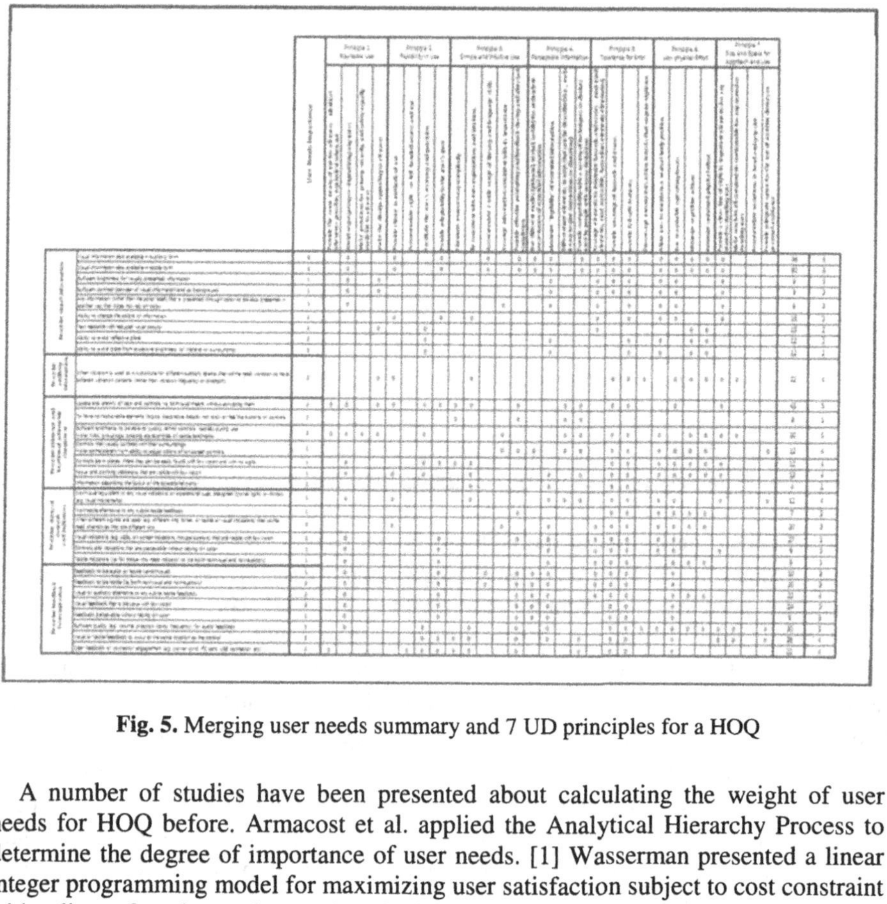

Fig. 5. Merging user needs summary and 7 UD principles for a HOQ

A number of studies have been presented about calculating the weight of user needs for HOQ before. Armacost et al. applied the Analytical Hierarchy Process to determine the degree of importance of user needs. [1] Wasserman presented a linear integer programming model for maximizing user satisfaction subject to cost constraint with a linear function and procedure for normalizing the relationship ratings between customer requirements and design requirements. [13]

3.2 Application of QFD

The product of comparison matrix needs to be applied to the HOQ, a tool for QFD, to complete the design methodology for universal design. A generic and typical HOQ looks like one shown in Figure 6.

Since we limit the scope of use of QFD only to extraction of critical engineering characteristics through the detailed use of user needs, the consisting factors such as

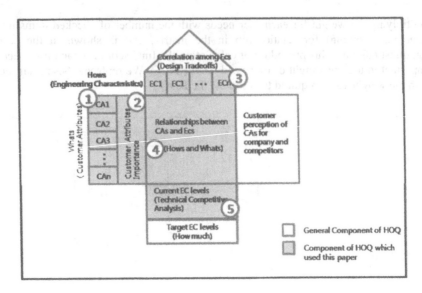

Fig. 6. Structure of a typical HOQ(House of Quality) [2]

customer perception of CAs for company and competitors, correlations among engineering characteristics, and target engineering characteristic level were excluded in our model.

For the consisting factors of the HOQ in Figure 6, user needs items are placed for Customer Attributes ①. For Customer Attributes Importance ②, the customer attributes of user needs need to have weight for each attribute. The final scores from a comparison matrix derived from 3.1 and 3.2 for acquiring the user needs scores by mapping user needs to 7 UD principles are used. In ③, Engineering Characteristics, detailed technology and design attributes for intended products are listed. For ④, relationships between CAs and ECs, the user needs in ① are mapped to the engineering and design attributes ③ and their relationships are quantified in scores. Current EC Levels ⑤ will add up all the scores in ④ multiplied by weights ②. The calculated values in ⑤ would provide a basis of engineering requirements that are going to be used in final product design, where only the engineering characteristics whose value exceeds a certain criterion would be used. [10]

4 Conclusion

This paper tried to establish a model for universal design process, which has been conceptually accepted only in principles and guidelines, by adapting user needs summary technical report so that the user accessibility needs can be reflected as critical engineering characteristics in product design.

The advantages of the product design process proposed in our study can be summarized as follows:

- The user needs summary technical report can easily summarizes the user accessibility needs of the people with disabilities and older people in using general IT products.
- Product designers and engineers can easily and promptly examine the user needs to provide accessibility to their products using only the required modules from the user needs summary.
- Product designers and engineers can easily understand the use problems in using their intended products by the people with disabilities and older people using the user needs summary.   .
- Product designers and engineers can visualize the solution for applying the universal design principles using our model.
- The comparison matrix can provide relationships required to substantialize the specific user needs by mapping them to the universal design principles.
- The weight factors used in the HOQ is objective since they are derived from thoroughly listed user problems.
- The critical engineering characteristics and their weighted values from the HOQ method would provide priorities for accessibility features to be reflected in products.

Acknowledgment

This research was supported by MKE, Korea under ITRC IITA-2008-(C1090-0801-0046).

References

1. Armacost, R.L., Componation, P.J., Mullens, M.A., Swart, W.W.: An AHP framework for prioritizing customer requirements in QFD: an industrialized housing application. IIE Trans. 26(4), 72–79 (1994)
2. Cohen, L.: Quality function deployment: how to make QFD work for you. Addison-Weseley, Readings (1995)
3. Demirbilek, O., Demirkan, H.: Universal product design involving elderly users: a participatory design model. Applied Ergonomics 35, 361–370 (2004)
4. Gargione, L.A.: Using Quality function Deployment (QFD) in the design phase of an apartment construction project. In: International Group for Lean Construction conference, pp 357–367 (1999)
5. Hauser, J.R., Clausing, D.: The House of Quality. Harvard Business Review, vol. 63 (1988)
6. ISO/IEC JTC 1 Special Working Group on Accessibility, Information Technology-Accessibility Considerations for People with Disabilities – Part 1: User needs Summary. ISO/IEC2007 (2007)
7. Kogure, M., Akao, Y.: Quality function deployment and CWQC in Japan. Quality Progress 16, 25–29 (1983)
8. Lowe, A., Ridgway, K., Atkinson, H.: QFD in new production technology evaluation. Int. J. Production Economics 67, 103–112 (2000)
9. Story, M.F., Mueller, J.L., Mace, R.L.: The universal design file: Designing for People of All Ages and Abilities. The Center for Universal Design (1998)
10. Teminko, J.: Step-by Step QFD Customer Driven Product Design. 2nd edn., St. Lucie Press (1977)

11. Vanderheiden, G.C., Vanderheiden, K.R.: Accessible Design of Consumer Products: Guidelines for the Design of Consumer Products to Increase Their Accessibility to People with Disabilities or Who Are Aging. Madison, WI: Trace Research and Development Center (1991)
12. Vanderheiden, G.C.: Accessible Design: A handbook for More Universal Product Design. Madison, WI: Trace Research and Development Center (1993)
13. Wasserman, G.S.: On how to prioritize design requirements during the QFD planning process. IIE Trans 25(3), 59–65 (1993)
14. Yamaoka, T.: A universal design method using 3 Point task analysis and 9 universal design items. Journal of Korean Society for Emotional and sensibility 5, 63–72 (2002)
15. The Center for Universal design, http://design.ncsu.edu/cud/about_ud/udprinciplestext.htm

Author Index

Lecture Notes in Computer Science

Sublibrary 3: Information Systems and Application, incl. Internet/Web and HCI

For information about Vols. 1– 4704
please contact your bookseller or Springer